RAGLAN

RAGLAN

From the Peninsula to the Crimea

John Sweetman

Arms and
Armour

Arms and Armour Press
A Cassell Imprint
Villiers House, 41-47 Strand, London WC2N 5JE.

Distributed in Australia by Capricorn Link (Australia) Pty.
Ltd, P.O. Box 665, Lane Cove, New South Wales 2066.

British Library Cataloguing-in-Publication Data: a catalogue
record for this book is available from the British Library

ISBN 1-85409-059-3

Cartography by Peter Burton

Designed and edited by DAG Publications Ltd. Designed
by David Gibbons; edited by Michael Boxall; printed and
bound in Great Britain.

Jacket illustration: *The Charge of the 17th Lancers at
Balaklava, 1854*. Reproduced by courtesy of the Director,
National Army Museum, London.

Printed and bound in Great Britain
by Hartnolls Ltd, Bodmin, Cornwall

CONTENTS

LIST OF MAPS

PREFACE: FAREWELL

'His funeral [cortège] was a finer sight than the Duke of Wellington's.' (British eye-witness) [1]

Tuesday 3 July dawned clear, bright and warm in the south-western corner of the Crimea. As the sun climbed higher and the temperature rose, scattered knots of uniformed figures began purposefully to converge on an isolated collection of low, white buildings with sloping red-tiled roofs, which housed the British military headquarters on a barren plateau high above the Plain of Balaclava south of the Russian naval port of Sevastopol.

The Siege of Sevastopol, centrepiece of the Crimean War between Russia, on the one hand, Britain, France, Turkey and Sardinia on the other, had been under way for nine months. Allied guns ranged constantly on the beleaguered suburbs, as enemy artillery in turn raked the invaders' trenches. Throughout the bitter previous winter the antagonists had faced piercing cold and near-starvation, while infantry forays further probed and tested one another's defences without clear advantage. The Russian commander in Sevastopol had been killed in action; the first French commander succumbed to cholera. Now the Allies were mourning the death of the British Commander-in-Chief (CinC), Lord Raglan, a 66-year-old Peninsular veteran, who had passed away during the evening of 28 June. Today his body would commence its last, sad journey to England. His colleagues – and, as it transpired, his enemies – would ensure that it did so with dignity and ceremony.

At 3 p.m. a 9pdr gun topped by a wooden platform, its four-wheeled carriage drawn by ten horses, approached the main building – fringed with swaying trees – through a wide avenue between stables, the tents of the Quartermaster-General's department and half-ruined outhouses. The gun-carriage moved steadily towards the three-sided courtyard at the north front of the old farmhouse, coming to a halt before the entrance to its west wing as infantry closed in protectively behind. Soon, selected representatives from the different armies began to gather in the tiny forecourt; 'the round hat and cock's tail' of the Bersaglieri and red-capped hussars prominent. General La Marmora, wearing a Sardinian bluish-grey uniform, was an early arrival, followed swiftly by the Turkish commander Omar Pasha, his fez studded with gold and decorated by a broad red ribbon and whose staff, mounted on distinctive Arab chargers with high saddles, were flamboyantly clad in cream trousers and coats topped by upright high golden collars. Clusters of officers in colourful dress gently jostled one another, while the whole uneven mass shifted and fidgeted whenever newcomers swelled the sober throng. 'Presently a more lively commotion was visible among the nodding plumes and curvetting (*sic*) chargers.' General Pélissier, in a cocked hat edged with white to denote a commander-in-chief, and General Canrobert, his predecessor in command, had arrived. Both showed outward signs of grief and reputedly, once the funereal column moved forward, Pélissier's uncontrolled sobs became distinctly audible.

Scarcely had the two French officers appeared than Raglan's coffin, covered in a pall and draped with the Union Jack, was borne from the doorway and slowly eased on to the wooden frame. The tense silence was broken only by the restless scraping of hooves and the faint, occasional tinkle of burnished accoutrements. At precisely 4 p.m. two field batteries of the Royal Artillery, on a knoll opposite the house, began a nineteen-gun salute. To the subdued strains of the Dead March from *Saul*, played by the combined bands of the 3rd, 9th and 62nd Regiments in an adjacent vineyard, the 'melancholy procession' set off on its seven-mile trek towards the French-held Bay of Kazatch, west of Sevastopol.

As it moved away, 100 Grenadiers of the Guard of Honour from the late CinC's own regiment presented arms, while to muffled drums the regimental colours were lowered. Meanwhile detachments of 50 men with one field officer, one captain and one subaltern from the Royal Sappers and Miners and each infantry regiment were drawn up in double ranks ready to bow heads and reverse arms along the mile between the British and French headquarters, a squadron of cavalry on the right of the line, another together with two artillery batteries on the left. Spaced between the Allied headquarters were the bands of the Sardinian Grenadiers and the British 10th Hussars. 'Behind these, and at both sides of the lines, the motley crowds of men of all nations and costumes looked on in silence.'

The six miles between the French headquarters, where another Guard of Honour presented arms, and Kazatch Bay was initially lined by sallow-faced Zouaves, each resplendent in a 'green shawl on red fez, over-hanging tassle, black jacket and red bags of trousers, yellow leggings and white gaiters'. Beyond them were the long coats and bearskins of the Imperial Guard, and infantry from the French I Corps. Close to the French headquarters were a battery of the Artillery of the Guard and a detachment of Sardinian lancers, their blue pennons stirring gently in the soft breeze. Like the British for the first mile, French bands were positioned at intervals over the second, longer portion of the chosen route to take up the Dead March as the solemn cavalcade passed. Puffs of smoke betrayed the minute-guns of the French field batteries fired from high ground to left and right of the road; and, as the cortège drew level, each regimental Colour dipped in salute.

The sombre parade that accompanied the coffin was led by two squadrons of the British 12th Lancers, followed by two squadrons of Sardinian Light Cavalry, four squadrons of French Chasseurs d'Afrique, four squadrons of French cuirassiers, two troops of French horse artillery and Major Brandling's I Troop, Royal Horse Artillery. Then came the 9pdr gun-carriage drawn by horses of Captain Thomas's C Troop, Royal Horse Artillery, the coffin's black pall fringed with white silk and crowned with the field marshal's cocked hat, epaulettes and swords together with a wreath of yellow *immortelles*, placed there by Pélissier in a touching, personal tribute. At the wheels of the gun-carriage, acting as mounted pall-bearers, Lieutenant-General Sir James Simpson (Raglan's successor in command) and Pélissier rode in front on the left and right, with Omar Pasha and La Marmora respectively behind them – as one officer said, 'four nobler fellows to bear a pall it would be difficult to find'.

Just behind the gun-carriage came the riderless brown bay Shadrach, which had carried Raglan at the Battles of the Alma and Inkerman, led by two mounted orderlies, in front of the late commander's immediate staff and relations, senior officers of the French, Sardinian and Turkish armies, the British commissioners to the individual Allied armies, British general officers and their staffs, staff of the British headquarters, one officer from each regiment of cavalry and infantry, two officers from the Naval Brigade, Royal Marines, Medical and Commissariat staffs, and three from the Royal Artillery. These were followed by the personal escorts of the four Allied commanders-in-chief, Lord Raglan's former escort (Captain Chetwode's troop of 8th Hussars), a battery of field artillery, two squadrons of the British 4th Dragoon Guards and a detachment of the Mounted Staff Corps. The entire escort was commanded by Lieutenant-Colonel J. E. Dupuis, Royal Horse Artillery, with Major-General W. Eyre in charge of the British infantry. As one observer put it, 'for mourners, he [Raglan] had the whole army, who had so often showed their devotion in obeying his commands, and the sincere regret of his brave allies'. Looking north-west from the French headquarters, the correspondent of *The Illustrated London News* 'watched the long line of the glittering procession, as it wound up and down the hills and hollows, rolling its side like a vast serpent'. One of those in that column less dramatically recorded that 'we wound our slow and melancholy way along the dusty road' past Kamiesch, whose own bay lay hidden beneath a forest of masts, to the neighbouring Bay of Kazatch. 'As a military spectacle, it was splendid,' wrote one onlooker; another thought it 'a beautiful sight'.[2]

The final approach to the wharf at Kazatch was flanked by detachments of Royal Marines and sailors from the Allied navies. Rear-Admirals Bruat and Stewart together with officers of the combined fleets formally received the coffin which was then lowered carefully into the launch of the British flagship and towed to *Caradoc* by boats from warships of the combined fleets. Minute-guns were fired from the columns of assembled warships, as British, French and Sardinian cavalry lined the embarkation wharf. When the laden launch left the shore of the Crimean peninsula, the troop of Royal Horse Artillery and the field battery, which had formed part of the procession, deployed on rising ground overlooking the bay to fire a final nineteen-gun salute. The flags of all the Allied vessels fluttered at half-mast in mute accord. 'And so, amidst everyone's sincere regrets, he was borne off in his coffin, till it arrived at the *Caradoc*, where it was hoisted on board, and we saw it no more.' Throughout the progress of the cortège from the British headquarters to Kazatch Bay, enemy guns in Sevastopol had remained strangely silent.[3]

Shortly before 8 p.m. *Caradoc* weighed anchor and moved slowly out into the Black Sea, while 'veteran generals and others who had liked him [Raglan] well stood bareheaded along the beach to take a last look at what covered one whose days had been cut short serving his country'. At the masthead of the steamer that had conveyed the deceased field marshal from Marseilles in April 1854 and, five months later, taken him on his crucial reconnaissance of the Crimean coast to select the Allied landing beaches, flew the poignant signal 'Farewell'.[4]

Thus the mortal remains of the Hon FitzRoy James Henry Somerset, First Baron Raglan, Privy Councillor, Knight Grand Cross of the Order of Bath, Colonel of the Royal Horse Guards (Blue), Commissioner of the Royal Military College Sandhurst and Royal Military Asylum Chelsea, Knight of the Orders of Maria Theresa of Austria, St George of Russia, Maximilian Joseph of Bavaria, recipient of the Tower and Sword of Portugal and the Turkish Imperial Order of the Mejidii First Class, holder of the Peninsular Gold Cross with five clasps and Silver War Medal with five clasps, began their last, joyless voyage to Bristol for eventual interment at Badminton, the Beaufort family home where Raglan had been born.[5]

ACKNOWLEDGEMENTS

I wish to acknowledge the gracious permission of Her Majesty The Queen to make use of material from the Royal Archives at Windsor. I should like, also, to thank Lady Sheila de Bellaigue and the staff of the Royal Archives for their kind assistance during my research. I am extremely grateful to His Grace, the Duke of Beaufort, for permission to use and to quote from the Badminton Muniments; similarly, to FitzRoy, 5th Lord Raglan in respect of the Raglan Military and Private Papers; and the Commandant, the Royal Military Academy Sandhurst, in connection with records of the Royal Military College. For use of manuscript sources in their care, I am indebted to the trustees and staff of Bristol Central Library, The British Library, Bodleian Library Oxford, Ealing Central Library, the Scottish Record Office, the National Library of Scotland, the National Register of Archives, the National Army Museum, Nottingham University Library, Newcastle University Library, Gloucestershire Record Office, Herefordshire Record Office, West Sussex Record Office, Wiltshire Record Office and Westminster School Archives. Extracts from the Palmerston Papers and Palmerston Letterbooks are published by permission of the Trustees of the Broadlands Archives; extracts from Crown copyright material by permission of the Controller of Her Majesty's Stationery Office.

My sincere thanks are due, as well, to a considerable number of people who have given me special help, advice and encouragement throughout this lengthy project, including: Andrew Orgill (Librarian, RMA Sandhurst); Peter Bird (Head of English, Salesian College, Farnborough); Dr P.B. Boyden (Head of Archives, Photographs, Film and Sound, National Army Museum); Mark Curthoys (Librarian and Archivist, Christ Church, Oxford); Mrs M. Dove; Miss M. Gooding (Local History Librarian, Central Library, Ealing); Dr T. A. Heathcote (Curator, The Sandhurst Collection); John Field (Librarian and Archivist, Westminster School), Mrs M. Richards (Archivist and Librarian, Badminton) and Philip Warner (former colleague at RMA Sandhurst). I must not forget, either, Mrs Dorothy Fox who struggled valiantly with my much-altered draft to produce the final typescript.

Above all, however, I am deeply indebted to the enthusiasm and commitment of two Portsmouth schoolmasters, Ted Washington and John Marsh, who many years ago persuaded a doubtful pupil that the study of history involved far more than tedious rote learning. To them, in lasting gratitude, I dedicate this book.

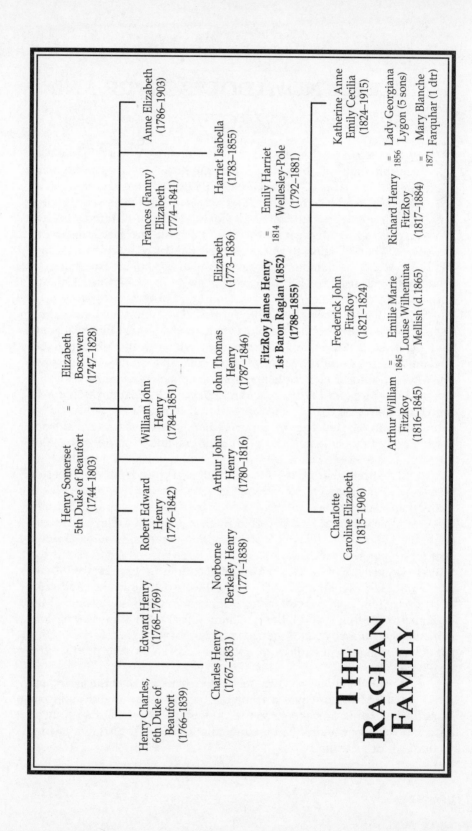

THE
RAGLAN
FAMILY

Henry Somerset
5th Duke of Beaufort
(1744–1803)
=
Elizabeth
Boscawen
(1747–1828)

Henry Charles,
6th Duke of
Beaufort
(1766–1839)

Charles Henry
(1767–1831)

Edward Henry
(1768–1769)

Norborne
Berkeley Henry
(1771–1838)

Robert Edward
Henry
(1776–1842)

Arthur John
Henry
(1780–1816)

William John
Henry
(1784–1851)

John Thomas
Henry
(1787–1846)

FitzRoy James Henry (1852)
1st Baron Raglan
(1788–1855)
=
1814
Emily Harriet
Wellesley-Pole
(1792–1881)

Elizabeth
(1773–1836)

Frances (Fanny)
Elizabeth
(1774–1841)

Harriet Isabella
(1783–1855)

Anne Elizabeth
(1786–1903)

Charlotte
Caroline Elizabeth
(1815–1906)

Arthur William
FitzRoy
(1816–1845)
=
1845
Emilie Marie
Louise Wilhemina
Mellish (d.1865)

Frederick John
FitzRoy
(1821–1824)

Richard Henry
FitzRoy
(1817–1884)
= 1856 Lady Georgiana
Lygon (5 sons)
= 1871 Mary Blanche
Farquhar (1 dtr)

Katherine Anne
Emily Cecilia
(1824–1915)

CHAPTER 1

CHILDHOOD, ADOLESCENCE AND MILITARY SERVICE (1788–1808)

'An active and intelligent fellow ... anxious to go on service'. (Duke of Richmond)[1]

On 30 September 1788 Elizabeth, 41-year-old wife of Henry fifth Duke of Beaufort, gave birth to her thirteenth child and eighth surviving son at the family seat of Badminton in Gloucestershire. The new arrival's brothers were Henry Charles, later sixth Duke of Beaufort (1766-1835); Charles Henry (1767–1831); Robert Edward Henry – more usually known as Edward – (1776–1842); Arthur John Henry (1780–1816); William George Henry (1784–1851); John Thomas Henry (1787–1846); and Norborne Berkeley Henry (1771–1838), who was deaf and dumb. Another brother, Edward Henry, had lived only five months (1868-9). Elizabeth (1773–1836); Frances Elizabeth – normally called Fanny – (1774–1841); Harriet Isabella (1783– 1855) and Anne Elizabeth (1786–1803) completed the immediate family.[2]

FitzRoy James Henry, baptized in a private ceremony at Badminton on 12 October, possessed a distinguished lineage. During the Middle Ages the Beauforts had enjoyed considerable authority until support for the Lancastrians during the Wars of the Roses lost them both possessions and influence. Two centuries later they partially emerged from political obscurity when Royalists in Raglan Castle stoutly resisted the besieging Parliamentarians. At the time of the Glorious Revolution the Beauforts also adhered to the Crown, but being staunch Protestants failed actively to support James II in the field. Thus not until Queen Anne's reign were they fully restored to royal favour.[3]

FitzRoy Somerset's mother was the daughter of Admiral Edward Boscawen who had held fighting commands throughout the world against the French and Spanish during the mid-eighteenth century, achieved a famous victory at Lagos Bay (1759) and, when Commander-in-Chief Portsmouth, signed the execution order for Admiral Byng. Member of Parliament for Truro and a Privy Councillor (both offices later held by Lord FitzRoy), in his professional capacity Boscawen sought to improve the health of seamen by increasing ventilation on board naval ships. His grandson would, in due course, likewise show keen concern for the welfare of men under his command.[4]

Besides Badminton, in 1788 the Beauforts owned Troy House on the River Trothy near Monmouth and supposedly haunted by a carriage and pair, as well as Stoke Gifford close to Bristol, which had been inherited by young FitzRoy's paternal grandmother. Blandford Park in Oxfordshire was used mainly for hunting, and Beaufort House at 5 Grosvenor Square, London, had been secured on a long lease. Tutors for the children were provided at all of these residences. The Duke's chaplain gave educational instruction at Badminton, and James Chew remained music master there throughout Lord FitzRoy's childhood. At Blandford Park and Stoke Gifford other music masters were employed on an occasional basis; and during April 1800 payment for a Latin master appeared in the Blandford accounts. The number and range of hired tutors increased markedly in London, partly because of the social demands of the annual season. Fees up to £30 were paid to a succession of drawing, dancing, writing, music and singing masters, several of whom were professionally distinguished, such as Dr (later Sir William) Parsons, Master of the King's Band, Dr Samuel Arnold, organist of the Chapels Royal, and the composer Samuel Webbe. Account books show that a harp and piano were available at both Badminton and Grosvenor Square. There is no evidence that Lord FitzRoy played an instrument or sang – activities almost certainly reserved to his sisters – but he did become an accomplished dancer; and he clearly grew up in neither an educational nor a cultural desert.[5]

The first specific reference to young FitzRoy after his baptism appears in the London house accounts for 11 June 1891, when Nurse Limden received £10.7.1 for looking after 'the child'. He was too young to attend the wedding of his eldest brother (Worcester) in the Archbishop's Chapel, Lambeth, on 17 May of that year. In middle age Lord FitzRoy recalled the liveliness of his early childhood at Badminton, the bustling activity of 'the horses, the carriages' and, enigmatically, 'the tea'. He remarked to his brother William that '... [I] cannot but sigh over bygone days', when every 'effort' was 'made to vary the scene and enjoy the sober pleasures of the country', possibly an allusion to the annual visits to Tetbury races and his father's passion for fox hunting. His paternal grandmother independently declared Badminton during FitzRoy's youth 'a kingdom free and happy', though she was less enamoured with the 'doubtful comforts' of some of the family's temporarily rented accommodation. With his distinctive ash-blonde hair, FitzRoy was indeed energetic and out-going. At Badminton on 30 September 1793 – and incidentally revealing that the entire family attended the church adjoining the house each Sunday – Mrs Boscawen wrote: '... [today] is a holiday, being one of the little one's birthday; 5 years old – a pretty little rogue'; and his father had underlined family affection a year earlier by specially riding over from a Volunteers' camp at Bristol for FitzRoy's fourth birthday party. Years later, quoting Raglan's daughter Charlotte, Josceline Bagot claimed that the Duchess of Beaufort deplored her son's preference for writing with his left hand and had it tied up to encourage more orthodox use of the right. If so, this natural tendency would prove invaluable after Lord

FitzRoy's loss of his right arm at Waterloo. FitzRoy Somerset does not seem to have been a tall youth; for the Prince Regent burst out laughing at his first levee, because his sword almost equalled his height.[6]

In 1795 FitzRoy joined his brothers Arthur, William and John at Goodenough's School in Ealing; and it is just possible that for at least part of his time there he stayed with his maternal grandmother, Mrs Frances Boscawen.[7] Goodenough House was a three-storeyed building with substantial single and double storeyed extensions. Situated on the north-east corner of Ealing's central crossroads, it stood in seventeen acres of land, that contained an abundance of mature trees, shrubs and ample open ground. In a contemporary print, boys can be seen playing cricket; and this may explain FitzRoy Somerset's later keenness to provide cricket grounds for soldiers' recreation. Almost certainly, as a lively youngster, he learnt the game at Ealing. Two years after FitzRoy arrived Dr Samuel Goodenough became Bishop of Carlisle, and control of the school passed to his nephew, William Goodenough. The boys went to and from Ealing by hired carriage which, depending upon the time of year and severity of the weather, cost between six and ten guineas for each journey. Initially, when FitzRoy left for school, his father gave him one guinea each term, a sum increased to £1.10.0 in 1799 and two guineas a year later. The Duke's Christmas present to each of his boys was £25 and occasionally he would send those at school an additional ten shillings during term time. FitzRoy and John left Goodenough's School in December 1801. Fifty-three years later Lord Stratford de Redcliffe added a postscript, in referring to a Greek as 'our old acquaintance at school'. As Lord Stratford attended schools in Wanstead and Hackney, east of London, prior to Eton and Lord FitzRoy went on to Westminster, the Greek must have attended Goodenough's before Eton.[8]

On 14 January 1802 the Duke of Beaufort settled a bill for £4.16.0 for FitzRoy's books and another for £8.4.0 to provide towels and shirts for John and FitzRoy (then aged thirteen) prior to their setting out for Westminster. They left Badminton twelve days later, each with his one-guinea allowance and an entrance fee of six guineas for the headmaster. William Rice received £14.8.0 for transporting them to London. John and FitzRoy were placed in the Under Shell form as 'town boys' and lived in a private boarding-house in Little Dean's Yard run by Mrs Clapham, where the annual charge for board, washing and lodging totalled £18.7.0, exclusive of £18.8.0 school fees. Included in this sum was four guineas for a single bed, which required each boy to supply two pairs of sheets and two pillowcases in addition to one dozen towels and one silver table-spoon. A quarter's notice had to be given before quitting the house, and 'cast off cloaths' were 'to be left for the servants'. FitzRoy and John followed their father, brothers Henry, Charles, Robert Edward and William to Westminster where among their contemporaries were the future politicians J. Cam Hobhouse, Lord John Russell and James Graham. George Bingham, later third Earl of Lucan, and Lord George Paget, both to be involved in the celebrated Charge of the Light Brigade, attended Westminster after Lord FitzRoy.[9]

Lord FitzRoy's days at Westminster were not uneventful. Reputedly one night in November 1802 the usher at Clapham's House was awakened by his screaming in the throes of 'some fit or dream' feigned to cover an escapade by his brother and a friend. A sixth-form contemporary at Westminster in 1803 remembered FitzRoy as 'a youth of fair and ingenuous countenance, with hair approaching flaxen' and drew attention to another incident that demonstrated 'that generous and kindly feeling in early life which accompanied him during the whole of his career ... It so happened that in what is the challenge or contest for places before passing into the shell form ... Lord FitzRoy took his brother's place, but immediately after the challenge was over, he went to Dr Vincent, the then headmaster, and begged as a favour that he might be permitted to exchange his place with his brother. He could not bear as the junior to stand before the elder. The doctor acquiesced.' A less likely version of this legend holds that the boys were assigned to different forms, and FitzRoy pleaded to be assigned to the same form.[10]

In the words of one contemporary, life at Westminster was not all *'couleur de rose'*. Lessons began at 8 a.m., the upper school being allowed twenty minutes for breakfast an hour later. At noon came a two-hour lunchtime, before afternoon lessons until 5 p.m.: prayers began and finished each session. This schedule was invariably worked on Monday, Wednesday and Friday: Thursday and Saturday were half-days, Tuesday sometimes devoted to half- or full-day 'play', when the boys themselves organized recreational activities. It is thus interesting to speculate whether, like Wellington, Lord FitzRoy learnt the art of battle on the playing-fields. Almost certainly, as at Ealing, he had the opportunity to play cricket. The formal curriculum comprised Latin, Greek, English, History, Geography and French; and boys had the right to listen to debates in Parliament, though no firm evidence exists that Lord FitzRoy did so.[11]

By January 1803 the Duke had increased each boy's term allowance to two guineas, poignantly giving each that amount on 2 October 1803 as they set out for London, nine days before he died. Expenses at Westminster, however, far outstretched the mandatory £36.15.0: on 28 February 1803 the Duke paid a bill from Mrs Clapham of £112.6.0 for the year 1802. Term accounts for FitzRoy's books and writing materials were settled directly with Messrs William Ginger & Son: £4.9.8 on 26 June 1802 and £3.15.0 on 25 January 1803 detailed, for instance, provision of an ink glass (3d), bottle of ink (8d), Greek and French grammars, works by Cicero and Horace, a lexicon and Book of Common Prayer. Another bill for 11/3 on 29 July 1802 included 6d for FitzRoy's watch ribbon and two shillings for gloves. Sixpence per month was paid for soap, and FitzRoy's monthly haircut cost one shilling. Apart from those for books, it seems probable that Mrs Clapham's annual payment involved money for the settlement of other bills. This supposition is reinforced by a receipt for £4.19.8 to Mrs Clapham on 10 March 1803 – after the Duke's payment to her on 28 February – from James Chubb, the locksmith, in respect of work for Lords John and FitzRoy up to 7 December 1802. Chubb had, for example, fitted locks to shutters, door and drawers and, evidently because the original keys had been lost, broken open a drawer and cupboard before then repairing the damage in November 1802. One other interesting bill, paid on 9 March 1803, showed £11 to a writing master for ten months prior to Christmas 1802, suggesting that FitzRoy may have received extra tuition after his arrival at Westminster. FitzRoy's stay there was short, however. Neither he nor John appear on the roll for 1804, and the probability is that their father's death on 11 October 1803 (in the same year that their youngest sister Anne died) led to withdrawal from the school. The outlay on the various Beaufort properties had proved onerous, so long-standing tutors such as James Chew lost their appointments, and the Duke left only a small annuity to each of his large family.[12]

On 9 June 1804 Lord FitzRoy joined the Army, still three months short of his sixteenth birthday. Need to raise money for the purchase of a cornetcy in the 4th (Queen's Own) Light Dragoons may also partly explain his leaving school. Between his time at Westminster (1802-3) and 1807, though, nothing positive is known of his life. He advanced to lieutenant by purchase on 30 May 1805 and it is just possible, though unlikely in view of contemporary practice, that he did serve with his regiment. *The Illustrated London News* afterwards commented: 'There can be no doubt that, like so many other scions of the aristocracy, Lord FitzRoy Somerset thus obtained his promotion with undue rapidity', but unlike others 'he was of the stuff whereof good soldiers are made'. In view of the French wars then in progress, quite apart from the family's financial straits, Lord FitzRoy is unlikely to have undertaken the Grand Tour as had his brother Henry earlier, though the possibility of a shortened version cannot be entirely discounted.[13]

Undoubtedly, however, while nominally serving in the 4th Light Dragoons, Lord FitzRoy nibbled at the edges of diplomatic life, which would again briefly entice him in years to come. From May until September 1807 he accompanied Arthur Paget, brother of the Earl of Uxbridge and a forerunner of FitzRoy's at Westminster, to the eastern Mediterranean. Thus, at the age of eighteen, Lord FitzRoy became acquainted with the Ottoman Empire (Turkey) whose fortunes almost 50 years on would shape his destiny and, indirectly, lead to his death.[14]

On 16 May 1807 the Foreign Secretary, George Canning, appointed Paget to 'a special mission' aimed at detaching Turkey from its alliance with France and at the same time encouraging the Sultan to make peace with Russia and Britain. The following day Canning suggested that negotiations be conducted on 'one of the islands in the archipelago' rather than at Constantinople where French influence was high. In little over a fortnight Paget and FitzRoy Somerset began 'a rather tedious passage of fifteen days' to join Admiral Lord Collingwood's fleet off Cadiz on 18 June. Two days later they sailed on in the battleship *Queen*, reaching Palermo on Saturday 4 July, subsequently calling at Malta and eventually arriving off the island of Tenedos on 30 July. The next day Paget wrote scathingly to his mother that 'my pen is unable to describe the Horror of the Place'. Ashore the new arrivals 'found the Town nearly reduced to ashes, the Island deserted by its former Inhabitants, dead bodies floating about the shore, and the air infected by those now lying unburied on the Island, not even water to be had, the wells having been destroyed etc.' Unhappily, on his return to the country in 1854, FitzRoy Somerset would discover that, dead bodies notwithstanding, Turkish hygiene had scarcely improved. He may well, then, have reflected on the accuracy of Paget's pessimism: 'I have little hope of being able to bring the wretches to any Terms ... it will be all the same an Hundred years hence, as they say'.[15]

Canning instructed Paget to make the most of knowledge about secret clauses attached to the Treaty of Tilsit between Napoleon and Alexander I of Russia, signed on 8 July, whereby Turkey would be reduced to Constantinople and its immediate European hinterland. 'Make our peace with Turkey as soon as you can,' he urged – a directive easily penned from the distant haven of Downing Street. On 22 August Paget left Tenedos in *Montague*, anchoring ten days later off 'Imbro' (Imbros, west of the Gallipoli peninsula), aware of growing French pressure on Turkey not to treat with him and aware also that Russia and Turkey were in the process of making peace. With Russia no longer actively engaged in hostilities against Turkey, Paget's position became uncomfortable and not a little dangerous: the Russian fleet withdrew its protection, and without its help the British squadron could not impose an effective blockade. Nevertheless, after conferring with Turkish officials, Paget hoped for formal peace. In vain. As the weather deteriorated so his mission ran metaphorically as well as actually into choppy waters. And his disillusionment heightened: 'There is not in any one of the Islands a House into which one could set one's feet – there is therefore no choice about remaining on board ship.' On 5 September Paget complained to Canning that he and his staff had been tossing in gales for five weeks and achieved nothing, as they battled between Imbros, Tenedos and occasional sterile visits to Turkish emissaries ashore.[16]

During these uncomfortable days FitzRoy undoubtedly did suffer – an active young man confined to anguished inactivity. At this time, however, he seems to have formed what was to become a lasting interest in moral philosophy. Paget was wont to meditate on the justice and nature of Man's mortality and the subject of Eternal Life. Writing to FitzRoy's mother from 'off Tenedos' on 25 September, he revealed: 'Poor FitzRoy is quite in the Dumps at having received no letter by the last arrival. Unfortunately I had already made him read Dr Beattie, otherwise I should unquestionably have consoled him with a few pages of it.' James Beattie, professor of moral philosophy and logic at Marischal College, Aberdeen, in the late 18th century, published works on aspects of Christianity and moral science which appealed to high churchmen to whose theological tenets FitzRoy would remain faithful throughout his life.[17]

Lord Fitzroy clearly made a powerful impression on Paget beyond his philosophical contemplations. 'He is a most excellent Lad – I have the sincerest Regard for him – But indeed you have no idea of the wretchedness of our existence; it is now I think seventeen weeks that we have not slept ashore, and to this moment, I don't know whether my friend FitzRoy can, but I know that I cannot guess what is to be the end of it all. We now and then get a walk on an uninhabited Island, which is the sum Total of our Recreations, and the winter months are approaching.' Somewhat wistfully he added: 'Pray bestow a thought on us during your Xmas Gambols.' FitzRoy had thus intrigued Paget not only by his personality, so that the older man could refer to their friendship, but also his judgement, allowing that FitzRoy might see a solution to their predicament that had eluded him.[18]

At length, after more frustrating and uncomfortable journeys back and forth, negotiations broke down irretrievably on 22 October when the Turks declined to 'renew the former Ties of Friendship' with Britain until a peace with Russia had been concluded. That would take at least an estimated four more months to attain; and failure allowed Paget's bitterness full rein. 'Instead of being received in a suitable manner ashore,' he complained to Canning, 'I was allowed to remain on board ship during the whole course of it [the negotiatory process], sometimes off Imbro [sic] sometimes off Tenedos, and at others off the Dardanelles, according to the State of weather and wind.' 'Even in the stress of weather', the Turks would not permit even a frigate to take shelter within the Dardanelles. 'Upon the whole I could not have experienced greater Inhospitality and Inattention among the most uncivilized people.' Hardly an alluring introduction to the world of diplomacy or to the Turkish Empire for FitzRoy. One other aspect of the sorry business had relevance; but only in retrospect. A fortnight before he finally admitted defeat Paget advised Canning that he did not believe that Turkey would fight France and Russia – following their accord after Tilsit – if Britain's assistance were confined to the Royal Navy. A commitment of ground forces was needed. Lord FitzRoy (as Raglan) would lead the Army Expeditionary Force when Britain and Turkey did eventually fight together against Russia almost a half-century later. Then, too, naval commitment alone would not suffice.[19]

Meanwhile FitzRoy Somerset returned to England in late 1807 after Arthur Paget's abortive mission and prepared to begin (or, possibly, resume) an active military career. On 5 May 1808 he obtained a company and the rank of captain in the 6th Garrison Battalion. Two months later he was in Ireland and about to sail for Portugal as aide-de-camp (ADC) to Sir Arthur Wellesley. Apologizing for a hurried letter, he wrote to his brother William on 12 July, hoping that 'my house is going on well' and urging him to feed corn to one of his horses 'to get him fat' during the coming winter. The location of Lord FitzRoy's house and indeed any details of an associated transaction are not known. Despite his haste FitzRoy typically concluded by expressing his affection for his mother and other close members of the family. That same day (12 July) he wrote a second, more lengthy letter to William aboard *Donegal*, explaining that he had dashed to the ship whose departure was imminent due to 'a fine fresh breeze'. He had acquired a horse from an officer in Ireland, which suggests that his appointment as Wellesley's ADC had been quickly arranged. Unfortunately the Master of Transport failed to send a boat to embark the horse so it was left ashore. Showing a special interest in the social round, Lord FitzRoy commented that the London season must be drawing to a close and that William would therefore soon be going to the country. Showing a maturity beyond his years, he proceeded to comment on his brother's plans to marry. He advised him not to sell out of the Army completely,

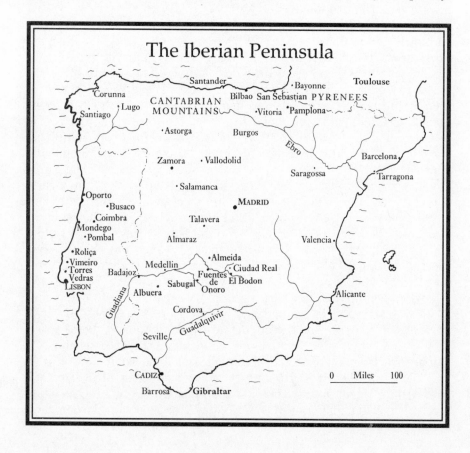

The Iberian Peninsula

but to remain on half-pay as a captain or field officer. If he decided not to marry, however, FitzRoy pressed him 'immediately [to] make application to the Duke of York and get some situation in the expedition which is to follow us from England'. He urged him to make a personal application backed by their elder brother (Lord Edward) 'and I doubt not you would immediately be appointed to the adjutant-general's staff'.[20]

FitzRoy Somerset was not yet twenty. None the less he was off to war in company with an experienced commander who, after taking part in the disastrous Flanders campaign of 1794, had commanded with distinction in India and the previous year had reinforced his military reputation in Denmark. In June 1808, after their royal family had been superseded by Napoleon's brother Joseph, eight Spanish provinces were in revolt. Wellesley had been poised to lead a military expedition to Venezuela, but persuaded the Government instead to appoint him 'to the command of his (Majesty's) army to be employed upon a particular service' – to free Portugal and Spain. Yet the prospect of campaigning in Iberia was far from inviting, though there FitzRoy Somerset would sadly experience many of the features (political, military and geophysical) that later would face him in the Crimea. High mountains, windswept, bleak plateaux were ruptured by sharp fissures through which rock-strewn rivers raced to the sea. Little vegetation relieved the featureless landscape baked by pitiless heat during summer, washed by torrential rain in spring and autumn and exposed to biting cold in winter. To compound problems for an army, most rivers and their interwoven mountains ran laterally east to west, roads were poor – many impassable during the rainy seasons; and there was little sustenance available from the land. Politically, Wellesley (as Chief Secretary for Ireland and with a brother – Lord Wellesley – shortly to enter the Cabinet) might have influence in his native land. But he would soon find himself embroiled with an unattractive range of Portuguese and Spanish political figures and his own government's anxiety to avoid long-term commitment and short-term expense. At Wellesley's side FitzRoy Somerset would, indeed, learn a great deal.[21]

He had not met Wellesley before being appointed to his staff through the influence of the Duke of Richmond. Nevertheless, during the passage across the Bay of Biscay, the General and the young officer struck up a friendship which would endure quite literally for a lifetime. Together they also worked to master the Spanish language, using Lady Butler's prayer book which had been given to Wellesley. Lord FitzRoy transferred to Crocodile with Wellesley, went with him to Corunna and on to visit Admiral Sir Charles Cotton farther south, before reaching Mondego Bay on 30 July. There, two days later, Wellesley's troops began to disembark. With an uncanny presage of Lord Raglan's later landing in Calamita Bay in the Crimea, strong winds and rolling surf delayed completion of the disembarkation for five days. Meanwhile Wellesley had been informed that he would only command the expedition until the arrival of a more

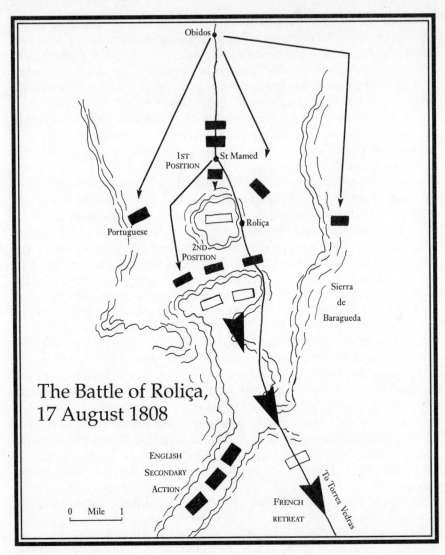

Obidos

1ST
POSITION

St Mamed

Portuguese

Roliça

2ND
POSITION

Sierra
de
Baragueda

The Battle of Roliça,
17 August 1808

ENGLISH

SECONDARY

ACTION

FRENCH

RETREAT

0   Mile   1

To Torres Vedras

senior officer (Lieutenant-General Sir Harry Burrard). He had, therefore, to explain his actions thus far to Burrard, pending his arrival; and he informed the naval CinC (Cotton) from his headquarters at Lavaos that he intended to concentrate his troops in that area because 'division of our forces' by landing some south of the River Tagus would be 'likely to be attended with bad consequences'. Early in 1855 Raglan would similarly deplore plans to divide the Allied forces in the Crimea. To Burrard, Wellesley further explained that, in consultation with Cotton during 26–7 July, it had been decided that the 'attack proposed' upon Cascaes Bay was 'impracticable' because Fort Cascaes stood out of range of the ships' cannon and could not therefore be silenced. Failure to do so would seriously prejudice the success of any landing operation. Similarly landing in the Paco d'Arcos in the Tagus estuary would be impossible without neutralizing Fort St Julian. Once more the parallel with Raglan's later experience in September 1854 is striking. He, too, rejected the proposed landing beach at the mouth of the River Katcha through fear of destructive enemy shore batteries; and Wellesley's predicament at this time may well have influenced that decision. Meanwhile Wellesley noted that all other beaches around the Rock of Lisbon had been ruled out. Mondego Bay, north of Lisbon and 'the nearest place which afforded any facility of landing', had therefore been selected.[22]

With a mixed force of 12,000 British in co-operation with 6,000 Portuguese and 1,500 Spanish under their own commanders, Wellesley began the 90-mile march south towards Lisbon on 10 August, knowing that strong enemy units lay in his path. Forty-six years later Lord Raglan would likewise undertake a 30-mile advance southwards towards Sevastopol from a northerly landing beach. Like Wellesley he would face defended enemy positions en route, have gathered sparse supplies from the surrounding countryside, and would use a coastal road parallel to the shore to keep in touch with his shadowing fleet. Five days after leaving Mondego Bay Wellesley's advance guard clashed with French outposts, in much the same way as Raglan's would encounter Russians on the Bulganek between the beaches and the River Alma. [23]

General Loison's main force withdrew towards Lisbon leaving a rearguard of 4,250 men, including cavalry and artillery, on a hill astride the main road at Roliça. Before Wellesley could attack, the French fell back across a stream to occupy another hill up whose steep slope any attacker must climb. The enemy position was protected at both ends by a gorge. Once across the river attacking forces could use four dry gullies although there was cover at the foot of each for determined defensive skirmishers. The Alma position in the Crimea, although on a much larger scale, would be very similar. Wellesley's initial attempt at double envelopment failed on 17 August, but after three unsuccessful frontal attacks the position was at last carried. Nevertheless the bulk of the enemy withdrew in relatively good order. Comparison with the later Alma action in the Crimea is indeed marked. Allegedly during the clash at Roliça, which was his first experience of action, Wellesley asked his young ADC 'Well, Lord FitzRoy, how do you feel under fire?' 'Better, sir, than I expected,' came the cool reply, which is said to have impressed his commander. On the following day (18 August 1808) by an administrative quirk FitzRoy's transfer into the 43rd (Monmouthshire) Regiment of Foot was gazetted.[24]

On 20 August, having resumed his advance on Lisbon, Wellesley reached Vimeiro Ridge, a line of hills astride the River Maceira, where he learnt that Burrard had anchored in nearby Maceira Bay. Burrard remained afloat, but forbade Wellesley to move further. Next morning, however, the initiative was seized by General Junot in a desperate attempt to stifle the British invasion. On a bright, sunny day he paid the penalty of trying to outflank Wellesley's superior numbers which were occupying the ridge and other high ground to the south, close to Vimeiro village. The French suffered heavy casualties and, moreover, lost fourteen guns to the British – a recognized mark of success in the field, which could not have escaped FitzRoy Somerset's notice. Another event that day may well have over-influenced him also. The British cavalry rashly pursued the enemy too far (as it would do also at Waterloo), suffered unnecessary casualties and almost incurred disaster. Wellesley would thereafter be cautious in his deployment of cavalry, as would Raglan in years to come, when he was in command. To Burrard, Wellesley emphasized that brigade commanders had responded individually to enemy attacks, and that British use of the bayonet had been decisive; as would be the case at Inkerman in November 1854.[25]

The day after the battle at Vimeiro Wellesley informed his brother that 'we gave the French an unmerciful beating yesterday', but revealed that yet another officer senior to him had arrived on the scene, Sir Hew Dalrymple. It was a prelude to an unhappy sequence of events whose repercussions would affect Wellesley and FitzRoy Somerset greatly within months. On 22 August Dalrymple ordered Wellesley to seek a ceasefire. Two days later Wellesley's anger spilled over in a letter to his brother, William Wellesley-Pole (Lord FitzRoy's future father-in-law). Dalrymple had forced him to sign the ceasefire: 'I wish that I was away from the Army. Things will not flourish as we are situated and organized; and I am much afraid that my friends in England will consider me responsible for many things over which I have no power.[26]

Furthermore Dalrymple determined to convert the temporary ceasefire into a formal convention; and FitzRoy Somerset was called upon to play a part in that process. On 27 August Wellesley wrote: 'Lord FitzRoy has been very useful to me, and I have this day lent him to Sir H. Dalrymple to go to the French headquarters.' Four days later the 'definitive convention' was signed. Thereafter Wellesley never ceased to protest that he had become embroiled in the controversial Convention of Cintra by obeying the order of a superior officer; and the affair rumbled on until a Board of General Officers met in London from November to December 1808, to inquire into the circumstances surrounding the Convention. In the meantime Wellesley had resumed his post as Chief Secretary for Ireland in Dublin and Fitzroy Somerset had returned to England. In accordance with the terms of the Convention French troops left Portugal for La Rochelle. Elsewhere on the Iberian peninsula, however, other French formations would soon expand their influence in Spain, push Sir John Moore back to Corunna, drive into northern Portugal and capture Oporto. Lisbon thus again came under threat; and once more Wellesley and his ADC would be called to the Colours in its defence.

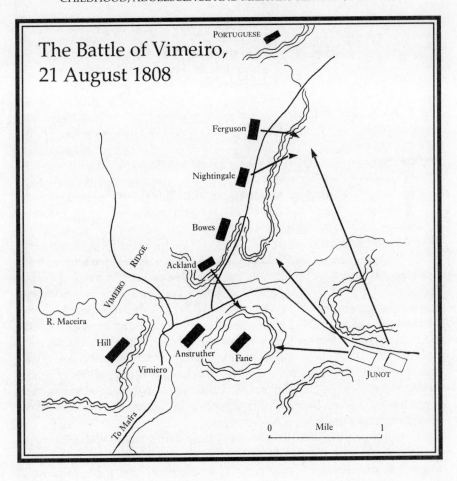

The Battle of Vimeiro,
21 August 1808

PORTUGUESE

Ferguson

Nightingale

Bowes

Ackland

VIMEIRO RIDGE

R. Maceira

Hill

Vimiero

Anstruther

Fane

JUNOT

To Mafra

0   Mile   1

CHAPTER 2

THE PENINSULAR WAR
(1809-14)

'He [FitzRoy Somerset] will one day be a great man, if he lives.'(Major, later General Sir William Napier)[1]

Three weeks before the French took Oporto in March 1809, Wellesley underlined the need to encourage Spanish resistance and effectively to organize the 70,000 militia and regulars under arms in Portugal. He recommended 'very extensive pecuniary assistance and political support' plus immediate British troop reinforcements.[2]

Events then moved swiftly. His baggage was stowed aboard *Surveillante* anchored at Spithead on Wednesday 12 April, but strong 'gails'(sic) prevented him 'and his suite', including FitzRoy Somerset, from joining the ship off Portsmouth until 11.30 a.m. on 15 April. *Surveillante* set sail for Portugal early that afternoon in 'light breezes'. At 5.20 p.m., however, a freshening north-westerly obliged the captain to 'come to' off Dunnose at the south-eastern extremity of the Isle of Wight. In the space of fifteen minutes the wind 'veered' sharply and conditions continued to deteriorate. However, both the captain's and master's logs recorded only 'fresh breezes' and 'squally rain' without any hint of alarm; and *Surveillante* got under weigh again at 12.15 a.m. on 16 April. The delightful story that the vessel nearly foundered, with Wellesley being warned to prepare to abandon ship, therefore appears to be apocryphal. What is not in dispute is that *Surveillante* experienced a very rough crossing of the Bay of Biscay and on 20 April fired shots to harass a 'strange sail', which turned out to be a Portuguese schooner. Two days later land was sighted and Wellesley went ashore at Lisbon.[3] Shortly aferwards he assumed formal command of the British troops from Lieutenant-General Sir John Cradock. That appointment, 'to be Commander of his [Majesty's] forces in Portugal', announced in Lisbon on 27 April, coincided with confirmation that FitzRoy Somerset would be one of his four ADCs.[4]

Wellesley determined to move to the relief of Oporto without delay. This time his advance would be northwards beyond the 1808 landing beach at Mondego Bay. En route he was appointed Marshal-General of the Portuguese Army, and during 10-11 May his troops clashed with French units near Villa Nova, capturing 60 guns – an astonishing first effort. Shortly afterwards Wellesley reached the Douro only to find that the road bridge had been blown up. By the time that sufficient troops had been ferried across to liberate the town the French had fled.[5]

Having captured Oporto and put Marshal Soult to flight in the north, Wellesley decided to deal with Marshal Victor's other French army, which entailed partly retracing his steps towards Lisbon, then striking eastwards into Spain. He was already discovering, though, how difficult the question of supplies would become. Plans to pursue Soult's forces after the victory at Oporto had been shelved because of lack of bread and no prospect of obtaining any 'for some days'. Once on the move eastwards he complained of insufficient money to pay for provisions and of lack of forage for artillery horses and mules: 'our Commissariat is very bad indeed,' he commented. In extremity, he removed Assistant Commissary Gordon from his post with Lord Edward Somerset's 4th Dragoons because of 'incapacity to perform his duty, and of making false reports'. Commissariat deficiencies continued to plague Wellesley during the Peninsular War and they would haunt Lord Raglan (FitzRoy Somerset) in the Crimea.[6]

As he made his way south from Oporto Wellesley revealed an interesting attitude towards the loss of guns to an enemy. Writing to Marshal Beresford (commanding the Portuguese in the field), he explained that he was not averse to building batteries on the upper Tagus, but that heavy guns should not be placed there, rather 'some guns of small calibre, which would be of no use to the enemy if they should fall into their hands'. This explains why Wellesley was keen to avoid loss himself and, at the same time, capture cannon to turn against the enemy as he would later do at Pamplona. Raglan's order that instigated the Charge of the Light Brigade during the Battle of Balaclava years later was, almost certainly, governed by this principle.[7]

During the summer of 1809 a curious incident took place. One day a Major Baker dined with Wellesley, and at the table Lord FitzRoy 'recommended' Spanish gypsies as 'useful spies'. Wellesley reacted sharply: 'I hate all humbug and consequently gypsies,' to which Lord FitzRoy surprisingly replied: 'I think you deceive yourself more than others... [because] you surely believe in their prophecies.' Another officer present observed that they only prophesied good; years afterwards, Baker recalled that a gypsy predicted correctly that Wellesley would die peacefully in bed. Days after the dinner Baker and FitzRoy Somerset were riding through a cork wood when they encountered the same gypsies. 'The youngest and prettiest girl ... greeted Lord FitzRoy Somerset but as she addressed him in a language he did not understand, he threw her a piece of gold and rode on.' Lord FitzRoy may not yet have been fluent in spoken Spanish, or the girl may have used an obscure local dialect. However, Baker tarried and the girl said 'in Spanish': 'Be grateful stranger that you are generous to a daughter of the wandering tribe of Egypt. Many battles shalt thou see with head erect, as Conqueror shalt thou lose thine eye or thine hand sooner than the Laurel Crown. Conqueror shalt thou be on this and on the other side of the great ocean and inherit the field marshal's staff of the most renowned of heroes. Thou shall fight as conqueror with those that are now thine enemies. Thou shall see and live thro' the War of Peace.' Cynics might easily dismiss gypsy forecasts, but this proved a fairly accurate summary of FitzRoy Somerset's future career. The gypsy, who predicted Wellesley's peaceful end, also said that he would die in the same year as Baker.[8]

Having advanced into Spain, Wellesley fought the French at Talavera on the River Alberche 60 miles south-west of Madrid. In that action one of Wellesley's other ADCs would be Lord Burghersh (afterwards Lord Westmorland), in 1811 destined to marry the 18-year-old sister of Lord FitzRoy's future wife; Lords Edward and John Somerset, FitzRoy's brothers, also took part. Lord FitzRoy very nearly did not join them. During the afternoon of 27 July 1809 Wellesley and his staff were in advance of the main force, surveying the terrain from the top of an old stone building when French skirmishers appeared. The British officers dashed down the stairs and galloped away followed by a stream of bullets. Unscathed they reached the main defensive position north of Talavera, dominated by the Cerro de Medellin which then unexpectedly came

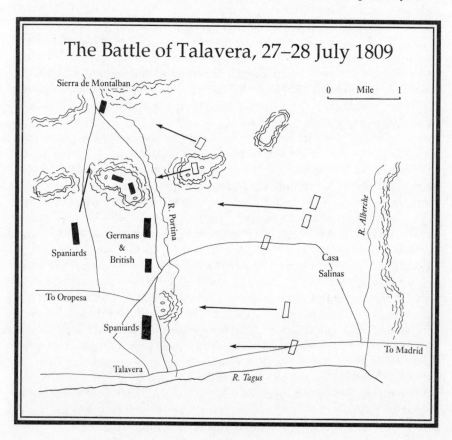

The Battle of Talavera, 27–28 July 1809

under attack late that evening. Four Spanish battalions fled the field leaving Wellesley's 20,000 British and Hanoverian troops to face more than twice that number of enemy under King Joseph, Marshals Jourdan and Victor. Vigorous counter-attacks recaptured the lost ground quickly and, despite artillery bombardments supplemented by repeated cavalry and infantry assaults, it was held throughout 28 July. By the close of that day the French had withdrawn across the Alberche, leaving their dead, 'twenty pieces of cannon, ammunition, tumbrils and some prisoners' behind. Wellesley wrote to his brother: 'I was hit but not hurt and my coat shot through. Never was there such a murderous battle!' Fortunately FitzRoy Somerset escaped unhurt, and he was among Wellesley's 'personal staff' to be commended.[9]

In fact, he was singled out by Wellesley who followed the practice of sending back to England with the battle dispatches an ADC for whom he especially desired promotion. After Talavera that distinction fell to FitzRoy Somerset. He was absent from the army for 'nearly nine weeks' during which time Wellesley had become Viscount Wellington and his army had withdrawn across the Tagus into Portugal. While in England Lord FitzRoy went to Badminton where one of his nieces recalled him 'in dear papa's sitting room ... he looked so thin – so pale – after all the hardships'. But she added that he greeted them with 'his own sweet smile ... and all of us children hurried to be embraced'. He enthralled them with his descriptions of the fighting in the Peninsula while they sat at his feet. During this time in England, he also impressed his future father-in-law, William Wellesley-Pole: 'Lord FitzRoy Somerset ... seems a fine lad,' he wrote to Wellesley in August.[10]

Lord FitzRoy returned to Wellington's headquarters at Badajoz during the first week of October, taking with him a new regimental cocked hat for Edward. He had been delayed 'a few days' by poor weather at Falmouth and brought out papers dated 21 September 1809 which contained 'accounts of the duel' between two Cabinet ministers, Lord Castlereagh and George Canning. They fought that morning on Wimbledon Common with Castlereagh shooting Canning through 'the fleshy part of the thigh' though not dangerously; apparently prompted by a letter to Canning from Castlereagh 'using many bitter epithets in many places and accusing him of gross deceipt [sic]' in manoeuvring to get him out of office. Lord Wellesley refused to act as Canning's second because Castlereagh had supported Wellington in the Peninsula. Wellington believed that this unfortunate episode would 'confirm in the minds of all Men the despicable opinions which they have had of the publick [sic] Servants of the State'. Aware of problems at home concerning formation of a new government following the fall of Lord Portland's administration, he noted that while political squabbles took place in England he was fighting to defend Portugal. 'I may be wrong,' he wrote to Wellesley-Pole, 'but the conviction of my mind is that all the misfortunes of the present reign, the loss of America, the success of the French Revolution, etc., are to be attributed in a great degree to the Spirit of Party in England.' This jaundiced view was scarcely cured by William's conclusion 'that [not] one man or horse has yet sailed to replace your losses', and the cynical addendum that 'we expect our armies to beat superior numbers without limitation'. Wellington's mistrust of politicians could not have been entirely lost on FitzRoy Somerset.[11]

Scarcely had Lord FitzRoy returned from England than he set out for Seville from Badajoz with Wellington before travelling on to Cadiz. He was clearly disenchanted, finding 'no sort of amusement' in the English camp and declaring to his brother Edward: 'I don't think a more disobliging people exist than the Spaniards.' By now combining the duties of Assistant Military Secretary with those of ADC, Lord FitzRoy had begun to acquire more responsibility, dealing for example with the appointment of a secretary to Major-General Doyle. But 1810 on the whole was not a good year for the Allies. Greatly reinforced and reorganized, the French took the frontier fortress of Ciudad Rodrigo and advanced successfully on Almeida in July. By early September in FitzRoy Somerset's words, 'everything indicated the immediate invasion of Portugal by the French army', and by the middle of the month Marshal Masséna had indeed swept into the Mondego valley. FitzRoy Somerset, Lord Edward Somerset, commanding the 4th Dragoons, and Lord Burghersh, fighting with the 3rd Dragoon Guards, then became actively involved in a lengthy rearguard action. Eight miles north-east of Coimbra Wellington deployed his divisions along the commanding ridge of Serra de Busaco which ran some nine miles north-east from the River Mondego. The flat-topped ridge gave ample opportunity for lateral movement and Wellington's headquarters in a convent to the left centre of the position offered him visual command of the battle from a rocky projection thereafter known as 'Wellington's knoll'. But his troops were so extended that he had to ride back and forth along the ridge during the day to encourage them. During most of that time FitzRoy Somerset shared the danger with him. Attacking in the mist, shortly after dawn on 27 September – as Russian columns would do at Inkerman in the Crimea – the French launched, according to Wellington, 'desperate' and repeated attacks against the British line in two places, but were repulsed with 'enormous' loss. Critically, when General Reynier threatened to break through between the British Generals Picton and Leith, Wellington brought up guns to take the enemy flank. Lord FitzRoy (Raglan) would use a similar tactic at the Battle of the Alma in September 1854. Having regrouped, the enemy seemed ready to outflank Wellington at Busaco so he withdrew during the night of 27/8 September.[12]

During the struggle at Busaco FitzRoy Somerset received his first wound after being 'repeatedly brought ... under galling fire'; and Wellington paid warm tribute to him and other members of his personal staff that day. Towards the end of the year other developments had major signifi-

cance for Lord FitzRoy. It had gradually become apparent that Lieu-
tenant-Colonel James Bathurst could no longer carry out the duties of Mil-
itary Secretary. Lord FitzRoy had been acting as his assistant for some
time, and one area of his duties concerned intelligence. Colonel Colquhon
Grant, who adopted many disguises including that of an American in
Paris to obtain information about the enemy, acted as Wellington's 'Chief
Scout' in the Peninsula. On one occasion his brother-in-law (Sir James
M'Grigor) was advised by Wellington: 'Go into the next room and desire
FitzRoy to show you the information from Grant enclosed in the dispatches to Lord Bathurst.' FitzRoy Somerset assumed *de facto* full responsibility on 19 September when Bathurst went home on sick leave. On 28
November 1810 the Army learnt formally from the Adjutant-General's
office at Cartaxo (Wellington's local headquarters) that 'all letters and
applications, hitherto addressed to the Military Secretary, must in future
be addressed to Lord FitzRoy Somerset by whom all warrants will be
countersigned till further orders'. With Bathurst at length declared unfit
to resume his duties, on 1 January 1811 a further General Order from Cartaxo announced: 'Captain Lord FitzRoy Somerset is appointed Military
Secretary to His Excellency the Commander of the Forces from the 25th
ultimo [Christmas Day].' His appointment at 22 and his retention of the
post for the remainder of the Peninsular War were mute tribute to his out-
standing qualities.[13]

The Military Secretary dealt with the CinC's confidential correspondence, so within days of his formal appointment Lord FitzRoy was
advising Wellington about the application of Lieutenant McInnes to purchase command of a troop of 2nd Life Guards. Thereafter similar matters
frequently demanded his attention and he also acted as Wellington's regular contact with subordinate commanders. His ease at establishing personal relations proved particularly advantageous, as did his clarity of
expression in writing and, above all, the complete mutual trust between
him and Wellington. There was never any doubt that he spoke for the
CinC and enjoyed his full confidence. During the winter of 1810/11
Wellington's field army sheltered behind the Lines of Torres Vedras
which had been planned and constructed in the previous twelve months.
The fortifications in the defensive lines were occupied mainly by Portuguese militia and two Spanish divisions, with a naval flotilla in the
Tagus estuary ready to pour fire into the advancing enemy over the
defenders' heads. This static situation allowed Lord FitzRoy opportunity
to establish a working relationship with divisional and regimental officers
without the immediate pressure of manoeuvre and action in the face of
the enemy. Later Sir William Napier paid fulsome tribute to his effective
contact between headquarters and battalion officers, whose relative youth
enabled the new Military Secretary to achieve an easy rapport with them.
In gaining their confidence FitzRoy Somerset learnt a great deal about
them and the state of their formations. In Napier's words: 'Lord FitzRoy

acquired an exact knowledge of the moral state of each regiment, rendered his own office important and gracious with the army, and with such discretion and judgement that the military hierarchy was in no manner weakened.'[14]

Once Masséna had retreated from the Lines of Torres Vedras in March 1811 Wellington again advanced northwards. He did so with a familiar warning from the home government. On 20 February Lord Liverpool (now Secretary of State for War and the Colonies) advised him that the Government was becoming very uneasy about the rising financial burden of the war: the 1808 campaign had cost £2¾ million, that of 1810 more than £9 million. The Government was 'unanimous' that expenditure on this scale could not continue 'for any considerable length of time'. It was therefore opposed to Wellington's accepting command of the Spanish armies which had been proferred. Operational co-operation might occur, but no joint command, which would imply long-term military commitment. Wellington must find some means of gaining Spanish support without the expense of sending a British army deep into Spain. Knowledge of this and like strictures meant that FitzRoy Somerset as Lord Raglan would not be entirely surprised by similar government missives when he held command in the Crimea.[15]

Shortly after beginning the advance Wellington and his staff came under fire from French sharpshooters while studying the terrain from a small hill near Condacia. Fortunately the enemy's aim proved inaccurate; and Wellington survived to cross the Spanish frontier early in April, having fought several minor actions against the enemy rearguard on the way, as FitzRoy Somerset recorded: 'During their retrograde movement many affairs took place at which I was present ... such as Pombal [11 March], Redhina [12 March], Casal Nova [14 March], Foz d'Aronce [15 March] and Sabugal [3 April].' With Wellington, Lord FitzRoy advanced 300 miles in 28 days. Behind them, though, due east of Lisbon, Marshal Beresford and his Portuguese troops failed to retake Badajoz which, surprisingly, had fallen to the French in March. On 16 April 1811, the enemy in the north having retired across the River Agueda, Wellington and his staff (including Lord FitzRoy) left the headquarters at Villa Fermosa and rode south towards Beresford so rapidly that Wellington wore out two horses and, in crossing a swollen river, lost two accompanying dragoons who were swept away. They reached Elvas in four days and forded the River Guadiana to reconnoitre Badajoz where some of their German escort were captured by enemy foragers. News of Masséna's renewed advance, however, sent Wellington hurrying back north on 25 April. Beresford meanwhile undertook a formal siege of Badajoz which he was obliged to lift on 12 May through lack of heavy artillery.[16]

While Beresford was thus engaged, Wellington faced the French at Fuentes de Onoro where FitzRoy Somerset yet again distinguished himself. Hoping to recapture Almeida in a fortnight, on 1 May Wellington nevertheless suspected that he might need to fight 'a general action in a day or two'. He was right. Two days later he encountered a large French concentration that seemed determined to prevent him from reaching Almeida. He deployed his forces along low hills behind the gorge of Dos Casas on the plain of Nava de Aver with Fuentes de Onoro on his right. The British line was dangerously stretched as Wellington fought to hold back the enemy; and for a brief period the village of Fuentes de Onoro did fall into enemy hands. FitzRoy Somerset described this episode as 'a very fierce struggle'. At one point Wellington and his staff were almost cut off by a regiment of French dragoons; and throughout the entire encounter, which was fought in extreme heat, according to Captain John Kincaid of the Rifle Brigade, FitzRoy Somerset displayed 'gallant bearing'. And, indeed, as a direct result of his performance at Fuentes de Onoro he was granted a brevet majority on 9 June, precisely seven years after being commissioned as a cornet.[17]

Once the Fuentes de Onoro action was concluded Almeida fell to Wellington; but he became concerned about Beresford's continued failure to take Badajoz. Feeling that, for the moment, the north was secure, he and his staff returned south. This time Wellington decided to direct operations personally; and by the close of May a second siege had begun. But again lack of heavy artillery proved a telling drawback and on 10 June he abandoned his own attempt to carry the fortress, though FitzRoy Somerset argued that the siege was 'interrupted by movements of the French' which required Wellington's urgent attention elsewhere. The lessons remained that siege operations must be stringently planned, the points of assault carefully chosen (Wellington suspected that the engineers had not served him well in this respect) and, above all, that heavy artillery be available. These lessons would be absorbed in the short term by Wellington in the Peninsula and in the long term by Lord Raglan before Sevastopol.[18]

Yet once more, then, Wellington had to hurry north where a large concentration of French forces under Masséna and Marmont seemed imminent; and this may well be what FitzRoy Somerset meant when he held that Wellington raised the siege of Badajoz because of 'movements of the French'. Recognizing the exposed position of his northern army, Wellington decided to withdraw into Portugal for another winter. On 25 September, however, Marmont caught the British rearguard on a plateau at El Bodon, six miles south of Ciudad Rodrigo, and only stubborn resistance prevented the French from breaking through to harass the main force behind. Lord FitzRoy was present at this battle.[19]

During the winter of 1811/12 Wellington's army was not destined to remain immobile behind the Portuguese frontier for long. In January it made an unexpected and successful advance on Ciudad Rodrigo, the fortress lying astride the northern road from Madrid to Portugal. An assault in the depths of winter took Marmont completely by surprise. On

7 January Wellington informed Lord Castlereagh that he intended to invest Ciudad Rodrigo; and the following day the siege began in earnest. Conditions prevented the French from reinforcing the garrison or effectively bringing up a relief force; and as the siege commenced Captain Kincaid noted 'a smartish frost with some snow on the ground'. For the defence of Ciudad Rodrigo the 2,000-strong garrison deployed 153 guns, had fortified three convents in the suburbs and built a strong redoubt on a hill outside the walls commanding the main approach road. By 16 January two of the defended convents had fallen as well as the isolated redoubt. Two days later Wellington examined two large breaches in the walls and decided to attack. Such was the surprise achieved that the leader of the 'Forlorn Hope' (Lieutenant J. Gurwood) received the sword of the Governor at his own dinner-table. The siege had lasted just twelve days.[20]

The success was marred by an orgy of looting and destruction which took time to control; and Wellington also had to undertake the melancholy task of writing to the next of kin of casualties. His brother referred to the acclaim that his victory had brought at home, which in turn led to an earldom. William Wellesley-Pole suggested that Lord Douro could be retained as the second title and that Arthur become Earl Wellington. Once the excitement and turmoil of the battle and its aftermath had quietened, FitzRoy Somerset resumed the day to day burden of administrative duties such as the countersigning of an authorization for payment of £584.15s.3d. to the Commissariat on 6 March following approval by the appropriate board.[21]

Wellington now turned his attention once more to Badajoz, standing on the left bank of the River Guadiana and commanding the southern approach road from Madrid to Portugal. He and his staff arrived on 9 March 1812 and seven days later the siege formally began. An enemy sally by 2,500 men on 19 March was repulsed in heavy rain, and the first major bombardment commenced on 25 March with 28 guns in six batteries; and that day capture of an important defence-work allowed more batteries to open fire closer to the walls. On 31 March 35 artillery pieces began 'with great effect' to create the necessary breaches. By 6 April three viable gaps had been made and Wellington issued orders for an assault on all three at 10 p.m. Captain John Kincaid of the 95th recorded: 'The scene that ensued furnished as respectable a representation of hell itself as fire and sword and human sacrifices could make it: for, in one instant, every engine of destruction was in full operation.' Persistence throughout that awful night was rewarded and by 10 a.m. on 7 April French prisoners of war were on their way to Elvas and the British forces were in undisputed possession of the fortress.[22]

FitzRoy Somerset could be well satisfied with his performance that night. As Military Secretary, he amended in his own hand Wellington's lengthy order to his commanders on 6 April, further to explain points that evidently had been queried, and emphasizing: 'The attack

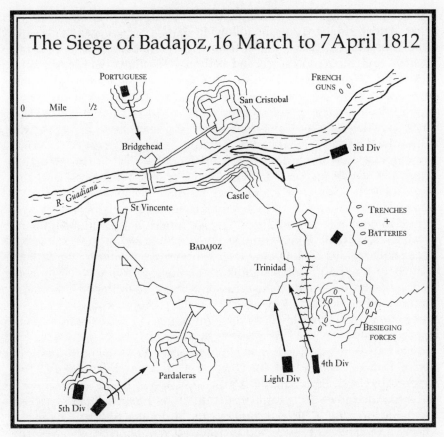

The Siege of Badajoz, 16 March to 7 April 1812

PORTUGUESE

FRENCH GUNS

San Cristobal

0   Mile   ½

Bridgehead

3rd Div

R. Guadiana

St Vincente

Castle

TRENCHES
+
BATTERIES

BADAJOZ

Trinidad

BESIEGING
FORCES

Pardaleras

Light Div

4th Div

5th Div

must not commence before 10 o'clock.' Once that attack had started he did not remain aloof. In fact the assaults on the three main breaches were initially driven back and not renewed until dawn, after Generals Picton and Walker had gained entry to the town by escalade at two other less likely points. During the darkness of the early morning, before the second attempt was made, FitzRoy Somerset 'became anxious to ascertain the real position of affairs ... [and] proceeded on foot without any specific orders from Lord Wellington towards the previous point of attack of the Lt and 4thDivisions', passing down the British trenches and over the counterscarp into the ditch in front of the wall. He was accompanied by only one other person. Unchallenged in the darkness and confusion he passed through the breach and across a plank which had been laid over a trench beyond and inside the wall. So he entered the town itself. Lord FitzRoy had been 'attracted by hearing French spoken in fluent abundance around him', and he perceived that the trench 'was filled with the enemy' in whose midst he had unwittingly arrived. He was 'in no way molested however but the conversational powers of the French among themselves seemed to have increased in proportion as their belligerent propensities had diminished'. Entering the town, which he knew well from the period when it had previously been in Allied hands, he discovered an officer (Captain Cameron) with a party of the Light Division also at large. Lord FitzRoy and Cameron's party then set out for the Governor's House 'where they found the females belonging to it in the greatest possible state of alarm and anxiety'. They insisted that General Phillipon had quit his quarters at 8 p.m. the previous evening (6 April) and had not been seen since. Leaving some of Cameron's men 'as a Safe Guard to protect the house and its lady inhabitants', FitzRoy Somerset walked on alone through the town and, astonishingly, met another lone British prowler – one of Beresford's staff officers, Lieutenant-Colonel William Warre – and learnt that the Governor had in fact taken refuge in San Cristobal, a detached fort beyond the River Guadiana. Lord FitzRoy and Warre agreed to go there, crossed the bridge over the river and climbed the hill towards General Phillipon's refuge where about 400 of the garrison of Badajoz had joined him. During their extraordinary progress through an enemy town at night in the middle of a battle, the two men (seemingly completely unsupported) came across a Portuguese drummer boy whom FitzRoy Somerset ordered to accompany them. Approaching the fort, in effect outside the main town, as daylight began to break, the three were understandably mistaken for French by some of Picton's men from the 3rd Division who had overrun an old Moorish castle at the north-east corner of Badajoz overlooking the town itself and the approaches to San Cristobal beyond. Fortunately the range was too great for accuracy; and the disparate three strolled unharmed uphill to the fort. Utterly exposed to enemy fire, 'Lord FitzRoy ordered the drummer to beat a parley – which with chattering teeth and in fear and trembling he obeyed.' The bluff worked and a French officer appeared under a flag of truce. No doubt the defenders reasoned that the bold trio constituted an embassy from the victorious British Army which now controlled Badajoz. Cut off as they were they could not know the true picture. FitzRoy Somerset 'at once suggested ... the convenience and propensity of an *immediate* surrender'. The Frenchman hesitated, wishing to contact the garrison's superior headquarters (that of Marshal Soult). Warre 'listened more favourably', but Lord FitzRoy insisted that 'nothing short of *unconditional* and *immediate* surrender ought to be listened to or would be sanctioned by his Great Chief'. After more brief exchanges and consultation by the French officer with the Governor, Phillipon surrendered, whereupon 'the chattering Portuguese drummer boy seized the goods and chattels of the French tambour as his rightful spoils of war ... Lord FitzRoy then invited Phillipon to accompany him to Ld Wellington which he did and the night's portentious struggle' was over. Phillipon and Wellington breakfasted together on 7 April. 'Thus Lord FitzRoy Somerset received the surrender of the Governor of Badajoz as Gurwood had previously taken the same functionary at Ciudad Rodrigo.' The facts of FitzRoy Somerset's actions at

Badajoz outshine the inaccurate but delightful embellishment that adorns later accounts which hold that he had passed through the smoking breach and galloped up to the drawbridge of San Cristobal to demand its surrender. Contemporary accounts are unclear as to whether FitzRoy Somerset or Warre received Phillipon's sword. It is more likely that it went to Warre, the senior officer, as the editor of Warre's letters claims.[23]

Of the fall of Badajoz, Wellington wrote to his brother William: 'I think that upon the whole it was the handsomest affair that I have yet been ... engaged in.' For FitzRoy Somerset it was, most certainly, one in which he displayed courage, initiative and sheer gall. Wellington recognized his achievement. He explained to the Military Secretary at the Horse Guards in London that he would have liked to send to England with the dispatches FitzRoy Somerset 'for whom I am very anxious to obtain the rank of Lieut Colonel [sic]; but it would really be so inconvenient to me, and to the public service, to be without him that I prefer to trespass upon His Royal Highness's [the Duke of York, CinC at the Horse Guards] kindness, and to ask him as a favour to promote him'. Although still a captain in the 43rd – now designated 'Light Infantry' – on 27 April 1812 FitzRoy Somerset, not yet 24 years old, duly became a brevet lieutenant-colonel.[24]

Staff officers with Wellington in the Peninsula certainly had to be good horsemen and fit. No sooner had Badajoz fallen than events 170 miles to the north once more claimed the CinC's urgent attention. He determined to take the offensive there to deal with Marmont's threatening force of some 40,000 men. So Wellington established his headquarters at Salamanca in June, having ejected the last French defenders after a ten-day resistance. Marmont, meanwhile, had been joined by about 6,000 reinforcements and in mid-July recrossed the River Douro to advance on Wellington. Several days of manoeuvring north-east of Salamanca now took place with Marmont seeking to cut Wellington's communications with Ciudad Rodrigo. On 18 July only swift action by the British cavalry saved Wellington and his staff from capture. Three days later the British took up a three-mile defensive position on reverse slopes outside Salamanca which Marmont fatally tried to carry by enveloping the British right. Over-extended, the French were open to successful counter-attack and by evening were in disarray and flight. During the battle Wellington rode constantly between his formations and on one occasion was struck by a stray bullet. For the most part he was accompanied by FitzRoy Somerset who went with him in the late evening to the ford of Huerta to witness the enemy's disorganized retreat. During the night many of the French did escape across the River Tormes, but the field belonged undoubtedly to Wellington who claimed some 15,000 French casualties and 7,000 prisoners – almost a third of Marmont's force, the French commander himself being mortally wounded – and eleven guns. To underline its pleasure Parliament voted Wellington £100,000 to purchase an estate, and the Crown created him a marquis.[25]

Apart from taking his young Military Secretary with him during the battle, Wellington showed extraordinary confidence in FitzRoy Somerset that day. Having made his preparations, and with Marmont's forces still advancing though out of range, Wellington said: 'Watch the French, FitzRoy. I am going to take a rest. When they reach yonder copse near that gap in the hills, wake me.' Whereupon he wrapped himself in his cloak and fell asleep. During the course of the battle Wellington reputedly rebuked FitzRoy Somerset for 'over-temerity' in exposing himself unnecessarily to danger. To the Secretary of State for War and the Colonies in London, Earl Bathurst, he especially praised Lord FitzRoy's performance at Salamanca; and his Military Secretary was with him when the triumphant British Army went on to take Valladolid on 29 July.[26]

With both the northern and southern approaches to Portugal now secure, Wellington pushed on to Madrid which he entered unopposed on 12 August 1812 to the acclaim of its inhabitants. Wellington formally received the keys of the city, but he was not destined to stay there long. The following month he moved 130 miles due north to the area of Burgos, to confront the French who had been rallied by Clausel after Marmont's death at Salamanca. Leaving Madrid on 31 August, he re-crossed the River Douro a week later to reach Burgos on 19 September. That night he attempted to storm the castle, but was beaten back although an outwork did fall. Failure to bring up sufficient heavy artillery yet again proved decisive. During the following month repeated efforts to take Burgos Castle, defended by some 2,000 determined Frenchmen, failed with heavy casualties incurred and the destruction of two of Wellington's three 18pdr guns. On 4 October a minor breach was made in the outer wall which British troops were unable to exploit; and seventeen days later Wellington abandoned the siege. His troops had suffered 2,064 casualties, the garrison a mere 623. As one soldier noted: 'To begin the siege of Burgos without shot and without a battering-ram ... you might as well have sent the boys of the grammar school to take the Castle of Edinburgh with pop-guns ...' There is some evidence that advice from the engineers was unsound and that their equipment was defective. Although present, FitzRoy Somerset had no direct responsibility for the débâcle, but the reasons for failure could not have eluded him.[27]

He shared the discomfort of the besiegers and their subsequent retreat to Salamanca, Wellington's old headquarters, where he was joined by the remaining troops from Madrid. But the French seemed set to cut them off from Portugal so once more Wellington fell back on Ciudad Rodrigo. With the men short of rations and a combination of fog and rain hampering progress, part of the force decided to try an alternative route against Wellington's orders and found their way blocked by an impassable stream. Questioned about Wellington's reaction to such insubordination, Fitzroy Somerset replied: 'Oh, by God, it was far too serious to say anything.' By 12 November Wellington's army had taken up winter quarters in the area of Ciudad Rodrigo close to the Spanish-Portuguese frontier. Wellington settled his headquarters at Petueja where 150 staff officers were billetted in 30 houses: only Wellington and the Prince of Orange had single rooms. But by the end of November he had moved to Frenada with the staff dispersed in nearby villages, which did not impress his Deputy Judge Advocate who, in the biting easterly winds and driving snow, 'found Lord Wellington's secretaries sitting with candles at twelve o'clock in the day, and burning charcoal fires'. [28]

Before Christmas, Wellington and FitzRoy Somerset together with a single dragoon orderly left Frenada for Cadiz. Travelling without baggage and with good horses, they managed 30-50 miles a day. Noting that they had left the winter quarters, Major Napier of the 43rd exclaimed that FitzRoy Somerset was 'as good as he [Wellington] is and nearly as clever as Lord Wellington himself; he will one day be a great man, if he lives'. Wellington's reason for such a lengthy journey was to give advice to the Spanish regency and cortes who were concerned about French intentions in the south. He and FitzRoy Somerset were greeted with pomp and ceremony which possibly explains why Lord FitzRoy pronounced himself 'much pleased' with the city. Indeed, this pleasure may at least partly have been induced by the flattering reception given to him and Wellington by the señoras and senoritas 'glancing from the chief to his secretary Lord FitzRoy Somerset (whose fine and ruddy countenance glowing with health and delight smiled on all around)'. They cried *'Mirar el Rubio '* ('look at the ruddy man') ... *'Hay que buenmoso muchado'* ('what a handsome youth') ... *'Que ojos picaron'* ('what roguish eyes'). Spanish women were, the observer continued, 'above the affectation of repressing their sentiments of pleasure or dislike and Lord FitzRoy Somerset was destined to hear his manly beauties praised with all the ardour of Spanish female character'. [29]

Wellington and Lord FitzRoy made their way back via Lisbon to Frenada where life was not altogether drudgery. In addition to dinner-parties, formal balls were held. On 15 March such an occasion occurred at Ciudad Rodrigo, seventeen miles from headquarters. Wellington and many of his staff, including FitzRoy Somerset, rode over during the afternoon. In the early hours of the following morning, with the ball in full swing, only the Quartermaster-General was prepared to accompany Wellington back to his quarters. The rest stayed on to enjoy the festivities. Speculation soon arose as to when the army would advance. In mid-April Deputy Judge Advocate Larpent noted that FitzRoy Somerset had sent his horses 'nearly a hundred miles off for grass' and therefore concluded that Wellington would not move in the second week of May as rumour predicted. News of General Murray's victory over Suchet near Alicante reached Frenada on 30 April 1813 and, unable to contain himself, Wellington rushed into his Military Secretary's room, exclaiming: 'Murray has beat Suchet, FitzRoy!' At dinner in headquarters on 4 May, however, Lord

FitzRoy told Larpent that the Spanish had exaggerated the scale and importance of the affair near Alicante. He also sent Larpent a pamphlet about Napoleon's retreat from Moscow in 1812 which, 'though not exceeding the Russian gazettes in the number of French prisoners, added several rather incredible details, such as the French crawling into the fires like gnats into a candle, without being sensible of their danger etc ...'[30]

On 9 May Wellington, accompanied by his personal staff, including FitzRoy Somerset and the Prince of Orange, set out at 2 p.m. for the 80-minute ride of thirteen miles to the Conde de Penne Villemur at Huero on the River Agueda, where he was to review the Spanish cavalry. The ceremony commenced at 3.30 p.m. and, as on an English parade, Wellington and his entourage passed in front and rear of the parade which then rode past him: some 700 Spanish plus a squadron of irregulars. At 5 p.m. Wellington set off back at a gallop and everybody kept up for about a league. But unlike Wellington the others did not have fifteen horses and Lord FitzRoy was among those who eased off to return more slowly, reaching Frenada at 7.15. The very next day Wellington carried out another review in his dress uniform as Colonel of the Blues and a week later (17 May) inspected the British Light Division, on each occasion accompanied by Lord FitzRoy. An anniversary dinner to commemorate the Battle of Albuera was given at headquarters for Marshal Beresford on 16 May. Staged in a tent, which proved, in Larpent's words, 'very comfortable', the occasion 'went off famously'. Full medals were worn to provide a 'glittering array' by the assembly of high-ranking British and Portuguese officers, their staffs, Wellington's personal staff and his heads of department. The following warm, sunny morning Wellington reviewed some 6,000 Allied troops near Espeja. Then, on 18 May, he and his staff rode six leagues in another direction to Friexada; and that day the army began at last to stir.[31]

Determined not to repeat the error of an inadequate siege train, Wellington now moved purposefully forward. Initially dividing his forces to mislead the enemy, and moving swiftly across country between the two separate wings further to cause confusion, he at length concentrated 80,000 men on the Douro early in June 1813. Moving his supply base to Santander on the Bay of Biscay and thus shortening his lines of communication, he determined to cut off the retreating French columns which had blown up the fortifications of Burgos before evacuating the area. The Allied advance was not without incident. At Zamora on 3 June Wellington and his personal staff were entertained by the inhabitants 'with a concert, lemonade, and ices, etc'. Wellington did not enjoy 'the time lost in singing praises to him', but as a mark of gratitude he gave a dance in the evening. One staff officer noted that 'the country was flat and rich in corn, meadows, etc., nearly all the way, but low and boggy and a hard march for men and baggage, etc.'. Accommodation en route was not always ideal, the temporary headquarters at Massa on 14 June being 'miserable'.

As Wellington and Beresford strolled along the main street there, FitzRoy Somerset sat against a wall, writing on his knees, while his four servants pitched his tent. Later several officers had to sit on the ground in a field to eat their food, as in Larpent's words 'the Prince (of Orange) and Lord FitzRoy, like two boys, were playing together'.[32]

Six miles west of Vitoria – a small twin-spired town in the foothills of the Pyrenees – King Joseph had deployed 50,000 French troops on undulating, wooded ground behind the River Zadorra and astride the road to Bayonne, facing south-west. But Wellington sent Lieutenant-General Sir Rowland Hill to capture the Puebla Heights on the enemy's left, as more troops crossed the river to attack the centre and others on the enemy right almost achieved a double-envelopment. As was his custom, with FitzRoy Somerset in attendance, Wellington carried out a reconnaissance on 20 June before launching these attacks the following day. Wellington and Lord FitzRoy were seen repeatedly riding across the battlefield on 21 June, coming up at the head of the Light and 4th Divisions just as Hill broke through the gorge of Puebla to take the Puebla Heights. Informed by a Spanish peasant of an enemy weak spot, Wellington and his Military Secretary then galloped off to bring up Kempt's brigade decisively in the centre. But, as Wellington later made clear to the Secretary of State for War and the Colonies, divisional and brigade commanders generally used their own initiative within his overall plan. The enemy was utterly routed: 151 guns were captured and 2,000 prisoners taken. Failure of the British cavalry hotly to pursue the retiring enemy led to later prolonged battles and sieges in the mountains, at least some of which might have been avoided. So panic-stricken were the French that King Joseph left behind a vast quantity of personal belongings, including valuable booty, and many ladies' carriages laden with baggage were also abandoned. Clearly Joseph had not anticipated defeat. Spectators watched from hills to the rear. The scene would be repeated at the River Alma in September 1854. The foe then would be Russian; the British commander Lord Raglan.

FitzRoy Somerset was commended for his 'activity and daring ... throughout the battle', and Wellington declared himself 'much indebted' to Lord FitzRoy on the day. It became evident, too, that Wellington had become exhausted by his activities – including such widespread travel and battlefield action – and that his personal staff to some extent protected him from undue labour during the pursuit of the French into the Pyrenees after Vitoria. His success in that battle did, however, bring him a field marshal's baton. There was an interesting postscript in London. To celebrate Wellington's success the Prince Regent arranged a vast fete and dinner at Vauxhall Gardens which was attended by some 10,000 guests. Unfortunately the organization proved less than perfect, and Henry Torrens complained to Lord FitzRoy: 'I am half-ruined by the expense, exclusive of having my carriage broken to pieces in the scramble.'[33]

Failure quickly to follow up success at Vitoria allowed the enemy to regroup. Nevertheless Wellington's forces soon invested Pamplona and also laid siege to the fortress of San Sebastian on the coast 40 miles to the north-west. Inability to storm San Sebastian successfully on 25 July led Wellington to opt for blockade until more ammunition and heavier guns arrived from England. Once this equipment came, following bombardment and breaching of the walls on 31 August, San Sebastian fell although some of the garrison held out in the castle for another nine days. As at Badajoz an orgy of looting and ill-discipline greeted the success.[34]

While San Sebastian and Pamplona were resisting, Wellington's forces were vulnerable to counter-attack, extended as they were between the two locations and needing also to screen the French frontier forward of the siege operations. When Wellington was at San Sebastian on 25 July, under Marshal Soult's overall direction, Generals d'Erlon and Clausel penetrated the Maya and Rçesvalles passes to converge on Pamplona. During the morning of 27 July Wellington and FitzRoy Somerset rode off north-west of Pamplona to survey the situation as news filtered through that British forces were giving ground. Wellington believed that the French advance between Pamplona and San Sebastian was designed to draw his troops away from both sieges. It failed because of decisive action by Wellington and swift riding by FitzRoy Somerset. Six miles from the British headquarters at Lesaca – swingeingly condemned by the staff as 'an unhealthy, smelly Pyrenean village ... swarming with fleas and flies' – at Sorauren CinC and Military Secretary very nearly came to grief. Shortly before 11 a.m. they reached the village to discover French forces deploying on the heights above to command the Lanz valley through which British troops were due to fall back on Pamplona. As Wellington explained to his brother, he arrived at Sorauren 'just in time to write the orders for the movement and collection of the Army, and to send them off before the enemy entered the village and closed the road. They were moving down to it from the mountain while I was writing the orders on the bridle with which Lord FitzRoy Somerset galloped off one way and I the other into the Camp. If I had been two mins [sic] later probably the position would not have been maintained; we should have lost the blockade of Pamplona and with it our siege of St Sebastian and other advantages.' Quite literally, therefore, as Wellington and his Military Secretary spurred away from the village at one end, the enemy entered at the other.[35]

While Wellington reached the safety of the heights and the protection of British troops there, FitzRoy Somerset made his lone way in heavy rain through nearby passes to warn the 6th and 7th Divisions. His action not only alerted the British troops to the impending danger, but led directly to redeployment of the reserve divisions and their success in the ensuing battles at Lizasso and Sorauren (28-30 July 1813), during which FitzRoy Somerset also distinguished himself at Wellington's side. Had

Pamplona been relieved at this time, 57 more cannon and 5,000 men would have been available to the enemy in the field.[36]

Stemming the French tide in the area of Sorauren, as Wellington predicated, not only ultimately allowed the siege of San Sebastian to be pressed, but that at Pamplona too. Key to control of the Pyrenees and entry to southern France, in the third week of June Wellington had laid plans to blockade Pamplona using 28 French 12pdr guns taken at Vitoria – underlining the practical reason for not wishing to lose artillery to an enemy in battle. The siege did not go according to plan and by mid-July Wellington was still not satisfied that it was close enough.[37] Even after the French threat of immediate relief had been removed at Sorauren, Welling-ton still could not break down the stubborn defenders. That is until he had a stroke of luck. He and FitzRoy Somerset were riding through a mountain pass in early autumn when they came upon a muleteer carrying a secret communication from the Governor of Pamplona to the French commander, Soult. The messenger mistook Wellington for Soult, pulled the scrap of paper from his mouth and gave it to him. It was in code. FitzRoy Somerset scanned the message, noted two or three vowels and quickly deciphered the whole. If unrelieved Pamplona would soon need to capitulate. With this intelligence Wellington could press the siege with confidence, especially as Lord FitzRoy made a transcript of the message and ensured that it reached the Governor, who thus knew that it had fallen into the wrong hands. On 31 October Pamplona surrendered.[38]

Meanwhile Soult was aware that Wellington would try to pene-trate the northern Pyrenees once San Sebastian had fallen and reasoned that he would do so parallel to the coast. The French, therefore, deployed in strength around the dominating Mount Rhune near the town of Vera, believing that the tidal flats of the River Bidassoa would protect their right flank. So Wellington would have to advance further inland. In fact, learning from local shrimpers that the flats were passable at low tide, he crossed the Bidassoa to outflank Soult's main position on 7 October. The French commander withdrew with little loss and reformed south of the River Nivelle, strengthening his position with a series of fortifications. Wellington felt, nevertheless, that Soult's sixteen-mile front must be thinly spread in places. So, in deep snow, on 10 November the two flanks of the Allied forces probed the enemy line to suggest double-envelopment, then Beresford decisively attacked the centre. By early afternoon the enemy line had broken, but dusk fell before Wellington could fully exploit his advantage. Although Soult lost 4,351 men and 51 guns on the Nivelle, he was able to slip away in darkness to regroup between the sea and the River Nive. To the Secretary of State for War and the Colonies, Wellington wrote: 'I received the greatest assistance in forming the plan for this attack, and throughout the operations ... from Lieutenant-Colonels Lord FitzRoy Somerset and Campbell.' The Military Secretary himself sent details of the battle to Wellington's brother Henry, the British Ambassador in Cadiz. On Sunday 29 November 1813, his headquarters now established at St Jean de Luz, Wellington and his staff attended a drum-head church service on the sands by the sea. 'It was rather cold work,' complained Deputy Judge Advocate Larpent.[39]

The momentum of Wellington's advance had slowed, partly because the two wings of his army (coming from San Sebastian and Pamplona) had to be co-ordinated for a thrust on Bayonne, partly because of fears that Spanish indiscipline might undermine his efforts in France. So, although for a month no serious fighting was taking place, the work of the Military Secretary did not slacken. Larpent noted that FitzRoy Somerset 'certainly deserves promotion ... [he] gets through a great amount of business with little assistance, and always quite in public, almost [sic] in a common coffee or lounging room, in the midst of talking, noise, joking and confusion'. At length, early in December, the army began to close on Bayonne south of which the enemy were entrenched. Initially the French attacked those troops under Sir John Hope, moving parallel to the coast, on 10 December. After making little headway Soult transferred his attention to Hill's smaller force on Wellington's right flank. On 13 December he attacked this between the Rivers Adour and Nive. At first the enemy made some progress, but after Wellington's arrival on the field Hill's men steadied, the 6th Division put in a telling counter-attack and the Battle of the Nive was won. The French still held Bayonne which would be invested by Hope as Hill and Wellington drove north-eastwards deeper into France to menace Soult's lines of communication. That advance, however, lay in the future – in 1814. Meanwhile FitzRoy Somerset was again formally praised by Wellington for his performance on the battlefield of the Nive; and until fighting resumed, Wellington and his staff enjoyed as full a social life as possible under the rigorous circumstances of a campaign. On 27 December 1813 they went hunting with hounds.[40]

In the New Year 'a certain communication' was opened with Bayonne: 'French watches, rings, trinkets and silk dresses' were traded in the British camp. 'We carry on war in a very civilized manner,' Larpent observed. The foxhounds were in action frequently, and Wellington and his personal staff used to promenade by the sea almost daily in late afternoon. Larpent enigmatically referred to 'the exertion of walking to which we men of business are accustomed to take at a true twopenny postman's trot'. FitzRoy Somerset's energy and sense of fun remained noticeable. During a memorable dinner at headquarters he asked for the Prince of Orange by his nickname 'slender Billy', and received the reply from further down the table that the Prince was indeed present and would be pleased to take a glass of wine with him. Their personal friendship established in the Peninsula would continue until the Prince's death years later.[41]

In mid-February 1814 as Hope passed west of Bayonne via the mouth of the Adour to invest the French stronghold unexpectedly from the north, Hill forced his way across the river's tributaries to skirt Bayonne to the east. Recognizing the danger of this manoeuvre to his lines of communication, Soult concentrated a strong force at Orthez, 35 miles east of Bayonne. The main French force occupied a dominating ridge north-west of Orthez, with other troops deployed to cover the approaches to the town itself. Wellington's initial assault on the main position early on the morning of 27 February failed to make progress, but towards midday he ordered another which was aided by Hill's attack on the enemy left. This combined assault carried the day. The country proved unsuitable for vigorous cavalry pursuit and, although beaten, many of Soult's troops managed to escape and regroup twenty miles farther back. The battle though short had been fierce – 'a desperate stand', according to Larpent. At Wellington's side throughout the day, FitzRoy Somerset yet again received Wellington's approbation in his post-battle dispatch.[42]

After the encounter at Orthez, Soult retired to Toulouse, almost 100 miles farther east, a strategic road centre and the main enemy arsenal in southern France. To reach Toulouse Wellington had to make a deep southern detour to skirt impassable mountain regions, adding another fifty miles to the march. En route his staff were immersed in the day-to-day round of planning and administration, relieved by such events as the commemorative dinner at the temporary headquarters at Grenade in honour of the fall of Badajoz where Lord FitzRoy had so distinguished himself. During his march Wellington had been reinforced by British and Portuguese cavalry, but closing on Toulouse independently from the north 18,000 men under Beresford became temporarily isolated after crossing the swollen River Garonne. Fortunately they were not attacked. Soult was preoccupied with organizing the defence of Toulouse, which was effectively protected by the Garonne and a canal on three sides with Mount Rave – ideal for artillery domination of the area – on the fourth. Strengthening existing fortifications, Soult constructed an elaborate system of inter-connected trenches and redoubts on Mount Rave, which was thus the key to the city.

At 5 a.m. on 10 April Wellington launched his assault. Probes by Picton from the north-west and Hill from the south-west deflected attention away from the principal attack on Mount Rave. A prolonged and bloody struggle took place there, with French counter-attacks in column against the Allied deployment in line decisively repulsed. When darkness closed in Soult abandoned the high ground, as Hill drove into the southern suburbs of Toulouse despite stubborn and costly resistance. Needing to replenish his supplies of ammunition, Wellington failed to renew the battle on 11 April, but that night Soult withdrew from the area. On 12 April 1814, therefore, Wellington triumphantly entered Toulouse with FitzRoy Somerset, who again earned praise, beside him. The last of 24 major or minor encounters fought by Wellington in the Peninsular War (at the vast majority of which Lord FitzRoy had been present) was over.

Tragically, it had been unnecessary. That same evening Wellington learnt of Napoleon's abdication on 4 April. Thus do the lives of men hang upon the speed of communications.[43]

On the evening of 12 April a huge celebratory dinner was held at the Prefecture. Wellington's health as *'Liberador del Espagna'* was proposed by General Alava, who would remain a friend of Lord FitzRoy's in after years, and toasts were drunk to Louis XVIII. Much cheering punctuated the proceedings, many English officers wore white cockades, the new French Constitution was read out and the culmination of events was the inevitable ball. These celebrations helped at least for a time to override memories of the fierce struggle just past and unpleasant duties in its aftermath. Major Coghlan had been wounded and captured at Talavera, but subsequently escaped to rejoin Wellington, only to be killed on 10 April at Toulouse. His body was then temporarily buried, but exhumed two days later and reinterred in the Protestant cemetery. Lord FitzRoy was among those to pay 'the last tribute of respect to his remains'. This was only one of many melancholy burials.[44]

Soult's formal surrender on 17 April was greeted by a *Te Deum* in Toulouse and, to Larpent, 'a most strange, noisy, military and religious ceremony attended with all the drums and military band'. On 30 April Wellington and FitzRoy Somerset set out for Paris where they arrived on 4 May just in time for the Allied victory parade and for Lord FitzRoy to meet his future wife. On 10 May, the day that he was created a duke, Wellington announced his intention of returning to Toulouse 'in order to carry into execution the convention with the French and the order of the Government for the expedition', before travelling on to Madrid. His instructions from Castlereagh were to 'prevail upon all parties [there] to be moderate, and to adopt a constitution more likely to be practible [*sic*] and to contribute to the peace and happiness of the [Spanish] nation.' He 'hoped to be able to do much good by this journey' and did not therefore expect to reach England until the end of June. Five days later he wrote to his brother Henry from Toulouse for post horses to be ready at specific points en route. He anticipated getting to his old headquarters at St Jean de Luz on 18 or 19 May and, going via Vitoria and Burgos, to reach Madrid on 23 May. 'God send that I may be in time to prevent mischief,' he added. The Spanish General Alava, FitzRoy Somerset and Lord FitzRoy's future father-in-law went with him.[45]

Wellington found that the whole of Spain, except Cadiz, had declared for Ferdinand VII who was now firmly on the throne. The duke did influence part of the army to support Ferdinand and he went some way to improving relations between the King and the Cortes. Although he had thus been instrumental in ensuring peace within Spain, Wellington remained uneasy that Ferdinand had evidently set aside the draft liberal constitution – something that would lead to further political unrest in the country and a separate mission by FitzRoy Somerset nine years later.

Wellington and Lord FitzRoy reached Bordeaux on 10 June, then travelled on to Paris and eventually London where they arrived on 23 June. Soon afterwards Wellington went to Portsmouth whence he had sailed in 1809 – where the Prince Regent, Emperor of Russia and King of Prussia were reviewing the fleet, though not apparently with Lord FitzRoy. Later, though, they would both attend the national thanksgiving service at St Paul's. Professionally, on 25 July 1814, Lord FitzRoy transferred from the 43rd Light Infantry to become captain and lieutenant-colonel in the First Foot Guards. His military apprenticeship had been successfully completed.[46]

Successive editions of *The Army List* recorded, somewhat inadequately, that FitzRoy Somerset was present at the Battles of Fuentes d'Onor (*sic*), first siege of Badajoz, 'the brilliant affair' of El Bodon, the siege and capture of Ciudad Rodrigo and Badajoz, the Battle of Salamanca, capture of Madrid and Retiro, the 'driving' of the enemy from Valladolid to Burgos and the siege of Burgos Castle. He also took part in 'various affairs on the retreat from Burgos to the frontiers of Portugal', the subsequent advance in 1813, battles of Vitoria and the Pyrenees, the action of Irun, passages of the Bidassoa, Nivelle and Nive. Then came the advance in 1814, Battle of Orthez and Toulouse 'and every other affair which took place'. For all of this he was awarded the Peninsula gold cross with five clasps (Fuentes d'Onoro [sic], Badajoz, Vitoria, Salamanca, Pyrenees, Nivelle, Nive, Orthez and Toulouse) and Peninsula silver war medal, also with five clasps (Roliça, Vimiero, Talavera, Busaco and Ciudad Rodrigo). He was a 25-year-old who had not even seen action six years previously.[47]

CHAPTER 3

DIPLOMACY AND WARFARE
(1814-15)

'You are aware how useful he has always been to me.' (Duke of Wellington)[1]

Neither Wellington nor FitzRoy Somerset would stay long in England after their return from the Peninsula. On 5 July 1814 the Duke was appointed British Ambassador to France. Travelling via the Low Countries, he toured the fortifications on and near the French frontier under the guidance of his former ADC, the Prince of Orange, Crown Prince of the new Kingdom of The Netherlands. Eventually, on 22 August, he reached Paris and two days later presented his diplomatic credentials to Louis XVIII.[2]

Within days of his arrival Wellington re-crossed the Channel to attend FitzRoy Somerset's wedding. Lord FitzRoy had been appointed the Duke's Secretary of Embassy, a post for which he was well-suited being fluent in written and spoken French. During the evening of 6 August 1814, at her father's house (3 Savile Row, London), FitzRoy Somerset married by special licence Emily Harriet, 21-year-old second daughter of William Wellesley-Pole – Wellington's elder brother, destined to become the third Earl Mornington.[3]

The bride's charm and vivacity were widely acknowledged, though malicious tongues hinted at a more flirtatious temperament. Certainly her early portraits suggest a sense of fun and physical attraction, qualities which FitzRoy Somerset was apt to remark in the opposite sex throughout his life. He did, in modern parlance, have an eye for a pretty woman. If rather highly strung, Emily was a celebrated contemporary beauty; she and her sisters Priscilla and Mary being dubbed 'the three graces'.[4]

Lord FitzRoy had met his future wife when she accompanied her parents to Paris in the spring of 1814 to see Priscilla, Lady Burghersh, following the defeat of Napoleon. FitzRoy Somerset went with Wellington to Paris after the Battle of Toulouse and 'for the first time' saw Emily while dining in the Duke's company with the Wellesley-Poles. Within a few days 'he had formed that attachment to her which glowed in his heart till the last moment of his life, and which I am firmly convinced never waned for one moment,' Priscilla later wrote. She recounted how her father travelled with Wellington and Lord FitzRoy to Madrid after their short stay in the French capital, and he was 'much struck during the journey with the merits of the young ADC'. She was evidently ignorant of her father's earlier praise of him to Wellington after Talavera and may have been unaware that Lord FitzRoy could have seen Emily, however fleetingly, at that time. An earlier acquaintance cannot therefore be entirely ruled out. None the less, soon after returning to England FitzRoy Somerset asked for Emily's hand. The match was not financially attractive, for his father had left an annuity of just £600 to Lord FitzRoy, payable moreover only during the son's lifetime. 'Very much admired and courted', Emily might have done better. Priscilla recorded her father's positive reaction: 'I had rather see my daughter married to him, than to the richest Duke in the kingdom, so admirable do I think his conduct and disposition. Besides which, with his talents and industry, and high character, he is quite sure to become a most distinguished man.' She added: 'My father's affection and respect for him were as constant as his own affections. To the day of his death my father consulted him on everything, and he left him his executor.' Moreover, Priscilla claimed, 'those who had doubted very soon came to the opinion we all agreed on, that she [Emily] was the most fortunate of women in her marriage'.[5]

By late November the newly-weds had settled into a house close to the Barrière de Clichy in the Montmartre district of northern Paris, where they played a full part in the diplomatic and social activity of the Embassy.[6] Lord FitzRoy, though, did not relinquish his military career, remaining captain and lieutenant-colonel in the Grenadier Guards. In Paris he quickly became officially involved in a delicate matter with the French authorities. A British subject complained to Wellington that papers in his possession had been seized at Villejuif by order of the Minister of Police, although he was travelling to Italy on a British passport. Wellington believed, however, that the papers included letters from 'discontented and disaffected persons at Paris to others of the same description in Italy'. Lord FitzRoy was required to investigate the affair. He met the Minister of Police and agreed with him that the seal on the packet of papers and letters taken at Villejuif had not been broken. A settlement was then worked out whereby the Minister returned to the man 'all his own papers and all sealed letters directed to Englishmen', but kept other correspondence. On FitzRoy Somerset's advice Wellington rejected the claim that any seals had been previously tampered with and argued that, on the contrary, the plaintiff had contravened the law. The sealed letters ought to have been sent via the post office. Thus Lord FitzRoy assuaged French sensitivity.[7]

More serious security problems, meanwhile, had already begun to affect the Embassy, as anti-Bourbon feeling gave rise to open demonstrations and threats against Wellington's life because his victories had helped to put Louis XVIII on the throne: towards the end of October shots were fired at him during a military review. Early in November, Wellesley-Pole referred to Cabinet concern for his brother's safety: its members were 'not justified' in delaying the Duke's withdrawal from the French capital and Wellesley-Pole confessed to 'uneasiness in his mind' until Wellington had left France. Wellington declined command of the expeditionary force to the United States, and towards the end of December he learnt from Castlereagh that he was to replace him as British representative to the Congress of Vienna.[8]

On 3 January 1815 Lord FitzRoy discovered from the Duke of York that 'in consideration of your Lordship's eminent Services' the Prince Regent had conferred upon him 'the distinction of Knight Commander of the Most Honourable Military Order of The Bath ... But your Lordship is not to wear the Insignia of the Order until you shall be authorized by further and sufficient authority so to do and, when you shall receive the Insignia, you will return to me [as Commander-in-Chief] the Medals, or other Badges, heretofore conferred upon you, which are to be considered as superseded by The Decoration of the Bath.' Six days later Wellington wrote to the Under-Secretary of State at the Foreign Office: 'Lord FitzRoy Somerset ought ... to have a credential to enable him to act here' (Paris) in the Duke's absence; and Lord FitzRoy's authorization as 'Minister Plenipotentiary' in Wellington's stead was signed by the Prince Regent on 18 January. After visiting London to confer with the Government, Wellington left Paris at daybreak on 24 January 1815. By then FitzRoy Somerset had assumed responsibility for his ambassadorial duties, though his formal assumption of the powers was not without incident. After Wellington had gone he discovered that the Duke had taken with him the key to the 'office box' which contained the Prince Regent's authority for him to hold office. Sending a messenger after Wellington would have caused embarrassing delay, so Lord FitzRoy personally broke open the box, informing the Foreign Office how and why he had done so. He subsequently reported to Lord Castlereagh – now Foreign Secretary in London – that on 7 February he had presented his credentials to Louis XVIII who 'expressed in animated terms his firm reliance on the friendship and attachment of HRH [sic] the Prince Regent' and his desire to strengthen the bond 'which at this moment so happily exists between the two nations'.[9]

Almost immediately the new Minister Plenipotentiary had to deal with a delicate situation. Castlereagh informed him that the Princess of Wales, estranged wife of the Prince Regent, intended to be in Paris during March on her way back to England. Lord FitzRoy must not receive her nor 'be instrumental in causing Her Royal Highness to be received by the French Court'. However, Castlereagh continued: 'You will not consider yourself thereby precluded from contributing by your endeavours to procure for Her Royal Highness all the necessary facilities for prosecuting her journey to England.' The Foreign Secretary observed that, due to the company that she had been keeping 'lately', the Emperor of Russia and the King of Prussia had both declined to see her in their countries and he hoped that the King of France would react likewise.[10]

Other difficult tasks soon fell to Lord FitzRoy. A dispute between the Admiralty Victualling Board and French Customs over seizure of live oxen, already paid for to supply a warship off La Rochelle; claims by the

French for goods seized at Genoa when the port surrendered to the British; and need to gain French approval for the appointment of a British vice-consul at Bayonne, all had to be negotiated. Lengthy and at times peremptory correspondence made Lord FitzRoy aware of the British Government's concern and that of Lloyd's at American privateers being allowed to tow British prizes into French ports: 'Your Lordship will not fail to avail yourself of the opportunity of making them [the prizes] a subject of representation to the French government and to require from them a satisfactory explanation of the facts'; which FitzRoy Somerset did promptly. Lord FitzRoy himself initiated action in support of British merchants who had been encouraged to supply goods to the Gironde on the written promise of lucrative indemnity, only to discover that an unpalatable administrative device had been employed to evade payment. He explained to Castlereagh: 'I think it my duty to protest in the strongest manner against the adoption of a measure not in accordance with the original agreement.' Early in February he asked the Foreign Secretary for guidance about the repatriation of British deserters discharged from the French army. Very quickly, therefore, he realized the scope of activity that would need his personal attention.[11]

One major duty was to keep the Government informed of developments likely to affect national security. Towards the end of January 1815 he alerted Castlereagh to the lukewarm attitude in France towards the restored Bourbon monarchy. Reporting the re-interment of the bodies of Louis XVI and Marie Antoinette in an elaborate state ceremony, he noted: 'The procession was not very numerously attended by the lower orders, nor was there I apprehend any very lively interest shewn in favour of the Royal Family.' Shortly afterwards he observed that commissioners appointed to ascertain 'the general disposition of the several provinces [of France] have returned and their report is by no means of a satisfactory nature': the people were not pleased with the measures adopted by deputies, and unrest could be detected. Farther afield he observed that in Italy Murat had used Neapolitan troops 'to intimidate the Pope' in a dispute, which awakened fears of renewed military action; and disturbances among the Swiss cantons might also be exploited by Napoleonic sympathizers.[12]

Dread of Napoleonic manoeuvring and latent sympathy within France proved well-founded. In the early hours of 7 March news reached Vienna that the former Emperor had escaped from Elba on 26 February. Prince Metternich divined correctly that he would make for Paris and began an intense round of negotiatons to ensure that an Allied army under Wellington would gather in The Netherlands to oppose him. In France news of Napoleon's movements at first remained unclear, not least, as Lord FitzRoy informed Castlereagh, because 'thick' weather prevented effective operation of the telegraph system. On 14 March, however, he wrote to Wellington, 'I see no reason why it should be at all expected that Napoleon should not succeed.' The French Minister, Fouché, similarly predicted that the Emperor would be restored after Napoleon landed near Fréjus on 1 March and quickly advanced to Grenoble. From Brussels the Prince of Orange, then commanding the Allied forces in The Netherlands, informed 'my dear FitzRoy' on 15 March that he was sending a special envoy to Paris. He asked his Peninsular friend to pass on to Dutch diplomats information about Napoleon's progress, which he obtained from the French authorities, so that a courier could then be sent back to Brussels. The Prince continued: 'I think it might be of moment to propose to the King whether he would like any co-operation on the part of our troops and of the Prussians under General Kleist, which I know to be willing to move in concert with me and which amount to about 50,000 men.' Pessimistically, he feared that most of the troops in the frontier fortresses were 'ill disposed' and liable to defect to Napoleon. His father, the King of The Netherlands, wished to replace the suspect garrisons with Allied troops and he wanted FitzRoy Somerset to discuss with the French government its reaction to this proposal, as well as the possible use of Prussian and Allied troops under the Prince of Orange in support of Louis XVIII. On these two matters he urged Lord FitzRoy to let him know 'without delay their [French] way of thinking'. In any case he was moving 'some of my troops towards the frontiers. This is more to satisfy the Belgians that I am not asleep than on any other account. They are very much allarmed [sic] but prove well affected'.[13]

FitzRoy Somerset meanwhile kept Castlereagh informed of Napoleon's progress as it became clearer. Noting news of the landing, the Foreign Secretary asked him to transmit to Louis XVIII the Prince Regent's 'deep and earnest interest ... in the effective suppression of this daring attempt to disturb His Majesty's Ligitimate [sic] Authority'. Other European powers would be invited to join Britain in opposing Napoleon. As the possibility of his restoration became ever more likely, Castlereagh wrote: 'Your duty is to follow the King, wherever he goes.' If Louis XVIII were to fall, however, Lord FitzRoy must return 'home', as 'you are accredited' only to him. Remaining in Paris with Napoleon was out of the question. Acknowledging the gravity of the situation, Castlereagh suggested that Charles Bagot and McKenzie of the Embassy staff be sent 'on leave of absence' forthwith, adding: 'Had you not better prevail on your wife to return to England?' The Foreign Secretary, with a hint of exasperation, acknowledged Lord FitzRoy's explanation that the French government was keen to deal with Napoleon without foreign aid. Castlereagh underlined strong support for the Bourbons and the gathering of foreign forces on the French frontier, but 'we consider the question of actual interference as one that requires the utmost delicacy and deliberation'.[14]

Independently Wellington expressed concern about Napoleon's activities, sending Lieutenant-Colonel Sir Henry Hardinge to France to report on his movements through 'His Majesty's Minister at Paris' to

Vienna; and the Duke did receive regular intelligence from FitzRoy Somerset. On 26 March he informed Castlereagh that Lord FitzRoy's letter of 17 March (received the previous day and enclosing copies of FitzRoy Somerset's dispatches to Castlereagh of 15 and 16 March) contained a letter from Hardinge at Basle which claimed (correctly as it transpired) that Marshal Ney had defected to Napoleon. Matching this allegation with other information received from Lord FitzRoy on 15, 16 and 17 March, the Duke dismissed as unreliable news of Ney's having changed sides. But Wellington soon learnt of the grave situation in France from Lord FitzRoy in letters of 18 and 19 March. Napoleon had reached Fontainebleau where he had indeed been joined by Ney and his troops; and Louis XVIII was about to quit Paris.[15]

Six days after FitzRoy Somerset warned Wellington that he would succeed, on 20 March Napoleon re-entered the French capital which the Bourbon Court had already vacated in haste at 1 o'clock that morning. Later, in rebutting criticism from the radical politician and Westminster contemporary J. Cam Hobhouse, Lord FitzRoy produced a 'statement of my conduct' during the preceding three weeks. Once news of Napoleon's landing reached Paris, 'it was the object of Lord FitzRoy Somerset to procure & transmit to his Government the best information he could obtain of Napoleon's movements, of the measures of the French Government to oppose him, & of the probable result of his landing & advance into the interior of France.' Accurate details about Napoleon's progress proved difficult to obtain. 'But he [Lord FitzRoy] can confidently state that he *was* prepared for the result': reference to his dispatches – not published and not therefore available to Hobhouse – would prove 'that his view of affairs was by no means an incorrect one'.

'Two or three days' after the first news reached Paris, 'the Members of the Corps Diplomatique' undertook to meet 'once or twice in each day'. At 'one of their *earliest* conferences' they determined to demand information from the French Minister for Foreign Affairs about the 'progress of Buonaparte & the intention of the King'. They also displayed a mixture of prudence and concern by requesting passports 'in order that they might be entitled to quit Paris if His Majesty should decide to leave his Capital'. A wise precaution. They knew their man. Louis XVIII was unlikely to face Napoleon. FitzRoy Somerset noted that the passports were supplied, which showed that the foreign ambassadors did not intend to remain in Paris after the King left. However, at 7 a.m. on 20 March, the day that Napoleon entered Paris, M. de la Valette directed that no member of the *corps diplomatique* should be provided with post horses. None of the corps could have left earlier because M. de Jaucourt's message that Louis proposed to leave at once did not reach them until later that morning, when he had already gone. FitzRoy Somerset immediately applied for post horses, planning to follow the King in accordance with his instructions; but he learnt that now he must apply to de la Valette. He duly made the necessary application, to be met with further bureaucratic obstruction. Writing to Castlereagh on 20 March he reported that 'the white flag has been removed from The Tuileries ... As soon as I can get horses I propose to follow His Majesty' to Lille, where Louis wished the *corps diplomatique* to join him. On a personal note, he thanked the Foreign Secretary for his concern 'about Lady FitzRoy, but she will not leave me'. Meanwhile de la Valette referred him to the Duc de Rovigo who 'declined to interfere'. The following day, 21 March, he wrote to the Duc d'Otranto requesting new passports (the Bourbon ones no longer being valid) for himself, his family and staff to join Louis XVIII. This move, in turn, failed; and he next wrote – in precisely the same terms – to the Duc de Vicenza. Hobhouse criticized these applications for passports to Napoleonic officials, but Lord FitzRoy pointed out that other members of the *corps diplomatique* followed a similar procedure and that they all eventually obtained new passports on 25 March.

In view of these facts FitzRoy Somerset utterly refuted Hobhouse's charges of his 'want of political presence of mind', the 'discredit' that he had brought upon the British nation by his actions as its representative, his participation in the 'panic which drives Man, Woman & Child to the Coast' and that he had undergone 'a terror ... [which] the Usurper's Armies had not inspired him with'.

Lord FitzRoy emphasized 'that he never felt either perplexed or confused, or that his mind was unequal to the responsibility of the situation which he was called upon to fill'. He was confident that 'the Gentlemen who acted under him, & the Members of the Corps Diplomatique' would support this view. He concluded his written defence: 'He [Lord FitzRoy]) really believes that Mr Hobhouse could never seriously intend to bring such accusations against him and trusts that he will lose no time in contradicting them.' His urbanity thus did not desert him even in the face of sharp personal attack. When compiling this document he did not mention that his first request for post horses during the morning of 20 March was specifically denied pending Napoleon's arrival; or that four days later, after considering his further submission on 23 March, Napoleon agreed that he should go to England via Dieppe.[16]

With his pregnant wife, Lord FitzRoy immediately left Paris, not for Dieppe but Calais which he reached 'about noon' on 28 March. He reported full details of his attempts to leave Paris to Castlereagh, adding that he remonstrated about being directed to Dieppe and received permission to travel instead to Calais. He fully intended to join Louis XVIII who was now at Ghent, not Lille, without returning to England. The remainder of the *corps diplomatique* had been given passports for 'Strasburgh'(*sic*). On the road from Paris to Calais Lord FitzRoy had noted soldiers with the red cockade and he had heard that 'large bodies of troops have been moved through Paris and have taken the roads leading to Belgium, and that Napoleon was expected to set out yesterday for that frontier'. Next day,

29 March, still at Calais he reiterated evident French determination to capture 'Belgium'. He estimated, however, that Napoleon would remain on the defensive 'till his army is in a better state of equipment', especially artillery. More broadly, he believed that only 'the lowest orders' had greeted Napoleon with enthusiasm, most other Frenchmen were suffering 'deepest consternation', with the inhabitants of Calais 'in despair'. 'Soon after daylight' on 30 March Lord and Lady FitzRoy reached Ostend by steamer and the following day joined Louis XVIII at Ghent. There he learnt that a more experienced diplomat, Sir Charles Stuart, was to be appointed Ambassador to the French Court in exile. On 1 April Sir Charles presented his credentials to the King and the following day Lord FitzRoy took his formal leave of him. He did not relinquish his post without commending the work of the Hon Major Percy and Mr Hervey to Castlereagh, before setting out for Brussels to rejoin Wellington as his Military Secretary.[17]

Wellington reached Brussels on 4 April shortly after Lord and Lady FitzRoy; and soon his Military Secretary was immersed in the burden of his many duties. On behalf of Wellington, he wrote to M. Caulincourt in Paris requesting permission for the Duke's belongings, which were still there, to be sent to England. On the Duke's behalf, too, he communicated with Hardinge, now British liaison officer with the Prussian commander, Marshal Blücher. In May he became involved in the compilation and dispatch of the many communications by which Wellington, in overall command of the Allied troops, deployed men to block Napoleon's possible routes into the Low Countries which the Emperor was confidently expected to attack. At a more mundane level he dealt with complaints by Commissary-General Dunmore of fraudulent claims by Dutch citizens in connection with supplies for the army, and he wrote to the Foreign Office in London about safe conduct for a vessel to convey his own baggage to England from Rouen. Meanwhile the further instructions concerning his KCB, promised on 3 January, had been issued by the CinC at the Horse Guards. In sending the 'ribbon and badge' which the Prince Regent wished FitzRoy Somerset to wear, the Duke of York informed him that he would not be invested with, or entitled to wear, the Ensign or Star until he became a major-general. On 14 May, however, recognition came that FitzRoy Somerset had now fully resumed his military career. Castlereagh noted that, with the appointment of Sir Charles Stuart as Ambassador to the King of France, Lord FitzRoy's position as Minister Plenipotentiary 'virtually ceased'. The Prince Regent acknowledged that his 'diplomatic duties' had 'temporarily' ended – an interesting hint that a civil career might later be resumed. Castlereagh assured him that the Prince Regent had expressed his 'satisfaction with the conduct which you have held in your Employment under my Department and in particular at the Zeal, Intelligence and Discretion which your Lordship manifested during the short but critical period in which you were engaged as His Majesty's Minister Plenipotentiary to the King of France'.[18]

During April, shortly after arriving in Brussels, FitzRoy Somerset encountered his old Westminster schoolfellow, J. Cam Hobhouse, who wrote to him from his hotel seeking a staff appointment for his brother Benjamin; and when he and Lord FitzRoy subsequently met by chance in the street, Wellington's Military Secretary promised to do what he could. Then, despite the near-certainty of hostilities with France, on 10 April Hobhouse called on Lord FitzRoy to announce his intention of travelling to Paris, ignoring warnings from Wellington and Lord FitzRoy. Three days later Hobhouse reached the French capital and there recorded details of interviews with Lady Kinnaird and Mrs Bailly Wallis during which allegations were made about Lord FitzRoy's conduct when Napoleon returned to Paris in March. Notwithstanding their acknowledged friendship and Lord FitzRoy's promise of assistance in Brussels, Hobhouse would subsequently publish these disparaging criticisms, leading to the strong reaction and threat of further action by FitzRoy Somerset.[19]

Meanwhile, personally and professionally, June 1815 would be distinctive for him as a letter on 6 June from Wellington to his brother, Wellesley-Pole, in effect presaged. An allied British, Hanoverian, Dutch, Brunswicker and Nassau army of some 80,000 men (including 13-14,000 cavalry) – FitzRoy Somerset later calculated that 75,975 were available at Waterloo and another 4,000 were lost at Quatre Bras or on 17 June – and 168 cannon was anticipated. Wellington also explained that 'Mrs Pole is very well & Emily is getting on.' For in Brussels at 9.30 a.m. on 16 May Lady FitzRoy had given birth to her first child, Charlotte Caroline Elizabeth. As mother and daughter nursed the infant, FitzRoy Somerset was with Wellington who early in June became acutely aware of French troop concentrations close to the border with The Netherlands. Broadly, the Prussians were deployed under their own commander, Blücher, to cover Ligny, with Wellington responsible for the road from Charleroi to Brussels and, separately, Mons. For Wellington was concerned lest Napoleon try to outflank his allied force to its right, parallel to the sea. As with Napoleon's progress towards Paris in March, reliable intelligence of enemy movements was hard to come by. On the evening of 12 June FitzRoy Somerset received information gleaned from a French traveller that about 100,000 infantry had already concentrated in the area of Maubeuge together with 'a very considerable corps of cavalry'. Napoleon's arrival at Avesnes, thought to be imminent, would be the signal for hostilities to commence. But Wellington did not believe (he was wrong as it turned out) that a French forward movement would occur soon.[20]

Nevertheless a clash could not be avoided indefinitely and, on learning that his brother-in-law (Charles Bagot) had been appointed Minister Plenipotentiary to the United States, Lord FitzRoy wrote: 'I think it desirable that you should not quit England till such events have occurred here, as may enable you on your arrival at the seat of Government to throw cold water upon any disposition on the part of the President (James Madison) to renew his connexion with Buonaparte.' FitzRoy Somerset felt that the Americans might oppose Britain again if Napoleon were victorious. He added a personal note, thanking Bagot for his 'cordial assistance', when Lord FitzRoy was in Paris.[21] Yet an immediate threat seemed so remote that he gave Sir Galbraith Lowry Cole (commander of the 5th Division) permission to get married in England on 15 June. And he dealt calmly with routine administration, finding time to recommend that a diplomat about to visit England be well looked after and introduced to the Foreign Secretary. Coincidentally, 15 June provided an example of how poor communications might affect military deployment. Major-General Dörnberg sent a message to FitzRoy Somerset from Mons at 9.30 a.m.: 'A man who was yesterday at Maubeuge says all the troops march towards Beaumont and Philippeville, and that no other troops but National Guards remain at Maubeuge. I just hear the Prussians were attacked.' The letter reached Lord FitzRoy at 9 p.m. By then other information had sharply deflated complacency. Napoleon was, indeed, on the move. Threats to Mons and the right flank had been deceptive. Marshal Grouchy was closing on the left and Ligny, Marshal Ney striking north in the centre from Charleroi.[22]

FitzRoy Somerset's account of events that day shows how Wellingon's appreciation of the military situation changed drastically. 'About five o'clock in the afternoon the Duke of Wellington while at dinner received from the Prince of Orange, who was up at Braine le Comte, a report sent to His Royal Highness from his advanced posts ... informing him that the French had attacked the Prussian advanced posts on the Sambre ... The Duke immediately directed the Quartermaster-General (Colonel Delancy [sic]) to send orders for the Troops to assemble at the Headquarters of their respective Divisions & to be in readiness to march at the shortest notice.' Specifically these orders applied to the British 5th Division under Sir Thomas Picton (vice Cole), Brunswickers under the Duke of Brunswick and the Nassau contingent – all in or close to Brussels. 'Lord FitzRoy Somerset, who was at his own quarters, being informed of this intelligence went directly to Head Quarters. He found the Duke in the Park giving the necessary orders to those around him. He wished everything to be in readiness to move on in an instant; but was waiting for further information before he made a decided movement with any part of his army, it being of the utmost consequence first to ascertain the point to which Buonaparte directed his operations.'

At 'about 10 o'clock' FitzRoy Somerset in conversation with Wellington remarked: 'No doubt we shall be able to manage these Fellows [the French].' The Duke replied that 'there was little doubt of it provided he did not make a false movement'; and he reinforced this opinion by ordering the Quartermaster-General to ensure that the troops did not march 'till further information was received'. That night the Duchess of Richmond held a ball in Brussels, as arranged, on Wellington's advice: cancellation would have suggested alarm. FitzRoy Somerset and 'every British officer of rank' attended, including Wellington. The Prince of Orange, having heard no more from his outposts, with everything quiet on his front and 'probably not considering the attack on the Prussian outposts of much importance' went too. Wellington, less than impressed, advised him to return to his men forthwith. The Earl of Uxbridge and 'a great many cavalry officers' at the ball went back to their quarters before midnight. FitzRoy Somerset recorded that 'further reports reached the Duke in the course of the evening' from Lieutenant-Colonel Sir Henry Hardinge with the Prussians, 'which determined the Duke to order British troops on the right' to march westwards. Another messenger, from the Dutch chief of staff (General Constant), arrived at about 1 a.m. with more news of events north of Charleroi. Ney had attacked the lone Allied brigade commanded by Prince Bernard of Saxe-Weimar near Quatre Bras, the prominent intersection of the Namur-Nivelles and Charleroi-Brussels roads 21 miles south of Brussels. Unaware of the true weakness of Saxe-Weimar's force – possibly concealed in thick cornfields – Ney had camped for the night south of the crossroads. Wellington recognized his opportunity, as the last dress uniform left the ball in the early hours of the morning. The army was about to move.[23]

At 4 a.m. the three brigades of Picton's 5th Division paraded in the Park and, shortly afterwards, began to march out of Brussels singing 'The Girl I Left Behind Me' and other popular ditties. Followed by Brunswickers and the Nassau contingent, they took the high road to Charleroi through the Forest of Soignes, where they halted 'for a short time between the Forest & village of Waterloo'. Meanwhile, at 'about 8 o'clock', Wellington and his staff followed them, reaching Quatre Bras two hours later. As he passed the resting troops Wellington ordered them to resume their advance, which they did between noon and 1 p.m. On his way to the crossroads Wellington learnt more details of the action on the previous evening. Saxe-Weimar's brigade, having been driven out of Frasne, fell back north of Quatre Bras and lost contact with the Prussians farther east. The French, however, then withdrew to the south of the crossroads to a more secure position for the night. Early on the morning of 16 June, reinforced and now under the Prince of Orange, the Allied troops regained Frasne and all the ground lost on 15 June. When Wellington arrived at Quatre Bras, therefore, he found Prince William in firm control and 'only a few of the enemy in front, who occasionally fired a shot & a little popping musketry, but nothing more serious was at that time threatened in that quarter'. So Wellington, his staff 'and a small escort of cavalry' left Quatre Bras between 11 a.m. and noon for Blücher's position on heights overlooking St Amand and Ligny, villages occupied by the Prussians.

Blücher and Wellington studied the French columns advancing towards them, and the Duke promised Blücher 'all the support in his power' during the coming struggle. Knowing that the British cavalry, the rest of the Prince of Orange's corps, the Guards and Count von Alten's division were due at Quatre Bras at about 2 p.m., he then galloped back westwards, arriving at the crossroads close to 2.30. Using his spyglass 'attentively' he saw Ney's men again converging on Frasne; and 'in a few moments' the French attacked the Prince of Orange. But Picton's division had by that time passed through Quatre Bras, deploying 'on the left of the high ground leading to Frasne and Charleroi', some 6-700 yards south of the crossroads. As French infantry and cavalry probes intensified at about 3 p.m., Wellington became concerned about the security of Bossu Wood on Picton's right. Prince William assured Wellington that it was held by Nassau troops, a fact confirmed to FitzRoy Somerset by the Prince's Quartermaster-General. 'To the surprise of everybody,' wrote Lord FitzRoy, '*French* troops were seen coming out of the wood & were at first taken for Belgians.' In fact, the Allied defenders had been driven to the right and rear unseen.

Now French cavalry appeared to scatter nearby Belgian mounted units who fled northwards. In so doing they created confusion and panic. Supply carts turned back and some of the Belgians rode on into Brussels to 'spread the alarm'. When the French cavalry charged the Belgians, Wellington and FitzRoy Somerset were 'in front' and were very nearly taken. Spurring rapidly back towards Quatre Bras, they leapt over a bank, ditch and the crouching figures of 92nd Highlanders. 'On a worse horse', FitzRoy Somerset observed, 'he [Wellington] might not have escaped'; nor would have Lord FitzRoy himself. FitzRoy Somerset saw the Duke of Brunswick fall under enemy artillery fire; and he was sent shortly afterwards by Wellington to tell the 5th Division's regimental commanders to keep their troops in hand; as they were pressing forward too eagerly and losing formation. Major-General Kempt agreed that the troops 'were certainly not in hand', but quickly brought them under control. At one point in the battle Sir Andrew Barnard of the 95th approached Wellington for orders. FitzRoy Somerset detached himself from the knot of officers around the Duke and said: 'Barnard, you are wanted instantly. Take your battalion and endeavour to get possession of that village', pointing to houses on the rising ground south-east of Quatre Bras. According to an attendant officer (Captain Kincaid) Lord FitzRoy added: 'But if you cannot do that, secure the wood on the left, and keep the road open for communication with the Prussians.'

The Guards reinforcements arrived from Nivelles later than expected at approximately 5 p.m. and were ordered to drive the enemy from Bossu Wood, where they were menacing Wellington's right flank. In doing so they lost some 500 men, a high figure which drew a gentle reproof from FitzRoy Somerset; '... not perhaps going about it as a Rifle or Light Corps would have done'. But the French were pushed back along the whole line. At dusk they occupied a ridge two miles away, with low ground separating them from another rise held by Picton. Meanwhile firing from the Prussian direction had ceased; and at 9 p.m. Wellington and his staff left Quatre Bras for Genappe, farther north on the road to Brussels, where supper had been arranged at the inn. As they rode towards the village Wellington believed that Blücher had repulsed the French, calling him 'a d...d fine old Fellow'. At approximately 10.30 Captain Hardinge rode into Genappe, looking for a surgeon to attend his brother, Sir Henry, the liaison officer with the Prussians, whose hand had been shot off. Hardinge told Wellington that he had left the field between 8 and 9 o'clock: Blücher had suffered badly, there was 'considerable confusion' and small parties of Prussian soldiers were undoubtedly withdrawing. Hardinge could give no coherent nor definitive account of the situation and Wellington treated his views with some caution 'thinking that a young officer agitated perhaps by his brother being wounded, might have considered things worse than they were'. So confident was he of French failure that at 10.30 FitzRoy Somerset wrote to Lady FitzRoy in Brussels, assuring her that 'the Prussians & we have repulsed the French'. Wellington went to bed in Genappe between 11 p.m. and midnight, though his staff continued to write and dispatch letters in accordance with his orders. A courier arrived from Brussels at about 2 a.m. without any significant new information. The course of events on Wellington's left throughout 16 June remained obscure at the British Headquarters.

About an hour later, at 3 a.m. on 17 June, Wellington left Genappe for Quatre Bras. Once there 'immediately' he sent Sir Alexander Gordon with a squadron of hussars to discover what had happened to Blücher. Gordon returned at 'about 7 o'clock, with news that Blücher had withdrawn to Wavre. FitzRoy Somerset recalled that none of Wellington's staff knew precisely where Wavre was, believing that the Prussians had only fallen back a short distance. 'General Müffling (the Prussian liaison officer) was the person who opened the Duke's eyes ... "Ma foi, c'est fort loin!"' Suddenly Wellington realized that his left flank was dangerously exposed and decided to fall back towards Brussels, 'the worst troops first – Belgians, Dutch & Nassau – the Brunswickers, Hanoverians & British troops followed'. Lieutenant-General Sir Rowland Hill's troops in the Nivelles area were similarly to withdraw towards Brussels. Wellington's Quartermaster-General (de Lancey) rode off 'to make out a position in front of the Forest of Soignes'; and the withdrawal from Quatre Bras commenced 'about 9 o'clock'. Not until 2 p.m. did French cavalry and artillery approach from Namur to threaten Quatre Bras. By then only a rearguard of light troops, some cavalry and Wellington's staff were in range.

Wellington remarked to Uxbridge, commanding the cavalry, that 'it was of no use to wait, the sooner he got away the better, that no time was to be lost in getting off'. So between 2 and 3 p.m. Wellington and his staff left Quatre Bras and 'proceeded leisurely towards Waterloo'. According to FitzRoy Somerset, on reaching the inn of La Belle Alliance, Wellington was surprised to find that de Lancey had not chosen the ridge which ran astride the road there for the defensive position because it was 'too extended'. Instead he had 'marked out a position' on another similar feature a mile closer to Brussels, stretching from Braine la Leude across the Quatre Bras-Brussels road and eastwards for another mile, a total front of approximately two miles. Before taking up his appointment as ambassador in Paris the previous year, Wellington had surveyed this area, and he had ridden up that same road to Quatre Bras on 16 June. FitzRoy Somerset is quite clear that Wellington carefully organized the withdrawal from the crossroads: there was no panic. It is therefore unlikely that he did not fully and carefully brief de Lancey and quite possible that Wellington had outlined options to his Quartermaster-General unknown to the Military Secretary. For once, Lord FitzRoy seems to have misread Wellington's mood.

Troops were beginning to occupy the Mont St Jean position when Wellington arrived at about 4 p.m. He quickly saw that the right flank was vulnerable and ordered troops to be angled back in an 'elbow shape' from the château of Hougoumont in advance of the extreme right of the ridge towards Braine l'Alleud where infantry, a brigade of cavalry and a battery should also be deployed. As they reached the area the infantry were 'conducted to their respective stations' by staff officers; with the cavalry rearguard still covering the road, along which French cavalry and artillery soon appeared. At about 7 p.m. Allied cannon opened fire on the enemy, much to Wellington's annoyance as he wanted the extent and nature of his defensive dispositions to be concealed. After a brief exchange of salvoes the French withdrew beyond La Belle Alliance at about 8 p.m.[24]

In fact, during that night of 17/18 June the Allies completed their preparations along the ridge near the village of Mont St Jean. To reach Brussels Napoleon had either to carry this position or outflank it – hence Wellington's elbow-like deployment on the right. To Wellington's left (east) Blücher's Prussians were near Wavre, menaced by Grouchy's pursuing force but able to prevent a major outflanking movement. The bulk of Wellington's force was deployed along the ridge itself, forward in the château of Hougoumont or just in advance of the crossroads in the middle of the position from which Wellington would conduct the subsequent battle, in the farmhouse of La Haye Sainte. That farmhouse would play both a crucial part in the Battle of Waterloo and have a lasting impact on FitzRoy Somerset's life. The night after the retirement from Quatre Bras, Wellington, Lord FitzRoy and other members of the staff slept in the village of Waterloo behind the ridge on the Brussels road beyond the Forest of Soignes. As they did so French units converged on the lower, roughly parallel ridge on which La Belle Alliance stood. Napoleon, like Wellington, spent the night in a village (Le Caillou) behind the lines. Neither commander, nor his staff, was called upon to suffer the drenching rain and violent thunderstorm that swept the field during darkness, thoroughly soaking unprotected men and equipment and, critically, making the ground so wet that cavalry could not operate across it for some hours on 18 June.

Wellington rose between 2 and 3 a.m. on 18 June and wrote to the Duke de Berri at Alost, requiring him to stand fast until 'official information' had been received that Brussels had been evacuated and was in French hands. He should then make for Antwerp. Unfortunately, on receipt of this message Berri immediately set off for the coast. Wellington also wrote to the Governor of Antwerp urging him to admit women 'and others with their equipages into the Town'. He left Waterloo on horseback at about 6 a.m. and on his way to the front met a Prussian officer bringing Blücher's reply to a request from Wellington the night before for one or two corps in support. Blücher now promised to send them. Noting the arrival of 'a large cavalcade of officers coming at full speed ... [through] mud and slough', Lieutenant Rees Gronow (Picton's former ADC) recorded that 'Felton Hervey, FitzRoy Somerset and de Lancey were the last that appeared. They all seemed as gay and unconcerned as if they were riding to meet the hounds in some quiet English county.' Captain and Lieutenant-Colonel Lord FitzRoy Somerset, KCB, First Regiment of Foot Guards, rode a bay mare.[25]

Once on the Mont St Jean ridge Wellington went across to inspect the right, then down the slope to Hougoumont where he ordered Colonel Cooke to demolish part of the garden wall, raise 'a temporary rampart within it' for the troops to fire over and put an abattis across the nearby Nivelles road. FitzRoy Somerset explained that Wellington then rode up to the high ground without his staff to overlook the forthcoming battlefield at a time when 'two or three companies of Mitchell's Brigade' were there and 'videttes beyond them'. Because he drew particular attention to not being with Wellington on this occasion and his account of the battle is partial, it is reasonable to assume that the Military Secretary went with the Duke where other movements are described in Lord FitzRoy's later summary.

Following Wellington's personal reconnaissance, when French activity on the right was noticed, the 3rd Division withdrew from in front of the crossroads to the reverse slope behind the ridge, two brigades of artillery (twelve guns) were allotted to each division and a brigade of howitzers was placed in front of the Guards 'at the elbow' in the area of Hougoumont. The Duke then rode across the ridge to the extreme left and the village of La Haye. He was back in the right centre, west of the Brus-

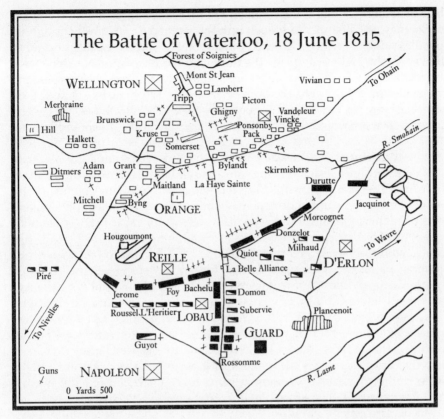

The Battle of Waterloo, 18 June 1815

sels road 'in front of the left of the Guards', when the battle started; and there he 'frequently' issued orders to the Prince of Orange in person. As 'things got on' he gave direct orders to other divisional and corps commanders, too, and was thus in clear command of events.

The Battle of Waterloo opened at 11.30 a.m. when French infantry, supported by artillery but not cavalry, attacked Hougoumont. Allied gunners brought them to a halt 'for a quarter of an hour', causing Wellington optimistically to exclaim: 'We have stopped them!' The enemy advance resumed, however, and some 800 Nassau troops fled from the orchard beside the château, but their place was quickly taken by Guards under Lord Saltoun. The first and second French assaults were beaten back, but in the third the adjacent wood fell. This opening phase of the battle, watched by Wellington from the ridge, lasted 1½ hours.

Seeing the French threaten to outflank Hougoumont to the west, Wellington moved the Coldstream Guards in line down to the Nivelles road. Throughout the day, dressed modestly in a blue frock coat, Wellington moved freely about the field, exposing himself and his staff to enemy fire. Shortly before 2 p.m., having witnessed the action around Hougoumont, he rode across to the elm tree on the right of the crossroads in the middle of the position. Here he saw the next major French attack develop east of the Brussels road. FitzRoy Somerset described the subsequent events in which d'Erlon's infantry were first held by Picton's 5th Division then successfully scattered by the British cavalry, in the somewhat disjointed and incomplete way that they must have appeared to him at the time. 'On the advance of the French, the 95th which was posted at [the] Quarry on the left of the road, & above La Haye Sainte, was withdrawn. The French attacked in three columns. They ascended and moved up to the hedge behind which Picton's division was posted, & were repulsed. Ponsonby's Brigade charged the French columns [Sir William Ponsonby's Union Brigade of heavy cavalry]. He was killed far in front of our line. The 12th Regt, Vandaleur's Brigade charged also; Colonel [Frederick] Ponsonby commanding it was wounded – at this time our Artillery were in the rear of the hedge. The cuirassiers charged Halkett's Brigade ... upon which Lord Edward Somerset [FitzRoy's elder brother] with the household troops charged the enemy. He went himself to the right of the farm of La Haye Sainte; many of the cuirassiers were killed near the wall of the farm; another regiment charged to the left of the farm or to the left of the chaussee (the Brigade crossed the chaussee inclining to the right [sic]), the brigade or part of it advanced a great deal too far, got into the position of the enemy near La Belle Alliance and suffered much [this, in fact, was when Sir William Ponsonby died].' In essence FitzRoy Somerset was recalling that phase of the battle, lasting from about 1.30 until 3 p.m., during which Picton's division held, then counter-attacked the enemy (Picton himself being killed), and Lord Edward Somerset's Household Brigade charged downhill to the right and left of La Haye Sainte, Ponsonby's Union Brigade even farther to the left beyond the Brussels-Charleroi road, the latter's pursuit being pressed almost disastrously too far.

La Haye Sainte came under separate attack from time to time, and certainly part of it changed hands more than once. This may explain why FitzRoy Somerset recorded that 'the French gained possession of La Haye Sainte & fired upon our troops from the upper part of the House' before 4 p.m., when the farm was not wholly lost for another two hours. 'About 3 or 4 o'clock', a captured cuirassier officer told Wellington that Napoleon was 'going to make a great effort with his cavalry', a warning of the succession of assaults launched by Ney on the Allied positions west of the Brussels road over the next two hours. In Lord FitzRoy's words: 'There were frequent charges of Cuirassiers, Dragoons & Lancers – they were repeatedly driven back by our Cavalry; they continued two or three hours. The great effort of the Enemy's Cavalry – no Infantry. Our limbers were drawn to the rear, the Guns were left in front.' In Wellington's view, Lord FitzRoy recorded, Napoleon was 'guilty of a great fault in not attacking with infantry also at the same time'. He continued his narrative: 'These charges were between La Haye Sainte & Hougoumont – The

Brunswickers were by degrees brought up some on the right, some on the left of the Guards – French infantry [a mistake for 'cavalry'?] advanced; they saw nothing but our guns – the Infantry were behind the crest of the ridge. The Duke said: "I'll be d...d if we shan't lose this ground if we don't take care." This ground was between Halkett's Brigade & the Guards; the troops were much thinned. The Duke advanced the Guards to take ground to their left towards Halkett's Brigade. He sent orders for Adam's Brigade & Mitchell's to be brought across the Nivelle [sic] road. The Duke went to Adam, made him form his Brigade in line four deep – with this Brigade the Duke crowned the crest of the Hill.'

These dispositions were scarcely completed when Ney launched another fierce attack, this time with cavalry, infantry and artillery. In this assault La Haye Sainte at last fell into enemy hands when the defenders of the King's German Legion ran out of ammunition. As the French infantry fought on past it to the main position on the ridge west of the road, 'Adam moved on the right of the Guards and advanced beyond the line of our Infantry; at that time all were exposed & suffered much from musketry as well as from the enemy's artillery. The Guards crossed the road [running along the crest of the ridge]; formed in front of it, three weak battalions of Halkett's Brigade did not reach the chaussee on their left. Adam had got rather too far forward with his Brigade which he was aware of before the Duke's order to fall back reached him. Lord F. Somerset [sic] told the Duke that our Troops did not fill the ground on the left of the Guards to the chaussee [Brussels road]. The Duke went to the Guards & made them take ground to their left.' In the course of ordering this reorganization, 'while riding by the side of the Duke, Ld F Somerset [sic] was wounded about 7 o'clock by a musket ball from La Haye Sainte'. Later accounts suggest, dramatically, that his right sleeve at the time was brushing Wellington's left arm and that, therefore, only an inch or two saved the Duke from the sniper's bullet. Not having seen the last two hours of the battle, FitzRoy Somerset concluded his account briefly. 'Half an hour after he [Lord FitzRoy] quitted the field, another heavy attack was made by the French Guards upon our Guards & Adam's Brigade by whom they were repulsed. After this, the Duke looked attentively through his glass & observed great confusion in the French Army. He said he would advance.' To his Military Secretary, he later remarked: 'I have never fought such a battle and I trust I shall never fight such another.' Lord Edward Somerset afterwards wrote: 'By all accounts, Brussels was in fine alarm & confusion, & every one except the Duke of Richmond's family quitted it. Lady FitzRoy went to Antwerp.'[26]

FitzRoy Somerset's wound proved so serious that he would be left with a permanent disability. Having dismounted he walked back to the building used as a field hospital. On a table, without anaesthetic, Dr John Gunning (surgeon-in-chief to the army) cut off his right arm above the elbow. Lord FitzRoy was so alert that he called for the severed limb to be returned: 'Hey, bring my arm back. There's a ring my wife gave me on the finger,' is one version of his words. Others include: 'Fetch me that hand, it has a ring on it that my wife gave me.' 'Hallo! Don't carry away that arm till I have taken off my ring.' ... 'Hello, boy! Look for my arm and bring it to me. Take off my wedding ring, slip it onto my left hand,' with a murmured addition: 'What would my wife say?'[27]

The following day, 19 June, Wellington compiled a comprehensive dispatch for the Secretary of State for War and the Colonies, Lord Bathurst. In it he drew attention to the gallantry of Lord Edward Somerset and wrote, too: 'I was likewise much indebted to the assistance of Lieut Colonel Lord FitzRoy Somerset, who was severely wounded.' In a private letter that same day, referring by name to the dead and wounded among the staff and senior ranks including FitzRoy Somerset, he wrote to Lady Webster of 'a most severe and bloody contest ... My loss is immense'. To the Duke of Beaufort he penned a more personal message: 'I am very sorry to have to acquaint you that your brother Lord FitzRoy is very severely wounded, and has lost his right arm. I have just seen him, and he is perfectly free from fever, and as well as anybody could be under such circumstances. You are aware how useful he has always been to me; and how *much* concerned I am for his misfortune ... I hope, however, that your brother will soon be able to join me again and that he will long live to be, as he is likely to become, an honor to his country, as he is a satisfaction to his family and friends.' Lord Edward Somerset also wrote to Beaufort. 'In so dreadful a battle, it was hardly to be expected that when so many of the family were engaged, all could escape unhurt; consequently we have to lament poor FitzRoy's wound, by which he has lost his right arm. I understand the ball entered near the elbow, and shattered the bone so much that the surgeons instantly decided to take it off. My friend Scovell was in the room with him, whilst the operation was performed, and he tells me he bore it so manfully that the Prince of Orange, who lay wounded in the same room, was not aware that the amputation had been made.' Lord FitzRoy was 'doing as well as possible'. At 8 p.m. on 19 June an express messenger brought Lady FitzRoy in Brussels news of the battle and her husband's wound.[28]

Lord FitzRoy was worried, quite naturally, that the severity of his wound would curtail or badly restrict his military career. But his more pressing desire was to reassure his family. The doctors, however, prevented him from travelling to Brussels for 24 hours. When he did so he gave 'my dear wife a relic of Waterloo' (a fan) – though whether this was a battlefield memento or not is unclear. What is certain is that from Brussels on 20 June he wrote a perfectly legible letter with his left hand:

> 'My dear mother,
> I am doing as well as possible. Emily will tell you the rest.
> Give my love to Fanny [his sister]
> > Your most affectionate son,
> > FitzRoy Somerset.'[29]

Understandably, family considerations dominated during the first weeks after Waterloo. On 23 June Wellesley-Pole reassured Emily: 'Nothing can surpass my feelings for dear FitzRoy, and that I take as strong an interest in him as any one Human Being can do in another.' Emily should not 'groan' at his misfortune, but thank God 'he has spared him to us'. He very much hoped that Lord FitzRoy's 'talents and his integrity' would still allow him to prosper. 'My house shall be ready for FitzRoy and you and your child for I shall insist upon your taking your old quarters when you return to London.' It was lucky, Wellesley-Pole said, that her mother was with her when Lord FitzRoy's wound occurred, as she had been able to help him as well. On 28 June FitzRoy Somerset wrote again to his mother at Muddiford: 'I fear you have been under the greatest uneasiness about me. Pray be assured that I am recovering as fast as possible, that I get stronger daily and that I do not suffer more pain than is usual in such cases.' He intended to leave Brussels in eight or nine days, reaching London on 11 or 12 July. 'Pray do not think of coming to Town to see me, as I intend paying you a visit immediately afterwards & it might be as well for both parties if we don't meet till I shall have recovered from the fatigues of the voyage.' He sent, as before, his 'kindest love' to his sister Fanny. Attached to this letter was a note from Lord Edward Somerset: 'I can assure you with perfect truth that what FitzRoy says is quite true. He mends wonderfully & I have no doubt that he will be able to move from hence in eight or nine days.'[30]

Lord FitzRoy's mother wrote to her daughter-in-law from Stoke Gifford on 3 July: 'I have read your letter [dated 26 June] again and again', not really believing that her son would be able to leave Brussels so soon: 'The warmest wish of my heart is to receive him here.' Wellington had written to inform her that the family would travel from Ostend to Gravesend, thus avoiding a rough journey by 'land carriage'. The dowager Lady Beaufort hoped that Lady FitzRoy had 'recovered and that seeing dear Fitz [sic] in such constant good spirits has restored yours'. She was glad that Emily had secured a wet-nurse for 'the little girl' whom she looked forward to seeing. 'I assure you that FitzRoy's misfortune has very much interested this neighbourhood. In the Bristol paper of last Saturday was a paragraph which announced with pleasure that he was so well recovered as to have walked out.' Lady Beaufort was puzzled as to how the paper acquired these details because she had not told anybody since her return from Muddiford. She had 'the comfort' of a long letter from Edward who 'felt much for FitzRoy and for you'.[31]

On reaching London, FitzRoy Somerset and his family did stay with the Wellesley-Poles in Savile Row. From there he wrote to his sister Fanny on 29 July, apologizing for not having contacted her since losing his arm, nor his mother after arriving in England. He had planned to refrain from correspondence 'till I could write a good hand, but as my progress is not sufficiently rapid to hold out any immediate prospect of attaining that object, I do not like being silent any longer'. He had seen their sick brother Arthur at Northwood and thought him better, though Arthur was 'low' in spirits. Of himself, 'my general health is good enough, and the wound is now become very small, but still does not heal'. He therefore did not know 'when I shall be liberated from this smoky city'. Charlotte was 'very well and is in my opinion a very pretty, nice child'. The FitzRoy Somersets spent that winter, 1815/16, at Badminton where Lord FitzRoy recuperated and compiled his account of the Waterloo campaign. His 17-year-old niece recalled that, for a long period, the Duke and Duchess of Beaufort were absent on family business at Stoke Gifford. 'I was therefore always with FitzRoy and Lady FitzRoy – in those days she was wrapt in him and both were so kind to me, we used to be together most of the day'; their lives were further enriched by the infant Charlotte.[32]

Meanwhile FitzRoy Somerset attained military preferment. Official note was taken of his 'arduous duties' in the Waterloo campaign and Wellington informed him that he had written to the Duke of York recommending that he be made ADC to the King. In fact, on 28 August he became an extra ADC to the Prince Regent and, on the same day also, following representations to Sir Henry Torrens, Military Secretary at the Horse Guards, he was promoted colonel in the army and lieutenant-colonel in the First Foot Guards.[33]

Awards and honours also came his way. He received the Waterloo medal – issued to all those with Wellington on 16, 17 or 18 June – and a number of foreign orders. On 2 August Wellington forwarded to him from Paris the Cross of a Knight of the Order of Maria Theresa 'which the Emperor of Austria has sent to me for you, in testimony of His Imperial Majesty's approbation of your services and conduct, particularly in the late Battles fought in the Netherlands.' The Prince Regent's permission to accept this was granted six days later. In late August and early September he similarly received the decoration of the Fourth Class of the Order of St George from the Russian Emperor and the Military Order of Maximilian Joseph from the King of Bavaria. In December came an award from the Portuguese Prince Regent of the Tower and Sword of Portugal for his 'courage' in the defence of the Prince's country. Nearer home, on 7 July he became a Freeman of the City of Gloucester 'as a tribute of Respect for his Gallant and continued Exertions during the War in the Peninsula, and the Spirited and Heroic Conduct displayed by him in the severe Battle and Glorious Victory obtained over Bonaparte in Person at Waterloo.'[34]

Arrangements were soon in hand for him to resume his original appointment in Paris, where Sir Charles Stuart was now ambassador while Wellington commanded the Army of Occupation. As early as 13 July 1815 Lord FitzRoy learnt from Wellington that Castlereagh would allow him to return to Paris if he so wished. Ten days later the Duke revealed that the Secretary of State had raised the salary of the Secretary of Embassy to £1,200 per year plus a housing allowance. He advised Lord FitzRoy not to 'surrender' the Paris post which was still open to him, before he secured another appointment. Indirectly Wellington encouraged him to take up an active administrative career again by praising his improving hand-writing. And, in a long letter of 12 October 1815 from Paris, he gave more advice about the future. He acknowledged Lord FitzRoy's doubts, expressed in a letter, about resuming the post of Secretary of Embassy. Wellington explained that he would remain in command of the British and Allied troops in France, prepared to take military action again if necessary. Renewed operations might, indeed, be necessary if the present unrest and air of political crisis were not resolved. But he cautioned him against spurning the civil appointment in favour of a military one. If he were to give up his 'diplomatick office', he could do so without 'any charge of caprice', because when he originally took it he was 'not aware of military employment' being possible. However, Wellington went on: 'If you do give it up in a period of Peace it will not be so easy to get another; whereas if you serve in Peace in the Diplomatic Office and quit it only in War, you have always a claim to be so employed on the Return of Peace.' Wellington admitted that these 'reflections ... may be erroneous', but they did represent his considered opinion. He would, though, be 'very glad' to have Lord FitzRoy again, if he wished to return to his 'military office' – presumably as Wellington's Military Secretary.[35]

In the event FitzRoy Somerset heeded the Duke's advice. Once recovered he would resume the post of Secretary of Embassy in Paris, having last left the French capital as Minister Plenipotentiary in March 1815.

CHAPTER 4

BUREAUCRACY AND POLITICS
(1816-27)

*'He had always discharged the duties of the situation in an unexceptionable man-
ner.' (Revd Dr Cardew)*[1]

During the autumn of 1815, while Lord FitzRoy and his wife
were living at Badminton and Charlotte was barely four
months old, Emily again became pregnant. Towards the end
of March 1816 the FitzRoy Somersets returned to London
where Lord FitzRoy intended to leave his wife with her
mother and go on to Paris which he plannned to reach in the first week of
April. 'But Emily bore the journey from Gloucestershire so ill', he
informed Wellington, 'that I was obliged to change my plans and to
decide to stay in England until after her accouchement.' On 6 May 1816 in
London, Emily presented him with a son and heir, Arthur William
FitzRoy, to whom Wellington agreed to 'stand as godfather'.[2]

Shortly before Arthur's birth some embarrassment about Lord
FitzRoy's income required resolution. Writing to Wellington from 53
Montagu Square, London on 21 April, FitzRoy Somerset noted that the
Government was looking at the staff of the army 'in order to diminish the
expenses'; and he was surprised to discover that he was still listed as
Wellington's Military Secretary. The Secretary of State for War and the
Colonies (Lord Bathurst) had sent for him 'yesterday ... and expressed a
wish that in order to prevent any notice being taken of it in the House of
Commons (it being generally known that I was appointed Secretary to the
Embassy at Paris) I should cause the omission of my name in the abstracts
after the 24th December 1815.' Lord FitzRoy assured Bathurst that he
would immediately write to Wellington to this effect because 'I did not
consider myself to have the smallest claim to the pay of the Military Secretary having accepted the Diplomatick Office'; in fact he had already written to the Duke intimating this on 15 October. He had therefore expected
his military allowance to be discontinued on 24 October and only realized
that this had not happened when he received a draft for his pay as ADC
up to 24 December while 'I was in the country.' Actually 'any attack that
might be made on me touching the affair of Secretary of Embassy must
fall to the ground as by the regulation of the Foreign Office my allowances
could not commence till ten days before my departure for Paris'. He nevertheless asked Wellington to delete his name from the staff list after 24
December 'and that you will accept my best thanks for your great kindness in continuing me on your Staff for so long a period after I had ceased
to perform the duties of the appointment'. In concurring Wellington

replied that he had intended Lord FitzRoy to receive his military allowance until he actually took up his diplomatic office.[3]

On 7 July 1816 Castlereagh forwarded to FitzRoy Somerset, already in Paris, his commission as 'the Secretary to His Majesty's Embassy at the Court of the Most Christian King'. It seems likely that during their second spell in Paris the FitzRoy Somersets lived at No 1 Avenue des Champs Elysées, which was closer to the embassy in Rue du Faubourg St Honoré than had been their old address in Montmartre. At about the time that he returned to Paris, the controversy over J. Cam Hobhouse's comments about FitzRoy Somerset's conduct in the French capital during March 1815 was resolved. Acknowledging that passages in the first edition of his book, *Letters from Paris*, might imply that Lord FitzRoy had not been aware of what was actually going on at that time, Hobhouse informed Colonel Ponsonby of the embassy staff that he had excised the offending sections from the second edition. Ponsonby nevertheless reminded Hobhouse that these 'could be construed as going beyond a critique of the conduct of the British Minister at the time of the King's leaving Paris' and that Hobhouse's information had not been gleaned from 'the best source'. To Lord FitzRoy, though, Ponsonby wrote a shade tersely that he had retained his written statement, but that as Hobhouse had 'done away with the very objectionable part ... you have no right to ask any more of him'. The first edition thus stayed in circulation, but FitzRoy Somerset's reputation does not seem to have suffered permanent damage.[4]

During the winter of 1816/17 Emily was into her third pregnancy and FitzRoy Somerset was dealing with the administrative tasks of his office. In December Wellington wrote to him officially concerning a paragraph in an edition of *Galignani's Messenger*, published every weekday morning in Paris and Cambrai, which alleged that a 'riot' had been caused in Reading by four drunken officers of The Blues. Wellington wanted Lord FitzRoy to question Galignani about his authority for the statement. If he had none he must publish a retraction and an apology; if he refused to do this Wellington would 'proceed against him'.

On 24 May 1817 a second son (Richard Henry FitzRoy) was born in Paris. During the final stages of the pregnancy Wellington warned Mary Bagot that her sister had not been well. He chided his niece: 'She [Emily] has two beautiful children, and most probably will have a dozen in a few years at the rate at which she goes on. I wish Priscilla could take a leaf out of her book or your book on this point!!' On 2 June Wellington's elder brother Richard, Marquis Wellesley offered his 'sincere congratulations' to Lord and Lady FitzRoy, expressing his delight at 'Emily's happy situation' and 'greatest pleasure' at being invited to act as godfather. He asked whether either Wellington or Sir Charles Stuart should stand in for him at the baptism in Paris. FitzRoy Somerset admitted on 18 June that both mother and baby were 'so weak', but happily this situation soon improved. Indeed before many months had passed Emily was pregnant again. Early in December, writing to Lady Burghersh, Wellington hoped that she would emulate her sister, Lady FitzRoy, who was expecting her fourth child in almost precisely three years in May 1818. Given the absence of a recorded birth a miscarriage may well have occurred. In another letter to Priscilla from Paris he observed: 'Mama [Mrs Wellesley-Pole] appears to me to be very well and in good spirits, and so is Emily: and for once in her married life, she is not in the way!!!' Mrs Wellesley-Pole could have been caring for Emily after the loss of her baby.[5]

FitzRoy Somerset continued to enjoy a close relationship with Wellington who corresponded with him frequently. In July 1817 from Mont St Martin the Duke referred to 'all these questions of foreign Police [which] are very awkward in reference to the Laws of Nations', warning that Britain should not get involved without firm public backing at home. This perhaps indicates that the question of a quasi-international European police force, later mooted at the Congress of Aix-la-Chapelle, was already under discussion. Four months later Wellington castigated the French government for throwing away 'the popularity which they might expect would attend to withdrawing of the army [of occupation]' by concentrating on increasing the size of its own army to the consternation of the Allies. 'I have never known so foolish a proceeding,' he exclaimed. Early in 1818 Lord FitzRoy expressed shock in detailing at length to his father-in-law, Wellesley-Pole, another attempt on Wellington's life on 10 February, as he arrived in the Rue Champs Elysées.

Later in the year, writing from his headquarters at Cambrai, Wellington discussed a proposal for 'the Sovereigns' to review Allied troops while attending the Congress of Aix-la-Chapelle. He believed that this would be unwise without first visiting the King of France; but that their going to Paris before withdrawal of the Army of Occupation would also be unwise. The planned review did not appear feasible therefore. Weighty issues of this nature were relieved by more personal matters. With one letter from Cambrai he sent 'a quarter of an immense wild Boar' which he had killed 'with my spear'. In November 1818, writing from the Congress of Aix-la-Chapelle where he had advocated withdrawal of the army of occupation, Wellington informed FitzRoy Somerset that he hoped to leave for Paris at the end of the month and see a play and go to the Opera before travelling on to England. He reached London on 20 December, notified Lord FitzRoy of his arrival the following day, and on 22 December wrote to say that Lord FitzRoy's mother-in-law had also arrived – with a cold but otherwise in good health.[6]

Lord and Lady FitzRoy would not remain long in Paris either. Wellington had returned to England to take up the post of Master-General of the Ordnance, officially on 26 December 1818. In this appointment he would command the Ordnance Corps (commissioned and non-commissioned ranks of the Royal Artillery, officers of the Royal Engineers and other ranks of the Corps of Royal Sappers and Miners – the so-called 'scientific corps' of the army – with its own promotion structure, Paymaster-General, hospital and transport services. Under this structure there were, in essence, two distinct branches in the British Army: the Ordnance Corps under the Master-General; and the cavalry and infantry under the Commander-in-Chief (CinC) at the Horse Guards. In addition to his military duties the Master-General controlled the civilian Ordnance Department which produced certain stores and equipment for both army and navy, and constructed and maintained fortifications and barracks at home and abroad. Although not appointed for his political views, the Master-General often sat in the Cabinet to proffer military advice; Wellington did so on succeeding the Earl of Musgrave. The day-to-day administration of the Ordnance Department was conducted through the Board of Ordnance, nominally though rarely presided over by the Master-General. The Board had its own Secretary, but the Master-General also had a personal Secretary to assist and advise him in his military and civilian capacities and more especially to handle confidential correspondence. It was this latter appointment – Secretary to the Master-General – that Lord FitzRoy was destined to fill. His past experience as Wellington's Military Secretary amply qualified him for the post.[7]

Scarcely had Wellington become Master-General than, on 3 January 1819, he wrote to Fitzroy Somerset revealing that he had spoken to the Prime Minister 'respecting your removal to the Ordnance'. Liverpool anticipated no difficulty, but Wellington thought that a delay of 'about two months' would occur. He explained that any petition against Lord FitzRoy's going to the Ordnance must be lodged within fourteen days of Parliament's being notified of the intended appointment. Parliament would be sitting on 10 February and a petition would then have to be heard. 'In the meantime we must help the situation and place you in the Ordnance as quiet [sic] as possible.' The salary of the Secretary to the Master-General was 'about equal' to that of the post currently held by FitzRoy Somerset. Wellington pointed out that the Ordnance vacancy was at home, not abroad, and that the Embassy appointment involved 'political risks'. Moreover the Ordnance post would carry a pension; and he recommended Lord FitzRoy carefully to weigh the respective merits of the two positions. Not surprisingly, FitzRoy Somerset opted for the home post and took up the appointment after the death of Sir Felton Hervey. Still serving as an extra ADC to the Prince Regent (King George IV in 1820), six years after going to the Ordnance he was promoted major-general on 27 May 1825 and thus was able to enjoy the full benefits of the KCB awarded to him ten years previously.[8]

Wellington's involvement in Cabinet business meant inevitable devolution of Ordnance work on his secretary. In June, September and November, for example, Lord FitzRoy returned to Paris 'as the Duke's emissary'. And doubts soon arose about Wellington's health, thus adding to his burden. 'The Duke is I hope well but he is dreadfully thin, and aged in his appearance'; and there is some evidence that Wellington's increasing deafness was made worse by bad treatment two years later. Coping with a constant stream of requests for favours in particular tested Lord FitzRoy's patience, but he apparently dealt with them quickly and courteously, as Lieutenant-Colonel (later General Sir) William Napier generously acknowledged in 1825: thanking him for responding rapidly to a personal query and, referring to a similar reaction following a request for help from somebody in Gibraltar, Napier wrote that such responses 'would be extraordinary coming from any other quarter, but your accurate knowledge of everything that does or has belonged to the Army enables you to *do* before others can *think*'. Napier went on to note that FitzRoy Somerset would know he was 'no flatterer' and not therefore prone to such sentiments. 'But I should be wanting both to you and myself if I failed to express my admiration of the warmth with which you assist the services of the individual, neither has the delicacy with which you have upon so many occasions kept back all appearance of personal protection been unobserved by myself or those numerous claimants whatever at different times found a sure friend in you when they could find none elsewhere.'[9]

The role of the Ordnance in supplying forces overseas kept FitzRoy Somerset alert to foreign developments. In 1824, for instance, he was acutely aware that 'trouble' was brewing in the West Indies and that there was concern about 'our relations with South America' which might require increased military action. Closer to home, he inadvertently saved Wellington from personal danger. In February 1820 the so-called Cato Street conspirators, somewhat grandly aiming to murder prominent members of the Cabinet and seize London, sent James Ings to assassinate Wellington as he left the Ordnance Office in Pall Mall. Unfortunately for Ings on the chosen afternoon, FitzRoy Somerset came up to walk with the Duke across Green Park to Apsley House, thus shielding him from his would-be assassin. Later that year, faced by a restless crowd hostile to George IV's plan to divorce Queen Caroline, Lord FitzRoy heard the rhetorical taunt: 'Well, you who have lost a wing, what do you say to it?'[10]

In June 1822 FitzRoy Somerset became involved on the periphery of a potential family scandal when his nephew, the future seventh Duke of Beaufort, quietly married his dead wife's half-sister. After the event Henry sought his uncle's advice. Lord FitzRoy could do nothing to dampen public speculation that the union would be declared void; and the fact that the new Marchioness of Worcester was his own wife's first cousin further complicated the matter. Legally the issue was not resolved until 1835. Otherwise, domestically Lord FitzRoy experienced joy and tragedy in rapid succession. A fifth child, Katherine Anne Emily Cecilia, was born on 31 August 1824; but, on 26 November Katherine's young brother, Frederick John FitzRoy (born 8 March 1821) died. Meanwhile, on

23 September Lord FitzRoy's eldest son Arthur was formally appointed Page of Honour to George IV in place of Charles Bagot 'to have, receive and enjoy the Salary allowed by the Establishment of our Stables, with all other Allowances as usual'. The appointment would date from 5 August, though Arthur was not sworn in until 18 December 1824. He heard too from Burghersh that Priscilla had given birth to another boy, which 'made me and Emily very happy'. He was 'exceptionally flattered' to be invited to become 'one of the little gentleman's godfathers', accepting 'with pleasure'. Lord FitzRoy looked forward to seeing Burghersh, his wife and family in England the following spring; he himself was anticipating shortly 'a quiet season' in the country. He meticulously remembered anniversaries. On 16 May 1826, for example, he wrote to Charlotte from his mother's house at Stoke: 'This morning at half past nine Your Pugship was eleven years old. I am very well pleased to have such a nosie little girl and I am willing to admit that you have justified the observation of your mama, who at the very moment of your birth cried out "dear little love".'

He hoped that Charlotte would continue to be 'the comfort and happiness of your dear mother and me', asking her to accept the Book of Trades which Emily would give to her on his behalf. He added that Miss Talbot had been married that morning in Stoke church and 'looked very well'; and that Charlotte's grandmother was 'pretty well'. He signed his letter 'your most affectionate father', betraying the deep feeling for all his children that characterized his dealings with them. Their mother tended to be more severe. In thanking Charlotte for a letter in July 1826, Lady FitzRoy nevertheless corrected her English: 'My Brothers, Kitty and I ... not me'; though she did express sorrow that Charlotte had been sick on the way back from Aunt Priscilla's house.[11]

FitzRoy Somerset made a brief but inauspicious entry into politics during these years. In 1818, while still holding the Embassy post in Paris, he had been elected as an MP, though not without some alarm. Perhaps influenced by Wellington's condemnation of Party faction frequently expressed in the Peninsula, he was never closely associated with any specific political grouping, although he was designated 'tory' in election literature in Truro for which his maternal grandfather and great grandfather had sat in Parliament. He himself triumphed there by a single vote in the 1818 election, which prompted the opposition to demonstrate violently. Lord FitzRoy and other guests had gathered in a house opposite the hotel where a celebration dinner was to be served. 'A furious mob', according to one account, attacked the house, smashing the windows with stones and causing the shutters to be closed for the protection of those inside. So ugly did the scene appear that Lord FitzRoy was advised to escape via a ladder into the backyard, scale a neighbouring wall and proceed across the nearby green to enter the hotel unseen from the rear. He rejected such ignominy, reputedly saying: 'No, no! we will go out the same way as we came in; only let us keep together, and we shall make our way through the crowd. When the front door was opened the crowd fell silent and at first did not attempt to bar the party's way. Jostling soon took place, though, and a blow was aimed at Lord FitzRoy, whereupon his assailant was upbraided for seeking to strike a one-armed man. With some difficulty Lord FitzRoy reached the haven of the inn 'where he passed a merry evening with his friends, laughing over the adventure of the day'.

Two years later another election brought a different result. Sir Hussey Vivian (another Peninsula veteran and later Master-General of the Ordnance) secured outright victory; FitzRoy Somerset and Vivian's fellow-whig tied for the second seat which required another contest. On the day before the ballot supporters of the whig, Lieutenant-Colonel Gosset, secured the appointment of two sympathetic burgesses to fill existing vacancies in the corporation, knowing that another double (tied) return would otherwise occur. The procedure by which this election was carried out remained dubious but the parliamentary contest went ahead. The Revd Dr Cardew proposed Lord FitzRoy as a fit and proper person to represent the borough. 'He had always discharged the duties of the situation in an unexceptionable [sic] manner; he was besides recommended to them by splendour and rank as a branch of one of the most illustrious families in the country, and was connected with another noble family, the head of which was the Recorder of the Borough, from whose friendship the Corporation in particular, and the inhabitants of the town in general, had derived many advantages.' In seconding Lord FitzRoy's nomination John Thomas reminded those present that 'they should not forget that he had not only fought and bled for his country but that he was the grandson of that Cornish hero, Admiral Boscawen.' In vain FitzRoy Somerset's supporters protested about the votes of the new burgesses; and Gosset was preferred. Six years later Lord FitzRoy regained his seat, but did not contest the 1829 election.[12]

Lord FitzRoy first took his seat at Westminster in time for the election of a new Speaker, Manners Sutton, on 14 January 1819. He did not sit for Truro in the session which began on 31 March 1829; so the total length of his two spells as an MP (nominally 1818-20 and 1826-9) amounted to a little over five years, during which he took no active part in any debate. His name appears in Hansard only as an elected member and, on one occasion, in a division list. This does not necessarily signify neglect of his duties; Hansard rarely published the names of those voting with the majority. At 3.30 a.m. on 13 May 1828 he voted against a motion to consider 'adjustment' of the laws against Roman Catholics, which was carried to add impetus towards Catholic emancipation. This may well have dissuaded him from contesting the next election. Unlike his brother, Lord Edward, he did not switch to support for the change; and he was no longer sitting for Truro when the crucial Commons' approval of the Catholic Relief Bill went through in the following year. It is surprising, though, that he did not defend his brother Charles whose conduct as Governor of the Cape of Good Hope came under attack several times in the House during 1826 and 1827. Lord Edward did speak out, and it may be that the family settled on him as Charles' sole champion.[13]

Farther afield Lord FitzRoy entered the arena of international politics when he 'attended' Wellington 'to Vienna and Verona in 1822'. The accord between the powers that had overcome Napoleon in 1815 had been threatened by the determination of Prussia, Russia and Austria – abetted by France, subsequently admitted to their counsels – to interfere in the internal affairs of another country if in their opinion its condition menaced political stability. In practice this meant a *carte blanche* to put down any political movement liable to embarrass a ruling despot. Ferdinand VII faced serious domestic opposition, but Britain was reluctant to sanction external interference in the Iberian peninsula, particularly as French troops were likely to be sent in to support the absolutist king. A re-run of the Peninsular War was not inconceivable.[14]

As Britain's plenipotentiary to the European congress planned for the autumn of 1822, Castlereagh (lately created Marquis of Londonderry) intended vigorously to oppose French interference south of the Pyrenees. Following Castlereagh's suicide, Wellington took his place and FitzRoy Somerset went with him to Vienna. On arrival they found that the meeting would instead be held at Verona in Italy. The attractive geographical setting of marble basilica and stately houses could not obscure the futility of Wellington's position. The other nations were determined to pursue an interventionist policy and perfectly willing to allow French forces to implement it. Wellington and FitzRoy Somerset left Verona, before the congress officially ended, on 30 November.[15]

The dispatch of French troops into Spain in support of Ferdinand seemed increasingly likely, so on their way home Wellington and Lord FitzRoy called on the ailing Louis XVIII, offering mediation. That offer was subsequently refused, but Canning, who had succeeded Castlereagh as Foreign Secretary, was keen that an attempt be made to forestall external intervention in Spain. A visit by Wellington could be provocative, but Lord FitzRoy might travel to Madrid less conspicuously to convey the views of Wellington in his capacity as a Spanish grandee, Duke of Vitoria. As Lord FitzRoy left England in January 1823, diplomatic representatives from Prussia, Russia and Austria were recalled from Spain at their own request, and Louis gave strident notice of France's willingness to intervene by massing troops along the Pyrenees.[16]

FitzRoy Somerset's mission therefore looked hopeless from the outset, but Wellington had drawn up a comprehensive memorandum for him. 'It is important to make the Spanish feel, first, that they cannot get rid of their King without exciting the hatred, indignation and enmity of all Europe ... [secondly] the power and prerogative assigned to the King in the system should be such as to enable him to perform his duties.' Essentially Wellington looked to establishing 'internal tranquility' and the avoidance of 'perpetual successive insurrections' by dissatisfied sections of the population. '... the Spaniards who really desire the peace and welfare of their country must look to an alteration of their constitution which shall have for its objects to give the King the power of executing his office.' Lord FitzRoy was, thus, asked to persuade supporters of the liberal constitution to grant more power to Ferdinand. An agreed amendment, Wellington believed, would solve the current crisis and ensure future stability. He held that such a settlement would remove any reason for French intervention. Lord FitzRoy should make it clear that 'the very foundations of social order and government are in a state of risk': in the present uncertainty, trade, public and private revenue could not be guaranteed, nor could 'the army or any of the public servants or establishments' be paid. 'I happen to know that the principal monied people in Europe will not lend their money in Spain until they shall see a system prevail in that country which will afford some hope of the re-establishment and permanence of peace and good order.' Unless 'some settlement of her internal dissension and distractions' be found, Spain could not deal effectively with 'her revolted colonies' in South America. Lord FitzRoy had in truth been given an impossible task. Despite his familiarity with the country he lacked Wellington's prestige and influence, and his brief verged on the arrogant. Sending him may have seemed politically wise, but the mission was inevitably doomed and grossly unfair to him. His hopeless position was underlined by Canning who, on 6 January, reiterated the private nature of the undertaking, which should not in any way detract from the work of the British Ambassador, Sir William à Court. Wellington's views 'as the friend and well-wisher of Spain' moreover must not be conveyed as being those of the British Government.[17]

As he toiled through heavy snow to reach Madrid on 21 January 1823, Lord FitzRoy must have pondered on his slim chances of achieving anything. 'Every horse worth five shillings has been stolen by the *facciosos*,' he complained. His correspondence with Wellington from 22 January until 20 March bore out à Court's contention that he had 'not much chance of success'. 'The country is in a sad state and the people are ruder and more unaccommodating than ever,' he wrote pessimistically soon after he arrived. He soon confirmed, too, à Court's discouraging assessment that it was 'quite impossible to prevail upon any party to act in concert with the King'. Lord FitzRoy observed that 'the only amusing thing that I have heard is that the priests have persuaded the *facciosos* that the Constitutionalists have *ravos*'. Ferdinand 'was sorely affected with gout – whether of the diplomatic kind or not', and unable to meet him. Lord FitzRoy doubted the King's sincerity or that generally he was respected.[18]

Early in April he decided to return to England empty handed. Acknowledging with regret the inevitability of the decision, à Court felt that his efforts had been pointless for at least two months. 'It was then [February] made clear to me that nothing would be conceded here till

78

force compelled a concession and especially so that France having once been brought into action would no longer listen to any intervention nor consent to treat otherwise than directly with the Spanish authorities.' Sir William agreed that the 'amicable suggestions' for reconciling Ferdinand and his reforming opponents from himself and Lord FitzRoy had been 'useless'. In noting that he and Lady à Court would 'both feel the loss of your society very sensibly', à Court concluded: 'I need not say how much I regret being deprived of your assistance, for I never concealed from you how great an advantage I considered it to have such a witness of my conduct and such authority to bear me out in accuracy of my statements. Most happy shall I be, if fortune should ever throw us together again upon public Service.' French troops duly crossed the frontier shortly after Lord FitzRoy left Madrid, quickly suppressed opposition to Ferdinand in that area and, despite a defence organized in part by Lord FitzRoy's erstwhile Peninsula colleague General Alava, had overcome the last pocket of resistance in Cadiz before the close of the year. It was scarcely Lord FitzRoy's fault that his one and only independent foray into international politics had ended in failure; the cards were always stacked heavily against him. It is a measure of his integrity and devotion to duty that he should have sought to resolve such an intractable situation.[19]

Three years later he went abroad again, this time to the Russian capital St Petersburg; and on this occasion once more with Wellington. Tsar Alexander I died on 1 December 1825 and early in the following year Wellington went as Britain's official representative to attend the coronation of his successor, Nicholas I. The hidden agenda for the visit involved the co-ordination of common action with Russia against Turkey in support of the Greeks, currently struggling for independence from the Ottoman Empire.[20]

Lord FitzRoy had no direct influence on the nature or outcome of these discussions, but his account of the visit is interesting in its own right. On 6 March he wrote to his sister Fanny at their mother's house at Stoke, explaining that they had arrived in the Russian capital four days previously, having taken six days to travel overland from Memel. There had been a lot of snow, though not enough to warrant mounting the carriages on sledges. Once the frontier had been crossed the Russian roads were good and the postillions drove fast. On arrival he had been 'very much struck with the grandeur and magnificence of this Town. It may certainly be considered the finest city in Europe.' Wellington was the only field marshal present and was treated 'like a prince', being received by the new Emperor and his family 'in the most marked and flattering manner'. The Duke and his suite, including Lord FitzRoy, were lodged in a house provided by the Emperor and allocated carriages and horses to ride. Lord FitzRoy was delighted to renew his 'long-standing friendship' with the Prince of Orange who was also there for the coronation. He occasionally breakfasted with him and found Prince William 'in no degree altered', as kind as when they were together in Spain. Having inquired after her, the Prince 'expressed great regret when I told him how long and how hourly my mother has suffered'. At St Petersburg Lord FitzRoy had ample spare time, though he had not so far been into a shop. Fur was a popular commodity, but very expensive and he already had a North-American bear skin pelisse bought in London for 'nearly £50', which kept him 'warm as toast'. In fact it had not been particularly cold since their arrival and the temperature in the house was normally 50 degrees Fahrenheit, ensured by stoves in every room with more in the hall and on the staircase to eliminate draughts. The Tsar attended Guard Mounting virtually every morning, though his predecessor would not be buried until 24 March. Lord FitzRoy estimated that the new Emperor was 'about thirty', the Empress 'twenty-five to twenty-seven'. Both were 'handsome'. 'She has a remarkably good figure and a very interesting countenance ... She knew all about me and Lady FitzRoy and was extremely civil and gracious.' Ironically this Tsar and Tsarina would still be in power when Lord FitzRoy invaded their kingdom at the head of British troops in 1854; and Russian failure in that campaign would supposedly contribute directly to Nicholas's death.

Lord FitzRoy concluded his long letter with comments showing his concern about individuals at home. He was delighted to have just received Fanny's letter of 13 February explaining that his mother was 'tolerably well' and that Gertrude was 'so comfortable'. He was 'ashamed' not to have given Maria Talbot anything before her marriage and would bring back some frankincense from Russia. The only way for their brother John to be made a Lord of the Bedchamber was for Beaufort to apply directly to the King, by-passing the politicians; but Lord FitzRoy in an unusually tart observation doubted that Beaufort had the 'courage' to do so.[21]

Lord FitzRoy also wrote that day to his eldest child, Charlotte, whom he addressed by one of her nicknames, 'Cuddy'. It was 'extraordinary' that since leaving England nobody had asked whether Charlotte had a 'pug face or a sore nose or ... trick of sucking your fingers ... or of crying when Papa speaks loud'. Chidingly he went on: 'Well, miss, I am obliged to you for those long letters which you have thought of writing to me and which you would have written if Betty had not upset the ink and if [illegible] had not gone to Chelsea without leaving paper out, which was very provoking of her.' Disappointment that his children did not write regularly when he and they were apart would often appear in his letters to them. Now he explained to his elder daughter that he had seen the Emperor and Empress of Russia – 'handsome people' with a girl of eight months, 'who holds her head as well as Miss Kitty', two other girls 'and a nice boy about four years old'. He would soon be heading home. In the meantime he hoped that 'my dear Pug Face will soon be well'. She should take care of her mother, 'do all you can for her' and 'kiss Miss Kitty for me'. It was, despite its slight irony, a typically paternal letter.[22]

Lord FitzRoy wrote again to Fanny on 16 March, expressing concern that no letter had been received from England since hers dated 13 February. He had heard from the Bagots in The Hague, with 'favourable' news of Lady FitzRoy on 24 February. However, to Fanny he wrote: 'It is worrying not to have heard of her from herself'; and it was also 'a matter of great regret to me that I have no news of my brother'. 'The Common Post' had been functioning well for others in the Duke's party and he could only assume that his mail had been directed via the less reliable Foreign Office system. He was 'pretty confident' that they would be leaving St Petersburg on 1 or 2 April and that, if the roads proved satisfactory, they would reach England about 23 April. However one of the roads on ice used on the way out had now broken up and others were melting. He was not therefore sure whether they would travel via Warsaw and Dresden or Mechlin. Lord FitzRoy favoured the former because he had already seen Berlin, although that road would almost certainly be the better. He did not 'envisage the journey with much delight', the only advantage being that England was 'at the end of it'. 'I cannot bear being so far from home'; and he reiterated the promise in his previous letter: 'My mother may rely upon my running down to Stoke as soon as I can after I get back.' He hardly enthused about the social round in St Petersburg: 'We have by no means a gay time of it here. As I believe I told you in my former letter, no Russian House is open, and therefore the only society which is open to us is that of the *corps diplomatique*, which consists of eight or nine women of different ages and some thirty men.' There was, he observed, 'nothing very remarkable' about any of them: 'The best of the Ladies is the wife ... of the English Secretary of Embassy. She is not pretty but she is lively and agreeable.'

The Imperial family, he explained, had left St Petersburg on 11 March for the country house of the late Emperor, where his body arrived the following day. This would be conveyed to St Petersburg 'with great pomp and ceremony on Saturday [18 March] next [followed by the Emperor and Empress on foot] and deposited in the great Shrine for a week and then the funeral is to take place.' The burial would occur in the fortress on the other side of the river, necessitating yet another procession to Lord FitzRoy's dismay: 'I wish it was all over, for I dislike these melancholy ceremonies.' Enigmatically, he added: 'But I believe they are useful in this Country.'

In the short time since the Emperor had left St Petersburg for the country house, FitzRoy Somerset had been sight-seeing – 'certainly one of the most fatiguing amusements I know'. He was further impressed by the 'prodigiously fine' Imperial palace with its splendid art collection, founded on Catherine the Great's acquisition of pictures from Lord Cholmondeley for 'a trifling' of their real worth. His mother would know more about this matter, he believed. Grand Duke Michael's palace, although only partially furnished, was 'very splendid', with its rooms so remarkable in size and beauty that they surpassed 'anything we have in England'. The College of Mines contained 'a great many curiosities' and, although he was professionally interested in the Arsenal, he felt that details of its contents would not excite Fanny. Lord FitzRoy had also seen the Tauride or Summer Palace, with its 'immense ball room', 'considerable garden' and gravel walks in an annex roofed over so that one was not exposed to the elements. For somebody so averse to the exercise Lord FitzRoy had seen a lot of the city that had so impressed him, and his remarks were by no means culturally trite. As ever, he ended the letter with a thought for his family: 'Pray say something that is kind and affectionate to my mother and assure her that I am most anxious about her, and that I look forward with pleasure to the time when I shall be able to run down to Stoke and see her.' In a letter to his brother-in-law, Sir Charles Bagot, Lord FitzRoy explained that 'we are lodged in the *Hotel des Appanages*, which was in your time, I believe, in the possession of Gourieff', reiteratng that he and Wellington had been cordially received by the Imperial family, several of whom expressed 'the high opinion they entertain of you and Mary'. The previous day he had visited the Malmaison Gallery: 'What a curious picture is the Paul Potter!' he exclaimed – reference to the representation of an Aesop Fable depicting a scene where men are being hunted by animals. He declared himself 'very much struck with the town' and described a pleasant meeting with Count Nesselrode (Russian Foreign Minister) and his wife, who both enquired 'most kindly after you'. Mischieviously he added that the 'ladies are so vicious in their taste as to fancy you *un tres bel homme! Ah Dieu, quel mauvais gout!*'[23]

A little behind schedule, FitzRoy Somerset was at Dover on 27 April. There he wrote to Fanny his last account of the visit to St Petersburg because he would be too 'fully employed' to do so once he reached London. He recalled writing to her from Riga on the morning of 9 April after dealing with dispatches all night, but that letter has not survived. From Riga it took five days to reach Warsaw across 'the very worst roads I ever passed in my life'. In an allusion evidently familiar to Fanny, he likened them to 'the deepest part of the Lower Woods' and could not imagine why they were classified as 'roads'. The wheels sank deep into mud, which 'splattered' the carriages and there was difficulty in obtaining satisfactory replacement horses on the way. Nevertheless they arrived at Warsaw on 14 April, the coaches 'none the worse for wear', and stayed at the royal palace. That evening Wellington and Lord FitzRoy dined 'tête-à-tête' with Grand Duke Constantine and his wife. Although 'elder brother' of the present Tsar of Russia, Constantine had renounced all claim to the throne on marrying his wife, who was not of royal blood and could not therefore become a grand duchess. In his younger days Constantine had the reputation for a violent temper, but 'he has altered very much' under the influence of his wife, who was known within the royal family as 'Sage de Paix'. Lord FitzRoy confessed: 'I do not think I was ever more taken with any Lady than I was with the Princess ... Without being pretty she has a most interesting and expressive countenance, added to which she has the best and most engaging manners, and as much consideration as one could wish.' He thus enthused about a 'pleasant' dinner, even though the Grand Duke appeared to think that Wellington was extremely deaf.

He described Warsaw as 'a very pretty town' on the left bank of the 'very fine' River Vistula, though he had no time to explore it. Wellington was due to review Polish troops on the morning of 15 April, but the weather proved too poor; and 'towards midday' they continued their journey. That day the roads were satisfactory, but during the ensuing two days proved 'exceptionally bad', differing from those east of Warsaw only because they were pure sand, not mud and sand. Twenty-two horses were used on Lord FitzRoy's carriage between Warsaw and Frankfurt-on-Oder; and further difficulty occurred with replacements before they drove into Berlin on the afternoon of 18 April. At this point in his letter he included an anti-Semitic passage, which may only have reflected contemporary High Church opinion at home. 'The whole of the country through which we travelled from Mittau to Warsaw is infested with swarms of Jews, who are of the most filthy appearance and wear long beards ... [indecipherable] it would take all the scrubbing burghers to be found in London to make one of them decently clean.'

On 19 April Wellington and Lord FitzRoy rested in Berlin where they dined with 'the King ... [being] treated by him and his family with marked kindness'. Leaving Berlin on 20 April, Wellington reviewed 'Prussian Guards' formed up outside the capital some ten miles along the route to Weimar where they dined with the Grand Duke, travelling on to reach Frankfurt-on-Main on the night of 22 April. The roads were now good and 'we went merrily' on to Bonn, though the subsequent leg to Liège (reached on 24 April) was 'tiresome'; and the following day Lord FitzRoy's carriage had to be 'put to rights' in Brussels. None the less, on the way to Calais 'yesterday', the four wheels again 'gave way' and he was detained while further repairs were carried out. Mobile again, he then found Lord Douglas 'in the middle of the road with his axle tree in two', so FitzRoy Somerset 'brought him on' to Calais where they arrived only fifteen minutes after Wellington. They could have embarked at once or delayed until 4 o'clock that morning [27 April], which the Duke preferred. They thus landed at Dover at 8.30 a.m., 'having had a very pleasant passage, except that it rained hard. But I mean we were not sick, which is more than half the battle.' Given his aversion to most roads abroad, dislike of absence from home and evident caution about sea travel, Lord FitzRoy could not have looked forward to excursions of this nature. Nor could he have entirely relished returning to domestic worries. News of Lady FitzRoy, not received at St Petersburg, had since come through. He feared that he would not find his wife well, for she 'has had a very painful attack of *Rheumatism* and was for ten days unable to walk'.

She was, he believed, now free from pain, but the illness had upset her 'very much'. He concluded by sending 'kindest love' to Elizabeth and Arthur whom he hoped were 'greatly well'.[24]

Back in London Lord FitzRoy resumed his work at the Ordnance, interrupted occasionally by duties of domestic importance. During 1826 Priscilla stayed at Apsley House while recovering from serious illness. In July she went with Emily to convalesce in Margate, and the following month Wellington arranged for an Admiralty vessel to take her to the continent. FitzRoy Somerset travelled to Deptford to confirm that the designated ship would be suitable and, if so, to liaise with his sister-in-law about the date of departure and port of destination. Little could he have realized as he did so that within eight months a political upheaval would end his stay in Pall Mall for a quarter of a century.[25]

CHAPTER 5

MILITARY SECRETARY, THE HORSE GUARDS (1827-42)

'My unqualified approval of the manner in which you have carried out the arduous duties of your highly important office.' (Lord Hill, 1842)[1]

In January 1827, on the death of the Duke of York, Wellington became CinC as well as Master-General – a unique combination of offices which caused even more Ordnance administration to fall on Lord FitzRoy. But on 13 April Wellington resigned both posts when George Canning became Prime Minister; and FitzRoy also left the Ordnance. The diplomat, the Hon F. Cathcart, observed that the King did not replace Wellington at the Horse Guards, leaving the way open for 'the Great Captain to return when the sulk is a little over'. To Bagot he added: 'In that case, the FitzRoy Somersets will come right again, as he will of course be Military Secretary. In the meantime I am very sorry for them. I know how hard it is to be obliged to turn out of a comfortable house and to trust to chance and politicks for another.' During the summer, efforts to persuade Wellington to resume at the Horse Guards failed. Lord FitzRoy argued that he should not 'accept the Command [again] but with full satisfaction ... or without receiving a full apology from Mr Canning' – a reference to Canning's determination to oust Wellington from the Cabinet which precipitated his twin resignations. Unexpectedly, on 8 August Canning died. Lord Goderich replaced him as Prime Minister and Wellington did then again become CinC. Shortly afterwards the Adjutant-General (Sir Henry Torrens) died and a reshuffling of the staff allowed Lord FitzRoy to join Wellington as Military Secretary. He would serve in that post from 28 August 1827 until 30 September 1852. As J.H. Stocqueler, historian of the Horse Guards, has pointed out, FitzRoy Somerset's experience of civil and military administration combined with his 'benevolent nature ... and accomplished manners, well-fitted him for the post'.[2]

He would indeed require urbanity in full measure during the next 25 years. The CinC exercised extensive responsibilities, controlling all regular infantry and cavalry and, when embodied, reserve forces in the United Kingdom. He was responsible for supplying troops and reinforcements for overseas commitments, together with officers to fill command and staff appointments. Once in the field troops might not be under his direct orders expeditionary force commanders answered to the Secretary of State for War and the Colonies – but he remained, in general terms, responsible for the discipline, welfare and promotion structure of the Army. At the Horse Guards in 1820 the CinC supervised an establishment of 21 civilian clerks in addition to military personnel, but in practice the burden of routine administration devolved upon three personal staff officers: Adjutant-General (discipline), Quartermaster-General (plans) and Military Secretary. Of the three the Military Secretary arguably enjoyed the most extensive authority. All confidential correspondence to and from the CinC and all communications with other government departments (including those connected with the East India Company) passed through the Military Secretary. Henry Torrens believed that no subordinate office of the Crown involved so much 'labour, importance, variety of matter and incessant confinement'. During Lord FitzRoy's years at the Horse Guards the physical frailty of Hill and, later, Wellington gave the Military Secretary enhanced *de facto* influence and a posthumous tribute that 'during a peace of 40 years, he reserved to England the nucleus of an army'.[3]

There was indeed much to be done. Despite peace in Europe in 1815, leading to the traditional quest for post-war military retrenchment, British troops were soon marching to the sound of the guns in Canada, China, Africa, India, Burma, Ceylon and New Zealand. At home the demands of securing national defence and public order did not diminish. But the entire administrative process was vastly complicated by a proliferation of civilian and military agencies, both within and outside the Horse Guards, with which the Military Secretary had to deal on the CinC's behalf. A Parliamentary Select Committee concluded that 'effective and economical conduct of military business is divided among too many officers totally separate and independent of each other'. FitzRoy Somerset had to negotiate what a future CinC would term 'this curious Chinese puzzle-like system'.[4]

Wellington's first spell as CinC lasted from January until April 1827. His second was only marginally longer. In January 1828 he became Prime Minister.[5] Holding that the CinC did not interfere in political matters, the Duke at first believed that he could combine the two posts. Persuaded otherwise, he appointed Lord Hill to the Horse Guards.[6] Hill had not been in good health since suffering a serious attack of 'bilious fever' in 1817, and was so low in the seniority list that Wellington proposed that he should be 'Senior General upon the Staff, performing the duties of Commander-in-Chief [rather] than Commander-in-Chief ... The only real difference is in pay, which is not of much importance to you.' Hill formally took charge on 16 February 1828; and FitzRoy Somerset remained as Military Secretary to provide continuity.[7]

As Henry Torrens had forecast, however, his new post involved the clerical equivalent of hard labour. Even when Lord FitzRoy left London for Badminton or holiday locations such as the Isle of Wight, official correspondence followed him. He wrote to Charlotte from Badminton on 24 September 1830 about 'a very heavy post of 59 letters besides those for signature', and, similarly, on 10 January 1834 that he had dealt with 50 letters that day. A major part of this correspondence involved communications to Hill at his home, Hardwicke Grange, or the Horse Guards' staff in

London, either conveying decisions or sending draft letters: on 3 October 1835 he sent eight draft letters from Dover to Hardwicke Grange for Hill's signature. On occasions (and certainly in 1836 and 1837) he was at his desk in the Horse Guards on Boxing Day. Writing to Hill from Badminton on 24 December 1837 he revealed – in response to two letters from Major-General Sir Willoughby Gordon at the Horse Guards that day – that he would leave for London on Christmas Day, expecting to arrive soon after 6 p.m., because the situation 'in North America [Canadian unrest] was causing alarm'. Especially when Hill was away from the capital, Lord FitzRoy coped personally with urgent matters: in advising the CinC that there was no need for him to hurry back, on 20 January 1834 he listed the problems under active consideration and pointed out that he was sending Hill only papers 'which will not give you much trouble'. In September 1836 he mentioned to Wellington that the family's departure for Dover would be delayed until after the Monday morning mail had arrived at the Horse Guards. Duty first.[8]

At the Ordnance FitzRoy Somerset had had no more than a mild foretaste of the deluge of issues concerning promotion, patronage, requests for personal favours and day-to-day business that would engulf him in Whitehall. In December 1834 Colonel Richard Egerton, Hill's private secretary, forwarded a plea from Major Champain's uncle for his nephew to be appointed 'second lieutenant-colonel' to the 9th Regiment. The uncle conceded that there might well be 'numerous applicants of more service and older standing'; but Champain had exhausted his personal funds in purchasing every step to the rank of major, which he had held for 'nearly six' years, two of those in command of the depot. Lord FitzRoy explained to Egerton that the question of a second lieutenant-colonel of the 9th had not formally arisen and even if it did Champain had scant chance 'in the present circumstances of getting the promotion': entering the Service as a half-pay ensign in 1817, he had not obtained a regimental appointment for a further two years. FitzRoy Somerset was asked by Hill for advice in a painful case where the grief-stricken mother of Lieutenant W.I.B. Webb, cashiered for fraud in southern Africa, appealed for clemency on the grounds that her son had been stranded without money to get home. The Military Secretary regretted that no grounds for leniency existed. Not that he was always negative, the story being recorded that 'a poor officer' of the 43rd applied for Lord FitzRoy's help in gaining advancement for his son, 'a junior clerk in a public office'. The boy went to see the Military Secretary in some trepidation, only to be greeted warmly by FitzRoy Somerset who shook his hand and spoke highly of his father. Lord FitzRoy did make representations 'in the proper quarter', the young man secured promotion and eventually worked his way up to become head of a department.[9]

The scope of the Military Secretary's work under Hill required dealing with such diverse matters as a detailed plea from Major-General

Sir Jasper Nicholls that he had a net annual pension of merely £155 to support a wife, nine children and servants, whereas a retired clerk from the Navy Pay Office with similar length of service received £160 per annum; a supplication from Sir Samuel Brown 'for a regiment'; the King's request for removal of the garrison commander at Plymouth; rival claimants for a staff post in Corfu; the relative attributes of candidates for the governorships of the Royal Hospital Chelsea and Royal Military College Sandhurst; disciplinary controversies after a guardsman read publicly a printed article on 'Military Bullyism'; allegations of gagging as a punishment in the 84th Regiment; a tedious search for a 'ball cartridge firing' area for the Guards, settling finally on Wormwood Scrubs; a dispute as to whether the King or CinC should convene a board of inquiry into possible financial irregularities in the Household Cavalry's accounts; and, delicately, uncertainty as to whether Hill would be invited to the celebratory dinner at Windsor in January 1842 following the royal christening.[10]

At times FitzRoy Somerset wielded considerable personal influence over military appointments. When William IV favoured General Hodgson as colonel of the 4th, Lord FitzRoy argued persuasively that Sir George Walker had better qualifications; and Hill supported him. In January 1837 the CinC agreed that Sir Hussey Vivian should become colonel of the Royal Dragoons, leaving a vacancy in the 12th Lancers. The Military Secretary submitted to the CinC a list of possible replacements with an analysis of their qualities, 'omitting Sir Loftus Otway and two or three others whose claims you would not be disposed to entertain'. Goldie had not served in Great Britain and 'speaking quite confidentially' he thought that Lord Melbourne (the Prime Minister) might object to one of the other candidates. This left Need and Cumming. The latter, Lord FitzRoy noted, was rich; the former was not. FitzRoy Somerset's preference thus became evident; and Hill subsequently announced that he had come 'to the conclusion that Cumming is the best person to recommend for the 12th Lancers'. Lord FitzRoy then saw Melbourne, who had no objection to the appointment, so the necessary papers were prepared immediately for Sir Henry Cumming and Sir Hussey Vivian to sign.[11]

Financial considerations lay behind FitzRoy Somerset's advice not to allow Seaton to transfer from the colonelcy of the 94th to the 52nd, because his current regiment was '200 men stronger' and on the Indian establishment where 'the emolument ... [is] much greater'. Similarly he cautioned against appointing Sir FitzRoy Maclean to the 45th, which 'might gratify his feelings ... but it will not benefit his pocket'. His views on the appointment of a Deputy Assistant Adjutant-General in Dublin were based, though, on professional fitness. In August 1841 Lord FitzRoy reported to Hill that four applications had been received for the vacancy. Two had never before held staff posts, another had spent eleven years on half pay 'and I question his efficiency as a mounted officer in the field'. The fourth, Captain Sterling of the 73rd – 'a very clever man and highly qualified' – had 'unquestionable' fitness. Hill chose Sterling.[12]

In order to proffer sensible advice on overseas' appointments FitzRoy Somerset needed to be aware of the army's wider commitments. He could thus confidently counsel Hill to communicate personally with Melbourne about the command of troops in North America. The King had told him at Windsor that 'it was in contemplation' to replace Major-General Sir John Colborne as Lieutenant Governor of Upper Canada, 'abruptly' with a civilian, Sir Stewart Mackenzie, because Colborne had been lax in communicating with the Colonial Office in London. Lord FitzRoy 'took the opportunity to tell the King that in my opinion no officer in the employment of the publick ever devoted himself more exclusively to the discharge of his duty than Sir John Colborne'. Colborne was not in fact dismissed; but he later offered to resign his office, coincidentally as military command in Canada was coming under serious discussion. FitzRoy Somerset noted that Lord Glenelg had 'admitted' to the King that, in view of the unrest in Upper and Lower Canada, it would be 'desirable' for a General of standing to take command of forces there – in other words, to create a purely military command to 'infuse the Canadians with respect'. In May 1836, having been replaced in his political appointment by Sir Francis Head, Colborne took up the military command of Upper and Lower Canada. The influence of the Horse Guards and – given his unprompted testimonial for Colborne – of FitzRoy Somerset may be inferred in this arrangement.[13]

More routinely, personal interviews formed an integral part of the Military Secretary's work. In August 1837 he reported to Hill a 'long conversation' with Colonel Harvey who was 'disposed to speak warmly of his grievances'. Lord FitzRoy treated him 'with good humour'. Eight months later, however, there took place 'a long and by no means agreeable interview with Lieutenant-Colonel Delancey'. Delancey had thought that Lord FitzRoy would offer him command of the King's Dragoon Guards and was 'sadly taken aback' to be informed that Sir Charles Dalhousie had expressed displeasure with him. The interview became so tense that FitzRoy Somerset called Sir John Macdonald (the Adjutant-General) to his aid; but to no avail. Delancey demanded an 'investigation' so Lord FitzRoy was left with the unenviable task of approaching Dalhousie for more details of his objections. On another occasion Lieutenant-General Sir Latimer Widdrington accused Lord FitzRoy of not forwarding his request for the colonelcy of a regiment to Hill, and was dissatisfied with the Military Secretary's diplomatic response: 'His Lordship has not been unmindful of your wishes, but the difficulty with regard to their accomplishmant continues too great to admit of his giving you such an answer as would be agreeable to you or himself.' This failed to quieten Widdrington who took his case to the government. But Howick (the Secretary at War) advised the Prime Minister (Melbourne) that he would not interfere in a matter of army patronage which remained the province of the CinC.[14]

Lord FitzRoy was, however, able to smooth a number of ruffled feathers and ease the way through other bureaucratic minefields. Lieutenant-General Sir John Hamilton wrote to Lord FitzRoy expressing 'many, many thanks' for the 'truly kind letter' which revealed that Hamilton was *not* entitled to Peninsula prize money. Pleading that he had been 'repeatedly advised' to apply for the award, Hamilton wanted all his letters on the subject 'quashed' and 'destroyed'. The case of Colonel Goldie also required tact. Goldie approached Hill from Templeman Barracks, Tipperary, through Egerton, explaining that he had a continuing chest complaint which involved on occasions spitting blood, although this had eased recently. 'Our surgeon tells me, however, that I must expect to have a return of it next winter unless I can get to a milder climate for the cold season.' Enclosing a long memorandum from the surgeon, Goldie asked for a Mediterranean posting. His letter was passed to FitzRoy Somerset who replied judiciously. It would be impossible to secure a regiment in the Mediterranean in time, but he suggested that Hill might allow Goldie to go on leave early in the autumn: 'I have a high regard for and a high opinion of Goldie and I shall be very sorry to see him give up the command of his regiment.' And his sensitivity was evident – as well as the value of an excellent memory – in dealing with a series of distasteful attempts to defraud Wellington. Asking the Duke to forward a 'begging letter' from a Lieutenant-Colonel Cole of the 45th, he recalled a Cole in that regiment who had only been a major. Shortly afterwards he informed Wellington that a 'soi-disant Captain Erskine' had been apprehended by the police who were actively seeking 'Lieutenant-Colonel Cole': 'Our great object is to punish these swindlers without obliging you to appear against them.'[15]

Royal personages caused particular professional problems. Drawing Hill's attention to the pending arrival of the Duke of Cambridge's son in England and the undesirability of his appearing in Hanoverian uniform, FitzRoy Somerset revealed that Cambridge wanted him to become a colonel in the army without 'any regimental commission', though he was not averse to his being seconded to the Guards or Rifle Brigade. As a result Prince George went to Gibraltar for his training under Lieutenant-General Sir Alexander Woodford. Woodford explained to FitzRoy Somerset that the Prince's previous association with the Jäger Guard in Hanover would stand him in good stead and that once he had mastered the British style of drill, 'interior order and economy', he would be brought on to the field officers' roster with command of light companies on field days. Shortly afterwards Lord FitzRoy warned the CinC that the Duke of Cambridge himself, as Colonel of the First Regiment of Guards (Grenadiers), sought to invoke an order of Charles II to take command of the Brigade of Guards. Hill somewhat mildly hoped that the Duke would 'not persist in his intentions'. There was difficulty, too, over the King's natural son, Lieutenant-Colonel George FitzClarence, who wanted promotion. When

William IV told him that Hill could not agree, FitzClarence evidently 'betrayed much violence' and FitzRoy Somerset regretted that the King had suffered this 'annoyance', adding: 'I wish I may have an opportunity of speaking to Lieutenant Colonel FitzClarence. I think I could shew him that he owes it to his father to cease pressing for his promotion at the present moment.' On 7 October 1838, Lord FitzRoy did have 'a very long conversation' with FitzClarence who refused to back down, insisting that the King agreed with him, but admitting in the broadest way that he had *no military claim whatever* and that his case rested solely upon his relationship to the King. Acknowledging Lord FitzRoy's strenuous efforts to resolve the problem, Hill sympathized with his sense of failure.[16]

Notwithstanding Lord FitzRoy's scrupulous apolitical stance in his work, in 1833 a disaffected former cavalry officer caustically concluded that 'the CinC and his numerous co-adjutators are the personal friends of former CinCs ... [and] are *rejetons* of tory growth'. Patronage, in particular, incurred the ire of the writer. Lord FitzRoy – possibly a direct target, being a friend of a former CinC (Wellington) – undoubtedly did prefer acquaintances or their relations, but not at the expense of professionalism and certainly not for political purposes. The pamphleteer vehemently opposed flogging and he may have taken exception to FitzRoy Somerset's defence, in October 1832, of a commanding officer's retaining the right of 'instantaneous punishment' following reports of a mutiny in the 7th Regiment. The Military Secretary argued that, if not, 'the Army would in a short time become an Armed Rabble and a nuisance instead of a benefit to the Country.' It is possible, however, that the ex-officer merely objected to the military conservatism which led FitzRoy Somerset to show less than enthusiasm when the Admiralty proposed that 'the Marines ... come under the CinC': 'I do not see how actually they can be so more than they now are and I would recommend that the question should be cautiously dealt with.' His sympathy for Wellington's argument that the present musket – effective in firepower and the right length for bayonetting – did not need replacement may similarly have been deplored. But it was not politically biased. He was, in practice, careful to emphasize that an officer must be apolitical: '... any show of political feeling in an officer must affect and prejudice his desire of a Military Appt [*sic*]'.[17]

FitzRoy Somerset did become closely involved in a successful rearguard action against attempts by whig politicians to reform the 'Chinese puzzle-like' army administration and, at the same time, bring command of line regiments and the Ordnance Corps under one officer. But he did not do so from a tory perspective. Rather he reinforced his contention that the Army must professionally be divorced from close political direction. During Lord Hill's time at the Horse Guards proposals for reform found expression in the findings of official bodies, culminating in the Howick Report. In 1833 the Duke of Richmond's Royal Commission recommended that a Board under a civilian member of the Cabinet should supervise 'the civil business' of the War Office, Board of Ordnance, Pay Office, Comptrollers of Army Accounts and Commissariat – the Treasury department responsible for army land transport and certain supplies – and that the CinC should take over the military duties of the Master-General. These proposals were not implemented; indeed they were neither published then nor debated openly. Four years later the Duke needed to summarize his findings for Howick. Howick felt that Richmond's resignation from Lord Grey's government in June 1834 might have killed his initiative. In view of the fierce opposition to Howick's own recommendations, a vigorous covert campaign of lobbying – which involved the Horse Guards – is more likely. Two changes of government in 1834 produced a fertile environment for delay. Almost simultaneously with Richmond's investigations, FitzRoy Somerset on behalf of the CinC personally met the Secretary at War (Edward Ellice) to fend off his vigorous suggestions for economy at the Horse Guards, especially in the Quartermaster-General's department.[18]

The search for economy and efficiency in military administration would not die, however. Howick's Royal Commission rejected Richmond's conclusion as being 'no adequate remedy to that which we consider the chief defect of the present system, namely the want of one authority having an efficient control over the whole military expenditure of the country and responsible both for its amount and for the manner in which the sums voted by Parliament are applied.' It therefore concentrated on consolidation of political control and recommended in its report of 21 February 1837 that the powers of the civilian Secretary at War be vastly enhanced: 'The greater part of the authority with reference to the Army, which at present belongs to the Secretaries of State should for the future be vested in the Secretary of War ... he should be the person to communicate on all points with the CinC on behalf of the Administration and be immediately responsible to Parliament for all measures of the Government with reference to the Army.' Specifically he would exercise 'general superintendence' over the CinC and Master-General. Edward Ellice's successors would thus find their quest for economy among the CinC's staff much easier to achieve and, not surprisingly, military antagonism to Howick's report became marked.[19]

FitzRoy Somerset certainly played a part – possibly an important co-ordinating role – in that opposition. In March 1837 Wellington wrote strongly to him, claiming that the Crown's authority would suffer: 'This measure will transfer the effective command of the Army from the King to the House of Commons – of which body the Secretary at War will be the most powerful Member ... This new *Leviathan* ... [would control] everything relating to the Political Command – the pay – the movement – the equipment – the stationing – the barracks – the stores – the arms – the forage and provisions of the Army'. The Duke concluded forcefully: 'The most serious point of this affair is that it takes the Military Power of the

State totally and entirely out of the hands of the person exercising the Royal Authority; and places it in the hands of one member of the House of Commons and of the Cabinet.' Potential damage to the royal prerogative and, more widely, the equilibrium, whereby command and control of the army had been divorced since the seventeenth century, would be dangerously upset.[20]

Lord FitzRoy, at least in general terms, supported this position because at the height of the storm over Howick's recommendations William IV's Private Secretary (Sir Herbert Taylor) assured Lord FitzRoy that his views and those of Wellington had been communicated to the King. As a consequence William IV had emphasized to Melbourne the adverse effect on the royal prerogative if Howick's Report were adopted. None the less on 30 December 1837 FitzRoy Somerset warned Wellington that 'the adoption of the report on the Military Departments is seriously contemplated'. At a meeting the previous day between Hill and Melbourne, he explained, the Prime Minister had promised to forward to the Horse Guards a copy of the Draft Order in Council which would implement the proposals. Before this reached Whitehall, taking Lord FitzRoy's advice, Hill decided on another approach to Melbourne. And once Hill had studied the Draft Order the Military Secretary collated his comments and passed them to Wellington – the implication being that this represented the basis of Hill's further arguments to Melbourne.[21]

Hill also wrote to Howick, and Wellington again communicated with Melbourne during the opening days of 1838, making his celebrated comment that the CinC would not henceforth be able to 'move a corporal's guard from hence to Windsor without his [Secretary at War's] approval'. Melbourne made Howick aware of these further expressions of disapproval. Thus FitzRoy Somerset acted as a link between Wellington and Hill, and he made Sir Herbert Taylor aware of his own qualms. Indirectly, through these correspondents, his views were conveyed to Melbourne and the King. The strength of Lord FitzRoy's personal influence cannot be accurately gauged, but remained evident. Howick's proposals were quietly shelved and Melbourne admitted to an uneasy Howick that military disquiet had contributed to their withdrawal.[22]

An incident in 1834 offered a glimpse of effective political constraint. Returning from a stay in Nassau, Sir Francis Head compiled a memorandum on the training of the Prussian Army. Presenting a copy to Lord FitzRoy at the Horse Guards, Head asked him why such a proven system of instruction, command and 'the minutest details necessary for the subsistence and movement in the field' could not be adopted by the British. 'For some seconds', FitzRoy Somerset 'appeared unwilling or unable to answer my plain question: at last, calmly shrugging up his left shoulder and the stump of his right arm, he replied "Joseph Hume"' – the persistent radical opponent of military expenditure.[23]

The behaviour of one commanding officer during Hill's time at the Horse Guards caused the CinC and his Military Secretary very serious concern. (Twenty years later he would again prove embarrassingly troublesome in the Crimea.) Lieutenant-Colonel Lord Brudenell (from August 1837, seventh Earl of Cardigan) purchased command of the 15th King's Hussars in 1832 and, as a consequence of his domineering manner and violent temper, soon found himself at odds with his officers. Twice during the autumn of 1833 he put Captain Wathen under arrest, and on the second occasion a court-martial ensued. Wathen was vindicated and on 1 February 1834 by a General Order of the CinC Brudenell was removed from his post. Brudenell refused to accept the justice of his removal and began to lobby vigorously for another regiment. In this process Lord Hill, FitzRoy Somerset, certain political figures and Wellington became embroiled. Through his sister, married to Queen Adelaide's chamberlain (Lord Howe), Brudenell also sought support from the Court.

To some extent Lord FitzRoy's position was difficult, for he knew Brudenell socially and had stayed at the family home of Deene Park in Northamptonshire. Nevertheless he exercised detached professional judgement throughout his dealings with Brudenell at the Horse Guards. In conveying the King's refusal to grant Brudenell a court-martial or court of inquiry, he advised the aggrieved officer that he might later secure Horse Guards' support if he would behave in a restrained manner. Brudenell could not. It was alien to his nature. He continued to pester Lord FitzRoy who in September 1835 reported two further interviews with him to Hill: 'They did not have any satisfactory results,' he drily commented. 'On the first occasion, he hardly gave me the opportunity to speak ... But on the last I distinctly told him that your Lordship considered that you must not recommend him for employment at the present moment, assuring him however that you had every disposition to meet his wishes when it might be practicable.' That, possibly, gave Brudenell the impression of ultimate Horse Guards' sanction. FitzRoy Somerset revealed that Brudenell believed he had the support of Howick, the Secretary at War, though Lord FitzRoy wondered how he could have formed that opinion. In accordance with Hill's wishes the Military Secretary had seen Melbourne, and the Prime Minister would write to Howick asking him whether he were 'ready to fight the battle in the House of Commons'. This stemmed from Lord FitzRoy's having told Melbourne 'as I had previously told Lord Brudenell that the question was one upon which there should be a complete understanding between the CinC and the Govt'. During the following month the Military Secretary whimsically reported: 'Lord Brudenell favoured me with another of his disagreeable visits yesterday [13 October]. I confined myself to telling him that you could not recommend his appointment to the 11th Light Dragoons.' Brudenell wanted to know why and Lord FitzRoy 'undertook' to write to Hill. When FitzRoy Somerset was out of London – on holiday with the family at Dover – Brudenell pursued his case via the mail, enclosing in his letter the copy of another addressed by Vivian (the Master-General) to Sir Henry Hardinge; but as Vivian mentioned neither Melbourne's views nor those of Hill, Lord FitzRoy considered this letter 'quite useless'. Before leaving London FitzRoy Somerset had seen Brudenell yet again: 'The interview was not a very long one nor can I say that it was an agreeable one'. With a hint of exasperation the Military Secretary emphasized that Hill must see Brudenell himself when the CinC returned to London.

In the New Year, possibly through decisive Court intervention, Brudenell was gazetted commanding officer of the 11th Dragoon Guards, after he had again officially seen Lord FitzRoy on 19 January 1836. The appointment caused a storm in the press and the radical MP, Sir William Molesworth, unsuccessfully attempted to get a select committee 'to enquire into the conduct of the Commander-in-Chief of the Forces' in making the appointment. Sir Henry Hardinge, however, wrote effusively to Hill: 'Your decision to reinstate Lord Brudenell to active service is one of the most popular acts of your military administration ... and I congratulate you on the termination of a matter which from various causes was from the outset one of great difficulty and delicacy.' Hill thanked Hardinge for the 'kind terms with regard to my conduct on Lord Brudenell's restoration to full pay'. Hardinge and Hill were deluding themselves, however, if they thought that trouble with Brudenell had ended. Lord FitzRoy's advice counselled caution. He knew the man better.[24]

For three years Cardigan (as Brudenell now was) remained out of the limelight, mainly because he went to join his new regiment in India. In 1840, the 11th – soon renamed the 11th, Prince Albert's Own Hussars because they had formed the escort to Prince Albert from Dover to London on his way to marry Queen Victoria – were back in England. And trouble soon began. Cardigan clashed with Captain John Reynolds, who was arrested for allegedly drinking porter from a black bottle at a mess dinner contrary to his Commanding Officer's orders and publicly reprimanded by the Inspector-General of Cavalry; and another officer (Captain Richard Reynolds) who was court-martialled and cashiered. He gained a reputation, generally, for harassing and verbally abusing others. On 12 September 1840 he fought a duel on Wimbledon Common with one of the 11th's former officers, Lieutenant Harvey Tuckett, which led to Cardigan's arrest and release on bail. Lord FitzRoy reported, in regard to the latter episode, that the Adjutant-General (Macdonald) '... is sadly vexed and annoyed at this Cardigan business', adding: 'I was always of the opinion that the duel was an injudicious *complication* and so it proved.'[25]

Scarcely had Cardigan been released on bail following the Tuckett affair than he put another of his subalterns, Lieutenant William Forrest, under arrest for a minor offence, which caused Forrest to complain formally to the CinC. Writing to Egerton on 29 September Lord FitzRoy explained that 'I thought at one time Macdonald had better see Lieutenant

Forrest ... I dropped Macdonald a note to suggest how he might tackle it.' But, as the arrest had occurred on 18 September and no action had subsequently been taken, he felt on reflection that an interview would no longer be appropriate. FitzRoy Somerset was not wholly condemnatory of Cardigan: 'Cardigan mismanaged this matter to my idea grossly, but it was too much of Lieutenant Forrest to complain of insulting language when he disobeyed an order before Lord Cardigan spoke to him at all.' This was an overstatement of the situation which concerned a minor problem about access to personal accommodation; but Lord FitzRoy may not have known the full facts. Nevertheless Cardigan had, in two regiments, clashed with junior officers in such a way as to make his judgement, at the very least, suspect. Lord FitzRoy now betrayed a prejudice that must have been nurtured with Wellington in the Peninsula and which was severely to damage his relationship with the press in the Crimea: 'The hell hounds of the press are let loose upon Cardigan and the Horse Guards.' *Ergo*, officer and institution were being ill-used. In the event Forrest was censured. Enigmatically, a correspondent to the radical *Morning Chronicle* referred to 'obligations of a very peculiar nature existing between Lord FitzRoy Somerset and the Earl of Cardigan', possibly alluding to their aristocratic and social connections. Lord Hill, though, made his position clear: 'I am thoroughly sick of the 11th! And all that belongs to it.'[26]

Seemingly immune to criticism, Cardigan remained a prime target for the press; and he was reviled when he appeared in public theatres at Brighton and in London. On 16 November Lord FitzRoy warned Egerton to alert Lord Hill about a letter from a field officer in *The Times* of that day, 'which is calculated to give great offence to Lord Cardigan'. In mid-December Cardigan disciplined a junior regimental surgeon which caused Hill to rebuke him in writing. Later that month, refused permission by Cardigan to attend the senior department of the Royal Military College Sandhurst, Captain John Reynolds – of 'black bottle' fame – applied for permission to sell out. FitzRoy Somerset became closely involved in an attempt to resolve this latest fracas. He met Reynolds' uncle privately, in the hopes of mediation, and he evidently met Reynolds on more than one occasion. On Boxing Day 1840 Lord FitzRoy wrote to Hill about 'another meeting' with Reynolds at which Macdonald was present. Reynolds refused to withdraw his resignation 'unless you [Hill] allow him to go to the College and in arranging this for him we must take care not to give life to the supposition that you have any motive in wishing him to continue in the service' – possibly to avoid further adverse publicity, if the press focused on his resignation to Cardigan's further discomfort. Reynolds would call again and 'in the meantime', he explained to Egerton, 'Sir John [Macdonald] has written to Lord Cardigan to state what are his objections to Captain Reynolds' going to Sandhurst.' The situation was still unresolved a fortnight later when FitzRoy Somerset went to Stratfield Saye to discuss the matter with Wellington. Eventually

Reynolds did go to Sandhurst, though not before 'the hell hounds' had sniffed out some of the details for malicious publication. In mid-February 1841 Cardigan at length stood trial before the House of Lords for his part in the duel with Tuckett and was acquitted on a technicality. FitzRoy Somerset had no part in this process, but he attended the celebration dinner given by Lord Adolphus Fitzmaurice at St James's Palace on 18 February, together with the Duke of Cambridge and his son George (later one of Raglan's divisional commanders in the Crimea).[27]

Cardigan had yet to reach his nadir of notoriety. On the morning of Easter Sunday, 11 April 1841, the 11th Hussars attended divine service in the riding-school at Hounslow and shortly after this finished were marched back again to the same place to witness a flogging. *The Times's* indignation at 'the atrocity committed by Lord Cardigan' aptly summed up the ensuing outburst in press and Parliament. Melbourne advised Hill that Cardigan should be removed from command, but in the event Wellington argued that legally Cardigan had been correct, though guilty of 'a great impropriety and indiscretion'. Despite the furore Cardigan remained in post. Before the end of the year Lord William Paget had written to *The Times* threatening to take Cardigan to court for allegedly having an affair with Paget's wife – and this unsavoury episode would drag on until December 1843. Meanwhile, on 18 April 1842, the findings of Captain Richard Reynolds's court-martial were annulled and he was appointed to a captaincy in the 9th Hussars.

There has been a suggestion that Wellington was overruled in this matter, the government being determined that Hill should right a perceived wrong. Surviving Somerset papers imply otherwise, hinting that the initiative may rather have come from the Horse Guards in Hill's absence, with Wellington's agreement. On 29 March 1842 FitzRoy Somerset wrote to Egerton that 'the Government [is] quite with us in this Reynolds affair' and further that the Duke had approved a 'draft letter' for the Queen – apparently concerning Reynolds's vindication and reinstatement. On Wellington's advice, Lord FitzRoy had shown this to the Prime Minister, Sir Robert Peel, who wanted it to remain a purely military matter without the politicians being 'brought into it'. Sending that draft to Hill, FitzRoy Somerset recommended that the CinC write on 'letter paper' with the date at the bottom, let the Military Secretary have the draft back and advise him whether the Reynolds papers should go into a 'separate box', which Lord FitzRoy himself favoured.[28]

Cardigan was proving an undoubted irritant, but potential and actual civil unrest were even more acutely claiming Lord FitzRoy's attention at this time. Shortly after commencing his tenure at the Horse Guards he cut his administrative teeth on a quaint issue. In October 1828 Wellington expressed 'great anxiety' about possible disruption by Portuguese troops at Plymouth. Under their own officers they could use their weapons 'at very short notice without our previous knowledge'. The Portuguese, Wellington explained, were 'very quiet people', but their troops were paid and directed by 'the vilest set of vagabonds that ever assembled in any country'. The garrison at Plymouth was 'very weak' and there were few means to reinforce it. Wellington wanted an appreciation of the situation from FitzRoy Somerset, evidently feeling that the armed Portuguese could cause havoc. The Duke suggested that separation of officers and men, with only 'a few hundred' men remaining at Plymouth, would reduce the danger. He then detailed instructions of how the garrison commander, General Cameron, should protect the dockyard and deploy the garrison, ensuring that 'a few held pieces in the Salients of the Lines' were present 'every night'. Interestingly, he further suggested that the mayor and 'police' might help Cameron by 'keeping an eye' on the Portuguese. Nine days later Wellington, referring to a subsequent report from Lord FitzRoy, acknowledged Cameron's opinion that the Portuguese troops themselves were not the primary problem and that the garrison commander confidently had the situation under control. Once more, however, Wellington deplored 'the desperate blackguards who direct them, who reside in London and who would do us any mischief in their power'.[29]

The Plymouth incident remained localized; but more widespread security worries were looming, exacerbated by a lack of effective civil police outside London and need for troops to maintain law and order. Radical agitation and growing dissatisfaction with the electoral system combined to create pressure for parliamentary reform, which frequently spawned violence in both urban and rural areas of the country from 1830 to 1832. Lord FitzRoy believed that the High Sheriff of Buckinghamshire over-reacted in demanding extra troops in December 1830, but he acknowledged to Melbourne that serious disorder had taken place elsewhere and during the ensuing ten months troops were often moved to trouble spots principally in the south and west of England. There, mobs frequently rampaged through the streets to attack the houses or even the persons of those considered unsympathetic to reform. Wellington, among others, suffered: returning from the Mint on one occasion, he was forced to flee through Lincoln's Inn Fields and, on 27 April 1831, the windows of Apsley House were shattered. On 5 December 1830 he warned FitzRoy Somerset that he had 'heard of disturbances in the Town [London] tomorrow night the 6th ... from several quarters'. Had the Horse Guards been made aware? 'I have however taken my precautions.' The army's peace establishment ought 'immediately' to be completed and 'cadres [prepared] for the reception of the Pensioners with Veteran Battalions'. A ballot for the 'English and ... Scotch militia' should be held, and additional Corps of Yeomanry raised which would 'possibly prevent much mischief'. Wellington would not call out the pensioners until the last moment, but he would prepare officers to receive them and collect arms and accoutrements at their depots. The cost of this whole exercise would be about £300,000.

While Parliament, the House of Lords in particular, procrastinated on reform, ugly scenes were enacted and more troops were called out. Furthermore, throughout this period Wellington (though out of military and political office) kept constantly in touch with Lord FitzRoy about military support for the infant Metropolitan Police. From Walmer Castle, in November 1831, too, he noted that a Court of Inquiry had been established into the conduct of the military in Bristol where considerable damage was done during riots. He hoped that the Horse Guards was aware of unrest in the Birmingham area and had placed 'a good officer', who would not panic, in charge of the small-arms factory at Weedon. 'Remember (and Bristol is an example) that an Army of Stags with a Lion at the head of it is better than an Army of Lions with a Stag at its Head.' Wellington's concern about Birmingham may have been prompted by a report that the Scots Greys (later part of Raglan's Heavy Brigade in the Crimea) had declined to put down a reform riot there because the people had a just cause. Overall, internal security problems did not abate. The following year Lord FitzRoy referred to proposals from Colonel Charles Rowan (Metropolitan Police Commissioner) to contain a particular outbreak, in which 'they will make a display of strength ... [and]) many of them will be armed'. Lord FitzRoy was confident that 'his [Rowan's] arrangements are admirably calculated to stop the progress of the mob westwards'.[30]

The so-called Great Reform Act of 1832 quelled unrest but only for a short time. Before the decade was out Chartism had brought renewed violence, a whiff of a possible *coup d'état* and great hullabaloo surrounding presentation in 1839 of the first Chartist petition. Home security again topped the military agenda. An attempt on Queen Victoria's life in 1840 brought a letter from King Louis Philippe of France, congratulating her on her fortunate escape. The attempted assassination of the Queen on Constitution Hill, so near to Buckingham Palace and Apsley House, underlined dangers in the capital. After a lull the Chartists amassed signatures for a second petition to Parliament in 1842. This time, very serious outbreaks of violence – especially in the industrial north of England – triggered preventive troop deployments. To Egerton, FitzRoy Somerset wrote: 'These are queer times.' And in August the 3rd Battalion, Grenadier Guards, were sent to Salford during Chartist 'disturbances' and remained there until the following November.[31]

In his letter of 5 December 1830 to Lord FitzRoy, Wellington alluded to the problems overseas which could involve British units. Events across the Channel, in France and the Low Countries, were especially worrying. In July 1830 a revolution in Paris overthrew Charles X and a month later riots in Brussels signalled the break-up of the Kingdom of The Netherlands. Before the new independent Belgian state was established, France would be tempted to interfere once more in the area. Shades of Waterloo, fifteen years on. In May 1831 Wellington, in a confidential letter to FitzRoy Somerset, expressed belief that international pressure would achieve a solution to the Belgian question without resort to troops. In the following year, however, Lord FitzRoy informed Hill that military intervention might well be necessary. The Dutch were about to put down Belgian resistance by force, and Palmerston had called to see FitzRoy Somerset at the Horse Guards. The Foreign Secretary thought that the French would advance to support the Belgians and that the British Government might wish to react similarly. Were two or three battalions available, if required? Hill's Military Secretary advised Palmerston that only the Guards and Rifle Brigade depots could be considered; and he proposed that in addition a company be withdrawn from each of three battalions in southern Ireland. Although he had mentioned a force of two to three battalions Palmerston left FitzRoy Somerset with the firm impression that only a small body would be committed. On reflection, and after Palmerston had left the Horse Guards, Lord FitzRoy wrote to him suggesting a force of merely 1,500 men comprising the 9th Regiment – already empowered to embark – and about 300 men from Ireland. Hill, at Hardwicke Grange, authorized Lord FitzRoy to organize the necessary force without waiting for his return to London. In the event British troops were not sent to the Low Countries. After intense diplomatic activity the separate Kingdom of Belgium was eventually recognized internationally in 1839.

Already tension between France, which backed Mehemet Ali in his adventures in Syria, and other European nations supporting Turkey was threatening to spill over on to the European mainland. War again seemed possible. On 23 October 1840 FitzRoy Somerset at Dover reported that 'there was a salute fired this morning and shortly after the French packet left harbour with a flag in addition flying. So I suppose Guizot is on his way to Paris to help form an administration which is to save Louis Phillipe from destruction and Europe from an unnecessary war.' Both judgements were to prove correct.[32]

Meanwhile the Iberian peninsula yet once more warranted attention. In July 1830 Wellington wrote a 'private and confidential' letter to FitzRoy Somerset revealing that the Spanish ambassador had shown him papers 'which prove that there exists at this moment in London an organized conspiracy for the purpose of producing a revolution in Spain'. Some 'disaffected' Spanish officers had recently received money from the City to assist their passage to Rio de Janeiro, but instead they planned to land in Spain. In fact the Carlist Wars would simmer south of the Pyrenees for some years. Despite lack of official involvement Lord FitzRoy received intelligence from Colonel de Lacy Evans about the British Legion's – fighting in support of the Queen of Spain against Don Carlos – having executed a successful attack on the Carlist Lines 'in the immediate vicinity of San Sebastian'. And Major-General Sir Alexander Woodford explained to FitzRoy Somerset that the 'Carlist Party' was gathering strength in southern Spain where the Queen's cause seemed to be weakly supported. In 1837 concern for control of the Straits of Gibraltar caused Lord FitzRoy to take note of correspondence between Sir John Fraser and Sir Hussey Vivian (the Master-General) about possible British military occupation of Ceuta on the North African coast.[33]

Even farther-flung locations required the Military Secretary's attention. Lord FitzRoy welcomed the Government's intention to replace the East India Company's garrison on St Helena with British Army infantry and artillery. But he queried whether the displaced officers, who would lose their appointments, should receive half or full pay and whether the Company ought to be financially involved in the settlement. The position of English officers in Persia (where Russian influence had increased since the Russo-Persian War of 1826-8) was creating alarm. And, in January 1838, FitzRoy Somerset forwarded to Hill a draft letter concerning troops for Botany Bay. Later that year he supported the move of the 96th 'at once' to New South Wales, asking Hill for permission to submit 'this arrangement for the Queen's approbation'. In a letter to Egerton on 9 October 1838 he passed on the news that the 'Burmese Question' had been settled 'by the appearance of two frigates off Rangoon' – a delightful example of gun-boat diplomacy. He recorded the success of British troops in China, notably their capture of Shanghai: 'All is rose coloured in that part of the world whilst it is as black as ink in Afghanistan', he wrote to Egerton in February 1842. Worried about possible Russian influence to the detriment of British India, Lord Auckland had deposed the Amir of Afghanistan in favour of an unpopular British puppet. Internal unrest escalated. Lord FitzRoy explained to Egerton that the explorer Sir Alexander Burnes (temporarily commanding Afghan forces loyal to Britain in Kabul) and his brother had been 'murdered', other 'officers and detachments ... surprized'. Optimistically he wrote: 'As far as I can ascertain no serious misfortune has befallen either of the Queen's regiments and as long as they continue we may hold up our heads.' Such were the vagaries of communication that before FitzRoy Somerset penned this letter almost 15,000 men, women and children had been slaughtered or captured attempting to reach the safety of India. Later in 1842 a punitive expedition would be needed to rescue other prisoners, relieve isolated garrisons and sack Kabul to underline British displeasure.[34]

Appointment to 'the command in India' created further problems. In August 1838 Lord FitzRoy reported to Hill that two candidates had turned down the post. The refusal of the second, Lieutenant-General Sir Thomas Bradford, might well make Hill 'feel annoyed'. FitzRoy Somerset wanted to know 'by return of post' whether he should offer the appointment to Sir John Lambert or try Bradford again, but warned Hill that 'Bradford being a widower with several daughters growing up, I suppose he has made up his mind not to leave them if he can avoid it.' Given discretion by Hill to persist with Bradford or contact Lambert before he left

Paris for Italy, Lord FitzRoy opted for Lambert, explaining that 'I don't know his age but he is apparently in good health.' Lambert became the third officer to decline the post. 'What is the next step to be taken?' the Military Secretary inquired. He enclosed a draft letter for Hill to the President of the Board of Control, Sir J. Cam Hobhouse. For the crisis had emanated from Hobhouse's desire to replace Sir Henry Fane. FitzRoy Somerset suggested that Hill might again write to Bradford, possibly inviting him to travel from his Morpeth home to see Hill at Hardwicke. Lord FitzRoy was 'much concerned' about failure to fill the position; 'notwithstanding that the List is overloaded with General Officers there are none who are equal or willing to take upon themselves high and responsible appointments'. Subsequently Hill did write to Bradford, but received another rebuff, so Fane remained in India. FitzRoy Somerset drafted a letter to him from Hill with Hobhouse's approval, which would be forwarded to Fane via Malta, Egypt and the Postmaster at Bombay, expressing clear concern about his conduct. Hobhouse, with whom Lord FitzRoy had personally discussed the matter, remained committed to Fane's replacement, and in October the Military Secretary advised him that 'local rank is very frequently given to enable an officer to exercise a High Command with the utmost advantage to the Service but not to put him over his Senior'. This ploy Hill considered might be 'desirable considering the present very critical state of affairs in India'. If Hobhouse agreed Hill would write to Fane asking him to retain the command 'for a time' – until his successor could be appointed.

In November Lord FitzRoy referred specifically to a clash between Fane and the Governor-General. Anxious to establish the legality of what had transpired, he advised against approaching the East India Company's Court of Directors, preferring to use Horse Guards' resources. He undertook to arrange for staff to 'search the adjutant-general's office' for relevant records and the pages of the *Annual Register* for precedents. 'My notion', he wrote, was that the Governor-General 'had full right to interfere in the organization of the Field Force', but that Fane ought to have explained 'the former practice' to him and that what Fane proposed 'was in accordance with it'. Lord FitzRoy's dismay at Fane's action became clear: 'Far from doing so Sir Henry admits the *novelty* and loses the advantage ground he could have stood on.' He ought to have argued in a paper the wisdom of what he intended to do, supporting this by his own experience, but he did not – and Lord FitzRoy was perturbed about 'the violence of his [Fane's] language'. A year later the affair was still rumbling on. 'It is extraordinary that Fane should not regard Lord Hill's letter of the 11th. of May as an intimation of the desire of the Govt. that he should at once leave India. He really is the most pig-headed general I ever had to do with.'[35]

Westwards, across the Atlantic, unrest continued. In January 1838 Wellington advised FitzRoy Somerset to press for an increase in depot strength, pessimistically concluding: 'I am afraid that the Government will make no augmentation of their Force and treat the Canadian affair as a little war', adding his oft-misquoted remark: 'There is no such thing as a *little war* for a great Nation.' In April FitzRoy Somerset forwarded to Wellington extracts from a letter of Lieutenant-Colonel Taylor in Montreal, criticizing 'the yielding policy towards the French or Canadian party'.[36]

In truth, continued dismay at failure to pacify Canadian rebels and resolve difficulties about the government of Upper and Lower Canada raised active questions about Colborne's future once again – this time as a military commander. Reporting on a conversation with Lord Melbourne at a dinner that day, FitzRoy Somerset revealed that the Prime Minister wanted to replace Colborne with either Sir George Murray or Sir James Kempt, favouring the latter because of his 'most intimate knowledge of the country'. Melbourne would like Hill quietly to sound out Kempt's willingness to accept as a service to his country. An open refusal would embarrass the Government. Lord FitzRoy subsequently revealed that Kempt had become dangerously ill, was not expected to live long, and that the Government had accepted Hill's advice to invite Colborne to remain in command. Early in November FitzRoy Somerset wrote sharply to Egerton about Lord Durham's report on the future of Canada: 'Lord Durham's proclamation is the most egotistical production I ever read'; and later that month he believed that 'affairs have assumed a very ugly appearance in Canada'.[37]

That concern did not solely involve internal affairs. The prospect of hostilities with the United States over disputed boundaries caused unease for some years, and FitzRoy Somerset became the recipient of comments and plans about possible action. In 1841, for example, he forwarded to Wellington a plan of attack on the United States sent to him by Mr Cowell, on which Colonel Napier had commented. Cowell suggested that a naval blockade of New York should be followed by seizure of Slatern Island with 15,000 men, and the cutting of the Erie Canal from Canada. In view of the reasons underlying the American Civil War twenty years later, it is interesting that Cowell based his plan on the antipathy of Southerners for the North and their willingness to break from the Union rather than lose the cotton trade with Europe. He hoped that cutting the Erie Canal would ultimately damage northern industries and bring those states to their knees in two years. Lord FitzRoy explained that Napier had serious objections to Cowell's project. Intelligence to hand suggested that Georgia, Alabama and the Virginias would not break from the Union. Napier doubted the political wisdom of siding with Southern slave-owners and could not see the practical advantage of occupying Slatern Island. He preferred his own plan, put forward two years previously, of encouraging a revolt of slaves in the South.[38]

FitzRoy Somerset's correspondence with Wellington about Canada once again illustrates the fact that behind Hill the Duke retained very real influence at the Horse Guards. For Lord FitzRoy he was something of an *éminence grise*; but his own insistence upon being consulted also emphasized the reality of his professional reputation. Military matters were of prime importance to him. When FitzRoy Somerset discussed with him the incidents of fatalities caused by bayonets in off-duty affrays, Wellington believed that the wearing of side-arms off duty should cease. But he advised the Military Secretary to wait for 'ministers' to raise the matter rather than take the initiative. In an exchange of letters with Herbert Taylor, William IV's private secretary, following Lord Grey's attack on the retention of flogging, Lord FitzRoy gave considerable weight to Wellington's views and noted that a compromise to restrict the number of lashes awarded had been worked out to 'satisfy' Parliamentary critics. The Duke's views on broader issues of military action were certainly canvassed. During the Afghan crisis FitzRoy Somerset reminded Egerton of Wellington's 'wise' dictum: 'Great operations undertaken without sufficient means are always likely to end ill.' And the Duke offered more direct criticism of plans in India. The scheme to seize Oude in 1833, he argued to FitzRoy Somerset, would be impracticable because an increase in European troops would require that augmented establishment for the British Army be voted in London. In 'the present climate of opinion' that would be impossible. To Lord FitzRoy he also speculated on the possibility that the British might 'come to blows with the Russians in India' – reflecting contemporary obsession with the 'Great Game' and dread of a threat to the Khyber Pass.[39]

Somerset family matters required Lord FitzRoy's attention, too. On 20 February 1831 his difficult brother, General Charles Henry Somerset, died at the Bedford Hotel, Brighton, where he had taken up residence after returning from the Cape of Good Hope in controversial circumstances. He had survived attempts to remove him – partly through Edward's defence of him in Parliament in 1828-9 – from his posts of Governor of the Cape of Good Hope and Commander of its forces. During the twelve years that he held those offices he had quarrelled with many influential people including the poet Thomas Pringle, Bishop Burnett and his own Lieutenant-Governor, Sir Rufus Donkin. He had, a critic remarked, an 'unfortunate history', yet in his 'own cross-grained dictatorial way' sought to fulfil his duties conscientiously. Buried at Hove, not at Badminton, he left a 9-year-old son, Poulett, by his second marriage, who would be one of Lord FitzRoy's ADCs in the Crimea.[40]

During these years FitzRoy Somerset's children were not neglected either. He continued to be an attentive, if at times demanding, correspondent when apart from them. The brothers and sisters wrote to one another frequently as well, referring to their parents, and the whole family used pet nicknames: Cuddy, Puggins, Pug or Pug Face (Charlotte),

Lilla, Kittens or Kitty (Katherine). In June 1828, while staying at 'Went-worth's' in Surrey – bounded by Sonning Hill, Chertsey, Bagshot and Egham – he explained to 'my dear Pug' that Arthur would visit him and Lady FitzRoy the following day, go to the races and return to his school at nearby Laleham that evening. In August of the following year Arthur wrote from Laleham to 'my dear Cuddy' at Stable Yard, St James's. Arthur subsequently entered the Royal Military College Sandhurst in 1830, stayed for more than two years, but did not graduate. Cadets who satisfactorily passed four designated subjects (arithmetic and mathematics; French; fortification; military drawing;), achieved a 'College recommendation' for a free commission. A second category allowed cadets to be 'withdrawn' by their friends or family, either because they had no prospect of passing all four subjects or because they had enough money to purchase a commission. A third group involved those 'returned to his friends' – that is, thrown out – although they too could purchase. Arthur was not expelled. He was admitted as No 34 to 'B' Company, Category 'B' – on reduced fees as the son of a serving or former officer of the army or navy. He was then thirteen years and nine months old, height 5ft 0¼in, the son of Major-General Lord FitzRoy Somerset, KCB. On 10 May 1832 Arthur was 'withdrawn by his father': he had done well in French, arithmetic and mathematics, but had reached only the second class in military drawing and failed to pass any examination of the prescribed five in fortification. Nevertheless on 18 May 1832 his commission as an ensign and lieutenant in the First Foot Guards (his father's regiment) was acquired without purchase.[41]

Nor was FitzRoy Somerset's younger son less of a problem at this time. Richard matriculated at Christ Church, Oxford on 4 June 1835 and went into residence in the Michaelmas Term. In December the Dean and Canons nominated him to a studentship – roughly equivalent to a scholarship in other colleges – which carried an annual emolument of £25 and certain other benefits, such as priority in succeeding to college livings. Theoretically studentships were awarded on the basis of intellectual merit, but complaints of nepotism and influence were rife. Somerset family connections may well have been important. In fact surviving records of Richard's work show annotations such as *'non satis'*, *'male'* and *'parum'*. He did not return to Christ Church in the autumn of 1838. The reason seems to have been as much financial as academic. Three warrants were issued against him by the University which claimed jurisdiction in such matters, after he had been obliged to leave Christ Church for New Inn Hall (popularly known as 'The Tap' and a refuge of undergraduates ejected by their colleges). The outcome of these actions – possibly seizure of goods in default of payment – is unknown. But it is certain that the Dean and Chapter of Christ Church, noting that 'Somerset Student of this House not having proceeded to the Degree of Bachelor of Arts on the last day of Hilary Term, ordered that his Student's place be declared void from that day, viz., the 23rd day of this Instant March [1839].' In short, he failed to gain a degree and, like many other undergraduates who had disgraced themselves, Richard would soon find himself packed off to one of the colonies.[42]

Lord FitzRoy had good reason to be displeased with his younger son. It is just possible that the loan of £1,000 obtained from Hoare's Bank in London in 1837 and repaid by instalments over the next six years was connected with Richard's debts. But it is more likely that it related to Arthur's purchase to lieutenant and captain on 24 February of that year. Then, after serving as ADC to Lieutenant-General Sir Edward Blakeney in Ireland, towards the close of 1841 Arthur, aged 24, was detached from the 1st Battalion, Grenadier Guards, to be Military Secretary to the new Governor-General of India. Charlotte described the confusion of his departure from England on 8 November in a letter to Richard, then in Ceylon. Arthur had stayed in London with the family for two days and planned to travel to Plymouth by steamer from Southampton on 4 November. Lord FitzRoy checked the details personally with the railway company, and Arthur together with two ADCs set out from London at 1 p.m. He reappeared at 10 p.m. 'very much disgusted' because on arrival at Southampton he discovered that the steamer was not sailing until the following Thursday. So on Friday 5 November he left for Bridgwater by the Great Western Railway, taking the chance of finding transport from there for the 90-mile journey to Plymouth. His baggage weighed 12cwt. Evidently, though, the quest at Bridgwater proved successful.[43]

While at sea, Arthur wrote to Richard in Ceylon to begin a weighty correspondence between the brothers that reveals occasional glimpses of their relationships with their father. While anchored in Madras Roads, on 21 February 1842, Arthur speculated about Lord FitzRoy's future: 'What odd reports there are about my lord's coming to India and again of his going to the Ordnance office.' He would be 'surprized' if FitzRoy Somerset went to the Ordnance. The post was not suitable for somebody of his age (54) and, moreover, he might hope to obtain the Horse Guards: 'It is unlikely that Lord Hill would remain much longer as he is getting very old and must be tired of his office.' The following month, intimating that he had suffered financial setbacks while in Ireland, he added that 'I am still under a black cloud', cautioning Richard not to mention his depression in letters to England. Arthur was evidently desperately unhappy in India: 'I have literally no companions.' He went on: 'If I were not in debt and had £300 a year besides my pay I would resign this moment', adding: 'For God's sake say no word of this to a living soul.' And it soon became clear that, having got himself into financial difficulty, he dreaded the idea of Lord FitzRoy finding out. For he had left Ireland in debt, which had enraged his father. 'You will be sorry to hear that my lord at home has cut me and refuses to write to me – though I trust he will come round in time.' 'I am anxious to keep it [the breach] from my Lady and so is Lord FitzRoy', who would be 'more angry' if he knew that Arthur had told Richard. Furthermore, if Lord FitzRoy learnt that Arthur had incurred further debts a reconciliation would recede even farther.[44]

Arthur's depression did not lift quickly: 'The only thing that prevents me from cutting my throat is the prospect of our marching up the country' to Ferozopore, he wrote in June. However, the news from England was soon 'more agreeable'. Lord FitzRoy had received Arthur's letters from the Cape of Good Hope and Madras which 'pleased him much'; and Arthur's maternal grandfather (Lord Mayborough) had also written a 'kind letter'. In the third week of June he confirmed that more letters had arrived from the family in England.[45]

Lord FitzRoy's correspondence with his daughters was less fraught and often more utilitarian. When Charlotte was twelve, Lord FitzRoy wrote 'to my dear Pug' from Wentworth's, congratulating her on a 'beautiful' letter to him, which 'everybody breakfasted on', explaining that her 'mama ... [was] too idle' to write and asking her to 'tell Miss Kitty that she is a very nice young lady and that I send her my love'. The following year he wrote an 'immediate' letter to her from Badminton, explaining that due to 'horrible roads' the journey to Gloucestershire had not ended until past midnight: fortunately, Charlotte's grandmother and grandfather had not then returned from dining with the Duke of Gloucester. Lord FitzRoy had left his gun in London and Charlotte was instructed to send to Mr Moor, the gunmaker in St James's Street, for it. 'Get somebody to fetch old William from the stables and make him pack those things in the upper part of my portmanteau, which John has orders to bring.' John must be careful of the gunpowder and not to forget to include as well his boots from Hoby's, jacket and trousers from Layfield's. 'My green slippers', which William forgot, must be brought, so must the 'new roadbook' from the little drawing-room or possibly the bookcase near the maps and 'the India rubber off my table'. In a postscript he remarked: 'There is such a quantity of flowers here.'[46]

In September 1830, again from Badminton, he mentioned that despite the rain, yesterday 'we had some fine gallops ... and I hope to have a good ride today'. Lady Mary, he revealed, had a 'very pleasing voice' and a 'very good' manner; Lady Blanche rode with them every day. 'Badminton looks well', he noted, adding 'I dress in the room next to that in which I was born.' However his 7-year-old daughter petulantly reminded him from Brighton in November 1833 that he could be negligent: 'My dear Papa, I am very angry with you for not having written to me since you went to Town. Miss Alexander and myself both think, that if you wait until Charlotte is married to write to her you may wait a long time. I have not been idle while you have been away, for I have learnt what you could *never* teach me, that is to tell the hour by the Clock. I have had some very nice rides in the Country and a very pleasant companion to accompany me. Adieu my dear Papa, Your dutiful Child, Katherine Somerset.' That same year an unidentified correspondent also alluded to matrimony. 'Very sorry' to learn that Kitty was still suffering from fever, he or she noted that Charlotte was 'always good natured' and did not 'grumble'. Referring to an unnamed beau, the writer added: 'I cannot help thinking that poor Charlotte has a much better chance of turning out well with him than if she remained at home.' The inference was that otherwise she might become a household drudge dominated by her mother. Next day, Charlotte was due to drive out to Bond Street with Lady FitzRoy to go shopping.[47]

Despite Katherine's girlish tantrums, FitzRoy Somerset clearly did not habitually forget his daughters while away from them. In January 1834 he described a shooting expedition, when he failed to spot many pheasants and 'only killed four, five hares and one woodcock'. Then heavy rain forced the large party to create its own indoor entertainment. 'I am glad', he concluded 'to hear that your mama is pretty well and that Miss Kitty had removed her fatigue and the top of the eau de cologne which affected her so quickly.' From Goodwood in January 1841, signing himself 'P.A.P.A.', Lord FitzRoy thanked 'my dearest Kitty' (aged sixteen) for her long 'epistle'. They had arrived at Goodwood from Mr Maxes's (an hour's journey) to join a large party. The weather was fine but cold, and there had been snow in the night. In June 1841 Lord FitzRoy wrote to Charlotte from another country house asking her to 'give orders' for the cabriolet (light carriage with two wheels) to meet him at Paddington Station at 5.15 p.m. None of these family letters dealt with matters of substance. In December he reported that Lord Hill was 'unhappy' with the shoot at Hardwicke Grange. Only about a dozen pheasants had been found: Lord FitzRoy killed 'some' and a solitary woodcock. Lord FitzRoy's form of address to his elder daughter often reverted to 'My dearest Pug', even when she was nearing thirty. From the Horse Guards in May 1842 he was 'charmed' to learn from her welcome note written at the station that she had arrived at Farnborough 'sain et sauf.' The weather in London was 'raining more or less' and Kitty, he noted, was waiting for a shower to pass before venturing out. Two days later, in a letter not apparently addressed to one of the children, FitzRoy Somerset displayed a slightly tetchy tone. 'My picture' had cost his friend Sir George Scovell 'something to the tune of one hundred pounds'. 'None of my family have ever desired my picture, not even my late brother Beaufort who was very fond of me or his chivalrous son who made his campaigns with me ... Scovell therefore stands alone in this particular and deserves to be honored accordingly.' A touch, perhaps, of parental melancholy. As an afterthought he appended a list of future parties and noted that Kitty was being escorted during the forthcoming season.[48]

Family correspondence affords only the occasional glimpse of Lady FitzRoy whose health had begun to fluctuate. She did not always accompany Lord FitzRoy to country house parties and not infrequently undertook prolonged seaside holidays in hired houses. Sir Willoughby Gordon and FitzRoy Somerset separately referred, in January 1834, to Lady FitzRoy's having remained in London while Lord FitzRoy was 'in the country'. Writing to Hill in August 1837 FitzRoy Somerset explained: 'We have taken a house at Dover from the 26 and propose to go there on the 28 or 29', though Lady FitzRoy would travel in advance of her husband. She stayed at 28 Marine Parade long after he had returned to the Horse Guards. The following autumn she went to Kent again, and this time she was unwell. In September Wellington revealed to Priscilla that Emily was staying at Walmer Castle with him, suffering from 'an acute rheumatic fever with some appearance of gout'. On 30 September in a letter to the Duke of Cambridge from Dover, FitzRoy Somerset explained that Lady FitzRoy was 'more comfortable, suffering very much less pain and I trust that by degrees she will get the better of her attack, but it has been a severe one'. Already sixteen days in bed, she was likely to remain there for another week.

Writing to Egerton at Hardwicke Grange from the Horse Guards on 9 October 1838, he explained that Lady FitzRoy had somewhat recovered, but that he was 'still anxious to get back' quickly to her: 'Her chief pain is now behind the eyes which at times annoys her very much'. Two days later he was again in Dover and reported that 'her eyes are in a state of considerable pain'. By the end of the month she was complaining about 'a good deal of rheumatism' as well as her eyes, and 'of feeling beaten and weak'. Progressing only slowly, she had under her daughter's guidance 'been several times out airing'. 'Miss Somerset', he rather formally explained to Egerton, 'has been all attention to her mother during her illness' without much thought for herself. Over the years Charlotte would indeed be attentive, but her mother's temperament held her and the rest of the family in thrall. Perhaps that is what Charlotte's unknown correspondent from Essex had feared. She needed a husband in order to break away from the state of pseudo-serfdom that afflicted so many unmarried Victorian ladies.[49]

Louise Dessoulavy, a Swiss friend of Charlotte's from childhood, writing the following year, remarked on Lady FitzRoy's recovery from what must have been a serious illness. In so doing she afforded a a glimpse of the beauty and vivacity of bygone years. Louise recalled that she used to sleep in the same room as Charlotte. 'Waking once in the middle of the night and fancying I saw some beautiful fairy princess, I peeped through the curtain to see if it was still a dream when I saw your Mama just arrived I suppose from a soirée. She had on a beautiful turban which suited her delightfully indeed – a great deal better to my thinking than the court dress.' She once saw her beautifully arrayed in full dress and Lord FitzRoy resplendent in uniform after returning from a levee: Louise was clearly impressed in those days with the style and grace of the FitzRoy

Somersets. In referring to the marriage of Lord Douro she observed 'though I had much rather it had been your own'.[50]

Illness, death and the weather were constant topics in correspondence, reflecting the harshness of contemporary life. In September 1835 Lord FitzRoy referred to a serious attack of dysentery affecting his mother-in-law, Lady Mayborough, which made her daughters Emily, Lady FitzRoy and Priscilla, Lady Burghersh, alternately 'very unhappy' and 'distressed'. At one stage the daughters spoke of 'a gleam of hope'; though the mother would actually make a full recovery. Writing to his brother William, in March 1836, about the death of their eldest brother, he referred to 'dear Beaufort's solid unostentatious merits' and 'the extent of the loss which the brother and sisterhood have sustained by his death. For the last few years he saw but few out of his own family and it may with truth be said that his moments of relaxation were all spent with us.' FitzRoy Somerset went on to underscore the value of family solidarity: 'We have now no connecting link, no *point de réunion* but we must make the best of it.'

In a letter to Hill from the Horse Guards in January 1837, having dealt with necessary business, he produced health bulletins on the Duchess of Gloucester and Willoughby Gordon, adding that Lady Farnborough had died. To Wellington, after discussing the Howick Report, he described a temporary illness of his sister-in-law Priscilla, and Emily's care for her. Two days earlier Priscilla's 15-year-old daughter Louisa had succumbed to typhoid; and, at the time of writing, Lord FitzRoy could not anticipate that Lady Burghersh would in fact retire in utter dejection to St Leonards for almost a year. That scarcely improved Emily's own state of mind. Just before Christmas 1838 he expressed condolences to Egerton on the loss of his nephew, characteristically adding a special word of sympathy for 'poor Mrs Tarleton and her daughters' at the death of 'a fine young man'. In the same letter he referred to a report that four officers and ten men had been drowned in a 'rough sea and bad weather' when returning with their regiment from Ireland, though a hasty postscript explained that later news identified horses and not men as the victims. Writing to Egerton from Gosport in 1842, almost exclusively concerning professional matters, he concluded: 'My poor brother William has had the misfortune to lose his eldest daughter, a very nice girl of Charlotte's age.' And few letters lacked reference to the weather.[51]

During Lord Hill's tenure at the Horse Guards Lord FitzRoy appeared to suffer from only minor ailments and there is no indication that his physical disability hampered him. He rode frequently and for shooting or using a spyglass he had a special harness for his shoulder and good arm. Once while staying at Goodwood he wrote to Kitty about catching 'a bad cold' and mentioned that he had taken medicine to relieve 'a pain I had between my shoulders, but I am still much *exhausted*'. He could not say why he had caught cold, because he had not got his feet wet or indulged in more than 'pleasant exercise'. Later that year, December 1841, he apologized to Charlotte for not having written the previous day as illness had forced him to go to bed early: in the evening he had felt 'suddenly very uncomfortable in the stomach and very queer altogether', so had missed dinner. But generally his health appears to have been good. He enjoyed riding and horses were something of a passion. He approached his brother William on behalf of Robert Fagel 'the Dutch Minister at Paris, one of the best fellows alive and a great lover of an English horse'. Fagel was 'now creeping towards sixty' and required a docile horse; so Lord FitzRoy requested 'further particulars of the one-eyed bay horse'. On another occasion he asked Egerton whether 'Miss Julie' were intending to sell a horse which he thought might suit Lady Caroline Maxse. His dealings in this respect were not always successful. A horse recommended by him for which Lord Mayborough paid 150 guineas died at exercise three months later.[52]

Fitzroy Somerset was by no means a desk-bound bureaucrat. Apart from absences from London for family holidays, such as one with Wellington at Walmer in September 1841, his attendance – often prolonged – at house parties bore witness to his energy. He often went to Badminton, Goodwood, Wentworth's, Copt Hall, Maxse's and Lord Hill's home at Hardwicke Grange. On at least one occasion (December 1839) he stayed with the Duke of Cambridge at Cardigan's residence Deene Park, in Northamptonshire, some 100 miles from Badminton. This visit, following on from a stay at Badminton, meant that he was absent from the Horse Guards for almost a fortnight. Surviving family correspondence for 1835 shows that during part of April and May he was at Wallmouth Hall, Gloucestershire, late in May at Hardwicke Grange, during much of October and November at Dover and for part of November and December at Badminton. In addition he apparently played his part in the London season, attended such functions as the Cirencester Ball, and went to the races. Occasionally he dined with the Queen at Windsor; and in July 1840 he went to a state ball at Buckingham Palace.[53]

During Hill's time as CinC several honours, appointments and promotions fell to Lord FitzRoy. Despite having persuaded Hill not to recommend him to the colonelcy of the 43rd in December 1829 because of his comparatively junior position on the general list, on 19 November 1830 he accepted the colonelcy of the 53rd Regiment of Foot. Hill explained to Lord FitzRoy that the vacancy had occurred with his own appointment to the Horse Guards and that the King had 'ordered' Hill to recommend FitzRoy Somerset to him, because he 'has, in His Majesty's opinion by his gallant and distinguished service in the Field and his able, assiduous and exemplary discharge of the arduous duties of Military Secretary, so well merited the mark of His Majesty's favourable approbation'. Hill supported 'Lord FitzRoy's just claims to this reward', which Wellington also upheld; and he dismissed any objection that the appointment was premature. Shortly before Hill left the Horse Guards FitzRoy Somerset was appointed a Commissioner of the Royal Military College Sandhurst. The Royal Warrant was signed by the Secretary at War, Sir Henry Hardinge. Meanwhile, on 23 June 1838, he had been promoted lieutenant-general: and, in common with other holders of the Waterloo medal, in 1840 was allowed two years' additional service.[54]

One special civil honour fell to him as well. On 30 January 1834 Wellington was installed as Chancellor of the University of Oxford. Later that year, in June, Lord FitzRoy became an honorary Doctor of Civil Law (DCL). Although not personally present, 'because my stomach has been sadly out of order ever since I have been in London', the Duke of Beaufort described the event from eye-witness accounts: 'Dr Philimore in introducing FitzRoy did so with great taste, and particularly mentioned the loss of his arm, which when the company saw, by the shifting of the gown he had on, when he went to make his Bow to the Chancellor after the Degree was conferred, acted like an electric shock, and there was such a Peal of Applause as was hardly ever heard before. The Bishop of Gloucester told me the other day that it was quite affecting.' Philimore's address of presentation was indeed flattering: 'Most illustrious Chancellor, and eminent Proctors, I present to you a nobleman of the highest military character, Lord FitzRoy Somerset, brother of the Duke of Beaufort, one of the chosen Officers of the King's army, and a Knight of the Order of Bath – A guest indeed worthy of all favour and honour from us, as well for the high ancestry, which enobles him, and his own military reputation, as for the close and intimate bond, which during so long a period and so constantly, unconquered leader, connected him with you – Brought up in your very tent from his first youth, he was present as adviser and friend, in all those labours and vigils, in all those actions and operations, which ever so vigorously executed by you in liberating Europe and to crown all, he it is, who, in the battle of Waterloo, doing his duty bravely as a soldier, received, as you see, those severe wounds – Joyfully therefore and gladly I present him to you in order that he may be admitted to the honorary degree of a Doctor of Civil Law.'[55]

Early in 1843 Hill's health began to cause acute concern: unable to travel to Windsor in January to greet the King of Prussia, he remained at Hardwicke; and the following month FitzRoy Somerset expressed his regret that the CinC was 'suffering irregularity of the bowels'. Ever more of Hill's official business devolved upon Lord FitzRoy so that he was virtually directing the Horse Guards during the first eight months of the year. During a brief period in April Hill returned to his post, but a combination of illness, the burden of Indian affairs in the wake of severe troubles in Afghanistan and the death of his brother affected him so much that he found it 'so painful and tiresome for me to write'. In a bid to recover strength he took possession of Coleham House at Fulham where FitzRoy Somerset had a distressing interview with him on 7 July. Not only was

Hill's body wracked with pain, but his eyesight had now become badly affected. He talked about resigning his post 'sooner or later', but would not authorize his Military Secretary to act positively as yet. Anxious to keep Lord Hill informed of military developments and out of human compassion, Lord FitzRoy continued to visit Fulham; and three weeks later Hill asked him to speak to the Duke of Wellington about possible retirement from the Horse Guards. That same day, 28 July, Wellington went to Coleham House and both he and Hill agreed that resignation was inevitable. Next day Wellington informed Hill that Sir Robert Peel, the Prime Minister, had been appraised of the situation, would tell the Queen and make formal arrangements for a successor after Parliament had been prorogued. Almost immediately Hill left London and on 9 August transmitted his written resignation to FitzRoy Somerset, who was devastated: 'To separate from him after having enjoyed his confidence so many years was very painful and it was also a sad blow to lose the assistance and co-operation of our friend Egerton,' he wrote to his son Richard.[56]

On 10 December 1842, four months after his resignation, Lord Hill died at Hardwicke Grange. He was buried at Hadnall church, four miles north-east of Shrewsbury. During his years at the Horse Guards the War Office had seen eleven Secretaries at War. More significantly, perhaps, in his later survey of the Horse Guards J. H. Stocqueler admitted that it was impossible to determine how many of the measures carried through for the benefit of the army – including introduction of garrison libraries, rewards for distinguished service, reform of punishments in prison – in the fourteen years of Hill's command originated with the CinC, his staff or the War Office. The files of his Military Secretary show that, in reality, Hill spent a good deal of time at Hardwicke Grange.[57]

When Lord Hill resigned, speculation arose about his successor. Lord FitzRoy was neither experienced nor senior enough to be considered. But his future depended upon the whim of the new CinC. The approbation of Hill, meanwhile, was abundant. In a private letter from Hardwicke Grange he expressed 'my unqualified approval of the manner in which you have carried on the arduous duties of your highly important office during the long period we have acted together. I felt from the first that I might place the fullest reliance upon your judgement and ability and that feeling the experience of so many years has only tended to strengthen and confirm – I honestly believe that it has been your constant endeavour to support the best interests of the Service of which I have been the head, and in all matters connected with your Department to bring before me the claims of individuals with fairness and impartiality.' A handsome tribute, for which Hill apologized as 'this very imperfect expression of my feelings' because of his poor health.[58]

CHAPTER 6

WELLINGTONIAN TWILIGHT, THE HORSE GUARDS (1842-52)

'No doubt he [FitzRoy Somerset] was the most popular man in the Army.'(Sir John Fortescue, 1927)[1]

The Prime Minister (Sir Robert Peel) advised Queen Victoria that Sir George Murray, Sir Edward Paget and Lords Londonderry, Combermere and Beresford were 'in line' to succeed Hill. All were full generals with extensive active service, command experience and, in most cases, additional diplomatic or political background. Despite Arthur's filial optimism in February, FitzRoy Somerset was neither senior nor experienced enough to challenge realistically for the post.[2]

In fact Peel did not adhere to his own list. He recommended Wellington; and in his last General Order dated 15 August Hill duly named the Duke as his successor. Yet, patently, Wellington was no longer physically strong. For some years he had been deaf, and in 1841 had opted to act as Minister Without Portfolio rather than hold a specific post in Peel's new cabinet. There must, therefore, be more than a suspicion of a titular reward for the ageing hero, appointed by letters patent to be 'Commander-in-Chief ... during the term of his natural life'. Remaining with him as Military Secretary, FitzRoy Somerset observed: 'I hope we shall not overload the Duke with business and so injure his health.'[3]

Once more, however, as in 1828 questions were posed about Wellington's occupation of the Horse Guards and continued presence in the cabinet, albeit now in a lesser role than that of Prime Minister. Peel 'apprehended that there was no constitutional rule against the tenure of a seat in the Cabinet by the CinC', and the matter was dropped. Curiously, when Peel resigned Wellington believed that he could not continue at the Horse Guards because he would be politically opposed to the incoming premier (Russell). The Queen persuaded him otherwise, appealing to his loyalty; and Sir John agreed to Wellington's remaining in post. These exchanges illustrate the belief that the Army persisted as something of a royal preserve and, throughout Wellington's tenure of the Horse Guards, an uneasy truce existed between the Palace and those who wanted more overtly to bring the Army under direct political control. For FitzRoy Somerset the atmosphere could not have been relaxed.[4]

Wellington also kept a tighter rein on his staff than Hill. The Military Secretary seems not to have asked Hill's permission to be away from London. Yet he did so frequently of the Duke. After Wellington's return the pattern was quickly set. In September 1842 Lord FitzRoy informed

114

Kitty, then with the rest of the family at Ryde, that Wellington was coming to London prior to attending Windsor and that he must therefore remain at the Horse Guards, though he hoped that the Duke's business with him would be concluded the following morning, in time to catch one of the afternoon trains to Portsmouth. However, he might need to wait until Wellington had returned from seeing Lord Hill. 'Expect me when you see me.' The last ferry from Portsmouth left at 7.45, 'but pray beg my lady not to wait dinner for me'. The following month he told Charlotte that he could not guarantee to accompany Lady FitzRoy out of London because he did not know of Wellington's intended movements. Whether the Duke would attend a Privy Council at Windsor the next week was unclear, but he would certainly be in London for the Cabinet meeting on l November. Therefore, it 'looks as if I should not have much of a holiday'. Towards the end of December Wellington wrote to FitzRoy Somerset: 'I can have no desire that you should not go to Badminton. I have signed all the letters.' The Duke expected to be regularly in touch with business when out of London. In January 1845 from Stratfield Saye he thanked the Military Secretary for keeping him informed daily of what had been happening at the Horse Guards. Later that year Lord FitzRoy explained to Charlotte that, as the Duke would not be 'leaving Town until next week', he could only join the family in Dover for the week-end. On other occasions the Duke made it clear that he expected Lord FitzRoy to be at the Horse Guards when he returned from Walmer Castle, and FitzRoy Somerset wrote: 'I conclude we are safe for some little time from the issue of any other Ordinance de la Reine from the Colonial Office, and therefore would request your permission to be absent myself for ten or twelve days from Friday next.' He explained that he wished to make two visits either side of London, and that he would therefore call into the office to deal with pressing matters when he crossed the capital between them. As late as 1849 – indicating that his keenness in this respect had not faded – Wellington wrote from Walmer that he had 'no objection' to FitzRoy Somerset 'quitting London'; and in August Lord FitzRoy told Charlotte that he would be kept in London until the Duke left at the end of that particular week.[5]

It would be utterly incorrect, however, to conclude that FitzRoy Somerset merely looked to Wellington's absence to escape from the office. As under Hill, he continued to work hard. In January 1847 he wrote to his daughters from the Horse Guards at 'past six', explaining that he found 'plenty of work' waiting for him that day and more interviews had still to be conducted. Three years later he noted how a heavy work schedule ('an awful list') had meant a delayed and hurried dinner before going to the theatre with Kitty.[6]

Whether physically at the Horse Guards or not, Wellington laid down precisely what his Military Secretary must do. Orders from the field commander did not easily fade away. A volley of short notes during 1843 required Lord FitzRoy to consult the *London Gazette* and 'other sources' for details of losses in Afghanistan and China, as the Duke must make a statement to the Lords 'in the course of a few days'; detailed the exact procedure for collecting the late Lord Hill's Gold Stick and insignia of the Order of the Bath; and dictated arrangements for forwarding correspondence to Belvoir Castle where the Duke was staying temporarily. With a hint of reproof, in a letter timed at 6 p.m., he wrote on another occasion: 'I called at the office on my being up from the House of Lords ... Will you be so kind as to let me have at as early an hour as may be convenient tomorrow morning all the ... reports on the present operations. As I must read them before I go to the Cabinet.'[7]

Wellington not infrequently pressed for information urgently, as on this occasion; and he could react testily if it were not rapidly produced. In September 1845 while at Walmer, he asked his Military Secretary to secure Ordnance Survey maps of Kent, Sussex and Surrey from the Quartermaster-General's department. Ten days later a brief, sharp note conveyed displeasure at their non-arrival: 'I should be very much obliged to you if you will urge them to send me the maps which I desire to have, as soon as it may be practicable.' Evidently this letter was passed on to the Quartermaster-General who wrote in pencil on the back: 'Five of the sheets could not be purchased being out of print – They have this morning been received from the Ordnance Map Office at Southampton and I have every hope that the whole will be completed this week.' Whether this mollified the CinC or not is unclear.[8]

In spite of his desire to exert closer personal control, in practice Wellington frequently referred matters to Lord FitzRoy for action and decision. Following the 'sad' death of Colonel Gurwood, Wellington asked FitzRoy Somerset: 'What shall I do with the office in the Tower?' Could he suggest a 'steady old officer' of colonel or even major-general rank? On occasions Lord FitzRoy exercised considerable, possibly excessive, influence over promotions and appointments: in November 1846 Wellington left to him the final selection of all necessary promotions to lieutenant-colonel and above. In his near contemporary history of the Horse Guards, J.H. Stocqueler asserted that the conduct of courts-martial was delegated to Military Secretary and Judge Advocate General, with Wellington intervening little. Certainly they did directly discuss the establishment of Courts of Honour in 1843. For five years Lord FitzRoy corresponded intermittently on behalf of Wellington with the Governor of the Royal Hospital Chelsea and the Office of Woods and Forests following publication of a report from Her Majesty's Commissioners for Metropolitan Improvements recommending increased public access to the hospital gardens, relinquishment of exclusive use of the adjacent Burton's Court and construction of roads to the north and south of the Hospital to replace existing paths. FitzRoy Somerset had tactfully to explain the CinC's objections on the basis of security and quiet for the old soldiers. Eventually a satisfactory compromise was achieved through Lord FitzRoy's diplomacy; and Wellington's agreement was conveyed to Lord Carlisle at the Office of Woods and Forests on 29 January 1850.[9]

One distinguished historian, not unsympathetic to the Duke, has described Wellington's last decade at the Horse Guards, when he was having difficulty in mounting and dismounting his horse, as 'a mixture of sleep and irritability'. An exaggeration, perhaps. Nevertheless, even when in London, he reputedly rode the short distance from Apsley House to Whitehall infrequently and stayed at the Horse Guards only briefly, leaving no later than 4 p.m. His insistence upon receiving regular information from his Military Secretary and, in turn, Lord FitzRoy's reluctance to leave London, may indicate that it was FitzRoy Somerset who was guiding the Headquarters' staff during those ten years. In his standard volume on the workings of the War Office, Captain Owen Wheeler has pointed out that much of the work of the Adjutant-General during Sir John Macdonald's long tenure of that post (1830-50) fell to FitzRoy Somerset; and to Macdonald's successor – Sir George Brown – Lord FitzRoy expressed relief that 'the Duke will be saved the pain and annoyance' of dealing with a disciplinary case, which had been resolved without reference to him. Stocqueler and Sir Frederick Maurice later concluded that many of Wellington's duties at this time had, indeed, been carried out by others. Stocqueler, for instance, cites FitzRoy Somerset's memorandum about the introduction of a formal examination before professors at Sandhurst for first commissions.[10] He goes on to credit Lord FitzRoy with boosting the role (and income) of unofficial tutors or coaches. Asked for advice on how to prepare for the new test, Lord FitzRoy replied that a certain amount of judicious cramming would suffice. Explaining the mutual respect between Wellington and her brother-in-law, Priscilla Westmorland explained that 'the D never spoke of him but as "Lord FitzRoy". How often has he said to me, "What does Lord FitzRoy say?"' She maintained – no doubt with a tincture of exaggeration – that he deferred to FitzRoy Somerset 'on all military matters, especially during the latter years'. 'I cannot say anything till I have asked Lord F what he thinks. He will know the state of the case (or, he knows all these things) much better than I do,' Wellington was apt to say.[11]

By 1847 the diarist Charles Greville had recorded concern about the Duke's being frequently in 'a fitful uncertain state and there is no knowing in what humour he may be found ... he is sometimes very amiable and good humoured, sometimes very irritable and morose', adding: 'All this is very unlike him.' The implication clearly was that the Duke's health was deteriorating still further. Reminiscing later, Lord Granville wrote: 'Towards the end of his life, he became sometimes irritable', adding that on some days even FitzRoy Somerset dare not approach him. On those occasions Lady Douro, Wellington's daughter in-law, would act as intermediary between the CinC and his Military Secretary.[12]

Internal security proved a persistent issue during Wellington's third term at the Horse Guards. Lord Melbourne (former Prime Minister) and Sir James Graham, the Home Secretary, were among those who stressed the dangerous condition of unrest in 'the manufacturing districts' of the Midlands and the North, where several disturbances in support of Chartist claims did occur in 1842. Six years later Chartism once more posed a potential menace to law and order at a time when revolutions had begun to affect the European mainland and unrest in Ireland was again causing special concern. Wellington, as CinC, determined the overall strategy for containing trouble, subject to political direction. But Lord FitzRoy clearly organized the tactical response.[13]

A Chartist gathering on Kennington Common, followed by a procession to present the third Chartist petition to Parliament, signalled a possible flash-point in London on 10 April 1848. A week earlier, therefore, cavalry and infantry reinforcements were moved into the capital, and on 8 April the Deputy Adjutant-General discussed with the Military Secretary placement of troops on roofs in the Strand, and at 'Bethlehem hospital' midway between Whitehall and Kennington Common and well-placed to cover Westminster and Blackfriars bridges. Already, two days previously, Lieutenant-Colonel Alexander Tulloch, Military Superintendent of the Enrolled Pensioners, had agreed to deploy 800 pensioners to protect important establishments such as the Tower of London and the Bank of England.[14]

Lord FitzRoy's involvement in the anti-Chartist precautions escalated from 8 to 11 April, Sunday the 9th proving especially busy. A long memorandum outlined policy for the following day. Police would be on Kennington Common but no opposition would be offered to unarmed people. If the Chartist procession sought to reach Parliament its leaders would be told that all bridges had 'sufficient force' to prevent a crossing. No objection would be made to 'a small number of persons' accompanying the petition. If the procession tried to force one of the bridges it was 'confidently anticipated' that the police could cope, but troops would be close by to assist the police on authorization of a magistrate. One hour after the petition had been taken over one of the bridges in accordance with the restrictions imposed, small numbers of people should be allowed to return north of the river, except via Westminster Bridge. From the Horse Guards FitzRoy Somerset wrote to Tulloch transmitting the Home Secretary's desire that pensioners also be sent to 'the Mansion House, Custom House, North Western Railway, the Museum and the Pantechnicon.' Later that evening, from Stanhope Street, he issued orders on Wellington's behalf to the officer commanding Bethlehem Hospital whose temporary infantry garrison would be joined by two squadrons of the Life Guards and four guns. A magistrate was to be at Bethlehem on 10 April in communication with the police at Kennington, 'so that the commissioners may know where to send to should they require the assistance of the Military'. Also that evening Tulloch informed Lord FitzRoy that he had written, as 'directed' by him, to Sir Denis Le Marchant, Under-Secretary of State at the Home Office, and had met Major-General Brotherton. He and Brotherton 'have waited to see you and secure your final orders ... but as you have not arrived' Tulloch intended to take three companies to Blackfriars Bridge on the Monday morning and put himself under Brotherton's orders. Brotherton subsequently explained to FitzRoy Somerset that, with the full co-operation of residents, he placed 'the veterans' in private houses at the northern end of Blackfriars Bridge with regular troops nearby ready to support them and the police.[15]

In a comprehensive memorandum Lord FitzRoy detailed the deployment of troops held in barracks and at locations such as Somerset House, ready to support the police – as at Blackfriars Bridge – at reserve positions like Bethlehem Hospital and the prison at Millbank. In all, on 10 April, sixteen squadrons of cavalry, nine battalions of infantry and twelve guns were ready to intervene if required, apart from the 800 pensioners and 4,012 police (including those manning seven boats on the Thames). All were in position by 10 a.m. In the event the occasion passed without serious trouble, and at 2.15 p.m. on 11 April Lord FitzRoy conveyed to Tulloch the approval of the Home Secretary for all pensioners 'to return to their homes', including those guarding the Bank of England and the Mint. On 13 April he told Le Marchant that troops sent to Millbank 'by the Secretary of State's orders' were to be withdrawn and the following day asked the Under-Secretary to express Wellington's thanks to those members of the public who had made their houses available near Blackfriars Bridge or had allowed cavalry to occupy their private stables. He re-emphasized that the troops had been held ready 'until their Services should be called for in aid of the Civil Authorities'.[16]

The feared unrest did not therefore materialize in London, but FitzRoy Somerset had to ensure that potential trouble elsewhere could be contained. On the very day of tension in London, 10 April, he learnt that Major-General Sir William Warre at Chester was too ill to take command in Liverpool. He immediately, in Wellington's name, dispatched a special messenger to St Leonards ordering Major-General Shaw Kennedy to Liverpool 'at once [to] place himself in communication with the Civil Authorities and take charge of the troops' in place of Warre. Lord FitzRoy also ordered Brigade Major Gordon at Chester to go to Liverpool and put himself under Kennedy's command. The Military Secretary received confirmation that six companies of infantry were to be conveyed by non-stop train from Portsmouth to the depot at Weedon on 10 April and that additional troops had been drafted to Nottingham. At 8 a.m. on 10 April the Horse Guards was informed that troops and artillery had been sent, at the request of the South-Western Railway authorities, from Gosport to protect Nine Elms Station.[17]

Fears of public disorder were not altogether quelled during the spring, however, for in June Wellington warned FitzRoy Somerset about the possibility of arms being seized from military depots at Woolwich and Deptford. He also cautioned that meetings, where people were armed, should be watched by troops. The depths of the CinC's unease were expressed in a lengthy letter to the Marquis of Anglesey, Master-General of the Ordnance, on 17 June. 'I am very sensible to the danger of our position ... My opinion is that we shall have to contend with Mobs, armed with pikes, and Fire Arms of all descriptions!' Wellington then made clear that he feared a revolutionary uprising: 'I have considered seriously of the means of defending the Sovereign and the Monarchical Institutions of the Country against this danger in its new form.' He had therefore ordered Sir Edward Blakeney in Dublin to identify houses that would be taken over to give sufficient fields of fire to control a rampant mob, and he instructed commanders in London and Liverpool to take similar precautions: 'I shall [therefore] know in what houses to post men with arms in order to secure the passages, through the several streets and communications.' Those responsible for public buildings such as the Bank of England and the British Museum had been warned to prepare for their defence. Once more Wellington had outlined a strategy. His injunction to Lord FitzRoy about the military depots, and the Military Secretary's activity in April suggest that in the event of trouble FitzRoy Somerset would have been intimately involved in any military deployment. So 1848 was a busy year.[18]

Dread of French invasion, coinciding with a domestic revolutionary uprising, lay behind Wellington's concern. Parallel to the Chartist problem, the 1840s had witnessed periodic outbursts of panic such as that following publication of a pamphlet by the King of France's son in 1844 which the Duke dubbed 'an invitation and provocation to war'. During the previous year French influence in Ireland had proved particularly worrying, though Lord Monteagle assured FitzRoy Somerset that, apart from a little unrest in County Clare, the country was 'tranquil'. Perhaps understandably, politicians and generals alike fretted about the parlous state of coastal defences. In 1848 Wellington complained to Lord FitzRoy about press publication of confidential correspondence on the subject between him and Sir John Burgoyne, which could only heighten public disquiet. It must therefore have been something of a relief for Lord FitzRoy to organize troops for ceremonial duties such as the funeral of the Dowager Queen Charlotte.[19]

For events farther afield offered neither more solace nor military stability. Problems in Canada continued; and in April 1845 William Williams did not press in Parliament for troop reductions in view of more trouble about the Oregon boundary with the United States. Wars in India, China and Afghanistan caused political repercussions even after their formal conclusion; so that men were kept ready for any renewal of hostilities. Tsar Nicholas I's visit to England in mid-1844 to discuss foreign affairs and to allay fears about Russian expansion did to some extent reduce tension. But any thoughts of paring forces in the Mediterranean or, as the situation temporarily improved there, Canada, were balanced, as FitzRoy Somerset reminded Lord Grey, by the need to cope with Kafir disturbances near the the Cape of Good Hope and send reinforcements to New Zealand. Lord FitzRoy did have one special overseas duty, tinged with deep personal regret. His former Peninsula colleague, the Prince of Orange, had become Willem II of The Netherlands on the abdication of his father in 1840. In March 1849 he died at Tilburg and a month later Lord FitzRoy attended his funeral in The Hague. He was succeeded by his son Alexander who was crowned Willem III – he was the same age as Lord FitzRoy's younger son, Richard. FitzRoy Somerset was treated with 'very great kindness' in The Netherlands and, writing to Westmorland, referred admiringly to Willem III's wife: 'The young queen is one of the most agreeable queens I ever met with.'[20]

In his administrative dealings with others FitzRoy Somerset's tact and consideration did not desert him. In 1842, at the instigation of his son Richard, he approached the Duke of Buckingham for assistance in reconciling Captain Fisher of the 95th (a staff officer at Kandy in Ceylon) with his father, the Revd John Fisher. Eventually, on 3 November, Lord FitzRoy could record his 'great pleasure' at the successful reconciliation which he had engineered. His role in the unsuccessful suit of Prince Henry of The Netherlands for the hand of Princess Mary, the Duke of Cambridge's daughter, was equally conciliatory. Cambridge acknowledged Mary's coolness, but feared giving offence. He agreed with Lord FitzRoy, though, that she must be convinced of happiness with a life-long partner. Two years after the original exchanges FitzRoy Somerset advised Prince George, who had by then succeeded his father as Duke, that the rejected suitor 'clings to the hope that Princess Mary's decision is not irrevocable'. Indeed Prince Henry appears to have re-opened correspondence with Cambridge through FitzRoy Somerset in 1852.

Lord FitzRoy's tact was called into play in 1845 to cope with a serious professional problem. He agreed with Sir Robert Peel and Sir Henry Hardinge that 'great difficulty will arise' if Sir Charles Napier were to be passed over for the Bombay command. But Lord FitzRoy suggested that it could be explained to him that the Governor-General had nobody suitable to go in his place to Scinde where the Government held him 'in the highest regard'. He further suggested that the local rank of lieutenant-general be conferred on Napier with an increase in salary. FitzRoy Somerset had investigated the question of salary and it would be possible to pay Napier as a general on the staff and as Governor of Scinde. The CinC Bombay received an annual salary of £8,300: under these arrangements Napier would receive in Scinde £7,000 in his civil capacity, £1,300 in his military – the same sum. Lord FitzRoy suggested that he prepare the necessary documents and forward them to Wellington for signature the next day. Eventually this solution was accepted and Napier was duly promoted; but he would resign the governorship of Scinde in 1847.[21]

In spite of the evident added restrictions imposed by Wellington, FitzRoy Somerset maintained a busy social calendar. In January 1843 he was shooting at Copt Hall and referred also to a dinner engagement with the Morningtons. On 22 November 1843 he revealed that Culling Smith and Sir John Macdonald had dined with the FitzRoy Somersets the previous evening and that Macdonald had eaten heartily until 'My Lady' congratulated him on his improved appetite. Thereafter the Adjutant-General ate little. That evening he was dining elsewhere, hoping to meet the Woronzovs; Lady FitzRoy would eat with her parents; both would dine at Savile Row the following day. From Wilton on New Year's Day 1845 he reported 'beautiful weather ... and good sport', noting that 22 guests were expected for dinner. The next day he recorded another 'splendid day's sport', but explained that he must hurry to finish the letter so that the servants might have their ball. December 1845 saw him at Savernake where the perils of taking part in shoots were underlined. Lord FitzRoy described visiting a beater who had been seriously injured and might require a second operation. 'The poor man' had at least four children (the number seen by FitzRoy Somerset) and his wife looked 'old'. Because of this accident the house party did not shoot on 14 December but instead went over to Tottenham for lunch, Lord FitzRoy sharing a coach with Lady Malmesbury and Lady Bruce. They all examined the new house being built for the Bruces. Only one wing had so far been finished, but Lord FitzRoy believed that the end-product would be 'altogether splendid', with the lake 'quite beautiful'. To Charlotte he signed off 'à demain, Papa'. Six days later he was at Goodwood, not apparently having visited the Horse Guards in the meantime. He outlined another accident to Kitty. 'A brisk northerly wind' had 'made the pheasants fly with much rapidity' and he had missed many, 'little to my credit'. Within an hour of the commencement of the shoot, his loader, however, 'had a serious accident which occupied some time and caused us all much anxiety and annoyance. He was following me when he unfortunately placed his foot on the stump of a tree which was as slippery as glass. One of his feet slipped and the other somehow or other gave way and the man fell crying out that his leg was broken.' He was made as warm as possible and taken home 'in the game cart', while somebody rode to Chichester for a doctor. The man (named Cobden) kept a public house near Halnaker, and once the day's shooting had ended Lord FitzRoy went to see him. Apparently the small bone near the ankle was broken and the man had to rest 'quiet for three or four days'. Thus the accident was not 'serious', but 'a misfortune'. FitzRoy Somerset concluded his letter with a request that Lady FitzRoy arrange a house party for Christmas Day, and a reference to another party at Copt Hall. Before leaving Goodwood on 21 December he reported 'droppings of snow', which did not interfere with 'good sport': 'I killed twenty-eight or twenty-nine [pheasants], two or three of which were not picked up, a woodcock and a partridge, but then I had the front seat of the dress circle and got much more shooting than others.'[22]

That allusion indicates an active interest in the theatre, which was not always rewarded. He explained to Charlotte on one occasion: 'You never saw any thing so horrible as the performance at the Adelphi ... I came away before Norma, which I am told is better worth seeing than anything else.' On another occasion, after dinner, he and his sister-in-law, Priscilla, at his suggestion went to the Haymarket, arriving after 10 p.m., to see part of 'Who's Gone Friend?' and 'a very good farce', 'The Jacobite', in which the leading actor [John Baldwin Buckstone] gave a 'capital performance', before returning home at 1 a.m. Incidentally Lord FitzRoy remarked that after a little over six hours in bed he got up to vote for Lord March in a Parliamentary election. In November 1850 he recorded that, after dining with his daughter, he and Kitty had gone to the Lyceum. During this period only a single reference to literature appears in surviving papers though this does not necessarily prove lack of interest. Writing to Kitty in January 1846 he explained that Charles Somerset would travel to Badminton in a few days. If Lord FitzRoy had finished the eighth volume of 'Monte Christo [sic]' by then, he would take it with him. The inference was that he had read the first seven volumes – no mean feat. Of the eighth he remarked somewhat disparagingly: 'So far I have got in it, it is tiresome, very poisonous, etc. ...'[23]

FitzRoy Somerset's health still seems to have been generally good, though mention of a number of minor afflictions appear in his correspondence. Writing to his younger daughter in September 1842 he referred to a pain in his side which had troubled him for some time but had now subsided 'and thus I think the Drafts have done me a great deal of good'. Three years later he explained to Charlotte that he had delayed travelling to Badminton from Dover because of 'the pain which has fallen almost without interruption since yesterday', possibly the same ailment. Certainly, in May 1846, reporting discomfiture from an upset stomach, he added 'that malaise brought on the old pain in my side and put me quite *hors de combat*'. Later stomach trouble was mentioned once again when he told Kitty that '*mon intérieur* is right again'. A passing reference to trouble with his feet on one occasion may have merely signified tiredness after a long day's shooting. Twice he mentioned toothache which necessitated a visit to the dentist, though on neither occasion was an extraction found necessary. In fact, in February 1850 Cartwright, who had 'migrated from Sackville Street to Savile Row, looked carefully over my mouth and pronounced that there was nothing wrong in any of my teeth and seemed satisfied that the sensations I complained of would pass away. He said that I took excellent care of my teeth and refused a fee.' A year later, similarly, Lord FitzRoy reported: 'Mr Cartwright is quite satisfied that there is nothing wrong in the tooth. He examined it very carefully.'[24]

During the 1840s FitzRoy Somerset suffered two injuries that may have left him with prolonged discomfort; for a year after the first incident he still 'found galloping and the jumping quite hard'. In January 1843, possibly while riding, he damaged his arm. His doctor [Hume] later believed that leeches ought to have been applied immediately after the accident so that 'the coagulated blood which now presses upon the extremity would have been dispersed'. Hume recommended a bandage and 'the occasional application of eau de cologne or other cold stimulant'. When Hume bandaged Lord FitzRoy he 'put me to acute pain when he touched the one point underneath the arm, which had been so tender from the first'. That night he slept well and woke at 7.30 a.m. He could not get his riding-coat on *'aussi tout ça va bien'*. The following day he informed Charlotte that he had experienced 'a good deal of pain' during the previous evening and had removed the tight bandage. He used 'my lady's lotion' on the arm last night and that morning and it had lost its 'tight' feeling. Almost exactly two years later he reported that 'my career of amusement has been checked'. Just before the end of a day's shooting at Goodwood on 6 January 1845, 'I sprained or ruptured some of the tendons of my right leg in erecting myself to go up a steep bank', and ten days later was 'still lame' even though using a heel two inches taller than usual. Three months afterwards the lameness remained. In 1851 he revealed that medical advice suggested 'medicated cotton upon my arm and I shall do so directly' – though it was not clear whether this referred to continuing trouble from the 1843 injury, difficulty with the stump or another accident. That year, also, writing to Richard the Duke of Cambridge noted that he had recently seen Lord FitzRoy 'looking a great deal better than when you left [for Hanover] and complaining less of rheumatism'; an indication that perhaps after all, at this time, FitzRoy Somerset was not in first-class health.[25]

There was no doubt, though, that professional difficulties were real. Especially towards the close of his time at the Horse Guards Wellington's perceived conservatism invoked growing disquiet. Writing to FitzRoy Somerset on 8 December 1845, he dismissed a proposal to grant additional pensions to selected NCOs, arguing that nomination would be difficult. The backbone of the British Army, he claimed, was the officer, 'the man of education, manners, honor, and other qualities acquired by the education which English gentlemen receive.' Men looked to their officers, and the decline of the Spanish and Portuguese armies was due to 'nothing but the want of education of their officers'. The present system, therefore, should not be changed: improvement of incentives for NCOs ought not to be encouraged. In 1850 a disparaging pamphlet circulated, openly a satire upon Wellington with a frontispiece: 'Thus saith the Duke – thus hath the Duke inferred.' In a wide-ranging assault on the whole administration of the Horse Guards, making use of cartoons as well as prose, the authors castigated Wellington for forgetfulness and blind adherence to aristocratic interest. One section, in particular, by inference attacked Lord FitzRoy, suggesting that he was simply a clerk. Furthermore, the writers declaimed: 'When we behold persons verging in years towards the completion of a century buoyed up by the fulsome sycophancy of parasites'; and they referred to 'an old gentleman in his declining years', who naturally leant upon people of his own generation whom he had known over a long period of time in the Service. Such a scurrilous, anonymous tract might be ignored. Yet in that same year the Secretary at War (Fox Maule, later Lord Panmure) circulated a confidential memorandum calling for administrative reform, which indirectly also cast aspersions on the running of the Horse Guards. Lord John Russell adopted a gentler approach, though his overall aim remained the same. To Prince Albert he argued: 'It may be useful if your Royal Highness will see him [Wellington] from time to time in relation to the Army ... [which] may overcome the indisposition to change which he naturally entertains.'[26]

The common theme of these several criticisms centred on Wellington's anachronistic grasp of military affairs and, by implication, his Military Secretary's inability – possibly unwillingness – to influence him otherwise. Lord FitzRoy's own view on flogging and duelling – issues of fierce debate during the mid-1840s – have not survived. But his anti-liberal sentiment may be judged from a note of April 1849 to Westmorland, British Ambassador in Vienna, that he 'indeed rejoiced at Radetsky's success'. 'I have been an Austrian throughout,' he added, though 'a little uneasy about your King's acceptance of Imperial dignity', recognizing that this may have been a move to curb military aspiration to power: 'I have been told I do not know how truly that your army shewed symptoms of ambition.'[27]

Throughout these years, no matter what difficulties and disappointments he faced, Lord FitzRoy gained strength from his family. He was especially proud of his two daughters, enthusing to Richard about Kitty's being presented at her first royal drawing-room and later how popular she was at the London balls. He praised Charlotte for her 'good qualities and cheerful disposition'; and he acknowledged both girls' care and devotion to him and Lady FitzRoy. He wrote proudly of Kitty's being 'the youthful queen' and Charlotte 'the sweet Lady Grace' in an amateur theatrical performance at Badminton and, on another occasion, referred to 'great doings and play acting' by both girls at another country house. He vastly enjoyed their company and was delighted when both accompanied him to Badminton in January 1844. When they were away from Stanhope Street he admitted to loneliness. Kitty rode to hounds twice with him in December 1843 which prompted special pleasure. To Richard he explained that Charlotte would be bridesmaid to Miss Foley at her forthcoming wedding and how, on 6 June 1845, both girls attended a fancy dress ball given by the Queen at which they 'had looked to great advantage'. He did betray to his younger son, though, a trace of traditional paternal concern: 'Nobody has yet bidden for your sisters but I can with truth say this that whoever gets them will get a treasure ... Duty is their first object. They are indeed a great blessing to us.'[28]

Lord FitzRoy was not, however, an ultra-indulgent father. He issued clear instructions to Charlotte to arrange for a coach to meet him at Paddington Station on 15 December 1845 and at London Bridge a week later following visits to Badminton and Goodwood respectively. On each occasion it must arrive sharp at 1 p.m. He could be pernickety to the point of fussiness. In January 1843 when he was in London and the girls at Badminton, he reminded them each to pay their laundry bills of £1. 4s. 6d. and not leave that to Beaufort. Later that year he wrote pointedly to them about not having thanked Henry Somerset for his presents to them before they left London: 'Pray repair this omission as soon as you can.' After discussing with Charlotte a letter from Colonel Harry Smith in India about Arthur, he ended his letter to her with an admonition not to reveal what he had told her to Arthur: *'Mind this.'* Charlotte was then 28. Of Kitty he demanded in January 1844: 'Have you sent haybills to Richard and Arthur?', presumably for horses being stabled in England on their behalf. If not, Lord FitzRoy would do so himself. When Charlotte was almost 33 he wrote a detailed letter to her about travelling to London from Badminton. He was pleased to learn that she had 'fixed a day for returning to London', and added: 'Pray give the coachman 5s. for washing his carriage.' She should take the barouche to Chippenham station for the 1.30 train which would reach London at 4.50. If she did not pick up Emilie and her maid on the way and the Duke's horses had to take them to Chippenham, she should give the boys a reward of 5s each. Mysteriously, in 1852 he chided Charlotte: 'If you had the opportunity, you would be an inveterate gambler.'[29]

As the years went by Lady FitzRoy became something of a trial to them all. She seemed to suffer from a succession of ailments which put the family to considerable inconvenience. At this time Lord FitzRoy's hair – if not the ash-blonde of his youth – remained fair; hers was thick, light-brown with traces of grease and dandruff. No portrait from this period exists to confirm or deny her continued physical attractiveness. But, certainly, her vivacity had gone.[30] And she did seem unlucky. Towards the end of 1842 she suffered an unfortunate accident, being badly shaken 'by a fall upon her head of one of the sun blinds in the great room over the drawing-room in Deal Castle' where her parents then lived. FitzRoy Somerset explained to Richard that she was helping him to get the blind up when 'suddenly the frame and blind fell and the corner of the former passed down her forehead and made a deep sharp cut in it'. At first Lord FitzRoy did not realize the extent of the injury until blood spurted which he had difficulty in 'quenching'. He sent for a surgeon 'who immediately drew the cut together and assured us that no inconvenience would result from the accident'. This happened on 25 November, but she was able to travel to London on 1 December though necessarily had 'to keep herself very quiet for a while'. Three months later Lord FitzRoy reported that 'your mama sometimes complains a little of her head', indicating that the injury had not yet completely healed. Later in 1843, perversely, a family visit to the seaside was cancelled: 'My lady fancies that sea air makes her rheumatic', he observed. He regretted that the annual family pilgrimage would not take place. The following year he was unable to persuade his wife to go to Badminton with him to join the girls: 'She complains of a pain in her back and hates exertion'. The early months of 1845 were traumatic for Lady FitzRoy. On 2 February her sister, Mary Bagot, died; twenty days later her father died and, as a result, Lady Mornington became ill. Not surprisingly, perhaps, FitzRoy Somerset explained to Richard: 'Your mama's health has suffered a little but I trust rest and quiet will soon restore her.' The following month he confirmed that these were 'not lively times' for his wife. In June she was, according to Lord FitzRoy, still 'a bit low in spirits'. These could not have been lively times for her family either. In July she was persuaded to go to Dover for her health, but soon returned. FitzRoy Somerset explained that, contrary to Dover where she complained constantly, Lady FitzRoy made no mention of 'rheumatic pains' in London. That, at least, was comforting.[31]

Extensive correspondence with Richard, when he was in Ceylon and later Hanover, revealed the same tetchiness at non-receipt of letters that Lord FitzRoy displayed with the girls. He constantly nagged his younger son for not writing. Scarcely had 1842 opened than FitzRoy Somerset declared himself 'disappointed' that the November mail had brought no letter from Ceylon, though admittedly those of September and October had. He was sure that the fault was not Richard's. He recognized on other occasions that delay had been caused by a build-up of mail in Ceylon before dispatch or been due to 'violent winds': at best, a letter took almost two months to arrive. However, in general, he reproached his son with a succession of complaints: in August 1843 he noted that the Marseilles mail had not brought a letter and hoped that the Falmouth one would produce something for his sisters: 'I am not happy if you do not write to somebody every mail.' A similar rebuke went off early in December when the Marseilles mail again proved barren: FitzRoy Somerset hoped that the Southampton mail would not. His unease remained at the end of the month: no letter since 21 October, and to receive one 'relieves me of the fidgets', that Richard might be ill. In mid-1844 he again expressed unhappiness: he had thought the Marseilles mail had left before the Ceylon mail of 20 May had reached Bombay, but on inquiry discovered that this was not so. So he could only hope that the Southampton mail would be more fruitful. In March 1845 the complaint was that no letter had arrived since 7 January. Two months later, in acknowledging a letter of 22 March, he underlined that neither he nor Richard's sisters had received anything by the previous two mails and, he emphasized again, that he would prefer Richard to write by every mail. The following month father complained to son of no letter since 16 April. On Christmas Eve he invoked the girls: 'Their backs are up in annoyance', because Richard had not written to them 'for months'. Far away, Richard could not have been encouraged by this querulous torrent, even though it represented paternal concern lest he should be unwell or otherwise injured.[32]

Lord FitzRoy did praise Richard whenever he learnt of his good progress. In June 1844 he wrote that he had been told that 'you are not only a perfect gentleman but an *excellent* man of business'. A year later he professed pleasure that, on his return to England, Arthur Talbot had given a 'most flattering account' of Richard; and in October 1845 he again indicated his delight that Richard was spoken of well 'and I have no doubt that under all circumstances you will continue to give me satisfaction' – the voice of a caring father. However, that care extended to pressing Richard to work hard. He reminded his son 'that before you went to Ceylon you had the reputation of being an idle dog and that habits of indolence are acquired with much more ease than they are shaken off.' 'Be industrious,' his father urged him. There is some collateral evidence that Richard was something of a socialite and ladies' man. Writing from the Foreign Office in London, where he was confined to 'this blessed shop scribbling', Augustus Paget in light-hearted vein described 'capital fun' on Derby Day, with Colonel Anson pocketing '£25,000 or more' when his horse Attila won. He went on to portray other meetings with the clear indication that he and Richard had enjoyed such events in the past. He inquired whether Richard were getting his share of elephant rides; and Lord March, writing from Regent's Park Barracks, inquired: 'Have you broken many hearts in Ceylon?' Years later when Richard's engagement was announced, Augustus Gore wrote to him recalling their 'adventures' in Ceylon and asking whether Richard still saw any of a list of acquaintances from that time. The impression given by Gore was that he and Richard had led a busy social life. The cryptic postscript, 'Do you ever see anything of Mrs Maclean now?', could well have been insignificant. Certainly, though, when he did become engaged, to Lady Georgiana Lygon, another 'unhappy' woman was 'disappointed' and fled to Scotland. Of his social life in Ceylon, however, the certificate of his entry to the St John's Lodge, Colombo of the Freemasons on 8 April 1847 (Year 5847 in Masonry) represents the only firm evidence of activity.[33]

Lord FitzRoy displayed paternal sympathy when Richard was 'thrown into sad affliction by the untimely end of Miss Layard', which cast a shadow of gloom over the entire English circle in Ceylon. He professed no objection to the prospect of Richard's becoming a member of the Managing Committee of the Savings Bank – 'when you are in the chair with a wig on, you will be a very respectable character indeed' – and expressed delight later that he might become a director of the Bank of Ceylon, a 'flourishing concern'. Lord FitzRoy showed pleasure in details of a trip to Kandy which Richard undertook in the course of his duties. But he was 'much annoyed' that Arthur had invited Richard 'on a pleasure excursion' to Bombay and, further, to the frontier of the Punjab 'to attend Lord Ellenborough on his interview with the Sikh Government'. Richard's prime responsibility was to carry out his own duties in Ceylon. 'You are in office and must do the duties of that office so steadily and constantly as that you may acquire regular habits of business, recommend yourself to your superiors and enter by your good conduct a claim to advancement' – a peremptory caution, which he would repeat two years later.[34]

In fact his younger son's work in Ceylon caused Lord FitzRoy a great deal of anxiety. Richard had gone there after his father had persuaded the Governor, Sir Colin Campbell, a Peninsula veteran, to find him an appointment as a personal favour. Lord FitzRoy declared himself 'delighted' when Richard indeed acquired a position and urged him to repay Campbell's kindness by his industry. The Governor, he pointed out, would give him a good grounding in public business. Within months he learned that Richard had become 'assistant government agent' with an annual salary of £300 and travelling expenses of £100 – a great distinction, Lord FitzRoy observed, for 'a young civilian'. The cautious father then emerged. Richard should send home his surplus salary which would be wisely invested to guard against 'a rainy day'.

Before the close of 1842, however, FitzRoy Somerset expressed alarm at an unpleasant development. 'No trace' of Richard's appointment to the Ceylon Civil Service could be found in the files of the Colonial Office in London. This became manifest after Lord Stanley, the Secretary of State, had been upset by a petition from Ceylon signed, among others, by Richard. Lord FitzRoy had explained that Sir Colin Campbell received written authorization from Lord John Russell (Stanley's predecessor in office) to take Richard with him and appoint him to a suitable post. FitzRoy Somerset asked Richard to show Sir Colin this part of his letter and to ask the Governor whether Lord FitzRoy's memory were correct. Apparently Sir Colin confirmed this sequence of events for in March 1843 – acknowledging Richard's letter of 21 January, which arrived late because of 'violent winds' in the Mediterranean – FitzRoy Somerset announced that Stanley had accepted the validity of Richard's appointment. Evidently the father had worked hard in London on his son's behalf. He did not conclude his encouraging letter without a mild homily. Richard should seek to be a good civil servant, grow rich and not get into debt. Indeed, professionally, Richard appeared to be settling down well. A year later his father expressed pleasure at a report from Sir Colin of how well Richard was doing, such that he had been given more responsibility. 'This affords me the highest satisfaction. I hope you will earn still further claims to his particular and good office and will establish yourself the reputation of an excellent man of business', in the sense of professional ability.[35]

A cloud, however, was on the horizon. In October 1844 FitzRoy Somerset acknowledged that Richard had purchased 200 acres of land, intending to plant coffee. He trusted, though, that Sir Colin had been fully consulted, for 'the golden days of Coffee Planting in Ceylon are gone'. Potential trading losses soon proved but one snare. Two months later Lord FitzRoy was warned of a rumour in London that civil servants were to be barred from entering into speculations such as Richard's coffee plantation, as this would deflect them from their proper duties. Early in 1845 Stanley did apply stringent restrictions on colonial civil servants holding land. FitzRoy Somerset sympathized with Richard's consequent dilemma, hoping that he would obtain an 'advantageous' price for his 200 acres, but anxiously inquiring about progress in the coffee venture. In April he wrote that, despite representations (by implication from himself and others), Stanley would not modify his order against civil servants holding land: 'Rely upon it that those who propose to profit by it are waiting to make purchases at a reduced rate,' he warned. A slight breathing-space quickly ensued. Two months later Lord FitzRoy wrote that 'by accident' he had heard that Stanley had prolonged the time for decision in Ceylon from six to nine months, when civil servants had to decide whether to sell or remain in office. If Richard opted to remain a civil servant he would have another twelve months to sell. No further mention of the matter appears in FitzRoy Somerset's files; and it is possible that the issue lapsed when W.E. Gladstone replaced Stanley in December 1845.

Stanley – perhaps in the aftermath of the unpopular petition – appeared, at least temporarily, to have blighted Richard's career also. Referring to Richard's letter of 10 June 1845, he read 'with regret' that Sir Colin had not recommended Richard as 'acting government agent' because he felt that Stanley might object. After being assured that he would get the appointment, it must be 'a sad disappointment', though Richard appeared 'to have behaved like an angel'. He believed, nevertheless, that 'my friend Campbell' would swiftly make amends in some way; and an opportunity to do so occurred before the close of the year. Mr Gibson, the Assistant Secretary in Ceylon, returned to England and Lord FitzRoy hoped that Sir Colin would recommend to Stanley that Richard replace him, possibly on a permanent basis: 'I will try to find out what Mr Gibson's intentions are, but it will be very difficult to do so.'

With Stanley out of office prospects seemed likely to improve. But in February 1846 Lord FitzRoy was still referring only to the prospect of Richard's becoming Assistant Secretary, wishing that he could secure 'something decent' for him in England: 'It is very difficult indeed and I dare not indulge any sanguine expectations,' he continued. However, he would look around; though Richard must not abandon Ceylon until something firm had been arranged. 'My dear boy,' he went on, '[you] have been fully five years abroad'; and Sir Colin would probably be returning to England in 1847. If he did so Richard should approach him for leave of absence and accompany him, but on no account resign. Reporting 'a serious conversation' with Sir James Graham, the Home Secretary, who promised to speak to the Prime Minister (Peel), in April Lord FitzRoy revealed that he was making strenuous efforts to place Richard at home. A month later he reported no progress with Graham; and this particular initiative appears to have foundered when Peel's government lost office in July.

In January 1847 Lord FitzRoy noted Richard's provisional appointment as Assistant Secretary in the absence of Mr Gibson then still in England. The new Secretary of State for War and the Colonies, Lord Grey, had promised Lord FitzRoy that if Gibson did not return Richard would be confirmed in the post. He hoped to have firm news of this by the next mail: 'In the meantime though I do not like to encourage hopes the fulfilment of which do not depend upon myself, I cannot help saying that the chances are more for than against you.' None the less a decision had not been reached three months later. Grey had still not decided between Gibson and Richard – suggesting that Gibson wanted to return. 'If I were a betting man', Lord FitzRoy wrote, he would back confirmation of the provisional appointment which Sir Colin had made. An auditor, he felt, would support this view – presumably on the grounds that two salaries were currently being paid for the same job, those of Gibson (absent) and Richard (in Ceylon).[36]

In his letters to Richard, Lord FitzRoy also touched on political and security issues at home. In September 1842 he observed that he had had 'a very hard season', partly as a result of the Chartist disturbances. In the spring of 1844 he reported a 'tremendous' nine-day debate on 'the Irish question', with a 'very satisfactory' ending whereby the whigs 'got nothing by their motion'. Six months later he professed to being 'astonished' that the Law Lords had overturned a conviction of Daniel O'Connell for his inflammatory 'preachings' in Ireland. Commenting on 'the Corn Question' early in 1846, he noted that it 'has given rise to a great deal of ill blood and many of Sir Robert Peel's several supporters are opposed to him upon it ... A sad pity and [it] will go far to break up the Conservative Party' – an interesting use of the new political terminology of party, and a perceptive judgement. In May his comments were even more pointed. 'The state of politics is detestable,' he exclaimed. Despite 'furious protectionists' Peel held that repeal of the Corn Laws would be carried through both Houses. However, 'God knows what may happen afterwards ... Sir Robert Peel's Government is surrounded by difficulties'; a masterly understatement.[37]

Foreign affairs, too, attracted comment, not least – as he pointed out with reference to India in 1842 – because deployment of troops overseas was referred to the CinC through him. He discussed 'the great and glorious news' of Generals Pollock and Nott in Afghanisatn and 'the highly advantageous treaty of peace' in China, all of which 'has afforded universal satisfaction and is viewed as of immense importance to the interest of the Country'. These successes would secure 'our Empire in the East' and, by opening up trade with China, 'give an impulse to our trade and lead to a better state of things in our manufacturing districts'. They would help to dampen 'little stirrings' in the industrial Midlands and they might persuade 'our immediate neighbours, the French, to be more wary how they enter into a quarrel with us'. In this latter hope FitzRoy Somerset was quickly disappointed. In August 1844 he drew attention to 'an awkward question pending with France', because French officers had been guilty of 'gross outrage' against a British official in Tahiti. The French press had become very agitated: 'what will come of it God knows', but he believed that a compromise would be reached with compensation offered to Britain. Furthermore the Prince de Joinville seemed bent on provoking a war with Morocco which would make the supply of fresh provisions to Gibraltar difficult. By September, as he had prophesied, having been 'on the brink of war', the British and French governments had settled the Tahiti dispute.[38]

At times Lord FitzRoy professed shortage of money. He wrote in 1845 to Richard: 'All that I have in the world has been spent buying the house in Stanhope Street and I have still some thousands to pay on that account.' Great Stanhope Street, due east of the Stanhope Gate entrance to Hyde Park, stretched a mere 100 yards between Park Lane and South Audley Street, approximately 100 yards south of the Dorchester Hotel, 300 yards from Apsley House and within easy reach of the Hyde Park rides and Rotten Row. Close to Grovesnor Square and Berkeley Square, it lay just north of Piccadilly with direct access to Green Park and St James's Park, across which the Horse Guards could be reached. It was therefore admirably placed for Lord and Lady FitzRoy. Number 5 Great Stanhope Street, a substantial four-storeyed terraced building with an impressive portico protecting the front door, was also well-suited for entertainment and the demands of the London season.[39]

Lord FitzRoy appears, however, to have been over-anxious about his finances which, according to his banker, were never noticeably strained. Having paid off his loan of 1837 in June 1843, he borrowed a further £7,500 in July 1844, which he cleared in 1852. This loan enabled him to pay £8,400 to Lord Abingdon, which could have been the purchase of the lease of 5 Great Stanhope Street to which he referred, for 'buying' did not necessarily refer to acquisition of freehold. He did, though, sell £5,000 worth of securities in 1849, enabling him to pay that sum to his solicitor, Mr Walford; but the nature of this transaction is not now clear. Messrs Hoare, Lord FitzRoy's bankers, would not have been aware of private transactions. Possibly through temporary financial need, Lord FitzRoy sold his horses (one for 100 guineas) in 1842. Nine years later he took great care in seeking to acquire another horse. He explained at length to Kitty how he and Charlotte had been negotiating to secure one of three. He hoped to obtain a mare from Dublin through a friend, another horse closer to home having been rejected because of 'a strong halt'. Should the Dublin transaction fail 'there is an end to my chances of getting an 'orse [sic]'. Enigmatically, he added: 'But what is the use of my having one' – perhaps because he travelled mostly by carriage or train. He eschewed one of the proffered horses because it was 'unequal to my weight' – lack of riding might explain an expanding waist-line. In 1852 he had to sell more securities worth £16,000, to make 'part payment of Mr Hatcher's mortgage', the precise nature of which is obscure.[40]

Inevitably, given such a large family, Lord FitzRoy dwelt heavily on the fortunes of its members, beyond the immediate circle based on Great Stanhope Street. Lord Mornington, Lady FitzRoy's father, figured prominently for three years as his health gradually deteriorated. The first indication of impending decline came in December 1842 shortly after he succeeded to the title. FitzRoy Somerset reported to Richard that he was unwell: 'The seat of his disorder is in the prostate gland (take care in your answer not to allude to this by name) brought on it is said by riding at his time of life. He has been told that he will never be clear of this trouble and has been forbidden to ride again – a sad mortification to him'. When Lord FitzRoy stayed at Deal Castle – Mornington's residence – his father-in-law did not once dine with the family in ten days: 'I am sure you will grieve for him.' By the end of the month Mornington was travelling in a new brougham 'as easy as a Sedan chair and very comfortable'. But three months later, because of his health, he gave up Deal Castle, moving to a house at Roehampton so as to be nearer to his doctor. The move, however, did not help significantly. Lord FitzRoy noted in May that he expected to dine and sleep at Roehampton on occasions, the house being only seven miles from Stanhope Street; and evidently other members of the family were similarly keeping an eye on him because Lady Mornington was not particularly robust. Early in 1844 Mornington appeared to rally (FitzRoy Somerset's letters to his son in Ceylon recorded only an attack of influenza) and in July he leased Orleans House at Twickenham for six months. In August he had a bad fall there. Not having been up a certain flight of steps before, he was unaware that the door opened outwards, which caused him to fall back down the steps. It seems that he never fully recovered from the shock. By January 1845 his condition had given rise to serious concern, and he died on Saturday 22 February. Two days later Lord FitzRoy gave Richard a graphic account of his last three days. Mornington was buried at Grovesnor Chapel, South Audley Street, on 3 March 1845: the list of those attending the funeral was long and distinguished, the new earl having returned to England on his father's death.[41]

Never strong, after her husband's death, the dowager Lady Mornington now became a special worry. On 1 August 1845 Lord FitzRoy told

Charlotte that she was not eating much, 'seemed very feeble' and her hands were 'lamentably thin'. She 'engaged' 21 Marine Parade, Dover, in order to convalesce. Seven weeks later, however, Charlotte learnt that her grandmother was 'very critical', yet in four days she miraculously recovered to be declared 'out of danger'. In July 1847 Lord FitzRoy recorded 'another attack'. When Dr Wilson arrived, though, he discovered that his patient had devoured half a box of biscuits. So Charlotte was discouraged from sending any more to her. Five months later FitzRoy Somerset described how he had dined with his mother-in-law. She 'seemed pretty well ... but the new set of teeth disfigures her very much and gives her the appearance of making grimaces'. In August 1849 she was again eating 'sparingly' though on this occasion the reason may have been an infectious disease. For Lord FitzRoy added that, after a 'tolerable night', 'the skin was peeling off'. That crisis also passed. The following year came yet another 'attack'. On a visit to her, he considered her to be very ill, though her nurse told him that she was well but 'drowsy'. 'After the first certainty [she] did not know me, taking me for my brother Charles and asking after Lady Charles.' This was the first time that she had not known FitzRoy and when he mentioned Lady Westmorland (her daughter Priscilla), she said: 'Let me see, who is Lady Westmorland?' Lord FitzRoy thought her much thinner, as she lay on a sofa. Eventually, to the distress of her immediate relatives, she died on 23 October 1851.[42]

There were a good many other family illnesses. In October 1842 Lord FitzRoy's eldest brother Henry, sixth Duke of Beaufort and another former ADC to Wellington in the Peninsula, seemed well. Lord FitzRoy dined with him to test a new cook, whom he declared 'not *cordon bleu*', and reported that the Duke and Duchess went to the races at Newmarket next day. The following year, however, Lord FitzRoy revealed that Beaufort's gout had not been cured by a visit to a German spa. Noting that Beaufort was in London to present his daughter Lady Blanche at her first drawing-room in the spring of 1845, Lord FitzRoy remarked on his relative immobility. By August 1845 he was worse, 'walking very badly and looking anything but well'; and, shortly before Christmas, FitzRoy Somerset wrote to Charlotte: 'Poor Beaufort I fear is very ill and I very much doubt whether he can get well unless the Duchess gives up directing the physicians.' Possibly she was persuaded to do so, for the Duke survived another three years.[43]

Two of Lord FitzRoy's brothers died at this time, however. In August 1842 he warned Richard that Edward 'lies at the point of death', explaining that he had suffered from a heart complaint for some time and had had a 'violent attack' recently in Geneva. His condition had deteriorated alarmingly during the past few days, and FitzRoy Somerset expressed concern for the fate of his girls if he should die. Within days he informed Richard that his uncle Edward had indeed died shortly after 2 a.m. on 1 September. The funeral would be on 8 September and Lord

FitzRoy had ordered a spray in commemoration. Once again he wondered what would become of his 'poor daughters'. Next John appeared to be 'far from well'. His cough was better, but he had a tumour between the legs, and violent rheumatic pains in the shoulders and back of the neck, 'it is said from the inactive state of his liver'. A brief period of remission followed, but by July 1846 he had suffered a relapse. From then on decline accelerated. By early September he had moved from Bristol to Weston Super Mare in the hope that the sea air would help. Visiting him, Lord FitzRoy regretted that the cure was not working and little hope of survival now existed. John could no longer walk and could scarcely turn over in bed. 'This is a sad affliction to me for I dearly love him and he was the companion of my youth and all our early recollections are the same.' Richard was John's 'favourite' and he was sad that he had not come home to England that year. In the third week of September John was still holding out but could not stand without assistance. Yet he had improved slightly to the point that, with the aid of a manservant, he could progress a few steps. Writing to Richard towards the end of that month, though, Lord FitzRoy revealed that he had lost 'my dear brother' on 3 October. Having travelled to Weston Super Mare the day before, unaware that the end was nigh, he was with him when he 'breathed his last'. 'I have lost a most affectionate brother', and Richard, too, would undoubtedly miss him. John left his family nothing other than Lady John's 'fortune', the interest on which exceeded £300 per year. Lord FitzRoy, none the less, suspected 'a great deal of debt all occasioned by her extravagance and folly', while John was frugal in his tastes and manner of living. Another brother, William, became ill in 1850. He dined with Lord FitzRoy on 26 September, but ate little. His doctor the following day recommended that he see a specialist, and the result of that consultation was awaited. But William never fully recovered and died at Clifton on 14 January 1851. Meanwhile Priscilla's son George had died in June 1848. His passing, Lord FitzRoy believed, was a 'heavy shock' to his father, but 'his life was a burden to himself', increasingly less able to communicate and therefore to enjoy society. 'Latterly his daily existence was a blank solitude.' His brother, Ernest, had been very attentive to him and, writing to Westmorland, FitzRoy Somerset exclaimed that Ernest would be 'a most worthy successor' to the title of Lord Burghersh.[44]

The sudden death on 2 February 1845 of Lady Mary Bagot, sister of Emily and Priscilla, shocked Lord FitzRoy: 'she bore her sufferings with much patience and resignation and was sensible to the last', he wrote to Richard, adding that, as with his brother Edward, he was concerned about her 'poor daughters'. In fact one of Edward's daughters (Blanche) married her first cousin, the Revd Charles Locke, to Lord FitzRoy's mild disapproval: 'His means are very small and he can make no settlement upon her but he has some prospect of preferment in the church.' Less depressing items of family news were that the new Lord and Lady Mornington had bought the former house of Lord FitzRoy's niece, Blanche Galloway, in Grosvenor Square. In 1842 FitzRoy Somerset reported that the Westmorlands were in Berlin – 'a very dull place' – George Fane, their son, occupying the London house. Ernest, with 1st Battalion, The Rifle Brigade, in Malta, and Francis (later as Lord Burghersh, Lord FitzRoy's ADC in the Crimea) at Sandhurst, were 'doing very well'. He was mildly disapproving of another nephew – William's son Henry – who had returned from Van Diemen's Land (Tasmania) with a wife and two children. His spouse, Lord FitzRoy remarked, was 'less beautiful' than reports had suggested.[45]

Early in 1849 Lord FitzRoy's advice about the military career of the new Lord Burghersh was sought. On 8 February he wrote to his brother-in-law, noting that the previous day Burghersh had called at the Horse Guards 'and we have had a good deal of conversation upon the course he should pursue for the future'. There was no prospect of 'employment on the staff at present'. Lord Cathcart, about to take command of the Northern District, had two sons and a son-in-law to place as ADCs. Moreover with Ernest's marriage 'on hand' he ought not to risk being sent abroad and Lord FitzRoy's 'best idea' would be to 'effect an exchange into the Guards'. It so happened that 'very recently' the Queen's equerry, Colonel Berkeley Drummond, had called upon FitzRoy Somerset 'to enquire by desire of Prince Albert' whether he knew of a captain 'anxious of entering His Royal Highness's Regiment'. Lord FitzRoy had mentioned this to Ernest who said that he would be 'most happy' to make such a move, and the Military Secretary put him 'in communication' with Drummond. 'Upon every view of the case,' FitzRoy Somerset wrote, the Prince would like Westmorland's eldest son in his regiment, and Ernest's impending marriage together with 'the delicacy of his constitution' dictated that 'the Guards is the branch of the Service that would suit him best'. Drummond was 'very anxious that no time may be lost in obtaining your decision', so Lord FitzRoy was including all the relevant information in this letter. As a postscript, he hoped that 'Ernest's choice of a Bride is acceptable to you' and that his marriage would bring happiness to Westmorland and Priscilla.

On receipt of Westmorland's approval the Military Secretary 'immediately' contacted Drummond, who took the Prince's pleasure. His command that Ernest should exchange into the Guards would be 'laid before the Queen without loss of time'. Ernest was extremely pleased and planned to visit his parents in Berlin, not having seen them for some time. Lord FitzRoy did not regret having advised Westmorland to put Burghersh into the Guards. He explained in March that the exchange would not improve Ernest's income. A lieutenant in the Guards received 7s.10d. a day, a captain of a line company 11s.7d., 'exclusive of the contingence allowance' which just about doubled the pay. To this must be added his loss of ADC's pay and allowances, probably totalling £250 per year. However the Guards position was eminently suitable, and Lord

FitzRoy trusted that Westmorland would be 'very kind to him'. 'Courting costs money', especially when a couple lived so far apart. The financial situation did apparently create second thoughts, though, for in April Lord FitzRoy informed Westmorland that a vacancy in the 56th was no longer available and that, in any case, the regiment was possibly destined for the West Indies – neither a popular nor a healthy posting. He hoped, therefore, to hear that Ernest had joined the Guards in Chichester as arranged. Admittedly little prospect of a staff appointment existed there, but Ernest would probably not like the 'billing and cooing' required to secure one in the Guards.[46]

Lord FitzRoy's letters were peppered with comments about individuals that were in themselves revealing of both subjects and author. He noted to Richard that his younger son's friend, Lord March, was to marry the eldest daughter of Algernon (Algy) Greville, a Waterloo veteran and Wellington's private secretary. The 'flirtation' had been going on for some time, but the proposal and acceptance had only just occurred. The wedding would take place as soon as a settlement could be worked out, which Lord FitzRoy enigmatically suggested might take 'a long time'. The details appeared to take three months to settle, for FitzRoy Somerset witnessed the nuptials at St George's Church on 28 November 1843. March looked 'grave', 'the bride was well dressed but she cannot be said to be pretty though she has laughing eyes and fine teeth'. She proved rather fertile however. In October 1845 Lord FitzRoy reported that 'she lies in for the second time at the end of the year' and that, when March dined with him, he remarked that 'she must give him a colt foal this time'. Lady March duly obliged. Meanwhile FitzRoy Somerset reinforced his view that people should not marry young, believing that Lady Georgiana, about to be wed, fell into that category. He disapproved of another union for different reasons. The marriage of Lady Charlotte Augusta Frederica Somerset (daughter of his nephew, seventh Duke of Beaufort) to Baron Neumann – currently Austrian Ambassador to Britain, at sixty-three, thirty-five years her senior and reputed to be the natural son of Metternich's father 'out of some low woman' – he dubbed 'queer'.[47]

When travelling outside London Lord FitzRoy made extensive use of the railway. Train services were particularly convenient for short journeys to Dover or Portsmouth en route to the Isle of Wight. And, leaving Paddington at noon, he could reach Badminton five hours later – considerably quicker than by road. He noted that by catching the 4.30 train he would reach '"the Wells" (how vulgar) at 5.55.' With some amazement he explained that the journey from Coventry to Stanhope Street took a mere two hours, that to Brighton from London by 'express' just over an hour. The Age of Steam had its advantages and comforts: returning from Portsmouth in 1842, he reported 'a very prosperous journey'. Shortly after Christmas 1851 he left Wilton at 1.30 and reached Goodwood at 5 p.m., not without incident. 'I was very nearly late from Portsmouth, the train from Salisbury having arrived there only just as the Chichester train was starting.' 'The first stop after Salisbury' an acquaintance got into his carriage, leaving at Bishopstoke, possibly for Sir Francis Basing's. Without revealing details, Lord FitzRoy explained to Charlotte that their conversation was 'wholly political', involving consideration of the government's actions – an incidental glimpse of Lord FitzRoy's willingness to discuss political issues in private.[48]

On 28 August 1844 the 53rd Regiment embarked for India where at Peshawar on 13 March 1852 Lieutenant-Colonel W.R. Mansfield presented new Colours on behalf of its colonel. In regimental orders that day Mansfield expressed 'great pleasure' at receiving 'the commands of Lord FitzRoy Somerset' to send the old Colours to him so that they could be placed in St Chad's Church at Shrewsbury over the monument to those officers and men who had died during the Sutlej campaign. And, during these years, honours fell directly to Lord FitzRoy himself. He became a Grand Chevalier of the Military Order of Maria Theresa of Austria. Metternich, the Chancellor of the Order, forwarded the medal inscribed with Lord FitzRoy's name and a letter of congratulation, hoping that the award 'will serve as a lasting memorial of the acts of bravery for which Your Lordship was received as a member of the Order'. Lord FitzRoy's letter of thanks to Metternich was written in perfect French. At home, on 24 September 1847, he received the Knight Grand Cross of the Order of the Bath (KGCB); and, in May 1848, Adolphus, Duke of Cambridge, sent to him a Star of the Grand Cross of the Bath 'as a mark of regard and esteem'.[49]

Lord FitzRoy's relations with his elder son remained cool, though, and Arthur tended to communicate with him through one of his sisters. From Agra in May 1843 he described to Kitty his humdrum daily life, punctuated by occasional excursions such as one to the Taj Mahal at sunrise. He concluded, however, by trusting that his father's arm and mother's head were 'quite well now'. 'Tell my lord', he wrote, 'I have nothing to tell him so will spare his eye and the Honourable Company's paper'; not an encouraging preface to a request for Lord FitzRoy to send him 'a selection of books both French and English, Historical, Rhetorical, Political, Military, etc. ... I think there is now a new edition of Madame de Sévigné'. By August, however, Arthur seemed to have cheered up, apologizing to Richard for not having written regularly while he was on the move during the summer, but noting that he was now settled back in Calcutta. Before long, too, he was in action and had suffered serious wounds. In London, Lord FitzRoy confessed to being in a 'miserable state of suspense' following news of a battle at Maharajpore printed in newspapers and the accompanying dispatch revealing that Arthur had been wounded. Eventually letters did come from Arthur to Lord and Lady FitzRoy separately, and the surgeon who had attended Arthur wrote too. FitzRoy Somerset explained to Richard that evidently 'poor Arthur had a very narrow escape, but he conducted himself under fearful circumstances with great spirit and presence of mind'. His wounds should heal: 'We have every reason to be satisfied that he had such an opportunity of distinguishing himself. We have too every right to be proud of the terms in which he is spoken of in Sir Hugh Gough's dispatch.' Lord FitzRoy thought that Richard 'must have suffered much uneasiness in consequence' of not knowing fully what had happened, though he hoped that this deficiency had now been repaired.[50]

Details of Arthur's injuries soon emerged in his correspondence with Richard and Lord FitzRoy. Writing to his brother on 9 January 1844 he explained that three sabre wounds were 'healing', though one had caused a 'narrow squeak for my right leg', and a musket-ball had passed through his arm above the right wrist. He went to a hill station, Simla, to recover; but he remained in 'great pain' from his leg and henceforth would always walk with a limp. Nevertheless he reassured his father that his arm was recovering. In June Lord FitzRoy learnt that Arthur was, according to medical reports, 'going on well', but that in future could only cope with 'a quiet sort of horse', which had made him 'low'. FitzRoy Somerset – no doubt drawing on his own experience – believed that there was no cause for 'despondency'. 'Only a few months' had passed since he had been 'so desperately wounded', and it might take one or two years to regain full fitness. Somewhat touchingly, and belatedly, Lord FitzRoy planned to send bandages to Arthur with 'somebody going out tomorrow [8 June]'. In a further letter to his father Arthur gave 'a good account of himself'. He remained lame, was able to walk a fair distance, but had not yet mounted a pony.[51]

In the meantime Lord FitzRoy had become unnecessarily and unreasonably agitated by reports in the *Morning Herald* of 6 March 1844 about two fierce battles to capture Gwalior which involved heavy losses. 'God grant that Arthur has escaped,' he exclaimed; although there was no chance – given his medical condition – that he could have been involved. Arthur was promoted to major on 30 April 1844; and, a month later, the astonishing news broke that Lord Ellenborough would be replaced as Governor-General by Sir Henry Hardinge – the Peninsula veteran and former Secretary at War in London. FitzRoy Somerset explained to Richard that despite opposition from the Government the East India Company's Court of Directors had dismissed Ellenborough for 'incivility and disregard of their orders'. He declared: 'It really is too bad', for Ellenborough had done a lot for India since his arrival in February 1842. The Charter of the East India Company expired in 1854 and Lord FitzRoy believed that actions such as this – stemming from an ability to act without reference to Her Majesty's Government – would be critically examined then. Hardinge would leave England as soon as possible, and Lord FitzRoy explained that Arthur would be appointed to his staff – a direct result of parental lobbying of a former colleague. Later Lord FitzRoy revealed that Hardinge would travel via Suez and Ceylon to Madras, and hoped that Richard might see him at the Ceylonese port of Galle. Whether Richard did so is not known; but in October 'still thin and weak', Arthur expected to make the long journey to meet 'his new master' at Madras.[52]

During the first half of 1845 Arthur's health and his spirits revived; and on 5 July he wrote somewhat dramatically to Richard: 'You will I dare say *not* be surprized to hear that I am going to be married immediately to Mrs Mellish', widow of an East India Company officer. Sir Henry Hardinge, although 'most kind', could not be at the ceremony lest it be thought that he sanctioned the marriage, 'yet he promises to make the best of it and to do all he can to allay my father's displeasure – I suppose I am not to be considered a good judge in this matter but I can with justice and safety assure you that poverty is the only drawback to this alliance'. Arthur was telling Richard, because his *'friend* Maddock did his best to make mischief about *her* when he was in Ceylon' by trotting out 'an old anecdote'. The marriage would be in Calcutta on 8 July – long before Richard would receive the letter – and the couple had been lent a 'very pretty house' for the first few weeks of their new life. Arthur fervently hoped that his 'dear wife' would be accepted by the family and looked for support from his only brother. Because of his marriage he would have to stay in India 'some time longer'.

Despite the claimed poverty – possibly referring to the lack of dowry that Mrs Mellish brought – in September Arthur wrote enthusiastically about the strength of his stable and the worth of his horses. But behind his bonhomie lurked persistent unease about the family reaction to his marriage. With obvious relief he thanked Richard on 29 October for writing 'so kindly to my wife', which underlined his brother's habitual kindness. They had arrived at Agra after three weeks in Meerut to find letters from his father and mother. Lord FitzRoy's was 'milder than I expected', though he emphasized that Arthur had undermined his professional prospects by marriage. 'Heaven knows how', Arthur remarked, 'unless my father intends in his official capacity to punish an act which in his eyes is connected with my publick character as an officer. He has already *punished* me for my debts by refusing me what was given to Wood, who is *three* years my junior in the Army.' He went on to explain that 'Wood is now a full pay lieutenant-colonel and as for me any chance of a lieutenant-colonelcy seems smaller every day – perhaps some ten years hence I may reach that rank – and then only when half the Regiment has purchased over my head.' There was some consolation from Lady FitzRoy: 'My mother's letter was kind enough. She has promised to use all her influence with my father in our favour.' He reiterated that the letters were 'kinder' than he had reason to expect, but no message of any kind had been sent to his wife: 'Had she been a perfect stranger less notice could not have been taken of her.' This had 'wounded' and 'hurt' her 'not a little'. Moreover his sisters had taken no notice of 'me or her'. Surely, he complained, his sisters, whatever the circumstances, ought to send 'kind words', something which had 'wounded me more deeply than I care to confess'. Richard was the only member of the family to show any affection: 'I shall never forget your kindness.' Yet once more Arthur appeared thoroughly depressed.

To Richard Lord FitzRoy also expressed forceful views. 'Arthur's marriage was indeed a surprize to me and a sad one too ... Arthur through life has been deaf to good advice and all prudent considerations, has always indulged his own fancies without the smallest regard for the feelings of others, and has at the same time been easily led by evil counsellors.' A *cri de coeur* from a frustrated father, unwilling perhaps to acknowledge that his son had reached adulthood. However Lord FitzRoy admitted to Richard, 'it is said' that Arthur's wife is 'a sensible person' and may therefore 'be the means of preventing him from doing foolish things'. The father could not resist appending a homily for his younger son: 'I hope it may please God that you may come home a single man and that you may be so fortunate as to marry a person who may be agreeable to your family and secure your happiness.'[53]

Arthur acknowledged Lord FitzRoy's letter of 7 September early in November. Addressed to 'my dear father', it covered twelve sides of writing-paper. Poignantly, it would reach Great Stanhope Street after Arthur's death. 'Your letter of 7th September was far more kind and more indulgent than I had any right to expect.' Yet FitzRoy Somerset had commented 'severely on the importance of the step I have taken and spoken in terms of strong approbation of my conduct in this instance' as another example of Arthur's trying 'to render myself independent of your will'. Arthur was a major, aged 29. The son hoped that 'sooner or later' his father would look more favourably on his marriage. Both he and his wife would work for a reconciliation, which was their 'earnest desire ... [and] anxious wish'. The thought of gaining 'your approbation is never absent from our hearts'. Arthur went on – perhaps with a touch of insensitivity – to laud the 'kindness' of Hardinge and the notice that he took of the new Mrs Somerset. He referred to a 'long letter' he had written to his mother in which he gave details of his wife's family. It was 'not a little gratifying' to reveal that her family was 'noble, indeed more so than most'. Emilie Marie Louise Wilhelmina was, in fact, the daughter of Baron de Baumbach of Hesse. Arthur did not lay stress on such matters, but Lady FitzRoy 'seemed very anxious on the subject'. Despite various military manoeuvrings, Arthur assured Lord FitzRoy that 'there is no prospect of a fight'; but at Allahabad a large number of soldiers had succumbed to cholera. Richard, Arthur noted, wrote 'frequently' and had also written a 'most brotherly and affectionate letter' to his wife. The implied criticism of Stanhope Street could not have been missed. Writing to Richard from Camp Shakabad on 30 November, Arthur noted Hardinge's intention of contacting Lord FitzRoy officially, as Military Secretary, and to advise him 'that he took the liberty of an old friend to tell him that he *ought* to get me a lieutenant-colonelcy next year'. Arthur believed that if an Adjutant-General's or Quartermaster-General's staff vacancy occurred in India, he should get it, and 'no one could accuse him [Lord FitzRoy] of *jobbing* for doing so'.[54]

Arthur's prediction that no fighting would break out proved false. Sadly, on Christmas Eve 1845 as, unknown to him, his elder son lay mortally wounded, Lord FitzRoy wrote to Richard in critical vein, drawing close attention to Arthur's previous shortcomings and the injustice of his current complaints. His irritation came through clearly; and, incidentally, he revealed Arthur's penchant for getting into debt. Arthur should not be upset at Wood's promotion. Robert Wood was 'certainly a lucky dog' but he had borne 'with perfect good humour' Arthur's nomination as Military Secretary to Sir Henry Hardinge, a post that he had had every reason to expect given his number of years as Hardinge's private secretary. Before leaving England Hardinge had arranged for Wood to acquire an unattached brevet majority. On arrival in India, a major of the 80th was found willing to exchange, which gave Wood field pay. He had now purchased a lieutenant-colonelcy in the regiment on the retirement of Narborough Baker after 39 years' service. This move could not have been achieved without money 'which Wood has but your brother has not'. Lord FitzRoy made it clear that this state of affairs was Arthur's own fault.

He went on to explain the reason for Arthur's move to India. 'Arthur had been very extravagant at Dublin to an extent that I little [illegible] of and I thought it desirable to get him on Lord Ellenborough's staff which with the assistance of Sir Henry Hardinge [the Secretary at War] I accomplished'; which explains why Hardinge so readily retained Arthur when he replaced Ellenborough. '48 hours [*sic*] before he sailed he employed Major [illegible] to inform me that he had debts I knew not of and that unless a large sum was raised he could not go. So I agreed to advance the money. I paid the insurance of his life for the first year and he departed after which other debts and bills made their appearance.' Lord FitzRoy went on to explain that 'he could not then have exchanged from the Guards without a frank explanation of the causes to the Duke of Wellington', which would have damned him 'for ever'. Moreover an unattached majority was not available and, even if it had been, Lord FitzRoy would have had to raise the money 'which I could do only at a great sacrifice after he had so repeatedly disregarded my advice and incurred such large debts'. But even if Arthur had exchanged into a regiment in India he would still only be a regimental captain with no money to purchase advancement.

FitzRoy Somerset continued even more critically: 'With regard to the payment of his debts he has made no great effort, let me tell you for the last fourteen months he has not sent one farthing to pay the insurance of his life and in 1844 he sent but £300 and the money he got for his wound ... From the first he rejected my advice with scorn which was to send home monthly half of his pay.' Furthermore 'what think you' that Arthur 'ordered out' four hand whips each £17 and forgot to pay for them? He received a brevet majority after the only action in which he had been engaged: 'This he has not only not thanked me for but never even acknowledged'. Clearly the elder son had thoroughly upset his father. 'If Arthur's name had been Smith or Jones, he would never have been Military Secretary either to the present or late Governor-General.' Arthur was very lucky, and those officers who kept telling Richard that his brother should have been a lieutenant-colonel long ago had no conception of 'his follies and extravagances'. 'The anxiety he has caused me is not to be told and whenever I see the good Mr Cox [army agent] I positively feel humiliated and ashamed so little has he kept his word with him.' Not surprisingly Lord FitzRoy advised Richard not to get 'embroiled' with Arthur 'on these matters' lest he become associated with his brother's suspect financial affairs. This sad letter, given its timing, revealed a depth of bitterness and despair rarely seen in Lord FitzRoy. At the very least his elder son had, in his eyes, utterly let him and the family down.[55]

Within six weeks FitzRoy Somerset was exhibiting concern of a different nature. 'We are all anxiety for news from India.' Reports were filtering through that the Sikhs had crossed the Sutjeh and government dispatches were awaited via the Marseilles mail: 'I trust to God that Arthur is safe.' On 23 February Lord FitzRoy learnt that, far from being safe, Arthur had died of wounds received at the Battle of Ferozeshah. Next day he wrote to 'My dearest Richard and now my only son.' Sir Henry Hardinge, though politically superior to the CinC India, fought as Sir Hugh Gough's second-in-command. In a letter on 23 December he described to Lord FitzRoy 'a very hard fought battle' at Ferozeshah (ten miles from the camp at Ferozepore) in which an entrenched Sikh position of 108 guns and 50,000 men under French officers had been stormed with the capture of 90 enemy guns. Unfortunately, 'your gallant son has been dangerously wounded', and Dr Walker, who was attending him, 'trembles between hope and fear'. 'Every possible attention' was being given to him, and he was occupying the same tent – ironically – as Robert Wood. 'I saw him when I came in and considering him as my own son, I kissed his forehead – when he forgot his own pain and danger to talk of his friend, my Boy'. Arthur Hardinge was with him when he was wounded and fetched a surgeon. Sir Henry Hardinge was 'greatly attached to him [Arthur Somerset]', whom he considered 'daringly gallant'. 'I cannot tell you how deeply distressed I am by his dangerous state.' On Christmas Day, from his headquarters nine miles from Ferozepore, Gough himself wrote, referring to 'your gallant son', who 'although shot through the lungs is doing very well – and promises to recover rapidly'. Gough admitted to basing this assessment on reports: he had not visited Arthur. Two days later Hardinge sent grimmer news. 'My fears have proved true – your brave son is no more what can I say to console you?' Perhaps with understandable exaggeration given the circumstances of grief, Hardinge emphasized his 'many fine qualities, which would have ripened into maturity and made him a distinguished officer. He had an accurate eye and great quickness for Troops and in our social circle he was an universal favourite from his kindheartedness and aimiability.' Arthur had died in the arms of Hardinge's elder son, Charles. 'I really cannot write on this subject it quite unmans me,' continued the Governor-General, who had attended 'your dear son's funeral in the burial ground here', the service being conducted by 'my Chaplain'. Shortly afterwards Gough wrote: 'I mourn to have to retract the favourable view' of Arthur's progress; 'your noble son died regretted by the whole Army.'[56]

Other tributes reached Lord FitzRoy. Lieutenant-Colonel Thomas Ryan of the 50th, wrote: 'The gallant and chivalrous Major Somerset received his death wounds in the ranks of the 50th Regiment, while cheering on the men on their rush upon the enemy's trenches on the 21st. We had shaken hands but a moment before.' An extract from a letter by Colonel Thomas Reed of the 62nd also found its way to FitzRoy Somerset: 'Poor Somerset, you will grieve to learn, died of his wounds. He was a noble fellow and the admiration of this army.'[57]

Almost two years after his son's death Lord FitzRoy received a detailed account of his passing. Writing from a quiet bungalow with 'magnificent scenery' and an unrestricted view of snow on the horizon north of Simla, Sir Henry Hardinge explained that his son, Arthur, had been staying with him recently and told him about Arthur Somerset's conduct at Moodkee (an action on 18 December) and Ferozeshah. Sir Henry had asked his son to commit his memories – based partly upon conversations with Arthur Somerset – to paper, and this document was enclosed in Hardinge's letter, accepting that this might 'excite' FitzRoy Somerset's grief.

On 18 December 1845 the British force had scarcely reached camp at Moodkee when intelligence came in of the enemy advance. Unattended by any of his staff, the Governor-General immediately galloped off to raise the line. His staff later tried to find him: Arthur Hardinge succeeded, Somerset did not and became engaged in the action elsewhere. The 31st Regiment had difficulty in engaging Sikh guns which were harassing the British positions. The regiment's commanding officer had lost his horse and dismounted, so the civil officer on the field ordered Arthur Somerset to take command, which he did 'admirably', rallying the men and urging them to attack the gun positions with fixed bayonets. He personally led the bayonet charge on horseback from the front when some of the men hesitated to move forward. At this point Arthur Hardinge joined him and both friends rode through the guns 'with no other mischief' than that a

Sikh gunner slashed open the quarters of Arthur Somerset's horse as he galloped by. One gunner stood in their way, but Somerset ran him through before they wheeled to the right and regained friendly lines.

At the later battle of Ferozeshah the Governor-General sent an order by Somerset to Major-General Sir John Littler, but Arthur returned in time to advance on the enemy's camp with Hardinge's staff. Sikh fire fell accurately on this part of the line, causing many staff casualties. Arthur Somerset and Arthur Hardinge rode off slightly to the left where the 50th was advancing. As they approached the Sikh camp with the 50th, dust and smoke was so dense that objects ten yards away could hardly be distinguished. Crossing into the Sikh entrenchments, Arthur Hardinge drew Somerset's attention to a small tent about fifteen yards away. As he did so 'a volley of musketry' streamed from it. Hardinge's horse was killed under him and Somerset fell to the ground. Running to him, Hardinge found his clothing saturated in blood. 'On my expressing my fears that he was dangerously wounded, he replied faintly that he would be better if I opened his coat, which I did.' Hardinge and a private of the 50th carried Somerset about 100 yards to the rear and laid him under a bush where a passing surgeon attended him. With regret the surgeon concluded that, as the wound was in the lungs, it would probably be fatal. Hardinge could do no more, so left Somerset in the care of the surgeon who promised to secure a litter for him.

On 23 December Hardinge and his father (the Governor-General) rode into Ferozepore and went to see Somerset who had been moved to a large tent within the fort, which he shared with Wood. 'He seemed very glad to see us, and in cheerful spirits, though very feeble.' Because he needed to be quiet Arthur Hardinge did not visit him again until the Thursday (25 December), when Somerset asked him why the guns were firing. 'I found him perfectly self-possessed but rather nervous, and as I feared that my presence might increase this excitement I stayed but a very short time with him. He died the same evening.'[58]

One other unsigned and undated account of Arthur's fate reached Lord FitzRoy. The writer recorded that just before he joined his regiment on the morning of 22 December, 'I found poor Major Somerset. He had lain on the field all night and was quite benumbed with cold. I got him a Doctor and a dhooly [litter] and left a Sepoy with him of my Regiment with orders not to quit him till he was safe in Cantonments. The man came to me afterwards and reported he had taken him to my house and thence in to the Field-work. I shall never forget the noble Somerset's ghastly appearance when I went up to him as he sat cowering over a few miserable embers with a group of Camp followers. I asked him where he was wounded and he counted five on his fingers and pointed to his breast, which was covered with blood. I sent off a horseman to tell the Governor-General, but I don't know if he did so. I mention all this about him, as I believe you know his father. I never saw him before, but he seems very much regretted by all who knew him.' These harrowing details could scarcely have brought much relief to Lord FitzRoy. Of more comfort, perhaps, was a letter from the Duke of Cambridge to Charlotte in which he confessed to being 'greatly shocked', 'sad and melancholy' at the loss of an 'excellent fellow', whom 'I had the greatest regard for'. And Lord FitzRoy evidently did take comfort from his relations, such as his 12-year-old nephew Boscawen (William's son), whom he thanked for 'the feeling and sympathy you have manifested for us on this distressing occasion'. Even then, he added a note of personal encouragement to him and his brother Aylmer: 'I hope you both strive to learn as much as you can and thus evince your gratitude to your father for the pains he takes to ensure you a good education.'[59]

On 2 April 1846 the Prime Minister (Sir Robert Peel), while officially moving a vote of thanks to those engaged in the battles of Aliwal and Sobraon (January-February 1846), paid an extraordinary tribute to Arthur in the House of Commons. 'I grieve to say that Lord FitzRoy Somerset has been deprived of his son – a gallant young man, who if he had been spared for the service of the state, would have well supported the honour of his name, and proved himself worthy of his father by high military talents as well as by acknowledged bravery. Lord FitzRoy Somerset, the father of this distinguished man, accompanied the Duke of Wellington throughout the whole of the Peninsular War. He was present at almost all the battles which took place during the glorious campaigns in Spain and Portugal; and now when in his official character he will find it his duty to distribute rewards and honours amongst the soldiers who have obtained for this country so much of that pleasing duty will be clouded by the recollection that he has lost a son who, though young, gave every hope and promise that if his life had been spared he would have proved an honour to his name and his country. Although the rank of Major Somerset placed him at some distance from those whose deaths I have been lamenting, yet in some consideration of the services of his father, I have been induced to dwell more particularly upon the loss of his son; and I trust it may be some consolation to the wounded feelings of his family that we should, as it were, create this public record to the memory of Major Somerset.' In the Lords on 5 May 1846 Glenelg went farther. He supported 'some memorial worthy of a great nation' to record those who had fallen in the First Sikh War, including 'Major Somerset, whose career had been brought prematurely to a close, when it might well have been hoped that he would have added more lustre to a name already known to history [Cheers].'[60]

Once Arthur had been buried in the Ferozepore cantonment cemetery, however, his affairs had to be put in order. Unfortunately his grieving father discovered that past habits of insolvency had not been shaken off. 'I was much annoyed', he wrote to Richard on 8 June 1846, 'at getting by the last mail a letter from a Captain Grove telling me that poor Arthur owed him £150.' FitzRoy Somerset had sent a copy of the letter to

Bob Wood and asked him to investigate. If Wood were satisfied he must pay it out of Arthur's estate: 'I could not undertake to pay it myself.' Two months later Lord FitzRoy reported that all Arthur's effects had been sold. Wood had settled all known debts and when other expenses in India had been cleared nothing would be left.[61]

The Somerset family had yet to meet Arthur's widow and ensure that she was provided for. On 7 March Lord FitzRoy wrote to Richard: 'This is a dreadful blow to us all but the person most to be pitied is his poor widow.' However letters from Mrs Currie and Wood had 'afforded great relief to my mind'. When Arthur's wife heard that he had been wounded she insisted on setting out for Ferozepore, but was deterred by other wives. For, as FitzRoy Somerset observed, had she completed her journey, she would have found her husband 'not only dead but buried'. 'Mrs Somerset' planned to go to Calcutta in mid-March, thence by steamer to Ceylon where she would wait for news from England. Referring to Richard's 'affectionate disposition and your love for Arthur', Lord FitzRoy expected his son to treat her kindly 'as you would a sister whose cup has been full of sorrow'. He enclosed a 'few lines' for her and asked Richard to convey 'my kindest feelings towards her'. Wood had told him that she intended to live with her mother in Germany, but would 'stay a short time in England if she hears we are inclined to make her acquaintance'. Lord FitzRoy wanted Richard to assure her that 'we shall be most happy to do so and to greet her with all affection'. He revealed that Hardinge had generously advanced her money for the voyage; and she must let FitzRoy Somerset know the amount. Richard should give her more if she were still short of money. 'Everybody speaks highly and kindly of her': Lady FitzRoy and the two girls intended to write to her in Ceylon, where she ought to arrive 'roughly when you get this letter' (mid-April). Mrs Somerset's departure from India was delayed however.

Early in April Lord FitzRoy, quoting information from Wood, observed that she was 'quite broken and her health has suffered very much. I cannot say how I pity and feel for her.' 'I would dain hope', he went on, that the journey from Suharampur to Ceylon would refresh her 'in mind and body', as would 'your affectionate kindness' and the letters from 'the four Somersets' which Richard would hand to her. Another letter to Lord FitzRoy from Hardinge had praised her: 'I grieve that we have to make her acquaintance under such painful circumstances which must be still more distressing to her poor thing than to us.' A month later FitzRoy Somerset wrote that his daughter-in-law was spoken of 'in terms of the highest praise' by those who had met her, and asked Richard to 'give her our most affectionate regards and wishes'. He then added something of a bombshell: 'Macdonald has heard that she is with child.' This letter crossed with one from Richard which affirmed the high regard in which 'my poor brother' was held by superiors such as Hardinge and Gough. He would go to Galle on 11 May to greet 'my poor sister-in-law' from the steamer, which arrived the following day having left Calcutta five days earlier that month because of the impending monsoon. He anticipated that Arthur's widow would travel to England now that she was certain that Lord FitzRoy would receive her. Like him, he had heard universally good accounts of her.[62]

Such were the vagaries of the mail – a letter taking six weeks to reach England from Ceylon – that Lord FitzRoy received Richard's letter of 22 April early in June, with news that Mrs Somerset had missed the April steamer from India, having arrived at Calcutta too late because of illness. By now Lord FitzRoy hoped that 'the painful meeting' would have gone well. Meanwhile he returned three letters from Mrs Somerset to Richard which his son had enclosed in his last letter and which had all been read 'with painful interest'. Mrs Somerset was fated not to have an easy passage to Ceylon. Richard's journey to Galle in May proved fruitless because his sister-in-law had remained in Calcutta awaiting a letter from Richard which Sir Herbert Maddock by 'an oversight' had failed to deliver. Lord FitzRoy felt sorry that Richard had made two unnecessary journeys (April and May) and that the 'poor thing' must by now be quite distressed. He noted from her latest letter to Richard that she probably would not travel quickly to England, but would remain in Ceylon, getting to know Richard and 'reposing her mind and body after what she has suffered'. Arthur's widow did eventually reach Galle by the June steamer, and Lord FitzRoy thanked Richard for letters from him and her, dated 15 June, though he noted that his daughter-in-law had neither written to Lady FitzRoy nor 'my daughters', a somewhat formal way of referring to sisters in a father's correspondence with his son.

On 24 August he reported to Richard that Mrs Somerset had reached Malta and would proceed to Southampton where the Duke de Melfort would welcome her and inform Lord FitzRoy of her arrival. He asked Richard to pass on his gratitude to Sir Colin Campbell for his kindness to Mrs Somerset during her stay in Ceylon. In fact she reached London during the afternoon of 26 August. Arriving home later that day, Lord FitzRoy found a letter saying that she was staying with the Duke de Melfort's sister, Lady Davies. As he explained to Charlotte, then out of London with her aunt Priscilla, he 'immediately' rode over to the house 'facing the park directly opposite the one Lady Westmorland lived in in the Bayswater Road'. He was ushered into the drawing-room where the Duke de Melfort, Lady Davies and Mrs Somerset awaited him. He thought that he would be left alone with his daughter-in-law when the other two left the room, but they returned. So he was unable to have any real conversation with Mrs Somerset and 'was obliged to talk "la pluie et le beau temps"' with the Duke. 'The poor thing was very much affected ... [and] annoyed' at this development, following him to the door when he left and speaking there 'for a few minutes'. Her face had been burned by the sun 'and she wears the mark of suffering a good deal'. She wore no cap, had cut off 'her back hair ... and therefore did not look to advantage'. He arranged for her to visit Lady FitzRoy at noon on 27 August. When she arrived he took her from the carriage to the drawing-room at 5 Great Stanhope Street where Lady FitzRoy had asked to see her alone. Approaching the room 'she trembled so violently that I did not attempt to say a word to her'. Lady FitzRoy and her daughter-in-law were together for 'nearly two hours' and, though 'painful' for both parties, the meeting went off satisfactorily. That evening she dined with the FitzRoy Somersets. When the Somerset girls returned to Great Stanhope Street on 29 August they, like their mother, 'took to the poor widow amazingly'. She was 'extremely pleasing', Lord FitzRoy thought, though her health was not good which was 'not to be wondered at'.

He had not yet had a confidential conversation with his daughter-in-law so knew nothing of her long-term plans. But she had spoken 'in the most gratifying and affectionate terms' of Richard and been grateful to Sir Colin Campbell for his kindness. The final reference to her in Lord FitzRoy's correspondence is on 24 September 1846. 'We continue much pleased with our poor widow,' he reported, but were alarmed 'that her constitution is seriously shaken' by her suffering: 'I do not know whether she has actually spit blood since she landed but she has had frequent palpitations and occasionally coughs a great deal.' The doctors believed the cough to be 'nervous' and that her lungs were not damaged. With care she should eventually recover. At that moment she was at Brighton – possibly with the family on holiday. Thereafter no mention of her is to be found in the family archives. She may well have gone to Germany to live with her mother. Despite Macdonald's assertion that she had been or was pregnant, this seems unlikely. Thus closed another chapter in Lord FitzRoy's life. The *Annual Register* would later recall Arthur's 'brilliant career in India'. Undoubted hyperbole. There, and previously, his elder son had caused FitzRoy Somerset considerable heartache. Perhaps that was in part the result of the father's reluctance to accept his independence in adulthood.[63]

Between Arthur's death and news of it reaching England, Lord FitzRoy faced a difficult personal decision. On the last day of 1845 the Secretary of State for War and the Colonies, W.E. Gladstone, wrote via Wellington, as CinC, offering him the Governor-Generalship of Canada, but giving him little time to consider the implications of the post. Whoever accepted, 'Your Lordship as I earnestly hope', must leave no later than the February mail packet 'whether he might prefer that mode of conveyance or not'. The very next day, 1 January 1846, Lord FitzRoy replied in a 'secret' communication from Great Stanhope Street: 'I have very little acquaintance with the nature of the duties that devolve upon the Governor-General, the system of administration established or with the country itself; but I well know that his path is beset with difficulties and I have no reliance on my power to overcome them; nor do I feel that I should to any extent justify the confidence you are willing to repose in me.' He insisted that he had, therefore, been 'swayed by publick consideration' and his own sense of inadequacy. But the root of Lord FitzRoy's reluctance may have been more personal. Admitting 'private and domestic' considerations, he aded: 'My absence from the Country at this moment might be productive of serious inconvenience to my family and myself.' His wife had still not fully come to terms with Arthur's death and there were other difficulties involved in arranging for her and the children to travel to Canada at such short notice. Moreover the health of Louisa (his late brother Edward's unmarried daughter) was causing concern. Undoubtedly family considerations were important, though a professional reason for refusal should not be lightly discounted.

No evidence exists that the Duke of Wellington exerted direct influence on him to decline, but he did express concern to Priscilla that her brother-in-law might accept. Lady Westmorland said that she had not discussed the matter with him but was sure that he would not leave Wellington 'for any situation'. The Duke mused: 'I don't know; it is a high situation and a very important post at this moment, and if the Govt. urges it, he may think it his duty to go.' Insisting that 'I have not said one word to bias him,' he nevertheless remained 'very anxious to know what he would say'. On learning that the offer had, indeed, been declined, Wellington told Priscilla 'I don't know what I would have done if he had [accepted]'. Next day Priscilla relayed these words to FitzRoy Somerset, which prompted tears to well in his eyes. Noting that reaction, Lady Westmorland recorded: 'He [Lord FitzRoy] never made *professional* or fine speeches; but where he loved and esteemed, his whole being, his look, his voice, seemed to overflow with tenderness and kindness.'[64]

The annual Waterloo Banquet, attended by 80 guests including the Prince Consort and FitzRoy Somerset, took place at 7.30 p.m. on 18 June 1852 at Apsley House, amid sumptuous surroundings adorned by silverware, Dresden china and glittering chandeliers. Prince Albert left at 10.45 after the final, fourteenth toast; then Wellington and Lord FitzRoy went on to the Duchess of Beaufort's reception. The Duke appeared to be in fine form. Three months later, on Tuesday 14 September 1852, as the FitzRoy Somerset family were preparing for dinner a rumour of Wellington's death reached Great Stanhope Street. Lord FitzRoy immediately went the short distance to Apsley House but obtained no further elucidation. Then at 10.30 p.m. a servant arrived from Kent to confirm, in Charlotte's words, 'the great calamity'. Next morning FitzRoy Somerset went to Walmer and the following day reported to the Duke of Beaufort that 'his countenance was placid'. Wellington had been 'quite well' on the Monday and had arranged to meet Lady Westmorland in Dover on the day that he died. His last illness had been 'awfully sudden'. Lord FitzRoy was, as Emily told Priscilla, 'dreadfully affected'. In thanking the Duke of Cambridge for his 'sympathetic' letter, he referred to 'the affliction' caused by 'the loss of the great man to whom I was so much attached and with whom I had been so long connected'. During the following month Queen Victoria twice noted Lord FitzRoy's continuing distress. He explained that 'he fancied the Duke's ear had had something to do with it [his death], for hard substance had formed itself there, which the Doctor had wished should be removed, but the Duke would not allow it'. And, on 30 October, after dinner at Windsor, he 'talked much of the dear old Duke', showing the continuing sense of loss.[65]

When Wellington died FitzRoy Somerset had been at the Horse Guards almost exactly 25 years. Throughout that period he had discharged his duties efficiently and, latterly in particular, shielded his friend and superior officer in his old age. Sir John Fortescue's later tribute was not misplaced: 'No doubt he [FitzRoy Somerset] was the most popular man in the Army. His gentleness, courtesy and tact were a proverb [and] were extended equally to officers of the highest and lowest rank.' But he had been so long associated with Wellington's regime that much of the criticism levelled in later years at the Duke's alleged lethargy and administrative sloth inevitably reflected upon him. Ellesmere's lines about Wellington's funeral did not help in this respect: 'Though time and death have scored the page with many a stroke severe,/The roll-call is not read in vain, while FitzRoy answers here.'[66]

CHAPTER 7

DISILLUSIONMENT, THE ORDNANCE (1852-3)

'I have considered it my duty to accept [the Ordnance].' (Lord FitzRoy Somerset)[1]

Despite lack of command experience, limited time in diplomatic posts and association with military conservatism, Lord FitzRoy entertained serious hopes of succeeding Wellington at the Horse Guards. The names of seven candidates including his were 'freely mentioned in society'. *The United Service Gazette* neatly pinpointed the Marquis of Anglesey's weakness: 'Is he not too old?' Indeed, he was. The one-legged veteran who (as Uxbridge) had led the Household Cavalry at Waterloo, had already turned 84. Lord Seaton (Sir John Colborne), another of Waterloo vintage, was 76. On the other hand, the Queen's cousin, the Duke of Cambridge at 33 seemed 'too young', the Prince Consort agreeing that 'he would carry no weight with the public'. Another septuagenarian was Sir John Fox Burgoyne, a vastly experienced soldier. But, as a Royal Engineer and Ordnance officer, the administrative system precluded him from commanding troops of the line and cavalry. Prince Albert himself came into the reckoning – not for the first time. In April 1850 the Prince had written at length to Wellington who had suggested amalgamation of the offices of Adjutant-General and Quartermaster-General into one Chief of Staff so that Prince Albert could succeed the Duke as CinC. Apart from the danger that the amalgamation would lead to abolition of the post of CinC, 'the maintenance of which is of the utmost importance to the Crown', if Prince Albert went to the Horse Guards he would become 'an executive officer of the Crown, receiving the Queen's commands through her Secretaries of State'. In September 1852 the Prince rebuffed the Prime Minister (Derby) when he revived the idea.[2]

Two possibilities thus remained: Lord FitzRoy and Lord (formerly Sir Henry) Hardinge. Both were Peninsula veterans and both, curiously, had been maimed in the Waterloo campaign. Hardinge at 67 was almost four years the senior; but he had a wider military, political and administrative background. FitzRoy Somerset lacked Hardinge's political experience (in office at home and abroad), and he had not served in the field since 1815. Nevertheless he was Wellington's acknowledged *'alter ego'* and, in the atmosphere of acclaim following the Duke's death, it might indeed 'seem but meet that the present system of command should be prolonged in his person'.[3]

In fact, Lord FitzRoy's close association with Wellington – quite apart from any shortcomings in overall experience – proved decisive. Prince Albert revealed that he and Derby had settled the matter at Balmoral after he had 'declined the offer' to become CinC himself. Not only was Wellington's successor determined, but a number of other appointments and awards agreed. Constitutionally the Prince Consort's involvement in this settlement of affairs seems, at the very least, strange. None the less Prince Albert revealed that he and Derby were sharply aware that 'we must not conceal from ourselves that many attacks on the Army which have been sleeping on account of the Duke will now be forthcoming'. Change must be pursued. So Lord FitzRoy would not succeed. 'We agreed', wrote Prince Albert, 'that for the loss of *authority* which we had lost with the Duke, we could only make up by increase in *efficiency* in the appointments to the different offices ... Lord Hardinge was the only man fit to command the Army'. He had once acted as Wellington's second in a duel, but latterly did not have the close association with him of Lord FitzRoy which in the end proved an overwhelming disadvantage.[4]

From Balmoral, on the same day that the Prince Consort compiled his memorandum, Lord Derby wrote to FitzRoy Somerset. As he read the long 'confidential' letter, Lord FitzRoy could not have anticipated its central core of personal disappointment. Derby began by noting that Wellington's death 'has come upon us all suddenly', and that Lord FitzRoy would particularly miss one with whom he had 'for so many years [been] on terms of such confidential intimacy'. The Prime Minister had, he revealed, taken Her Majesty's pleasure 'upon the various arrangements which have to be made'. It was necessary to 'obviate the extreme inconvenience which would arise from any protracted suspension of so important an Office as that of Commander-in-Chief' – and FitzRoy Somerset, given the tone of the communication thus far, might justifiably have expected good news in the next few lines. Instead, Derby revealed: 'I have therefore written by the messenger who takes this to signify to Lord Hardinge that he should take upon himself the command of the army; and I am further authorized by Her Majesty to perform a duty very acceptable to myself by requesting you to undertake the duties of Master-General of the Ordnance'. Derby went on hastily: 'Her Majesty has also been pleased to approve of my recommendation to confer upon you at the same time, should it be agreeable to you to accept it, the honor of a peerage, as an acknowledgement of your very faithful and valuable services; and as a tribute of respect to the memory of the late Commander-in-Chief, manifested in an honor conferred upon the Officer with whom he was in the habit of the closest public and private intimacy.' The Prime Minister ended what was undoubtedly a numbing letter: 'I trust that there will be no difficulty upon your part in accepting the arrangement which I am authorized to offer you and in offering which I am at once gratifying my own personal feelings and I am persuaded acting for the good of the service.' Its ingratiating tone could not conceal the acidity of the message. Queen Victoria subsequently noted Lord FitzRoy's deep disappointment 'at not becoming Commander-in-Chief' in his letter to Derby accepting the Ordnance. On 22 September 1852 Lieutenant-General Viscount Hardinge was officially appointed to the Horse Guards.[5]

Next day FitzRoy Somerset wrote to Richard, 'much concerned' to tell him that his connection with the Horse Guards had ceased. Summarizing Derby's confidential letter in which he had been offered the Ordnance and a peerage, he explained: 'I have considered it my duty to accept.' In doing so, however, he had also expressed to Derby 'my disappointment that a junior officer has been placed at the head of the Department in which I had so long held an important situation to the satisfaction of the Duke, Lord Hill and the publick and with the frequently expressed approbation of the Government.' In two sentences the mask of parental aloofness and professional urbanity slipped: 'You may imagine my feelings when I read Lord Derby's communication. I will not dwell upon them.' That admission to his son must have been hard. Similarly he admitted his desolation to Beaufort. Thanking him for his 'kind letter', he had 'great satisfaction' in noting that 'you share in those feelings of mortification and disappointment under which I labour at the preference that has been given to Lord Hardinge.' Writing from the Horse Guards, he pointedly explained: 'I shall not be here in a publick capacity after to-morrow morning.' Nevertheless, amid his own despair, he thought of his stricken relative; expressing sorrow that there was 'little hope of regaining the use of your legs'.[6]

Hardinge's appointment prompted no great outcry in favour of Lord FitzRoy; rather the contrary. His association with Wellington's supposed administrative lethargy seemed confirmed as a drawback. *The United Service Gazette* believed that 'in many respects the change at the Horse Guards will, we suspect, be found advantageous to the Service' – predictable after it had previously sponsored Hardinge as 'one of our finest soldiers ... unwearied in the performance of official duties, earnest in the cause of improvement ... equally great in the field and in the Cabinet'. Lord FitzRoy's 'gentle courtesy' signalled his disqualification: 'The Horse Guards has for too long a time been dominated by a variety of influences, none of which should have been allowed any weight in the adjustment of Military appointments ... [with] a country MP, an old friend, a plausible woman' holding sway. The diarist Charles Greville wrote: 'I have no doubt that the Court insisted on having Hardinge, who is a great favourite there.' Yet Lord FitzRoy had had frequent contacts with the Queen during his stay at the Horse Guards and had dined at Windsor on more than one occasion, staying overnight. Both he and Hardinge were thus on good terms with the Court. The reasons why Lord FitzRoy did not succeed Wellington must be sought elsewhere. Hardinge's wider experience provides the key.[7]

Greville also argued that 'the appointment of FitzRoy Somerset would have been more popular than that of Hardinge ... with the Army'; but there is no firm evidence to support this. It would, most likely, have been 'popular', but the comparative to the detriment of Hardinge is less sound. When Lord Palmerston left the War Office, as Secretary at War, after eighteen years, the clerks reputedly wished to show their relief by lighting candles in the windows. He had not been popular with them. As FitzRoy Somerset vacated the Horse Guards, the Deputy Secretary of State wrote a personal letter of appreciation to him and enclosed one from the War Office staff 'whose good fortune it has been in the performance of their Publick Duty to be brought into personal communication with your Lordship'.[8]

FitzRoy Somerset officially became Master-General of the Ordnance on 30 September 1852. Following his departure from the Horse Guards he had stayed for a short time in a hotel at St Leonards while his London home underwent alterations. He was not hopeful that the appointment would be long-term: 'I cannot in the present state of the parties but view my tenure of the Ordnance as most precarious.' Lord FitzRoy thus underlined that, as Derby's letter of invitation demonstrated, the post was held subject to government approval. *The United Service Gazette* saw a particular advantage in Lord FitzRoy's translation to the Ordnance. The possibility of amalgamating the Horse Guards and Ordnance under a single board like the Admiralty, thought likely in 1850, was now 'remote'. Little did the writer realize that 'remote', in this case, would prove highly elastic. Yet at the time the judgement did not seem misplaced. In February 1852 Anglesey had left the Ordnance aged 84. Using that criterion, Lord FitzRoy had many years to serve. Meanwhile, in keeping with normal practice, he took a nephew, Major Lord Burghersh, to Pall Mall with him as his ADC.[9]

Ironically, at the Ordnance FitzRoy Somerset succeeded Hardinge, reputedly a reluctant holder of that office where he commanded for only seven months. When Anglesey left the post Hardinge apparently advised Lord Londonderry to seek it and was surprised when offered the Ordnance himself. Responsibility for national defence at time of tension with France meant that the Master-General needed to tour fortifications; but organizations such as the Royal Carriage Works and Royal Laboratory also came under him. Although the Lieutenant-General of the Ordnance could deputize, Lord FitzRoy's new responsibility did involve much office work: apart from administration directly concerned with command of the Ordnance military forces, the Master-General officially chaired meetings of the Board of Ordnance four times a week.[10]

Over the second provision in Derby's letter from Balmoral, he hesitated. As his correspondence with Richard indicated and his inability to finance Arthur's extravagance proved, Lord FitzRoy was not rich. The expense of a peerage seemed daunting. Prince Albert wrote to Derby: 'It would be a great pity if Lord FitzRoy were to be obliged to decline the Peerage on account of poverty', indicating that FitzRoy Somerset had already raised this drawback with the Prime Minister, who had then informed Queen Victoria. Prince Albert acknowledged that Lord FitzRoy would feel 'mortified' if a grant were made from public funds: 'Under the circumstances ... the Queen would herself bear the expenses of the fees'. So much for Lord FitzRoy's not being favoured at Court. The sensitivity of the matter was acknowledged, for Prince Albert continued: 'If this were to hurt Lord FitzRoy's feelings, you could easily manage it so that he need never know from what source the £500 came. The Queen leaves the matter in your hands.' No further hint of the issue appears in his surviving papers, so the precise outcome remains obscure. But on 18 October 1852 Lord FitzRoy Somerset assumed the title of Baron Raglan of Raglan, Monmouthshire, taken from the old family holding, Raglan Castle. Letters of congratulation at his elevation went some way to consoling the new Lord Raglan. Yet he could still be self-deprecating. To the Marchioness of Cholmondeley he observed that her father 'would have smiled at the idea of my being a peer and would have asked what is to become of Richard'; raising, perhaps, the suspicion that reluctance to accept the honour may have had more to do with diffidence than money. The pain of being torn from the Horse Guards remained acute: 'Separation from those with whom I have long acted and whose career has been my study and my care is most painful to me but I must endeavour to reconcile myself to the change and to discharge my new duties with efficiency.' Incidentally, the date of this letter (30 September) shows that the question of acceptance of the peerage had been quickly settled. Derby could only have received the Prince Consort's letter seven days earlier. From the Foreign Office, the Permanent Under-Secretary of State, Henry Addington, offered his congratulations on 'well merited honours'.[11]

Meanwhile, on 24 September Lord FitzRoy received the GCB and on 16 October became a Privy Councillor. Despite continued regrets he settled in quickly at the Ordnance. 'I get on very well at the Ordnance and all the Offices of the Department appear anxious to meet my wishes and to shew that my appointment is agreeable to them,' he wrote in late November. And he was kept busy. 'The work is heavy and the interruptions are so frequent at the Ordnance that I have much to do at times. Still I do only care about the constant employment and all I have to regret is my separation from an office where every thing was familiar to me.' The Department's annual budget grossed some £3 million; for example, the number of barracks needing to be maintained in the United Kingdom and overseas amounted to 584. A total of 14,200 Ordnance troops were voted for the year 1851-2.[12]

The state of 'home defences' proved the main worry. Several critical memoranda by military and political figures such as Sir John Burgoyne, Palmerston and even Wellington during the previous decade had met with general apathy; and the Ordnance failed to secure funds for improvements to any meaningful extent. The French *coup d'état* of 2 December 1851 rapidly deflated complacency and Palmerston's colourful denunciation of 'our great dockyards' being defended 'with broomsticks and pitchforks' appeared less absurd on examination. Arriving in Pall Mall, Raglan discovered that his predecessor (Hardinge) had recently urged a review of coastal batteries now that ships could travel at 8-10 knots even in unfavourable wind conditions.[13]

Scarcely had Raglan taken office than the Queen asked the Prime Minister (Derby) to elicit his opinion and that of other responsible authorities (including the CinC and the First Lord of the Admiralty) about the state of national defences. Shortly afterwards, early in November, Prince Albert approached Hardinge to consult Raglan and produce a summary of the actual resources available for immediate defence and estimate the cost of necessary improvements. Independently, Grey noted Clarendon's alarm at the build-up of naval and military forces across the Channel where 'the common talk of the French army and of his [Louis Napoleon's] entourage is about the *"descente sur l'Angleterre"* and occupation of London'. In a more sober minute the Board of Ordnance noted information that, 'for several seasons', a French warship had been seen off the Scottish coast and the captain been heard to boast 'that he knew more of the places where troops could be landed than any of the inhabitants of that country'.[14]

The new Master-General very quickly prepared a comprehensive paper showing 'the immediate wants' of his department, which he forwarded to Derby. In essence £16,700 was needed to provide ammunition for 250 9pdr and 12pdr field guns, more labour to produce small-arms ammunition, 10,000 additional ammunition boxes, the purchase and equipping of more 10in guns. Authority to proceed with the relevant contracts was urgently required. 'About' £10,000 could profitably be spent quickly 'upon works of defence' – principally on the Isle of Wight and near Sheerness – but overall Raglan estimated that some £50,000 ought to be spent on defence works. The Royal Artillery required augmentation of 2,000 men and 1,000 horses for maximum efficiency. He subsequently sent Prince Albert a copy of the memorandum and noted that the Government had agreed to print it for circulation.[15]

Raglan soon discovered that neither unanimity of opinion nor strong positive support could be assured however. Rejecting Sir James Fergusson's call for strengthening coastal defences, a correspondent to *The United Service Gazette* in December 1852 declared that, even if the coast were 'walled like a garden' the best defence would be to blockade enemy harbours: 'We must attack rather than defend: that is our system.' The absurdity of this nostrum, given the number of possible enemies and consequent wide range of potentially hostile ports, was self-evident. The editorial the following week re-emphasized defensive weakness: only 'bull-dog courage' existed to save British shores from 'insult'. Indirectly acknowledging the work of the Ordnance, though, in January 1853 *The United Service Magazine* paid tribute to improvements in defence already in train. None the less *The United Service Gazette* and Burgoyne, in another comprehensive memorandum that same month, remained pungently on the offensive: coastal defences, especially around the dockyards, were too weak. Fears about French intentions were also voiced in the Commons during February. And Sidney Herbert, the Secretary at War, wrote: 'There are at Dunkirk, Calais, Boulogne, Havre and Dieppe steamers enough to tow over 75,000 men in sailing vessels in one trip', estimating that £30,000 would make Portsmouth safe from any associated *coup de main*.[16]

Concern about national defence led to an interesting planning commitment in which Raglan was closely involved as Master-General. The impetus for a more formal consideration of national defence policy may have come from Queen Victoria's suggestion in October 1852 that the Prime Minister consult the CinC, Master-General, First Lord of the Admiralty and Home Secretary. Shortly afterwards Derby's government resigned and not until early in 1853 did this, or a similar idea, gain substance. Then the Home Secretary (Palmerston) appears to have taken the initiative. Correspondence between him, Hardinge and Aberdeen (the new Prime Minister), together with a later statement in Parliament by Hardinge, suggests 'three or four' informal meetings took place during the early months of 1853 before co-operation with France, rather than potential antagonism, prevailed. That little tangible evidence survives of this planning committee, comprising military and civilian authorities, does not obscure the fact that it did convene however informally. It may, thus, be seen as the tentative, short-lived forerunner of that concept of consultation and co-operation which found expression in the Committee of Imperial Defence a half-century later.[17]

Whatever the strength or effectiveness of this *ad hoc* defence committee, Raglan's attention was necessarily focused on the need to strengthen the fortifications of particular locations, and the proceedings of the Board of Ordnance, which he chaired, show that positive remedial action did take place. In February 1853 *The Illustrated London News* summarized the activity already under way. At Dover 'batteries, breast-works, defences, etc., will be shortly placed in that state of old, when Dover was one of the first posts and strongest garrisons in England'. At Folkestone, 'the surveyors of the Ordnance have been making surveys during the week around the battery, down the face and along the foot of the cliff'. An 'ordnance survey' was being made of Rye with a view to establishment of a battery there; and at Pembroke alterations were taking place to accommodate 32pdr instead of 24pdr guns to make the battery 'most formidable'. Martello towers along the Sussex coast were 'to receive an armament forthwith'. The environs of Portsmouth harbour were to be considerably strengthened, notably at Gosport and Hilsea with further earthworks, 'preparatory to erection of a permanent fort' at Browndown on the Solent. However, only a single 32pdr at Exmouth existed over the 130 miles between Bristol and Plymouth in the West Country: interestingly, this report is contained in Lord Raglan's private files.[18]

Money for improvements was not readily available. In December 1852 the Board noted that 'want of funds' precluded improvements at Devonport, and early the following year a proposal to construct more barracks in the vicinity was attacked as 'unnecessary expense' by an anonymous correspondent. A counter-proposal to build in stone instead of brick met the objection that this 'would be disadvantageous with reference to strength, comfort, economy and space'. The allegedly poor condition of the Pembroke defences much exercised the Ordnance. In October 1852 the Adjutant-General at the Horse Guards penned a formal complaint which by mid-1853 had borne fruit with Ordnance action. Lack of money affected necessary improvements to the old naval port of Falmouth. Indeed, the Board expressed anxiety in general about the 'towers and batteries on the coast of the Western District', which must be put into 'an efficient state'. Palmerston suggested that Raglan might apply to the Treasury to use £22-23,000 surplus from the Home Office for 1852-3 for the repair of coastal forts.[19]

In the north-west, protection of Liverpool was similarly put at risk by lack of funds. There the corporation had to provide money for the construction of new forts. And Raglan informed the Duke of Buccleuch that, unless local assistance were forthcoming, 'little chance' existed of improvements at Granton. The Ordnance was not self-financing. In October 1853 a thorough report to the Master-General about the state of defences in Scotland was characterized by the comments on 'Leith Fort' being 'improperly called' a fort, and 'merely a half-moon battery in barbette for light guns'. Fort George may have been 'excellent', but Fort Charlotte boasted one invalid gunner and a corporal. It all made depressing reading and, in the absence of an obvious threat north of the border, little could be done. That was not true of the east and south-east of England, especially when, as *The United Service Gazette* noted, relations with Russia also were deteriorating. Newhaven, as well as Dover, received attention; so variously did Harwich and Eastbourne. Lack of money restricted work, though the Treasury did give special authority to repair the Cinque Ports' defences. The Channel Islands, close as they were to the French coast, needed swift, added protection and, for their defence, finance became more readily available. Land on Alderney was purchased to build new fortifications and there was considerable discussion at the Ordnance about the nature of works there and on Guernsey.[20]

The strengthening of the fabric of fortifications was of little use if they were insufficiently manned or armed, as the report on Leith and Fort Charlotte illustrated. When he became Master-General in February 1852

Hardinge discovered only 'forty or fifty' usable artillery pieces in fortresses. Eleven months later *The United Service Gazette* alleged that visitors to England for Wellington's funeral became aware of the country's defensive weakness. This impression was effectively challenged in Parliament by Sir George Pechell who quoted an 1849 report to argue that some 14,691 guns (from 13in mortars to 9pdr pieces) were actually available and, with others repaired, 23,963 could be made serviceable. The crucial point was not number, but calibre. With warships, 'especially French', now faster and more heavily armed, coastal fortifications must have 56pdr guns. That case seemed unanswerable. Thus improvements in artillery as well as the construction of required fortifications went ahead. Raglan's role in this was not passive. He chaired many of the Ordnance meetings that made the relevant decisions, and corresponded with other interested authorities in his official capacity. He also toured the country examining fortifications. In July 1853 he visited the Channel Islands, Plymouth and Portsmouth.[21]

Raglan proved mindful of the need to improve the system for supplying military weapons, which fell within the remit of the Ordnance. He declared himself before the Parliamentary Select Committee on Small Arms to be 'not satisfied with the present mode in which the supply was obtained' and that it was 'unsafe for the country to go on' with a contract system. He supported establishment of a government factory at Enfield. In 1851, he explained, the Board of Ordnance had taken preliminary steps 'to procure 28,000 rifled muskets' and entered into contracts in February 1852. The muskets were not delivered until November 1853. This delay came at a time when the Adjutant-General had complained officially about defects in existing muskets. But Raglan was not slow to defend his department if he felt that it had been badly treated. This is illustrated by his reaction to proposed amalgamation of the Ordnance and Army hospital services, in effect entailing abolition of the separate Ordnance organization. When Master-General, the Marquis of Anglesey had resisted this suggestion and the Report of the Select Committee on Army and Ordnance Expenditure published in July 1851, which favoured it, had not been followed up. However the similar findings of a War Office Commission of Inquiry had been approved by Hardinge when Master-General; and, on 4 December 1852, the Secretary at War was charged with the preparation of a Royal Warrant effecting amalgamation. Raglan, on learning of this, reacted strongly. He informed Hardinge at the Horse Guards that he 'was not aware that you had officially consented' to amalgamation and that he must 'look carefully' to ensure that Ordnance medical officers were not brought 'even indirectly' under the War Office. Hardinge subsequently argued that for some years co-operation had existed between Army and Ordnance medical officers in practice and that he was opposed to abolition of Ordnance regimental hospitals. Whether or not Raglan had caused him to modify his views is unclear, but the Royal Warrant, when finally issued on 14 February 1853, allowed for administrative cohesion through one overall Director-General and continued separation of the two medical corps. The Ordnance officers therefore remained subordinate militarily to the Master-General. It was an uneasy compromise which appeared to owe much to Raglan's intervention of December 1852.[22]

The Master-General's opposition to this proposed medical reform did not signal obdurate antagonism to all change in the Ordnance, where he sponsored economy and greater efficiency. The 1853 Estimates were £17,500 less than an average of the years 1845-50. Early in 1854 examinations for Ordnance clerks were made compulsory, and the duties of the Principal Storekeeper were reviewed when he assumed a new title 'Comptroller of Stores and Principal Storekeeper'.[23]

Despite these beneficial changes and evidence that the Department could adjust to short-term military requirements, criticism – apart from Joseph Hume's eternal search for financial restraint – was not muted. The poor quality of clothing issued to the troops came under fire, and the Board's reluctance to place long-term contracts for supplies and military equipment was attacked before The Select Committee on Small Arms in the spring of 1854. Raglan stayed at Pall Mall less than sixteen months, but the evidence suggests that he had at least made some progress in attaining more departmental economy and efficiency during that time. In fact the Treasury Committee of Inquiry, which reported in December 1853, paid tribute to the effectiveness of reform. Thus, on the eve of the Crimean War, the Clerk of the Ordnance could claim with some justification in Parliament that the Department was in good order. The total cost of the salaries of officers and officals at Pall Mall and all subordinate establishments such as the Royal Laboratory at Woolwich amounted to £71,369. In eight departments at Pall Mall, the number of clerks to deal with the widespread business of the Ordnance at home and abroad totalled 153. The War Office, with far less responsibility, had 119.[24]

Beyond his responsibilities at the Ordnance, Raglan became involved in a contretemps between Hardinge and the Adjutant-General (Sir George Brown), yet again as mediator. Shortly before going to the Ordnance, in late September 1852 when he was still FitzRoy Somerset, he had tried to persuade Brown that there was no 'organized conspiracy' against him at the Horse Guards. Brown had clearly hinted at resignation in a letter to Lord FitzRoy, who had hoped that nothing would occur to deprive the Army of Brown's experience in the post of Adjutant-General. He had surmised that Brown's report of a conversation with Grey to Wellington, which it was his duty to convey, had caused offence. Whether this were the root cause of the trouble or not, it soon became apparent that the Duke of Cambridge had complained about Brown's showing certain correspondence to Hardinge. Lord FitzRoy had supported Brown, and the discord quietened. Temporarily. In January 1853 Brown was again on the point of resignation and Raglan once more tried to dissuade him from precipitate action. On the day that Raglan wrote and before his letter reached Brown, the Adjutant-General drafted his resignation to Hardinge. That draft was not sent, so Raglan's advice appears to have had effect. If so it only achieved a delay, because in December Brown submitted the draft of 24 January 1853 with slight modifications. Essentially, he could not work with Hardinge. Neither Raglan nor other officers at the Horse Guards such as Richard Airey – who would prove a stalwart support to Raglan in the Crimea – could reconcile the Adjutant-General and his CinC.[25]

The previous month Brown, Hardinge and Raglan had seen Hardinge's predecessor at the Horse Guards laid to rest. Wellington's funeral procession was indeed magnificent; and Raglan, as Master-General, officially took part in the melancholy advance to St Paul's Cathedral on 18 November 1852. At 7.30 a.m. the cortège set out from St James's Park – the body having lain overnight in the Audience Room of the Horse Guards – via Constitution Hill, Piccadily, St James's Street, Pall Mall, Cockspur Street, Charing Cross, the Strand and Temple Bar to the Cathedral. Amid the vast array Raglan rode in one of the private carriages allotted to the group that included the Secretary at War, the Chancellor of the Exchequer and the Secretaries of State for the Home and Colonial Departments, following the band of the 2nd Life Guards and immediately behind the 'Banner of Wellesley' carried by a lieutenant-colonel and supported by two captains on horseback.[26]

Almost exactly a year later a family tragedy also caused Raglan distress. He watched Henry, seventh Duke of Beaufort, son of his late eldest brother and only three and a half years his own junior, deteriorate to the point where he did not recognize even his close family before his death in November 1853. Raglan explained to Priscilla that because of pressure of work he had been unable to respond to the telegraph summoning him to Badminton until twelve hours before the end. The Duchess and her daughters 'were all, poor things, in the deepest distress', and he therefore returned to London on the afternoon of Beaufort's death to avoid being in the way: 'I always consider on such painful occasions that nothing is more distressing than the meeting at meals.' Beaufort, he revealed to his sister-in-law, had been in 'great suffering' at Cowes in August. By October, when Raglan spent two days at Badminton, he was enduring frequent bouts of intense pain relieved only by doses of laudanum. During these attacks he was almost in tears, but with the medication seemed to recover. However, 'these violent neuralgic pains were succeeded by violent gout and being attended with fever confined him to bed for nearly the last fortnight and rendered him unable to feed himself'. Despite his ills Beaufort had remained cheerful. He was a sad loss to his family and friends 'as well as to me particularly ... He and I lived very much together in early life and we continued united in the recollection of former times and associations.' 'After a cold journey' Raglan reached Badminton again at 3 p.m. on 23 November in preparation for the funeral the next day at which 30-35 people were expected, including Lord Howe. Beaufort's daughters had been 'quite grateful' for a letter from Kitty, and Raglan urged his other daughter, Charlotte, also to write to them. The new eighth Duke of Beaufort was Raglan's great-nephew, Henry Charles FitzRoy.[27]

Despite chiding her for not writing promptly to her Beaufort cousins after their father's death and, on another occasion, fussily instructing her by letter from Eaton Banks to have a good fire in the front room of Great Stanhope Street on the afternoon of his return to London, Raglan clearly adored Charlotte. If she erred in not writing to Badminton in November 1853, she clearly did offer sympathy at that time to her father: 'A thousand thanks for your kind and affectionate letter,' he wrote. 'It is as you are under all circumstances, a great comfort to me and I rejoice in having you as my daughter.' A month later he addressed her as 'my dearest Good as Gold'.[28]

Despite the fact that Richard was settled as Private Secretary to the King of Hanover, towards the close of 1853 Raglan for some reason sought to get him appointed to the Ordnance. Lord Aberdeen explained to Lord John Russell that the office of Secretary to the Master-General had always been filled after 'some sort of concert with the Head of Department', and that Raglan had put forward his son. Aberdeen observed that his own son ought to change his appointment to further his military career, but he would not advance his name for this purpose – a hint of disapproval that Raglan might be guilty of nepotism. And, in fact, the Prime Minister rejected Raglan's request, pleading that a military man must be appointed. Thus the post remained open until December 1853 when it was filled by another officer. Raglan had not objected, nor indeed pressed Richard's claim. This was hardly a dereliction of parental duty. As a civilian Raglan must have known that his son's case was weak. However, all other attempts – dating back to his talks with Sir James Graham in 1847 – to gain Richard employment in England had failed too. The chance of getting him appointed to the Ordnance must have been slim, but it may show the measure of his anxiety to have his only surviving son close to him as he (Raglan) entered late middle age.[29]

Lady Raglan, meanwhile, continued to cause worry, not simply because of her real or supposed physical weaknesses but because she no longer seemed able to cope adequately with management of the household. More and more fell on Raglan and Charlotte. The food at Great Stanhope Street, Raglan complained to Charlotte, was 'execrable, abominable'; and 'My Lady is in great distress about her Establishments. Mr Roberts' footman will not come.' In the spring of 1853 Raglan wrote to Charlotte from the Egertons' noting that he had made a list of all the bills that had to be paid, which he would discuss with his daughter on returning to London. Meanwhile she was not to bother her mother. Unlike Lady

Raglan, he himself appeared not to ail seriously. During his years at the Ordnance only one indisposition seemed worthy of comment. In January 1853 he wrote to Charlotte: 'Still much cold about me but Hume told me this morning that my pulse was regular and my tongue clear'. Nothing much to note, perhaps. The following day, from Windsor Castle, he admitted to coughing 'a great deal' in the night, but less that day. He added: 'I have not felt comfortable and was worried for nearly two hours with that nasty palpitation (say nothing about this) which makes me feel poorly always.' Evidently increased heart-rate – possibly caused by anxiety – was not uncommon and, on this occasion, dissuaded him from shooting with the Prince Consort even though the weather was fine.[30]

In general, as at the Horse Guards, Raglan had a busy social life, often mixing business with pleasure. Visits to Windsor were never purely social. Within a month of taking office in Pall Mall he wrote to Charlotte, then with her mother near Hastings, that he was to attend a 'Grand Dinner' for foreign generals in either St George's Hall or the Waterloo Gallery. Raglan suggested that his wife should travel to London by train on the morning of the dinner, so that 'I might embrace her before I start'. He then issued detailed instructions as to where to find the necessary clothes and clean linen and how to pack them in either Charlotte's or her mother's 'imperial': 'I forget if my weights are at St Leonards or not.' During the visit in January 1853, when illness prevented him from shooting, he noted that they would be dining early to be in time for 'the play', though whether this involved family theatricals or a professional production is not clear. However he revealed that he had completed his conference with the Prince that day and had 'just now' independently heard details of 'a dreadful incident' on the day before. Miss Ricardo and her fat French maid had been thrown from their carriage when the horses started at a train's whistle in the station. The maid's leg had been so badly broken that amputation had been necessary; and Miss Ricardo was 'in a crazed state'. The incident had not prevented a ball that evening, held in the Town Hall not the Castle: 'I hope to God Beaufort will not be the worse for the madrigals,' he observed. The sad news that morning was that the maid had died.[31]

Towards the end of March Raglan and Kitty were at Eaton Banks, Egerton's home near Tarporley in Cheshire, where they had 'a couple of hours ride' together and nearly got lost in the forest in 'bitterly cold' conditions. They had had, he explained to his elder daughter who was in London looking after her mother, a 'small shower of snow to remind us that it was not absolutely mid summer'. But on this occasion and others he did not refer to post arriving or letters to be dealt with, as had been the case when he was Military Secretary at the Horse Guards. The Master-General's absences from his office seemed more relaxed, though there were the inevitable official calls for his presence. Thus on 31 March he asked Charlotte to refuse an invitation to the London Hospital Festival on his behalf. During a visit to Badminton later that year he commented on the poor weather which would keep him 'close to my chair all the day'. He mentioned going to church the previous day, which is the only firm reference to attendance at divine service in his papers at this time. However, to infer that he was not a regular attender would be wrong. On this occasion he linked the visit with meeting specific people. Normally no such reference would be necessary; and obituaries later made it clear that Raglan was a devout communicant. In closing this letter Raglan observed that Lord Howe would be shortly attending a Masonic fete at Leamington. Quite why Raglan should mention this to Charlotte is obscure. But the reference and the fact that Richard was a Mason tentatively suggest that Raglan may also have been one. There is no direct evidence of this however.[32]

After attending a review at Woolwich at which his horse Miss Mary, who would go with him to the Crimea, 'behaved well', Raglan went to Windsor again at the close of October for another working social engagement. A week later he recorded visiting the Drury Lane Theatre to see 'The Horsemanship' and dining at White's with 'Francis [Burghersh] and Bob Dundas'. The following day, 9 November, a visit to Lord Frederick and Lady Charlotte Calthorpe (his great-niece and daughter of the seventh Duke of Beaufort) was discussed and an invitation was received from Lady Howe for a shooting party on 28 November with 'dancing for the daughter who is with me'. Lady Raglan still eschewed social engagements. In December Raglan was at another shooting party which provided 'no great sport' but at which he killed a woodcock. Among the guests was a Miss Honeywood who apparently had known Richard at Isleworth. Raglan asked that, if room were available, Lady Raglan should invite Granville Somerset to stay at Stanhope Street. Despite Raglan's reticence about his sporting achievements, 'an old sportsman' expressed himself 'astonished at the quick manner in which he knocked over the rabbits' and another commentator recorded that 'at a party of young officers in 1853' assembled in the country by one of his nephews, Lord Raglan was declared to have been 'the liveliest boy of the lot'.[33]

His work at the Ordnance was also held in high esteem. 'An officer' wrote in 1853: 'In the execution of my public duties I have become acquainted with the sentiments and feelings of several military officers of the highest rank, and with those of numerous senior officers of the army; and they have brought me in contact with retired officers, their widows and families. From all these I have gathered the universal opinion of the strict sense of duty and considerate feeling for others (especially for those of the unfortunate) which have always actuated Lord Raglan in his public and private capacity.' On 5 February 1853 *The Illustrated London News* similarly praised Raglan's professional efficiency.[34]

Events in the Balkans that brought Russia and Turkey into conflict and had military implications for Britain, began to cause concern as

1853 progressed. During the late summer the situation in the region noticeably deteriorated; and on 29 September Aberdeen informed Queen Victoria at Balmoral that he could not leave London because 'the aspect of affairs in the East becomes more serious every day'. The Russians deployed to cross the Danube and penetrate the Balkans en route to Constantinople. Turkey declared war early in October, but Aberdeen still opted for neutrality, proclaiming 'great apprehension ... [that] this country should be irrevocably committed to a course, the consequences of which cannot be foreseen and may be most calamitous'. During October repeated Cabinet meetings reviewed the course of events and Queen Victoria left Balmoral five days earlier than planned. In general, nevertheless, there was no strong pro-war feeling, although individuals such as Palmerston favoured military intervention. All that changed when news came through that on 30 November a superior Russian fleet had used explosive shells to devastate a small Turkish squadron in Sinope Bay with the loss of 5,000 lives. Russia and Turkey were at war, yet 'the massacre', as the British press dubbed the action, thoroughly enflamed public opinion.[35]

The inexorable train of events that would lead to British troops landing in the Crimea had begun. As Raglan enjoyed that Christmas with his family, he little knew that it would be his last in their company. Nor could he have guessed, ensconced as he was at the Ordnance and neither in a field nor strictly army command, that in the Queen's words 'an attack on Sebastopol, of which the papers speak' would soon be of intense personal and professional interest to him and, ultimately, cost him his life. The waters of the Ordnance may have been placid. Those of the eastern Mediterranean would soon, for him, prove distinctly stormy.[36]

CHAPTER 8

ADVANCE TO CONTACT
(JANUARY-AUGUST 1854)

'Here our preparations for the great operation are continuing.' (Lord Raglan, Bulgaria, 1854)[1]

On 3 January 1854 British and French naval squadrons entered the Black Sea, with orders that 'all Russian vessels, other than merchantmen ... should be required to return to Sebastopol'. Neither Britain nor France was as yet at war with Russia, but Clarendon, the Foreign Secretary, acknowledged that 'Her Majesty's Government do not disguise from themselves ' that this action 'may at no distant period' lead to an outbreak of hostilities. Rumours of an army expeditionary force began to circulate in London as the press accelerated its bellicose clarion calls. Apart from awareness of the need to provide men and matériel in the event of the war, at the Ordnance Raglan was essentially remote from this activity. Not for long.[2]

Soon the Inspector-General of Fortifications and Commander of the Royal Engineers (Sir John Burgoyne) left England to survey the area around Constantinople in company with a French engineer (Colonel Ardent) in case Allied troops were called upon to defend the Turkish capital. Other officers went separately to the Danube area. As an Ordnance officer Burgoyne received his orders through Raglan and reported to him. Hence the Master-General conveyed the Cabinet's 'request [to] Sir John not to go beyond Constantinople, but to turn his back on the Black Sea'. Yet almost imperceptibly an attack upon Sevastopol rather than defence of Constantinople or resistance to Russian forces along the Danube had become the nodal point of Allied thinking.[3]

In December 1853 Sir James Graham (First Lord of the Admiralty) had argued that command of the Black Sea could only be secured by 'the entire destruction of Sebastopol with its naval and military establishments and all their contents'. Sailing into Sevastopol Bay on 6 January 1854 *Retribution* took the opportunity to survey the defences. Captain Drummond's report struck a pessimistic chord: entrance to the harbour could be sealed off by the Russians to prevent naval broadsides from silencing shore batteries or destroying the dockyards. Only a land force could achieve success. Drummond speculated that a landing north of the harbour might neutralize the dominating Star Fort and make positions south of Sevastopol Bay untenable. Before leaving England for his reconnaissance Burgoyne took a similar view: 'Sebastopol was not open to attack by Sea, unless the land Defences be taken by an Army equal to cope with the

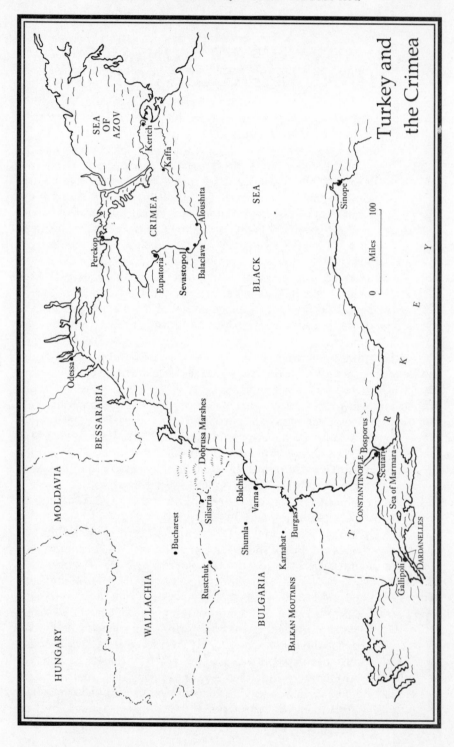

Turkey and
the Crimea

Russian garrison.' With a sketch of Sevastopol by an Austrian officer to hand, Graham agreed with Burgoyne that a naval assault would be 'madness': 'It is a second Gibraltar.' But he went on to show that political opinion was veering sharply towards combined action: 'There is no reason to apprehend any rashness of naval enterprise, unaided by an army'. Like the Secretary of State for War and the Colonies, the Duke of Newcastle, he foresaw an expeditionary force in association with the fleet. Sevastopol had now very much become the prize.[4]

As the war clouds gathered Raglan quite unexpectedly found himself appointed to command the Expeditionary Force. Ironically his close association with Wellington which had cost him command at the Horse Guards determined his selection for the Crimea. Whatever the views on Wellington's latter-day attitude to military reform, the Duke's reputation as a general had survived intact. In his absence, his disciple must serve. The *Morning Chronicle* referred, in approbation, to 'he who all his life was the right arm of Wellington', and Westmorland (echoing words from *The Illustrated London News*) observed that throughout the Peninsular campaign and at Waterloo Raglan had been at Wellington's side. Hardinge expressed the 'strong conviction' that Raglan was best suited to lead 'a British force to the East' because of his 'great professional experience under the Duke'. Despite these enthusiastic references, though, Raglan had never led troops in battle. But his keen eye for ground had been proved frequently in the past, and according to one commentator: 'He was a good and bold rider and a capital shot notwithstanding the loss of his right arm.' His energy, quickly demonstrated on his appointment, led *The United Service Magazine* to declare: 'The time is approaching when the place of this great soldier will be at the head of our army in the field.' A.W. Kinglake, later chronicler of the Crimean War, argued that despite his age (65) 'in general his well-braced features, his wakeful attention, his uncommon swiftness of thought, his upright manly carriage, and his easy seat on horseback, made him look the same as a man in the strong mid-season of life'. Clear in speech and fluent in French, his natural caution made him an ideal choice to deal with a touchy ally. He could quickly put men at their ease and inspire fierce loyalty, which perversely could dissuade his staff 'from conveying to him an unwelcome truth'. Men, Kinglake believed, 'tended to become his courtiers'. *The United Service Magazine* seemed justified therefore in proclaiming that his qualities marked him out for command of the expeditionary force. Tact in dealing with allies, learnt in the harsh realities of the Peninsula, figured high on the list of his attributes.[5]

When the prospect of taking command was broached early in February, Raglan consulted 'two or three of his principal officers in confidence' and they urged him to accept. His own strong sense of duty virtually predetermined that course, but his brother-in-law recorded Raglan's special conviction that he must ensure the defence of 'our ancient Ally ...

the Turkish empire'. Westmorland's wife, however, admitted to being 'quite upset' at the prospect of his appointment, adding: 'I dare not think [that] my son will have to go with his uncle'. Her sister Emily, she revealed, was in a state of 'great agitation'. Once the command had been confirmed Priscilla referred to 'the distress into which I am thrown', curiously expressing doubts not publicly voiced about Raglan's fitness: 'Under any circumstances I should deeply regret seeing Fitzroy, at his age and with his indifferent health, undertake a life so different from that he has been accustomed to for thirty-eight years.'

After having been assured that Raglan would accept the command, Hardinge recommended him to Newcastle who warned the Queen that he would 'probably' take her pleasure after the Cabinet meeting on 11 February. The CinC confirmed his verbal recommendation of 7 February in a letter to Newcastle the following day, maintaining that 'the officer the best qualified to be sent with a British force to the East would be Lord Raglan ... He possesses great professional experience acquired under the Duke, and he has for this service personal qualifications most desirable in a chief who has to co-operate with a French force. His temper and manners are conciliatory, and he would command the respect of Foreigners and the confidence of our own force.' But the Secretary of State expressed his own reservations about Raglan's fitness for the post because of his lack of 'experience of the personnel of the army' and want of recent active service. None the less, noting Queen Victoria's provisional support, on 13 February Newcastle wrote: 'The Cabinet warmly approved the appointment of Lord Raglan to command the expeditionary force now preparing for the East', thereby indicating that his objections had been overridden. Newcastle's initial lack of confidence in Raglan may explain his persistent cavilling once the campaign got under way. On 18 February, as 'General Officer Commanding the Forces eastwards of Malta', Raglan received authority under the Mutiny Act to convene courts-martial, but sentences must be in accordance with 'the said Act of Parliament and Articles of War' and transmitted through the Judge Advocate General. Three days later his appointment was officially confirmed with promotion to the local rank of General 'whilst so employed'. The method by which Raglan was appointed illustrates the roles of the CinC and the Secretary at War in the selection for an expedition of senior officers down to and including brigadier-general. Hardinge submitted recommendations to Newcastle who usually agreed on behalf of the Cabinet before the CinC sent the names to the Queen for formal approval. Newcastle, supported by his Cabinet colleagues, had the constitutional right to reject a poposed officer.[6]

A stalwart supporter of Raglan's later recalled, with justification, that 'the most zealous advocate of "Administrative Reform" will allow that in the opinion of the nation at large, at that time, to say the least, the right man was chosen for the right place ... The public papers of every shade of political view' agreed. On the day that Raglan's appointment was confirmed, the Duke of Cambridge wrote to Richard: 'There is not a man in the Army under whom I would rather serve ... I think he is pleased with the appointment himself and there is a lot more opinion as to the excellence of it. All say that Lord Raglan is just the man for the job.' Professional, press and public opinion therefore welcomed the appointment, but one minor hitch did occur. It appears likely that, in discussion with Hardinge, Raglan asked for Brown as his second-in-command. The CinC made it clear to Newcastle that he could not personally recommend his former Adjutant-General for that appointment. His 'punctilious' adherence to regulations might be admirable in barracks, but not in the field. Furthermore, in his view Brown did not 'possess those qualities of judgement, temper, skill and foresight' for the second-in-command of an allied force that would include the French and the Turks. 'The Government [is] at liberty to take any other course as circumstances arise', but Hardinge would not support the choice of Brown before the Queen.[7]

Newcastle noted that the Cabinet agreed on the dispatch of 10,000 troops to Malta on the afternoon of 8 February and that he would consult Hardinge and Raglan the following day before laying final details before Queen Victoria. Two days later he informed her that he and the two officers had agreed on the general shape of the force and 'the Duke of Newcastle has therefore issued directions to the Admiralty to hire steam transports' so that men and equipment could be at Malta within a month of the Cabinet decision. Hardinge would let Newcastle know 'in a day or two' which regiments would form the 2nd and 3rd Divisions, the Brigade of Guards already being allocated to the 1st Division. Somewhat optimistically Newcastle recognized that more than 10,000 men would be needed if a 'trial of strength' with the Russians developed, but he expected that the additional men could be amassed with 'great alacrity'. Naïvety marched constantly with the Duke of Newcastle.[8]

Raglan was not entirely without influence over the composition of his force, and he was besieged by individuals, their families and sponsors. Over appointments to the Commissariat – whose Commissary-General William Filder was merely 'attached' to the Expeditionary Force and remained under the Assistant Secretary to the Treasury – he had no control. Military posts were different. In mid-February Lady Raglan informed her brother-in-law that Raglan 'is quite overwhelmed with business and seeing *hundreds* of persons and is sure he shall not have a moment to himself today'. The *Morning Herald* reported that Sir George Brown and Colonel Richard Airey had 'both volunteered to accompany Lord Raglan in any situation whatever ... officials at the Horse Guards have all expressed their desire to be employed in any manner whatever under their late most gallant chief, Lord Raglan'. On 11 February the Duke of Cambridge wrote in his diary: 'Very busy all the day at the Horse Guards with a view to being employed with the Army to go to Turkey.' Four days later he noted that Newcastle told him he had succeeded.

In fact Cambridge's ultimate appointment to command the 1st Division had an interesting background. Queen Victoria recorded that he saw her and Prince Albert in 'a great state' on 13 February: 'He said he would feel having been disgraced were he not allowed to go. We agreed with him and promised to do all we could.' Later that evening Aberdeen dined at Buckingham Palace, in turn agreed with the Queen, but observed that 'the Cabinet are averse to his going', presumably because he was a member of the royal family. Aberdeen, however, had 'told' Newcastle that if Hardinge and Raglan approved 'and George were *not* 2nd in command', the Prime Minister would 'take the responsibility' of giving Cambridge an appointment himself. Lord Cardigan later recalled: 'I did not lose any time in applying for command in the Cavalry.' Francis, Lord Burghersh and Raglan's nephew, asked to go with his uncle, who suggested the post of either Military Secretary or ADC. Lady Raglan, writing to Westmorland, revealed that his son 'entirely prefers the latter, for he is not fond of writing'. Raglan would be 'very happy' to have Burghersh, and Lady Raglan hoped that Westmorland would not object. The Westmorlands (despite Priscilla's deep-seated anxiety) agreed and Burghersh duly became one of Raglan's ADCs, his second choice.[9]

Raglan certainly had strong, perhaps decisive influence over who should serve on his staff. On 21 February 1854 the final list was drawn up: Lieutenant-Colonel T.M. Steele (Military Secretary) and four relatives as ADCs: nephews Major Lord Burghersh and Captain Poulett Somerset; great-nephews Captain Nigel Kingscote and Lieutenant Somerset Calthorpe. A fifth, a relation by marriage and later Steele's assistant Military Secretary, Lieutenant Leicester Curzon would be added later. Airey declined the post of Quartermaster-General offered to him by Raglan, preferring to command a brigade in the Light Division; but Lord de Ros agreed to serve in that position. James Estcourt – in Rome when he learned of the proposed expedition – declared an interest in the Quartermaster-General's post, but was appointed Raglan's Adjutant-General.[10]

Later Hardinge claimed that Raglan had not only selected his own personal staff, including the Quartermaster-General and Adjutant-General, but 'the greater portion of his brigadiers'. Following Hardinge's advice, the Cabinet did not recommend Brown as second-in-command, and Raglan appears to have accepted this without demur. Other appointments did cause some controversy, two of which would have a lasting effect on Raglan's reputation. Hardinge apologized to Newcastle for recommending the appointments of Lord Lucan and Brigadier-Generals Torrens and Goldie to the Queen without reference to him. The Duke, although empowered to do so, chose not to ask for cancelllation of the appointments. Newcastle's biographer later quoted Raglan's great-nephew, Somerset Calthorpe, as telling him that Raglan had not been consulted about the appointments of either Lucan or Cardigan. Calthorpe maintained that Raglan protested strongly to Hardinge about placing in close professional proximity two such irreconcilable men whose antipathy for each other was well-known. But the CinC overruled Raglan's objections – with unfortunate long-term consequences.[11]

While he laboured to complete preparations for the expedition and, as Master-General, also supervise details of the Ordnance involvement, Lady Raglan reported: 'My Lord is remarkably well and in high spirits and so I do not like to worry him with my objections and feelings upon the subject', adding: 'I still entertain *a slight* hope of peace and that he may not have to go at all!' 'At all events', Raglan did not expect to leave England until at least the third week in March.[12]

Meanwhile, as Burgoyne and Ardent reached Turkey to carry out their defensive survey, speculation about possible aggressive military action was rife. Cambridge believed that neither Britain nor France could allow the Russians to occupy Constantinople and that Austria also had much to lose by an extension of Russian power. If 'Germany' (*sic*) sided with these three, the problem could be settled 'without much trouble in a great conference'. On the other hand if Germany backed Russia 'a flame will have been ignited' which would lead to 'a war of nations'. Britain had made herself ready by voting additional troops and completing the Guards regiments up to 100 men per company. Within days, however, Cambridge was arguing that Prussia and Austria ('the German powers') would remain neutral, 'but I am inclined to think that we must have War'. Lord Stratford de Redcliffe, writing from Constantinople, enclosed a plan 'by a British officer' for offensive action across the Danube into Wallachia and Moldavia via the Dobruja marshes, which, like Cambridge's comments, is in Raglan's surviving files. Whether this had any influence on Cardigan's later 'bare-backed' reconnaissance in that area is a moot point. Closer to home Colonel Hugh Rose produced 'Reflexions on the employment of a British and French Force in Turkey', rather vaguely concluding that 'the auxiliary Force is to be employed against Russia as an aid to the Turkish Forces, either as a Reserve or as an attacking Force'.[13]

In February Raglan received more papers about Russian strength and the geography of the Crimea. Brown summarized the prevailing ignorance of conditions in Turkey when he wrote to Airey: 'The style of the country is so like Spain, that I should say that very nearly the same arrangements which suited there would be recommended for Turkey.' On a sketch map of the defences of Sevastopol dated 'November 1835' de Ros wrote: 'It is believed that the Lines have long since been fully completed and made stronger than when this report was written.' From the Foreign Office Henry Addington sent Raglan a memorandum compiled by Major-General A.F. Macintosh and summarizing his knowledge of the Caucasus area, Bulgaria (gleaned during a journey from Constantinople to Shumla) and the Crimea, including a report on the defences of Sevastopol as they were in 1834. 'No ships are built at Sebastopol, but great activity prevailed in improving the Harbour and Defences, which when completed would raise it to the Rank of a strong Fortress.' Heavy seaward defences already existed and plans were then in hand to enhance others around the town. Macintosh identified three other features which, unknown to Raglan at the time, would have an important bearing on the campaign. 'The soil around Sebastopol is rocky and consequently difficult in excavation.' The harbour of Balaclava was 'narrow and deep', furthermore the heights above the Monastery of St George (to the south) gave a commanding view of Balaclava and Sevastopol. The Allied expeditionary force would come to appreciate these observations as well. At the end of February and early in March the Foreign Office sent Raglan details of troop movements in the southernmost port of Russia forwarded by the British Ambassador in Berlin and the Prussian Ambassador in St Petersburg. Meanwhile Raglan and de Ros visited Paris and learnt of Napoleon III's plans to attack Sevastopol.[14]

On 10 February Aberdeen declared: 'I, for one, deny ... that war is inevitable ... I will not abandon the hope of maintaining peace.' That same day a Quaker peace delegation met the Tsar in St Petersburg to reiterate the Christian ideal of peace among all men and the great suffering that would ensue from war. Their mission failed and the members returned to London on 23 February. Bizarrely, the following day Queen Victoria suggested to Aberdeen that a threat from France might still be the more real: 'Who can say it is impossible that our own shores may be threatened by Powers now in alliance with us?' In discussing augmentation of the Army by 15,000 her Prime Minister, also on 24 February, added a rider: 'If commencement of the war should take place ...'.[15] The failure of the Quaker peace initiative, however, signalled the demise of realistic hopes of peace; and already virtually irreversible steps had been taken to pave the way for war. On 21 February troops were authorized to proceed to the Mediterranean; four days later the 2nd Battalion, The Rifle Brigade, cleared Portsmouth, and on 27 February the advance guard of the Scots Fusilier Guards entrained for the South Coast. Thereafter sailings were frequent from Portsmouth, Southampton, Plymouth and later Liverpool. By now the nations' respective ambassadors had been recalled from London and St Petersburg; and on 27 February Clarendon issued an ultimatum requiring the Tsar to undertake within six days to evacuate his troops from Moldavia and Wallachia by 30 April: 'refusal or silence ... [would be] equivalent to a declaration of war'. Next day *The Times* published full details.[16]

Even as the warlike preparations went ahead, Raglan continued to discharge his duties at the Ordnance. Ironically, as one writer later pointed out, 'while engaged from morning till night in personally superintending and directing the most necessary armaments at Woolwich, he was accused of wasting time at home'. In retrospect this constant personal commitment seems to have been exaggerated, but he did discuss with Gladstone (Chancellor of the Exchequer) the placing of long-term equipment contracts with the Ordnance, and the provision of 'Army rations' – especially bread and meat – in the United Kingdom. During February, too, the issue of the 1851-pattern Minié rifled muskets proceeded satisfactorily – a tribute to the Department's efficiency. The Deputy Adjutant-General at the Horse Guards expressed satisfaction that the 2nd Battalion, The Rifle Brigade, had been wholly equipped, and all other regiments had received at least 25 stands per company, making some 3,000 in all. With the likelihood of the 1853 pattern becoming available shortly, it was 'not expedient that any more [1851 pattern] should be issued on the present occasion'.[17]

While abroad Raglan would retain control of the Ordnance. When notifying Queen Victoria of the Cabinet's approval for his command of the expeditionary force, Newcastle had noted that 'it would not be necessary, at least for the present, that he should resign his appointment at the Ordnance' – an indication perhaps of an anticipated short campaign. Raglan was considered by the Government 'the proper person to decide who should fill the office of Lieutenant-General of the Ordnance during his absence'; and he recommended Sir Hew Ross. This caused adverse comment in Parliament, but Gladstone explained that although Raglan's advice had been taken, the decision was solely that of the Government: 'This was an act that had been done by the Crown in the exercise of its prerogative in reference to an office of very high class.' Technically this was so, but effectively Raglan had exercised patronage on Ross's behalf, to the chagrin of supporters of Sir John Burgoyne who felt that he should have been preferred. Later, without supporting evidence, the Revd C.E. Kennaway maintained that Raglan had resigned the Ordnance on appointment to the expeditionary force command 'at once ... but, *at her gracious Majesty's express desire*' – for the Queen knew how small his fortune was, notwithstanding his long service – he was prevailed on to retain it.[18]

In the meantime attempts to secure a settlement short of war continued to weaken. In mid-March Russia's refusal to respond to Clarendon's ultimatum or deal positively with further proposals from Prussia, Austria, France and Britain, acting in concert, became clear. On 10 March Raglan obtained more reports on Russian troop movements from the Foreign Office via the Prussian Ambassador in St Petersburg, and towards the end of the month he received a detailed letter from Athens. The British Consul there quoted evidence from 'a person on whom I can confidently rely' that the Russians were going to send 25,000 men across the Danube to Sofia, thence into Macedonia in the hope of encouraging a general anti-Turkish rising. He claimed that the Greek royal family was in touch with the Tsar and was prepared to instigate military action against Turkey should this occur. And he appealed for 'a few English and French Regiments in the Turkish Territory ... to neutralize and check the plans which are maturing in this country'. Two days later news arrived from Paris of grave French concern about the crossing of the Danube by strong Russian forces, and on the last two days of March Newcastle forwarded to Raglan further information from the Foreign Office about Russian military activity in the Black Sea area.[19]

Sevastopol, not unnaturally, received close attention. On 2 March de Ros had reported a conversation with a French newspaper editor who had referred to Sevastopol as being of *incontestable faiblesse*. 'He [Yonval] said those were only "phrases" intended to convey to the world, *for the public good*, that the boast of the Russians that Sevastopol was impregnable had no real truth in it!!!' Thus may the public be misled and pressure be put on politicians to act unwisely. Shortly afterwards Raglan learnt from Lord Cowley (British ambassador in Paris) that 'some time back' the French had directed their ambassador at Constantinople, General d'Hilliers, to investigate the possibility of 'attacking Sebastopol with success'. He favoured landing troops to the north of the port, but he admitted that high ground to the south offered a better opportunity to command Sevastopol, whereas the terrain to the north was 'below the place'. If there were a landing to the south, it should be at Balaclava from which good roads led to Sevastopol. D'Hilliers had heard that the garrison numbered about 40,000, but admitted that intelligence was 'very vague'; and he was extremely cautious about reports that the population of the Crimea was hostile to the Russians. He had learnt from 'the Seraskier' that the Turks could only promise 10,000 infantry, 3,000 cavalry and thirty artillery pieces, if required to invade the Crimea.[20]

By mid-March Britain, France and Turkey were looking to a commitment each of some 5,000 men for an invasion of the Crimea. But Raglan emphasized to de Ros that the nature of any action by Britain and France depended on Burgoyne's report. Writing to Raglan from Constantinople on 8 March, Sir John cautiously supported a show of strength in the Mediterranean – presumably involving the current concentration of troops at Malta – but advised against moving to Turkey. Nevertheless plans to entrench around the Turkish capital were considered in London and declared 'excellent' by the Prince Consort. Burgoyne, possibly in the light of domestic enthusiasm, went on into Bulgaria, though his keenness for operations east of the Mediterranean scarcely heightened. The port of Varna through which troops must pass and be supplied, 'does not afford shelter either against certain winds or against certain Russians, should the latter be inclined to make mischief' he observed. In a memorandum to Lord Stratford de Redcliffe on 22 March, Burgoyne specifically disapproved of an attack on the Crimea.[21]

But British troops were sent to Turkey. On 17 March Newcastle informed Raglan that the 2nd Battalion, The Rifle Brigade, and two companies of the Sappers and Miners were ready for immediate embarkation from Malta; and on the 30th the first troopships cleared Valetta for Gallipoli.[22] The French had already dispatched some 15,000 troops with two Generals (Canrobert and Bosquet), so Sir George Brown, a 'British officer of corresponding station', commanded the British contingent proceeding 'to the scene of operations at Gallipoli ... in advance of the army under Lord Raglan'. Brown's force was to dig in preparatory to Raglan's arrival, Brown himself must ensure that the Commissariat amassed 'the necessary supplies'. On arrival he was to report to Her Majesty's Ambassador at Constantinople, though he would be 'neither under His Excellency's orders, nor dependent on him for instructions as to your proceedings'. In his order to Lieutenant-General James Fergusson, commanding at Malta, to embark the troops, Newcastle admitted to no 'accurate information' about the number of vessels available for this task but 'assumed' that 4,000 men could be transported. Neither precision of information nor planning had thus far characterized the operation.[23]

Brown left England on 23 March and wrote to Raglan from Paris next day. He had had an inauspicious start to his journey. At Dover the water had been too low for the packet to berth alongside the new pier so passengers were rowed out. The same ignominious procedure took place at Calais. In Paris Brown had visited Lord Cowley and Marshal St Arnaud, who would command the French contingent; Brown was not impressed by him. Brown explained that the train journey from Calais to Paris had taken seven hours, Paris to Marseilles (arriving 26 March) three days by road. He arrived at Malta on the 29th. That day Raglan wrote to him to say that the declaration of war had been published the previous day and that it was 'very desirous' that troops be moved from Malta to Gallipoli – an unnecessary duplication of orders. On arrival in Turkey Brown should contact the British Consul in the Dardanelles immediately. Brown thus had slightly conflicting orders from Newcastle and Raglan, though Raglan's had not reached him before he left Malta on 31 March.[24]

As Brown and the advance guard sailed eastwards Raglan's own position and that of his staff consolidated. With increase in size of the original force, Lieutenant Leicester Curzon, The Rifle Brigade, was appointed an extra ADC on 13 March. Nine days later Raglan received the Queen's Commission, countersigned by Newcastle, but forwarded to him by Hardinge, 'as Commander of the Forces to be employed in the Dominions of the Sublime Ottoman Porte'. Prior to this, when details of his pay had been transmitted to him, Raglan had been described as 'commanding the Army on a Particular Service'. Sir John Kirkland from the Ordnance had then explained that the Secretary at War had authorized him to pay Raglan £459.18s.8d., representing 50 days' pay plus embarkation allowance, less £13.16s.4d. 'income duty', and an additional £452.10s.0d. as an extraordinary field allowance from 1 January until 30 June 1854, making a total of £912.8s.8d. Similarly, Steele (Military Secretary) would receive £46.2s.4d. plus £45.5s.0d. (£91.7s.4d.), each of the ADCs £23.1s.2d. plus £31.13s.6d. (£54.14s.8d.).[25]

While preparing to follow Brown to Turkey, Raglan acknowledged a letter from his sister-in-law in Vienna: 'I love you very much, and look forward to the time when we may meet again with the greatest pleasure' – a wish sadly never to be fulfilled. But he did not feel 'that it would be thought right' for him to travel to Vienna, though he had secured Government approval for her son (Burghersh) to do so. In his letter Raglan sent details of Priscilla's legacy from her late mother, Lady Mornington: £2,658.6s.7d. in cash (with Messrs Coutts), 'flute linen' valued at £2,009.19s.11d. and £13,000 in stocks. It is not clear whether Emily received a similar legacy or that this was the gross amount to be divided between the two surviving daughters. Either way, Lady Raglan could no longer plead poverty.[27]

The relationship of the three Allied armies destined to take the field in the Crimea had now been uneasily settled. On 2 March Raglan had explained to Cowley that, on his insistence, Newcastle had agreed to keep the armies 'separate as much and as long as possible'. And ten days later, when national representatives signed a tripartite treaty (due for ratification six weeks hence) formalizing 'Military Aid ... in defence of the Ottoman territories in Europe and Asia against Russian aggression', joint consultation between the three independent Allied commanders-in-chief in the field was also agreed. Hence St Arnaud, commander of the French, asked to see Raglan in Paris before setting off for Turkey, holding that there was no need to await the return of Burgoyne and Ardent before deciding the 'dispositions and destination of Allied troops'.[27]

Russian failure to respond to Clarendon's ultimatum of 27 February resulted in the declaration of war to which Raglan had referred in his letter to Brown of 29 March. Two days earlier Queen Victoria had sent a message to both Houses of Parliament saying that she felt 'bound to afford active assistance to her ally the Sultan against unprovoked aggression', and the next day the official declaration was published in *The London Gazette*.[28] As yet Raglan was still in England. Not for long. On 5 April he received instructions from Hardinge couched in precisely the same terms as those issued to Wellington in 1809. 'Her Majesty having been graciously pleased to appoint Your Lordship to the command of a detachment of her army to be employed upon a particular service, I have to desire that you will be pleased to take the earliest opportunity to assume the command of that force, and carry into effect such instructions as Your Lordship may receive from Her Majesty's Ministers' – in effect, the Secretary of State for War and the Colonies under whose direct control Raglan now came. Nevertheless Raglan would be obliged to keep the CinC informed of all 'military transactions' and notify him of vacancies to be filled. Hardinge added: 'As in so distant and so extended a command, my Instructions can of course be only general, Your Lordship must consequently on occasions necessarily act on your own judgement and discretion.' Not quite Pontius Pilate. Interestingly, in view of later developments, Hardinge anticipated a sickness, as distinct from casualty, rate of 30 per cent in the expeditionary force.[29]

Five days later Newcastle formally appointed Raglan in the Queen's name 'to command the army ordered for service in Turkey', making clear that 'your correspondence will be conducted direct with me'. He would leave 'you free to act according to conscience ... [though] I do not claim for myself any freedom from responsibility for what you may do'. The Secretary of State went on: 'Much must necessarily be left to the free exercise of your own judgement and decision on the spot'; but in practice Newcastle laid down Raglan's course of action fairly rigidly and thereafter frequently offered detailed comments on tactics and strategy. In the letter of 10 April Raglan was instructed to proceed to Unkiar Skelessi (in Asia Minor), leaving Brown with 5,000 men at Gallipoli, preparatory to sending troops to prepare 'lines of defence in front of Constantinople between the Black Sea and the Sea of Marmara'. Raglan must 'consult' with the French 'upon all occasions' and also the Turkish commander (Omar Pasha) so as 'not to interfere with his operations'. Vice-Admiral Dundas, commanding the British fleet, would 'co-operate ... so far as the means at his disposal will enable him to do so', though he was not in any way under Raglan's direction. This diversity of responsibility in the theatre of war would make neither for easy planning nor for conduct of operations. Moreover from the outset Raglan was warned by the Secretary of State that a landing in the Crimea seemed likely.

Referring in a secret communication to his official 'dispatch of this date', Newcastle ordered Raglan to make 'careful but secret inquiry into the present amount and condition of the Russian Force in the Crimea and the strength of the Fortress of Sebastopol'. His 'first duty' would be to prevent a Russian advance on Constantinople, but if the enemy made no 'onward movement it may become essential for the attainment of the objects of the war that some operations of an official character should be undertaken by the Allied armies ... No blow ... struck at the southern extremities of the Russian Empire would be so effective for this purpose as the taking of Sebastopol', and with it the destruction of the Russian fleet. Raglan must secure information because Newcastle admitted that 'on many points ... little or nothing is at present known in England'. What were the landing possibilities, had the defences been strengthened since they had been 'lately' (January) inspected by Captain Drummond? Newcastle believed that Sevastopol's main water supply was eight miles from the port: what were the extent of the stocks in Sevastopol? These and other detailed questions were listed, with little (if any) appreciation of the geographical distances, terrain, or other problems involved. The Duke noted that the siege train would not reach Turkey until three to four weeks after the troops. The inference was that Raglan would have completed his intelligence-gathering by then and be ready to attack the Crimea. So much for armchair strategists.[30]

After a farewell audience with the Queen, Raglan left London by train for Dover with the Duke of Cambridge during the evening of 10 April. A crowd of some 300 cheered them off. The 78-year-old Duchess of Gloucester explained to Lady Westmorland that she 'made a great exertion to see dear Lord Raglan' before he departed. 'It was a painful parting for me. He looked well, but fatigued with business and in good spirits.' He was 'quite charming' to the Duchess, but became 'quite unnerved' when he spoke of 'Lady Raglan and his daughters'. Raglan and Cambridge crossed the Channel in the steamer *Vivid* during the early hours of the following morning to be formally greeted at Calais by the mayor before entraining for Paris where according to Cambridge they arrived at 9.30, though Raglan put the arrival at between 8 and 9 a.m. They both agreed, however, on the warmth of their reception. Raglan explained to Richard that after 'a very good journey' they were accorded 'all honors at the station' where the Minister of War (Marshal Vaillant) and Cowley met them. Travelling from there in the Imperial carriage and escorted by a detachment of Guards – 'the smartest regiment of Cavalry in the Emperor's service' – he and Cambridge saw the Emperor and Empress at The Tuileries after breakfast together with the Grande-Duchesse de Baden, Prince Jérôme (destined to serve in the Crimea) and Princess Matilde. That evening the two British officers dined in a party of fifty in the Galerie de Diane of the former royal palace, 'and the whole thing was magnificently done'. Cambridge also attended the opera that evening and it is possible that Raglan accompanied him.

The next day (Wednesday 12 April) Raglan went to the Palace again in an Imperial coach, then mounted and rode with the Emperor to review 25 battalions, 42 squadrons and 36 pieces of artillery on the Champs du Mars. To reach the parade-ground they had to ride two miles, and 'what is a great novelty in Paris there were numerous cries of "*Vive l'Angleterre*"'. The parade was 'superb', the cavalry 'very efficient, well mounted and move well', the infantry 'in general ... small but active and intelligent with very soldierlike appearance'. To Sir Hew Ross he enthused about the artillery. The Emperor was proud of the 12pdrs which had been bored up from 8pdrs; and Raglan suggested that the Ordnance might try boring up an English 9pdr. That evening and the following, Raglan again dined at The Tuileries. During the afternoon of 13 April he had a private interview with the Emperor, whom he had known in London as the French exile Louis Napoleon and had taken to meet Wellington at Apsley House. Although shown Napoleon III's instruction to St Arnaud, according to Kinglake Raglan avoided all questions of command, control and strategy, concentrating on the practical disposition of the two forces in Turkey. After the private meeting the two men joined Prince Jérôme, Cambridge, Marshal Vaillant, St Arnaud and de Ros. Like Raglan,

St Arnaud deflected attempts to discuss hypothetical situations, concentrating on practical problems. The generals, he maintained, could deal with difficulties on the spot as they arose. The French did have special reservations about the Turks whom they believed only possessed good artillery, fearing too that their commander (Omar Pasha) might embarrass them with his unorthodox military style. Raglan exerted his diplomatic charm to effect, and possible difficulties of this nature were, as St Arnaud agreed, not pursued. On Saturday 15 April he dined with Prince Jérôme who was 'magnificently lodged at the Palais Royal'.[31]

Meanwhile, in a private letter to Raglan in Paris on 13 April, Newcastle assured him that if 'occasionally assailed' by an 'exacting public', the Secretary of State would shield Raglan from 'their ill humour'. He went on to promise him intelligence about the defences of Sevastopol, and the same day advised Queen Victoria that he (Newcastle) was in the process of drafting 'a secret dispatch' to Raglan concerning an attack on the Russian naval port. Thus, from an early stage, a military assault on Sevastopol was officially under consideration.[32]

Raglan left the French capital on the morning of Tuesday 18 April; Cambridge departed later that day, intending to travel via Vienna and Corfu. From Marseilles on 21 April Raglan described to his sister-in-law Priscilla his somewhat eventful journey south through France. He travelled by train to Chalon-sur-Saône where the railway ended and he was 'obliged' to go down the Saône by boat to Lyons. On reaching Lyons, because of the 'lowness of the water in the Rhone' he went on by carriage with his ADCs, de Ros and Major Wellesley, plus all his baggage. The carriage proved 'rough' and 'noisy' and the journey therefore 'very fatiguing'. Having left Chalon between 5 and 6 a.m., they reached Valence just before midnight, then travelled further to Avignon on 20 April, arriving just too late for the train. When the party eventually reached Marseilles that evening a gale prevented all sailings and the adverse weather continued next day. The local forecast was that it would be the same next day: 'This is unfortunate and very tiresome,' Raglan mused. His estimate that he would leave Paris on 17 April and Marseilles three days later, enabling him 'to be able to shake you [Brown] by the hand on the 29th', before moving swiftly on from Gallipoli, seemed already well adrift.[33]

In fact the bad weather delayed sailing from Marseilles for 36 hours until late on 22 April. After a rough, 66-hour crossing Raglan reached Malta during the morning of 25 April. He stayed there only twelve hours, long enough to change to the steamship *Emu* because *Caradoc* had engine trouble; and, incredibly, he landed at Gallipoli a day ahead of schedule (early on 28 April). With Mrs Estcourt, wife of his Adjutant-General, he strolled unostentatiously from the landing-stage to the town where he met Brown, and sailed that evening for Constantinople. The following morning he reached the Turkish capital, reporting to Hardinge on 30 April that, although as yet without artillery or sufficient 'warlike stores', Brown was 'going famously at Gallipoli'. Heavy rain and strong winds on 29 April had prevented Raglan from crossing the Bosporus Straits to Scutari on the eastern shore, his immediate destination. Already de Ros had secured Raglan's approval for the housing of the reinforcements 'in excellent barracks' – not so gracious on closer inspection – 'notwithstanding the intended destination of Unkiar Skelessi'. Thus Raglan intended to establish his headquarters at Scutari. Nigel Kingscote, who had arrived in Constantinople on 24 April, fleshed out Raglan's account in writing to Richard. Confirming that Raglan, Steele and Poulett Somerset had arrived early on 29 April, he remarked that Raglan looked 'very well'. Kingscote thought that Raglan and Steele would remain for two or three nights in the British Embassy before moving to 'a house the other side of the water at Scutari'.[34]

While Raglan was in Paris British warships had been in action. On 13 April *Furious*, seeking to withdraw the British and French consuls from Odessa, was fired on by shore batteries. Other vessels close by retaliated the following day and, on 16 April after arrival of reinforcements, Dundas pounded the defences with a 900-gun broadside. A ten-hour bombardment on 22 April devastated Odessa's military installations leaving 200 dead and 900 wounded, but five damaged British ships were towed to Varna. Nigel Kingscote, with Raglan at Constantinople when details of the action arrived, commented that the fleet had 'the honor of opening the ball with Russia', and a peaceful outcome to the overall dispute now seemed remote.[35]

Information about Russian troop strengths and dispositions continued to be sparse however. Writing to Raglan in Paris, Newcastle had confidently predicted that 'several consuls and vice-consuls in the neighbourhood of the seat of War' would send copies of their reports to the Foreign Office directly to Raglan, who was instructed to transmit them in turn to the French. By the end of April very little useful information had been gleaned from these quarters. Earlier that month Assistant Commissary-General Smith had written to the Treasury from Constantinople: 'It is said in authentic quarters that there are 70,000 Russian troops in the Crimea, and that Sebastopol is so well defended by both land and sea as to render it impregnable.' Sir Charles Trevelyan wrote in the margin, 'my belief is that this is a studied Russian illusion', forwarded Smith's report with his own comment to Newcastle, who in turn sent it to Raglan. Stratford de Redcliffe provided more depressing figures for Raglan. The Ambassador in Constantinople estimated 120-140,000 Russian troops in Moldavia and Wallachia, plus possibly another 20,000 in Bessarabia, backed by strong cavalry and artillery. Furthermore the Turks had withdrawn from the Dobruja to fall back on Shumla, leaving only irregular cavalry in the marshland. If this sparse information had even only a passing acquaintance with reality, the task facing the Allies was formidable.[36]

Lack of firm information about Russian troop strengths did not curb extravagant ideas about the deployment of Allied forces. Brigadier-General Tylden (Raglan's commanding engineer) and the Prince Consort favoured an advance forthwith to Varna; Burgoyne believed that various attacks on Georgia, across the Danube and against Anapa could be carried out in addition to invasion of the Crimea. And the British Consul in Athens sought involvement in Macedonia. Raglan courteously thanked him for the latter thought, but explained that no current plans existed to occupy 'any detached fronts ... by Her Majesty's Government'. However, doubts about the fighting ability of his Turkish ally could not have helped Raglan. From Belgrade Consul-General T. de Fonblanque noted that he had been instructed to communicate with Raglan 'especially upon Military Subjects', and with obvious reluctance therefore sent extracts from a report by him to de Redcliffe of 25 April: 'Many persons – presumably competent to form a judgement, and undoubtedly free from Russian bias in arriving at it – confirm my belief that the Sultan's troops can only be depended upon for the purposes of desultory warfare, and the defence of Lines.' Not very encouraging.[37]

At this time though, as ever, Raglan's family proved both an abiding support and an affectionate commitment. From Paris he wrote the first of a series of long letters to his children, which sustained both them and him in the ensuing, traumatic months. Of them all Charlotte proved the most favoured correspondent possibly because as his elder daughter she had been a special comfort to him as her mother visibly wilted. Charlotte, however, was ill during the early part of April and Kitty wrote to her father as soon as he left England. On 12 April Raglan thanked her 'for your affectionate letter' which contained news of 'your dear Mama and dear Howes ... Charlotte I am confident is going on well though I fear it may be some time before she is quite well'. He continued: 'You will I know take care of her and your dear Mama', referring without elaboration to the 'sad shock' that Lady Raglan had recently endured. Kitty must take care of herself because she had endured a difficult few weeks coping with the family problems. 'I will always take care of myself,' he added. He excused his short letter by explaining that the review that day had taken four hours and that he still had much correspondence to deal with: 'God bless you my dear Kitty, Your affectionate Raglan.' Writing to Richard and Priscilla, he showed continued concern about his daughters, especially Charlotte, who on 17 April appeared to be making 'some progress', though remaining weak, seven days later to be improving 'though not rapidly'. In the middle of the month, Lady Raglan was insisting that Kitty go to bed early because of her obvious fatigue; but towards the end of April Raglan could assure Priscilla that 'Emily and Kitty are pretty well.' Thus, during his first month away, he wrote at length to Richard, Kitty and Priscilla, showing deep concern about Charlotte's condition. Given

Charlotte's nervous prostration when Raglan died, her illness may well have been linked to his departure from London.

Because Raglan's correspondence with his wife has not survived, the number and nature of his letters to her in April or later cannot be gauged. On the day of his departure he did write a practical letter to 'my dearest Emily'. As he had changed his name since making his will in 1842, he had made another 'precisely to the same effect'. Mr Robert Dundas had replaced the late Duke of Beaufort as one of the 'executees'. 'I have thought it best to leave everything to you having every confidence that you will do what is right by our children, but wishing to shew them a proof of my affection, I beg you to give dear Charlotte and dear Kitty one thousand pounds each and also the same sum to dear Richard as soon as arrangements can be made for that purpose and these can I hope be effected without difficulty, as independently as the assurances upon my life, I have stock standing in my name.' He concluded: 'I shall be anxious also that you should give each of my children some memento of me and that you should retain something of me, and regard it always as having been mine ... God bless you and them, Your most devoted and affectionate Raglan.'

Other legal affairs had also to be put in order. His sister-in-law, Priscilla, later wrote: 'It is *incredible* to how many persons he was executor, trustee, and guardian, and how he found time in the midst of all his business to attend to so much for other people.' She added: 'Before he left England ... [he] placed in separate drawers all papers relating to separate trusts, and all in the most perfect order.'[38]

Raglan would need the stability of a devoted family in the months ahead, not least because friction with the French soon occurred notwithstanding the pomp and promises of his stay in Paris. The medical and supply deficiencies identified by Brown and W.H. Russell at Gallipoli, irrationally but understandably given the tradition of Anglo-French hostility, began to be ascribed to Britain's ally. The French, arriving in force first, had unfairly stripped the countryside and commandeered the best accommodation. On 17 April Burgoyne warned Raglan that French behaviour at Gallipoli could prejudice the good effect of the dispatch of the Allied force. Friction would be disastrous. Hence Raglan's first General Order from Constantinople on 30 April noted: 'The Army will be, for the first time, associated with an Ally to whom it has been the lot of the British nation to be opposed in the field for many centuries.' There was a need, their commander reminded his men, 'to co-operate most warmly' with them now. The fact that Raglan issued the order in these terms testified to the insidious potential for discord. It would not be the last time that his powers of conciliation would be called upon.[39]

On the first day of May, Brown obliquely poured scorn on the French at Gallipoli in reporting to Raglan the arrival of Prince Jérôme, 'the least prepossessing specimen of Royalty'. More seriously, soon after St

Arnaud reached Turkey he sought quickly to expand his command at the expense of Raglan and, to some extent, the Turkish commander (Omar Pasha). He first argued that the Turkish irregular cavalry (the Bashi Bazouks) should be brought under French command then, dramatically, on 11 May called on Raglan to claim that the Turkish government had placed its entire field force (including Omar Pasha) under his control. Raglan mildly observed that his orders required him to act separately and that Stratford de Redcliffe appeared unaware of subordination of the Turks to St Arnaud. Two days later Colonel Hugh Rose, British liaison officer with the Turks, informed Raglan that St Arnaud was persisting with his claim that the Sultan had given him command of the Turkish Army. That day (13 May) also, the French and British commanders met Lord Stratford in Constantinople. St Arnaud had produced plans for absorption of Turkish formations into French divisions and the dismounting of 1,500 Bashi Bazouks to provide much needed horses for the French, claiming that the Sultan had agreed. Raglan pointed out the impracticability of splitting up the Turkish Army, which was then actively engaging the Russians along the Danube. Both he and Stratford de Redcliffe referred to the formal treaty of alliance, which placed each of the Allied armies under separate national command; and Raglan confirmed to Newcastle that the British Ambassador had persuaded St Arnaud to adhere to the tripartite agreement: 'The Marshal saw that our opinions were stronger than our expression of them,' he enigmatically added. But the French commander did not give up. On 23 May Lord Stratford warned Raglan that St Arnaud had arranged an interview with the Sultan at the Palace of Tziraghan at 11.15 a.m. the next day and advised Raglan to be present. Frustrated once more over the Turkish Army, St Arnaud suggested that in view of French numerical superiority he should exercise ultimate authority when the British and French forces acted together. Raglan patiently pointed out that he was under the orders of the British Government.[40] In fact, independent of St Arnaud, Raglan had quite properly quickly established contact with the Sultan. On 4 May he had a private audience with him at noon; and on 24 May Raglan and the Sultan reviewed the British force on the occasion of the Queen's Birthday Parade. On 27 May, however, Raglan suspected that St Arnaud had not yet abandoned hopes of 'acquiring the chief command'. Time would confirm the accuracy of this fear.[41]

During May the British Expeditionary Force began to take shape. On 1 May Raglan's General Order noted that Her Majesty had been 'graciously pleased' to appoint certain officers to staff appointments and, in outline, published details of the formations soon to be expected. In a dispatch to Newcastle the following day, however, he explained that he was unable to raise irregular cavalry because of lack of horses. Indeed, worry about a shortfall in cavalry prompted Raglan to ask William Monsell (Clerk of the Ordnance) 'to prevail upon the Duke of Newcastle' to send him the 10th Hussars from Bombay. Hardinge expressed his approval of Raglan's arrangement of his divisions and brigades, and Rear-Admiral Edward Boxer notified Raglan that he had been ordered by Dundas to liaise with him about 'a movement of the British Land Forces [which] will in all probability take place very shortly.' Nine days later Boxer received his warrant as Admiral Superintendent 'from the entrance of the Dard-anelles to the East Entrance of the Bosporus at the Black Sea', in effect con-trolling the passage of shipping and provision of transport. Unfortunately for Raglan's peace of mind, Boxer's warrant specifically made him respon-sible only to the Admiralty or a superior naval officer. Towards the end of May more British reinforcements arrived. By the end of the month all the infantry of the first four divisions – with the exception of the 42nd High-landers – had reached Turkey. Of the cavalry, the 8th Hussars and 17th Lancers had arrived, together with the First Division of the Royal Artillery. The rest were anticipated shortly.[42]

Raglan had by now settled into his headquarters near Scutari. The day after he arrived in Constantinople, having spent the night at the British Embassy, in the evening he walked to the Bosporus, 'took a native boat with three rowers who had two sculls each and went over to Scutari'. Before the light faded and it was time to return, he visited Sir George de Lacy Evans and also the three large barracks 'inhabited by three of our regiments and millions of fleas and other vermin'. The horses, though, he noted, were 'pretty well'. The following day (1 May), hearing that a house had been secured for him close to the troops and having bought eight baggage animals or servants' horses, he went over to Scutari again 'rowed by ten men with a flag at the bow'. Once ashore, he mounted his horse Miss Mary and accompanied by de Lacy Evans, Sir Colin Campbell, Major-General H. J. W. Bentinck and his own staff 'except Calthorpe who did not appear I do not know why', he visited the camp. 'Soon after three' he looked at the chosen house, close to the sea, for which sentries would be provided by nearby Guards' units. The house was a wooden two-storeyed building with kitchen and stables attached. The male and female quarters were separated, though 'each contains a good deal of accommodation'; and Raglan would occupy the female side which 'looks clean'. However he 'immediately' arranged for a fatigue party to clean the stables. While Raglan was at the British camp, Prince Napoleon arrived in Constantinople and 'has been lodged by the Sultan in a magnificent palace on the Water'. Raglan recrossed the Bosporus on the evening of 1 May to meet the Prince: 'He received me most kindly and has a good manner and a pleasing countenance', looking 'a good deal' like his sister, Princess Matilde. That evening, too, the Belgian, Spanish, Sardinian and Neapolitan Ministers dined at the British Embassy where Stratford de Redcliffe urged him to remain. Raglan was certainly comfortable there, but he was separated by the Bosporus from his troops. Nigel Kingscote, therefore, began the transfer of Raglan's luggage to the new headquarters on the eastern side of the Straits during the morning of 2 May and that evening Raglan dined there for the first time.[43]

Raglan admitted, however, to being uncomfortable in the climate. 'The sun and the cold wind have already attacked my face notwithstanding that I had got a white coton [sic] umbrella which Cator gave me and which everybody used at Malta,' he told Charlotte. He was, though, pleased with his staff. 'I never saw a finer fellow than Steele. I am very much pleased with Poulett too who made himself very agreeable during the voyage.' Bentinck 'is beyond measure proved of his command ... Sir Colin Campbell is delighted at my having placed him at the head of the Highland Brigade only one regiment of which is as yet [1 May] arrived.' Richard Airey had been put in Brown's division as he had requested. Raglan settled into 'the wooden house' quickly though not without problems. Reaching the new headquarters late on 2 May, he found Kingscote 'in despair' because the cook had not appeared. 'The poor devil' had landed at Scutari and 'for a long while' could not find anybody to tell him where Raglan lived. Eventually he did arrive and produced 'an excellent soup and under the circumstances a very tolerable dinner'. At that meal, served at 7 p.m. on 2 May, for the first time Raglan had four ADCs and Military Secretary together. 'The whole five made themselves very agreeable and we sat till past eleven not drinking but talking. I could not have had a better lot.' Soon they and Raglan were hard at work. But at the end of the month Kingscote showed himself disillusioned with the house which had seemed so pleasant: 'The sooner [they left] the better as we are sick of this place besides I do not think the house we are in is healthy as all of us have been seedy chiefly with diarrhoea whereas nothing can be more healthy than the people in camp have been.' Raglan was rather 'seedy' at present, but on the whole 'really wonderfully well', especially as he did enough work 'for a dozen men in writing and seeing people'. He was getting exercise, using 'the old mare' when visiting troops (such as the formal inspections of the Light and 1st divisions 16-17 May) and Shadrach for 'a quiet ride'. Kingscote noted that two Frenchmen had been attached to the headquarters for liaison duties, but both remained in Constantinople. So far as security was concerned, 'my Lord is as you know as close as wax'. Apart from him, the Military Secretary and Assistant Military Secretary [Curzon], 'we know nothing' at Headquarters.[44]

In the middle of the month the British liaison officer with Omar Pasha reported to Raglan from Varna that, on 15 May, Russian troops had crossed the Danube and the following day had laid siege to the fortress of Silistria. Shortly afterwards Raglan provided more details for Hardinge. By the third week of May the Russians had 70,000 men 'on this side of the Danube'. They had invested Silistria, were firing on it from an island in the river and had already attacked the outworks. Captain (later Lieutenant-Colonel) L.A. Simmons further reported that the enemy had extended operations to attack Jelauli Tabia in a heavy hailstorm on 24

May, but had been repulsed. These developments caused 'so much appre-hension that Marshal St Arnaud and myself have determined to move our Forces to Varna, and in front of it, although from the want of means of Transport, we are not yet in a state to take the field, or act on the offen-sive.'[45]

Raglan had already been to Bulgaria on a reconnaissance. On Thursday 18 May he, Steele and Kingscote travelled to Varna where Raglan held a Council of War with St Arnaud and Omar Pasha. On the Saturday morning the three commanders decided to go to Shumla, the Turkish headquarters. The large party set out, all riding 'except the three great swells', who went in carriages with Raglan's 'like a large tea chest'. At first the country was beautifully open, then gradually brushwood built up to a height of seven to eight feet. From 4 p.m. onwards rain poured down, making the unmetalled road 'like a ploughed field'. As night fell they reached a deserted village whose inhabitants had fled through fear of Cossacks and Turkish Bashi Bazouks. The staff had nothing to eat nor any shelter, being forced to lie down in the open in wet clothes. 'Luckily' Raglan had bedding with him and occupied a habitable room which he shared with Omar Pasha. Resuming the journey at dawn, they arrived at Shumla at about 10 a.m., the commanders having reviewed 6,000 Turkish troops on the outskirts of the town. After breakfast and a couple of hours' rest, Raglan and his staff 'rode through some of the encampments and round a good many of the forts'. 'We were wonderfully struck', Nigel Kingscote recorded, 'with the Turkish troops; though badly clothed and tough-looking men, they are stout and they move most capitally quickly and quietly and they have proved they can fight for I believe that at Silis-tria they are fighting well.' The Turkish commander made a most favourable impression on the whole British contingent. 'Omar Pasha is a capital fellow ... He is a sporting looking fellow and sits well on his horse in a plain grey frock coat and long jack boots, he is fond of horses and made my Lord and Marshal St Arnaud a present of one each.' The horse that he gave to Raglan was 'a beautiful grey Arab of the highest caste and is perfectly quiet'. Pleased though he was with the gift, Raglan would rather not have had it, for he had to give to Omar Pasha in return the chestnut mare which he had bought just before leaving England. Raglan left Shumla on Monday morning and, with a change of horses half-way back, reached Varna at 9 p.m. He arrived at his headquarters near Scutari at 1 p.m. on Tuesday 23 May, having been away for almost six days. 'The whole expedition' was 'hard', but Kingscote believed that Raglan was none the worse for his considerable exertions.[46]

The lengthy reconnaissance had allowed Raglan to assess both the terrain of Bulgaria and the situation in the area of the Danube and the Balkans. Writing to Hardinge, he estimated that 45,000 Turks were in a well-fortified camp at Shumla, and praised their military qualities. He emphasized, however, the true worth of the reconnaissance: he had made the acquaintance of 'Omer [sic] Pasha with whom I am much pleased'. That was a bonus, and would prove helpful when negotiating with the successive French commanders in Bulgaria and the Crimea. Moreover he had been able to reassure the Turkish commander that the Sultan was not planning to dismiss him.[47]

Raglan did enjoy personal advancement at this time. Following the death of the Marquis of Anglesey, he became 'Colonel of our Regiment of Royal Horse Guards Blue' on 8 May, while still Master-General of the Ordnance and, officially, 'Commander-in-Chief of the Eastern Army'. Hardinge's justification to the Queen for this appointment was impressive: 'General Lord Raglan during the Peninsular War filled a most important situation on the staff of the late Duke of Wellington, and since the close of that War, from the period of the Battle of Waterloo, where he lost an arm, he has given eminent proofs of unwearied zeal and great ability in Your Majesty's Service, especially during the many years he has conducted the arduous duties of Military Secretary since which Your Majesty has been most graciously pleased to confer upon him the appointment of Master-General of the Ordnance, and recently to entrust him with the Command in the Field of a large proportion of Your Majesty's Army serving in the East.'[48]

Professional recognition of this nature gave Raglan satisfaction, though he did decline the formal offer of the Order of the Mejidie from the Sultan. And his family, also, continued to afford him pleasure and comfort. One long letter to Charlotte from the British Embassy in Constantinople was completed over four days. In this he describes in detail his arrival, movements since reaching the Turkish capital and occupation of his 'wooden house' near Scutari. He mentioned more personal matters. His 'canteen is the admiration of every body', but the staff at Stanhope Street had forgotten to pack two silver cups – one given to him by 'poor Alava', the other belonging to 'poor Arthur', which had been sent back from India by Bob Wood. Could Charlotte arrange for these to be sent on? He wanted her also to arrange for 'the *second* edition of Mansel', which Raglan thought he had put in the bookcase at home, to be forwarded to him, so that he could give it to Lord Stratford. His bed in the headquarters building was 'excellent' and his sleeping room 'comfortable', even though 'it has eleven windows in it!!' That afternoon [3 May] he had recrossed to Constantinople. He and Lord Stratford had then travelled by Sedan chair to the French Ambassador's. General d'Hilliers he found to be 'a gentleman' about his own age, who 'has lost rather more of his left arm than Hardinge'. He would be giving a ball on the following Tuesday, and he asked Raglan to invite British officers. The dinner on 3 May was to welcome Prince Napoleon. Some 40 to 50 guests were present. Sitting 'between a Turk who spoke no language but his own and the Sardinian Minister who is not a lively bird', Raglan was 'bored'. Apart from de Lacy Evans, Raglan and Lord Stratford were the only Englishmen present, though he did note 'a very nice young Prince of Wurtemburg [sic], an officer in the Austrian Navy'. As soon as he emerged from dinner Prince Napoleon 'lighted a cigar and many others followed his example' to Raglan's evident distaste. He was afraid that his full dress uniform would smell of smoke and had asked his servant Ferdinand to air it. Continuing the letter at 'night' on 4 May, Raglan thanked his elder daughter for her letter received that morning. 'I rejoice my dearest Charlotte to hear that your health is daily improving', and that she was making 'wonderfully rapid progress' after such 'a sad illness'. On 30 April, the day after his arrival in Constantinople, he had written 'a volume' to Lady Raglan and noted that he had also written to her 'or one of you' from Avignon and Marseilles. News of his departure from Marseilles on 22 April had been telegraphed to England, so no doubt Charlotte had read about it in *John Bull* the next day [Sunday]. He concluded, 'Yours affectionately PAPA' – a touching gesture – and apologized in a postscript of 5 May that he had been 'too interrupted' to compose 'a long letter' to Lady Raglan, noting enigmatically that Lord Lucan had arrived.[49]

Like Prince Napoleon, the Duke of Cambridge was given a formal welcoming dinner by the Sultan. Raglan attended as one of the guests. He never betrayed any sign of dismay that one of his subordinate commanders, as a member of the British royal family, should be accorded special treatment, including superior accommodation to his own. When Cambridge's original 'fine castle' on the European side of the Straits proved 'inconvenient', another palace was made available near Scutari. Given Raglan's dissatisfaction with his own house, it must all have been galling. Yet Cambridge remarked specifically that 'Lord Raglan is very kind, friendly and splendid'. At no time, then or later when Cambridge's health led to prolonged absence from duty, did Raglan intimate in any way that his royal subordinate disturbed him, though the situation could not have been easy.[50]

During the last week in May and the first half of June Allied troops left the Straits for Varna and its immediate vicinity. But lack of supplies soon forced the British to move further inland, and before the close of June St Arnaud complained to Raglan that French and British commissaries were bidding against one another to secure local produce. Nigel Kingscote pithily identified the soldiers' plight: 'Bread is our greatest difficulty here as it is all sour.'. Nor had promised equipment arrived from England: on 15 June Raglan complained to Hardinge that the 3rd Division remained 1,500 Minié stands short. Ten days later he drew Newcastle's attention to a deficiency, which would plague him throughout the campaign: 'The means of [land] transport form our principal want and a most serious one.' There would never be sufficient carts and drivers available for hire.[51]

Sea transport also caused problems. Requirements could only be passed to the appropriate Admiralty department in England or to Admiral Boxer in the Straits. In turn, civilian vessels had to be chartered – neither easy, nor cheap. As early as 8 June Newcastle warned Raglan that the charters of several ships obtained for four to six months by the Admiralty were now running out; comforting news for a general seeking to build up the strength of his force prior to engaging the enemy. Raglan had to apply to Boxer for *Caradoc* to take him from Scutari to Varna on the afternoon of 15 June. Twelve days later de Ros similarly requested transport from Boxer for four Turkish battalions and twenty pieces of field artillery 'destined to join Lord Raglan' and now ready. That same day de Ros thanked Raglan for attempting to resolve difficulties that had arisen between him and Admiral Dundas – possibly over transport – 'in the midst of so much business', though de Ros feared that Dundas did not seek a reconciliation. He added that 'whispers' were in circulation in London against him (de Ros) which may have been the first signs of the strain that would lead to the Quartermaster-General's premature return to England. At home the War Office asked the Admiralty to provide steam transport to convey the second battering-ram to Turkey – unlikely, therefore, to arrive until early August.[52]

In his correspondence Raglan mentioned only minor health problems. On 9 June he admitted to Kitty 'some trouble' with his stomach after returning from his reconnaissance to Shumla. From the beginning of that week he had experienced 'symptoms of diarrhoea', which made him 'uncomfortable', so that Lord Stratford offered him accommodation; and he went over to Constantinople on the afternoon of 8 June: 'I was very poorly all yesterday [8 June] and had no desire to do any thing but play the part of Lord Sprawl.' 'Today' he felt much better, with the diarrhoea almost stopped and himself 'nearly right again'. The headquarters house near Scutari, despite its initial attractiveness, had proved 'furiously hot' and very unhealthy. 'The situation is low and on the beach where all the filth of Constantinople is driven either by the wind or the current and so great is the abominable smell thereof that for the last ten days I have been driven from the room I used to sit in and have been forced to receive and transmit business in my bedroom.' Staff Surgeon Henry Mapleton, Raglan's private physician, believed that 'the heat, the stench and the situation combined to affect my stomach', urging him to accept Stratford de Redcliffe's offer. Raglan did not think that he would return to Scutari. Leicester Curzon had travelled with him, and other staff officers crossed the Straits when necessary. Indeed Raglan remained at the Embassy in Constantinople until he left for Varna, by then having shaken off the diarrhoea. There was, however, an indication that his arm was troubling him when he went for a drive with the Secretary of Embassy (Lord Napier) and Curzon to 'the sweet waters'. The road proved 'neglected', so that he was shaken up and returned to the Embassy shivering in spite of a warm cloak. This experience led to a return of pain in his arm and shoulder, 'which I have been suffering from' and he passed an 'unpleasant' night. Raglan seemed now to be suffering transient pain from his arm quite regularly.[53]

Enduring problems caused him discomfort in another sense. Despite an agreed plan for Allied concentration in Bulgaria, St Arnaud had called on Raglan at 7 a.m. on Sunday 4 June to say that he proposed to send one French division to Varna and concentrate his remaining troops behind the Balkan range with their right resting on the sea at Bourgas and his own headquarters at Aidos. St Arnaud suggested that Raglan deploy his men inland near Bournabat on the French left flank to maintain Allied solidarity. It soon transpired that French troops were already marching overland north-west of Constantinople to reach the planned position. Raglan strongly disapproved; and St Arnaud therefore put his reasons in writing in Raglan's presence. If the British and French each only had one division near Varna, they could not be expected to support Silistria and would not therefore be embroiled in Turkish operations over which they had no real control. St Arnaud maintained: 'The safety of Turkey is not in Silistria; and it is necessary to aid and succour the Turks in our own way.' The following day Colonel Trochu visited Raglan to reinforce his commander's view, confirming that Bosquet's division was already on the march. Raglan told Trochu that he did not intend to deploy any British troops behind the Balkans. The Allies' best plan must be to support Omar Pasha, aiming to relieve Silistria. Firmly Raglan explained that if St Arnaud could not agree he would keep the bulk of his force east of the Bosporus in readiness to embark for Varna. At length, on 10 June, Colonel Rose informed Raglan that the previous day St Arnaud had agreed to adhere to the original plan. Raglan's firmness – albeit applied with courtesy – had been decisive. To Newcastle he made it clear that he was determined to stand by his word to Omar Pasha. In acknowledging Raglan's dispatch of 10 June announcing that St Arnaud had 'consented to revert to the original intention of placing the main body of the Allied Armies in Bulgaria ... [in] an effort to relieve Silistria', the Secretary of State praised Raglan's determination not to move until he acquired this French commitment.[54]

After dining with St Arnaud on the evening of 20 June Raglan sailed for Varna where he arrived at 2 p.m. the following day. Lord George Paget 'immediately' waited upon him, invited him to dinner and provided a boat to get ashore where Cambridge and Brown were waiting. Three of his ADCs (Burghersh, Kingscote and Poulett Somerset) had arrived the previous day in *Emperor* with the horses, and had not noticed *Caradoc*'s arrival, so they were surprised when Raglan appeared at the house. Generously he observed: 'To be sure they had been up since daylight landing the horses and baggage and their vision might have been a little obscured'. Steele, Leicester Curzon and Somerset Calthorpe had travelled with Raglan in *Caradoc*. Raglan described 'an animated' scene at Varna where the bay was 'full of English, French and Turkish ships of all

Above: The extensive grounds of Badminton, family residence of the Duke of Beaufort where Lord FitzRoy Somerset was born and subsequently buried in the vault of the attached church.

Right: Lord FitzRoy Somerset acted as the Duke of Wellington's Military Secretary during the Peninsular War (1808-14) and at Waterloo. he became Wellington's secretary at the Ordnance (1819-27) then Military Secretary at the Horse Guards (1827-8 and 1842-52).

Left: The Horse Guards, viewed from Whitehall, from where the Commander-in-Chief controlled the British Army, and where Lord FitzRoy Somerset acted as Military Secretary, 1827-52.

Right: The Spanish frontier fortress carried by British troops in April 1812, where Lord FitzRoy Somerset distinguished himself by persuading the French Governor to surrender.

Left: Nicolas Jean de Dieu Soult (1769-1851) rose to be a Marshal in the French Army under Napoleon and commanded the forces opposed to Wellington in the Peninsula until 1813. In later life he became a prominent politician.

Right: Henry Pelham Clinton, fifth Duke of Newcastle (1811-64), Secretary of State for War and the Colonies (1852-4), then Secretary for War (1854-5); he was responsible for the political direction of the Crimea Expeditionary Force commanded by Raglan.

Far right: Robert Stewart, Viscount Castlereagh and Marquis of Londonderry (1769-1822), Secretary of State for War and the Colonies (1807-9), Foreign Secretary (1812-22), replaced by Wellington as British plenipotentiary to the Congress of Vienna, 1815.

Above left: Lieutenant-General Sir George de Lacy Evans (1787-1870), Peninsula and Waterloo veteran, commanded the British Legion during the Carlist Wars in Spain (1835-7) and the 2nd Division in the Crimea.

Above: Lieutenant-General George, second Duke of Cambridge (1819-1904), grandson of George III and cousin of Queen Victoria, commanded the 1st Division at the Battles of the Alma, Balaclava and Inkerman in the Crimea. Later field marshal and Commander-in-Chief of the British Army.

Left: Lieutenant-General Sir George Brown (1790-1865), Peninsula veteran and former Adjutant-General at the Horse Guards. A strict disciplinarian, he commanded the Light Division in the Crimea. Later promoted general and appointed CinC, Ireland.

Above: Lieutenant-General Sir Richard England (1793-1883), commanded the 3rd Division in the Crimea after a distinguished military career in the colonies. Promoted full general in 1863.

Above right: William Howard Russell (1820-1907) made his name reporting Irish problems in the 1840s, went to the Crimea as *The Times'* war correspondent. His critical dispatches 'opened fire on Lord Raglan' and his staff, but brought Russell lasting fame.

Right: Lieutenant-General George Charles Bingham, third Earl Lucan (1800-88), commanded the Cavalry Division in the Crimea, where his tempestuous relationship with his brother-in-law, Cardigan, may have contributed to the destruction of the Light Brigade, for which Raglan censured Lucan.

Above: Having advanced from the landing beaches, on 20 September 1854 the Allies were faced with strong, entrenched Russian positions on high ground south of the River Alma. Dominating the post road on the enemy right lay the heavily fortified Great Redoubt, which the British 1st Division carried after climbing a steep bank and advancing up Kourgané Hill under fire.

Below: A small port on the eastern shore of the Bosporus opposite Constantinople, where Raglan established his first HQ. Better known as the site of British hospitals, whose standards of hygiene and provision for the wounded were deemed unacceptable by the press.

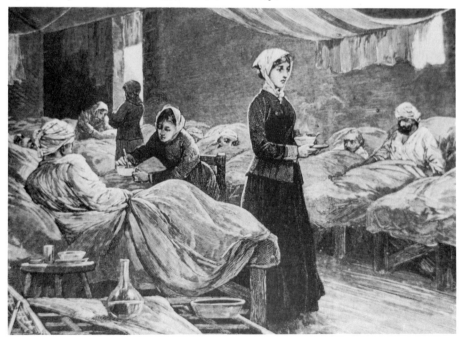

Right: Florence Nightingale (1820-1910) trained as a nurse despite family opposition. In November 1854 she and other nurses reached Scutari, where her forthright criticism of conditions displeased military authorities but earned her the praise of the soldiers as 'The Lady with the Lamp'.

Below: Colonel de Todleben, commander of the Russian engineers at Sevastopol, was responsible for strengthening the city's defences after it had become clear that the Allies would attack from the southern uplands. His energy in repairing damage held the Allies at bay for a year.

Below right: Prince A.S. Menshikov, CinC of Russian forces in the Crimea, assured the Tsar that he could hold the line of the River Alma. Despite the reverse there and further setbacks at Balaclava and Inkerman, he remained in command until February 1855.

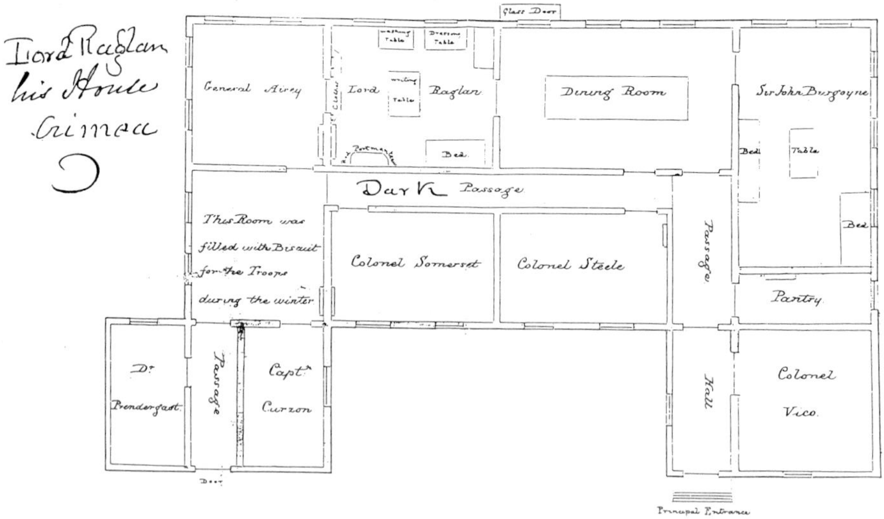
Lord Raglan his House Crimea
Glass Door
Washing Table
Dressing Table
General Airey
Lord Raglan
Writing Table
Bed
Dining Room
Sir John Burgoyne
Bed
Table
Bed
Dark Passage
This Room was filled with Biscuit for the Troops during the winter
Colonel Somerset
Colonel Steele
Passage
Pantry
Dr Prendergast
Passage
Captn Curzon
Hall
Colonel Vico
Door
Principal Entrance

Above: Plan of Lord Raglan's house in the Crimea

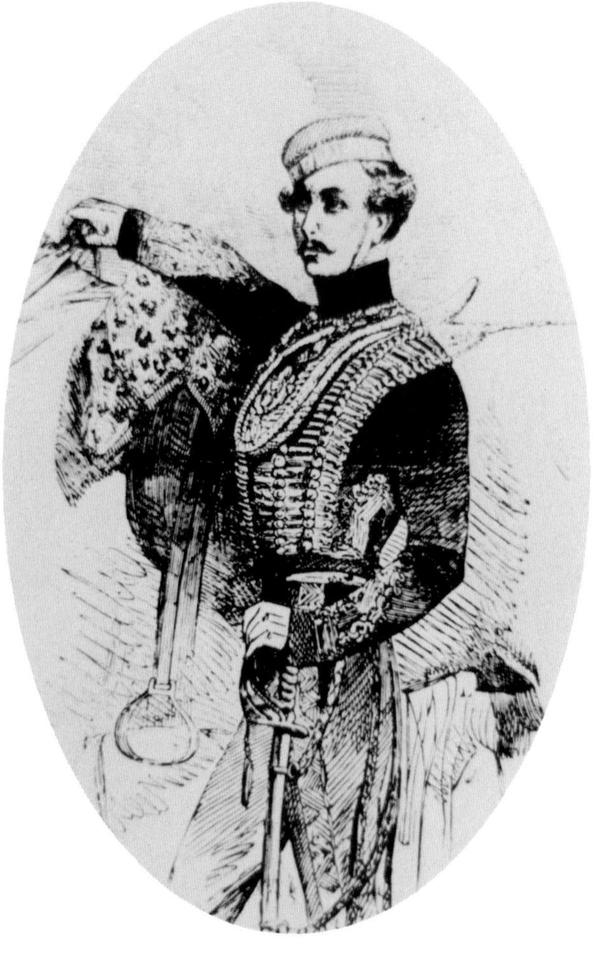

Left: Captain Lewis Edward Nolan, an accomplished horseman and author of books on cavalry tactics, carried Raglan's order to Lucan, which prompted the Charge of the Light Brigade, from the ridge overlooking the Plain of Balaclava.

Above: British guns in action before Sevastopol. On the extreme left the Woronzov Road runs to the head of Dockyard Creek. The line in the centre is the Second Parallel; the Malakov defence-work lies to the far right.

Right: The narrow harbour of Balaclava, showing steam and sailing vessels. The light railway and tidy wharf place this scene in 1855, after the early congestion had been eased. The old Genoese fort at the harbour entrance is in the background.

Right: Fiercely engaged on the right of the Allied line overlooking the Tchernaya valley, the Guards were initially obliged to give ground. Reinforced, they successfully defended their Colours before again advancing decisively.

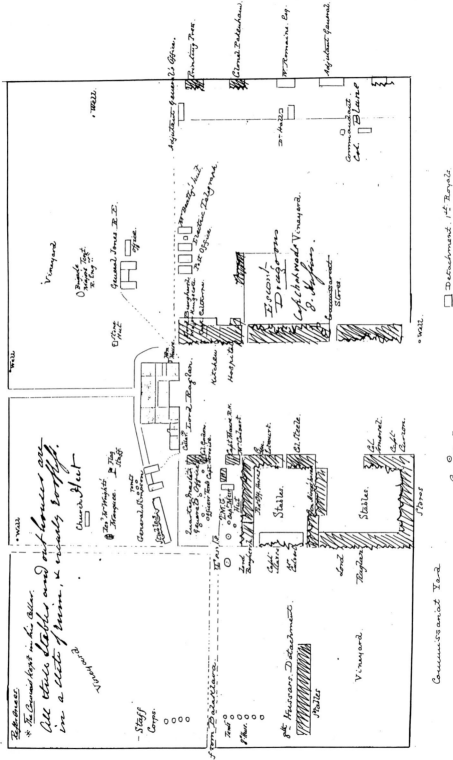

Commissariat Yard.

Grand Tent.

☐ Detachment 1st Royals.

Left: Plan of Raglan's HQ in the Crimea, showing proximity of all major commanders, stables and offices.

Above: Commanded by Brigadier-General J.Y. Scarlett, on the morning of 25 October 1854 the Heavy Brigade attacked uphill against 2,000 enemy cavalry advancing across the Woronzov Heights towards Balaclava, putting them to flight at a cost of 78 casualties.

Below: This scene shows the Heavy Brigade attacking right to left through the remains of the Light Cavalry camp, as Tartars plunder it. Balaclava harbour is in the background, Kadikoi village in the middle distance.

Left: During the celebrated Charge near Balaclava, in reality only two regiments formed the first line, one alone the second and two more the third. However, enemy dispositions are fairly accurate. The Woronzov redoubts lie in the middle distance, Balaclava in the background.

Left: The farmhouse at Khutor, on the upland 1½ miles south of Sevastopol and 4½ miles north-west of Balaclava, occupied by Raglan on 5 October 1854; he was to die there eight months later.

Right: This contemporary engraving shows 'the Guards working in the trenches before Sebastopol'. Labouring duties, in addition to their involvement in the siege, exhausted the men and undoubtedly contributed to the high rate of sickness during the winter of 1854-5.

Left: On Sunday 5 November 1854, 57,000 Russian troops with 222 guns in support were ordered to drive the British off Mount Inkerman on the extreme right of the Allied siege lines. Stubborn resistance and the intervention of two 18pdr guns frustrated this plan at a cost of 635 British dead and 1,938 wounded.

Above left: Lord FitzRoy James Henry Somerset served as Military Secretary during the Peninsular War and at Waterloo, where he lost his right arm. In 1852, he was created Baron Raglan before his appointment eighteen months later to command the Crimea Expeditionary Force. Promoted full general in June 1854 and field marshal in December, he died in June 1855.

Above right: Maréchal Le Roy de St Arnaud (1798-1855) initially commanded the French forces in the Crimea. Raglan resisted his attempts to secure overall control of all Allied troops. St Arnaud contracted cholera shortly after the Battle of the Alma and died before the siege was properly under way.

Top left: Jean Jacques Pélissier succeeded Canrobert in command of French forces in the Crimea in May 1855, and immediately established a good working relationship with Raglan. Fierce and energetic, despite Napoleon III's objections, he quickly agreed to the Allied expedition to capture Kertch. Grief-stricken at Raglan's death.

Top right: François Certain Canrobert took over from St Arnaud as French CinC in the Crimea in September 1854, but resigned in favour of Pélissier eight months later.

He accompanied Raglan on his reconnaissance of the Crimean coastline before the Allied landings and later gave his name to the hill on which No 1 redoubt stood, north of Balaclava.

Bottom left: Rear-Admiral Sir Edmund Lyons (1790-1858), experienced sailor and diplomat who had held senior appointments at Athens and Stockholm, was second-in-command of the Mediterranean Fleet at the outbreak of the Crimean War. He worked closely with Raglan before and after he

succeeded Vice-Admiral Dundas as commander of the supporting naval force.

Bottom right: Vice-Admiral J.W. Dundas (1785-1862) commander of the British fleet in the Black Sea during the Crimean War, but independent of the land force commander (Raglan). 'Opened the ball' by bombarding Odessa in April 1854, but failed to make any impression on the Sevastopol defences. He never established a warm working relationship with Raglan, and was replaced by Lyons early in 1855.

Top left: Omar Pasha, the
Turkish CinC, drove the
Russians back across the
Danube before taking
command in the Crimea.
There his troops were mainly
used in defensive positions,
but they successfully beat off
a determined enemy attack on
Eupatoria in February 1855.

Top right: As Lord FitzRoy
Somerset, Raglan attended
the coronation of Tsar
Nicholas I in St Petersburg in
1826. Confident of defeating
the Allied invaders in the
Crimea, despite the Alma

defeat, Nicholas refused to
abandon Sevastopol.
Depressed by failure to
dislodge the Allies, he reputedly died of a broken heart in
February 1855.

Bottom left: An experienced
engineer, Lieutenant-General
Sir John Burgoyne (1782-
1871) was already 71 when
sent to survey the Turkish
defences around
Constantinople early in 1854.
He subsequently joined
Raglan's staff in the Crimea
and was influential in advocating the flank march east of

Sevastopol prior to mounting
siege operations from the
south.

Bottom right: With a domineering manner and fierce
temper, Major-General James
Thomas Brudenell, seventh
Earl of Cardigan, established a
reputation as a harsh disciplinarian. Constantly at
loggerheads with his brother-
in-law and superior officer,
Lucan, and not noted for calm
judgement, he showed great
physical courage in leading
the Charge of the Light
Brigade.

Above: The Redan defence-work lay immediately ahead of the British trenches. Both it and the Malakov, farther east, in front of the French, had to be carried before Sevastopol could be taken. On 18 June 1855 British troops suffered heavy losses in attempting to capture it, and Raglan was personally devastated by their failure.

Below: The scene outside the British HQ on 3 July 1855, as the gun-carriage carrying Lord Raglan's coffin prepares to leave for embarkation at Kazatch. Note troops with reversed arms.

denominations', landing men, horses, equipment and supplies all day, so that the narrow streets were packed: 'All sorts of people mixed up indiscriminately some drunk, some sober, some quiet, some noisy'. British troops encamped outside the walls were not allowed free entry to Varna, only 'fatigue parties dressed in smock frocks, artillery wagons buying forage', but these 'all assist in adding to the confusion and the diversity of the streets'.[55]

Raglan's 'family' now totalled ten, including the two French liaison officers and Dr Mapleton 'who is a very nice fellow and was very amiable and constant in his attendance upon me when I was poorly ... he toiled up to the Embassy every day to see me, and frequently had to wait a long while before he could find me unoccupied'. His 'horse establishment' had been expanded with purchases – including a mule from Sir Colin Campbell – to twelve. Shortly after his arrival Raglan expressed distaste to Charlotte about Varna being 'a very nasty place'. He had been allocated a clean house, but one 'entirely without furniture', with only 'what may be termed the landing' on which to take meals. His small writing-room faced west, had no blinds – so that it was 'hardly habitable' in the afternoon 'and looks out on a dung heap'. Lord Raglan, it seems, was not altogether a happy general.[56]

In June overt signs of the anticipated friction between Lucan and Cardigan surfaced. Their significance, however, has been magnified with hindsight. Cardigan undoubtedly erred in approaching Raglan directly for permission to accompany advanced cavalry regiments to Varna. Routinely Raglan passed the request to Lucan (Cardigan's superior officer) asking him to make the necessary arrangements. In doing so he therefore tacitly approved of Cardigan's action, which caused Lucan to bristle and to reprove Cardigan for by-passing him. Once in Bulgaria, though, Cardigan perversely acted as an independent commander, reporting to Raglan not Lucan, who remained 150 miles away from him at divisional headquarters near Scutari. Lucan, perfectly correctly, objected; and the British CinC instructed Cardigan to keep his divisional commander fully informed of his activity. Technically Raglan ought to have referred the matter to Lucan once more before communicating with Cardigan. Realizing this, he sent de Ros to pacify Lucan: no slight had been intended. Cardigan persisted in claiming 'a separate and detached command', appealing to Raglan that he should therefore deal directly with the British CinC. He forwarded this plea through Lucan, who appended his own comments. W.H. Russell argued later, with the benefit of retrospective vision, that Raglan ought to have recognized at this point that the two men could not work together. According to Calthorpe, Raglan already fully realized this but his objection to their appointments had been overruled by Hardinge. He now had to make the command structure work, asking his Adjutant-General to communicate with both men. To Lucan Estcourt wrote on 20 June that 'the misapprehensions which Lord Cardigan has entertained of the nature of his command, have been rectified by private communication from me'. Raglan had never granted Cardigan any degree of independence: the Earl had assumed it due to his detached position. Estcourt went on: 'You [Lucan] may and ought to visit detached parties, and look to their efficiency in every respect for which you are responsible to Lord Raglan.' Lucan replied that Cardigan had, in effect, been insubordinate; and a further letter from Estcourt emphasized that Raglan felt that the position had now been made clear to all concerned, moreover privately. His conclusion to the letter of 20 June summarized Raglan's view: 'I [Estcourt] have not returned you an official letter in answer to yours because the misapprehension being corrected it is better to consider the question as never having arisen in a formal shape.' In retrospect Raglan could be accused of assuming an ostrich-like posture, but beside the myriad of issues with which he was confronted this was a relatively minor disagreement best dealt with 'privately' by senior staff officers such as de Ros and Estcourt. Unease within the Light Division, where Brown was 'very unpopular' according to Kingscote, for his insistence on rigid discipline, was contained without fuss.[57]

Meanwhile, at home, a major administrative change had been carried out which directly affected Raglan. The ministerial duties for 'War' and 'the Colonies' were divided. On 10 June Sir George Grey became Secretary of State for the Colonies, and Newcastle took the new office of Secretary of State for War, thus continuing to exercise control over Raglan. He claimed to have received no clear definition of his new duties and, later, that he had no office of his own until December. Two days after the Order in Council, which established the fourth Secretary of State, Newcastle left the Colonial Office building and the following day (13 June) complained to Raglan about the 'confusion of change of office', so that it was 'impossible to give you any instructions'.

Curiously Henry Drummond, Lord Melville's influential grandson, originally felt that the government was dragging its feet over the issue because 'the Duke of Newcastle's personal vanity is involved in the matter, and that he will not give up his share of the meddling', by surrendering either colonial or military affairs. Drummond urged Lord Grey to pursue the division eagerly, arguing further that a military officer ought to head 'the Military Department of the Empire' – the new War Department. He mentioned Raglan as the possible first holder of that office. While not entirely ruling out a military man, in reply Grey emphasized that generals rising to the head of their profession usually eschewed change. Though he did not mention Raglan by name, the shadow of his association with Wellington's military conservatism evidently persisted. Indirectly Raglan confirmed Grey's suspicions when he wrote to Priscilla on 15 June: 'How I hate all these new fangled notions.' He continued, practically, to evaluate how the change would affect his army, and in particular the transport system on which he relied so heavily. 'The Minister of War will have no more power than the Secretary of State. The most important duty when there are troops to convey by sea is the obtaining means of transport. This will still rest with the Admiralty whose authority cannot be encroached upon' – the ragged edge of mounting frustration. Moreover Raglan was free from Newcastle's bureaucratic attentions for but a few days. On 28 June the new Secretary of State for War belied any suggestion of real flexibility of action. Unless Raglan had already acted upon 'the suggestion' in previous private letters from him or in accordance with 'the general discretion' given in his orders, he should move Sir Richard England's 3rd Division from Gallipoli to Bulgaria.[58]

While this important political change was taking root in England, on 24 June Omar Pasha informed Raglan that the siege of Silistria had been raised during the night of 22/3 June. A garrison of some 12,000 men, supported by a brigade of Turkish light cavalry harassing the enemy lines of communication, had defeated 50,000 Russians, whose last assault on 22 June had been driven off with heavy loss including the wounding of Generals Gorchakov and Shilder. To Kitty, Raglan described the moment when the dramatic news arrived. During the evening of 24 June Cambridge and a party of sixteen were dining with him and just getting up from table when letters arrived from 'Choumla' (sic). Seeing one marked 'urgent', he thought that Silistria had fallen. He was therefore 'agreeably surprized' to discover that the siege had been raised and enemy troops were recrossing the Danube. The Duke of Cambridge concluded: 'We imagine it must be owing to our arrival here in force, and to the firm language and attitude assumed by Austria.' He felt that a Russian withdrawal from the two provinces and a negotiated peace was now possible; the inference being that the Allied forces might soon be on their way home.[59]

It was not to be. In a letter to Grey on 27 June Sir Charles Wood focused on the next move: 'Now comes the Sebastopol question and that turns on whether the French can go forward.' The British government had already determined on an assault. *The Times* had not relaxed its pressure for the attack and news that the Russian threat to Silistria and the other Danubian fortresses had receded made troops available for an invasion of the Crimea. As Wood indicated, the political will for invasion existed and the decision to press ahead followed swiftly after the news from Silistria. Already, on 8 June, Newcastle had privately paved the way. He did not believe the Navy's estimate of 120,000 Russian troops in the Crimea, declaring (without revealing his sources) that there were only 30,000 on the peninsula and another 3,000 at Odessa. He did not wish to press an attack on Sevastopol against the views of Raglan and the admirals, but 'all I say is that this is the thing to do and unless we destroy Russia's Black Sea fleet I do not see my way to a safe and honourable peace.' Similar arguments were later put forward in a memorandum by the Prince Consort.[60]

On 29 June, Aberdeen explained to Queen Victoria that the previous evening the Cabinet had approved Newcastle's draft to Raglan 'in which the necessity of a prompt attack upon Sebastopol and the Russian navy was strongly urged'. Later A.W. Kinglake implied that the decision to attack Sevastopol had been taken during that meeting on a warm summer's evening at Pembroke Lodge, Richmond, while many of those present dozed. Quite clearly the issue of attacking Sevastopol had been discussed often and Aberdeen showed that only approval of the wording of Newcastle's dispatch occurred at that meeting. Furthermore, already that day (28 June) Newcastle had written privately to Raglan warning him that an official dispatch was on its way and alerting him to its contents. In his letter to the Queen, Aberdeen maintained that the size of the force at Varna with the assistance of the combined Allied fleets 'appeared to be amply sufficient to justify such an enterprize'. A further 5,000 men were to be sent from England. Nevertheless Aberdeen managed to transfer the onus of decision from London to Varna. Although 'pressed very warmly and recommended to be undertaken with the least possible delay', the final decision would rest with the three Allied commanders. Newcastle's dispatch of 29 June reminded Raglan that his instructions of 10 April had directed him to ascertain the strength of the Russian forces in the Crimea and warned him that offensive action – particularly investment of Sevastopol – might be necessary. Russian retreat from the Danube had 'given a new character to the war'. Constantinople was now safe and the unhealthy nature of the Dobruja marsh area meant that 'any further advance of the Allied armies (in Bulgaria) should on no account be contemplated'. An attack on Sevastopol was of paramount importance. As Aberdeen had indicated, though, the burden of decision about that would rest with Raglan. The Government's confidence in him would continue 'unabated', Newcastle assured him, if 'upon mature reflection' it should be decided that Allied strength were 'insufficient': 'you are not to be precluded from the exercize of the discretion originally vested in you'. The Government would 'regret' any delay – so Raglan was only being offered the opportunity of postponement, not cancellation. The Secretary of State cautioned that delay would be dangerous because the Russian troops retreating from the two provinces could be 'poured into the Crimea'. Evidently forgetting the latitude of decision afforded to Raglan, he went on to suggest that Turkish troops, with British and French officers 'associated', should occupy the Isthmus of Perekop 'permanently' to prevent supplies and reinforcements reaching the Crimea. The military difficulties of attaining that objective – not least in gathering sufficient strength to do so and maintaining the forces while still advancing on Sevastopol – seemed utterly foreign to Newcastle. With the 'same object', Admiral Dundas should cut off the Sea of Azov. Turks might also be dispatched to the Caucasus. Having thus sketched out a fairly comprehensive pattern of operations – Perekop, Sevastopol, Sea of Azov and the Caucasus – Newcastle declined to express detailed opinions about the actual landing beaches 'at this distance', though with the blissful confidence of a distant civilian impressed upon the British CinC that he should land only 'in favourable weather'. Finally he reiterated that a 'safe and honorable' peace could only be achieved after reduction of Sevastopol.[61]

This dispatch would not reach Raglan for almost a fortnight, and its implication would require maximum co-operation between the three Allied commanders. Continuing problems with the French did not augur well for that. The difficulties that Raglan faced in seeking accommodation with his ally were, to some extent, underlined by Nigel Kingscote. In the narrow domestic context, the British CinC's ADC referred to the two French officers attached to the headquarters 'and a horrid bore they are, one is like a great fat cook, the other is a very good fellow but cannot speak a word of English'. Inborn prejudice, no doubt. More broadly the different style of leadership caused friction. 'Marshal St Arnaud [is] full of pomp and ceremony with a bodyguard of Spahis who are picturesque looking fellows. My Lord is such a contrast to the Marshal, the former hating a sentry to present arms to him', usually taking one ADC with him as opposed to St Arnaud's minimum of six. Sir Charles Wood noted that Westmorland believed that 'Raglan's imperturbable temper and good sense' had profoundly influenced St Arnaud, however, though Wood himself ungenerously did not give him 'so much credit'. Wood did, none the less, admit that Raglan's posture also had an impact on Napoleon III; and Lord Cowley revealed to Raglan on 29 June that the French Emperor now agreed that the Crimea must be the Allies' objective. How far Raglan did in fact influence this change of mind is very debatable.[62]

Until Silistria had been saved, the summit of British military activity in Bulgaria had amounted to drill, field days, inspections and weekly church parades. The day after Omar Pasha's dramatic missive arrived, as Calthorpe rode for Shumla with a message of congratulation from Raglan, Cardigan and the Light Brigade were dispatched to the Danube. With no time to pass orders through Lucan, Raglan 'immediately' (on the evening of 24 June) sent Burghersh and Poulett Somerset to Cardigan 'to desire that he would patrol as far as he could in order to discover what the enemy's left was about'. Both ADCs rode for half a day with Cardigan before returning to report to Raglan. Burghersh then set off again at 4 p.m. on 26 June to rejoin the reconnaissance, taking with him more detailed orders. The Light Brigade was ordered to go as far as Karajik, to the right of the direct line to Karasou, so as to confirm that all Russians had re-crossed the Danube. From Karasou Cardigan sent a brief report back to the cavalry camp at Devna on 30 June after which he and his regiments effectively disappeared towards the Dobruja marshes for more than a fortnight. Militarily, it was an unsatisfactory end to June. To all intents and purposes the Light Brigade was out of touch with Raglan; its activities unknown. For all he knew the troops might have been hit by the disease that was prevalent in the area and about which he had been warned, or encountered a superior Russian force with disastrous effect.[63]

In the meantime the diplomatic waltz played on. On 3 June Austria had delivered an ultimatum to the Russians to clear Moldavia and Wallachia and – more positively – eleven days later declared themselves ready to evict the Tsar's troops by force if necessary. Cynically, and fantastically, in the United States Karl Marx declared that once French troops were committed to Bulgaria, the Austrians and Prussians would declare for Russia and march on Paris. More realistically, especially in view of the Austrian commitment of 14 June, Raglan wrote to Priscilla: 'We are looking most anxiously for the active co-operation of your [Austrian] Empire. We are collecting ourselves in Bulgaria and hope the demonstration we are making may create a diversion in favor of Silistria.' Raglan's hopes seemed to have been realized, when Westmorland wrote on 26 June that the Austrian Emperor had indeed ordered his troops into Moldavia and Wallachia. Two days later Raglan received confirmation that the Porte had agreed to this move during joint consultations. How far Austrian pressure was directly responsible for the Russians withdrawing from Silistria and, subsequently, the two provinces is unclear. But the Austrian troop commitment north of the Danube ensured security of the Balkan region and thus removed another obstacle to Allied forces' leaving Bulgaria for the Crimea.[64]

Raglan's correspondence with his family continued to provide much needed solace during June. Although not frequent, his letters were long; and taken chronologically provide a progressive illustration of his feelings about events and people. Writing to Charlotte from 'near Scutari' on 5 June, in a letter begun 'two or three days ago', Raglan noted that he had received all her letters 'and your dear Mama's and dear Kitty's up to the 23rd and I am most obliged to you for them'. Movingly he added: 'They are an immense comfort to me.' In a letter full of personal and family interest, and not in fact mentioning the campaign at all, he expressed pleasure that Charlotte seemed to be gaining strength: 'I hope you will continue to take care of your dear self and will by degrees regain your strength entirely.' He was 'much shocked' to learn of the death of the Bishop of Bath and Wells whom he had hoped was recovering from a long illness. He recalled the many happy times that the family had spent in his and his wife's company. Four days later he wrote a twelve-sided letter to Kitty from Constantinople. Due to too much 'business' he had neglected her, 'and I have, I believe, behaved more shabbily to you than to any body else', repeating his pleasure at receiving letters from home expressed to Charlotte. He explained his current illness and the unhealthy nature of his quarters near Scutari. Noting that Lord Burghersh had received news of his mother's arrival in London from Vienna, he went on to discuss news sent to him by other correspondents such as Lady Georgiana Bathurst, including details of flirtations between family friends.

Glad that Kitty was keeping up her riding, he asked her especially to give his 'best regards' to Egerton and let him know how Egerton's eyes were. Would Kitty please thank 'MAMA' for the thermometer sent to him, which was greatly appreciated? He revealed, though, a sad development. 'De Ros looks very old and shabby and his costume occupies the attention and occasions [illegible] of all my staff. He is encompassed and enveloped in fleas but he is quite well and I fancy likes discomfort.' Unfortunately the Quartermaster General's eccentricity would soon become manifest in the mental illness of which it was as yet an unrecognized symptom.[65]

A short note to Richard, received by him on 2 July in Hanover and answered in turn two days later, thanked his son for two letters in May and congratulations on his father's appointment to the colonelcy of The Blues. Briefly mentioning his impending departure for Varna, he referred to 'desolate' Bulgaria and went on: 'We are not yet compleat in our means of transport nor in our cavalry, but in other respects the army is in fine order.' Touchingly he enclosed a cheque for £50, a sum which he would continue to send 'every four months'. Three days later, after arriving in Bulgaria, Raglan wrote a nine-sided letter to Charlotte. Given his sharp disillusionment with the port and his accommodation there, this lengthy communication had therapeutic qualities. He described the scene at Varna and the disposition of the troops, interspersing his information with family details. Augustus Calthorpe (Somerset's brother) was safe at Shumla and his mother should not worry that he was in any sort of danger. There was no enemy in sight of Varna or the British outposts and Raglan believed that none was within reach. Lady Erroll was the only lady in camp: 'She never leaves her husband poor thing. He can hardly be trusted to be alone. This of course is confidential', though not a flattering portrayal of the Rifle Brigade officer.

Raglan had received no letters since 20 June, though a mail was expected that day. Now that he had left Constantinople the mail would not be so regular, he observed: correspondence went overland from London to Marseilles, then by steamer to Constantinople where letters were handed to the Embassy, which arranged for forward transmission. Finishing this letter on 24 June, Raglan thanked Lady Raglan, Charlotte and Kitty for their letters of 8 June and also 'Aunt Priscilla' who was with them at Brighton. Raglan explained that Richard Airey had visited him on 23 June. He was 'quite well but the air and the sun have made sad havoc with his complexion and he is very, very grey.' Airey declined to stay long and refused anything but 'a glass of lemonade'. Raglan had enjoyed 'a capital dinner' with Cambridge in his tent the day before, prepared by a 'cordon bleu' cook. The Duke was dining with Raglan that day and would not fare so well. The tone of the letter was relaxed, as indeed was one to Kitty shortly afterwards. Acknowledging the arrival of all letters dated 13 June, he then mentioned to his younger daughter the raising of the siege of Silistria.

By a strange coincidence, on his way to carry Raglan's congratulations to Omar Pasha, Somerset Calthorpe met his brother Augustus travelling to Varna and eventually England for medical reasons. Augustus told him that Omar Pasha had left Shumla for Silistria, thus committing Somerset to a longer ride. Raglan explained that St Arnaud had given him a horse, which Nigel Kingscote rode (Raglan being too busy). The ADC thought that Raglan would not like the animal, it being high on his leg and having a 'very thick' neck. 'Miss Mary goes mad with fleas and I have not succeeded in getting a net,' Raglan went on. Completing the letter on 29 June, he mentioned a successful dinner with St Arnaud on 27 June, then gave a personal account of a 'sumptuous repast' aboard *Bellerophon* on Wednesday 28 June, after which the ship's company gave a concert which included a 'laughable farce' ('The Lottery Ticket') and a 'laughable interlude' ('Diamond Cut Diamond') interspersed with a collection of solos and choruses performed by selected artists. 'Was it not fun? They acted well and amused us amazingly.' William Hill, who acted women's parts in both the short plays, 'had a fist that would knock down an ox' and one of the other characters was required to take 'of her delicate hand!' De Ros, Raglan wrote, 'laughed manfully'. 'The quarterdeck was beautifully fitted and the groups of sailors most gracefully marked the outline.' At this stage the British CinC was clearly in good spirits.[66]

A letter to Lady Westmorland on 15 June gave a more intimate glimpse of the family at home. Thanking Priscilla for her 'very kind' letter of 28 May 'when you were so unwell and so unequal to any exertion', he understood that she was now recovering and should have gone to Brighton on 5 June: 'The air there always agrees with you and I hope that on this occasion it will at once set you up.' Exhibiting his usual solicitude, he noted how 'curious' it was that she usually became ill when first returning to England. Raglan was 'very grateful' to his sister-in-law for promising to take Charlotte to Brighton where the 'sea air' was 'all she requires to restore her nerves and remit her strength'. Charlotte had been 'very ill, poor thing' and he was sorry to hear that Kitty was 'thin' after experiencing an unspecified anxious time. 'Everybody' reported that Lady Raglan looked well 'at the Drawing Room' and Raglan thanked Priscilla for helping her. Noting, at that stage, the stout resistance of Silistria, where 'the Russians appear to have mismanaged their affairs most woefully', he dwelt on possible Austrian assistance to the Allies. He was pleased that Westmorland was highly thought of and that his efforts to influence the Austrians were appreciated. Raglan felt sure that, with her '*bonne tête*, tact and knowledge', Priscilla had played her part as well. He explained that Clarendon was 'a very agreeable man to deal with' and declared himself equally satisfied with Newcastle who, he hoped, would retain responsibility for 'War' when the new ministers were appointed – as indeed he did. Touchingly he concluded: 'Take care of yourself my dearest Priscilla, and when we have the pleasure of meeting let me find you flourishing.' Amid his many problems, family correspondence obviously provided oases of relief. In the professional context he also gained satisfaction from his promotion to General on 20 June. No longer was his rank purely local.[67]

As July opened Cardigan and the Light Brigade were still, to all intents and purposes, lost. Then a short report reached Raglan stating that the patrol had reached Karasou after five days riding, and on 3 July Cardigan reported that it was within two miles of the Danube at Bassora whence Cossacks had only recently retired and could still be seen north of the Danube. Eventually the Light Brigade returned to its camp at Devna, west of Varna, at 4 a.m. on 11 July, having ridden back via Silistria and Shumla. Eye-witnesses of their return noted that many of the men were walking their horses, and carrying saddles and harness, and that the brigade came into camp singly or in small groups throughout the day. Hence Cardigan's reconnaissance became known as 'the bare-back patrol' or 'sore-backed patrol' – an allusion to the state of the horses. Whatever its shortcomings, it had confirmed that in the area of Silistria and further east, no Russian forces were south of the Danube. Writing to Cardigan, Raglan acknowledged the importance of the reconnaissance and hoped that the experience 'will not prove injurious to your health and that of the officers and men under your orders'.[68]

Speaking to Fanny Duberly after his return, Cardigan expressed belief that the cavalry would now winter at Adrianople and that, by the time that the 1855 campaigning season arrived, peace would have been signed. His prediction proved wildly awry. For the major development during July concerned the decision to launch an invasion of the Crimea in order to neutralize Sevastopol with a combination of military and naval forces. Newcastle's private letter of 28 June, indicating that the official dispatch would shortly follow, arrived on 13 July and explained: 'The Cabinet is unanimously of opinion that, unless you and Marshal St Arnaud are not sufficiently prepared, you should lay siege to Sebastopol.' It evoked an immediate response from Raglan. The Allies were 'not sufficiently prepared' for such an enterprise and St Arnaud had actually been ordered by his Minister of War to move forward to the Danube in association with the French fleet if the siege of Silistria were raised. But Newcastle had assured Raglan that Napoleon III concurred in the British Cabinet plan to attack Sevastopol. Furthermore there was still a profound lack of information about enemy strengths and deployments, the French battering-ram had not yet left Toulon and the Turks were devoid of ammunition wagons, having only 24 rounds on each limber. To no avail; for the official dispatch, dated 29 June, arrived on 16 July. Raglan showed it to Brown who, like Raglan himself, had very grave reservations about invading the Crimea. The Light Division's commander believed that the Government was clearly determined on the operation and would replace Raglan if he demurred. Raglan, schooled in Wellington's belief that British generals must obey the wishes of legitimate civilian Ministers, recognized that professionally he must concur. In reality he had no room for manoeuvre; and his personal integrity would never have permitted him to abandon his army in the face of the enemy. When consulted, Brown allegedly said: 'You and I are accustomed, when in any great difficulty, or when an important question is proposed to us, to ask ourselves how the Great Duke would have acted and decided under similar circumstances.' Raglan undoubtedly did think along these lines. Like the Duke in the Peninsula, though, in acknowledging the orders on 19 July he emphasized that he was acting in deference to the Government's views, though scanty information existed about the enemy. Before Raglan's response to either his private or official letters had been received and before he knew that Silistria was safe, Newcastle in separate letters suggested a landing at Eupatoria, some 30 miles north of Sevastopol, and reiterated that the fall of Sevastopol would have an important 'political effect' on Austria. How facile military operations appeared on a small-scale map in London.[69]

The Allied leaders had now to fashion a viable strategy in the light of military realities on the spot. Not an easy task. St Arnaud's orders to advance to the Danube were rescinded; nevertheless Raglan noted that it would be 'a tough job'. The French battering-ram had still not left France and only part of the British 'battering-train' was in Bulgaria. On 14 July in a letter from Paris, Cowley revealed that French troops were embarking for a joint Baltic expedition with Britain – men whom Cowley believed should have been concentrated in the Black Sea area. A further administrative drawback was that, although the French admiral (Hamelin) came under St Arnaud, Dundas acted independently of Raglan. Raglan also pointed to lack of transport: the fleet could land the troops, but could not keep them supplied. And Omar Pasha was more interested in the Danube than in Sevastopol. For the Russians were still occupying Moldavia and Wallachia; and, on 12 July, Raglan explained to his daughters that the Turks were 'very near to getting a licking the other day in front of Rustuck [sic]' near the Danube. The Turkish CinC was very keen to cross the Danube in force and, as late as 26 July, Colonel Simmons advised Raglan that Omar Pasha was annoyed that his allies had not advanced to join him especially as (in the action referred to by Raglan) Turkish troops had already crossed the river. He felt that his men were exposed to counter-attack. Raglan and St Arnaud swiftly informed Omar Pasha that they were under orders not to advance in Bulgaria and urged him against committing men north of the Danube. On 29 July Nigel Kingscote voiced the continuing fear that, if the Allies went to the Crimea, the Russians would renew their southward march into the Balkans.[70]

So it was in neither a settled frame of mind nor unanimity of purpose that Raglan and St Arnaud convened a Council of War at the French headquarters on 18 July. The commanders of the two fleets and their respective seconds-in-command were present; but neither Omar Pasha nor any other Turkish representative attended. According to Kinglake, Raglan dominated the four-hour session, brushing aside any attempt to debate the wisdom of the operation and focusing attention on 'the time and the means'. The French argued that artillery must land with the infantry to provide immediate close support and that ten days would be required to construct the necessary 'flat-bottomed lighters' for guns and gun-carriages to be run straight ashore, so there would be time to carry out a survey of the Crimean coastline. Raglan does not seem to have mentioned Newcastle's suggestion of Eupatoria as a landing port. At this point the French had four infantry divisions plus cavalry and artillery support in Bulgaria. The British also had four infantry divisions (with a fifth on the way), one cavalry division and seven batteries of field artillery. Half the siege train was aboard nearby ships, the other half about to leave England. The Council of War had committed these forces to invading the Crimea and ordered a reconnaissance of the west coast north of Sevastopol to determine the most suitable landing beach. As Raglan explained to Stratford de Redcliffe, an attempt at deception would be made. Plans for an amphibious operation could not effectively be concealed – the building of the French artillery rafts alone would be indicative – but Odessa would be publicized as being the objective. It was a thin story.[71]

Raglan learnt that more troops and equipment were on the way from England. On 3 July Newcastle announced that the 'second battering-ram' was about to be embarked and that he had 'given orders' for cavalry reinforcements to sail. On 18 July Hardinge confirmed to Raglan that Sir George Cathcart had been appointed to command the new infantry division. Five days later Cathcart wrote to Raglan, noting that he had brought his own ADCs from the Cape of Good Hope, but asking that his nephew Augustus, serving with the 93rd Regiment in Bulgaria, might be added to his staff. Raglan then learnt from Newcastle that the Secretary of State, unasked, had raised a Mounted Staff Corps of fifty London police and Irish constabulary to assist him. They would be under Raglan's command, but with terms of service that made them liable to discharge when not wanted. Some sort of policing duties might be inferred from the background of the personnel, but Cathcart would give full information to Raglan on his arrival in Bulgaria about 'the formation and the duties'. The Secretary of State's flow of letters continued unabated. He acknowledged Raglan's news of his arrival at Varna three weeks after the event and rebuked Raglan on another occasion for sending his dispatches by normal mail and not by a Queen's Messenger. Raglan would have been well rid of such irritations.[72]

As July wore on more serious reservations about the invasion emerged. Sir John Burgoyne expressed his professional doubts about the enterprise, and the Commanding Engineer in Bulgaria, Brigadier-General Tylden, dubbed it 'a very rash undertaking' which would be 'lucky' to succeed. The Duke of Cambridge, 'appointed on the staff of the Army as lieutenant-general from 20 June', believed it 'a terrific undertaking' best left until 'next year'; to do so earlier would be 'rash'. A more junior officer, Henry Clifford, believed that the strength of Sevastopol's defences and the fact that such an assault had been openly discussed before and after the troops left England, rendered the idea dangerous: 'The least sanguine look upon the plan as that of a madman and the taking of the place as impossible.' Like Raglan, Tylden was concerned at the lack of firm intelligence about the enemy, but this did not appear to worry the reconnaissance party which set out in *Fury* to survey the west coast of the Crimea for a landing beach after the Council of War on 18 July. The primary need was to find a suitable place that was not dominated by Russian guns.[73]

On 21 July the Allied reconnaissance party, comprising Sir George Brown, General Canrobert, Colonel Trochu and engineer and artillery officers from both armies, steamed along the Crimean coast in *Fury*, commanded for the occasion by Sir Edmund Lyons. When the vessel ventured within a mile of Sevastopol shortly after daybreak, three enemy steamers could be seen getting under weigh, but these refrained from attacking when more Allied warships appeared. Nevertheless, according to Nigel Kingscote, 'one of the towers' did discharge six shots which broke two jars of butter belonging to the midshipmen's mess. Kingscote mused that, if more accurate, they could have killed two generals and an admiral. 'From daylight till sunset, they [*Fury*'s flotilla] ran up and down the coast within a mile and could see every thing down to two ladies bathing and a four-in-hand driving along the coast. Indeed they could see the people come to look at them and created no stir.' The two generals (Brown and Canrobert) decided on the mouth of the River Katcha, seven miles north of Sevastopol, as being a suitable landing beach and, on their return, communicated that recommendation to Raglan and St Arnaud.[74]

So far, so good. A further Allied conference was called on 28 July; again at the French headquarters. On this occasion Generals Canrobert, Martimpey and Brown were present, though Admirals Hamelin and Dundas were not. The French argued that defence of Turkey had been the expeditionary forces' objective and this had now been assured. Again, the danger of enemy troops re-crossing the Danube if the Allies descended on the Crimea, was aired. Raglan pointed to the determination of both the British and French governments to land in the Crimea. He acknowledged the paucity of information about the enemy, but stressed that time remained to rectify that deficiency. It was agreed, on his insistence, that preparations would go ahead, with embarkation planned for 30 July or 1 August. The rumour of an attack on Odessa was to be intensified and, as further deception, French troops were to advance into the Dobruja area. To a certain extent the deception was successful – if only among the Allies. On 29 July the Duke of Cambridge wrote to the Duchess of

Gloucester: 'It is supposed that we are to go somewhere by sea, but whether this is to be the Crimea or Anapa, I know not.' Stratford de Redcliffe too had succeeded in muddying the waters of comprehension by suggesting that Sir Colin Campbell take his brigade to the Caucasus. Confusing all this might be, but it was also unsettling.[75]

At least Raglan's plea to continue preparations for an invasion pending the acquisition of more intelligence seemed justified, when Charles Cattley produced a most comprehensive memorandum about the Crimea. Somewhat tortuously, he thought 'there can be no doubt Artillery might be transported' along the road from Balaclava to Sevastopol over 'undulating steppe', but he believed that Balaclava Creek was too narrow for a landing. In 1846 there had been 'no fortifications on the Heights at the back of the town [Sevastopol]' – that is, the southern upland. He had not been to Eupatoria, but felt confident that artillery 'might' be conveyed across the similarly undulating steppe via Tartar tracks southwards to Sevastopol. Cattley estimated that there were 70-80,000 troops in the Crimea, 40,000 of them in Sevastopol. If Sevastopol were to be attacked, the whole of the south-eastern coast ought also to be menaced 'to prevent the troops being withdrawn from such places as Kaffa and Kertch'. He understood that some 8,000 cavalry were in the Crimea and 'probably' some irregular 'Kazaks'. The total population of the peninsula was 200,000, mostly Tartars speaking a Turkish dialect and Muhammadan in religion. Cattley reckoned that they would have 'a strong anti-Russian feeling'. They could be approached prior to the landing through their 'moolahs or priests' via other moolahs in Constantinople. The Crimean Tartars might be useful as foragers. As to supplies, 'cattle and sheep would probably be found in plenty in the Crimea, but not corn. This latter probably might be seized at Beidiamsk or Taganrog in the Sea of Azov.' At first glance this all appeared promising, given Cattley's experience of the area while serving as consul at Kertch. In truth, though, the memorandum was hedged with qualifications and much of the detail was either out of date or pure supposition. The passages on the Tartars' allegiance and available supplies in the Crimea would prove to be utterly wrong. But Kertch, Balaclava and Eupatoria would all feature – to differing degrees – in the invasion.[76]

Meanwhile the supply and transport problems intensified during July. Estcourt, the Adjutant-General, argued that the Commissariat was 'very defective ... [because] there is a want of organization'. To some extent this was borne out by variations in the distribution of provisions in Bulgaria. On 14 July Brown explained to Raglan: 'We get excellent bread in the Light Division, but I understand that the Cavalry are by no means so well off, and that of the 2nd Division is execrable!' The basic problems lay with 'the contractor' and the content of the flour, not with the baking. Back in England *The Daily News*, drawing on reports from the front, also blamed 'our absurd system of throwing aside in peace the machinery we are compelled to make use of in war', favouring the French permanent organization. Raglan held that the system was defeating able men, though he did admit that rapid expansion of the Commissariat in time of emergency had led to recruitment of some inferior officers. Thus when William Monsell from the Ordnance queried whether the complaints against the Commissariat were justified, Raglan replied that the Department had insufficient personnel and some individuals lacked field experience.

One major complication, as a General Order of 6 July acknowledged, involved 'the Desertion of *Arabas* and other means of transport', possibly because the native drivers had not been well treated. Troops should change their attitude. This ploy clearly did not work, however, and on 31 July Filder advised Raglan that a strong escort of British troops must accompany the transport columns to prevent the native drivers from deserting. The worrying aspect of the deficiencies in supplies and land transport was that they were occurring in an ostensibly friendly country and under non-combat conditions.[77]

The probability of casualties in the face of the enemy lay some way ahead. Sickness – and in particular cholera – became a more immediate and potent concern in Bulgaria. Its devastation of the Allied ranks threatened seriously to undermine their military capacity. The invasion might not, after all, be possible. It would certainly have to be postponed. On 19 July cholera was confirmed in two blotchy, twisted bodies in the French lines, and three days later it had reached the British. Inevitably, as victims were transported to the hospitals there, it reached Scutari; and by 21 July an outbreak occurred among the 4th Foot at Gallipoli. Units were dispersed in an endeavour to reduce infection. On 25 July Raglan ordered Cardigan to move the two brigades of the cavalry division away from Devna. With troops now scattered in the hinterland of Bulgaria, the task of mounting an invasion had become immeasurably more difficult. Morale, too, had inevitably suffered. From Monastere, Airey informed Raglan that a sudden outbreak of cholera in his brigade had provoked 'some panic'.[78]

Other disasters scarcely helped. On 2 July a devastating hurricane swept through the camps, causing destruction of equipment and much personal discomfort. The behaviour of some Turkish troops towards local inhabitants shortly afterwards complicated inter-Allied relations, too, and made Raglan furious. He expressed his anger at the outrages to Stratford de Redcliffe on 19 July, and a week later bitingly informed him that British troops were having to protect Christians from attack. No doubt these events coloured Raglan's views of the military worth of the Bashi-Bazouks. Writing to Newcastle, he forcefully exclaimed: 'I have no wish to have any of them, and indeed would rather be without the assistance of such a force.'[79]

Nigel Kingscote declared himself 'bored to death' in Bulgaria and 'longing to go anywhere' because there was 'no amusement of any kind whatever' – a euphemism for lack of military action. He did, however, further qualify his comments by noting that the serious outbreak of cholera in the British and French ranks encouraged thoughts of rapid translation to combat elsewhere: 'Better to have them killed before Sebastopol than die like flies here.' The usual round of inspections and training took place in July: Omar Pasha reviewed the cavalry on 3 July, for instance. The summer heat, however, curtailed training. Raglan reminded Estcourt that the troops were not to exercise after 8 a.m., noting that the cavalry had recently been out until 9 a.m. or later. No doubt the hours of enforced idleness led to boredom, and rumours abounded; on 13 July a cavalry move to Vienna was confidently predicted. Most of the second half of the month was spent trying to stop the spread of cholera. In terms of positive military activity, July proved negative, once Cardigan's patrol had returned on the 11th. Psychologically, if not practically, preparations for the forthcoming invasion were poor.[80]

Amid the confusion, uncertainty and sickness, Raglan's qualities of persuasion, care and consideration remained constant. He was not, however, always successful. On 15 July he admitted failure to achieve reconciliation between Admiral Dundas and Stratford de Redcliffe, though it was, perhaps, a measure of his sensitivity that he had tried to do so. As his Adjutant-General noted, he 'works very hard ... he is very kind and considerate and affable'. He cared about individuals enough to request that interpreters be exempt from Income Tax – one of only eight letters that he wrote to Sir Charles Trevelyan at the Treasury during the campaign. When cholera struck, *The United Service Magazine* acknowledged: 'Nothing could exceed the interest which Lord Raglan manifested for the sick, or the efforts he made to mitigate, by sanitary and dietary measures, the virulence of the plague.'[81]

Despite the orders from London and Paris to prepare for invasion, the slim prospect that peace might yet prevail proved disturbing. On 10 July Omar Pasha informed Raglan that Austria intended to occupy Moldavia and Wallachia with troops once the Russians retired, in accordance with the agreement with Turkey signed on 14 June. Two days later Raglan wrote to his daughters explaining that, as yet, the Russians had not withdrawn from Wallachia and despite previous promises no firm indication had been given of Austrian occupation. Yet he was sufficiently optimistic to discuss peace prospects with Stratford de Redcliffe on 21 July. Perhaps he hoped that hostilities would not break out, so that he could hurry back to England where the Ordnance was again under threat. For in mid-July Sidney Herbert (the Secretary at War) told the Commons that he still held to views expressed 'privately' in March. The separate departments of the CinC and Master-General constituted 'a great evil'. All military troops should come under the Horse Guards.[82]

Raglan's own health remained satisfactory, though he clearly disliked the heat. Kingscote explained to Richard that he 'feels the heat a little but he hardly goes out in the sun which I think is a good thing and he has *oceans* to do without going out'. He made the same point to Kitty, though 'a nice breeze' off the sea, which died away at night, did to some extent relieve the worst heat. Raglan, he revealed, hardly ever rode for exercise; the heat took enough out of him without riding. Kingscote claimed that his uncle was 'flourishing', though his stomach had been 'a little upset'. The more serious indispositions of Scutari seemed behind him.[83]

August opened with good news. On the 2nd, the last Russian soldier recrossed the River Pruth to clear Moldavia and Wallachia. But the original dates (31 July or 1 August) for commencement of embarkation for the Crimea had also passed, as sickness and dispersal still affected the Allied troops. Much remained to be done before an invasion could be mounted; and diplomatic manoeuvring still created an atmosphere of uncertainty. Two days after the Russian withdrawal from the provinces, Raglan felt that the Tsar was 'dying to make peace', because his trade had been 'annhilated ... and his two fleets shut up in cages'. But the Allies 'want to strike a blow which if successful will probably make peace more difficult'. The Tsar would not wish to be humiliated, though Raglan mysteriously added 'after all he is right in the main'. From Paris, Cowley represented a more cautious opinion. The Russian withdrawal appeared designed to paralyse possible action by Prussia and Austria. Raglan himself reluctantly veered towards this view, in writing privately to Cambridge. 'I am afraid that Austria has placed herself in a fix and fears to have all the vengeance of Russia upon her back and possibly she may have discovered that whilst her immediate object is universal peace that of the western powers hallooed on by the English press is to attack and capture Sevastopol before any arrangement be entered upon or discussed.' Later in the month Raglan conceded that the Turkish government likewise rejected the Russian withdrawal 'as a token of peace' seeing it more as 'a device to detach Austria from active co-operation with the Western Powers', though he expressed suspicion about Austria's intentions, given her reluctance physically to commit troops to Moldavia and Wallachia. Eventually Austrian troops did enter Wallachia on 20 August, but there was very little realistic hope that the British would draw back. *The Times* had already prematurely announced departure of the armada from Varna, and Raglan writing to Richard believed that 'there is such a feeling against her [Russia] in England that it is very difficult for her [Britain] to enter upon the discussion of a peace or of a cessation of hostilities.'[84]

At the beginning of August Newcastle acknowledged that Raglan's decision to attack Sevastopol had been 'taken in order to meet the views and desires of the Government, and not in entire accordance with your opinion'. But the Secretary of State did then recognize the need further to reinforce the troops in Bulgaria beyond the formation of Cathcart's new infantry division. 'The time has now come', he advised Raglan, to remove the bulk of the remaining force from Gallipoli, especially as the French had already given orders to reduce their garrison to 200. Raglan was to consider himself 'authorised' to order recent arrivals at Gallipoli to join Cathcart, leaving only 50-100 men there. Newcastle himself sent troops from Corfu to Bulgaria. Underlining his commitment to an invasion, which seemed more and more likely to take place, Newcastle thanked Raglan for a copy of Brown's 'clear and satisfactory' report on his reconnaissance of the Crimean coast.[85]

Brown's choice of the mouth of the Katcha for the landing did not find universal favour, however. Sir John Burgoyne, while still in England, pronounced his horror at landing over a small open beach so close to Sevastopol, preferring one farther north. Invited by Newcastle to do so, he sailed for the east once more on 11 August. En route, in Greece, he produced 'my first rough copy of reasonings and speculation on proceedings for the attack on Sebastopol'. Basically he opted for a British and French landing at Eupatoria, with an additional 10,000 Turks descending on the south coast of the Crimea to divide the enemy's forces. On 29 August, two days after arriving at Varna, he developed this plan by arguing for a landing in the north, then marching the troops round Sevastopol to the east to bombard the dockyard, naval installations and town itself from uplands to the south. He did so merely by consulting a map which indicated 'a fine position between the valley that runs into the head of the harbour on one flank and near the Monastery of San Giorgio on the other. It appears capable of being given great strength.' He went on to explain that 'prodigious advantage' would be gained by securing Balaclava and 'perhaps one of the bays round Cape Chersonese' for the landing of supplies. He felt, though, that the whole enterprise was bedevilled by 'the advance of the season' and poor health of the troops. Like the French, therefore, he favoured postponement until the following spring. In all other respects he had sketched the plan ultimately adopted.[86]

That is not to say that the concept of a Crimean invasion was widely accepted. On 9 August Cambridge agreed that an operation was imminent 'possibly to the Crimea, to which place the good people of England seem quite determined to send us at all hazards and risks'. The following day Tylden, the commanding engineer, wrote a detailed memorandum for Raglan. The defences of Sevastopol had, certainly, been improved during the past two years and would no doubt be effectively manned. Moreover the winter season started in the Crimea in November – when the Allied navies would not be able easily to maintain station offshore – and any investing army would need to construct a proper trench system to protect itself; which would take time. 'Therefore, it is my opinion that the projected attack on Sebastopol, with our present resources at command is eminently hazardous, and will, at best, require a longer time to effect, than the present advanced season will allow.' Tylden, too, supported postponement until 1855. Strangely, ten days later and before Burgoyne reached Varna, estimating 70,000 Russian soldiers and 10,000 sailors in the Crimea, Tylden suggested a *coup de main* against Fort Constantine, which dominated Sevastopol harbour, with landings at Kaffa, Anapa and Eupatoria to cut off reinforcements. Once more Eupatoria figured in an appreciation of options. On 29 August de Ros explained: 'The more I think of the Crimea ... the more certain I am that Alma Bay between the Katcha and Eupatoria, north of Sevastopol, is too near Simpheropol and Batchki Serai, as well as Sebastopol, for any sound footing to be gained there without too great a risk.' He thus opted for Eupatoria, because it would be better to seize a town than risk landing on an exposed beach 'to the probabilities of masked batteries and other contingencies, prepared beforehand by an alarmed enemy, who has studied every form and feature of the ground and is well prepared'.[87]

Burgoyne had been right to underline the debilitating effect of illness. During the first week of August the sickness total in the British force had risen to 1,862 (7.73 per cent): on 7 August 257 were admitted to hospital at Varna, of which 112 died. During the second week, despite dispersal of units, 2,624 (9.73 per cent) were sick; and up to 9 August 345 had died of 'Asiatic cholera'. It had struck the fleets severely, causing them to put to sea, but *Britannia* still lost 139 of a ship's company of 985. Raglan told Richard that 'we have lost about 500 men and several officers', including two regimental commanders, but the French were more heavily hit. Cholera was not the only problem. 'A good deal of fever ... [has] pulled down officers and men', besides the inevitable strains of campaigning. On 21 August Raglan noted that the Duke of Cambridge had gone to Constantinople for health reasons.[88]

In the face of so many difficulties Raglan unreservedly praised his immediate staff. Writing to Charlotte, he declared: 'I like them all and my choice was a most fortunate one.' He was clearly fond of them. Nigel Kingscote was 'very sturdy' and 'very good company', though Raglan did not know previously that his nick-name was 'Old Square Toes'. Kingscote himself underlined to Kitty that the feelings were reciprocated. They were all devoted to making Raglan 'as comfortable as possibly can be done under the existing circumstances'. Her father was 'very cheerful', Kingscote assured her. Raglan had 'lots to do but always likes his evenings when nothing prevents him sitting and chatting with us'. Mapleton, the physician, had been feverish for the last few days, though, to Raglan's concern. 'Our party' now numbered twelve, including 'a Mr Calvert ... who knows the Crimea very well' and Tom Leslie, who appeared unexpectedly and would have had to sleep in the street had Raglan not shown 'compassion' towards him. Kingscote thought that, although an 'amateur', Leslie would go on with them. Raglan would only be able to take two horses with the initial landing party and had chosen Miss Mary and Shadrach. It was hoped that the others would be transported to the Crimea later. Prior to the operation Raglan had allowed Burghersh to visit Therapia 'for a lark'. Raglan's headquarters certainly seemed relaxed. He did, none the less, have to change his Quartermaster-General. From a hotel on the Bosporus, where he had originally gone to rest, de Ros warned Raglan on 20 August: 'My nerves are alas like a child's, and they send me into tears – a pretty bit of material you see for a QMG who ought to be made of iron.' Nine days later he announced that the doctors had decided that he must go back to England, as he kept falling prey to a succession of minor ailments, such as a sore throat.[89]

Meanwhile efforts were being made to provide Raglan with better intelligence of the Crimea. Kingscote referred to the arrival of Calvert. The government had, earlier that month, 'determined upon sending out to Turkey, for the purpose of assisting Lord Raglan by his knowledge of Russia and its language, Mr Charles Cattley'. Once there he assumed the name of Calvert lest the enemy should realize the extent of his experience, he having been a consul in the area for some time. He would ultimately prove his worth, producing reports throughout the winter and up to the time of Raglan's death on available supplies, Russian strengths and the nature of the terrain. He also interrogated prisoners of war and deserters. Above all he would run a Tartar spy network in the Crimea behind enemy lines, which generated valuable information on Russian deployments on the north side of Sevastopol, at Batchki Serai, Yalta and Simpheropol. His attachment to Raglan's headquarters during this period gives the lie to the received wisdom, uncritically repeated over the years, that Raglan eschewed the use of spies. Indeed, he and Stratford de Redcliffe discussed their use in August 1854. The Ambassador recommended a Greek to him, who had volunteered: 'The employment of spies, however dangerous, is I perceive at times necessary, and something must generally be risked in the employment of them.'[90]

Raglan's willingness to make Tom Leslie one of his household illustrates that kindness which endeared him to men of all ranks and which he showed in spite of the difficulties experienced in Bulgaria and, more precisely, in the run-up to the invasion. De Ros, waiting near Constantinople to return to England, thanked Raglan for his 'kind letter' and, with his departure imminent, wrote: 'Lady de R was so grateful to you for your note about me'. Writing to his daughters towards the end of August, he asked them to thank a list of people for 'kindly' writing to him and explain that he was unable to answer in person due to pressure of work. He noted that he had received a number of letters from relatives of 'poor Duffy', who had been sent home ill, thanking him for being so considerate. Raglan showed concern about friends in England, notably Egerton who had contracted a cataract of the lens, not the cornea as feared, and must take it 'quietly' until 'the organ is ripe for an operation'.[91]

Yet once more Raglan emphasized to his girls how much their letters meant to him, and his added regret that in going to the Crimea 'we shall be further from you. I shall feel much in the delay of your letters.' At present, 'it gives me much pleasure to hear from you and from your dear mama who is an excellent correspondent.' Despite the trial that Lady Raglan undoubtedly was to him, he remained devoted to her. Priscilla, too, proved a robust and regular correspondent during a month in which family illnesses abounded. In another touching personal gesture, he sent two scarves and two pocket handkerchiefs for her and her daughter Rose for 'your kindness to Emily and my girls'. In mid-August Raglan again expressed his gratitude to her for 'communicating with [Dr] Ferguson about dearest Emily and obtaining from him an assurance that her complaint is not dangerous'. Lady Raglan was about to go to Paris with Charlotte en route to Germany. Raglan wished that Priscilla could have gone with them because Emily had 'so little the habit of travelling'; and he was, therefore, 'most anxious' to hear when his wife and daughter had reached Paris.[92]

The condition of Lady Raglan and Charlotte dominated other family letters as well. Writing to Richard on 22 August he expected that his son would have met his mother and sisters before receiving the letter. Lady Raglan had 'been seriously ill and has been recommended to try the Ems waters'. Dr Ferguson had suggested, however, that Charlotte should not drink the waters, only bathe in them to enhance her strength. He hoped that both girls would improve their spoken German (a language they read well). Richard's presence at Ems would be 'a great joy and comfort to them'. To the girls, he wished that he were going to Ems with them, but 'rejoiced' that they were well enough to look forward to the journey. He did not know that day packets left Dover and had imagined them having to travel to Calais by night 'and I figured to myself that if the water was low in the harbour my Lady and Charlotte climbing up a steep ladder to their dismay'. The journey would now be over. But he hoped that, if the sea were smooth, they had gone via Ostend and Ghent 'with less fatigue'. Raising the hem of a curtain of past exasperation, he added: 'I see My Lady lift up her hands and eyes at all the unaccustomed inconveniences.' Raglan thought that cholera in the armies and fleets had abated, but addressed Kitty with the sad news that 'our poor friend Colonel Trevelyan was carried off in a few hours ... he was a most good natured excellent man', whose funeral Steele and Poulett had attended. He concluded by urging his daughters to take good care of 'dear mama', who would be very fatigued after the journey, and to make sure that she followed the doctor's advice. Lady Raglan probably would not like the change of food 'but novelty sometimes does wonders'. Charlotte must not try to walk too far: 'I do not like, my dear Charlotte, your still being weak.' And Kitty must not think that she was 'as strong as a bull and can live upon air and such luxuries'. 'I think of you all. Think you of yourselves' – an emotional homily from an anxious father, himself in the midst of danger and death. His last letter of the month to 'My dearest Charlotte' noted that he had written to 'your dear Mama' and Kitty, whose birthday fell on 31 August. Once more family anniversaries were precious to him. Raglan had been delighted to receive the letter describing the first day's journey 'in your passage across the Channel [when] you had not a ripple to disturb your stomach'. Did Charlotte remember when he had offered them 'fat pork', when the sea was not so smooth on one occasion? He was concerned about the dowager Duchess of Beaufort, who repeatedly suffered debilitating bouts of illness. Perhaps the measure of his affection and evidence of strain is best illustrated by his signing this letter to his 39-year-old sick daughter simply 'PAPA'.[93]

The question of Raglan's future after the war was raised by Aberdeen in mid-August. Following the death of the Marquis of Anglesey, the Queen had allowed the Prime Minister to offer Cowes Castle to Raglan 'as an agreeable residence'. It was, Aberdeen assured him, no longer a fortress: its character had completely changed. Another personal matter emerged during correspondence at this time. There is little firm evidence about Raglan's stature, portraits (especially group portraits) being unreliable. His son Richard was certainly more than six feet tall and Richard's sons were also about that height. Raglan seems, however, to have been shorter, below Wellington's known 5 feet 9 inches. Furthermore, in a letter to his daughters on 24 August he remarked: 'I don't much care for the change of uniform. The tunic is an awful thing for a stout gentleman with short legs.' It is just possible, though, that he was referring not to himself but a recent portrait of the late Duke of Beaufort. So the mystery of Raglan's stature may remain.[94]

Towards the end of August, with the worst ravages of cholera behind them though by no means fully eliminated, the troops began to concentrate once more in the Varna area; and preparation for the invasion gathered pace. On the 20th an Allied conference of military and naval commanders agreed to convey the troops, horses and equipment either in steam vessels or sailing ships towed by steamers, with 2 September fixed as the departure date.[95]

Embarkation began in earnest on 24 August. The French planned to take some 24,000 infantry and 70 pieces of field artillery, with the horses per gun reduced from six to four. Only about 100 cavalry would go with the initial landing party for escort duty. Most of the French troops would be conveyed in naval vessels, which assumed that they would not need to clear for action; in view of lack of recent Russian activity at sea, a justifiable gamble. But a gamble nevertheless. Approximately 5,000 Turks would be carried in their own warships and attached to the force under St Arnaud, who had thus partially achieved the overall command of his dreams. Rear-Admiral Sir Edmund Lyons supervised the British embarkation – the first 60 artillery pieces with a full complement of horses; 22,000 infantry; and 1,000 cavalry (the Light Brigade) in that order. A brisk north-easterly breeze delayed embarkation of the cavalry for a short time, otherwise the process went ahead smoothly. On 29 August Nigel Kingscote wrote to Kitty: 'We are all in great glee at the prospect of getting away so soon from this horrid place and of having something to do besides the bustle and activity of the embarkation gives one excitement.' In Raglan's words, 'the great expedition' was about to begin.[96]

It did so, at least in England, in a heady atmosphere of optimism verging on euphoria. Writing to Raglan, Newcastle declared: 'I will not believe that in any case British arms can fail.' When the British CinC voiced concern about suitable winter quarters for the troops in the Crimea, the Secretary of State blandly hoped that the taking of Sevastopol would solve his problem. The Duke of Cambridge still believed the enterprise 'a terrible risky one at this late season', adding ominously, 'but the government insists on it and the commanders have not got the courage to say no'. Unfairly the blame for possible failure was already being laid at Raglan's feet.[97]

CHAPTER 9

INTO BATTLE, THE CRIMEA (SEPTEMBER-DECEMBER 1854)

'The Queen cannot sufficiently express her high sense of the great services he [Raglan] has rendered and is rendering to her and to the country.' (Queen Victoria)[1]

Having embarked troops, equipment and stores, the tri-national armada aimed to concentrate in Balchik Bay, fifteen miles north of Varna, for the scheduled departure on 2 September. However, 'a strong breeze for several days previously, and ... a good deal of surf on the beach' slowed progress. Not until the afternoon of 4 September was embarkation complete, and the signal given for the British force to leave Varna. It sailed in the order (Light, 1st, 2nd, 3rd and 4th Divisions, then Light Brigade) as laid down in Raglan's instructions of 3 September: 'The invasion of the Crimea having been determined upon, the troops will embark in such ships as shall be provided for their conveyance, which will rendezvous at Baltschik [sic], and proceed with the combined fleets to their destination.' Publishing full details of the distribution of troops among transports, orders for landing and a map of the Crimea, *The Illustrated London News* speculated upon the landing spot: Eupatoria, Balaclava, Katcha (Brown's choice) or Kaffa, with the latter (following Macintosh) preferred.[2]

The armada did not, however, leave Balchik precisely as planned. When Raglan reached the bay during the morning of 5 September he discovered that St Arnaud in *Ville de Paris* had already gone. Worried about the different speeds of the ships, especially as Admiral Hamelin had belatedly announced that he could not provide enough steamers to tow all the sailing vessels, St Arnaud had set off independently with 36 French and Turkish sailing and steamships. Shortly before 5 a.m. on 7 September the last group of Allied vessels left Balchik [sic]. Just after midday St Arnaud dispatched a letter of explanation to Raglan from 'nearly twenty leagues to the north-east of Baltchick' revealing that, afraid of losing contact with Raglan, he was about to put back to rejoin the main force. St Arnaud regretted that the British CinC had not reached Balchik as agreed on 2 September. On the advice of Dundas he had therefore sailed three days later, as soon as orders had been issued for the main French convoy to proceed with Raglan; and he had been assured by the British admiral that Raglan would only be delayed by an hour. A further letter from Dundas on 6 September revealed that the British were still not under way, but a favourable wind determined Hamelin to continue to the rendezvous, 40 miles west of Cape Tarkan. Only the realization that by 12.30 p.m. on 7 September a dangerous gap of 'nearly 20 leagues' had opened up between *Ville de Paris* north-east of Balchik and Raglan, now made St Arnaud change his mind; and the following day (8 September) the ships carrying the two commanders at length met at sea. None the less, as the different vessels proceeded at their varying speeds towards the rendezvous, the armada was by now spread over a wide area, protected only by British warships which (unlike the French) were not carrying troops. Discord among the commanders and disruption of the armada had thus already occurred. Even more problems lay ahead.[3]

On 8 September Dundas boarded *Caradoc*, the steamer carrying Raglan, to tell him that St Arnaud wanted a conference, but was too ill to move from *Ville de Paris*. In the choppy sea the French three-decker was inaccessible to Raglan given his physical disability, so he sent Steele to represent him. At the conference that afternoon St Arnaud was joined by Hamelin, Admiral Bruat, Count Bouet-Williaumez and Colonel Trochu. The British party comprised Rose, the liaison officer, Dundas and Steele. The French produced another appreciation of possible landing spots, drawn up by senior officers advised by artillery and engineer experts. The mouth of the Katcha, Yetsa and Kaffa were considered. The author of the document (who remained anonymous) strongly opposed the current choice of the Katcha and, furthermore, eschewed any landing north of Sevastopol. The only feasible option was Kaffa – 100 miles to the east and separated from Sevastopol by mountainous terrain. But it lay in a large bay, had a secure anchorage and would avoid the hazard of landing over exposed beaches. Its situation dictated that any assault must be postponed until 1855, however. St Arnaud was too sick to debate the issue and the conference was adjourned to reconvene in *Caradoc* the following day, without the French commander but with Raglan presiding. Crucially, in reading out the paper, Trochu commented unfavourably upon it and supported the present intention. When both the French and British naval representatives also opposed any change in the operational plan, Raglan could easily scotch the entire notion. Nevertheless, evident unease about the Katcha – expressed here not for the first time – led him sensibly to suggest a second reconnaissance of the Crimean coast. As he did so he must have been fully aware of the number of references already made to Eupatoria and the anxiety to secure a port (such as Varna) to facilitate landing and resupply. By 9 September, therefore, as the Allied armada gathered at its rendezvous (from which masthead lookouts could see the Crimean coastline), expecting to make for the Katcha, the landing beach was in serious doubt.[4]

Early that day as the slower Allied vessels were still closing on the rendezvous, Generals Canrobert and Martimprey together with Trochu and French artillery and engineer officers joined Raglan, Brown, Lyons and Burgoyne in a party of twelve aboard *Caradoc*, which steamed towards Sevastopol supported by *Sampson*, *Agamemnon* and the French steamer *Prinoquet*. Shortly after dawn on 10 September the ships sailed past Sevastopol before rounding Cape Chersonesus and reaching the Genoese fort which marked the entrance to Balaclava harbour. Turning north once more, in Raglan's words they sailed 'so closely [to the shore] that Admiral Lyons and a Russian officer on horseback exchanged civilities and bowed to each other'. Passing Sevastopol for the second time on a 'fair, bright' Sunday morning as the bells rang out, farther north two rowing-boats put out from the reconnaissance flotilla to ascertain the depth of water. An alarmed Russian vidette 'on a prominent point loaded his carbine' and summoned cannon to his assistance, which fortunately arrived after the boats had returned. Progressively the mouths of the Belbec, Katcha, Alma and Bulganek rivers were examined, with Canrobert still opting for the Katcha which Raglan disliked because of its narrowness, proximity to Sevastopol – allowing enemy reinforcements quickly to amass – and vulnerability to artillery positioned on overlooking cliffs. Eupatoria appeared too small, but Raglan revealed that they remained immediately off the port for a considerable time, although 'men and women in their Sunday best clothes walked about without seemingly feeling any apprehension'. Having rejected Eupatoria and the other possible landing sites, Raglan chose a stretch of beach just south of Eupatoria. The superstitious might have queried its location (Calamita Bay), but Raglan considered it ideal. By the time that *Caradoc* returned to the main armada in the early hours of 11 September, Calamita Bay had replaced the Katcha and detailed plans were drawn up accordingly. In the course of a 'very interesting and exciting day', Raglan reported seeing 'a good many camps' containing possibly 20-25,000 men. He recognized that an additional garrison would be lodged in Sevastopol and other troops stationed inland at Simpheropol, Batchki Serai and other centres. Thus he was no longer seduced by estimates of modest Russian forces on the peninsula, but he considered the country more open than he had thought. Somerset Calthorpe expressed specific concern about Sevastopol: 'The fortifications looked of immense strength and appeared to bristle with guns.' Curiously, Lord Hardinge apparently told Newcastle that Calamita Bay was too close to Sevastopol, yet he wrote to Airey approvingly, adding that 'Katcher [sic] was too severe' with rocks and the cliffs giving the Russians too much cover.[5]

During the morning of Monday 11 September the armada (though still not fully concentrated) began to move again, sailing through showers of hail that day and the next towards the Crimea, with enemy territory off the port beam. By the evening of 12 September Eupatoria was in sight. Next day St Arnaud had recovered his vitality after five days of debilitating illness during which Kinglake alleges Raglan took effective command of the whole enterprise and laid down the place and timing of the landing. The impression of ruthlessness implicit in this contention is misplaced. Raglan never rode roughshod over his ally at any time, though he undoubtedly did greatly influence the Allied decisions during this critical period. He was not unsupported, after all, in rejecting the suggestion of Kaffa in 1855: French officers agreed with him. It is therefore difficult to accept Kinglake's contention that Raglan had overcome a French 'rebellion' in committing the Allies to the landing.[6]

Before disembarking in Calamita Bay, Eupatoria had to be secured on its northern flank. At noon on 13 September Steele and Trochu with Calvert (Cattley) as interpreter landed to request its surrender. The Governor audaciously replied that the troops might land at Lazzaretto but must consider themselves thereafter in strict quarantine. His temerity proved fruitless. The town was occupied by a small garrison next day, and remained in Allied hands throughout the war.[7]

Meanwhile, during the afternoon of 13 September the armada sailed south to anchor that night in Calamita Bay, though some ships did not close up until the early hours of 14 September. That morning the French would land to the right, the British to the left of a marker buoy placed opposite a salt lake near the Old Fort which lay inland of the more southerly beach. Unfortunately, during the night the buoy was set too far north, thus allowing the French the whole of the southern beach. Lyons discovered the error at daybreak. Rather than cause further disruption Raglan decided to adhere to the plan, so the British landed on the northern beach in front of the larger Lake Kamischlu. Thus the two armies (French, plus Turks, and British) landed a mile apart, though the narrow flanks of both beaches could be easily defended and naval vessels offshore commanded the low cliffs within range.

Throughout the morning of 14 September Allied troops landed in an atmosphere approaching gaiety. Corporal McMillan, a Coldstream Guardsman, reported 'the band ... on the Poop playing the national tunes'. But he also described some enemy resistance: 'It seemed the enemy expected us to land there'. Allied warships shelled Russian encampments and 'two or three small redoubts opened fire on the steamers but they could not reach them [because] their guns did not carry enough'. McMillan's account is at variance with others that graphically refer to a single Russian officer observing the landing from a headland while calmly taking notes; and, almost certainly, his account of naval actions were based on hearsay, referring to shelling of enemy positions farther south. Nor were all the troops confined to the beach area. Landing 'after dinner', the Coldstreams marched inland for '4 or 5 miles over a barren piece of country' with neither tree nor house in sight before bivouacking. All accounts agree, though, that the troops endured torrential rain without cover that night and that the French quickly and effectively pillaged most available supplies. Contrary to other reports that accuse Raglan of not allowing tents ashore until 17 September, the Coldstreams had theirs on 16 September. During the nights of 17 and 18 September Cossacks attacked the

Allied outposts, and cavalry were dispatched to scour the vicinity in day-light. They did manage to gather some cattle, but needed to drive off enemy cavalry on the way back. McMillan noted that the Russians started 'such large fires extending for miles' to deny the Allies supplies and that the Commissariat proved ineffective by issuing no sugar and only green coffee which the troops could neither grind nor roast. 'So we were obliged to be content with a drink of very brackish water.' For this, Raglan could not be blamed. He had consistently drawn attention to deficiencies in sup-plies for which the system, rather than individuals, was responsible.[8]

On the whole the British dealt more reasonably with the native Tartars from whom Raglan received an address of welcome, which he characteristically and courteously acknowledged during a meeting with local headmen on the afternoon of 15 September. But very few supplies and scant land transport were secured from the vicinity of the beaches: Airey gathered a mere 350 wagons with drivers. And not for five days were the Allies ready to move south. The French writer Baron César de Bazancourt blamed the long delay on British disorganization. In reality the last-minute alteration of landing beach had unavoidably slowed down disembarkation, and rough seas further delayed the landing of horses and equipment. The French had few cavalry: the British had to land a light brigade, including grooms and farriers, of some 1,000 men plus horses, accompanying stores and equipment. Field Marshal Sir Evelyn Wood (in 1854, a midshipman) later praised Raglan's choice of a low shingly beach protected by a salt lake inland and with flanks narrow enough for the fleet's cannon to cover. Thus the entire Allied force got safely ashore with-out incurring any loss through enemy action. By the evening of 18 Sep-tember Raglan had landed his entire army. Watching the exercise from aboard ship, Fanny Duberly succumbed to heady optimism. The Allies, she averred, would be in Sevastopol in a 'few days'.[9]

A narrow post road ran parallel to the sea towards Sevastopol across undulating ground and over several streams. Along this the Allies prepared to advance early on the morning of 19 September. In addition to Raglan's force, the French claimed to deploy 30,000 (though Raglan thought only 27,600), the Turks 7,000, making a grand total of 63,000 men and 128 guns. The only cavalry force was the British Light Brigade. The French had usually operated on the Allied right, and they now adopted that position with the Turks behind them; protected on the right by the sea. This meant that Raglan had to cover the exposed Allied left, enemy forces being likely to harass the invaders from the direction of Batchki Serai and Simpheropol. To permit his British force to meet any threat by deploying into line, Raglan kept his infantry divisions in two columns with (front to rear) on the left the Light, 1st and 4th Divisions, on the right the 2nd and 3rd Divisions abutting the French, with the cattle and bag-gage behind them. This would allow a minimum of two divisions to meet a threat from the front or left. Skirmishers were posted ahead, to the rear and on the left flank. Additionally Cardigan led two regiments of light cavalry in advance of the entire force, two other regiments covered the left and a fifth the rear. The artillery moved on the seaward (right) side of each division for protection against enemy attack. Because of the weak condition of the troops, many of whom were sick, Raglan allowed them to march without knapsacks, carrying their possessions in their blankets. Nevertheless the extreme heat of the late morning coupled with a scarcity of water caused many to collapse by the wayside, and the bands soon fell silent. Such was the troops' exhaustion that Lady Erroll and her French maid, mounted on mules, were soon virtually buried under a pyramid of discarded rifles. 'The day's march had been most wearisome,' Raglan noted that evening. A masterly understatement.[10]

Enemy troops lay in ambush beyond the Bulganek. Early on the afternoon of 19 September, in advance of his infantry divisions Raglan reached the north bank from which he observed Cossacks south of the river. He ordered the cavalry advance guard of 11th Hussars and 13th Light Dragoons under Cardigan, but with Lucan also present, to investigate. It discovered some 2,000 enemy cavalry drawn up on the crest of a hill, and British regiments therefore deployed into line as the Russians edged forward. Both forces threw out skirmishers and hostile action seemed imminent. But Raglan and Airey glimpsed the flash of bayonets in a valley beyond the rising ground and immediately recognized Cardigan's perilous position. Quickly Raglan brought up the Light and 2nd Divisions, two further cavalry regiments and 9pdr guns attached to the 2nd Division. Raglan then sent Airey in his name to require Lucan to retire the light cavalry screen. As he did so enemy guns opened fire, inflicting minor casualties; and British 6pdr and 9pdr guns replied, causing the enemy to retreat. Raglan had, thus, acted decisively in this first encounter on the Crimean peninsula, skilfully extricating his cavalry screen from danger. Of the Light Brigade, he wrote: 'It was impossible for any troops to exhibit more steadiness ... It fell back upon its supports with the perfect regularity under the fire of the Artillery, which was quickly silenced by that of the batteries I caused to be brought into action.'[11]

That night the bulk of the British force camped south of the Bulganek, the 4th Division and 4th Light Dragoons remaining on the north bank. By 19 September a dangerous gap of almost one mile had opened up between the British and French, and a Cossack patrol exploited this to capture a French liaison officer with Raglan's headquarters during darkness. Meanwhile Raglan and his staff occupied a post house where the Sevastopol road crossed the river to the right rear of the British position. According to Kinglake, Raglan 'placed the troops himself, fixing their exact position with minute care' to cover front, left flank and rear. The open (left) flank remained highly vulnerable although the Russians had already retired to strong defensive positions farther south.[12]

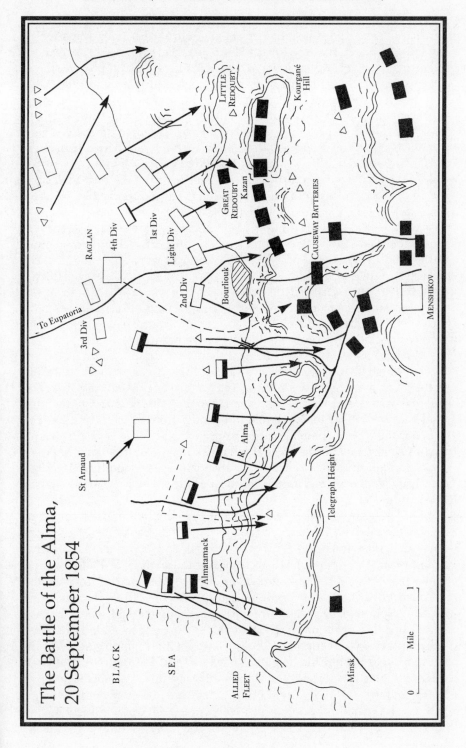

The Battle of the Alma, 20 September 1854

BLACK
SEA
ALLIED FLEET
Minsk

St Arnaud
R. Alma
Almatamack
Telegraph Height

To Eupatoria
RAGLAN
4th Div
3rd Div
1st Div
Light Div
2nd Div
Bourliouk
GREAT REDOUBT
Kazan
LITTLE REDOUBT
Kourgané Hill
CAUSEWAY BATTERIES
MENSHIKOV

0   Mile   1

Raglan had been warned by a report from *Terrible* on 15 September that enemy troops had concentrated south of the River Alma which ran into the Black Sea close to Cape Loukool. The ground on the northern (right) bank of the Alma down which the Allies must approach sloped gently, that on the southern bank rose steeply – in places to fifteen feet high before levelling off in a ledge prior to climbing again. High above the southern bank a series of uneven hills formed rolling downs which stretched inland some four miles from the sea. Dominating the northern approach slopes, these formed an ideal defensive position astride the Sevastopol post road. At the western end of the downs a 350-foot cliff abutted the Black Sea. Two miles further inland, and covering the post road from the west, stood Telegraph Height. Between it and Kourgane Hill (450 feet high) farther east, the post road after crossing the Alma climbed through a pass or causeway where additional field batteries were situated on convenient, detached knolls. Telegraph Height and Kourgane Hill, dominating as they did the post road and both well-fortified, were the centerpieces of the Russian defences; and only a single regiment supported by a half-battery of field guns guarded the western end of the downs. South of the river the ascending slopes were scarred by several gullies and covered by scrub which provided ideal cover for enemy skirmishers. Crossing the river to attack the Russians would thus prove hazardous. A steep, narrow track wound its way up the cliffs near the river's mouth, a ford at the village of Almatamack (one mile inland) led to a wagon road; three others farther east were less accessible to Telegraph Height, but passable. The main crossing point was, therefore, the wooden bridge carrying the post road near the village of Bourliouk, three miles from the sea. This, like the pass beyond it, was commanded by Kourgane Hill and Telegraph Height. East of Kourgane Hill the ground fell away making outflanking impossible. Although in theory Allied ships anchored at the mouth of the Alma could engage the enemy, in practice most of the Russian positions were in dead ground to them.[13]

These geographical features were apparent to the Allied commanders as they moved forward on the morning of 20 September. Hoping to delay the Allies for up to three weeks to allow reinforcements to arrive from Bessarabia – many of them troops withdrawn from Moldavia and Wallachia – the Russian commander, Prince Menshikov, fortified the so-called Great and Lesser redoubts, respectively with twelve and nine cannon supported by massed infantry, on Kourgane Hill where he also established his headquarters. He deployed more men and artillery on Telegraph Height overlooking the causeway. Other infantry and cavalry lay in reserve behind the heights. Vineyards north of the river had been cleared to give a better field of fire. In all, Menshikov commanded some 33,000 infantry, 3,400 cavalry, 2,600 gunners and 106 guns. Small wonder that, given the natural position that he occupied, he was confident of success. On the Allied right 37,000 French and Turkish troops were supported by 68 field guns and the fire of steamers offshore. Raglan, on the left, had some 26,000 men (including 1,000 cavalry) and 60 guns, but was out of range of supporting naval gunfire. When formulating their plans, however, Raglan and St Arnaud were essentially ignorant of Russian strength, their maps were 'imperfect', no information had yet been gleaned from spies and the only reliable observations came from warships in the Black Sea.[14]

During the evening of 19 September St Arnaud visited Raglan at his quarters by the Bulganek. Basing his plan upon naval reports, he proposed that, supported by naval gunfire, the French should carry the cliffs by the sea and effectively turn the entire Russian position. Raglan evidently did not strongly disagree, according to Kinglake, but events the next day suggest that he postponed a final decision on a plan of attack until he had examined the ground and the enemy position himself. Meanwhile, at the conference late on 19 September it was agreed that Bosquet's 2nd Division would set off at 5 a.m. on 20 September on the Allied right towards the two most westerly crossing points. The remainder of the British and French forces would leave the Bulganek two hours later, taking the divisions of Canrobert and Prince Napoleon to the three access routes to Telegraph Height, the British on the left to the area of Kourgane Hill and the bridge by Bourliouk village. A General Order issued from the 'Bivouac on the Bulganek' during the evening of 19 September required the British force to march at 7 a.m. the following morning, in the same order as that day after having closed to within 20 yards of the French left. The Alma lay five miles distant.

Shortly after the appointed hour Bosquet with the Turkish troops in reserve began to march. At 7 a.m. the rest of the French were ready. The British were not, although headquarters was officially 'en route' at 7.30. The delay did not stem from idleness. Throughout the night Raglan had protected the vulnerable Allied left flank, and his formations had to be manoeuvred into the order of march before they could move forward. Moreover the mile-wide gap that had developed between British and French troops the previous day had to be closed, and Raglan wisely insisted that his baggage train with its valuable reserve ammunition must be fully protected, which entailed even more reorganization. Furthermore, the line of the Bulganek occupied by the British ran obliquely to the line of march. Eventually, over an hour late, the bulk of the Allied force began to move. In front of the British Light and 2nd Divisions were 'small bands which played occasionally'. Raglan rode in front of 'C' Troop RHA with the Light Division, accompanied by 'a large staff' among which was Kinglake. By now Bosquet was well in advance on the far right, and at 10.20 the steamers opened up in his support. An hour later the main body halted about 1 1/2 miles from the Alma where the ground began to slope towards it.[15]

After they had halted, Raglan and St Arnaud conferred on a rise between the British and French troops using 'field glasses' to survey the enemy. A previous attempt to confer at 9.30 had been frustrated by the presence of Russian cavalry on nearby hills. No record exists of what was said, and only a snatch of conversation was overheard. Raglan evidently confirmed that in view of Russian cavalry strength and the nature of the ground west of the line of march, outflanking to the left would be impossible. He was thus committed to a frontal assault on Kourgane Hill which he considered the key to the whole Russian position. His eye for ground and the critical point of an enemy's deployment had not deserted him. As Raglan later explained to Newcastle, given the obvious strength of Kourgane Hill, Bosquet's assault on the Russian left and French capture of Telegraph Height were expected to precede the British advance in the area east of Bourliouk.

So, just after 1 p.m. (precisely at 1.10 according to one eye-witness) the bulk of the armies (less Bosquet's independent division) once more advanced. As they did so Russian skirmishers fired the village of Bourliouk and surrounding foliage, in Raglan's words 'obscuring their position and rendering a passage through it impracticable'; and to a large extent Russian cavalry movement beyond as well. After half an hour, the British halted again, deployed from column into line and lay down, this time in range of enemy artillery, while Raglan waited for the French to make the necessary progress against Telegraph Height. At 2 p.m., hearing gunfire to the right, a staff officer optimistically exclaimed that the French were warmly engaged. Raglan, however, with the voice of experience demurred. There was no exchange of fire; excited French skirmishers alone were firing. After another hour during which the troops lay exposed to enemy fire, St Arnaud brought up his reserve division (Forey); but it became clear that Telegraph Height would not be quickly taken. Following Wellington's practice, at this stage of the battle Raglan and his staff moved freely along the line in a 'plumed cavalcade', pausing to take observations apparently at leisure from time to time – activity which calmed inexperienced soldiers in the ranks. Especially near the post road, the Russians peppered the group with round shot and shell, but to no avail. At length, though, Raglan decided that his troops must move. They were beginning to incur unacceptable casualties, as they waited for the French to take Telegraph Height. The report of a French ADC may also have influenced Raglan to move forward for fear that his ally might retreat. At approximately 3 p.m., therefore, he ordered the British across the Alma.[16]

Brown's Light Division lay on the British left, with de Lacy Evans' 2nd Division on his right, the 1st and 3rd Divisions behind them respectively, Cathcart's 4th Division in reserve and the cavalry guarding the open flank. In the smoke and confusion of battle Brown failed to realize that the river under Kourgane Hill ran at an angle across his front, so as he advanced his troops squeezed the British 2nd Division against French troops to its right. Raglan saw potential disarray developing and sent an order to Brown to move to his left, following this by personally approaching one of Brown's brigade commanders, Codrington. Inexplicably the Light Division did not alter its line of march and thus became intermingled with 2nd Division. In the vicinity of the burning village of Bourliouk a round shot landed near Raglan but he was unhurt. Seeing the confusion of the Light and 2nd Divisions which were advancing towards the Great Redoubt on the western forward slope of Kourgane Hill, he realized too that the Duke of Cambridge's 1st Division was in effect moving east of Brown and was thus exposed to the full force of the guns in the Lesser Redoubt. He sent an ADC with the injunction to 'go quietly, don't gallop' to order the 3rd Division to move to the left. Evaluating the situation, Raglan had committed all but one of his infantry divisions; only the 4th remained in reserve. Together with the cavalry it was held back 'to protect the left flank and rear against large bodies of the enemy's cavalry which had been seen in those directions'. Raglan's caution appeared well justified.

At about 3.15, having set his divisions in motion, in his blue frock coat, white shirt, black tie and white plumed hat, Raglan rode across the river west of the post road up a narrow defile to occupy a low knoll on the lower slopes of Telegraph Height, approximately 800 yards south and 100 feet above the Alma. From there he could observe clearly the progress of the battle, unhindered by smoke from the burning village and discharges on the battlefield, looking directly towards Kourgane Hill ('the high pinnacle' in his words) and through the pass at the Russian reserves. The knoll was not altogether safe, attracting the attention of Russian skirmishers, who wounded two of Raglan's staff. Seated on the brown bay Shadrach, which proved restless under fire, Raglan had difficulty in using his spyglass from the saddle. Recognizing the ability to threaten the enemy from this spot, however, he sent Airey back for Adams' brigade from 2nd Division. In the meantime he hoped that the enemy would think that he was already supported by troops: 'Our presence here will have the best effect'; and Kinglake argues that, suitably deceived, Menshikov critically withdrew guns from the Great Redoubt to cover this supposed threat. Others felt that impending capture of the defence work by the Light Division prompted this withdrawal.

Kinglake notes that he then heard Raglan exclaim, 'Now, if we had a couple of guns here!', indicating that the author himself was on the knoll. Indeed, Kinglake records that during this whole period Raglan was so unperturbed as to discuss Shadrach's behaviour with him. Responding to Raglan's desire for guns, Lieutenant-Colonel Dickson immediately rode back down the gully. As he did so a French ADC arrived pleading for assistance. Kinglake noted how reddened Raglan's face was by the recent sun as he bent kindly to offer a battalion which was all that he could spare. Raglan remained calm, 'taking no more notice of the firing than if he had been at a review', according to Calthorpe. Yet, due to a misunderstanding, Light Division troops had withdrawn from the Great Redoubt. Others were pinned down by determined enemy fire, as the 2nd Division supported by England's artillery, sought to force the river in the area of the post road. The general situation was not, therefore, encouraging. At 3.40, however, two 9pdr guns from Turner's battery reached the knoll and, after initial difficulty, began successfully to engage the enemy. By 3.55 they were harassing the left of the Kourgane position and causing havoc among the Russian reserves. Shortly afterwards the 1st Division, having belatedly crossed the Alma, carried the Kourgane, though it would be a gross exaggeration to claim that the two guns on Raglan's knoll provided more than an additional aid to the brave action of the infantry further east. However, recognition of the worth of their contribution and the advantage of deploying Adams' brigade near the knoll underlines Raglan's ability quickly to analyse a battle situation. When Adams did arrive Raglan personally deployed his two battalions. But by then (about 4.30 – 'exactly 4.20' in one report) the enemy was in retreat and, after displaying the fresh troops for moral effect, he re-deployed them to the south-east, while sending Turner forward to fire on the fleeing enemy. As he did so Raglan left the knoll, rode across the post road and up Kourgane Hill to meet Cambridge. By 4.30, therefore, the British were in full command of Kourgane Hill, the pass (causeway) through which the post road ran and part of Telegraph Height, with the French abreast of the downs further west and Congreve rockets speeding the Russians on their way.

Aware of the cavalry's eagerness to pursue the enemy, Raglan was clear that he could not imperil the Allies' only brigade with 3,000 Russian cavalry still at large. He therefore sent Estcourt to forbid Lucan to attack: he must only escort infantry to the front. When some cavalry were seen to disobey, Raglan dispatched other staff officers to order them back. Later misinterpreted as lack of initiative and certainly disliked by the cavalry themselves, Raglan's action made eminent sense. Cambridge fully recognized Raglan's dilemma: 'Unfortunately we could not follow them up owing to lack of cavalry, otherwise they would have been cut off from Sebastopol,' he concluded. Retreating in disarray, the enemy had to funnel through a narrow gorge; and Raglan saw that they would then be susceptible to flank attack from French troops on Telegraph Height. Two requests for decisive action were sent, but the French did not attack. Raglan was in no position, following the heavy cost of taking Kourgane Hill, to move alone.

Kinglake would later criticize Raglan for not adopting 'a sterner method' advancing himself before the light faded at about 6 p.m. This would have obliged St Arnaud, who pleaded that his men's knapsacks had been left north of the river, to follow. That would have been totally unrealistic because patrols had reported a Russian rearguard with 30 guns two miles behind Telegraph Height. There was no guarantee, therefore, that had Raglan pushed on independently his men 'would have drunk of the Katcha [seven miles south] that night'. They might easily have been repulsed with further casualties.[17]

After the initial French refusal to forge ahead, towards 5 p.m. Raglan rode slowly down from Kourgane Hill through the ranks of the weary infantry and recrossed the Alma. The ruins of Bourliouk were still smouldering, though wounded were sheltering beneath its broken walls. Earlier, having been embarrassed to receive the cheers of his men as he rode through their midst, he now 'passed a long time, giving tender care to the sufferers'. When he was leaving the knoll, Kinglake noted the strain on Raglan's face; and that evening at 9 o'clock he dined in his small tent with the author. When Brigadier-General Torrens arrived in some distress, having cleared the landing beaches with the rearguard as ordered only to find that he had missed the battle, Raglan arranged a third place at the table. 'With kind, frank, thoughtful words Lord Raglan strove to soothe him,' Kinglake recorded. Raglan's own state of mind as he bivouacked among the troops on the heights above the post road that evening can only be conjectured, but French intransigence and, soon, the realization that 362 (including 25 officers) had been killed and 1,640 British troops were wounded or missing undoubtedly deeply affected him. Lyons later recalled the British CinC's words during a meeting with him at his headquarters above the Alma shortly after noon on 21 September: 'With the troops perfectly fresh and fit to march on and the weather very fine, I sent to Maréchal St Arnaud to propose that we should march on to Sevastopol and assault the place at once (to take our ground above the town, I forget which was the expression) and the answer to me was that the French troops were fatigued and cannot move on any further. That cannot be the real reason, as the march has not been long enough to fatigue the troops – but however as they cannot move of course I cannot either.'

Raglan's lack of understanding of the stresses of the recent battle seems strange: for these alone must have tired the men. Lyons may not, therefore, have accurately recalled Raglan's words, but the gist was probably right. Lyons suggested that St Arnaud, once more sick, either did not get the message or did not make the decision. No doubt from later experience, he caustically said that 'Canrobert would never take a decision' in his stead. Lyons fervently held that if Raglan's suggestion for swift pursuit had been acted upon, Sevastopol could have been taken by a *coup de main*. Only 2,000 men were there at this time, and a 'golden opportunity' had been lost to secure the prize 'in the week after we landed in the Crimea'. Lyons saw Raglan again next day (22 September) and found him 'in low spirits'. He had once more been rebuffed by St Arnaud, who rejected an immediate advance across the Rivers Katcha and Belbec. The

Allies might well force the 'strong earthworks on the banks of the river', St Arnaud admitted; but the casualties would be unacceptable.[18]

While the armies dallied, the dead were buried, the sick and wounded carried aboard ship. Raglan fretted, though compassionately he sent 500 Russian wounded by sea to Odessa. On 22 September a 'General After Order' congratulated the troops for 'their unrivalled efforts' on 20 September in carrying 'a most formidable position, defended by large masses of Russian infantry, and a most powerful and numerous Artillery'; noted that their 'spirited and successful attack ... cannot fail to have attracted their [French] notice and admiration' – a reminder of the alliance; thanked 'the Army most warmly for its gallant exertions ... [which] gloriously maintained the honor of the British Name'; and concluded that 'Lord Raglan condoles most sincerely with the Troops on the loss of so many gallant Officers and brave Men'. That same evening (22 September) Lord George Paget found his commander dining alone in the open and was invited to join him. Raglan complained to Paget of French inactivity, showing his irritation at 'their confounded too-too-tooing' – reference to fondness for martial trumpet calls. This reaction proffered further evidence of temporary despair.[19]

When the march resumed on 23 September the crucial decisions of where the troops were to go and how Sevastopol was to be attacked had still not been resolved: seizure of the northern suburbs with their dominating forts; or bombardment from uplands to the south? Initially the armies made for the Katcha and ultimately the north side of Sevastopol. En route Raglan's dispatch about the Alma battle was completed. His first notes, in pencil, were dated 21 September from 'Heights of Alma', and another more comprehensive version in his handwriting was composed during the next day from 'Camp on the Alma'. Steele, however, revealed that the dispatch was finalized 'at a house in the village of Katcha where we halted for the night' of 23 September. He went on: 'The greatest part of the dispatch which was sent to Govt was written under a tree above the Belbeck [sic] river before the flank march was decided upon by Leicester Curzon', though Steele clearly meant that Curzon had produced the fair copy. In his dispatch Raglan claimed that the Russians had been overcome at the Alma 'in less than three hours' – justified if counted from 1.30 when the troops lay down within artillery range.[20]

South of the Alma questioning of the few inhabitants still in the region established that the Russian retreat had not been halted. Thus, on 23 September, Raglan ordered Lucan with the cavalry and a troop of horse artillery to proceed south of the Katcha to occupy the village of Duvankoi, upstream on the Belbec and astride the high road from Sevastopol to Batchki Serai. Lucan complied with his orders, taking the village in a 'nook shut in between the bank of the river on one side and precipitous heights on the other'. At dusk, having confirmed lack of enemy activity in the area, Lucan withdrew to high ground close by.[21]

The main body was scheduled to advance again for the Katcha early on Sunday 24 September, but at 7 a.m. St Arnaud requested a delay of three hours to evaluate the intelligence that 'yesterday' the Russians had sunk seven warships across the mouth of Sevastopol harbour; and to allow reconnaissance of the new earthwork reported near the mouth of the Belbec. He was also concerned about reports of another battery in advance of Sevastopol's northern defences, which could menace the French. The march did recommence at 10 a.m., and the heights between the Katcha and Belbec were soon scaled from which Sevastopol could be seen before the troops began the descent to the Belbec. At this stage St Arnaud was clearly very unwell. Cardigan meanwhile scouted ahead, and beyond the Belbec he noted an 'impracticable' marsh plus a causeway dominated by enemy guns supported by infantry and cavalry. That evening, as the Allies camped near the Belbec, another conference took place. It was to be decisive.[22]

The precise sequence of events on 24 September is unclear, but evidently Sir John Burgoyne visited St Arnaud in the presence of the French commanding engineer (General Bizot) before the conference between the two commanders and their staffs at the French headquarters that evening. The central question concerned the strength of the Russian defences on the northern side of the bay and whether they could be carried by the Allies. Once taken, in theory, they could be used by the Allies to make the southern sector of the port with its dockyard untenable. At worst troops would then need to cross the bay under the cover of those captured northern guns to assault the southern defences. Among the enemy's northern defences before the Allies, the crucial work was Star Fort – an octagonal earthwork surrounded by ditch and glacis, overlooking the sea to the west and Sevastopol Bay to the south. In January 1854 Captain Drummond RN had declared this position the key: if captured 'the place [Sevastopol] would fall imediately'. Following the Allied landing in Calamita Bay, however, the Russian engineer Lieutenant-Colonel E. E. I. Todleben had strengthened its defences and, furthermore, deployed infantry in close support. Two more batteries had been thrown up to the north, one of which covered the mouth of the Belbec and so worried the French. There is no doubt that, on the right of the Allied line, the French were especially concerned about the strength of the defences in their path and the likelihood of Russian troop reinforcements on the northern side of Sevastopol. A Polish deserter heightened French fears by suggesting that approaches to Star Fort had been mined and that naval guns from the south could dominate the north of the bay. But Burgoyne had long favoured attack from the south and at his meeting with St Arnaud may well have pressed his point. Sir John must have been aware too of a report dated 22 September by *Sampson*'s captain, which detailed 'great exertions' to strengthen the shore defences in and around Sevastopol and that heavy guns on the north side had a range of some 4,000 yards. The flank march, as it became known, would avoid a frontal assault on the northern defences.

Arguments such as Burgoyne's that the north side was defended by an 'army', French fears about the strength of the fortifications and the contention that the north side had no safe harbour from which to resupply the Allies in poor weather appeared conclusive. Yet Burgoyne certainly, and Raglan probably, were mentally prepared for a southern attack from the moment of landing. To Newcastle on 28 September Raglan wrote: 'I have always been disposed to consider that Sebastopol should be attacked on the south side, and Sir John Burgoyne leant strongly to the same opinion.' On 21 September Burgoyne had produced a strong six-paragraph memorandum favouring operations form the south, rather than north, making use of Balaclava and 'the bays near Chersonese [sic]' for naval support and supplies. Kinglake revealed that Raglan spoke personally to two travellers, Oliphant and Oswald Smith, before leaving England, and was impressed by their separate opinions that troops landing in one of the bays to the south could successfully mount an attack on Sevastopol. For whatever reason, the decision to commence the flank march on 25 September was taken at the evening conference on the 24th on the Belbec during which St Arnaud sat rigidly in his chair. As he was leaving Raglan remarked that the French commander was obviously 'dying', an impression reinforced when he saw St Arnaud the next morning before the advance resumed.[23]

Leaving Cathcart's 4th Division and the 4th Light Dragoons on the Belbec to maintain communication with the fleets off the Katcha, Raglan planned to avoid the marsh identified by Cardigan, swing east to gain high ground at the head of Sevastopol Bay and reach the Sevastopol-Batchki Serai road near Mackenzie's Farm. The cavalry division (less the 4th Dragoons but plus the Scots Greys, who had landed at the Katcha) under Lucan was to scout ahead, supported by a battalion of rifles and a battery of horse artillery, through the wooded area leading to Mackenzie's Farm. Once he reached the Baktchi Serai road Lucan was to report to Raglan on enemy troop dispositions. The wooded area in front of the British, as they left the Belbec, was crossed by tracks that could be negotiated by the cavalry and artillery. But the infantry would have to move through the forest by compass. As soon as the British had established the line of march (Mackenzie's Farm – Tractir Bridge – Tchernaya – Balaclava) the French would follow.

Delayed for an hour by the tardy arrival of The Rifles, Lucan set off at 8.30 a.m., closely followed by Raglan and his staff. Unfortunately, at a junction of tracks, Lucan's guide led the cavalry along the wrong track. Ignorant of this error, the British CinC rode on to high ground close to the more easterly of two lighthouses at the head of Sevastopol Bay and, in bright sunlight, looked down the length of the bay to its Black Sea entrance and the sunken Russian vessels. After briefly studying Sev-

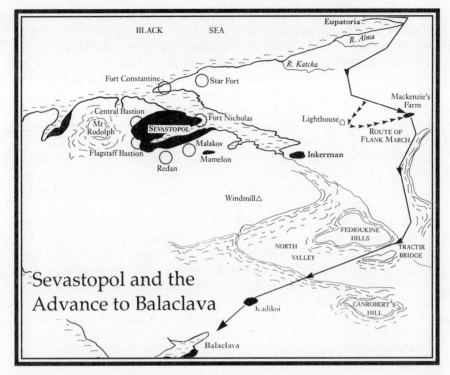

BLACK   SEA

Eupatoria

R. *Alma*

R. *Katcha*

Fort Constantine
Star Fort

Central Bastion
Mt Rodolph
SEVASTOPOL
Fort Nicholas
Lighthouse

Mackenzie's Farm

ROUTE OF
FLANK MARCH

Malakov
Flagstaff Bastion
Mamelon
Redan
Inkerman

Windmill

FEDIOUKINE
HILLS

NORTH
VALLEY

TRACTIR
BRIDGE

Sevastopol and the Advance to Balaclava

Kadikoi

CANROBERT'S
HILL

Balaclava

astopol itself, he turned aside and found his way through the forest to the right track for Mackenzie's Farm, expecting to fall in behind Lucan. He discovered only Captain Maude's battery of horse artillery and personally led it forward. When a clearing appeared Airey rode ahead to reconnoitre. After advancing a short way he raised his arm in warning. Raglan and the following small force halted.

Kinglake, an eye-witness, learnt that they had all but met the rearguard of Menshikov's army as it withdrew from Sevastopol. 'In a tranquil low voice', Raglan sent an officer to find Lucan and deployed his own hussar escort under Captain Chetwode as a forward screen. Meanwhile he and his staff gently backed down the lane and waited. When the cavalry galloped up – in single file because of the narrow track – Raglan called out with some warmth: 'Lord Lucan, you are late!'. Lucan pursued the Russians with the Light Brigade as Maude unlimbered his guns to fire on the enemy rearguard and Raglan dismounted to order the Scots Greys into nearby woods to cover the British flank. Having captured the enemy wagon train, Cardigan spurred on until Raglan recalled the cavalry which had left his headquarters defended only by Maude and the Scots Greys. Rebuked by Raglan for pursuing the enemy too far, Cardigan replied that he was no longer in command of the cavalry. The feud between the volatile brothers-in-law had not cooled. Raglan referred to his brush with danger and possible capture as an 'incident of war', but a thin line of trees alone concealed his weak position. On that the success of the flank march and perhaps the entire enterprise rested. Lucan may have, in reality, been not only late but too late to save his commander-in-chief. When the cavalry had once more taken the vanguard the advance continued though the Allied force was now spread over a wide distance: the British lst Division trailed Raglan's headquarters from the Belbec by 1½ hours, the French and Turks were following behind the last British formation. That night, having paused only briefly at old buildings (Mackenzie's Farm) on the heights east of Sevastopol – long enough, however, to have the sharp interview with Cardigan over handling of the cavalry – Raglan moved on to occupy a small deserted post-house beside Tractir Bridge, which spanned the Tchernaya as it flowed into Sevastopol Bay. He and his staff dined sparingly from the leg of a wild boar provided by Captain Thomas RA. As Raglan later explained to Newcastle, 'we were in a dangerous situation'. The invading troops were still dispersed along the heights east of Sevastopol; the British encamped on the lower slopes, the French above and some two miles behind. In reality the entire Allied force was straggling between the Rivers Tchernaya and Belbec. Most of these men, while remaining vulnerable to counter-attack, were without food or water. Fortunately thick fog reduced the prospect of enemy action. Small wonder that Raglan expressed relief when dawn broke and no attack had materialized, though at least one messenger from Cathcart was fired upon during the night as he approached Raglan.[24]

During the morning of 26 September Raglan crossed the Tchernaya and rode south into the village of Kadikoi, about 1½ miles north of Balaclava. Assured by inhabitants that the port was undefended, he advanced down a narrow road in front of his troops to the head of Balaclava Bay whose main wharves were masked by cliffs beyond a bend in the road. Suddenly a shot plunged into the water close to Raglan, propelled from an old castle overlooking the entrance to the harbour. Angry that he had been deceived by the villagers, he ordered the Light Divison, supported by horse artillery, to capture the heights above Balaclava harbour. As he took cover naval guns were heard engaging the fortification; and before troops had reached their objective above, the militia garrison surrendered. Raglan then rode forward along the track to the water's edge, where he watched a British warship enter the harbour. However, bearing in mind the line of march since Calamita Bay, the British theoretically ought not to have remained in Balaclava. Instead, wheeling right they should have continued north-westwards to take up positions on the left of the Allied line on the upland south of Sevastopol. Had this been done they could have used Kazatch and Kamiesch, west of Sevastopol, as supply ports. The French, on the right, could have used Balaclava. The course of the ensuing siege would have been different and the battles of Balaclava and Inkerman would not have been predominantly British affairs.

But Balaclava had appeared frequently in British appreciations of the Crimea hitherto and, when consulted by Raglan, Lyons strongly advised its retention. Canrobert (who succeeded St Arnaud in command late on 26 September) offered Raglan a choice on 27 September when the two commanders met 2½ miles north-east of the port on a detached feature thereafter known as 'Canrobert's Hill'. Raglan opted to retain Balaclava. Strategically, therefore, the British were left once more to defend the open (eastern) flank, as the French wheeled across their rear to occupy the Allied left on the upland. Kinglake maintained that the flank march was successful because, with St Arnaud ill, Raglan effectively directed the operation alone. It was the only time during the war that even *de facto* undivided command was exercised. Little could Raglan have dreamed how important Balaclava would become for his men and for how long its restricted waters would be needed to supply them. Its security, too, would cause him prolonged concern, of which a false alarm of impending attack on 28 September was but the first of many. To Lord Stratford de Redcliffe Raglan explained that this 'obliged me to leave my writing-table and remain on horseback several hours'.[25]

On 27 September the British followed their allies on to the heights, though for the time being Raglan kept his headquarters in Balaclava, in a small two-roomed house: one his bedroom, the other for business. Cathcart, having left the Belbec the day before, independently ascended the heights in the wake of the French farther north than the other British divisions. The upland south of Sevastopol (sometimes referred to as the Chersonese Heights), shaped rather like a heart, sloped from east to west, the eastern escarpment (Sapoune Ridge) being roughly 700 feet high and overlooking the Plain of Balaclava. The undulating ground had scant vegetation and few tracks, though the metalled Woronzov Road did cross its extreme eastern end, after climbing from the Plain, before entering Sevastopol. Only one break in the southern part of the heights gave access to Balaclava, the so-called 'Col' up which wound a single track. Once established on the upland the British would rely primarily upon this for the transport of men, supplies and equipment. South of Sevastopol Bay lay the main port with its docks, arsenals, stores, houses and public buildings. Essentially, 'Man of War Harbour' (the principal deep harbour) divided the military quarter to the west from the more residential suburb of Karabel to the east. Initially that harbour marked the line between British forces on the right (east) of the siege lines, French to the left (west). Thus the British – with roughly the same number of troops at first – would have to guard the approaches to Balaclava, protect the right flank of the Allies against the unknown mass of Russian troops gathering in the east, and play their full part in the immediate attack on Sevastopol. It was, evidently, a major commitment; but on 27 September not considered long-term. A *coup de main* still seemed probable.[26]

However, with the northern forts remaining in Russian hands and the line of sunken ships protecting the bay from naval incursion, Todleben concentrated on the southern defences. By 27 September a semi-circle of fortifications protected Sevastopol from that direction. An estimated 151 guns faced the Allies, supported by unsunken warships able to fire over the buildings of Sevastopol and a force of infantrymen, marines, local militia and seamen disembarked from the sunken vessels, all commanded by Vice-Admiral Kornilov. East of Man of War Harbour, protecting the Karabel suburb and immediately opposite the British, were from west to east, the Great Redan, Malakov Tower, Little Redan and four guns at the head of one of the many bays leading off the main inlet (Careenage Ravine). Later it emerged that only 23 of the 151 Russian guns were located in these works, that the Malakov – then a 'naked tower' without glacis or flanking batteries – was by no means the formidable obstacle that it afterwards became, and few linking entrenchments existed. But, if the defences of Sevastopol were as weak as Todleben and Kornilov claimed, that was not evident to observers on the southern upland. Against an estimated garrison of more than 20,000 and a Russian field army on the open flank beyond the Tchernaya, the Allies lacked both manpower and firepower to launch an immediate assault.

Kinglake, without corroborative evidence, described an alleged conversation between Raglan and Cathcart, when the British CinC visited the 4th Division's camp. 'Land the siege trains! But my dear Lord Raglan, what the devil is there to knock down?' The accuracy and even authenticity of this exchange may be in doubt, but such a view was certainly canvassed. To his wife, shortly afterwards, Cathcart wrote: 'If they [heavy guns] had all been up we might have taken the place. Now, we have given them time to prepare and land their ship-guns, and we must have a long regular siege.' By Cathcart's own admission, though, such an assault would have been a gamble: the Allies 'might' have captured Sevastopol. Interestingly, three weeks later W.H. Russell noted: 'We could have stormed with more chance of success when we first set down before the place. Yes, we could perhaps, but who was to know?' Nevertheless, according to Kinglake, on 27 and 29 September Raglan asked the French to mount a joint attack on Sevastopol with him. Canrobert declined, fearing 'any check or reverse ... [and] the safety of the whole army would be compromised'. French doctrine discouraged infantry attacks without preliminary artillery bombardment. Like the British, the French did not have that support on 27 and 29 September. Lyons and Airey apparently favoured an attack, Burgoyne and the French did not. Whatever his own views – and these are by no means clear – Raglan could not have attacked with British troops alone. An assault east of Man of War Harbour without one to the west would have been pointless and costly. A later claim by The Times that 'he [Raglan] appeared before Sebastopol; Sebastopol was his;

but he had not sufficient spontaneous energy to take it', constituted sheer fantasy.[27]

In response to a request from Raglan, Dundas sent ashore 1,000 marines with a complement of field guns, a naval brigade of 1,040 officers and men and six 68pdrs from *Diamond*. But because of the steepness of the escarpment, getting the heavy guns into action proved a lengthy process. Meanwhile Burgoyne expressed surprise that the Russians had determined to resist so strongly, implying perhaps that such an eventuality had not entered his calculations when advising the flank march. 'I was in hopes that the Russians would not have made this effort at resistance at Sebastopol, but they now seem determined to give us as much trouble as possible,' he complained to Colonel Matson (at the Ordnance in London) on 29 September, 'and accordingly we have to land all our heavy guns and siege equipments, and to drag them 8 or 10 miles over a mountain.' None the less he optimistically forecast bombardment of the walls of Sevastopol in a week, prior to a storming operation.[28]

Amid this critical activity the irritating, disruptive confrontation between Lucan and Cardigan did not abate. Lucan's strong objection to being left at Varna prompted Raglan to take him to the Crimea even though the Heavy Brigade remained in Bulgaria. Cardigan's hope effectively of an independent command thus vanished; and the brothers-in-law were exchanging acid letters even before the troops landed. Cardigan became further aggrieved because Lucan directed his brigade at the Bulganek, the Alma and during the flank march. Once the flank march had been completed, on 28 September Raglan dealt with a complaint by Cardigan about undue interference in the running of his brigade. The British CinC attempted to be firm, but conciliatory, appealing to reason: Lucan and Cardigan were 'both gentlemen of high honour and of elevated position in the country, independently of their military rank. They must permit me, as the Commander of the Forces, and, I may say, the friend of both, earnestly to recommend to them to communicate frankly with each other, and to come to such an understanding as that there should be no suspicion of the contempt of authority on the one side, and no apprehension of undue interference on the other.' It was both a sensible and sensitive appeal to better nature; and time would tell, utterly useless.[29]

October would be a month of fluctuating fortunes, the events of the 25th near Balaclava doing more than any other to colour and distort historical judgement on Lord Raglan. It opened, however, with congratulations on success at the Alma, which were then reflected in letters and dispatches throughout the month. On 1 October Raglan's 'telegraphic communication' announcing the victory reached Newcastle. Seven days later, as his uncle had done after Talavera, Burghersh reached London with the dispatch that had been completed on the Katcha on 23 September and which Prince Albert's private secretary described as 'one of the finest and most manly productions it has often been my good fortune to read ... written plainly and simply without any of the bravado that distinguishes our allies'. The following day *The Times* published Raglan's dispatch in full, and Hardinge immediately wrote congratulating Raglan on his triumph and the clarity of his dispatches. That same day Newcastle composed a private letter: 'Your fame is now established in history, God grant you may live many years to enjoy the reputation you have won.' His official dispatch of 10 October referred to Raglan's 'own distinguished service' in the Crimea, and expressed 'the sense which the Queen entertains of the valuable service which you have rendered to this country, and to the cause of the allies'. Responding to a personal letter from Queen Victoria noting the 'very gratifying news' of the Alma, on 27 October Raglan wrote: 'Lord Raglan begs Your Majesty to believe that his services will always be at Your command, and that Your Majesty's approbation will ever be his first ambition, the highest incentive to his exertion' – an apt summary of his concept of duty.

St Arnaud's dispatch of 21 September devoted four lines to the British contribution, two of them to Raglan: 'The bravery of Lord Raglan rivals that of antiquity. In the midst of cannon and musket fire he displayed a calmness which never left him.' A generous tribute, but overall paltry acknowledgement of the British contribution to the Battle of the Alma. It was perhaps fortunate that by the time this dispatch reached British eyes St Arnaud had died. To some extent this reduced anger. In Paris, where sketches in the press purporting to look inland from the fleet, reinforced the impression that the British in the distance were on the periphery of the battle, Lord Cowley formally protested at publication of the dispatch that implied that St Arnaud issued orders to the British troops deployed on the French left who, it said, delayed the entire operation by not being ready to move until 10.30. On 10 October the ambassador warned Raglan that the dispatch – with its anti-British interpretation – had caused consternation in France. Perfidious Albion; though Raglan suspected that St Arnaud exaggerated French casualties. One of the most interesting letters sent to Raglan at this time came from Combermere: 'There is one circumstance that militates against my full enjoyment of your brilliant success which is sincere regret that our beloved old chief had not lived to see you follow the course he would have traced and with decision, forethought and zeal, equal to his own.' That shadow of Wellington yet once more.[30]

The Alma, though, was in the past. Sevastopol lay ahead and preparations for the siege needed to be expedited. Airey was not sanguine of swift success: on 3 October he wrote privately to Hardinge: 'My own opinion is that we are here for the winter, maintaining only a strong position until we can be reinforced.' And Burgoyne admitted to Matson that the strength of the Sevastopol defences had indeed surprised him: 'We found the place surrounded by detached loopholed towers, crenelled walls, and earth bastions, with a good many guns mounted, and a tolerable garrison said to be 20,000'. British troops were 2-3,000 yards of hard ground, swept by Russian artillery and naval vessels, away from the defences. At an Allied Council of War on 7 October, the peril of attempting to cross this exposed ground was acknowledged. Raglan therefore decided that the long-range guns must be brought to bear in strength on the enemy positions in order to weaken them before an assault could be launched. Burgoyne gloomily commented that 'our position is one of extreme difficulty, and I do not perceive how we are to extricate ourselves'. His influence with Raglan, especially in view of the obvious engineering problems facing the Allies and the death of the commanding engineer Tylden, remained strong: 'He advises with me, and asks my opinion on almost all proceedings, before deciding upon his own.' With an artillery bombardment determined, during the night of 7/8 October two 'half-sunken batteries' about 2,800 yards from the enemy, were started for the Lancaster guns, in range of enemy ships at the head of Sevastopol Bay and the Malakov (known then as The White Tower). The French on their left had less trouble with the ground and moved forward to occupy Mount Rodolph. On 10 and 11 October under cover of darkness, the British seized the crests of the unmanned Green Hill and Woronzov Height (respectively 1,300 and 1,400 yards from Sevastopol) and established entrenched batteries there.[31]

Despite evident Allied weakness and Airey's pessimistic assessment that the forces might well be stranded on the upland throughout the winter, optimism in regard to the capture of Sevastopol increased. On 1 October Aberdeen advised Queen Victoria that 'the fall of Sebastopol cannot long be delayed', revealing that he had already planned for 'the immediate and entire destruction of the works' there and the occupation of the Perekop peninsula to enable the troops to winter in the Crimea 'in perfect security'. In fact, the very next day rumours of the fall of Sevastopol began to circulate in London. On 3 October and for the following two days The Times incredibly confirmed the news, quoting 'decisive intelligence ... from our correspondents at Vienna and Paris'. Similarly deceived, Napoleon III announced the Allied success to troops at Boulogne. On 8 October Sir James Graham penned a long, effusive letter to Raglan based on the assumption that Sevastopol had fallen. It was not tinged with modesty. Graham claimed that he had 'urged the policy of considering the conquest of the Crimea and the capture of Sebastopol as the object to which all our efforts in the East ought to be directed', before Raglan took up his command. The First Lord of the Admiralty continued: 'I could not anticipate so grand a result in so short a time. If the poor old Duke had lived to see your great triumph, how justly proud he would have been of Victories won by his Pupil and by his dearest and most trusted Friend. Indeed, he still lives in the Army, which he trained, and in the General, whom he taught to conquer.' Graham paid tribute to

Raglan's powers of conciliation: 'You have also been signally successful in the management of our Ally, which is not at all times an easy matter'.[32]

Newcastle, as Secretary of State for War, underlined the unreality of the mood in London on 9 October. Noting that Sevastopol 'may' already be in Raglan's hands, he had no doubt that it 'will' be by the time that his letter arrived. He did exhibit slight reservation, however, that the task might take longer; but added an extraordinary instruction. Vice-Admiral Dundas would be important in the event of a prolonged campaign. If he issued orders detrimental to the army, Raglan should persuade Lyons to disobey them. Quite unbelievable – and disgraceful. Raglan was being put in an invidious position, and there is absolutely no indication that he in any way heeded this advice. Meanwhile the battle for Sevastopol was far from over. As Raglan watched his guns ineffectively shelling the Russian fortifications on 17 October, he learnt that *The Times* had announced the fall of the city. He was furious. Next day he wrote with scarcely veiled rage to Newcastle: 'It is an injustice to our troops to view the accomplishment of the enterprise as an easy operation; and with the full determination to do everything to ensure success, I must still regard it as one of extreme difficulty, and of no certainty.' Realism, not pipe dreams. A week later Newcastle wrote less confidently, but managed to suggest that failure to take Sevastopol rested with Raglan. The Secretary of State acknowledged more difficulties than 'you had previously anticipated', but remained sure 'that the walls of Sebastopol are not more impregnable than the heights of Alma'.[33]

On 5 October Raglan had moved his headquarters from Balaclava on to the upland. He and his staff took over the abandoned farmhouse in which he would die at Khutor, north of the Col and east of the French headquarters, 1½ miles from Sevastopol and four miles north-west of Balaclava. Scavenging troops had been prevented from dismantling the roof just in time, and Raglan expressed his delight at 'a good house in the centre of the position, which is undoubtedly an immense advantage'. Adding that 'I hate a tent,' he remarked to Priscilla that he was the only one of the army not under canvas – a luxury enjoyed only until others laid claim to vacant rooms. The building comprised three small, connected wings surrounding a courtyard which was open on its fourth (northern) side. The whole structure ran roughly north-west /south-east, so that Raglan's spartan room in the southern wing looked towards the Monastery of St George and gained the benefit of evening sun. The British commander-in-chief's washing and dressing-tables stood beneath the single window; his writing-table, where he dealt with dispatches and from which he conducted meetings and interviews, lay in the centre of the room opposite its only entrance via a dining area to the west. Immediately behind the table another opening to the east led into Airey's room but was blocked by clothes' racks. Raglan sat at the table with his back to the

Quartermaster-General's room, with the window on his left. His iron bed rested in the angle near the entrance door farthest from the window.

Each of the building's protruding wings had an exit to the north, the western one designated 'principal entrance'. Within the house, the narrow connecting passages were officially described as 'dark'. A pantry was found in the west wing, another room 'filled with biscuit for the troops during the winter' in the east. Other rooms were occupied by Burgoyne, Colonel Vico (French liaison officer), Steele, Poulett Somerset, Curzon and Dr Prendergast. A hen-house abutted the wall of Vico's room and, bizarrely, a cow lived in the cellar under Prendergast's. The church and flagstaff were located on ground immediately south of the house within sight of Raglan's room. Beyond the two north entrances a broad avenue contained half-ruined outhouses which were used either as stables or, in the case of the more habitable, as offices and quarters. Other small outbuildings were occupied by Estcourt and other staff officers, the commissariat, printing press, post office, hospital and guard detachments. Four vineyards surrounded the house and three wells were easily accessible, and there was ample space for additional tents. Raglan had good reason to be pleased at the concentration of men, equipment and horses so close together. Even as he took up his new quarters, though, he found it necessary to justify the flank march and choice of Balaclava. To Stratford de Redcliffe he argued that the march had been perfectly successful and one 'for which the enemy was by no means prepared'. Balaclava was 'a beautiful harbour': to disembark reinforcements and equipment at the mouth of the Belbec under enemy fire would have been impossible. Nigel Kingscote also indirectly defended selection of Balaclava by stressing its deep water.[34]

By now the heat of September had most definitely faded as Calvert ominously warned about bitter Crimean winters. Writing to Newcastle on 23 October, Raglan enclosed Calvert's memorandum which stressed that 'in such weather no human creature can possibly resist cold during the night unless in a good house properly warmed; and in day-time unless warmly dressed.' Stand-to in biting winds at 5 a.m. had already proved less than popular.[35]

Raglan was well aware of the conditions under which his men were fighting. Kingscote noted that he went to the front line 'daily', and W.H. Russell reported that he had made a 'minute inspection' of the British trenches on 10 October. Three days later Mrs Duberly wrote that he had been in 'the foremost trench' until 1 a.m. under fire and that 'a rifleman standing near him had his head taken off by a round shot'. On 14 October during a snap night inspection he found to his dismay the covering party 'in the left trench' in an 'objectionable' state: the men were 'not only lying down but were wrapped in their blankets and their arms on the ground some little distance away'. He reacted swiftly, insisting that general officers of divisions carry out trench inspections in person. Vigilance must be maintained. When reports suggested that Russian reinforcements were converging east of Sevastopol, Raglan feared an assault on Balaclava and ordered the building of redoubts on the low Woronzov Heights, north of the small port, which divided the Plain of Balaclava into its two valleys. He overruled Brown's request that sharpshooters be removed from his division, because they attracted unwarranted counter-fire. They were annoying the Russians, which Raglan considered a bonus and a discouragement to their trench builders. As he remarked to his sister-in-law, 'a siege is a most tiresome operation'.[36]

One specific problem caused anxiety at this time. Sir George Cathcart had been given a dormant commission, allowing for him to take over command from Raglan should the need arise. Fortunately this had not been publicized, but Cathcart considered that he ought to be closely consulted about the conduct of the campaign. On 4 October he complained of not being admitted to Raglan's confidence, formally requesting an inverview. Ten days later he objected to Raglan's reproof about the slackness noted during an unannounced inspection. The area in question was not his responsibility, he claimed, but that of the 3rd Division. In a long letter he protested that he carried out inspections of the trenches night and day and that his devotion to duty could not truly be faulted. Fortunately for Raglan, though strangely belatedly, on 13 October Newcastle wrote to Cathcart asking him to surrender his dormant commission because it would be unfair to Brown to deprive him of command in an emergency. Given the Government's resistance to Brown as second in command to Raglan, Newcastle's request seems strange.[37]

The increasing prevalence of sickness began to cause serious concern as October advanced. On the 4th Admiral Boxer from the Bosporus officially informed Raglan that 710 sick had arrived at Scutari during the past five days, 'about seventy-five of which died on the passage', although 'about 500' invalids previously sent there had recovered. Further disturbed by reports of bad conditions in hospitals, Raglan asked Dr J. Hall (Inspector-General of Hospitals) for frequent detailed information about the numbers of sick, their condition, the state of their accommodation and comfort. Towards the end of the month Raglan informed Hardinge, however, that cholera cases continued to mount. Overall, although 'well fed', the men were in 'indifferent health' so that only approximately 16,000 infantry could be mustered. Raglan further pointed out to Newcastle that half of these were engaged in 'guards and working parties for the trenches' leaving 'something under 8,000 men ... available for the support of those in advance of a sortie, and for the maintenance of our position, which is assailable on our extreme right, and right rear'. By now *The Times* had seized upon the rising casualties and the apparent lack of adequate medical care for them. A provocative article on 12 October declared: 'The men must die owing to the medical staff of the British Army having forgotten that old rags are necessary for the dressing of wounds.' Russell fed the paper further damaging comment in his dispatches of 9, 12 and 13 October, in the latter graphically declaring that 'the manner in which the sick are treated is worthy only of the savages of Dahomey', moreover claiming (unjustly as it would later turn out) 'here the French are greatly our superiors'. In vain did Dr D. Menzies (Deputy Inspector-General of Hospitals at Scutari) protest that allegations of deficiencies in dressings were 'perfectly erroneous', because linen was always ready to be applied when 'necessary'. But the damage had already been done. The medical authorities in the East stood condemned and, by implication, Raglan with them.[38]

Newcastle assured Raglan that he appreciated the magnitude of his difficulties. Yet when the British CinC asked for winter clothing and huts, he forwarded a pamphlet by a Dr Lee praising the climate of the peninsula. The Secretary of State pronounced faith in Raglan's ability to overcome current problems with 'the wisdom and foresight which are the indispensable qualities of an able commander'. Yet he overrode Raglan's objections to the raising of 4,000 irregular Turkish cavalry by Colonel Beatson, quoting 'the determination ... [of] Her Majesty's Government'. Discouragingly, too, he wrote to Raglan that the Austrians might have been 'selfish' and actually in collusion with the Tsar, providing an excuse for the Russians to evacuate the Principalities and transfer troops into the Crimea. That must have been a great comfort for a commander whose troops had been halved through sickness. Raglan's reaction to another communication, suggesting that ships sailing from the Crimea to Constantinople should first call at Varna so that information could thus reach London in 'five or six days', has not survived. Extension of the telegraph link and subsequent speeding of messages to and from London served to make political control over him even tighter.[39]

Early in October Raglan received the copy of a letter from Colonel Fenwick Williams, British liaison officer (commissioner) with Turkish troops in Armenia, complaining that Lord Stratford de Redcliffe had studiously ignored 44 of his letters in succession. The fact that Raglan, engaged actively in the siege of Sevastopol, should become involved in Williams' troubles pinpointed yet another responsibility that had been unwillingly thrust upon him. Since August 1854 Williams had been officially placed under Raglan's direction. He had travelled to Varna for an initial briefing and been required by Lord Clarendon to send copies of all his dispatches to Raglan, rely upon him for military support and to pass his correspondence with the Turkish government through the British CinC. Patently he had, however, contacted Lord Stratford directly and was now calling upon Raglan for his assistance. Raglan appears at least to have interceded on his behalf, for on 16 December Williams would acknowledge Raglan's help, which in the circumstances of the war could not have been material, given Raglan's own pressing needs. Williams continued to keep Raglan informed of developments in his theatre, on 23 June

1855 informing him that the Russians had appeared before Kars in force. Williams represented another unnecessary burden, yet Raglan appears to have dealt with him sympathetically.[40]

The so-called First Bombardment of Sevastopol by 126 British and French guns began on 17 October, though the Russians pre-empted the Allies by opening fire shortly after dawn. Kinglake maintained that the signal of three shells was correctly fired at 6.30 a.m., but other evidence suggests that many Allied batteries responded to the Russians prematurely and individually. Moreover two lucky hits on ammunition magazines brought the French firing to a halt at about 10.30. Thereafter only 41 British guns engaged the defences. Crucially, the proposed simultaneous naval bombardment had not yet commenced. At 10.30 p.m. on 16 October Dundas had written to Raglan informing him that due to lack of French ammunition the fleets could not open fire until 10.50 a.m. on the 17th. Then, on the morning itself, the admirals changed their method of attack – preferring to bombard from an anchored position some 2,000 yards off the coast. So the fleets did not begin firing until 1.30 p.m. by which time the French guns on land had long been silent. Thus a co-ordinated bombardment of the Russian right never took place. The fleets achieved little, negatively proving that they could make no effective contribution to the attack on Sevastopol now that access to the harbour had been blocked. On land Raglan's batteries, having heavily damaged the Malakov, then hit the Great Redan close to which a magazine exploded at 3 p.m., killing more than 100 men and rendering most of the enemy guns useless. The Russian troops were then withdrawn behind the shattered earthwork; in theory a gap had opened in the enemy defences. Raglan proved reluctant to assault alone because the plan required a simultaneous attack on the Flagstaff position by the French. Airey maintained afterwards that, as late as 4 p.m., Raglan was prepared to launch an assault, but Canrobert refused to advance. Kinglake criticized Raglan – unjustly – for not pressing ahead independently. The British could have been caught in the narrow streets east of Man of War Harbour and been open to enfilade fire from batteries no longer engaged by the French as they advanced.[41]

Nevertheless, failure to follow up with infantry allowed the Russians to repair their defences overnight and, although the French opened fire on 18 October and both sets of Allied gunners continued to shell the Sevastopol outworks for another week, the bombardment had failed both as the preliminary to an assault and as a means of inflicting severe damage on the Russians. Raglan explained to Newcastle: 'The position which the enemy occupy on the south side of Sebastopol is not that of a fortress, but rather of any army in an entranched camp on very strong ground, where an apparently unlimited number of heavy guns, amply provided with gunners and ammunition, are mounted'. He might have added that the so-called Sappers Road, parallel to the Bay of Sevastopol north of the Allied right, allowed free passage of men and *matériel* between the

Mackenzie Heights and Sevastopol. While the bombardment proceeded in its decreasing effectiveness, Raglan rode up daily to the batteries from his headquarters. Revealing the dubious nature of some of his information, during this period Russell reported that 'on dit', which he claimed as an 'authority', noted that the Russians had asked for a day's truce to bury the dead, but Raglan had replied that he had 'no dead to bury'. Mrs Duberly noted another alleged refusal by Raglan. Reputedly he rejected a Russian request that houses containing wounded and flying a yellow flag should be 'exempt from fire' on the grounds that this was a ruse to protect magazines. No corroborative evidence for these claims was advanced by either writer.[42]

Away from the siege Raglan had always been acutely aware of the vulnerability of Balaclava. Warned of unusual enemy troop movements beyond the Tchernaya in the Chorgun area, at 10 a.m. on 18 October he rode to the edge of Sapoune Ridge. After studying the vicinity for an hour through their glasses, he and his staff decided that no immediate threat existed and returned westwards to observe the bombardment. But the potential danger had been underlined by the advance of Russian cavalry and infantry in fog on the redoubts along the Woronzov (Causeway) Heights, from which their Turkish occupants drove them back. Similar alarms occurred on 20 and 22 October though without any exchange of fire. Failure of the Russians to carry the line of redoubts on these occasions may have unconsciously invested those minor fortifications with more power than they actually possessed. Practically, the Russian probes proved of more value to the enemy than to the defenders.[43]

Raglan was not, therefore, unaware of either the importance or the vulnerability of his supply port, and the very real danger posed to it by Russian forces to the north and east. The narrow track down which Raglan had advanced on 26 September, before coming under fire, wound itself from Balaclava Bay through a gorge to the village of Kadikoi, situated approximately 1¼ miles north on the Plain of Balaclava. Due east of Balaclava, beyond the Marine Heights, lay the village of Kamara and still farther east the Baidar Valley. Parallel to the sea, immediately north of Kadikoi and at right angles to it, stood South Valley, some four miles west to east and one mile north to south. In turn the South Valley 'of coarse meadow land' was bordered to the north by the 300-foot-high Woronzov Heights (described by Russell as 'four conical hillocks, one rising above the other as they receded from our lines' on the upland) along which ran the metalled Woronzov Road from Yalta to Sevastopol. Half-way along the ridge the road dipped into the North Valley before climbing the escarpment of the Sapoune Ridge and thence to Sevastopol. The North Valley ran three miles west to east from the Sapoune Ridge to another group of hills abutting the River Tchernaya, where Russell noted that 'the valley is swallowed up in a mountain gorge and deep ravines above which rise tiers and tiers of desolate whitish rock, garnished now and then by bits of scanty herbage'. On its north side lay the low Fedioukine Hills, separated from the Woronzov Heights by 1½ miles. The North and South Valleys would be the scene of the forthcoming clashes. Menacingly, the Russian field army lay in the area of Chorgun, north-east across the Tchernaya and east beyond Kamara. Collectively or individually Russian forces from these directions posed a direct threat to Balaclava. From Chorgun the enemy could cross Tractir Bridge and the Fedioukine Hills as the British forces themselves had done. To guard against this, Raglan had caused the six redoubts to be constructed along the Woronzov Heights and manned them with Turkish militia; and these had barred the enemy's path on 18, 20 and 22 October. An attack from Kamara presented potentially greater problems because it could only be detected by forward pickets.

Of the redoubts, numbered 1 to 6 from east to west, five were spread over two miles (roughly 500 yards apart, though No 4 lay 800 yards from No 3), the sixth (No 1) lay on a detached rise (Canrobert's Hill) some 500 feet above sea level and almost 1,000 yards south-east of No 2. Because of the urgency of the situaton all the redoubts were rapidly built by Turks under British supervision, No 2 reputedly in one day; so not one of them was a strong fieldwork. Only four were armed with 12pdr naval guns, three in No 1, two each in the next three. On 25 October Nos 5 and 6 were unfinished and unarmed. No 1 had roughly 600 Turks in and around it, Nos 2-4 approximately 300 each. A British artillery NCO was in charge of each of the four redoubts whose 1,500 men and nine guns formed the outer defences of Balaclava. Raglan had also deployed the 93rd (Sutherland) Highlanders, less four companies detached to the area of Balaclava, a battalion of Turks and a six-gun field battery around Kadikoi. A total of 1,200 Marines were stationed on the heights due east of Balaclava harbour. Kadikoi and Marine Heights (at the time still called Mount Hiblak), supported by a total of 26 guns, formed the 3-mile semi-circle of inner defences of Balaclava. The inner and outer defences were commanded by Sir Colin Campbell who had led the Highland Brigade at the Alma. Above the Plain of Balaclava were the five British infantry divisions and Bosquet's French Corps of Observation. Conscious of the need to keep a close watch on Kamara and cover the South Valley approaches to Balaclava, Raglan posted the Cavalry Division below No 6 Redoubt at the western end of South Valley, 1½ miles north-west of Kadikoi. Both brigades (some 1,500 sabres in all) were supported by a troop of horse artillery and were under Lucan's command independent of Campbell. On 20 October Campbell pronounced himself satisfied with these arrangements. To Raglan he wrote: 'I fancy we are now very strong as well as secure,' though he admitted to being 'a little apprehensive' about a night attack. Including the cavalry, Marines, Turks and Highlanders, the defenders of Balaclava totalled some 4,500 men. Unknown to Campbell, across the Tchernaya Menshikov had 20,000 infantry, 3,400

The Battle of Balaclava, 25 October 1854

Chasseurs
d'Afrique

MENSHIKOV

RAGLAN'S POSITION

Lancers

4th Phase

Light
Brigade

4th Div

NORTH VALLEY

1st Div

3rd Phase

CAUSEWAY HEIGHTS

Woronzov Road
1st Phase

2nd Phase

SOUTH VALLEY

Heavy
Brigade

KADIKOI

93rd
Regt.
'Thin Red Line'

South
Valley

Kamara

REDOUBTS ⑥

0   Miles   1

Marines

Balaclava

cavalry and 2,300 gunners with 78 guns in the area of Chorgun. Russian
probings and patrols convinced Menshikov that Kadikoi was the key to
Balaclava. Its loss would menace the British flank, lay the port open to
direct attack and cut supply communications.

An hour before dawn on 25 October both cavalry brigades were
standing to as Lucan, his staff and Lord George Paget, commanding the
Light Brigade because Cardigan had not yet come up from his yacht at
Balaclava, cantered across South Valley towards the Kamara Heights. As
the sky lightened a staff officer pointed to two flags flying one above the
other on No 1 redoubt, the signal for 'enemy advancing'. Almost at once
gunfire confirmed that the redoubt was under attack; and Lucan sent an
ADC back to divisional headquarters. Joined by Campbell in the eastern
part of South Valley, the two generals decided that this was indeed a serious attack. As Campbell returned to Kadikoi, Lucan himself retired west
having also dispatched Captain Charteris to warn Raglan. Putting the
Light Brigade in reserve, the divisional commander led the Heavy
Brigade to the east and flamboyantly manoeuvred it as Maude's field battery crested the Woronzov Heights near No 3 redoubt. The enemy was
not to be deterred.

At 6 a.m. Nos 2 and 3 redoubts came under fire and shortly after-
wards, their commander wounded and their guns low in ammunition,
Maude's men were ordered out of the line, though a Turkish battery on
Sapoune Ridge and British heavy guns near Balaclava vainly tried to

reach the Russians. By 7.30 No 1 redoubt, outgunned and unsupported, had fallen; the defenders of Nos 2-4 redoubts then voted with their feet 'with their quilts and the rest of their simple camp treasures'. They could scarcely be blamed. In peril of being outflanked and overrun by vastly superior forces, their flight was understandable. According to Raglan the guns in the three 'lesser redoubts' had been spiked: but in truth the first phase of the Russian attack had gone well. Having dismantled No 4 redoubt the enemy concentrated in and around Nos 1-3. The scene was now set for the cavalry to carry Kadikoi and, after that, Balaclava.

Alerted by Lucan's ADC at approximately 7 a.m. – before No 1 redoubt had fallen – Raglan advanced to the edge of the Sapoune Ridge at the western end of North Valley: Russell wrongly put his arrival at 'soon after 8'. Raglan now overlooked the battlefield as Wellington had done from the ridge of Mount St Jean at Waterloo. Like the Duke, from his position he could evaluate the situation and dispatch ADCs accordingly. Concerned that the Russians were making an elaborate feint to draw off men from the siege lines, and unable to get a clear picture of the battle situation because of undulating ground, he nevertheless ordered Cathcart's 4th Division and Cambridge's 1st Division down to the Plain. Cathcart, the victim of a false alarm on 21 October, was reluctant to move, especially as his men were in the siege lines two miles from the escarpment. Cambridge's division lay in reserve overlooking the Plain. Raglan intended Cathcart to follow the Woronzov Road on to the Woronzov Heights across the western end of North Valley, while Cambridge marched farther via the Col into South Valley. Neither division could reach the plain before 10.30 a.m. To guard against a surprise foray from Sevastopol Raglan also put Sir Richard England's 3rd Division on alert. Independently assessing the situation, Bosquet sent two infantry brigades and eight cavalry squadrons down the Col to the western end of South Valley under the lee of the Ridge.

At about this time Raglan became concerned about the exposed position of the Cavalry Division and sent Captain Wetherall to withdraw it west: 'Cavalry to take ground to the left of the second line of redoubts occupied by the Turks' – that is, beyond No 6 redoubt, as Nos 5 and 6 effectively formed 'the second line'. Wetherall remained to see that what became known as Raglan's First Order was carried out. By 8.30 the stage was set for the second phase of the action, involving 2,300 Russian cavalry supported by 26 field guns advancing westwards along the North Valley 'against the enemy camp'. Four squadrons (400 men) were detached across the ridge close to No 3 redoubt, by then firmly in Russian hands. This force was halted and turned back by the 'Thin Red Line' of 700 British and 1,000 Turkish troops supported by a single field battery under Campbell's personal command. By 9 a.m. the second phase of the battle was over, but the main body of Russian cavalry meanwhile had continued its westward progress. Raglan's next (second) order would decisively affect the fate of this body, but when issued it referred to the Russian attack on Kadikoi.

From his eyrie Raglan could see that the Turks on Campbell's flank were faltering so he sent Captain Hardinge with a message to Lucan: 'Eight squadrons of Heavy Dragoons to be detached towards Balaclava to support the Turks, who are wavering.' But the the ADC took more than ten minutes to reach Lucan and by the time that the Heavy Brigade under Brigadier-General Scarlett had begun to advance across South Valley the action at Kadikoi had ended. The bulk of the Russian cavalry (almost 2,000 men), however, was already sweeping down over the Woronzov Heights into South Valley on Scarlett's left flank, close to the unoccupied No 5 redoubt. Attacking uphill in two waves and heavily outnumbered, the Heavy Brigade defeated the Russians in a sterling encounter. The inner defences of Balaclava had held.

Russell recorded that 'a cheer burst from every lip – in the enthusiasm officers and men took off their caps and shouted with delight'. Raglan 'at once' sent Leicester Curzon with the message 'well done' to Scarlett, who replied with dignity: 'I beg to thank his Lordship very sincerely.' In his dispatch to Newcastle, Raglan referred to the charge as 'one of the most successful I ever witnessed' – extravagant praise, *The Times* reminded its readers, 'from a General, who is not given to exaggerated descriptions'.

It was still only 9.30; and victory had not been without price, quite apart from the 78 Heavy Brigade casualties. Five hundred yards west of Scarlett's action the entire Light Brigade of 700 sabres waited – 'spectators' according to one embittered cavalryman. Cardigan later explained: 'I had been ordered into position by the Earl of Lucan, my superior officer, with orders on no account to leave it, and to defend it against any attack of Russians ... They did not, however, approach the position.' The Light Brigade none the less felt slighted, Cardigan and Lucan were once more at loggerheads, the divisional commander declaiming that he had actually told Cardigan: 'My instructions to you are to attack anything and everything that shall come within reach of you, but you will be careful of columns or squares of infantry.'

Above the Plain Raglan noted the beaten cavalry withdrawn to the eastern end of North Valley, Russian infantry in exposed positions on the Woronzov Heights and Fedioukine Hills. At about 10.15 he sent another (third) order to Lucan: 'Cavalry to advance and take advantage of any opportunity to recover the Heights. They will be supported by the infantry which have been ordered. Advance on two fronts.' Composed in the heat of battle, the message should nevertheless have been clear to Lucan. The 'Heights' could only be the Woronzov Heights which he had seen captured by the Russians, then occupying Nos 1-3 redoubts. The 'two fronts' meant Cathcart via the Woronzov Road into North Valley, Cambridge via the Col to South Valley. The two divisions would thus approach the redoubts from different angles. Wetherall had explained Raglan's First Order that day for Lucan to withdraw his division out of range, and the bearer of this message would have been fully aware of its meaning. Lucan's immediate action suggests that the order was, in fact, perfectly clear to him. He moved the Light Brigade to the head of North Valley, keeping the Heavy Brigade close to No 6 redoubt in the South Valley. Each brigade could then co-operate with an infantry division. But Lucan had no intention of attacking prepared enemy positions with cavalry until the infantry arrived. The capture of the Woronzov Heights was absolutely clearly in his mind at this stage, based upon Raglan's assessment (confirmed by Russian officers after the war) that enemy morale had suffered a severe blow through the Heavy Brigade's success. A swift British assault on the redoubts would have removed support from troops on the Fedioukine Hills and threatened to outflank those at the eastern end of North Valley. In his post-operational report to Newcastle Raglan explained that 'I directed the cavalry ... to move forward and take advantage of any opportunity to regain the heights, and it appearing that an attempt was making [sic] to remove the captured guns'.

The 1st and 4th Divisions did not reach the Plain as quickly as intended. Some accounts, possibly embellishing a footnote by Kinglake that infantry reinforcements were 'stated ... to be ready to undertake an attack' then, put infantry in Nos 5 and 6 redoubts at 10.30. W.H. Russell, writing later that afternoon, was even more precise. Maintaining that Raglan issued orders to Cambridge personally at 10 a.m. to put himself under Campbell's orders once on the Plain, Russell held that 'the Fourth Division took up ground in the centre between the two cavalry brigades at the western end of the Woronzov (Causeway) Heights; the Guards and Highlanders (1st Division) filed off towards the extreme right (South Valley) and faced the redoubts'. He timed arrival in these positions at 10.40. But Lucan insisted that they had 'not yet arrived', when he read Raglan's Fourth Order. Cambridge, with the longer march, made satisfactory progress. Cathcart did not. Raglan sent 'messenger after messenger to endeavour to find out where he was, and to learn the cause of his delay'. In fact, the 4th Division, instead of following the Woronzov Road, struck south-eastwards from the trenches towards the Col in the wake of Cambridge. The infantry could not, therefore, arrive simultaneously nor 'advance on two fronts'. By 11 a.m. they were in no position to advance on the enemy at all.

Meanwhile the lie of the land obscured much of the Woronzov Heights and North Valley from Lucan, positioned as he was between his two brigades. He, unlike Raglan, could not see that Russian artillerymen with horses and lassoes were about to tow away the captured guns from the redoubts. Although spiked, they could be repaired and used again against the Allies; furthermore, to surrender a gun meant admission of a lost battle in military convention. At about 10.40 Raglan dictated the

Fourth Order, which Airey wrote in pencil on paper balanced on his sabretouche: 'Lord Raglan wishes the cavalry to advance rapidly to the front, and try to prevent the enemy taking away the guns. Troop of horse-artillery may accompany. French cavalry is on your left. Immediate, R Airey.' Kinglake held that Raglan intended essentially to repeat the Third Order with emphasis on immediate action. Airey composed the order, but Raglan 'dictated some additional words which Airey at once inserted', possibly one or both of the last two sentences. Captain Edward Nolan, an accomplished horseman, carried the message, and as he left the upland Raglan ordered him to 'tell Lord Lucan the cavalry is to attack immediately'. Eschewing the Woronzov Road, he negotiated the steep slope under Raglan and reached Lucan in a little over five minutes. Nolan undoubtedly knew Raglan's intention, but it is quite possible that personalities now played a fateful role. Nolan had been openly contemptuous of the performance of the cavalry in the Crimea thus far, and had recorded his feelings in a diary. Moreover the antipathy between Lucan and Cardigan appeared to prevent rational discussion of the order, Cardigan in particular still smarting about the Heavy Brigade's earlier success. Lucan maintained that 'neither enemy nor guns' were in sight; and the exchanges between him and Nolan, which took place during those last desperate minutes before Cardigan set off up the North Valley shortly after 11 a.m., have been variously recorded. Undoubtedly Lucan asked Nolan for clarification. Kinglake (relying on Lucan's later assertions) describes how Airey's ADC retorted: 'Lord Raglan's orders are that the cavalry should attack immediately.' To which Lucan answered: 'Attack, sir! Attack what? What guns, sir?' The author further wrote that Nolan threw back his head 'and pointing with his hand in a direction which Lord Lucan says confidently was towards the left-hand corner of the valley' said: 'There, my lord, is your enemy; there are your guns.' Lucan's professional pride evidently stopped him from questioning the arrogant Nolan further and he then trotted over to Cardigan in the North Valley.

Yet, as Raglan later contended, read sensibly in conjunction with that sent at 10.15, the Fourth Order ought to have been clear. Issued with his orders by Lucan, Cardigan drew attention to the folly of charging the twelve Russian guns drawn up in advance of infantry and cavalry at the end of the valley, which were visible from his position: unhelpfully Lucan observed: 'I know it, but Lord Raglan will have it. We have no choice but to obey.' A less volatile officer might have reflected on 'to recover' in the Third Order and 'taking away the guns', not 'withdrawing his guns' which would have otherwise conveyed the meaning that Lucan ascribed to the order. The key word surely was 'the' not 'his'. Whatever he later claimed, Lucan knew that the enemy had captured the guns in the redoubts. Basing its conclusion on Russell's dispatch of 25 October, *The Times* referred to 'a written order, in terms that seemed to leave no discretion, to advance and recapture the guns in the hands of the enemy'. Lucan admitted to Raglan on 27 October: 'The Heavy Brigade having now joined the Light Brigade, the division took up a position with a view of supporting an attack upon the heights; when, being instructed to make a rapid advance to our front to prevent the enemy carrying [sic] the guns lost by the Turkish troops in the morning, I ordered ... '

Curiously, Henry Clifford reported a conversation with Cardigan two days later suggesting that the Fourth Order ran: 'Lord Lucan will attack with Cavalry, and prevent the English guns in the redoubts being taken away by the enemy' – precisely what Raglan intended, but surely not actually appreciated by Cardigan unless, in his terse exchanges with Lucan prior to the attack, he had tried to point this out. If so, the charge makes even less sense; and latter-day efforts to put the onus on Nolan appear even less credible. Kinglake, quoting 'an officer' who was one of the nearest of all the observers, argued that shortly after the advance began Nolan, who had opted to ride with the Light Brigade as Hardinge had charged with the Heavies earlier, spurred across Cardigan's front – confirmed by the brigade commander – at such an angle as to point to the Woronzov Heights as being the true objective. At that point he was killed by a shell splinter, as Russell observed from the Sapoune Ridge 'in advance of the Hussars, cheering them on'. Standing close to Raglan with General Buller, Henry Clifford held in two letters of 27 and 29 October that Nolan had been killed before the charge – strictly correct, as the brigade had not yet begun to gallop. Whatever Nolan's part in the débâcle, Raglan quite obviously did not intend Lucan to send the Light Brigade 1¼ miles down the valley, for its 673 men to be immortalized in Tennyson's celebrated verses. The fourth phase of the Battle of Balaclava ended at about 11.20; and the twenty minutes that it lasted have coloured History's judgement on Raglan's life. Russell placed the Charge between 11.10 and 11.30, but Kinglake's more detailed information suggests nearer 11 – 11.20. The difficulty in establishing the precise sequence of events and exactly what was said by individuals – crucially lacking an input from the dead Nolan – must affect any conclusion. Nevertheless Raglan's so-called Third Order (10.15) was undoubtedly understood. Half an hour later, from his observation point Raglan believed that the Woronzov Heights could still be recaptured while the enemy was preoccupied with withdrawing the captured guns. He did not have time to explain in detail to Lucan why he issued the Fourth Order. Like Wetherall, earlier that day, Nolan could be expected to answer any queries. Whether he did or not depends only upon Lucan's recollection of what passed between them. By the time Lucan recorded his memories he was defending himself from blame. At the time an eye-witness recorded that 'he [Raglan] hid his face in his hands on seeing from the Heights the inevitable destruction of the Light Brigade'.

Scarcely had the last trooper limped back than the recriminations began. A total of 113 men had been killed, 247 badly wounded, 475 horses killed and 42 injured. On their retreat the shattered remnant had been covered by the Heavy Brigade and French cavalry, which attacked Russian positions on the Fedioukine Hills. The British infantry made no forward movement until about 12.30, ordered by Somerset Calthorpe on Raglan's behalf to do so. Desultory fire continued throughout the afternoon, but no serious attempt was made to recover the redoubts, Raglan opting rather to concentrate on protecting Balaclava. Contrary to later accounts, he remained overlooking the Plain during the afternoon. In fact his elderly servant Ferdinand brought him his lunch on the upland. At 'about 4 o'clock', according to Russell, Campbell, Cathcart and Cardigan 'had interviews' with him and he 'evidently listened to their recitals with great interest'. His exchange with Cardigan surpassed mere 'interest'. Raglan reproached his Light Brigade commander: 'What do you mean, sir, by attacking a battery in front, contrary to all the usages of warfare, and the customs of the service?' Cardigan protested: 'My lord, I hope you will not blame me, for I received the order to attack from my superior officer in front of the troops.' Shortly afterwards Cathcart and Bosquet joined Raglan and, after 'a long conversation' all three rode down to the Plain to evaluate the situation on the ground. Raglan did not return to his quarters until after dark. Later that evening Lucan reported to him. Uncharacteristically and bitingly, thus exhibiting the depth of his distress, Raglan exclaimed: 'You have lost the Light Brigade', going on to emphasize that he intended an advance to the Woronzov Heights and recovery of 'our lost English guns'. Lucan afterwards claimed that Raglan added: 'Lord Lucan you were a lieutenant-general and should, therefore, have exercised your discretion and, not approving the charge, should not have caused it to be made.'[44]

A clear appreciation of the circumstances surrounding the Charge is complicated by different versions not only of what was said but the wording of the Third and Fourth Orders. The Third Order cited above is not that contained in Kinglake's main text. He printed the same first sentence, but offered then: 'They will be supported by the infantry which have been ordered [to] advance on two fronts.' In a footnote he explained that this was the form of the original order in Lucan's possession (of which Raglan retained no copy). That 'furnished by him [Lucan] to Lord Raglan' omitted the full stop and had 'Advance' with a small 'a'. As Kinglake points out, the 'clerical errors' make little difference to the meaning, although – as he knew of the original wording – it is strange that Kinglake used the slightly inaccurate version sent later to Raglan by Lucan. It is just possible that Kinglake misread Lucan's capital 'a'. In manuscript a capital 'a' can be a larger presentation of the lower-case 'a'. It is conceivable that there was no full stop, in fact. In the Fourth Order Airey used a dash in place of a full stop throughout. Lucan may not have made a clerical error after all. Strangely, in that Kinglake claimed to be quoting 'the copy which Lord Lucan afterwards furnished to Lord Raglan', Raglan himself offered another slight variation when writing to Newcastle: 'The cavalry to advance and take advantage of any opportunity to recover the heights. They will be supported by infantry, which has been ordered to advance on two fronts.'

In August 1855 *The United Service Magazine* published a further variation: 'The cavalry to advance and take advantage of any opportunity to recover the heights. They will be supported by infantry, which has been ordered to advance on two points [*sic*].' This makes no sense at all: from two directions, perhaps, but not 'on two points'. In truth, leaving aside the eccentric *Magazine* version, the slight difference in wording had no material effect. Lucan reacted as expected, except that he waited for the arrival of the infantry. Raglan made clear to Newcastle that he intended the cavalry to 'be supported by infantry', not 'to support the infantry', and that the cavalry ought to have advanced on receipt of the Third Order.[45]

The Fourth Order has received even more attention. Kinglake explained that Raglan did not retain a copy of it either – which, in the circumstances, is not surprising. On 26 October Lucan wrote to Airey: 'I enclose a copy of the order handed to me by Captain Nolan yesterday, as desired by Lord Raglan.' Unlike the Third Order, Kinglake does not admit to the version in his book (reproduced above) being different from the original. Yet Lucan later detailed a different form of words. 'Lord Raglan wishes the cavalry to advance rapidly to the front, follow the enemy [*sic*] and try to prevent the enemy carrying away the guns. Troop of horse artillery may accompany. French cavalry is on your left. Immediate. Airey.' And the actual handwritten order read: 'Lord Raglan wishes the cavalry to advance rapidly to the front – follow the Enemy & try to prevent the Enemy carrying away the Guns – Troops [*sic*] Horse Arty may accompany – French cavalry is on [unclear] left R. Airey Immediate -' 'Follow the enemy', which is a phrase not in Kinglake's text but included in an appendix, is crucial. No enemy can be *followed* unless in retreat or flight. If the phrase were, indeed, in the Order there would have been no rational margin for misunderstanding. Raglan offered to Newcastle a form, which purported to be that of the Fourth Order, but was quite obviously a paraphrase: '... The cavalry was to advance, and take advantage of any opportunity to recover the heights, and that they would be supported by infantry'. It did not include 'follow the enemy'.[46]

For whatever reason, however, Lucan did misconstrue Raglan's intentions: the cavalry was to 'follow' the enemy 'carrying away the (redoubt) guns'. Cardigan would not have seen the written order, only received verbal instructions from Lucan based upon it. The critical failure of communication thus occurred between Nolan and Lucan, both evidently resenting the other. Kinglake claims to 'follow Lord Lucan's written narrative'. Lucan may have produced more than one account, for Kinglake's words are a free adaptation of the text which Lucan sent to Raglan (substantially repeated when he addressed the House of Lords on his return to England): 'The aide-de-camp, in a most authoritative tone, stated that they were Lord Raglan's orders that the cavalry should attack immediately. I asked him where? And what to do as neither enemy nor guns were within sight? He replied in a most disrespectful but significant manner, pointing to the further end of the valley, "There, my lord, is your enemy; there are your guns." ' By Lucan's own admission he could see no guns and no enemy; and it is difficult not to conclude that, failing to obtain a balanced, full briefing from Nolan for whatever reason and having assumed that the far end of the valley was the objective, Lucan afterwards rationalized the content of those exchanges. None the less, why a lieutenant-general, of fierce and dominating personality, who had on more than one occasion shown himself sensitive to his rank and standing did not sharply order an arrogant captain to explain himself more temperately is astonishing. Reading Lucan's account, Kinglake may well have over-dramatized the encounter between Nolan and Lucan. A tragic misunderstanding remains the likely explanation. Lucan's attempts to justify himself at Raglan's expense have muddied the literary waters. Another version offered by *The United Service Magazine*, allegedly 'published' by Lucan, represented a belated attempt to justify the charge down the valley, but lacked authenticity: 'Lord Raglan wishes cavalry to advance rapidly in front, follow the enemy, and try to prevent their carrying away their [*sic*] guns. Troops [*sic*] of artillery may follow. French cavalry on the [*sic*] left. Immediate.'[47]

Rightly, as it transpired, Raglan sensed that the commander of his cavalry division would dwell unreasonably upon the event. He remained convinced that Lucan had erred. In private and official letters to Newcastle Raglan referred to 'a fatal mistake' deriving 'from some misconception of the order to advance', so that Lucan believed he must attack 'at all hazards'. He stopped short, nevertheless, of censuring Lucan; the charge had after all been technically well executed. In essence a mistake had been made, but the war must go on. On 27 October Airey (on Raglan's behalf) went to Lucan's tent to reason with him, assuring him that Raglan's report would not, in fact, blame him. There, for the moment, the matter rested.[48]

One other aspect of the Battle of Balaclava needs to be mentioned – the Woronzov Road. Kinglake maintained (and other writers have uncritically followed) that its 'loss would become a cause of cruel suffering to the English army', because supply transport could no longer use it. This implies that if Raglan were responsible for the reverses on 25 October, he could not escape blame for the privations endured by his men during the winter. But Captain Montgomery (42nd Foot) pointed out that to reach it wagons and men had to cross South Valley and then follow the longer route to the siege lines. Before the bad weather set in the shorter route via the Col was preferred. The Russians withdrew from the Woronzov Heights in December, and even then the Woronzov Road was not used. Conditions in the South Valley made any approach from Balaclava virtually impossible, but Raglan also feared danger from marauding Cossacks.[49]

Raglan's concern that the Russians might use a distraction against Balaclava to pour out of Sevastopol on to the upland was all too soon realized. Heartened by the previous day's victory, evidenced by the arrival of the seven guns taken from the Turkish redoubts, which prompted the singing of a Te Deum and a thunderous celebratory barrage directed at the Allied trenches at 9 p.m., the enemy next day (26 October) made a determined effort to dislodge the British from their positions on the right of the siege lines, in the Battle of Little Inkerman. De Lacy Evans' 2nd Division, supported by the Guards and artillery, drove back the Russians in an action lasting some three hours at a cost of 89 casualties as against 350 Russian casualties (including prisoners). Essentially this was a minor skirmish in which Raglan had no direct part, but the Paris correspondent of *The Times* reported that he had thanked Bosquet for hurrying to Evans' assistance, even though French troops had not needed to join the action. He further reported 'that there exists in all our relations an understanding and a cordiality worthy of remark ... This perfect understanding between the two Generals-in-Chief is, I need not add, a most important point.' Raglan's conciliatory treatment of his ally was showing profit. The Turks were also pleased, the Sultan awarding Raglan the Imperial Order of the Medjidie, First Class, for his contribution to the defence of Turkey, which this time he felt able to accept.[50]

Of Austria's persistent failure to fulfil the promise of intervention, Raglan could not conceal his dismay. Writing to Priscilla in Vienna, he recalled that a message from Baron de Hess to him towards the end of August had anticipated a declaration of war on 2 September and Austrian troops on the march six days later. If this had come about, as promised, and the Austrians had moved into Wallachia, the Russians would have been obliged to detach troops to cover them. This in turn would have prevented the enemy from sending 'thousands' into the Crimea via Odessa and the Perekop peninsula.[51]

Despite his many preoccupations Raglan's family was not forgotten. Thanking Richard for his letter from Ems with news that Lady Raglan and the girls were well, he expressed delight that his son was with them. His short letter, obviously composed in haste, noted that 'we have a serious job before us', and enclosed a cheque for £50 which would 'be due to you when you get this'. The caring father did not forget his offspring even under the stress of battle. Nor did he eschew his paternal duty: 'I regret the habit you have adopted of smoking,' he chided. Richard was 37. On 16 October Raglan at length responded to Aberdeen's offer of Cowes Castle. Like Raglan, Lady Raglan was 'very much flattered ... but unfortunately she has such a dislike to going upon the sea, that even the passage of the Solent would be most irksome to her and would render what would be otherwise a great enjoyment quite the reverse'. Lady Raglan's nervousness in this respect had evidently increased rapidly, for she had been used to taking the steamer from Portsmouth to Ryde in the past.[52]

For Raglan and the army before Sevastopol, November was dominated by two events: the Battle of Inkerman and a disastrous hurricane. The north-eastern corner of the triangular plateau occupied south of Sevastopol by the Allies featured high ground, roughly $1\frac{1}{2}$ x $\frac{3}{4}$ miles, and known to them as Mount Inkerman, to the Russians as Cossack Mountain. Bordered on the west by Careenage Ravine and on the east by the edge of the escarpment, access to it could be gained from north and east via three small ravines and two gullies. Roughly in the centre of Mount Inkerman stood Shell Hill which spawned two shoulders – East and West Gut. Four hundred yards from the southern end of the Quarry Ravine, 1,200 yards from Shell Hill and 30 feet higher than the hill lay the L-shaped Home Ridge which would become the focal point of the forthcoming battle. Here the probing of 6,500 'muffin caps' with four field guns in support had been repulsed on 26 October. But there were few defence works in the vicinity of Mount Inkerman, whose uneven terrain was spotted with brushwood, loose rocks and stunted trees, hampering movement and cramping artillery fields of fire. Just beyond the north-eastern extension of Home Ridge stood the empty Sandbag Battery – a 9-foot-high defence work with embrasures cut for two guns to engage enemy forces crossing the River Tchernaya below, but no banquette for men with smallarms to resist elsewhere. In front of Home Ridge, where the old post road emerged from the Quarry Ravine on to the plateau, lay a 4-foot-high wall of heaped stones known as The Barrier. On Home Ridge itself another loose-stone rampart, a mere two feet high, known as Herbert's Folly, offered meagre protection to field gunners. There were no entrenchments in the area, just the two rudimentary stone walls and the abandoned battery.

Here the British 2nd Division, temporarily commanded by Lieutenant-General J. L. Pennefather in the absence through illness of Sir George de Lacy Evans, deployed some 3,000 men south of Home Ridge or thrown forward in pickets. A mile further to the rear (south) stood the camp of the Guards Brigade and one troop of horse artillery, though a Guards picket had been established overlooking the Careenage Ravine. West of the Guards' camp – but divided from it by the Careenage Ravine – and about $1\frac{1}{2}$ miles from the 2nd Division lay the Light Division, and even further west, cut off by more ravines, were Cathcart's 4th Division (2 miles from Pennefather) and the 3rd Division, too far for intervention. Raglan's headquarters lay south of Home Ridge close to the siege-gun park. The broken nature of the ground made reinforcement of Pennefather's men difficult; and Bosquet's Corps of Observation overlooking the Plain of Balaclava was even farther south.

Already alarmed at the Russian attack of 26 October and further prompted by repeated pleas from de Lacy Evans for reinforcement, Raglan had examined the defences of Mount Inkerman. Discerning their essential weakness, he pressed Canrobert for the French division that he had promised. Burgoyne then took the French commanding engineer (Bizot) over the ground. Despite the evidence of Little Inkerman, Bizot argued that the area was too far from Sevastopol to warrant serious military attention. With, as Calthorpe observed, the 2nd Division 'much over-worked' already, Burgoyne detached British engineers from siege works farther west to raise the Sandbag Battery, which in the event was neither finished nor armed. At a Council of War on the very eve of the battle (4 November), Canrobert again undertook to send the promised division to the British right. Too late.[53]

On learning of the Russian advance from a 2nd Division staff officer, Captain J.A. Ewart, Raglan had quickly mounted his horse, recognizing that the threat was concentrated on the upland. But he was also mindful that unseen below him another advance on Balaclava might be in train or, alternatively, the action ahead of him might be a diversion to allow more enemy troops to break out of Sevastopol further to the west. He therefore sent word to Sir Richard England to be vigilant on the British left, and orders went to Cathcart and the Duke of Cambridge to move in support of 2nd Division. Arriving on Home Ridge at approximately 7.30, Raglan learnt that Brown and Cathcart had politely declined assistance from Bosquet; and he sent a staff officer, Lieutenant-Colonel Studholme Brownrigg, to reverse that refusal. French help would be welcome. His most decisive contribution to the battle, though, was to order up two 18pdr guns from the siege park. Realizing the preponderance of enemy artillery and its ability to reach deep into the British positions, he determined to bring these long-range guns into the fray. On being told that to get the guns across the rugged terrain would be 'impossible', he replied: 'I do not like the word "impossible".'[54]

During the battle Raglan and his staff remained on Home Ridge, exhibiting an air of calm. At one point, mail arrived from England and was quietly distributed, as shot and shell lanced through the pervading mist. Later Newcastle would chide Raglan for exposing himself to risk, but the British CinC would answer that he did not do so 'unnecessarily'. Admitting that the Russian guns were 'numerous and powerful', he could not 'keep clear of the line' if he wished to exercise his command. When the mist lifted he saw that the Russians were close to breaking through between the Barrier and the Sandbag Battery, so he sent Airey to Cathcart, requiring him to head off this peril. Cathcart, on the contrary, planned to advance on the extreme right in an attempt to turn the enemy left. Airey conveyed Raglan's specific order not to do so. The 4th Division was 'to move to the left (not right) and support the Brigade of Guards and not to descend or leave the plateau ... Those are Lord Raglan's orders.' Cathcart

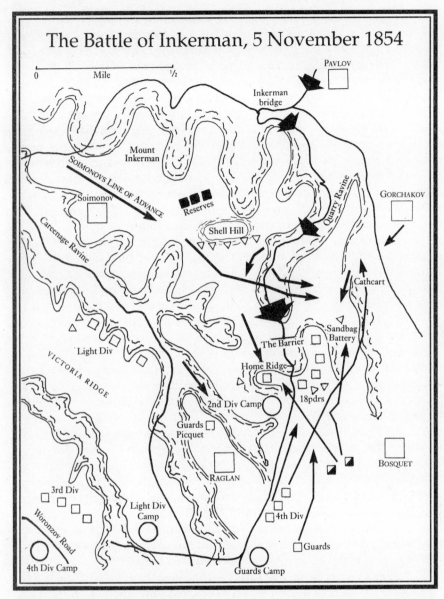

The Battle of Inkerman, 5 November 1854

disobeyed and took himself and many of his men to their death as he unwisely descended the plateau on the British right. Fortunately, as he tragically carried out this manoeuvre other 4th Division troops arrived on the field and Raglan ordered them to plug the gap, employing Calthorpe to guide them. This movement at approximately 8 a.m. was critical and represented another positive contribution by Raglan to that day's victory.

The Russian threat to Home Ridge remained, however, and the British CinC was delighted when French troops appeared in support, less so when they retreated under fire. He exhibited, according to Calthorpe, 'astonishment and annoyance' and, in fact, some enemy troops were then close to Raglan and his staff on Home Ridge. Moreover, shells were still falling close by. Raglan was chatting to Brigadier-General T. F. Strangways, veteran of Leipzig and Waterloo, when the artillery commander's leg was blown off, and several horses nearby were killed or wounded. Withdrawing temporarily to the reverse slope, Raglan reorganized his staff before calmly resuming his study of the action. Seeing the enemy falter, he sent an ADC to order the 55th forward; and the Russians were cleared from Home Ridge with bayonets. This advantage was pressed home by more British troops and the French, who had regrouped. Off Home Ridge, shortly after 9 a.m., the Russians remained dangerously established on Shell Hill and their guns decimated British and French troops who rashly pursued them north of Home Ridge.

At about 9.15 the guns ordered up by Raglan 1½ hours earlier arrived. Coming into action at 9.30 at the angle of the Home and Fore Ridges, the gun crews suffered heavy casualties. Raglan rode over and dismounted close by. Gradually the two 42cwt 18pdr iron guns found their line and range. As they did so Bosquet sent Raglan a message assuring him of support for Home Ridge, but in the event the French reinforcements went instead to the far right where two French battalions already engaged were under severe pressure. When Canrobert in turn requested assistance from Raglan, Nigel Kingscote on his behalf ordered Lord George Paget – again in command until Cardigan rode up from his yacht at Balaclava – to advance the Light Brigade which had been moved to the Chersonese upland since 25 October, in support of the Chasseurs d'Afrique. Raglan evidently acceded to Canrobert's request in the interest of inter-Allied co-operation, but militarily the manoeuvre was pointless. Ten men, survivors of the Charge, became casualties and the Brigade failed to come into action. At midday, still close to the 18pdrs, Raglan sent Calthorpe to discover the situation farther to his left. Pennefather reported that if reinforced the British would 'lick them ... to the devil'. Raglan translated this bellicose sentiment to Canrobert, who had joined him, to the French commander's obvious delight. Raglan then sent for Pennefather who received Raglan's praise 'beaming and radiant'.

Shortly after noon the 18pdrs exhausted the 100 rounds per gun that had been brought up and a pause occurred until another 200 arrived. Then the cannon resumed 'the tyranny', in Kinglake's colourful words. Certainly in his operational dispatch Menshikov referred to the effectiveness of the British 'siege artillery' that day, as did General Dannenberg – one of the divisional commanders closely involved – who paid tribute to the 'murderous fire of the enemy artillery', which prompted him to order a retreat at 1p.m. As the enemy fell back Raglan urged Lieutenant-Colonel Collingwood Dickson to take one of the 18pdrs forward of Home Ridge, but the rough ground defeated this intention. At 2.30 the Russians withdrew from Shell Hill, and at about 3 p.m. Raglan and Canrobert rode side by side to East Gut from which they could see the enemy streaming back across the Tchernaya. 'I have been attacked by 40,000 men,' Raglan remarked; and as Dickson rode up Raglan said to him: 'You have covered yourself with glory.' Paying due credit to subordinates was a positive aspect of his leadership, which makes his anger on 25 October all the more stark. His sensitivity was also evident. Nearby a wounded Russian soldier cried out for water. There was none. But Raglan supported his head with his left hand, offering comfort. The day had been won. A total of 10,729 Russians had been killed, wounded or taken prisoner. But 2,357 British were also casualties, 597 of them killed including 39 officers. Raglan had shown decisive leadership and could be justly proud of the victory. Calling for the two 18pdrs, lending moral support and encouragement to infantry and gunners by his orders and presence and ensuring French support on the right were invaluable contributions to the Allied success. Soldiers' battle it may have been. General's direction proved indispensable.[55]

Raglan's calm during the battle, when he was personally exposed to danger either on Home Ridge itself or its junction with Fore Ridge where the 18pdrs were situated, attracted favourable comment. Flamboyantly, and perhaps with the slightest hint of hyperbole, The United Service Magazine declared: 'In the thick of the fray the soldiers beheld their illustrious chief, calm and immovable as at a review, animating every heart by his great example. While the bullets fell in an incessant shower around him, and officers of the staff were struck down by his side, he continued to give orders with his customary sang-froid.' Compassion and judgement did not desert him under trying circumstances. Late in the afternoon Canrobert pressed Raglan to commit the Guards to a charge against the Russians in the Shell Hill area in company with French troops, many of whom had not hitherto been in action. Raglan later told Sir John McNeill that he demurred, knowing how worn out the Guards were after their strenuous efforts to hold the right of the line. Similarly Sir Edmund Lyons recalled that he had been with Raglan 'for some time after the battle began', but when Raglan came under fire he sent the admiral out of range, saying that it was not Lyons' duty to expose himself to danger on land. The equable nature of Raglan's behaviour was, perhaps, illustrated by one incident during 'the dreadful day of Inkerman'. Towards midday an elderly civilian was intercepted approaching the action from the south and was told sharply by an officer to be off. He replied that he was Raglan's servant: 'My master is not so young as he was; he must not do without his luncheon.'[56]

Writing to his daughters towards the end of the month, Raglan explained that because of broken telegraph wires his dispatch on the battle had been delayed, whereas Canrobert's reached Paris quickly. This ascribed to the French a larger share of the glory on that day than they deserved. Rather piquantly Raglan feared that the Government would believe that he had not sent a dispatch. In fact, when the Allied commanders had moved forward to the Shell Hill area to observe the broken enemy streaming back across the Tchernaya and after Raglan had explained the inability of the Guards to mount an effective pursuit, he asked Canrobert to attack the enemy with his fresh troops. In Sir John McNeill's later words: he 'implored Canrobert to follow up the Victory by pursuing them', pointing out that the Russians 'would be entirely annihilated'. McNeill further explained that Raglan 'always spoke with peculiar regret of his inability to follow up the Victory of Inkermann [sic] and expressed his conviction that had the French done so the Russian army would have been destroyed'. Lyons independently confirmed this sequence of events. Canrobert argued that the Russians were not so beaten as they appeared, acknowledging that the British did not have enough troops to mount an effective pursuit, but declining to move up the French right. Sir Edmund claimed that afterwards English officers at the French headquarters heard Canrobert regret on three separate occasions that he had not followed Raglan's advice. Canrobert allegedly had been caught muttering to himself that, had he done so and destroyed the Russian army, celebrations would have occurred throughout Europe.[57]

Clearly stock had to be taken of the Allies' position in the immediate aftermath of the battle. A Council of War on 6 November committed the troops to continuing the siege, but recognized the need to strengthen the defences of Mount Inkerman. Thus the focus of attention for the moment centres on defence against renewed enemy assault. Richard Airey, present at the Council of War, explained how Raglan insisted on holding the forward trenches and not allowing the Russians to advance on to the plateau, which would have made the Allied position untenable in the long run. Inevitably the French supply ports would be threatened, as would Balaclava. Recognizing the suffering among the troops that this decision must bring, in Airey's words, 'Lord Raglan grieved, but did not hesitate; for there was [sic] only one of the alternatives which could consist [sic] with the honour of the British army.' According to Calthorpe, de Lacy Evans urged Raglan to take a much more radical line: 'He [Evans] therefore gave it as his opinion that there was nothing to be done but for us to raise the siege, embark the troops in the best way we could, and evacuate the Crimea.' Everybody – British, French and Russian – now agreed on one thing: the siege would stretch into the winter. On 7 November Burgoyne, quoting authority from Raglan, wrote to the Assistant Inspector-General of Fortifications in London: 'There is every prospect of our wintering in this corner of the Crimea, without towns or villages to have recourse to, or any resources but what can be drawn from the sea.' A stark prospect. Ammunition, of course, would be very important, but so would 'cover'. On Raglan's initiative, material was being sought in Sinope and Constantinople to make 'sheds', but Burgoyne was pessimistic of success. He therefore urged Major-General G. S. Harding to make 'immediate' inquiries about the means of making sheds, possibly by stretching tarpaulins over wooden frames, and to arrange for necessary materials to be sent out from England. Meanwhile Raglan had asked Burgoyne to request another company of Sappers, 10,000 entrenching tools and 100,000 sandbags. Too little, too late. Neither men nor equipment could reach the Crimea before the New Year.[58]

Raglan, aware of the need to replace damaged artillery, arranged with Dundas for more naval guns to be landed and required a further supply of some 15-20 heavy mortars to come up from Malta. Once the decision to continue had been made on 6 November, considerable thought was given to the manner of conducting the siege. Four days later Burgoyne re-emphasized to Raglan the continued heavy losses on 'Inkerman Hill', not least from enemy heavy batteries. He therefore advised construction of an advance work to deal with Inkerman Lighthouse (at the eastern end of the Bay) and steamers anchored in the harbour. Pessimistically on 17 November he reminded Raglan that the 24pdrs from Malta would only replace damaged guns, without increasing the weight of the siege train and, moreover, deterioration in the weather and consequently the poor state of tracks to the front line would make their transit from port to gun position difficult. In addition to doubts about ability to press the siege in strength – Kingscote felt that at best the bombardment could not recommence 'in earnest' until mid-December – the Allies disagreed about points of concentration. Burgoyne still held that the Malakov was the key enemy defence work, whereas the French favoured the Flagstaff Bastion west of Man of War Harbour. On 25 November Raglan noted that Bizot strongly opposed altering the points of attack or constructing new works. In extending their parallels the French were close to the Flagstaff by the third week of the month and, recording that the Coldstreams were 'into the second parallel', McMillan wrote on 26 November: 'Getting very close to the Redan with our trenches.' Troops who attacked that work seven months later would find that statement relative. In reality, there was still a very long way to go.[59]

By now the army's situation had further deteriorated alarmingly as a result of the second major event of the month – a destructive storm on 14 November. From 6 a.m. for eight hours strong winds – of hurricane strength according to some reports – leavened by a thunderous downpour lashed the south-western corner of the Crimea and the surrounding coastline. Men, tents, animals and ships endured a period of extreme misery, discomfort and danger. Unsecured objects and loose boulders added to the perilous landscape of destruction. It was, Corporal McMillan wrote, 'one of the roughest days that ever man was out in ... we were all nearly perished ... Bearskins, caps, tin cans, blankets even knapsacks were swept off the ground and carried at railway speed into the valley'; a 'fearful gale' according to Nigel Kingscote. British headquarters withstood the worst excesses of the day, but neither Raglan nor his staff could venture out and every available corner of the house, adjacent stables and sheds was crammed with shivering men. Whatever the discomforts and dangers experienced by the men, the principal effect was a damaging loss of provisions and equipment. Twenty-one British vessels of various sizes and importance foundered that day from the mouth of the Katcha to the inner harbour at Balaclava. *Prince*, carrying a wide variety of stores including valuable warm clothing, and *Resolution* with more than ten million rounds of ammunition, were the most critical losses. Of *Prince* Raglan wrote to Newcastle on separate occasions, 'I feel the misfortune deeply' ... 'The destruction of that vessel is indeed a heavy misfortune.' Underlining the serious nature of the losses, on 15 November he pressed Newcastle for urgent replacement of lost supplies and ammunition; and three days later he persisted: 'You cannot send us too many supplies of all kinds.' Locally he ordered wreckage at Balaclava to be collected for the construction of shelters, and the hides of dead and slaughtered animals to be used as roof coverings after suitable treatment. Officers were sent throughout the neighbourhood to secure commodities from food to charcoal. Clothing naturally figured high on the list of requirements: in his diary, Kingscote recorded Raglan's 'every exertion' to obtain warm garments for his men.[60]

Lack of manpower to build a road was but one indication of the steadily decreasing strength of Raglan's army. On 3 November he formally and courteously wrote to Newcastle: 'I will not conceal from your Grace that I should be more satisfied if I could have occupied the position in considerably greater strength.' Put bluntly, he was short of men. Ten days after Inkerman the Cabinet considered Raglan's request for reinforcements with sympathy. If transport were a problem, Queen Victoria offered the royal yacht and Samuel Cunard undertook to provide troopships. Sidney Herbert supported the need to recruit into the army in an endeavour to meet Raglan's requirements, for there were no more serving troops available to send to the Crimea. It was hardly realistic for a new arrival on the upland, Captain Hedley Vicars, to complain towards the end of the month: 'We are anxiously waiting for Lord Raglan to storm Sebastopol; for, though we must lose many in doing it, yet anything would be better than seeing our soldiers dying there daily.' November proved a particularly depressing month for the haemorrhage of senior officers. Generals Cathcart, T. F. Strangways and Goldie had perished at Inkerman; and, as Poulett Somerset remarked, the rest were 'shuck' (shook). De Lacy Evans and Bentinck had been invalided home, the Duke of Cambridge was sick at Constantinople and unlikely to return to duty. Sir George Brown, Generals Torrens and Adams had all been wounded. The command structure of the expeditionary force had thus been disrupted extensively, three divisional commanders and the commanding gunner having been lost. Such was Raglan's plight that he asked the Horse Guards urgently for as many replacement officers and, in particular, generals 'as can be sent'.[61]

Nevertheless British success at Inkerman provoked an orgy of domestic celebration which brought Raglan instant acclaim. Congratulations almost literally showered upon him. Queen Victoria expressed to him her 'pride and joy' at 'the glorious but alas bloody victory of the 5th'. Her feelings of 'pride and satisfaction ... [were though] painfully allayed by the grievous loss'. She was 'most thankful' that Raglan had survived but chided him for rashness: 'The Queen trusts that he will not expose himself more than is necessary.' Her Majesty continued: 'Both the Prince and the Queen are anxious to express to Lord Raglan their unbounded admiration of the heroic conduct of the Army and their sincere sympathy in their sufferings and privation so nobly borne.' Thanking Raglan for his letter of 28 October, the Queen concluded: 'He [Raglan] has led the bravest troops that ever fought.' The Prime Minister (Aberdeen) wrote in similar vein: 'No words can do justice to my admiration of your conduct; and although my opinions are comparatively of little value, it must be satisfactory to you to know that they are shared by the whole country.' From Belgium King Leopold, recalling that they were 'old friends', observed how Raglan had 'gloriously distinguished yourself in a struggle of unusual difficulty and danger'. He added that 'our dear friend the Duke of Wellington' would have been 'happy' to observe the success of 'you, his near relation and ever faithful friend'. Major-General Charles Yorke, Military Secretary at the Horse Guards, also referred to Wellington's approbation when writing to Airey: 'What a man Lord Raglan has proved himself – we all think that the Duke his old chief, if he had found himself in a similar situation, could not have conducted matters better.' Five days after receiving Raglan's dispatch on the Battle of Inkerman, Newcastle wrote formally to him expressing many of the sentiments already conveyed in private correspondence, not least the Queen's pleasure at 'this important victory ... [and] Her Majesty's high appreciation of the noble exertion of Her Troops in a conflict which is unsurpassed in the annals of War for persevering valour and chivalrous devotion.'[62]

Such expressions of acclaim could not wholly mask unease about the mounting influence of *The Times*, especially through the dispatches of W.H. Russell which frequently contained unsubstantiated criticism and direct personal attacks on Raglan. Fortunately the British CinC was unaware of Russell's private letter of 8 November to his editor, John Delane, in which he declared unequivocally: 'I am convinced that Lord Raglan is utterly incompetent to lead an army through any arduous task', alleging further that he neither visited the camps nor was known to the troops. Raw meat to greedy leader writers. Raglan's own irritation surfaced in a letter to Newcastle on 13 November, drawing attention to an article in *The Times* of 23 October, which contained minute details of the disposition of the troops before Sevastopol: 'Invaluable to the Russians, and in the same degree detrimental to Her Majesty's troops'. Allied lack of ammunition, gabions and fascines had been revealed, as had the precise positions of Raglan's own headquarters, the powder mill and individual regiments. Recognizing that 'the writer' sought 'simply' to satisfy 'anxiety and curiosity', Raglan continued that 'the innocency of his [the writer's] intention does not diminish the evil he inflicts, and something should be done to check so pernicious a system at once.' 'I do not propose to take any violent step,' he informed Newcastle, 'though perhaps I should be justified in doing so.' He did intend to ask Mr Romaine (the Deputy Judge-Advocate) 'to see the different correspondents [in the Crimea] of the newspapers and quietly point out to them the necessity of greater prudence in future; and I have no doubt that they will at once see that I am right in so warning them.' He urged Newcastle similarly to approach 'editors of the daily press' in London urging them to 'expunge' from their pages information which might prove valuable to the enemy. The situation scarcely improved, though, and before the end of the month Kingscote was writing from headquarters castigating 'the humbug and untruths' perpetrated by correspondents for their papers from the front.[63]

Amid these and his many other troubles, Raglan faced renewed disruption over the Battle of Balaclava, once his official dispatch had been made public. As Nigel Kingscote explained, only the Military Secretary (Steele) and his assistant (Curzon) and 'I suppose General Airey' saw Raglan's dispatches before they were published in the press. Lord Lucan did not; and on 30 November he reacted violently. The temporary peace established by Airey's conciliatory conversation with him on 27 October was irrevocably (as it turned out) shattered. Lucan formally wrote to Raglan, referring to his dispatch 'given in the papers' which had 'just arrived from England'; and the British CinC's allegation that 'from some misconception of the instruction to advance, the Lieutenant-General considered that he was bound to attack at all hazards, and he accordingly ordered Lord Cardigan to move forward with the Light Brigade'. Furiously Lucan exclaimed: 'Surely, my lord, this is a grave charge and imputation reflecting seriously on my professional character.' 'I cannot remain silent,' he continued, feeling it 'incumbent on me to state those facts which I cannot doubt must clear me from what I respectfully submit is altogether unmerited'. He then detailed his version of the order, pointing out that after reading it he 'urged the uselessness of such an attack, and the dangers attending it'; to which 'the aide-de-camp' replied in 'a most authoritative tone' that Raglan's orders were to attack immediately. On being asked where 'as neither enemy nor guns were within sight', Nolan adopted 'a most disrespectful but significant manner, pointing to the further end of the valley'. When passing the instructions to Cardigan, the Light Brigade commander made 'objections ... in which I entirely agreed'. But Lucan considered that, even though a lieutenant-general, he did not

have 'discretionary power' to disobey a written order from 'my Commander-in-Chief', which would have 'been nothing less than direct disobedi-
ence of orders'. The British CinC, after all, 'from an elevated position' had
a far more commanding view of the battlefield.

Outlining the action that he had taken, not daring to disobey
Raglan, Lucan requested Raglan 'kindly to give the same publicity to this
letter that has been given to your report'. The flame of resentment had
thus been thoroughly fanned, and Raglan would not be free of the bitter
debate surrounding the charge throughout the remaining months of his
life. It was a far from comfortable manner with which to end the traumatic
month of November 1854. Strangely, a week previously Nigel Kingscote
had uttered strong views on the action in a letter to Richard Somerset,
showing that the incident still caused controversy at the front. The Light
Cavalry Charge had been 'very gallant but ought never to have taken
place and never would have had his Lordship's order been properly
obeyed. Lord Lucan made a sad mess of it and poor Nolan who took the
order and was killed would no doubt have been broke by court-martial
had he come out of it.' Kingscote added harsh words about Cardigan,
who 'can do nothing but talk about "his charge". I wish he would go
home, he is a perfect failure.' Writing to Kitty on 28 November, Kingscote
declared: 'Tell Charlotte she is "most sapient" about Lord Lucan as he
ought to have done exactly what she said, namely sent back to say that
such and such was the case but not a word must be said about it as my
Lord lets him and the Turks off very easy.' Not in Lucan's opinion.[64]

Neither Kingscote nor Raglan knew that another of the divisional
commanders also held strong views about one of the British CinC's dispatches and the whole tenor of Raglan's leadership. Still sick in Constantinople, the Duke of Cambridge penned a long, critical letter to his mother
on 30 November. 'Lord Raglan is an excellent man certainly but I admit I
do not think he is up to the job and is not the man to be in command of
the army. You have no idea of how everyone complains about him. He
certainly has a great deal to answer for including the disastrous day at
Balaclava and Inkerman, too. He was told before what would happen but
he did nothing to strengthen the position – besides General Evans and I
let him know our views every day but unfortunately without him paying
any attention.' Cambridge evidently remained unaware of Raglan's strenuous efforts to get the French to reinforce the area of Mount Inkerman
before 5 November, his keen awareness of the weakness of his extreme
right on the upland and lack of men to cover it. He went on: 'Well, now
the disaster has occurred and the position has been strengthened, but why
not before', the short answer being French reluctance. 'This has made
Evans and me quite ill, the anxiety of feeling that the day must and would
come, and I candidly tell you that I am very dissatisfied about my whole
position and about the general situation which is not as it should be. Lord
R is too reserved, he doesn't [sic] reveal his views to anyone and we gen-

erals are not treated by him as we should be in our position.' Cambridge had never been in battle before the Crimea. 'It isn't [sic] that he is not personally friendly and kind but he listens to no one and gives no information and that is very worrying in trying circumstances.' The inaccuracies and the transparent emotion of this outburst owed much no doubt to Cambridge's nervous exhaustion. Shortly afterwards the Duke commented on the number of officers 'going home as their health cannot stand it', including Cardigan who looked 'very poorly'. Cambridge also became incensed by Raglan's claim in his Inkerman dispatch that the Guards had been driven back. 'How Lord Raglan can say so, I do not understand ... Lord Raglan can't have seen it properly.' They withdrew rather from an isolated position, bayonetting their way through Russian ranks. Cambridge's dismay would fester, like that of Lucan's, for weeks to come. For the moment, however, he urged his mother not to say anything of this to 'a living soul'.[65]

Thoughts of people and family life in England continued to sustain Raglan as 1854 entered its last month. Writing to his daughters he declared himself 'very much grieved at the death of our dear friend Egerton ... [an] excellent man with every quality of a gentleman', who had shown such 'goodness' to them all during the family's annual visit to him and his wife, which allowed Raglan a 'few days relaxation from hard work'. Thanking 'my dearest daughters' for their letters, he gave them news of acquaintances serving in the Crimea, such as Tom Leslie who had been wounded and told Raglan before the 'ball was cut out', 'it is all right my lord'. He also responded to information from them, such as the death of Lady Disborne's son in an accident, recalling that his father and mother had been 'kind' to Raglan whenever he visited them, and asking Charlotte and Kitty to search in the Court Guide for Lady Disborne's address so that he might write to her. He signed himself 'Your most aff P A P A'. On Raglan's behalf Nigel Kingscote asked Kitty to go to Garrard's to see whether her father's worn dining plates could be made good with 'Electro Plate or whatever'. If so, the relevant items would be sent back to England, with a further request for 'much broken china and glass' to be replaced. One piece of good news was that Lady Raglan's health appeared, at least temporarily, to have improved, for she and Charlotte dined at Windsor on 4 December.[66]

In mid-December correspondence with Messrs Hoare of Fleet Street provided a rare contemporary glimpse of Raglan's financial affairs. He expected to pay off a £16,000 mortgage to the Duke of Hamilton in January 1855, and now planned to take over a £40,000 mortgage from a City merchant (Mr Thomson Hankey) on the estate of the Marquis of Ailesbury at East Witten, Yorkshire, which was being offered to him through Messrs Nicholl & Smyth of Carey Street. Once acquired the mortgage would yield half-yearly interest and rents of £4,600 per annum 'always most punctually paid'. This would constitute a sound investment:

'The security appears to be unexceptional and such as your Lordship may rest perfectly at ease about'. Raglan signed an order to his trustees in England to sell stock to provide the necessary capital, with the reservation that 'if there be enough without it, it had better not be touched'. His unnamed trustees would supervise the transaction and ensure that its provisions were carried out, using Messrs Hoare's professional services. Consulted in her London home on 13 December, following his letter to Messrs Hoare of 28 November, Lady Raglan pronounced herself 'very anxious' that Lord Raglan's wishes be carried out.[67]

Expressions of acclaim continued to arrive in the Crimea despite further whiffs of criticism. On 1 December the inhabitants of Melton Mowbray begged 'earnestly to record our deep sense of Obligation for such unparalleled Bravery under most trying difficulties', for which Raglan returned his 'most grateful thanks'. On 12 December he forwarded to his daughters 'my correspondence' with the Queen, Lord Aberdeen and the Duke of Newcastle in connection with his 'nomination' to be field marshal. He wrote that he felt 'most unworthy of such a distinction but everybody is most kind to me about it. The Queen's letter is most gracious. It is impossible to be more so, and Lord Aberdeen's expressions towards me and my services are not only most flattering but far beyond what I could expect in a man with so cold an exterior, tho [sic] I believe with a warm heart.' To Queen Victoria Raglan reiterated his devotion to duty: 'Such as they [his merits] are, however, they will always be at Your Majesty's command and it will ever be his pride as well as earnest endeavour to deserve Your Majesty's praise and approbation.' On 18 December the texts of the formal thanks expressed in both Houses of Parliament for the 'brilliant and decisive' victories at the Alma and Inkerman were sent to him, and three days later his field marshal's commission was finalized, counter-signed by Newcastle and 'entered with the Secretary at War' for the purposes of pay.[68]

During that third week in December Kingscote commented upon news of war fever in London amid scenes of great jubilation over the victory at Inkerman. On Christmas Eve Raglan published a General Order containing copies of dispatches from Newcastle to him expressing the Queen's delight at the success of Inkerman and her intention 'to confer a Medal upon all the Officers and Soldiers of the Army who have been engaged in the arduous and brilliant Campaign in the Crimea'. The medal itself would be inscribed 'Crimea' and clasps would be added for individual battles, whose names should also be henceforth shown on the Colours of those Regiments engaged. Ever thoughtful of the troops, Raglan highlighted in his Order a section from one of Newcastle's dispatches: 'Let not any private soldier in the ranks believe that his conduct is unheeded, the Queen thanks him, his Country honours him.'[69]

That General Order provided pre-Christmas cheer which was much needed. Raglan explained to the Queen that the 'weather and the consequent state of the roads and camps ... have impeded the conveyance and rendered the supply of the troops difficult and inadequate'. Shortage of fuel meant that on 8 December 'until further orders' it would be issued only to troops on the upland before Sevastopol, and eight days later a Board of General Officers was required to lay down the daily scale of fuel ration. A General Order of 10 December brought slightly better news than that, announcing free potatoes: 'Field Marshal Lord Raglan has the satis-faction to announce to the Army, that the vegetables that have been sent for their use are to be issued free of all charge, according to the instruc-tions he has received from the War Office.' The problem of how to convey rations to the troops remained, however; and Edward Hodge complained bitterly that cavalry horses had been detailed to carry up the daily rations from Balaclava. Estcourt, the Adjutant-General, exploded in a letter: 'Such roads ... such ground ... such a depth of mud'. Neither guns nor ammuni-tion could be moved to the siege lines, and the troops 'have been starved by the rotten mess of Trevelyan's pet Commissariat. They produce excel-lent provisions but they have no organized means of transport.' As soon as the roads worsened, no food arrived.

On 14 December Raglan addressed another terse communication to Commissary-General Filder: 'Something must really be done to place the supply of the army upon a more satisfactory footing or the worst con-sequences may follow. I receive complaints almost daily of some impedi-ment being thrown in the way of issues', citing an instance when an offi-cer arriving at Balaclava to collect the rations for his regiment was told that only a minimum of two tons of potatoes could be issued. 'I cannot help feeling that there is not infrequently a flippancy in the answers given without consideration,' he tartly concluded. This dreary picture may not have applied universally, particularly at headquarters. On 18 December Nigel Kingscote revealed that transport steamers from England had recently brought a saddle of mutton, English turbot and some corned beef for Raglan, which had been well received as Kingscote had killed the last sheep 'with no chance of any more for a week and only a few lean turkeys and geese to fall back on'. He explained to Kitty that he had written to Constantinople for beef and did not let 'the troubles' stop him from keep-ing a full pot. Similarly Hodge seemed more concerned about the 'exorbi-tantly dear' prices in Balaclava: 'ham 2s.2d. a pound, butter 2s. a pound, a small North Wilts cheese 15s., brandy 5s.a bottle'. At the end of the month he declared that 48s. for a dozen bottles of sherry was 'far too dear'.[70]

Concomitantly the medical services continued to create problems for Raglan. The swingeing criticism that had prompted the dispatch of female nurses such as Florence Nightingale to Turkey had to some extent abated. Lord William Paulet, exercising responsibility at Scutari, carried out a thorough inspection of the General and Barrack hospitals. Reporting his satisfaction to Raglan, he also praised Miss Nightingale and her staff for doing 'a great deal' for the sick and wounded. The impression that conditions at the Scutari hospitals had significantly improved appeared to be underlined by the Duke of Cambridge who enthused about the 'excellent' conditions there. But Paulet drew attention to the 'most dreadful state' of hospital transport from the Crimea: 'In the Avon steamer a number of men died, but I cannot find out who they were or what Regiment they belonged to.' Airey, after visiting the Balaclava General Hospital on 27 December, wrote critically to Raglan that he had seen no medical officer on the premises. Dr Hall's explanation to the British CinC that there had been a medical officer there but he had not recognized Airey seems distinctly thin.

On 31 December Florence Nightingale penned a devastating condemnation of the medical arrangements to Sidney Herbert, which pricked the balloon of local complacency. There was, she alleged, a total lack of order at Scutari, such that even the number of vacant beds or how much linen was available remained utterly unknown. Hygiene constituted a foreign concept. 'The vermin might, if they had but "unity of purpose" carry off the four miles of beds on their backs, and march with them into the War Office and Horse Guards.' Miss Nightingale, by temperament highly strung, wrote no doubt in the depths of temporary despair following a specific crisis, but her remarks more generally identified a lack of order which Raglan had appointed Paulet to rectify. He must have suspected that Paulet's early reports were over-optimistic, long before Florence Nightingale's sweeping condemnations.

Problems at Balaclava highlighted by Airey also weighed heavily upon him. In a General Order of 15 December he condemned publicly an incident, in which a medical officer was 'guilty' of leaving 'the sick, many of them in a very suffering state, ... in the streets for several hours, exposed to the very inclement weather'. Raglan sternly declaimed: 'The Commander of the Forces is sorry to have to animadvert very strongly upon the conduct of the medical department.' Small wonder that he wrote stingingly to Mr Romaine, Deputy Judge-Advocate: 'It is absolutely necessary that I should do all in my power to arouse the Medical Department to a sense of duty.'

The truth was, though, that the medical authorities, like the Commissariat and the Royal Navy, claimed primary allegiance to another authority in London, in this instance the Army and Ordnance Medical Department. In a long letter to its director, Hall rejected Raglan's complaint of insufficient hospital orderlies: 'I considered them sufficient for the charge, and I do still.' Similarly he held that the Purveyor provided 'ample for the wants of the sick', bitingly adding: 'It would almost appear as if His Lordship [Raglan] had been determined to find fault.'[71]

In the case of the Commissariat that situation marginally altered on 22 December when the Treasury relinquished its control to the Secretary of State for War. And, independently, Newcastle supported an initiative to improve transport between Balaclava and the siege lines by construction of a light railway by civilian labour. On 1 December the Cabinet resolved to contact Messrs Peto, Brassey & Betts with a view to 'laying a railroad from Balaclava to the camp before Sebastopol, principally in order to spare the incredible labour necessary to drag the artillery from the coast'. Indeed, an agreement was concluded swiftly with the firm to superintend 'a Civil Engineering Corps', which would build the proposed 'line or lines of rails'. Newcastle wrote to Raglan on 2 December announcing these plans: '300 skilled workmen' would have the railroad working within three weeks of landing in the Crimea, he confidently predicted. Four days later the Secretary of State suggested that Raglan might, in fact, provide 'such available labour to co-operate with the skilled workmen' – unlikely considering the parlous strength of the expeditionary force. Raglan responded positively, however. On 23 December he promised Newcastle that he would give every assistance to the new corps of civilian workers.[72]

As the Government came under increasing domestic pressure for its conduct of the war, however, Newcastle intensified his hectoring of Raglan. In the second half of December he peppered the British CinC with persistent volleys of complaint. The fact that some baggage remained at Varna exercised him, especially as Guards officers had apparently been wearing the same shirt for two to three months. There must be 'some neglect' in the Quartermaster-General's Department, too. 'An observer' had complained that ammunition was still aboard ship in Balaclava harbour because 'nobody thought it his duty to order its immediate discharge' – a fallacy, because Raglan had ordered it to be kept afloat to reduce risk of explosion. Noting Raglan's explanation about the state of the roads, he nevertheless observed that the 'same causes prevail in the French camp', yet there communications were in 'a much better condition'.

The Secretary of State would not let go. He had heard that insufficient nosebags were available, yet the French had no such deficiency and their 'horses are looking as well as when they landed'. Furthermore, 'the complaints of want of any regulation of method in the harbour of Balaclava are most disturbing'. So was Newcastle. His neurotic outpourings would have tested Job. For him even Christmas Day brought no rest and, so far as Raglan was concerned, little sign of charity. 'Private letters from the Camp received in Town two days ago' identified half rations for the troops, whereas plenty of food existed in Balaclava. No reflection on the reason for this or appreciation that transport difficulties might be involved. Carelessness 'in higher departments' must be the cause in the Crimea, not London, of course. Nor did the querulous stream abate as the year died. On 29 December Newcastle exclaimed: 'Complaints come in so thickly and so strongly ... relatives of officers [are] reproaching me for leaving the army to die away from want of proper care'. There lay the rub. It could not possibly be Newcastle's fault. Airey and Estcourt were 'not up to their work', because neither has sent 'any requisitions home to me or to any of the Military officers'. All the evils, Newcastle triumphantly proclaimed, were 'wholly attributable to these Staff officers'.[73]

How far Newcastle was reflecting the views of other politicians or how far he shaped them is unclear. But others were beginning metaphorically to desert Raglan, as well. Self-preservation and the retention of government office are powerful incentives to shift blame. Referring to Raglan's dispatches, which arrived in London on 23 December, Aberdeen observed to the Queen that they 'do not convey much information, but there is reason to fear that the sufferings of the Army are very great'. He went on dismissively: 'Local neglect and mismanagement appear materially to have added to the inevitable difficulties of the situation.' Granville personalized the problem: 'The War Office and the Cabinet derive no assistance from their general in the East,' he averred. By the end of the month the Cabinet was discussing the dispatch of officers to boost Raglan's staff – though no request had been received from him – 'especially to assist in the Departments of the Adjutant- and Quartermaster-General'. Lord Grey dismissed the posturing of Government Ministers as evidence of political manoeuvring. Referring to Newcastle and Sidney Herbert, he considered neither 'fit for taking a lead in so weighty a business as the conduct of a war, and they have the common fault of always looking for newspaper popularity'. At Raglan's expense. In this they may not have been alone.[74]

More parochially, Lord Lucan could not be quietened. He insisted that his letter of 30 November should be forwarded to Newcastle, which Raglan did reluctantly on 16 December. In his covering letter Raglan recounted the course of events surrounding the Light Brigade charge as he had seen them. Having failed, through Airey's further intercession, to persuade Lucan to withdraw the document, Raglan felt 'bound' to send it to Newcastle, at the same time 'submitting to you such observations upon it as I am bound, in justice to myself, to put you in possession of'. Lucan complained about the passage in Raglan's dispatch, which stated that Lucan mistakenly believed that he must 'attack at all hazards'. Raglan observed: 'His lordship conceives this statement to be a grave charge, and an imputation reflecting seriously on his professional character, and he deems it incumbent upon him to state these facts which he cannot doubt must clear him from what he respectfully submits as altogether unmerited.' Raglan firmly rebutted Lucan. 'Far from being willing to recall one word of it [the dispatch], I am prepared to declare, that not only did the Lieutenant-General misconceive the written instruction that was sent him, but that there was nothing in that instruction which called upon him to attack at all hazards, or to undertake the operation which led to such a brilliant display of gallantry on the part of the Light Brigade, and unhappily, at the same time, occasioned such lamentable casualties in every regiment composing it.' No hint of weakness, indecision or hesitation there.

Raglan remained resolute in his opinion. He emphasized that, in his letter, Lucan was 'wholly silent' about the previous order, 'merely' noting that 'the cavalry was formed to support an intended movement of the infantry'. Sternly, the British CinC observed: 'This order did not seem to me to have been attended to, and therefore it was that the instruction by Captain Nolan was forwarded to him.' There was, thus, absolutely no doubt in Raglan's mind that the Fourth Order represented a goad to execute the Third – 'to recover the heights'. Lucan 'must have read the first (Third) order with very little attention', Raglan argued, because he now held that the cavalry had been 'formed to support the infantry', whereas Airey's message had clearly required the infantry to support the cavalry in their recovery of the heights. Bitingly Raglan continued: 'So little had he [Lucan] sought to do as he had been directed, that he had no men in advance of his main body, made no attempt to regain the heights, and was so little informed of the position of the enemy that he asked Captain Nolan, "Where and what he was to attack, as neither enemy nor guns were in sight!"'

Lucan himself admitted this. 'The result of his inattention to the first (Third) order was, that it never occurred to him that the second (Fourth) was connected with, and a repetition of, the first'. Lucan considered an order to attack 'at all hazards', yet Raglan pointed out that the word 'attack' was not mentioned in either of the orders. Nevertheless, Lucan conceived that he must attack 'an unseen enemy, whose position, numbers, and composition, he was wholly unacquainted with, and whom, in consequence of a previous order, he had taken no step whatever to watch'. Raglan emphasized: 'I undoubtedly had no intention that he should make such an attack – there was nothing in the instruction to require it; and therefore I conceive I was fully justified in stating to your Grace, what was the exact truth, that the charge arose from the misconception of an order for the advance, which Lord Lucan considered obliged to attack at all hazards.' Raglan continued frostily: 'I wish I could say with his lordship that, having decided against his conviction to make the movement, he did all he could to render it as little perilous as possible. This, indeed, is far from being the case, in my judgement' – a damning indictment. Raglan went on to justify this stricture. Lucan had been advised that the horse artillery might accompany the cavalry. 'He did not bring it up.' Similarly, Lucan was informed that French cavalry were on his left: 'He did not invite their co-operation'. The whole of the heavy cavalry lay at his disposal, but by his own admission he 'brought up only two regiments in support'. Tellingly, Raglan then observed: 'He omits all other precautions, either from want of due consideration, or from the supposition that the unseen enemy was not in such great force as he apprehended, notwithstanding that he was warned of it by Lord Cardigan, after the latter had received the order to attack.'

Raglan ended his covering letter – which Lucan, of course, did not see – noting that he was 'much concerned' at having 'to submit these observations to your Grace'. He did not seek to 'disparage' Lucan's 'professional reputation', but he felt obliged to defend himself against Lucan's criticisms of his dispatch. Raglan had thus been forced to write at length 'in vindication of a report to your Grace in which I had strictly confined myself to that which I knew to be true'. He did not believe that his remarks 'could be viewed either as harsh or in any way grating of the feelings of his lordship'. In this, Lucan patently disagreed. Moreover Raglan's comments and opinions to Newcastle were so forthright that the matter could not be permitted to rest, once the Secretary of State had received Raglan's letter on 15 January 1855. For the moment, however, relative calm returned to the relationship between CinC and cavalry divisional commander. None the less this was an added burden which Raglan could have well done without as 1854 drew to a close.[75]

Yet, as the strains mounted, Raglan's health appeared unimpaired. In mid-December Nigel Kingscote assured Kitty that 'My Lord [is] very well indeed', having taken to riding Shadrach now that 'the ground is deep'. On the 30th he explained to Richard Somerset that the weather had been fairly mild of late, that Raglan was 'comfortable' despite the headquarters building being 'pretty ineffectual'. 'My Lord is particularly well,' he insisted, and writing to Richard from Constantinople on the last day of 1854 the Duke of Cambridge similarly commented upon Raglan's rude health. It was 'remarkable' how he carried 'the fatigues ... of this now protracted campaign'.[76]

CHAPTER 10

DEFEAT, DESPAIR AND DEATH
(JANUARY-JUNE 1855)

'My lord, I have passed a life of honor. I have served the Crown for above fifty years.' (Lord Raglan)[1]

Nigel Kingscote's prediction was that the weather in the New Year would be 'worse'. His bleak forecast proved uncomfortably accurate in a much broader context. For Raglan was about to enter the final six months of his life, during which the burden of political and military problems would increasingly tax his patience and endurance.[2]

Transport difficulties, already severe, intensified as the weather deteriorated. On 20 January Raglan explained to Queen Victoria that no Commissariat transport was available and the roads were impassable to wheeled vehicles. As Estcourt emphasized to Sidney Herbert three days later: 'Our only blot as I have often said before, and it is the beginning of all our serious difficulties, is the absence of an organized Military Conveyance Establishment.' Following a conversation with Raglan the previous day, on 20 January Lord Lucan advanced a detailed plan for 'a Muleteer Corps' of 5,000 mules divided into ten squadrons with an agreed complement of officers, NCOs and men and placed under his command to avoid friction with brigade commanders.[3] The idea remained stillborn, partly because, in the United Kingdom, alternative plans for a Land Transport Corps had been advanced, which owed much to Raglan's influence in the preceding months.[4] Meanwhile, Stratford de Redcliffe informed Raglan that James Beatty had reached Constantinople en route for the Crimea to begin preliminary survey work on the railway to the upland, though Lord Stratford's 800 'local labourers' provisionally hired by the British Ambassador to go with him declined to do so, 'discouraged by the weather, and the state of things in the Crimea'.[5]

Supply problems intensified, too. Raglan reminded the Queen: 'The Allied armies have no intercourse with the country and can derive no resources from it: and consequently all the requirements for the conveyance of stores and provisions, as well as the stores and provisions themselves, must be imported.' Lassitude in complying with requests not only engendered frustration but contributed directly to debilitating shortages at the front. Raglan pointed out to Newcastle that 'some months ago' Filder had been promised one hay vessel a fortnight from England, but by the end of January had received merely a single shipment. Not until 23 January had roasted coffee arrived. On 4 January Newcastle acknowledged Raglan's request for more hospital huts, dated 5 December. The

Secretary of State assured him that contracts were being drawn up for their supply and that 'no time will be lost' in dispatching them. Raglan explained to Sidney Herbert that when seven huts did arrive, they occupied 150 packages, each weighing 400 pounds. Herbert himself revealed that iron beds had arrived at Scutari, whereas the legs travelled in another ship to Balaclava. 'Whether the Ordnance people at the Tower are in fault or the Admiralty people who stow the ship I do not know, but it cannot be difficult to ascertain.' Not for the first time Raglan found himself the victim of an archaic system. At least one area of improvement could be identified. Raglan assured Newcastle that 'great progress is making [sic] in disembarking and issuing to the troops vast quantities of warm clothing of all descriptions'; and by 23 January he could report that the men were well-clothed. That, though, was only one problem solved. A week later, there was little point in Raglan authorizing attractive increases in rations – coffee, sugar, biscuit, meat and rice – if no means existed of getting them to the camps.[6]

　　While Raglan was grappling with these truly vital issues Newcastle subjected him to a renewed deluge of queries which often verged on the footling. The opening salvo on 1 January referred to the relative of a dying officer, who wanted to know 'how a Quartermaster-General [Airey] was likely to attend to his important duties who found time to write long private letters to at least half a dozen fine ladies in London' – among them, ironically, Lady Raglan and her daughters. In another dispatch that day, the Secretary of State referred to a complaint from Lieutenant-Colonel Tupper of the Guernsey Royal Militia that his son (an officer in the 38th Regiment) had not been moved to Balaclava as directed by a medical officer. Raglan should institute an inquiry about the incident. Five days later Newcastle generated a long, detailed list of accusations, involving sickness among the troops, 'starvation' among the animals and 'men in the trenches being on half, and in some instances, a quarter, rations for two or three days'. Among other 'numerous complaints' to reach the Secretary of State's ears was one about a detachment of Guards losing its way because no officer had arrived to guide it to the camp. Newcastle could not believe failure to issue supplies to the troops from Balaclava was 'entirely attributable ... to the badness of the roads or to the interruption occasioned by bad weather'. Sharply he concluded: 'I have for some time been painfully apprehensive that there has been either a want of foresight or ability on the part of some of your Lordship's staff, which has led to an amount of suffering and sickness amongst officers and men under your command which might and ought to have been avoided.' That same day Raglan expressed the 'greatest pain, regret and mortification' about Newcastle's unwarranted charges in a communication of 22 December. 'You observe that ammunition and clothes arrive in large quantities, but nobody considers it his duty to order its immediate discharge.' Raglan enjoined severely: 'Fortunately you have been wholly misinformed.'[7]

Newcastle's dyspeptic probing did not slacken however. Referring to a recent attack in *The Times* on Airey, and thus indirectly underlining the political influence of the press, he suggested that the Quartermaster-General be given a divisional command away from headquarters. Raglan's irritation began to show. Refuting yet once more unfounded attacks on his staff, he sensed 'that I no longer enjoy your confidence'. He went on with a tinge of reproof: 'My duty however to the Queen will induce me to persevere in doing my best to carry on the service to the utmost of my ability apart from all personal considerations.' Newcastle seemed unabashed. In the third week of the month he was peddling more jaundice 'upon the credit of a gentleman of high standing living in this country' concerning the poor reception and lack of accommodation for the 9th Regiment, whose men had to march through mud up to their knees in darkness. On 29 January, referring to his many dispatches urging 'the greater efficiency of the several Departments' under Raglan, he announced establishment of an inquiry by Major-General Knollys and Commissary-General Sir George Maclean in Paris into the organization of the French civil and military departments, requiring Raglan to institute a similar inquiry in the Crimea by a select committee of artillery, engineer and commissariat officers.

The following day Raglan replied to Newcastle's critical dispatch of 6 January. His tone of icy formality came close to outright rudeness, all the more telling given Raglan's habitual urbanity. 'I grieve indeed that your Grace should have entertained for a moment an opinion so fatal to the character and reputation of distinguished officers without inquiry from me or reference to them.' A devastating opening. He continued relentlessly: 'The Military Departments, my Lord Duke, have nothing whatever to do with the supply of provisions, the conveyance of them, or the care of the horses and mules employed in this branch of the service. These important functions rest exclusively with the Commissariat.' Nevertheless he defended Commissary-General Filder – whose own written comments he enclosed – who had been let down by non-arrival of promised supplies from England and hired Maltese and Turkish drivers who 'have been wanting both in zeal and industry'. Raglan protested that he had paid great attention to the matter of rations, on more than one occasion instituting boards of inquiry and otherwise determining levels of issues. He rehearsed old arguments about lack of transport, and the 'complete failure' of the Ambulance Corps. Like Filder, Airey dealt with Newcastle's long catalogue of complaints at length – such as those concerning the 9th Regiment and allegations that crucial baggage had been left at Varna – in a number of separate papers, which Raglan also enclosed. Newcastle's charges had caused Raglan the 'greatest concern'; and it is difficult to predict how the relationship between the CinC and Secretary of State would have proceeded had Newcastle not soon lost office.[8]

Raglan was, perhaps fortunately, unaware of relevant comments in Queen Victoria's diary: 'Lord Raglan enters *more* to detail, but still gives no satisfactory account of arrangements' ... 'in despair about Lord Raglan's imperturbability and impassebility [sic]!' ... 'giving no news, excepting that of continued illness'. Moreover, the Queen strongly supported Newcastle's most critical dispatch in January: 'The Duke has written a long and able dispatch to Lord Raglan, remonstrating and commenting in as kind a way as possible on the lamentable state of affairs – insisting on inquiry and amelioration. It is indeed highly necessary that this should be done.' At root, however, Queen Victoria only reflected the opinion of statesmen such as Newcastle, who failed properly to brief her or to defend Raglan.[9]

Newcastle's admission that *The Times* had shaped his opinion of Airey served to spotlight the continuing influence of that paper, and to some extent other publications such as *The Morning Post* and *The Illustrated London News*, which had correspondents at the front. Lord Granville noted on 26 January that he invited newspaper editors, including John Delane, to parties as a way of influencing them towards moderation: printed evidence suggests that the ploy did not succeed. Leader-writers continued to castigate the system that had resulted in 'the miserably led dozing hungry, naked and frostbitten in the trench'; and they followed Russell in continuing to compare British field hospitals adversely with those of the French. It was a short step, in keeping with Delane's social views, to see the army as 'the plaything of our aristocracy' and specifically to blame aristocratic direction of the war for all the evils in the Crimea. Sending out further reinforcements would only bolster failure, thus enabling Raglan and his staff 'to redeem their credit at the risk of another army'. In its correspondence columns, *The Times* of 13 January reopened debate about the military decision not to attack the north side of Sevastopol in September 1854, thus tacitly supporting the impression of incompetence at the front. Raglan bitterly condemned the paper's tendency to 'excite discontent and encourage indiscipline', doubting too whether 'the paid agent of the Emperor of Russia' could provide better intelligence 'than the correspondent of the paper that has the largest circulation in Europe' – reference to Russell's habit of describing troop dispositions and movements. There is no doubt that *The Times* did wield enormous influence in London. On 8 January Sidney Herbert warned Raglan of this, adding that, as a result, 'the position of the government here [is] very precarious'. More personally, Newcastle wrote to Raglan: 'I shall, of course, be the first victim to popular vengeance; and the papers, assisted by the tory and radical parties, have pretty well settled my fate already.'[10]

As Herbert and Newcastle had predicted, the conduct of the war led directly to the fall of Aberdeen's coalition government. On 26 January

Clarendon warned Stratford de Redcliffe that *The Times* was 'exciting the people almost to madness' and therefore carried direct responsibility for the current ministerial crisis. That day, too, Newcastle cautioned Raglan that a political storm was about to break, noting adverse public feeling about his continuing to hold office; and the following day, from Paris, Cowley blamed the 'infamous *Times*' for the break-up of the Government which he considered inevitable. On 26 January John Roebuck moved that a Select Committee be appointed 'to inquire into the condition of our army before Sebastopol and into the conduct of those Departments of Government whose duty it has been to minister to the wants of that army'. Four days later, at 1 a.m. on 30 January, the motion was carried; and Aberdeen's government resigned. For a few days, at least, political direction of the war would remain in limbo.[11]

Meanwhile, as the political crisis deepened during January, the hunt for military scapegoats intensified. In the Crimea Colonel C.A. Windham observed: 'On my honor as a soldier and a gentleman, I believe the fault is in our rulers here, not in the Duke of Newcastle.' Others, less circumspect, named Raglan. The Duke of Cambridge continued to write critically. From Malta he advised his wife Louisa: 'Poor dear Lord Raglan, he is an honorable man and gallant to a fault, but he is no General'; and, more pithily, he told his mother that 'as a General he is a nonentity'. While Cambridge was steaming towards England Captain R.B. Hawley reached Balaclava. In a series of swingeing letters he claimed to reflect opinion among officers already there. On 9 January he alleged: 'The army think little of Lord Raglan. He is too much of the office man and cannot forget his Horse Guards practice. The soldiers never see him. Canrobert is everywhere.' Another acid letter to his father eight days later claimed 'what you read in *The Times* is not exaggerated' ... 'All kinds of reports flying about ... one is that Lord Raglan delays the post to prevent our letters getting home'. The following day (18 January) he recounted details of a visit by Raglan – not without snide comment. 'The CinC, urged by our friend Russell of *The Times*, has now unwound himself from his winter sleep and come amongst us for the first time to-day.' Sardonically he went on: 'Let me relate his pattern dress [*sic*]: a light blue overcoat piped with scarlet, loose overflowing, gathered in by a strap behind, leather leggings capping his boots; and a black-and-white checked comforter finished his attire.' The ensuing passage was caustic to the point of venom: 'He seemed haggard. The crowd of soldiers passed him coldly and without recognition, though he asked a huge gunner, up to his ankles in mud, if his boots were thick and another if his coffee had sugar in it: kindly meant, but his feeble step and curved back told but too surely he had reached that period of life in which we all look forward to our allotted rest.' However, a week later, Hawley admitted to his sister that his impressions and much of his information had come from friends encountered in Balaclava, where he had arrived only on 1 January. At last, though, he was about to disembark, but not before emitting another anti-Raglan broadside. 'Lord Raglan expected to take the place [Sevastopol]', he confidently asserted, 'in a few days and did not ... having failed he has shown himself *quite* inadequate to his post. He minds *The Times*, though, and like a dormouse has unwound from his winter sleep and has shown himself *twice* to us.' Small wonder, perhaps, that opinion at home was hostile with such vitriolic, unsubstantiated and inexperienced views being so arrogantly propagated. Newcastle had demonstrated conclusively that second-hand gossip like this did have an effect in London.

On 20 January, Palmerston, destined soon to replace Aberdeen as Prime Minister, joined the chorus dismissing claims that poor weather 'unavoidable or unforeseen causes' were responsible for the army's plight before Sevastopol. The fault lay with the military leadership: 'He [Raglan] has shown himself deficient in that activity that care for the health and comfort of officers and men', and as a consequence of his patent shortcomings reinforcements were being 'sent to the slaughter and defeat and disgrace'. The Duke of Argyll took a similar line: '... to him [Raglan] we must trust in a great degree for the remedy of evils which he does not appear to see or at least to estimate, as we do'. Sir William Molesworth concurred with his Cabinet colleagues: 'The disgraceful and lamentable state of our army in the Crimea has been occasioned by the incompetence of the commanders.' All three Ministers, while deploring Raglan's alleged incompetence, nevertheless accepted that he could not be replaced. Charles Greville, not always a reliable source, none the less confidently recorded on 14 January: 'The Court [is] exceedingly alarmed and annoyed at Raglan's failure.' Two days earlier Queen Victoria recorded renewed charges that Raglan had 'frittered away' the army and that de Lacy Evans, now in England, was 'much discontented' at the conduct of affairs. 'All this is most grievous,' she remarked. Nor had the Duke of Cambridge been mollified by Raglan's response to his concern about the Inkerman dispatch, that he was 'sorry' the 'Brigade of Guards should be annoyed in the slightest degree'.[12]

Such a catalogue of condemnation appeared conclusive, Raglan's lack of ability beyond doubt. Yet, even as these carping criticisms were being penned, contrary opinions were forcefully expressed by many who had served in the Crimea. *John Bull* observed that 'the character and abilities of Lord Raglan have been so freely canvassed of late, that the individual opinions of [returning wounded] soldiers will be looked upon with no little curiosity.' It then republished details of interviews printed in the *Liverpool Mercury* of 19 January: 'I fought on the Sutlej [where Arthur Somerset perished] under Lord Gough and Lord Hardinge. They were splendid fellows, but there never was a General better liked by his soldiers than Lord Raglan' ... 'Why, the men thought he was far too much among the bullets' ... 'A braver man never breathed' ... 'There never was a better

General and right well every man in the army knows it.' *John Bull*, there-fore, concluded: 'The result of [these] inquiries would seem to show that his Lordship, notwithstanding the insinuations of his traducers, is actually idolized in the army.' Almost simultaneously, letters from before Sev-astopol concurred. Sir Edmund Lyons, acknowledging the 'insuperable difficulties' that Raglan faced, held that he was 'so kind, so brave, so reli-gious that people are surprized he should not *talk* of Providence in his Despatches'. Deploring the press attacks on Raglan, a sergeant declared: 'Lord Raglan has done everything for our comfort that lay in his power ... It is true we are suffering from sickness that is caused by the weather. I have yet to learn that Lord Raglan has power over that.' And an officer in the forward trenches noted that 'kind Lord Raglan was up here by day break this morning for a sortie, which was rather expected.' Writing from Taunton, where he was recovering from illness after returning from the front, A.W. Kinglake composed his own tribute: 'It was my fortune to be near Lord Raglan during some of those fleeting minutes which decide the fate of Armies, and the result was such as to impress one with the venera-tion for the Commander of the Forces which I can never feel for any other man living.' Lord Raglan was, thus, not without his supporters – notably those who had actually witnessed him in action.[13]

Despite the disturbing background of personal attack, Raglan still had to conduct military operations before Sevastopol and, in particular, grapple with need to mount another bombardment as a preliminary to storming the enemy defences. January opened with approval by Newcas-tle of Raglan's request to Dundas 'for supplies of heavy guns and ammu-nition and also for seamen to work them'. 'I am happy to find that the Vice Admiral felt himself enabled to accede to your application,' wrote the Secretary of State, a reminder that divided naval and military com-mand still bedevilled British planning. So did co-operation with Raglan's other allies. Although the French had not yet physically reinforced the Mount Inkerman area, as promised, on 1 January Airey secured Can-robert's agreement for them to attack the Malakov and Mamelon while the British concentrated on the Great Redan, provided that the British con-structed two additional flanking batteries of 23 guns in support. However, in reporting this to Newcastle, Raglan cautioned that, as French numerical strength rose with reinforcement, his own influence might correspond-ingly wane – another reminder to the Secretary of State about his lack of troops.[14]

By mid-January the French had still not moved; and only during the third week of the month did part of Bosquet's II Corps advance from its position overlooking the Plain of Balaclava to occupy Victoria Ridge and Mount Inkerman. But commitment to pressing the siege more closely seemed further in doubt, with the arrival on 27 January of an engineer officer (General Niel) at Canrobert's headquarters with authority from Napoleon III to 'advise' the French CinC. It soon became clear that the

Emperor was less keen to attack the Malakov than advance on the Russian field army across the Tchernaya. Raglan had been right to warn Newcastle of inter-Allied storms ahead. Nor had the French entirely given up the idea of assaulting the Flagstaff Bastion, rather than the Malakov, which had long been their wish. This may explain why Sir John Burgoyne produced a closely argued memorandum on 30 January re-emphasizing that the Malakov constituted the key to Sevastopol.[15]

Quite apart from Napoleon III's strategic ideas, which Niel had not yet revealed in detail, Raglan received other conflicting advice, advocating wider action. Despite firm preference for attacking the Malakov, on 15 January Burgoyne touched on the possibility of moving against the field army, Batchki Serai and Simpheropol. Sir James Graham, First Lord of the Admiralty, urged movement against the Perekop peninsula to cut off the flow of Russian reinforcements. Lord John Russell considered use of three Allied forces in the Crimea: one conducting the siege; another operating against the enemy field army; and a third using Eupatoria as a base against enemy lines of communication. Russell's scheme had a certain similarity to French plans, about to be canvassed. As Raglan pointed out in a memorandum attached to this letter, however, the possibility of two armies – engaged in the siege and in the field – had been discussed with St Arnaud in September 1854 and rejected for lack of men. The supply of reinforcements 'in driblets' ever since forestalled its revival. One encouraging development was news that promised Turkish reinforcements had begun to leave Varna at the end of January and Omar Pasha would come to the Crimea with them. All three commanders-in-chief would thus be in the primary theatre of war together once more.[16]

Amid all this Raglan did not forget Richard. 'I should think you must be looking for quarter day as a horse neighs for a feed of corn,' he wrote. 'I therefore send you a cheque for £50.' He thanked his son for 'magnificent ... [and] useful presents' of an eiderdown quilt and 'equally charming' padded waistcoat, for which he had 'every reason to bless you'. The weather was inhospitable and the gifts extremely welcome. He had heard 'indirectly' that Newcastle was about to do something for Richard in the way of a placement in England. Raglan was, though, rightly cautious: nine years had passed since 'the subject of your being provided for was first broached. I think our patience has been well tried.'[17]

At the front February opened with renewed optimism. Burgoyne secured Niel's agreement to his plans for the siege (concentration on the Malakov and Great Redan), which were subsequently approved in writing by both Allied commanders. So preparations for renewal of the bombardment were resumed in earnest, and on the 8th Burgoyne argued strongly for taking the Allied positions (in practice, the French) 1,200 yards in advance of the current ones on the right to counter any possible attack from the field army climbing on to the upland, as on 5 November.[18]

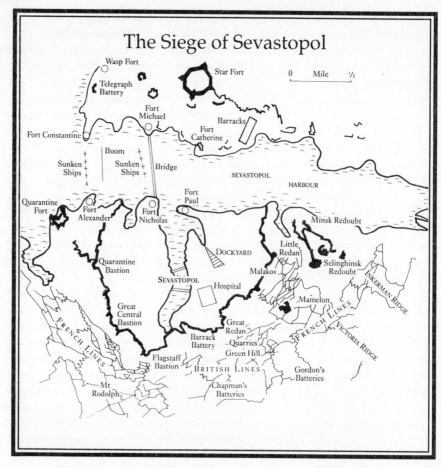

The Siege of Sevastopol

Burgoyne's precaution seemed sensible for the Russians began to construct new redoubts on land held by them north-west of Mount Inkerman, from which forays were unable to eject them. And they also further strengthened the Mamelon. On 20 February Stratford de Redcliffe alerted Raglan to a rumour that the enemy planned to attack during a snowstorm. Five days later Sir George Brown sent the CinC information from Codrington, one of his brigade commanders, suggesting that the Russians were massing for an assault in the Malakov area. Fortunately these proved yet further false alarms. Towards the end of the month the Russians sank six more ships in the entrance to Sevastopol harbour, thus destroying any hopes that they might not continue resistance. But, in the face of obvious need to pursue the siege, Raglan still lacked manpower. On 16 February Hedley Vicars explained that the 97th Regiment had been halved since 20 November and that the effectives in the British force scarcely exceeded 12,000. Four days later Newcastle's replacement as Secretary of State (Lord Panmure) somewhat unhelpfully informed Raglan that he hoped for 1,500-2,000 men from the Irish Constabulary Force so that 'your Brigade of Guards will rise Phoenix-like from the ashes'.[19]

Notwithstanding shortage of manpower and written agreement about prosecution of the siege, in mid-February the French advanced new strategic proposals which Raglan had to study. Canrobert suggested independent action against the Russian field army, Niel more specifically wanted complete investment of Sevastopol with Star Fort neutralized to the north and 50,000 men storming Mackenzie Heights. Fortunately, perhaps, at this stage Raglan did not know of plans to concentrate French reserves at Constantinople without committing them to the siege lines and the possibility of Napoleon III leading them in person in the field. Nor was he apparently aware that the Cabinet had unanimously rejected the Emperor's proposal to put the British force under French command.[20]

Arrival of Omar Pasha and the Turks in strength at Eupatoria did make Niel's option of an attack on the north theoretically easier to contemplate. By 11 February 26,000 infantry plus two batteries of horse artillery, with a third battery about to land, were under command there. Fortunately, as it turned out, for six days later they were in action, repulsing a determined Russian assault on Eupatoria, assisted by a few French troops and Allied warships firing over the heads of the Turkish defenders. Omar Pasha reported to Raglan and Canrobert that an estimated 36 battalions of infantry, six regiments of cavalry, 400 Cossacks, 80 artillery pieces and a number of horse artillery units had been committed by the enemy, who suffered 453 known dead, not counting bodies that may have been taken away in the retreat. Turkish reinforcements had arrived at Eupatoria just in time. Without them, it is difficult to imagine how the small garrison, despite naval gunfire support, could have held out against such a large force. The Russians now fell back, leaving the Allies the options of remaining static, attacking the lines of communication from Perekop or looking to an assault on the north of Sevastopol.[21]

Co-ordination of Allied strategy, whatever its form, must now be more difficult, however, given the rising number of troops and the presence of all three commanders in the Crimea. Almost inevitably signs of friction began to appear, especially as the French had by far the largest force and the Turks could claim numerical parity with, if not superiority to, the British. Raglan was in the weak position that he had presaged and which only his personality and experience could overcome. The rapport between the British and Turks built up in Bulgaria seemed to endure: Lieutenant-Colonel Neale forwarded a letter from Osman Bey in Varna to Raglan complimenting him on the high standard of discipline among the British and claiming that the citizens were sorry to see them depart. The personal, mutual respect between Omar Pasha and Raglan, forged in a spartan Bulgarian dwelling in May 1854, also endured. The French were not always so courteous. Bizot advised Marshal Vaillant (French Minister of War in Paris) that Niel had 'tried in vain to galvanize their [British] indolence'. Not a good omen for future co-operaton.[22]

Political changes in London and another Secretary of State for War presented an initial period of uncertainty, especially as discontent with conduct of the war had largely accounted for the fall of Aberdeen and Newcastle. But Raglan soon learnt that the new Secretary of State would be no less critical than the old. Panmure's first official dispatch on 12 February contained the old mixture of complaint, innuendo and down-right inaccuracy. Raglan was rightly dismayed when he received it sixteen days later. 'It would appear that your visits to the camp were few and far between, and your Staff seem to have known as little as yourself of the condition of your gallant men.' The familiar castigation of the Quarter-master-General and Adjutant-General followed. Panmure reserved his most biting comments for Raglan himself. 'I cannot find that your Lord-ship has been in the habit of keeping Her Majesty's Government acquainted, in a clear and succinct manner, with the operations in which you are engaged ... Your notices of the condition of your army are brief and unsatisfactory ... on the other hand, elaborate statements reach us from quarters which you denominate as unauthentic'. A familiar wail of lamentation ensued, culminating in a demand for regular fortnightly reports to him from every division: 'They will mention the condition of their [troops'] clothing; the amount and regularity of issue of their rations, the state of their quarters and the cleanliness of the camp in its several parts.' Panmure at the very least lacked finesse. Effectively, by demanding such detailed reports, he implied that Raglan was not doing his job. The Secretary of State did not soften his words in conclusion: 'I see no reason, from anything which has come to my hand, to alter the opinion which is universally entertained here of the inefficiency of your general staff.' Raglan could thus expect no easier ride from his new political master.[23]

There is no doubt that attacks on Raglan and his staff were esca-lating at home; and this to some extent explained Panmure's stringent outburst. Writing to Airey, Hardinge emphasized the strength of public opinion, based not only upon press reports but 'the letters of officers of rank' – Wellington's Peninsula 'croakers' once more. *The Times* was still prominent. It was no less effective for concentrating on targets already well-covered: Raglan's staff; medical arrangements; aristocratic 'trifling' with the troops in the Crimea. 'Their aristocratic general, and their equally aristocratic staff view this scene of wreck and destruction with a gentle-man-like tranquility ... [they would] return with their horses, their plate, and their china, their German cook and several tons' weight of official returns, all in excellent order, and the announcement that the last British soldier was dead.' On 12 February the paper made clear that it favoured Raglan's recall.[24]

Palmerston was less direct, but no less critical. In a memorandum to the Queen, the new Prime Minister explained: 'The opinion of the Cabinet seems to be that it is necessary to change the Adjutant-General and Quartermaster-General in the Crimea.' Shown government dispatches by Raglan, Estcourt confided to his diary: 'The burden of all was the displacement of Airey and myself'; though he and the Quartermaster-General strongly defended themselves in their detailed repudiation of the charges, which Raglan appended to his dispatch of 30 January. Burgoyne, too, was incensed. In a long memorandum to Raglan on 7 February he dismissed the complaints against the staff, and he commented to Colonel Matson at the Ordnance: 'The conclusion that seems to have been come to finally is that the errors and cause of every evil were *here* and not at home.' But, if Raglan could defend Estcourt, Airey and Filder, he had no means of protecting Burgoyne whose appointment to his staff had originated in London. Burgoyne was recalled and officially replaced on 24 February by Major-General H. D. Jones as Raglan's senior engineer adviser, although Sir John would not leave the Crimea until 20 March.[25]

Nor was that action the only initiative from England. If Raglan would not part with Estcourt and Airey, the operation of the staff must be made more effective in the eyes of the Government. The solution was to appoint a Chief of Staff. In his memorandum of 10 February, five days after taking office, Palmerston explained to the Queen that in view of the general dissatisfaction in England with the staff 'it would be desirable to send out an active and intelligent officer to act as Chief of Staff' between Raglan and his heads of department. Two days later he produced a 'Memorandum of Measures Taken to Establish a better order of things in the Crimea': Lieutenant-General Sir James Simpson would become the new Chief of Staff, with orders 'to inquire into the manner in which the Staff Officers perform their duties' and to carry Raglan's orders to the staff making sure that they were quickly complied with. On 19 February Panmure drew up comprehensive instructions which he described as 'novel' for Simpson based upon Palmerston's guidelines: 'It will be your business not only to convey to these [staff] officers the orders referred to but to see that these orders are speedily and implicitly carried into effect.' The Adjutant-General and Quartermaster-General were to report to Raglan through Simpson, who would also comment on the condition of 'the General Staff of the Army' to Raglan and Panmure, as Secretary of State. Recommendation of appointments to and removal from staff posts remained with Raglan, 'but you will not fail if you find any Officer in your opinion unfit, on trial, for the duties entrusted to him to report the same without fear or affection to the CinC'. Raglan's flexibility was, therefore, constrained, direct access of his staff officers to him curtailed and, in effect, his own performance by implication stood condemned. Simpson's appointment was a direct reflection upon him. The same day that he issued Simpson with his instructions, Panmure warned Raglan of his impending arrival, pleading that 'I must do something to satisfy the House of Commons.' On 19 February, also, in informing Raglan that

Simpson had left London that day Hardinge emphasized that the appointment of 'our friend General Simpson' was the only way to save Airey against whom 'the public cry ... [was] so great'. Hardinge had assured 'every authority' that he would have selected Airey, and by his words attempted to allay any fears by referring to Simpson's friendship with Raglan in the Peninsula. Nevertheless *The United Service Gazette* speculated that Simpson's appointment might be a way of allowing Raglan quietly to return to England, thus implying that Simpson had been sent to replace him as CinC. Queen Victoria privately noted otherwise. Simpson 'may be able to smooth down all difficulties which at this moment might be very serious, for it would be very difficult to appoint anyone in Lord Raglan's place. Lord Panmure feels, as we do, how valuable he is in his management of the relations with the French Army.' Simpson would thus fulfil the acknowledged administrative duties of a Chief of Staff. But the public perception would remain that the appointment reflected adversely on Raglan.[26]

In February the Commission of Inquiry sent out under Dr A. Cumming to investigate the state of medical provision for the Expeditionary Force produced its report. Conclusions such as 'we found the patients in the field hospitals generally in a filthy condition' and 'the privies are bad', coupled with adverse comparison between the British and French hospital transport, reinforced the overall impression of inefficiency and squalor. Palmerston, therefore, seemed justified in appointing a more powerful Sanitary Commission under Dr Sutherland to carry out more extensive investigation and to call for full co-operation from Raglan. The Prime Minister rightly feared obstruction from medical authorities in the field, but he evidently did not appreciate Raglan's limited authority over them. Emphasizing to Raglan the 'inadequacy of the Medical Staff', Palmerston held that the Sanitary Commission would 'put the hospitals, the port [Balaclava] and the Camp into a less unhealthy condition than has hitherto existed'. 'The Hospital at Scutari is become a Hotbed of Pestilence,' he alleged, moving on somewhat illogically to fear that 'your Camp will become one vast seat of the most virulent Plague'. Referring to the Commissioners, 'their mission will be ridiculed and their recommendations and directions set aside' unless Raglan supported them in 'the most peremptory manner'. As one who was charging the CinC with lack of authority and ability, Palmerston was now placing considerable reliance upon him to assist a Commission which at the very least indirectly reflected upon his own performance. On 19 February Sir John McNeill and Colonel Alexander Tulloch had been instructed to institute yet another Commission of Inquiry and to 'proceed to the Crimea in order to inquire into the whole management of the Commissariat Department'. *The United Service Gazette* welcomed the appointment and dispatch of these two Commissions. Engaged in the siege of Sevastopol, Raglan could have been pardoned for showing rather less enthusiasm.[27]

Towards the close of February better weather eased the overall supply and transport situation. Russell's dispatch of 19 February referred to more clement weather and better supplies: 'Provisions are abundant, hay has arrived, and fresh vegetables have been sent up to the front to check the scurvy.' The railway had made rapid progress to Kadikoi, and Balaclava had been cleaned up. Morale had consequently risen. The very next day, however, high winds and snow prevented a reconnaissance on the Tchernaya and, ironically in view of his encouraging dispatch, Russell wandered around lost for three hours. The next three days were, according to Estcourt, 'fine' and 'beautiful', heralding a more permanent improvement. During February, also, three ships loaded with clothing, food and other comforts (such as books, sweets and sheepskin coats) arrived at Balaclava under the auspices of the Crimean War Fund, administered in England by Lord Ellesmere. Raglan put some twenty civilian labourers, hired locally, at the disposal of the two commissioners, to supplement the labour force brought on the ships.[28]

Amid the plethora of complaints Raglan continued to attract fierce support from many who served under him. Burgoyne dismissed the 'unmerited' aspersions cast on his commander and argued that to blame Raglan for 'hardships and deprivations' was both 'illiberal and unjust'. He advanced a convincing defence on the grounds that the system was basically at fault and the Government, not foreseeing a long winter campaign, had inadequately prepared for it. Writing from the 'Balaclava Camp' on 1 February, an NCO of the 93rd (Hector McPherson), declared it the 'height of injustice to fasten blame on Lord Raglan', who deserved sympathy for having to combat 'obstacles' over which he had no control. McPherson had 'the fullest confidence' in Raglan and believed that he deserved more support from people at home. In England two days later, a letter from Lord Mount-Edgcumbe to *The Globe* (published, 5 February) quoted 'several' Marines who had returned from the Crimea, confirming that 'very frequently' Raglan had visited their camp at Balaclava. Raglan had addressed them, emphasizing the importance of their position and the 'confidence' and 'trust' that he had in them. One Marine had been in the Balaclava camp for eleven weeks: despite the distance from his headquarters, Raglan had ridden into the camp 'almost every day'. Another had personally seen him 'scores of times'. Interestingly, Mount-Edgcumbe quoted, too, 'an officer' who had written to his family: 'That it is quite time that Lord Raglan should be restrained, or his bodily health would suffer, for he was frequently seen on every part of the camp.' An unidentified general still at the front condemned 'the continued abuse of Lord Raglan ... [it was] so absolutely untrue and without foundation, all they say against him ... The army are quite unanimous on these points.' On this evidence personal support for Raglan from his troops was not declining.[29]

There was, too, corroborative indication of Raglan's habitual kindness and consideration for others. Lieutenant-Colonel Wilbraham, a staff officer, reported that, during an informal divisional inspection, 'he [Raglan] spoke to many of the men, who were there cooking their evening meal, and by his kind words and pleasant manner cheered the poor fellows, while they in their replies told him some useful truths'. Writing at the end of the month to Lady Elizabeth Orde, Charlotte relayed details of an incident that had been recounted to her by a civilian who had spent three weeks at the headquarters before Sevastopol. 'One morning one of the ADCs informed Lord Raglan that a soldier's wife had been confined in camp in what is called a *Dog Kennel Tent* (which is simply a hole dug into the ground and hoops of wood put on it with canvas stretched on them, similar to gypsy tents). Lord Raglan immediately, though it was a most awfully cold day and the tent was four miles off, determined to ride to see her. He filled the holster of his saddle with tea, filled a soda water bottle with brandy and water, ladened himself with a blanket and with a water-proof sheet given to Lord Raglan by the gentleman who warranted the fact, and thus laden Lord Raglan set off to see the poor woman, to whom he paid a visit in a place four feet wide and four feet high, and strange to say up to the time my informant left the Crimea, both mother and child were doing well, and Lord Raglan continued sending her little comforts.' A note appended to Charlotte's letter explained that, on his return to England, Nigel Kingscote recalled this episode vividly because 'violent wind and thick driving snow' could not deter Raglan.[30]

During February, Raglan's health evidently remained in the state that allowed him to undertake this ride in such adverse conditions. Nigel Kingscote assured Richard that his father was 'very flourishing and stands his work marvellously well though his mind at all events must have very great wear and tear'. And Charlotte, therefore, seemed justified in eulogizing about his health on 10 February: 'The only thing that keeps up our spirits is the comfort that God in his mercy preserves dear Papa in such good health and gives him strength to bear up against all the anxieties and cares he has to undergo and under all circumstances to preserve the calmness and equanimity of manner and what is still more wonderful I am told he is never out of humour. He works all day and half the night and rides about a great deal, sometimes even in that cold weather is on horseback six hours at a time.' On the last day of the month his elder daughter concluded: 'It is really wonderful to see how he takes all the additional care and annoyance it must be to see himself so vilified and abused.' He was not, to all outward appearances, wilting. Nor was his memory at fault. A senior officer in the Crimea paid tribute to his 'astonishing ... memory in every *detail* of the different Departments as they were administered under the Duke of Wellington during the Great War' and the fact that he had adapted them 'in modified form according to *present* circumstances in the clearest and most remarkable manner'.[31]

Despite the reassurances arriving from the Crimea of Raglan's health, his daughters were clearly concerned about the effect on him of the escalating criticism. Charlotte boosted her morale by contending that 'the *truth* will prevail', but she admitted that 'Papa is a good deal annoyed about it all, but more at the abuse lavished on those under him than about himself'. 'Poor Richard', she added, 'feels it a good deal.' It was a blessing that he was in Hanover, 'as he avoids hearing the numerous viperous and absurd stories which people take a pleasure in coming and telling us.' Raglan himself had little opportunity to write to his family in February. He apologized to Richard for a long-delayed reply to his request for advice as to whether he should resign his militia commission, suggesting that he do so in case the regiment were ordered abroad. In a telling conclusion, though, he wrote: 'I long to be at home. In the meanwhile God Bless you my boy.'[32]

The Balaclava affair would not die and this, with Cardigan in England already vociferous in his own justification, further multiplied Raglan's troubles. Recalled by Newcastle while he was still in office, Lucan left the Crimea with ill grace. On 24 February Raglan informed Hardinge that he had departed in high dudgeon, attributing his loss of command to Raglan's dispatch and subsequent correspondence with the Secretary of State. 'Now I confess that I did not expect that he would be recalled,' mused Raglan; rather a strange comment considering the severity of the his strictures and Lucan's violent reaction. Back in England, Lucan would stir up the press, Horse Guards and Parliament; and his feud with Cardigan continued there beyond the Crimean battlefields. That scarcely helped Raglan's cause. For, as Sidney Herbert observed, the change in mood towards Raglan since the award of the field marshal's baton had become most marked.[33]

In the Crimea, as March advanced, the weather continued to improve and morale naturally rose. Russell noted renewed energy among the troops, duck shooting on the upland and better supplies so that he anticipated murmurings that sufficient quantities of 'Godfrey's Cordial and Soothing Syrup' or 'Daffy's Elixir' were not available to the Grenadiers and Dragoons. Roger Fenton, the photographer, soon after his arrival in March wrote home about 'quite a farmyard at the Guards Camp', sumptuous evening meals and being woken at 4.30 a.m., 'when cocks and hens, sheep and lambs began their morning hymns'. Nigel Kingscote mentioned the 'elastic spirits of men, playing football, leapfrog – officers' spring races'. Referring to the great many divisional and regimental race meetings, both flat and hurdle, organized by the French and British, on 24 March Mrs Duberly wondered whether her journal should not be renamed 'Racing Calendar'.[34]

Yet from a military point of view March would prove sterile. On the 26th Panmure showed understandable concern at the 'slow progress' of the siege, suggesting to Raglan that its outcome was 'by no means certain'. The Secretary of State presumed that 'some sound military reason' existed for the French, having assumed responsibility for the Mount

Inkerman area, making no positive effort to dislodge Russian troops still holding high Ground above Careenage Ravine. He, however, could not see the logic for inertia. To some extent lack of Allied aggression could be explained by the need for the French to advance their trenches on the rocky right of the line and, as Raglan admitted to the Queen, despite the improving health of the troops, lack of men to fulfil British defensive siege duties. Furthermore enemy activity and potential strength constrained the Allies. 'Mr Cattley' who in Raglan's words 'has charge of the department of intelligence' estimated 40,000 Russians in Sevastopol, 90,000 in the field (including the small number still near Eupatoria), with 15,000 further reserves expected soon to arrive.[35]

During March the Russians were certainly not idle. The so-called 'White Works' – because the white rim of their diggings were seen by the Allies at first light – though more usually known as the Mamelon on the hill in advance of the Malakov were further enhanced to contain 22 cannon; and a new lunette of ten 24pdrs, covered by a further defence work of twelve guns, was completed above Careenage Ravine. The approaches to the Malakov were thus now formidable. During the night of 22/3 March the Russians were confident enough to launch their own assaults. Approximately 2,000 men advanced on the Right Attack and Gordon's Batteries, seeking to outflank the British position, while an estimated 5,500 attacked the French approaches to the Mamelon. Todleben later claimed that these probes were aimed to create maximum disruption and nuisance, but Kinglake suspected that a more ambitious scheme had been thwarted, possibly capture of the ridges sought on 5 November. At all events the night's skirmishing cost the Russians 1,300 casualties, the French 600 and the British 70 (including four officers dead). If Todleben's objective were simply to unsettle the Allies, though, he had enjoyed some success. Raglan assured the Queen that the attacks had been confidently beaten off, but Major-General Jones believed them 'very disturbing'. On 29 March, mindful of his need for more siege guns, Raglan sent for a fourth battering-ram from England.[36]

During March several proposals were considered for pressing the siege and, almost inevitably, more wide-scale actions. A conference on the 4th concentrated on the intensification of Russian fire on the Allied right. New enemy batteries, occupation of ridges south of Careenage Ravine and enhanced fire from steamers in the harbour all meant that an assault on the Russian left would now be more difficult. The French pressed for an exclusive attack on the Great Redan, but Raglan held that, without a simultaneous attack on the Malakov, this would be too costly and unlikely to succeed. Canrobert then suggested using 20,000 Turks under Omar Pasha against the enemy field army. Another Council of War two days later, attended by Raglan, Canrobert, Burgoyne, Bosquet, Brown, Niel, Bizot and Jones, looked at Burgoyne's plan to attack the new Russian works on the Russian left, principally the Mamelon. This was effectively a re-run of the negative debate of 4 March. Next day Burgoyne yet once more pressed the value of attacking the Mamelon to Raglan, alleging that Jones was now siding with the French idea to concentrate on the Great Redan. He reminded the CinC, too, that the French had agreed on 2 February to a dual assault on the Malakov and Great Redan. Raglan meanwhile successfully resisted yet another French ploy, reiterated when Canrobert visited him on 8 March, to bring Omar Pasha and the Turks to Sevastopol, contending that strategically they were much more useful at Eupatoria.

To Panmure on 10 March, Raglan pointed out that French reluctance – indeed, refusal – to move against the Malakov, as previously agreed, hamstrung plans for the siege and infinitely delayed the storming of Sevastopol. On 16 March Bizot at length accepted the need to attack the Mamelon; and it is likely that, four days before he left the Crimea, Burgoyne exerted decisive influence on him. Indeed, Burgoyne and Jones, as Raglan's professional advisers, were instrumental in defining the British position concerning the points of attack. Bizot, though, evidently had less influence on Canrobert than Burgoyne had on Raglan. To Sir John's intense dismay the French CinC remained sceptical and unsupportive. As Raglan warned Panmure, Canrobert was taking 'rather a gloomy view' of the future, fearing that when the Allies re-opened the bombardment, the Russians would advance against Kamiesch with 20,000 men and Balaclava with 40,000. The Allies, he felt, might well be 'overpowered'. Raglan and Lyons were 'surprized' at 'such desponding language'; and Raglan rather mildly noted: 'I ventured to express my opinion that the tone of his observations was somewhat serious.' Superficially, that reaction afforded a certain amount of credibility to Rear-Admiral Houston Stewart's contention that Raglan exhibited lack of strength in conferences. But Stewart may have been equating Raglan's polite form of words with infirmity of purpose. He was, after all, numerically in an inferior position, having recently asked the French to take over part of his siege responsibilities. Realistically his was a very weak hand, and he played it with consummate skill. He was a great persuader.[37]

Raglan's other ally proved ultra-sensitive on occasions. Having agreed to supply the Turkish troops at Eupatoria, after their arrival from Varna Raglan protested that Omar Pasha had distributed five days' flour to 16,000 paupers in the port. In response to a further request, Raglan ordered Paulet to forward 10,000 smooth-bore muskets and three million rounds of ammunition to Eupatoria on 12 March. A week later the Turkish CinC expressed his 'extreme gratitude' for supplies of bedding, ammunition, etc., and the attachment of British surgeons to his force. Yet he was soon complaining that the 26 officers and sixteen NCOs serving with his troops were not enough, especially as the defence lines around Eupatoria had been extended.[38]

In the meantime Panmure did not slacken his aggressive criticism. On 2 March he returned to the charge of Filder's having issued green coffee to the troops when roasted supplies were at Balaclava. Three days later, drawing attention to medical shortcomings, he sent Raglan a translation of a summary of Prussian medical arrangements published in *Die Zeit*. By now, Raglan had responded warmly to Panmure's charges in his initial dispatch of 12 February. Yet again he vigorously defended himself and his staff. Bad weather since 10 November had immeasurably affected operations, and he referred to his own misgivings about the weather and need to plan for a prolonged campaign expressed to Newcastle on 29 June and 23 October 1854. If sufficient reinforcements had been arranged he might well have been able to construct 'a stoned road'. When the bad weather 'set in' Turkish labour was used to repair the road from Balaclava towards the upland, but the men were 'not very efficient'. General Vinoy had been obliged to use French troops to repair the road west of Kadikoi. Raglan reiterated that he had every confidence in Airey and Estcourt, and had been assured by Filder that he had done his best under trying circumstances beyond his control. Raglan's conclusion to a lengthy survey of the campaign thus far and detailed refutation of Panmure's attack was dignified, but sharp. 'My lord, I have passed a life of honor. I have served the Crown for above fifty years ... I have served under the greatest man of the age more than half my life, have enjoyed his confidence, and have, I am proud to say, been ever regarded by him as a man of truth and some judgement as to the qualifications of officers ... My zeal and vigilance have never slackened, and I am wholly at a loss to conceive to what your lordship alludes in speaking of the strict routine of departmental etiquette.'[39]

Panmure remained unmoved. Writing privately to Brown on 15 March, the Secretary of State protested that he did not want Raglan dismissed – on the contrary, he held him in 'great regard' – but his 'lack of communication' in dispatches made it difficult for Ministers to defend him, when at home they were under attack 'day after day'. Newcastle had pleaded the same case. Neither of them seemed to have realized that Raglan was now not a uniformed scribe but a commander actively engaging an enemy in the field. The next day Panmure reminded the CinC that he (Raglan) was 'surrounded by a vigilant and an inquisitive and not friendly press ... [and] a vast number of your own officers have been in the habit of openly criticizing all that occurs in your camp in letters to their friends, which we hear daily quoted and hear daily read in Parliament'. Yet all Raglan had done was to 'despise', but not 'deny', what was reported. And, unabashed, on 19 March he replied to Raglan's dispatch of 2 March. Referring to 'the storm of popular indignation' that he must face, Panmure emphasized that Airey, as Quartermaster-General, was responsible for the state of communications between Balaclava and the camp. He dismissed Raglan's allegation of ill-founded criticism: his information came not from *The Times*, 'but from eye-witnesses of the scenes'. He, as

Secretary of State, could dismiss Airey and Estcourt, though he would not do so. Panmure thus indirectly inferrred that he could dispense with Raglan as well. He did not query his personal devotion to duty but doubted 'whether all the necessary precautions were taken for maintaining that army in the most perfect efficiency' – a scarcely veiled implication that Raglan had been inefficient. He repeated unease at the lack of description in Raglan's dispatches and steadfastly refused to reveal the identity of Raglan's 'slanderer', which would be 'a base breach of confidence in me to betray'. Condemned by persons or person unknown. The sting yet remained. Panmure's duty was 'to the army ... [and] the country', not solely Raglan. That must have boosted Raglan's confidence no end.

Nor would the issue of coffee go away. On 24 March Raglan noted that Filder had not lost time in distributing roasted coffee when it eventually arrived on 23 January; and he reminded the Secretary of State that 'some months ago' the Commissary-General had been led to expect a floating bakery complete with bakers, but as yet there was no indication that it had even left England. Sidney Herbert, whom Raglan counted as a friend, complained that, as Secretary at War, he had been blamed for 'the management of the war' even though he had 'no authority'; and he, too, remonstrated with Raglan for not providing the Cabinet with information or seeking to refute the 'stories'. This applied to Raglan's private letters as well as official dispatches. Government Ministers, Herbert claimed, had been forced to rely upon copies of Canrobert's dispatches or those from General Rose, liaison officer at French headquarters. He joined in the condemnation of Raglan's staff and quoted evidence of Florence Nightingale's dissatisfaction with the medical system. *Et tu*, Sidney. At the end of the month Panmure claimed to Simpson that 'the feeling against Raglan is subsiding'; though from the tenor of the correspondence the CinC would hardly have guessed it. Queen Victoria's comment on Raglan's reply of 2 March to Panmure's criticisms summarized a latent strand of opinion: 'It is natural that Lord Raglan should be pained and hurt at all that has been said and written but he seems wonderfully unconscious of his own defects.' The erosive impact of continuous carping at home was self-evident.[40]

In two long letters to Priscilla Raglan revealed how deeply adverse comment had affected him. '... he [Lord John Russell], I hear from Emily, was shocked to find his late [Cabinet] colleagues dropped me in the mud without making an effort to get me out of it ... I can even now hardly comprehend the extent and violence of the abuse that has been heaped upon me. *The Times* took up the attack of the Crimea, the ministers acted upon the same impulse, and both one and the other being unwilling to bear the blame thrust it upon me, and have striven to make me responsible for the climate, the season, the want of tents, the sickness and the labors of the troops and all the hardships of a winter campaign.' Lady

Westmorland was a trusted confidante, and he went on to demonstrate that he had, in some respects, reached the verge of despair, despite outward appearance of calm. Newcastle, whom he had believed to be a firm supporter, had deserted him: '... from the time the tide turned against me, I received no expression of sympathy or assurance of support from him but long letters came in upon me every mail!!' Wellington had suffered 'vulgar abuse', 'but then he was not abandoned by the Ministry of the day'. Clearly the newspapers had nettled him: 'The licentiousness of the Press is in itself an impediment to the due administration of an army.' His sense of isolation was underlined in his conclusion: 'I must be honest ... and am determined not to lose my character under any circumstances by any act or evading of my own.' On 26 March he repeated poignantly, 'I have deeply felt the desertion of others' and, significantly, in discussing the prospect of success for peace negotiations, he wrote: '... all I can wish for is peace and release from a burden which is hard to bear from a press-ridden country'. 'You cannot write to me too often,' summed up Raglan's sense of abandonment. Sir George Brown, reassuring Charlotte about her father's health, added: 'He tells me they [worries] keep him from rest at night, but if such is the case the circumstance does not appear materially to affect his spirits or to impair his equanimity.' Brown declared: 'Never was any poor man so unreasonably or unjustly assailed by calumny as he has been by those vile newspapers.'[41]

In view of his feeling of rejection Raglan might have resented Simpson's appointment. Instead he ensured that the new Chief of Staff was welcomed and treated with both personal and professional courtesy. His Adjutant-General, though, was certainly not happy. Simpson's appointment, he believed, meant that 'Lord Raglan and all of his Staff have been shabbily used in Parliament.' If his CinC felt dismay he did not reveal it. He enthused to the Queen about the arrival of Simpson, 'who he doubts not will render all the assistance it may be in his power to afford'. He was, uncharacteristically, less supportive of another Government decision. The whole concept of the expedition was 'extremely open to criticism' and possibly 'lightly undertaken', he observed to Lord John Russell on 26 March. Six months of stalemate in the Crimea lay behind that assessment. In a broader context he warned the Queen about 'wresting the command of it [the army] from Your Majesty ... and placing it under the more immediate controul [sic] of Parliament' – allusion to pressure for bringing the CinC at the Horse Guards more clearly under the Secretary of State for War.[42]

Lucan had by now reached England and had demanded a court-martial following Raglan's conclusions on his conduct of the Light Brigade's Charge. Hardinge refused because Lucan had been recalled as 'a good understanding' between him and 'the General Commanding in the Field' was 'indispensable' and quite obviously no longer attainable. Denied that avenue of publicity, Lucan resorted to the House of Lords where he found surprisingly little sympathy. And he went beyond more consideration of his own case. Filder complained bitterly to Raglan about Lucan's misleading evidence to the Roebuck Committee. None of this eased Raglan's or the minds of his friends and family at home; for Lucan's attacks on Raglan were compounded by the press. Burgoyne recorded that Raglan had shown him a copy of *The Morning Chronicle* of 1 March, which contained a sharp article: 'He says that his wife and daughters are dreadfully cut up by the abuse at home, and we can hardly wonder at it, when we recollect that two or three months ago, they were cheered at the railway station, as the relatives of the hero of the day!'[43]

Indeed, Raglan remained sensitive to the state of his children, and in particular the fortunes of his son, Richard. Writing to him in Vienna, he enclosed '... something for your *mieux plaisirs*. It will enable you to buy something for your mama and sisters.' Raglan hoped that while there Richard would 'have the opportunity of making the acquaintance of Lord John Russell, who is very kindly disposed towards me and will perhaps give you a helping hand'. In a stilted, though normal, fashion he wrote: 'I am very much obliged to you for all your letters', regretting that he had been unable to reply to everyone. 'God be with you, my dear Richard. Your most affe [*sic*] father Raglan.'[44]

Surprisingly, perhaps, Raglan's health continued to give no cause for concern. Leicester Curzon assured Charlotte that, in spite of the 'worry and annoyance' of the adverse comments 'at home', he had 'never looked in better health ... I see him almost daily ... Never was any poor man so unreasonably or unjustly assailed by calumny as he has been by those vile newspapers.' As CinC, Raglan was 'irreplaceable'. On 14 March Sir John McNeill commented at Balaclava: 'Lord Raglan is looking ten years younger than when he left England and is a great favourite with the men, and much respected by the officers' – evidently not all the officers.[45]

As March drew to a close Raglan certainly appeared buoyant. Major-General Jones recorded that an inter-Allied conference on 25 March set the re-opening of the bombardment for 2 April, with Niel offering to lend 20 wagons to bring up ammunition. Thus, the following day, Raglan informed Lord John Russell that he hoped to have enough ammunition to recommence the bombardment at the beginning of April, though he did add a note of caution: 'The French have not yet stated definitely what the immediate object of the renewed attack is desired to be', fearing that they might still opt for west of Man of War Harbour, not the Mamelon. He need not have worried. Jones confirmed, on 29 March, that Bizot and Niel had consented to a detailed programme of operations, which allowed for simultaneous ground attacks on the Great Redan and Mamelon/Malakov area following the bombardment. Airey paid tribute to Raglan's patient 'conferring' with his allies in wearisome all-day meetings, which achieved this harmony. Niel's doubts, particularly about a rapid assault before further sapping, had been overcome. On Monday 9 April 501 Allied (101

British) guns commenced the Second Bombardment of Sevastopol, in poor visibility caused by mist and rain.[46]

But already Raglan had become aware of renewed preference for wider operations. On 3 April he revealed knowledge of an unexplained concentration of French reserves in Turkey, which he must have guessed presaged operations beyond the siege: 'What a body of French troops collecting at Constantinople is for I cannot divine.' Two days later Simmons wrote to Clarendon, indicating that the commitment of Omar Pasha and Canrobert to an attack on Sevastopol from the north predated the Second Bombardment. On 2 April Simmons personally told Canrobert that Omar Pasha favoured this alternative strategy because he feared 'the practicability of taking Sevastopol from the south without a great loss of life and time'. The British liaison officer advised Clarendon that 'General Canrobert added that he also was entirely of the same opinion as to the importance of Eupatoria [as a base for such an operation] and that if necessity should arise and he had any force disposable he should be quite prepared to combine a portion of his army with that of His Highness to take the offensive from Eupatoria.' A copy of this letter went to Raglan, thus giving him ample time to prepare a response by the time that he met his fellow commanders.[47]

At their meeting on 14 April the three CinCs, together with their artillery and engineer advisers, Pélissier, Brown and Lyons (as independent British naval commander), agreed that no immediate assault on Sevastopol was possible; indeed, the French (except Pélissier) wanted priority given to the complete investment of the Russian port. The three CinCs and Lyons then met alone, and Raglan persuaded Canrobert and Omar Pasha to continue the bombardment, though at a reduced level so as to conserve ammunition, and to extend the duration of the cannonade. Niel, who was not present, subsequently criticized Canrobert for failing to press the Emperor's more grandiose plans. The following day (15 April) Brown presided over a meeting at the British headquarters in which British, French and Turkish representatives (Simmons being one of the latter) considered the whole range of possible siege and field operations in detail. It is reasonable to assume that Brown presented Raglan's views.

He held that 90,000 men were needed – exclusive of the siege train and cavalry – 'to secure' the present position before Sevastopol. General Martimprey argued that currently the French had 114,000 in the Crimea which, if non-effectives attached to hospitals and other support tasks were deducted, effectively totalled 90,000. So Canrobert proposed to retain 50,000 in the siege lines, making 40,000 available for field operations. Brown explained that the British had 15,000 before Sevastopol and 5,000 at Balaclava 'calculated upon the same principal [sic] as the French'. Additionally, the Sardinians had promised 15,000 and Omar Pasha could deploy 25,000 in the field as well as defend Eupatoria. There were, thus, 155,000 available overall, which could produce 90,000 (55,000 French,

20,000 British and 15,000 Sardinians) before Sevastopol and a field force of 65,000 (40,000 French and 25,000 Turks).

The Turkish military representative (Sefer Pasha) pointed out that Omar Pasha did not consider his men suitable for the trenches and still strongly favoured an attack on the north of Sevastopol using 'the sea coast as a base'. The Turkish CinC felt, too, that the French had proved reluctant to attack 'the enemy's works', which suggested that the present siege tactics would not quickly succeed. This relatively low-level conference made no executive decisions, but it served to keep the strategic considerations alive. Then, on 16 April, Raglan learnt why Canrobert had been prevaricating, when his French colleague revealed part of a letter from Napoleon III limiting his powers of negotiation: 'Do what you can, but do not compromise yourself' – in other words, agree to nothing positive.[48]

This, and the restraining presence of Niel, no doubt explains why, on 16 April, Canrobert agreed to attack the Mamelon, but three days later changed his mind. Raglan's patience was yet again sorely tested, and he must, too, have wondered what story Canrobert was feeding to Paris. On 21 April he expressed surprise to Cowley at the Ambassador's letter of 3 April, which showed belief in the French capital that British lethargy had caused delay in reopening the bombardment. He protested that consultations between artillery and engineer officers of the two armies had taken place 'frequently' and that, on 14 March, Jones had reinforced Burgoyne's view that the Mamelon must be taken prior to a successful assault. Then, incredibly, at another conference during the morning of Monday 23 April British and French artillery and engineer officers proposed that, if no investment of Sevastopol occurred within ten days, the port should be assaulted. That evening Canrobert met Raglan privately for two hours at the British headquarters and they agreed to intensify the bombardment once more on 26 April and attack Sevastopol in the most appropriate way – considerable room for manoeuvre here – two days later. Unknown to Raglan, though, in letters to Napoleon III next day, neither Canrobert nor Niel showed themselves so determined or so committed. Raglan may not have been entirely surprised – even if unaware of these reservations – when Niel arrived at the British headquarters on the morning of 25 April, less than 24 hours before intensification of the bombardment was due. He announced that the French generals were unanimously in favour of postponing 'offensive operations against Sevastopol' until the French reserves at Constantinople (due to embark on 10 May) should arrive. In vain Raglan pointed out the inconsistency of the French position, given their agreement to a bombardment and assault. Later that day Canrobert wrote formally to Raglan requesting postponement of the plans agreed on 23 April until arrival of the French reserves. So the proposed Second Bombardment petered out. Its demise was closely linked with French and Turkish preference for a strategic initiative apart from the siege lines. Raglan's major problem was to persuade his allies that deflection of attention and strength from the siege would weaken their overall position, not strengthen it. The main hope of success lay in pressing forward into Sevastopol, not marching on Mackenzie Heights or closing on Simpheropol. That would be an unnecessary dissipation of effort and, incidentally, create major supply and transport headaches.[49]

This unpromising picture was further complicated by Omar Pasha. Essentially he intended to gather all Turkish forces in the Crimea under his personal control, including those attached to the French and British before Sevastopol, so that he could use Eupatoria as a base for offensive operations. Nevertheless the month of April had opened with high hopes of co-operation. On the 3rd Raglan and Canrobert jointly asked Omar Pasha to come to Balaclava with a Turkish division; and two days later 14,000 Turks duly embarked in British and French ships at Eupatoria. But, possibly unknown to Raglan then, Simmons re-emphasized to Clarendon that the Turkish CinC still wanted to concentrate his men at Eupatoria, reinforcing them with the Egyptian division. He therefore envisaged only 'temporarily' commanding at Sevastopol 'for a period which he does not imagine will exceed ten or twelve days'. Given his reservations about Turkish troops occupying the trenches, it may well be that he anticipated the Turks acting in reserve until the British and French stormed Sevastopol. Whether or not this were so, Omar Pasha certainly intended to return to Eupatoria with all the Turkish troops, there to be reinforced by '20 or 24,000' of the Allies and so be 'in a position ... to threaten seriously or occupy some part of the Russian lines of communication with Sevastopol'. He had been assured that the French would provide return transport from Kamiesch, together with necessary rations.

Kinglake asserts that initially Raglan remained initially unaware of these bilateral arrangements, but when he was made aware of them he argued vigorously for keeping the Turks at Eupatoria as a menace to the Russian lines of communication, further arguing that more Turkish troops could not be accommodated before Sevastopol. But the Franco-Turkish axis apparent at Allied conferences during April seemed rooted in these commitments. On 8 April, following a letter from Simmons, Raglan must have suspected something. Simmons explained that Omar Pasha had ordered the Egyptian division from Constantinople to Kamiesch and would dispatch 6,000 more men from Eupatoria (making 20,000 in all) once the French had sent to Eupatoria the Turks now serving before Sevastopol. These somewhat complicated arrangements did seem to promise two divisions before Sevastopol – one from Eupatoria and the other from Constantinople. The arrival of the Turkish commander in person at Kamiesch on 8 April appeared most promising. And, eight days later, Simmons summarized the Turkish deployment: 20,000 near Sevastopol; 30,000 at Eupatoria.

Then, at the inter-Allied conference of 22 April, reports of renewed Russian activity near Eupatoria prompted Raglan and Canrobert to agree that Omar Pasha should return there with 'a portion' of the troops that had recently sailed south with him. Ostensibly he left behind the 7,300-strong Egyptian division, a brigade of 3,000 under Colonel Ogilvy and an unspecified number directly under Raglan's command around Balaclava. But these figures were optimistic: the Egyptian division had arrived at Sevastopol, but a British estimate on 25 April put its strength there at only 4,817. Simmons made clear that the Turkish CinC wanted even these withdrawn to Eupatoria, where he still intended to concentrate his entire force. Meanwhile relations between Omar Pasha and his Minister of War at Constantinople had again deteriorated. Omar Pasha refused to tender advice on the deployment of Turkish troops in the Caucasus, arguing that nothing had been done during the winter to counteract Russian penetration. By implication the politicians had been idle.[50]

But not in northern Europe. During mid-April Napoleon III visited England, and on the 16th Panmure warned Raglan that, because of the allegedly low morale of the French troops, the Emperor intended to visit the Crimea. At a so-called Council of War at Windsor on 18 April, attended by the Prince Consort, Palmerston, Cowley, Panmure, Vaillant, Walewski and Burgoyne (who in vain raised objections), he reiterated his intention of doing so and advanced an elaborate scheme of operations. Napoleon proposed that Omar Pasha with 30,000 Turks should hold Eupatoria. A further 30,000 plus 30,000 French, all under Canrobert, would continue the siege. The 20,000 British would be withdrawn from the siege and combined with 15,000 Sardinians, 5,000 French and 10,000 Turks to form a field army of 45,000 infantry, cavalry and artillery under Raglan. A second field army (dubbed the 'Army of Diversion') would total 70,000 and be entirely French: 45,000 withdrawn from the siege and 25,000 reserves from Constantinople. The organization of the three armies plus the garrison of Eupatoria was agreed at Windsor, despite the gross over-estimation of available Turkish troops; and their strategic deployment was further determined at a second Council of War held in Buckingham Palace on 20 April. Raglan would cross the Tchernaya to take the high ground around Mackenzie's Farm, though he had not in any way been consulted about the feasibility of such a risky action. An even more improbable operation was envisaged for the 'Army of Diversion': the 45,000 French troops withdrawn from the siege would march eastwards beyond Balaclava – with its flank unprotected – to the port of Aloushita to join the Constantinople reserves. The combined force would then advance northwards, separated from Mackenzie Heights by about 25 miles of broken country over numerous mountains and through countless vulnerable passes towards Simpheropol. In this latter venture, the French army would be joined by Raglan whose victory must be assumed. The two Allied field forces (Raglan's plus that from Aloushita) would thus overthrow all Russian forces north and east of Sevastopol to complete its investment.

Evidently Napoleon's personality dominated the two Councils of War, though there must be a suspicion that the more balanced military minds present believed that the unreality of the plans would quickly cause their abandonment. Writing to Raglan, Panmure felt sure that once Napoleon appreciated the problems on the ground, he would take the Aloushita army, which he intended to command in person, to join Raglan east of Sevastopol, enabling Sevastopol to be invested more closely. Fortunately all these fantasies came to nought; but not before Raglan had had to experience more anxiety.

Within a week of leaving London, on 27 April Napoleon informed Canrobert that he would not after all be coming to the Crimea, though he sent detailed instructions to the French CinC. He still envisaged Raglan taking the Mackenzie Heights and the French Simpheropol; though he urged Canrobert to 'consider it coolly with Lord Raglan'. Yet more delicate negotiations were thus in prospect in the wake of the failed Second Bombardment. There was, at least, one encouraging piece of news. Having landed earlier that day at Balaclava and been conducted around Allied positions there and on the Plain, General La Marmora, the Sardinian CinC, reached Raglan's headquarters early in the afternoon of 9 April.[51]

Before Napoleon's more extreme ideas faltered, Panmure again attacked Raglan's staff, in the light of the proposed summer operations. In the immediate aftermath of the Windsor and London meetings, he informed Raglan that he and Marshal Vaillant were not confident that bombardment would be successful. So they decided that field operations must take precedence, for which the efficient organization of supplies and transport would be crucial. Panmure therefore urged that Filder be replaced by Colonel Tulloch and that Airey and Estcourt should also go; but he stopped short of taking responsibility for any such changes. Once more the onus of decision would fall on Raglan: 'I cannot impress too seriously upon you the very grave responsibility which you assume entirely to yourself in continuing Generals Airey and Estcourt in their present positions.' And political attacks were not confined to the Secretary of State. Ellenborough (the tory former Governor-General of India) joined Panmure in calling for removal of Raglan's staff. In defence of them, however, Raglan received support from an unusual quarter: Simpson, his new Chief of Staff. On 16 April he declared to Panmure that Raglan was the 'worst used man I have ever heard of', his staff 'very much vilified ... nor have I any fault to find with Airey and Estcourt', noting only in passing that the line 'distinguishing their respective departments was not so distinct as it ought to have been'. Ten days later Simpson reiterated these favourable comments. He had, he explained to Panmure, arrived 'with some degree of prejudice against them [the staff] created in my mind by the gross misrepresentations current in England'. Now, 'I do not think a better selection of staff could be made.'[52]

Lord Stratford de Redcliffe chose April to spend several days in the Crimea at Raglan's headquarters. Anxious to examine all aspects of the Allied positions, he was conducted over the battlefields of Balaclava and Inkerman and visited front-line trenches. But, mindful of the Ambassador's safety, Raglan forbade Lord Stratford's guides to allow him to come under fire. That order was strictly enforced, but on an excursion to the French headquarters Lord Stratford did persuade General Rose (later Lord Strathnairn) to take him to trenches under fire. Fortunately he survived unscathed.[53]

Practical problems with the new railway added to Raglan's worries, and here, too, Panmure's ill-informed missives were less than soothing. On 13 April he complained that 'intelligence' revealed that although the track had been completed to Kadikoi on 17 March, it was not yet fully in use for Commissariat stores, which was to be 'reprehended'. The truth was that the railway had not proved entirely satisfactory. On 6 April details of a serious accident emerged. Because of the 'inability to break [sic] the train of wagons', which were carrying a detachment of the 71st, one soldier was killed, twelve men and three officers injured. Then, scarcely a month following completion to Kadikoi, many of the sleepers had to be relaid after heavy rain. Acquisition of local labour for menial tasks caused headaches. A General Order of 6 April optimistically declared: 'Twenty-five Eupatorians have been provided for each Division for the purpose of cleaning the whole of the British Camp', with a disciplinary structure under a military officer or NCO laid down. Later that month Simmons explained to Raglan that he had engaged a further three companies each of 50 Tartars under an officer on the same terms as those 'last sent'. He would dispatch yet another company as soon as possible to complete the 200 required by Raglan. But there is little evidence that this locally recruited labour proved satisfactory, rather the contrary as complaints about the state of the camps continued.[54]

At home, the Select Committee sponsored by Roebuck had settled into its routine of questioning. Although individuals such as the Duke of Cambridge pointed to the iniquity of the administrative system rather than individuals and the Queen wrote to Raglan deploring concomitant newspaper attacks on him, the CinC's reputation was by no means enhanced. Estcourt complained that many of the witnesses had left the Crimea before the severe winter, but the cumulative effect of criticism was of little help to the expeditionary force or its commander in April 1855. Essentially the Sevastopol Committee concerned itself with Christmas past. And the impression of ineffective military leadership in the Crimea gained credibility through the fulminations of Lucan, still seeking to justify himself at Raglan's expense. Airey, possibly reflecting headquarters' opinion, referred to the 'fine work' going on in England through the machinations of the Committee and Lucan. Admitting that Lucan did not admire him – 'that's pretty plain' – he none the less felt that he must 'write to show him up, which is so tiresome'. He hoped that he would never see Lucan again, 'but I'm afraid I shall'.[55]

Of more immediate concern was personal fitness and its impact on staff work. Ill-health again dogged Airey, 'my eyes are almost out – very dim indeed,' he admitted to Charlotte. Raglan, in contrast, flourished: 'Lord Raglan is wonderfully well and wonderfully strong – he incites my admiration for I am really as weak as an old cat.' The CinC's strength, while so many were wilting around him, and after such a rigorous winter, could only be marvelled at. His family remained a solace and a comfort to him. Airey assured Charlotte that 'Lord Raglan [is] always thinking of you all.' He 'longs' to be home. And on 24 April the thoughtful father wrote to his elder daughter: 'There is nothing to be had for your birthday here and therefore I send you a cheque for £20 with which you and Kitty may buy what you like in celebration of the 16 May a day to which I owe a beloved daughter for whose virtues and affection I owe to Providence.' He added gratitude for her letter of 6 April, which arrived 'yesterday', and a fervent prayer, which betrayed the longing alluded to by Airey: 'God bless you my dear Charlotte may you have many happy returns of it and may I pass your next birthday under the expression of your beaming countenance.'[56]

Despite his various difficulties Raglan ended April on a buoyant note. He informed Sir George Brown that he and Canrobert had discussed a combined expedition to Kertch, at the eastern extremity of the Crimean peninsula and guarding the entrance to the Sea of Azov. A successful descent would allow the Russian lines of communication from Rostov and other eastern supply centres to be effectively cut. The defenders of Sevastopol would therefore be deprived of valuable quantities of supplies and reinforcements. The future – with renewal of the bombardment also under discussion – seemed eminently more hopeful.[57]

Indeed the month of May was dominated by two attempts to execute the Kertch expedition, a change in command of the French forces in the Crimea, arrival of the Sardinians in force, another threat by Omar Pasha to resign and, not least, fierce fighting along the siege lines before Sevastopol. It was not characterized by re-opening of the bombardment. Nevertheless the month began in such a promising fashion as to justify Raglan's optimism. An obituary later claimed that 'to his [Raglan's] genius we are ... indebted for the brilliant expedition to Kertch'. The writer may have been guilty of hyperbole; but undoubtedly Raglan did overcome Canrobert's reservations. Having originally accepted the idea on 29 April, the next day the French CinC expressed doubts, based upon a report of strong Russian forces in the area. Raglan replied on 1 May, arguing that only a *coup de main* was intended to destroy defences commanding entrance to the Sea of Azov and that an Allied force of 10,000 would prove adequate, given that the enemy would not be concentrated. Canrobert's immediate response accepted Raglan's reassurances, announcing that he was issuing 'orders for the prompt embarkation' of 8,500 French troops. The following day Raglan gave instructions to Brown, whom Canrobert had agreed should lead the Anglo-French force, even though the British contribution would be considerably less than their ally's. The expedition, comprising 56 vessels, set sail in the early evening of 3 May. The national squadrons were commanded by Admirals Lyons and Bruat. Brown (under orders from Raglan) required the Kamiesch flotilla at first to steer north-west from the Chersonese peninsula towards Odessa, changing course only after dark at 9 p.m. Interestingly, McMillan noted in his diary: 'An expedition has sailed to some part of the Crimea but no person seems to know where.' Unfortunately Canrobert received a number of discouraging telegraph messages from Paris throughout the day. At about 10.30 p.m. he rode over to Raglan's headquarters, convinced that he must recall the expedition. He eventually left Raglan at 1 a.m. on 4 May; as the British CinC explained to Lyons in a letter shortly afterwards: 'I persuaded him upon the understanding that he relinquished his intention of doing so at my instance.' Canrobert needed a plausible excuse.

Raglan was not left long in peace. At 2.15 a.m. a French ADC arrived with the news that another telegram from Napoleon III confirmed that the Emperor would not now be coming to the Crimea, but that Canrobert should concentrate his forces once the Corps of Reserve arrived from Constantinople. A more self-confident commander might have continued with the Kertch expedition, concentrating only after the Constantinople force had reached the Crimea, and claiming that the order could be thus interpreted. Canrobert was not made of such stern stuff. The ADC told Raglan that his CinC had already prepared a message to be dispatched by boat, recalling the French troops; and Raglan sat down to write a letter to Lyons, which he sent at 2.45. In it he gave his full backing to Brown and his 3,000 British troops to continue independently. In the early hours of 4 May the Allied armada anchored within reach of its objective. But Admiral Bruat felt unable to ignore his recall; and Brown believed it unwise to proceed alone. So the expeditionary force returned ignominiously. As Raglan informed Panmure, the troops involved were incensed.[58]

The abortive Kertch venture indirectly claimed a distinguished casualty. On 19 May Canrobert informed Raglan that he had resigned command of the French forces in favour of Pélissier – an arch-supporter of the siege – and that he himself would take over Pélissier's corps. In transmitting the news to Panmure Raglan explained that Canrobert was 'very much weighed down by anxiety' over the Kertch recall. Significantly, Canrobert's formal letter of resignation referred to moral and physical fatigue over a period of nine months, though he had only been in overall command for 7½ months since succeeding St Arnaud. Raglan's appointment dated from 10 April 1854, and he had been involved in appointments and preparations for almost two months before that. Panmure was among those to castigate Canrobert, in the wake of his resignation, for 'vacillation and indecision of character'. Raglan did not join the round of condemnation, although he more than any other individual had suffered directly from the former French CinC's vicissitudes. On 19 May Jean Jacques Pélissier succeeded Canrobert and advised Vaillant: 'I have already seen Lord Raglan. Upon our general course of action we are in perfect accord.' And there is strong evidence that, from the beginning, the two CinCs established a good personal and working relationship, though Kinglake's assertion that Raglan exerted decisive professional influence over Pélissier is questionable. The fierce, energetic and dogmatic little Frenchman was a strong personality in his own right. He had already given Raglan support at inter-Allied conferences in respect of pressing the siege. That preference would now become crucial. Within days Kingscote was writing that Pélissier 'has begun very well'. After accompanying Raglan on the Queen's Birthday Parade of 24 May, he 'came to an impromptu lunch here afterwards which he wound up with a short speech and drank à la Victoria'. Kingscote did not continue so politely: 'He is so fat and has so short a neck he will go off like a ginger beer bottle.' None the less, he had created a favourable, professional impression.[59]

The new French CinC quickly made his mark on the siege. There had been little advance since French troops had captured enemy rifle pits before the Central Bastion on 1 May, an action which Raglan believed 'very brilliant'. Following a long, unsuccessful and costly struggle with the Russians around new enemy positions on 22 May, Pélissier ordered another assault the following night, which proved successful. Nigel Kingscote argued that such leadership had been sadly lacking in the past, and that Pélissier's determination would prove exhilarating. On 25 May Canrobert crossed the Fedioukine Hills with his corps to clear enemy troops from the west bank of the Tchernaya. Protecting Canrobert's right flank then were 15,000 Sardinians who had been placed under Raglan. Their recent arrival proved timely, Major-General Jones advising Raglan that the ground in front of the British 'is now studded with Strong Rifle Screens, connected with each other by Trenches of Communication'. The plan of attack agreed on 23 April was now invalid. Ejection of the enemy from the Quarries (opposite the British) and Mamelon (before the French) must now be a separate operation preliminary to assaulting the Great Redan and the Malakov. All Pélissier's energy and Raglan's tact would be required to ensure that these positions were attacked, and the available forces not frittered away on dashing, but ultimately pointless, peripheral enterprises.[60]

The attraction towards other schemes was, to some extent, reinforced by the nominal strength of the Allies. Raglan had objected previously to transfer of Turks from Eupatoria, partly on the grounds that only a limited number of troops could be accommodated in the Sevastopol/Balaclava area. Relying upon figures put forward by Niel on

20 May, Kinglake held that at that time 224,000 Allied troops were south of Sevastopol – though a closer examination suggests that, at least, the Sardinian and Turkish figures were inflated and it is unlikely that there were 32,000 British effectives. On 5 May Jones had produced an analysis of Allied strength and dispositions, estimating a combined overall strength of 213,000 (including the garrison of Eupatoria) and a British deployment of 25,000. Nevertheless, the restricted nature of the siege lines dictated that there must be something of a surplus, which encouraged the speculation of wider strategic use.[61]

Almost inevitably, Napoleon's proposal for three forces under-pinned associated inter-Allied discussions in May. Niel visited British headquarters on 4 May to explore its implications, urging Raglan to con-sult Canrobert about implementation. The British CinC demurred on the grounds that he had not yet received instructions from his Secretary of State. The following day, however, he advised Panmure that the plan was 'open to many objections'. Communication between the three forces would be difficult and 'the enemy might fall in great force upon one body without the one next it [sic] being able to render it assistance'. Three days later he added that a besieging force of only 30,000 French and 30,000 Turks would be at serious risk to fatal counter-attack by a garrison of 37–42,000 men, including those in the northern suburbs who, under the Emperor's plan, were not due to be attacked. Should the garrison success-fully break out, Kamiesch and Balaclava might well fall. Raglan preferred to press the siege and have Omar Pasha, supported by the French cavalry, advance from Eupatoria towards the north side of Sevastopol.[62]

This was not a promising background for a conference on 12 May, when Omar Pasha (who had travelled from Eupatoria), Canrobert (still then CinC) and Raglan met to discuss the Emperor's ideas. Canrobert explained that Pélissier would command the siege element, and he would take charge of the force emanating from Aloushita. Both Raglan and Omar Pasha strongly opposed this scheme, but Canrobert felt unable to gainsay his own Emperor's wishes. Two days later the three CinCs met again, and faced with Canrobert's obduracy, Raglan provisionally agreed to the idea of the three armies, but persuaded Canrobert to advance from Baidar on Batchki Serai, not from Aloushita towards Simpheropol. This would ensure that Canrobert was deployed on Raglan's right flank as he attacked Mackenzie Heights, thus avoiding the dangerous division of the two forces in the original plan. However, correspondence from Raglan to Panmure on 15 May made it clear that the compromise might never be put to the test. Before any field operations could begin, the siege position must be guaranteed and the supply ports secured. Raglan did not feel that the Emperor had made full provision for this; and, as he informed Pan-mure, neither Canrobert nor Omar Pasha would undertake to 'guard the English trenches' if Raglan were to vacate them for the Mackenzie Heights. So Raglan noted that four British divisions would have to remain there. Essentially, therefore, neither Raglan's compromise of 14 May nor the Emperor's basic plan could be implemented; for Raglan's field force depended upon participation of all available British troops, leaving the siege to the French and Turks. Raglan's inclination to temporize had proved sound.[63]

Pélissier, once in command, soon killed off Napoleon's hopes. He confirmed his prime commitment, oft expressed in the past, to the siege. No field operations should be undertaken until Sevastopol had fallen and unlike Raglan, who favoured limited action by Omar Pasha from there, he eschewed any aggressive activity from Eupatoria, preferring a defensive posture. He did agree to clearing the west bank of the Tchernaya – which Canrobert achieved on 25 May – but he saw the Karabel suburb of Sevastopol as the key. In practice this meant advancing against the Mamelon/Malakov and Great Redan. He saw no real prospect of overcoming the defences west of Man of War Harbour on the Allied left. Nevertheless, to avoid rousing Russian suspicions, he continued to probe in the vicinity of the Central Bastion, while ordering Bosquet to clear enemy counter-approaches on the Allied right. He had thus effectively destroyed Napoleon's caprices. In a telegram to Marshal Vaillant, he was quite explicit. Field operations from Aloushita or Baidar were impossible because of the nature of the country, and 'direct investment' after capturing Mackenzie Heights alone would be 'very uncertain' and probably costly. 'I have come to an understanding with Lord Raglan for the carrying of the [enemy] counter-approaches [and] for the occupation of the ground on our right home [sic] down to the Tchernaya.' Meanwhile an Allied Council of War on 20 May confirmed that the siege would indeed take precedence, and eight days later Jones reported to Raglan on a meeting, chaired by the French CinC, at which Pélissier firmly undertook to assault the Mamelon. On 29 May Jones further explained that detailed plans had now been made for the French to attack the Mamelon while the British took the Quarries. Inter-Allied co-operation seemed assured.[64]

That soon had tangible manifestation. At the Council of War on 20 May, one day after assuming formal command, Pélissier assented to remounting the Kertch expedition, aiming not only to capture the town but permanently to garrison it. In his messsage to Vaillant the following day he announced that 'Lord Raglan has asked me to renew the operation against Kertch.' Pélissier thought that to comply would be the best way of healing 'the wound they [the British] received from the recall of the former expedition ... [and to] restore that harmony which is in one word the great necessity of the time'. Despite subsequent pressure from Paris he adhered to his decision. Raglan reissued orders to Brown on 21 May, and next day some 7,000 French, 3,000 British, 5,000 Turks plus detachments of engineers and an escort of 50 British hussars set sail from Kamiesch and Balaclava, intending to rendezvous off Cape Takil (20 miles south of Kertch) at dawn on 24 May. The expedition went off smoothly, with the troops landing unopposed and moving on to seize Kertch and nearby Yeni Kale, as Lyons took his fleet into the Sea of Azov. Brown reported this progress on 25 May to Raglan, who two days later instructed him further to take Anapa and Soudjak-Kale, south-east of Kertch on the Circassian coast. Thus, on 29 May, Raglan enthused to Queen Victoria over the 'complete immediate success' of the expedition, which would cut off vital enemy supplies.[65]

Yet another initiative, aimed at deflecting political criticism, had meanwhile been announced in London. Prompted by Ellenborough, Panmure admitted on 3 May that a 'Corps of Navvies [was] ... under consideration of the Government ... for carrying on the general work of the army', which had thus far fallen on soldiers. He was, however, extremely vague about the true nature and composition of the proposed body. On 25 May he elaborated a little more in a letter to Raglan. 'The Army Works Corps' of 1,000 navvies would be raised by Joseph Paxton, come under the Commanding Engineer in the Crimea, but have its own civilian officers. Panmure did not know at this stage, that on hearing in the Crimea about this further support corps Raglan had written to him raising objections; and, in fact, no navvy reached the Crimea until after Raglan's death. In the meantime Raglan himself reopened the question of a medical support corps. A Corps of Hospital Orderlies had become essential because of the drain of effectives to tend the sick. He underlined his concern for other administrative matters, too, by urging the dispatch of 30 covered bread wagons and the creation of an 'establishment for the custody of Engineer Stores'. On his initiative a local exchange of prisoners of war was effected. So Raglan was by no means lacking energy after eight months of conflict.[66]

Not that Palmerston subscribed to a favourable view of the British CinC. 'Raglan will never of his own accord make any change; he is a creature of habit, and in himself wanting in that energy which would be required for the making of changes,' he bitingly observed to Panmure. Rear-Admiral Houston Stewart was rather more generous. He wrote to the Duchess of Somerset from *Hannibal* off Sevastopol: 'Lord Raglan's health is good and his temper and spirits quite remarkable. He often puts one in mind of Bedford's description of good Lord Salisbury on the eve of the Battle of Agincourt in Henry V. "Full of Kindness as of Valour/Princely in both!"' Indeed Raglan found time to answer Lord Kilmaine's anxiety on behalf of his son, expressed in a letter to him of 21 April; and he praised effusively the efforts of the Hon Algernon Egerton and Thomas Tower properly to distribute the stores, comforts and books provided by the Crimean Army Fund: 'I speak the feelings of the many thousands who have so largely benefitted by your exertions,' he assured the two commissioners based in Balaclava.[67]

As Stewart had indicated, Raglan's health continued to bear up remarkably under the strain; he was, according to Nigel Kingscote on 26

May, 'very well'. He rode regularly and at length. Kingscote described one ten-hour excursion on Miss Mary, when Raglan and his staff 'rode round the whole position which is beautiful and so picturesque ... one small valley which we overlook reminds me of England with its timber and hedgerows and the foliage is most beautiful and I never saw anything to equal the brilliancy and quantity of the wild life flowers.' At one point during this ride Raglan and his entire staff refreshed themselves from 'a fountain in a very picturesque spot'. However, as ever, Raglan did not appreciate the hot weather which, Kingscote observed, failed to put him in the best of humours.[68]

The saga of the Ordnance Department, as it evolved during May, upset him even more. It gradually became clear to him, as Master-General, that the Government had set in motion the irrevocable process of disintegration; and that he was powerless to influence it. On 7 May Panmure wrote to Raglan about Government plans to consolidate 'the Civil Departments of the Army', giving no details but indicating that the changes would be 'unpalatable' to the Ordnance. Eleven days later – with the Master-General having had no opportunity to offer a prior opinion – the Secretary of State announced the break-up of the Ordnance: the military Ordnance Corps would transfer to the command of the Horse Guards, the Secretary for War would assume 'supreme direction of, and be responsible for, the administration of all the business' of the Ordnance Department carried out hitherto by the Board's civil members. On 21 May Raglan could only feebly and ineffectually protest: 'I am much concerned to hear that the government have determined to propose the consolidation of the military departments and to break up the Ordnance Office.' He went on: 'I believe that the change will be the reverse of beneficial to the public. From the number of hours I was obliged daily to devote to the public business of the department I am quite satisfied that a Minister of War could not efficiently discharge it and at the same time perform the higher duties which devolve upon him as Secretary of State.' Inevitably much of the work would pass to subordinates 'and hence confusion and dissatisfaction may be expected to arise – perhaps an oblique admission that Raglan did not himself delegate, which Estcourt had inferred when noting that, on appointment of Simpson as Chief of Staff, heads of department such as he no longer had to wait on Raglan for decisions. As to the Ordnance Corps, Raglan argued that the transfer would be 'an imperfect measure', with officers being in the 'disagreeable position of having two masters' (CinC and Secretary of State for War), a contention only sustainable if the CinC were seen as an independent figure directly and solely responsible to the monarch. Panmure, however, maintained: 'I am convinced it [abolition of the post of Master-General] will lead to far more celerity of action in all matters touching the war.'

Sir Thomas Hastings (Principal Storekeeper of the Ordnance) wrote to Raglan regretting 'the extinction of the Board of Ordnance', which he contended had worked well in providing 'Ordnance, Military and Hospital Stores' for the Crimean force, and predicting that the proposed manufacturing arrangements would not work. No doubt Raglan would have agreed; but he could do nothing with Hastings' arguments from afar. To Ross, still nominally Lieutenant-General, Raglan ventured that the promotion of Ordnance officers by selection rather than seniority would prove unsatisfactory. It was all too late. Panmure's plan for reorganization had been submitted to the Cabinet on 2 May, approved and forwarded to the Queen on 10 May; and the Board of Ordnance was abolished by letters patent on 25 May. At least Raglan had the personal consolation of being formally 'granted, 15 May 1855, Her Majesty's Licence and permission to accept and wear the Imperial Order of the Medjidie of the First Class, which the Sultan had been pleased to confer on him as a mark of His Imperial Majesty's approbation of his distinguished services before the enemy during the present war'.[69]

Morale of the troops improved markedly with the weather. On 17 May the 2nd Division staged a series of horse races, and, a week later after the Queen's Birthday Parade with its cavalry review attended by Raglan, Pélissier and Omar Pasha 'with a very brilliant staff', sports were held for the troops on the Plain of Balaclava. Militarily, too, the month ended on a high note. On 31 May Raglan indicated that he had briefed Lieutenant-General Pennefather and Major-General Codrington for an assault on the Quarries by 1,000 men, supported by another 800 to exploit captured enemy trenches. The detailed plan of attack would be laid down by Jones. One discordant note had been sounded, however. Omar Pasha threatened to resign for 'ill health' because of dispute over command of the Turkish troops, which dated back to the agreement in February 1855 between the Porte and the British Government over placement of a Turkish division under Raglan. This and other perceived slights from his own government had profoundly upset Omar Pasha, just as the siege was about to resume in earnest.[70]

June, which would quite literally culminate in personal tragedy, opened well for Raglan. Admittedly, to his annoyance, Brown reported that despite his sending cavalry patrols into the towns at regular intervals, local Tartars and Turkish troops had systematically looted Kertch and Yeni Kale. But, militarily, the Kertch expedition had been most successful; and the subsequent sweep on the Sea of Azov by naval forces equally worthwhile. On 2 June Lyons informed Raglan that 'nearly 500' enemy vessels had been sunk, enough flour and corn destroyed to feed 100,000 men for four months. Furthermore a combined British and French force of 3,000 men had taken Soudjak-Kale and Anapa on the Circassian coast despite Napoleon III's instructions to Pélissier not to participate. Fortunately, the French CinC had turned a deaf ear, but Raglan wrote in some despair to Panmure on 12 June: 'I fear that much inconvenience may arise if his Imperial Majesty pursue [sic] the system of forbidding operations that may have been determined upon.' Withdrawing from the Sea of Azov, Brown left 7,000 men (mainly Turks) to guard the Straits of Kertch before sailing westwards again. Raglan generously praised the achievements of the expedition and, in particular, drew Panmure's attention to 'these gallant exploits of the Navy [which] have spread joy in our camps'.[71]

Before Sevastopol, the siege continued, though not fiercely enough for Jones. As the month commenced he produced two memoranda for Raglan. He argued that originally a temporary halt to operations had been called until the French 'Corps d'Armée' arrived from Constantinople. That had now been in the Crimea 'some time', yet the enemy still had free access to Sevastopol and could be seen unhindered taking in 'wagons and large quantities of gabions, etc.'. The British trenches were now so close to the enemy that heavy casualties were being incurred 'daily'. Positive action must be undertaken swiftly, and Jones reminded Raglan that the Allied conference of 23 April had agreed that 'it is indisputable either to assault or to attack the Positions of the Enemy without delay'. Nothing of note had been achieved since that meeting, and the enemy could be observed strengthening his defences around the city. Jones further complained that the British Left Attack was exposed to enemy grape during the day and rifle fire at night.[72] There were, however, broader considerations, which to some extent constrained action. Despite Pélissier's lack of enthusiasm, Napoleon III's strategic illusions had not altogether evaporated. Pélissier referred to 'a dreamer' in Paris, mesmerized by 'general maps' and 'geometric lines'; but the Emperor could not be utterly ignored. On 5 June Napoleon telegraphed to Pélissier: 'I give you the positive order to abstain from throwing your strength into the business of the siege before having invested the place,' a tactic which Niel had consistently pressed on Pélissier. Napoleon unequivocally continued: 'So concert measures with Lord Raglan and Omar Pasha for taking the offensive and operating whether by the Tchernaya or against Simpheropol.' Undeterred, Pélissier replied that he was 'to see Lord Raglan today (with whom, by the way, I am in perfect accord)' to finalize assaults on the outlying Russian defence works before Sevastopol.

Pélissier's firmness was commendable, but Napoleon's obsession with field operations remained worrying. The fact that Raglan and Pélissier had established a first-class working relationship from the outset no doubt helped. Kingscote observed that 'General Pélissier seems to get on very well with my Lord but who does not with a man of such wonderful temper as his.' He added, somewhat mischievously in his letter to Richard: 'Why Canrobert did not drive him mad I know not and if he did not the Government did their best to do so.' The ability to cope with French CinCs of such differing temperament was marked. Lyons said that Canrobert had admitted to Raglan that he did not have the courage to order his men into hopeless situations, hence he could never countenance an assault on Sevastopol. A curious allegation emerged during June. Sir Charles Wood, First Lord of the Admiralty, regretted that Raglan had not accepted the combined Anglo-French command on the departure of Canrobert, to which Raglan replied: 'I was not aware till you mentioned it that Canrobert or Pélissier had offered me the chief command. If they had I should have refused it, being convinced that no English officer could wield such a command with advantage to the Service, or the smallest degree of comfort to himself.' Wood may, therefore, have been reflecting discussion in London and assumed that Raglan had not only been involved, but had declined. One other command dispute at least had been resolved. On 5 June Raglan acknowledged Stratford de Redcliffe's work in getting Omar Pasha to withdraw his latest threat of resignation.[73]

So on the eve of the Third Bombardment the three Allied CinCs were secure in their posts and determined to co-operate. At 3 p.m. on 6 June, watched by Raglan and his staff for three hours from a convenient knoll, Allied artillery commenced firing. Howitzers kept up the cannonade during the night and at dawn on 7 June the entire range of batteries re-opened, spreading fire west of Man of War Harbour, as well as concentrating on the Karabel suburb. Rockets signalling the ground assault were fired on Victoria Ridge at 6.30 p.m. The intention was that the French, whose trenches were closer, would take the Mamelon, and the British would then advance on the Quarries. French troops overran their objective and its defence works so rapidly that, rashly – and unwisely – they swept on towards the Malakov. Here they were thrown back, chased through the Mamelon and forced to retake it again. Meanwhile, Raglan, who had watched the attack from the Woronzov Ridge, put his own part of the plan into operation. Two separate columns of 200 men attacked the flanks of the Quarries, others being ordered to silence adjacent positions. The Quarries were stormed successfully at 7 p.m. and the Great Redan was brought under small-arms fire. 'It was', Kingscote informed Richard Somerset, 'one of the grandest and most soul stirring sights ever seen especially when it got dark. The enthusiasm of our men was great and in the midst of the roar of the cannonading when our men attacked the sailors manned the parapet and gave three such cheers as were distinctly heard above the din.' That night the Russians launched a vigorous counter-attack, recapturing the Quarries for a short period, and throughout the next 24 hours made repeated efforts to throw the British back. During that day, though, Raglan had remembered to write to Brown at Kertch giving him news of the Allied successes. A final Russian assault shortly before dawn on 9 June failed, partly as a consequence of British deception in persuading the enemy that more troops were coming up. By 10 June the French had secured the area of the Mamelon; and the Third Bombardment had thus been followed by a successful assault. The French incurred 5,443 casualties, the British 671 (including 47 officers); and the French had captured 67 'heavy' and six light guns.

McMillan recorded the re-opening of the bombardment on 6 June, 'such a roar of cannon I never heard', and noted that the officers were betting 10:1 that the British would be in Sevastopol 'by tomorrow night'. That was not to be; the unpalatable fact was that, although important objectives had been secured, the formidable Malakov and Great Redan still lay ahead. Failure to subdue all the enemy flanking batteries continued to cause British troops in the Quarries some embarrassment. Nevertheless, Jones informed Raglan that on 10 June Allied artillery and engineer officers met to consider the feasibility of further progress, so that momentum was not lost.[74]

Renewal of the bombardment overrode all other considerations. The Malakov and Great Redan must be carried. On 16 June, Jones produced a detailed analysis of the construction, bomb-proof magazines and depth of surrounding ditches of the defences destined for attack. The Fourth Bombardment, clearing the way for that assault, was planned for 17 June, but this time the cannonade would not be prolonged. And on the 17th Raglan issued a memorandum to his general officers ordering the attack on the Great Redan to begin 'shortly after daybreak' on 18 June. The time and mode of the signal would be notified later. In his instructions, Raglan explained that Jones had been instrumental in drawing up the plan of attack. Three columns would be employed. The officer commanding the first column must maintain contact with the French troops 'acting in the Middle ravine upon the Malakov Tower Building', and be prepared to support them as and when necessary. Each of the three columns would be led by an engineer officer and a detachment of Sappers and Miners with ladders and cutting tools 'for removing abatis, palisades or any other obstacles'. A general officer would command each of the columns, with Brown in overall control. Raglan optimistically foresaw little resistance; as part of the overall plan, French units would demonstrate against the Tchernaya. The stage was set. After the gains following the Third Bombardment, as reflected in Raglan's orders, hopes of success ran high. That evening of 17 June, however, would be the last time that Lyons saw Raglan alive.[75]

The Fourth Bombardment started at daybreak on Sunday 17 June. Exclusive of the fleet, approximately 600 Allied guns engaged all along the line from the Quarantine Fort in the west to the Point Battery in the east. The shells from 114 French and 166 British guns fell in the Karabel suburb alone. By sunset, the western defences had been hard hit and farther east, beyond Man of War Harbour, the Barrack Battery, Great Redan, Gervais Battery, Little Redan, Malakov and Point Battery had, according to Todleben, been 'reduced to a nearly hopeless state'. During the morning Pélissier visited the British headquarters, and the two CinCs agreed that, after a lull during the night, the bombardment would be renewed with vigour at 3 a.m. next day, the infantry attacks commencing two hours later. The precise time of the assault would, as Raglan informed

Panmure, depend upon the French 'commanding officer on the spot', but 5 or 5.30 a.m. seemed likely. During the evening of the 17th, however, the French unilaterally changed the plan to an assault at 3 a.m. without preliminary bombardment. Kinglake describes how Raglan returned from visiting his divisional camps to discover the alteration in plan, when Jones brought the news to his headquarters. A letter in the Raglan files from Canrobert (the corps commander) to Raglan on 17 June notes that Jones had represented Raglan at an inter-Allied conference where the time of 3 a.m. was decided; and Jones confirmed later that Canrobert had initiated the change. So, late on the evening of 17 June Raglan found that either he must remonstrate with Pélissier or fall in with the new French arrangements. He decided that the latter would cause the least disruption, especially as fresh orders must already have been issued to the French troops. Thus at about 9 p.m. Raglan was obliged to issue amended orders so that his men would be in position before sunrise, their movement covered only by intermittent artillery fire throughout the cloudless night. The Allied activity did not, therefore, go undetected; and it is possible that burning ships in the harbour further illuminated their movement. Moreover the Russians had managed to repair most of their damaged works, especially in the vicinity of the Great Redan. By 2 a.m. on the 18th both attackers and defenders were ready. The last major assault under Raglan's command was set to begin.[76]

At about this time, Pélissier left his headquarters to ride towards the Victoria Ridge and the right-hand Lancaster battery, although he would not reach his chosen position before 3 a.m. Raglan and his staff opted for the Mortar Battery of the third parallel on the Woronzov Road. Having left their horses in sheltered ground, they were there before daybreak. The signal for the three French divisions to assault the Malakov and associated works would be 'a bright jet of rockets', fired on Pélissier's order. But Russian guns opened up before Pélissier arrived on Victoria Ridge, and a trail of light from a burning enemy fuze was mistakenly seen as the signal for attack. The French right division went forward, therefore, before 3 a.m. and came under fierce fire. The other two divisions did not move until Pélissier sent up his rockets, and then only after a delay. The French thus attacked in a disjointed fashion, made little positive headway and suffered heavy casualties. Raglan watched the French and noted that enfilade fire from the Great Redan was devastating them. Despite the daunting odds, he determined to advance. As he explained next day to Panmure: '... when I saw how stoutly they were opposed, I considered it was my duty to assist them by attacking myself'. Significantly, he added: 'I am quite certain that, if the troops had remained in our trenches, the French would have attributed their non-success to our refusal to participate in the operation.' Allied solidarity and the very future of the alliance, he felt to be at stake. The British CinC decided to attack the Great Redan from a distance of more than 400 yards without further preliminary bombardment. Brown directed the battle, but Raglan determined its course; and he remained in the line of fire from the Russian work throughout the action.

Predictably, perhaps, the attack was brave but unsuccessful. The two flank columns advanced unsupported, and, although engineer ladder and sack parties pushed forward under withering fire from the Great Redan itself and the Barrack batteries, few men actually got into the Great Redan and even fewer survived. Essentially the two columns attacked independently, torn apart by enemy grape; and heavy officer casualties further disrupted the command structure. From his position behind Colonel Yea's right-hand (eastern) column, Raglan witnessed the carnage: 'I never had a conception before of such a shower of grape as they poured upon us from the Russian works,' he wrote to Panmure. Of the 500 infanteers who advanced with Yea (himself killed), 313 became casualties; and the engineers and sailors, plus unauthorized 'volunteers' who had found their way into the trenches that day, also suffered heavily. The reserves incurred severe losses as they came into action. Raglan, accompanied by Jones, witnessed the whole scene. While most of Raglan's staff, on his orders, sheltered beneath the parapet of the Mortar Battery, Raglan and Jones peered over it. Jones, beside the CinC, was hit in the head, Raglan was unscathed. To cover the retreating troops, as they made their way back over the open ground, Raglan ordered the artillery to bombard the Russian defence works. The enemy was quickly silenced, and Kinglake maintains that Raglan intended to launch fresh troops while they were thus subdued. However, an officer close to Raglan paints a different picture. Major C.H. Malan of the Royal Fusiliers, wounded in the attack and not recognizing the CinC in a trench, told him, on being asked, that the British had been 'thrashed'. He maintained that Raglan left the trench to talk to an ADC. Despite the fact that the trenches were 'crammed with fresh troops', he determined not to attack again: 'No troops could live under such fire as this. I never saw anything like it in the Peninsula', he reputedly declared; and Malan 'was much struck by his kind face, his calm manner and his empty sleeve'.

Raglan rode over to see Pélissier. A body of French troops had taken the Gervais Battery and some actually reached the outer suburbs of Sevastopol; but, unsupported, they had to retire. This swayed Pélissier. He and Raglan agreed that the day was indeed lost. Pélissier withdrew his men from the field at 7 a.m. and an hour and a half later they had regained the relative safety of the trenches. The remnants of the British columns had already retreated, but a small detachment that had reached the head of the Man of War Harbour pulled back as late as 5 p.m. The final appalling total of British casualties, including sailors, was 1,505. The Great Redan and Malakov, undoubted keys to Sevastopol, remained untaken. That a few French troops certainly reached the outskirts and some British possibly – McMillan claimed to have seen 'silver plate, a

General's Cocked hat and Sword, three pigeons in a cage besides some more things' that had been taken from 'Sevastopol' – was scant consolation.[77]

Raglan felt the losses deeply, as he revealed in his account of the action written to his wife on 19 June. The British were met by heavy fire, 'particularly grape'. Few reached the Redan, he claimed, and none got in. 'In short, the operation failed, as well as that of the French, and we have to deplore the loss of many valuable officers and men ... *You* may imagine my disappointment at this failure! It is a great misfortune.'[78] He showed similar strain, to a lesser degree, in other correspondence. In expanding on his 'great disappointment' to Sir Charles Wood, he expressed mild criticism of Pélissier: 'The French General could not consent to make the assault general or indeed to attack the Town itself.' When the French did not make enough headway 'I felt bound to commence our attack', but the British troops ran into a 'murderous' fire: 'no body of troops could face it and exist, and this fire proceeded from points which it was hoped our batteries had effectually cut down'. The losses were 'sadly considerable', though he concluded with the stirring phrase beloved of generals – the troops were, nevertheless, in 'excellent spirits'. To Panmure Raglan wrote: 'I confess that I anticipated a very different result, and my feeling was participated in by both armies ... The failure of yesterday is a great affliction to me and a sad disappointment to the army.' A strange, unsubstantiated claim has appeared in later literature that Raglan said after the débâcle of 18 June: 'I shall never return home. I should be stoned to death.' However, there is no doubt that the reverse did most seriously affect him. Somerset Calthorpe and others at headquarters noted how his appearance visibly changed, and a Coldstream Guards officer, having emerged from an interview with him shortly after the action, is credited with exclaiming: 'Do you not see the change in Lord Raglan? Good God! He is a dying man.'[79]

That remark, like Raglan's own reference to the risk of stoning, may well be apocryphal, but by his own admission he did feel something akin to despair. On the very day that British troops suffered so horribly before the Great Redan, Roebuck presented his report to Parliament. It was a watered down version of what the forceful radical would have liked, but critics seized upon its findings to vilify Raglan. Five days after the Redan operation Hardinge warned Airey that the report 'contains the infamous attacks of Roebuck against Lord Raglan'. *The United Service Gazette* in summarizing the report, contrived to blame Raglan not only for administrative and operational shortcomings, but for supplying the Government with such sparse information that the gathering of reserves was not viewed at home as a high priority. These were a collection of half-truths and canards, whose effect upon a disappointed man towards the close of June can only be hazarded. They could not have raised his morale.[80]

Nor could the continuing saga of the Ordnance, which it later emerged most certainly did cause him deep personal and professional distress. Throughout June yet more comment and revelation reached Raglan. Echoing Raglan's own opinion, Ross complained to him: 'I am astonished ... that any gentleman new to a great office [Panmure] should consider himself equal to discharging the duties of the Master-General, Minister at War, Minister for War and Commissary in Chief ... Great confusion must issue ... There never was such folly.' Moreover Panmure simply brushed aside Raglan's protests: 'The change at the Ordnance is effective and I am sorry to hear that you anticipate so much confusion from it,' he wrote on 4 June. Before he received that dismissive communication, Raglan wistfully repeated his views to Richard. 'The overthrow of the Ordnance without any ceremony is a sad blow to the efficiency of the publick service and to me personally and I cannot say how much it grieves and annoys me. I like the business of the Ordnance so much and I got on so well with every body there that I deeply regret my separation from the departments. How one man is to do the duty of the departments which the Minister of War has caught hold of I cannot imagine. He will be a powerful man in the country and all the patronage will be disposed of politically and there will be the devil to pay. Alas, Alas !!!' By Raglan's restrained standards this constituted a very emotional outburst, underlining the deep-seated personal effect that the change had upon him. All hope of reprieve vanished with the signing of an Order in Council on 6 June revoking the letters patent of the Master-General and his principal officers and vesting their powers in the Secretary of State for War. The next day Hardinge declared his opposition to the changes to Raglan, holding that the Ordnance had been 'most efficient and admirable' in its arrangements during the war and maintaining that its abolition had a purely 'political object'. Raglan might have pondered, given his strong adherence to the apolitical nature of the Crown's command of the armed forces, the long-term implications of that political control.[81]

It was noticeable that, throughout June, despite his many tribulations Raglan still exhibited his customary thoughtfulness for others. When Mr Rawlinson, of the visiting Sanitary Commission, was 'grazed' by an enemy cannon-ball in the trenches, Raglan made available his own carriage for the wounded man 'to be moved down to Balaclava'. And his consideration did not fade during and after the traumatic events of 18 June. He found time to reassure a Portsmouth widow, Mrs Carpenter, that her husband had died 'as he had lived a most gallant soldier'; and, indeed, such was his evident compassion that Houston Stewart observed that, in spite of his 'most difficult and harassing duties, Lord Raglan writes with all his uncommon equanimity and consideration for others'. Several accounts survive of Raglan's visiting the wounded immediately after the Redan action. One relative explained how 'Lord Raglan called at his [cousin's] tent to inquire after him before he returned to his own quarters on that sad day'. Raglan also visited Lieutenant Cave RN in his tent and insisted that, when he 'was able to move', Cave should have the use of Raglan's 'own carriage'. During the last week of his life, an ADC described how he went through the hospital at Balaclava and 'spoke to almost all of the men, looked at their wounds and often with much tenderness re-arranged their bandages with his own hands and comforted some who were about to lose their arms by saying he had been without his right arm for forty years and did very well, see. He used to go through *all* the worst cholera and worst fever wards, however infectious they might be, *that* never deterred him.' Three days after the abortive attack on the Great Redan Raglan called to see Sir George Brown who was sick, and Brown later recalled with emotion: 'This was the last intercourse with my dear friend, and much respected Commander.' Three days before he died Raglan wrote a private note to Thomas Tower, one of the Crimean Army Fund's distributors, now back in England, thanking him for his efforts on behalf of the troops.[82]

There was no doubt, however, that Calthorpe and other close observers were correct. Raglan had now begun to wilt visibly. Airey saw that the deaths of his last surviving sister Harriet on 1 June, 'poor Estcourt' and Captain Charles Bowles of the 10th Hussars in quick succession 'affected him deeply'. The loss of Estcourt, in particular, proved devastating. The Adjutant-General had shown signs of cholera on 21 June and died three days later. He was buried early next morning (Monday 25 June) in the cemetery adjoining headquarters, but in the words of a later report, 'Lord Raglan whose nervous and circulatory powers were beginning to give out, was kindly prevented from attending the funeral by his personal staff.' Later that day he knelt alone by the graveside. It was the last time that he would leave the headquarters building alive. In truth, he had been unwell for some days.[83]

Dr Joseph Prendergast noted diarrhoea symptoms on 23 June and the following day 'weakness' resulting from lack of food and 'anxiety of mind caused by the death of General Estcourt'. By the evening of 25 June Raglan 'was much better ... [having] passed the day at his usual avocations [except riding]) diarrhoea apparently having ceased'. Prendergast recorded that he 'took nourishment and even dinner with appetite. This night slight alteration of voice observed as on a former occasion.' But he seemed stronger on 26 June. Then during the night of 26/7 June and whenever Raglan slept thereafter, Prendergast noted involuntary oozing of 'feculent fluid'. On 27 June, the diarrhoea had returned and by the evening the 'tongue [was] slightly furred for the first time'. Doctors John Hall and Thomas Alexander also examined Raglan 26-7 June and, according to Prendergast, concurred in the treatment initially of arrowroot wine and stringents, then lead acetate and opium pills every two hours. His biographer later claimed, however, that Hall's unease caused Alexander to be called in, though Alexander sided with Prendergast. On Thursday

28 June after early optimism, alterations occurred in Raglan's 'pulse, breathing temperature of surface [and] all indicated approaching dissolution'. At 3.30 in the afternoon the first signs of severe gastric pain appeared, by 5 p.m. the 'pulse could not be counted' and the 'tracheal rattle set in'. Raglan remained conscious only until 6 p.m. 'From this time till 8h 40m, the moment of decease, he almost imperceptibly got feebler and expired without pain.'[84]

Prendergast's bald summary was fleshed out by the observations and recorded impressions of others. On Saturday 23 June, the day that Estcourt died, a violent thunderstorm brought torrential rain and an oppressive atmosphere. That day Raglan began to show marked signs of weariness to his staff. Nevertheless, he worked hard on four dispatches and a long private letter to Panmure, visited the camps and hospital. In the evening he saw Estcourt for the last time and entertained Lord George and Lady Paget to dinner. He wrote, for instance, an appreciation of the siege for Panmure, in which he feared that Pélissier would henceforth confine his attacks to the Karabel suburb, given need to carry the Malakov. But Raglan held strongly that the town (left) front beyond Man of War Harbour must be kept under pressure otherwise the Russians would be able to switch troops easily. The following day (24 June) he wrote to Pélissier to arrange a meeting between them to discuss future operations, and answered Pélissier's inquiry about his health with *'rien de grave'*. Kinglake contends that he did not attend Estcourt's funeral next day for fear of breaking down before his troops, but Dr H.F. Smith's explanation seems more likely: he was ill. But he did deal with his correspondence, especially a dispatch dated 11 June from Panmure, which only arrived that day; and he notified Hardinge formally of Estcourt's death, recommending that Lieutenant-Colonel Pakenham take his place.

On Tuesday 26 June Raglan began work in his room as usual, dealing with letters and drafting a dispatch to Panmure in which he deeply regretted increasing sickness among the troops. He then felt mildly unwell, Prendergast advised him to lie down, and he missed dinner. The content of Prendergast's later summary showed no anxiety at this stage; and this lack of acute concern is borne out by Airey's letter to Charlotte that day. He conceded that 'as Lord Raglan is ordered to lie down and not occupy himself you may all be frightened'. They should not worry. 'The heat has been terrific for the last few days, which has overcome him, and put him out of order, but I have the satisfaction of telling you, that it is nothing else – I have seen the Doctor a dozen times today, and he assures me it is merely the heat, and if he will consent to lie quiet, on his bed, and not write or do any business [interviews] he will be quite right in a day.' Airey went on to show his own feelings. 'I am anxious about him, I hate to see him anything but natural & well – and joyous – but he's a difficult patient.' Airey's confident account of Raglan's condition at this time and Prendergast's subsequent timetable of events was sustained by Calthorpe's account to his mother. On arriving for luncheon on 26 June, he discovered that Raglan 'had gone to lie down, not feeling well', but was so little concerned that Calthorpe did not mention the fact in a letter home. Although it was not thought strictly necessary to do so, his staff did not 'like to leave him alone', so Nigel Kingscote sat up with him 'the first part of the night' and Leicester Curzon the last part. He did not seem better the following morning, so a cautionary message was dispatched to Lady Raglan, though as his condition appeared to improve a more encouraging one went to her in the afternoon.

Calthorpe sat with him during the night of 27/8 June: 'He [Raglan] slept a great deal through the night at about 4 had some soup and at 5 Thursday morning being in a most tranquil sleep', Calthorpe left his uncle and went to bed. When he got up at 10 a.m. Calthorpe learnt that Raglan was 'very much better' so another message to this effect went to Lady Raglan. He and the rest of the staff heard nothing more until they assembled for an early dinner at 3.30 'at which time they dined in hot weather, when his servant came in and called the Doctor saying his Lord was not so well'. Even then the doctor showed no alarm, though by 5 p.m. the pulse was so low that he warned them that Raglan was 'sinking fast'. Calthorpe doubted that Raglan knew anything after 5 p.m. Calthorpe's mother observed that her son mentioned neither diarrhoea nor cholera, but maintained that Raglan did not suffer then or during the final illness: 'The only thing observable the whole time was that he had a dislike of food, was depressed and unaccountably weak'; and it seemed 'that the frame gave way from all the mind had gone through'.

Kinglake argues that the final illness, which developed on 26 June, bore no relation to the upset of 23-4 June. This, however, assumes that Raglan had recovered by 25 June, which is not borne out by medical evidence. Kinglake, who later interviewed Airey at length, recorded one specific incident on 28 June. At about 4.30 p.m., when it became obvious that Raglan would not recover, the Quartermaster-General quietly asked him: 'Sir, you are ill; would you not like to see some one?' Raglan demurred, and Airey asked again: 'Sir, you are very ill would you not like to see some one.' A faint 'no' came from the tired figure on the narrow iron bed. Recognizing the gravity of the situation, Airey framed his third question more positively: 'Sir, you are very ill; whom would you like to see?' 'Frank,' came the reply. But his nephew, Burghersh did not arrive until after Raglan had sunk into unconsciousness. As his life ebbed away, the sun slowly dipped beneath the horizon.[85]

To some extent, the validity of this version of Raglan's last illness is challenged by Lady Westmorland, quoting letters from her son. During 28 June Burghersh told her his uncle had been 'dangerously ill' the previous day: 'he was better this morning but is now much worse'. This appears to undermine the contention that no serious concern arose until late on 28 June or that Burghersh was not close-by that day. 'Faintness' became evident at 3 p.m., and Lady Westmorland's firm account places Burghersh there at the time and until Raglan died. 'Francis, who did not leave him, held him in his arms, and it was there his spirit fled at half-past 8 – not having spoken again – looking as if asleep, with an angelic smile on his lips. He had neither sickness nor cramp nor any pain. Death came so gently that even the doctors did not perceive the actual moment.' On 25 July, specifically referring to a letter from Burghersh before he left the Crimea, Lady Westmorland described how her son had derived great strength from Raglan's devotion to him and 'also that he was able to be near him to his last breath; and that that dear man knew him: for when he seemed dazed, not having spoken or moved for a long time, the doctors said to him, "Lord Burghersh is near you". Then he said, "Ah, Francis, come nearer; lift me up." Francis took him in his arms, and he did not say another word.' Burghersh sent his mother a lock of Raglan's hair, evidently not that preserved in the Raglan archives, for Priscilla remarked that her brother-in-law had 'got very white since I last saw him'.[86]

In recording the death scene, the Chaplain did not single out any action by Burghersh. 'The room was small with little furniture in it, Colonel Poulett Somerset and Lord Burghersh on one side of the neat, narrow camp bed, Dr Prendergast at its head, Colonel Steele and General Airey on the other side. I stood next, close to the dying hero. As I uttered the words, "Peace to this House and all that dwell in it", all fell on their knees. At the close of the heart-searching service, I placed my hand on the broad handsome forehead of the noble soldier and commended the departing Soul to the keeping of God. A few minutes after, the great man went to his rest. Colonel Steele then asked me to pray that those present might be strengthened. I did so, and heavy grief sat upon the hearts of all who joined in that solemn appeal to Heaven for aid.' Kinglake quotes Wright in slightly different terms, though not substantially so, except that he places Lady George Paget in the room 'seated at the foot' of the bed, and identifies the service conducted by Wright as 'The Solemn Order for the Visitation of the sick'. Calthorpe put Simpson, the remainder of the headquarters staff and Lord George Paget outside the open door of the small room in the dining area. Burghersh cut off a piece of his dead uncle's hair for the family: it was fair, though no longer ash-blonde, with tiny streaks of silver. The next day a General Order announced Raglan's death, slightly inaccurately at 9 p.m. on 28 June, and noted that Sir James Simpson would assume command of the expeditionary force.[87]

The words 'Lord Raglan is dead' had already passed quickly round the camps the previous evening, and as an officer recorded: 'The shock was great', – the more so, because he had seemed well. The writer recalled how, when he had last seen him shortly before, Raglan had called him over to inquire about a Russian officer held prisoner at the Monastery of St George, and had appeared perfectly normal. Captain Baillie, Lord Rokeby's ADC, registered disbelief at Raglan's passing, not realizing that he had been 'seriously ill', and described how he and Rokeby rode to headquarters to see 'once more ... the dear old man, with the same placid countenance in death as he had had in life'. Although Simpson had taken over command, speculation was rife as to who would, or could, permanently replace Raglan. Writing to his father on 30 June, Henry Clifford noted that 'it is easy to find fault', but that 'as a Commander, I see no one to replace him'; although Hardinge, Lord Gough, Sir Harry Smith and Sir Colin Campbell – not Simpson – were all being canvassed. The dilemma was underlined by the words of an anonymous officer quoted in Parliament: 'If those who have been so lavish of their virulent, scurrilous, and undeserved abuse of poor Lord Raglan will now have the goodness to point out a successor who can efficiently fill his place they would save much trouble.' Not a bad epitaph.[88]

On 29 June came moving personal homage from Pélissier in a General Order. Having noted that all those who knew Raglan would pay tribute to his calm, noble, pure and stoic qualities, not least during the demanding battles of the Alma and Inkerman, he went on to declare his own sense of loss of a 'companion in arms ... with whom he had always found a loyal and affectionate empathy'. He and Canrobert went to British headquarters to pay their last respects. That day, too, Pélissier wrote to Lady Raglan, and the following day Napoleon III sent his formal regrets. Panmure asked Robert Dundas, a family friend, to express 'my deep sympathy' to Raglan's widow, as the Secretary of State did not know her personally. Steele, Military Secretary in the Crimea, wrote a letter full of feeling to Lady Raglan. 'One of the last times I rode with him, the men ran on all sides to cheer him; he was mobbed by soldiers who never give a cheer unless it comes from the heart, and with these he was greeted on all sides.' Steele then reassured Lady Raglan about Raglan's death: 'He passed away without a sign of pain, without a muscle distorted, and bearing the same kind look at the end.' On board *Hannibal* Admiral Houston Stewart recorded: 'At 9 p.m. on the 28th, the kindest, most considerate and bravest of hearts ceased to beat. The loss here is looked upon as irreparable.' And Leicester Curzon wrote to Charlotte 'how sincerely and deeply I feel for you at the loss of your noble Father ... I can never forget, even to my dying day, the kindness I have experienced at his hands. He will be ever present in my mind as a light of what is great, good and noble.' In London, Hardinge published a laudatory General Order which, he explained in a letter to Richard, had been written 'by the Queen's desire, and in which I have endeavoured to convey to the Army the eminent Services of your illustrious Father, and the brilliant example he has set to the whole Army by his talents and virtues'. Richard may have reflected that his father's last letter to him had enclosed his usual quarterly cheque and an apology that 'I ought to have sent [it to] you before', ending with 'God Bless you, Yours most affectionately.'[89]

Thus Raglan passed away, though his body had as yet to be returned to England for burial. The manner of his death would continue to cause debate. As late as 1873 the Chaplain, Wright, contended: 'In June 1855 he suffered from a slight attack of cholera, which became at last violent and carried off the great soldier on the 28th June 1855'; and cholera as the cause of death has ever since found intermittent favour with authors. But, from the front, Captain Hawley firmly informed his father that Raglan had died of dysentery not cholera. This was believed, too, by *The Wolverhampton Journal* in its editorial of 7 July. Noting that Raglan was 'reputed' to have succumbed to cholera and further doubting the virulence of his diarrhoea, independently the surgeon Dr H.F. Smith was also quite adamant: 'There was really no symptom of cholera present: no vomiting, no cramp ... no cholera countenance, there was, I heard, some weakness of voice, but without the "whisper" peculiar to cholera'. He did not, therefore, believe that cholera killed Raglan, nor did he think dysentery had either. The diarrhoea had not been 'distressing in frequency' and 'evacuations' amounted to only four or five in 24 hours, nor were there other symptoms of dysentery. Thus he concluded, 'we must look for some other cause'. Smith drew attention to 'the mental strain' and the likelihood that Raglan maintained 'a thoughtful cheerful countenance' despite inner sorrow. Immediately prior to his death, the additional burden of the failure on 18 June and Estcourt's death weighed heavily upon him: 'General Estcourt loved Lord Raglan, as one Brother loves another, and I have every reason to know that that love was reciprocated.' Smith argued that Raglan's symptoms showed that 'his disease may therefore be described as a case of acute mental anguish, producing first great depression, and subsequently complete exhaustion of the heart's action – or, in other words, a gradual cessation of the powers of the circulation, from continued mental anxiety and suffering'. In layman's terms, Lord Raglan died of a broken heart; and in the months to come ample evidence emerged to support this non-medical conclusion.[90]

Epilogue:
Burial and Memorial

'In action chivalrously brave - serene in adversity and success - noble in his address and loyal in his dealings.' (Lady Raglan)[1]

Raglan's death came as a shock to his family in London. Robert Dundas, Viscount Melville's son and one of Raglan's executors, dined with Panmure until after 11 p.m. on 28 June, by which time no further 'intelligence' had been received beyond an optimistic message earlier in the day. Then the Secretary of State left word on his way back from a ball at 2 a.m. on 29 June that Lord Raglan's 'health was going on well'. So Dundas called to see Lady Raglan after breakfast to encourage her. He found her in an anguished state of mind, as he told Lady Westmorland later that day. 'Lady FitzRoy is convinced that his illness is partly owing to the very great vexation and annoyance that he has felt about the abolition of the office of Master-General and Board of Ordnance.' Raglan had been particularly upset because the changes took place 'without any reference to him ... he wrote to her in the last letter, of the 16th, she received from him yesterday very fully on this subject stating that he does not speak of it to anybody about him and sees clearly that he is very much hurt and mortified about it and most justly so'. Hardinge had recently taken credit publicly 'to himself' before the Sevastopol Committee 'for improvements at the Ordnance', when he was Master-General, 'though he did nothing'. Furthermore Panmure had created new posts for his relatives, whereas Raglan had been unable to find an appointment in England for his only surviving son.

Next day, 30 June, Dundas justifiably claimed to Lady Westmorland that he himself had had 'an unhappy day'. For, while at breakfast, Panmure's private secretary arrived to announce receipt of another telegram, which had not yet been fully deciphered, but it clearly referred to Raglan's death. Dundas hurried to Panmure's house in Belgrave Square where two communications from Simpson had now become clear. The first described the deterioration in Raglan's condition, and death at '25 mins to 9 o'clock last night'. The second dealt with the return to England of 'the remains' which Panmure and Sir Charles Wood had already decided should be brought home in *Caradoc*. Panmure asked Dundas to break the news to Lady Raglan; and he left for Great Stanhope Street with copies of Simpson's two telegrams dated 29 June. On the way he saw Kitty riding in St James's Park, but did not approach her. 'I found Lady FitzRoy at home in the act of writing to him. She immediately asked if there were bad news. I told her there was, the worst possible. She was very weak, stunned, and it was some time before she could say "tell me all about it", which she repeated at intervals several times before she really was able to attend to any detail. As soon as she could read I gave her the copy of the telegraphic dispatches.' Dundas went on to explain the second communication, revealing that the necessary orders had been issued to bring the body to England. Lady Raglan asked Dundas to cancel her plans to travel via Calais to Ems 'next week', and to intimate that she would probably go at the end of July. She then locked the door of the Drawing Room, and Dundas stayed with her to compose the required letters concerning her travel. When Kitty returned from riding, she could not open the Drawing Room door, went to the street door to feed the horse and came back. Lady Raglan was 'in distress' as to how to tell her daughter the sad news, and at length Dundas agreed to open the door and speak to Kitty. 'I did so the best way I could, but it was like inflicting a cruel wound upon that poor girl.' She displayed 'more firmness than expected' and, like her mother, said little. When Dundas had completed the correspondence Kitty and her mother begged him to go upstairs to tell Charlotte, 'for neither of them felt able to open the thing to her'. Charlotte exhibited 'the same steadfastness' and he remained with her until Kitty at last joined them.[2]

All the members of Raglan's immediate family soon showed signs of distress. On 2 July a telegram arrived from Richard stating that he would leave Hanover that night. In a letter to Lady Westmorland the following day, after Richard's arrival at Great Stanhope Street, Robert Dundas revealed that Lady Raglan was 'very low', and that 'Richard is much distressed, especially being in that house without his father'. Although the girls were behaving 'as well as possible ... they are thoroughly good girls', they and their mother had been 'upset' at the arrival on 2 July of Raglan's letter of 19 June, telling them about the attack on the Great Redan. Such was their grief that Dr Ferguson, the family physician, prescribed medication for Charlotte and Richard. Added pain was then caused by the necessary legal formalities. On 3 July Raglan's will, which had been made on 7 April 1854, was read. The bulk of the estate went to Lady Raglan; Major-General Berkeley Drummond and Robert Dundas having been appointed executors. The family residence, 5 Great Stanhope Street, had been leased since 1834, and stables in Derby Street, Mayfair, had similarly been acquired later. There was, too, the lease on the Marquis of Ailesbury's estate in Yorkshire, recently taken on. His father did have a Law Life Assurance policy, though its terms are obscure. There were thus a number of financial obligations which Richard inherited.[3]

On 5 July Lady Raglan wrote to her sister. 'Oh! my dearest Priscilla *what* can I say to you? You were so attached to him,' ran her grief-stricken opening. 'After having been so well for fourteen months, escaping the perils of war and borne with the utmost patience and temper all the calumnies pressed upon him, to think of his being carried off in three days! ... Charlotte and Kitty are in the deepest affliction and so is poor Richard who is very unwell ... I was alarmed for Charlotte who nearly died of her Father's going away'. Lady Raglan referred to 'my unhappy self', who had not been aware of Raglan's 'dispositions' but who approved 'our old friend' Dundas as one of the executors, adding: 'I hope dear Francis will come over directly never to return to that dreadful place!' She had received 'great kindness and sympathy' and 'many offers of houses in the country', besides a suggestion from her nephew Julian Fane that she might drive down to Osterley for the day to 'sit out in the air'. She could not, however, leave London and when she did would go 'straight to Germany ... for a few weeks'. Poignantly, she had received two further letters and two 'photographic pictures' from her late husband on 4 July, showing that he looked well: 'not the least thinner or greyer'. Lady Raglan's postscript further underscored her anger at the treatment of her late husband: 'I shall always have the better feel [sic] that the breaking of the O [sic] and the ungracious way he was removed from it mortified him beyond measure and his disappointment too of the late failure of Sevastopol built the foundation for his fatal illness.'

Eight days later Kitty told her aunt that Charlotte remained 'still unequal to writing'. Kitty described, too, how 'the terrible fright ... fearful blow ... bitter affliction' had borne down her mother: 'We do all we can to support and comfort her.' 'From the moment he left us I can truly say Mama never had him out of her thoughts for one moment and her whole occupation was writing to and hearing from him seeing the people who had either come from him or [were] going to him and thinking what she could send to conduce to his comfort, and as she herself says the great occupation of her life is gone.'

It was impossible to express the kindness of Dundas or Westmorland and his son Julian, who visited them daily. The family were comforted because Raglan had been surrounded by staff such as 'Francis and Nigel' for whom 'he truly had the affection of a father'. Richard was 'a great comfort' to Lady Raglan, but he himself 'has been terribly cast down and is very unwell'. However the doctor said that he and Charlotte were improving. They all appreciated Lady Westmorland's own grief, and they looked forward to seeing her. 'It is such an unspeakable comfort that dear Francis is coming, it will be such an unspeakable blessing for you.'[4]

Entries in Queen Victoria's Journal show how the tragic course of events had taken the royal family equally by surprise. On 28 June, 'my coronation day', the Queen recorded that on rising she received a telegraphic dispatch from Simpson, timed 3.30 a.m. on 27 June, 'which rather alarmed us'. Noting that Raglan 'has been taken ill with fever and diarrhoea on the 24th', the Queen wrote that he had been confined to bed and – adding details not preserved elsewhere – 'in the opinion of the medical officers he will not be able to resume his duties for a fortnight, as he will require absolute cessation from all work'. Panmure had explained that this would cause no difficulty. For although Brown was sick, Simpson would prove a 'safe' temporary commander. The following day, more favourable news brought 'great relief'. Then came the gradual unfolding of the devastating story on Saturday 30 June. During the morning, Sir Charles Wood called on the Queen at Buckingham Palace, found her in the garden, and told her that telegraphic news from Admiral Stewart 'alluded to, but did not announce, the *death* of poor Lord Raglan! We were dreadfully shocked and startled, though we could not quite credit it.' Still uncertain, half an hour later the Queen learnt that Panmure had arrived to see her. 'I felt at once *what for* – to announce the sad news of this grievous and most truly tragic event ... which greatly distresses us'. Now in no doubt that Raglan was, indeed, dead, Queen Victoria confided her imme-diate thoughts at the 'sad loss' of somebody with 'inestimable qualities', exhibited by no other eligible person for the command, 'added to which his name, his experience, his birth – his very conciliatory manners and aimiable character, give him such might with the French'. It was 'too cruel and heartbreaking' that he would not return 'in triumph' to be 'rewarded for all his anxieties and sufferings ... Poor dear Lord Raglan – he still remains the victorious General, who led the bravest of armies though God saw fit to deprive him of *that* glory, which would have been his reward, had he lived to take Sevastopol!' She detailed the contents of Simpson's decisive telegram of 29 June: 'Lord Raglan had been going favourably until 4 in the afternoon yesterday, when very serious symptoms made their appearance. Up to 5 o'clock he was conscious but from this time his strength declined almost perceptibly until 20 m [sic] before 9, when he died.' 'Painfully impressed by to-day's sad news', the Queen 'wrote to poor Lady Raglan', mourning the loss of her 'noble, gallant and excellent husband ... We both feel *most deeply* for you ... We both most anxiously hope that your health and that of your daughters may not materially suf-fer from this dreadful shock.' Prince Albert delivered that letter in person to Great Stanhope Street, asking that he and the Queen be kept informed of Lady Raglan's state.[5]

Lady Raglan replied to the Queen on 3 July. 'Though scarcely able to hold a pen', she could not delay in expressing 'our most grateful acknowledgement for the kind sympathy evinced by Your Majesty and the Prince to us under the sad, sad calamity with which we have been inflicted'. Evidently the Queen continued to correspond sympathetically with Raglan's widow, for on 12 August from Bad Ems Lady Raglan thanked her for a letter with an important enclosure that had just reached her: 'My lamented husband would have had the greatest pride and satis-faction in receiving this [Crimean] medal from Your Majesty's own hands ... My dear Charlotte is still weak and nervous, but I hope the change of air and scene will soon set her up.'[6]

Other personal messages, invitations and visits also went some way to alleviating the family's distress. Sir John McNeill, alluding to 'what on public as well as on private grounds I must consider a great calamity', offered his condolences. He hoped that the family 'will derive consolation from the reflection that he died as he had lived and as he desired to live and to die devoting the whole energies of his pure and elevated nature to the service of his country'. The Duke of Cambridge, acknowledging that Richard had been 'quite ill' since returning to England, wrote expressing his sympathy on two occasions. From Spain came a moving tribute from former colleagues during the Peninsular War, on whose behalf FitzRoy Somerset had 'fought generously ... against our misfortunes and distress for many years in England'. The seventeen signatories asked that their 'grief, the truest and bitterest sorrow for his untimely and unexpected decease' be conveyed to 'those whom it may most concern ... our deep condolence for this loss'. From the Light Division camp in the Crimea, Codrington wrote: 'I need not say how strong were both my public respect and private feelings towards him.' And King Leopold of The Belgians declared: 'Lord Raglan I knew well and much ever since 1814, and he was a great and sincere friend.' Closer to home, Lady Elizabeth Orde recorded that officials at the Ordnance were disturbed to enter the room where they had been used to seeing him. She also mourned the loss of 'our dear, dear uncle ... to ourselves as a family'. Airey wrote again from the Crimea to Charlotte noting that he was 'so anxious about you all ... that I have become quite nervous, which I never was before. I am sure that day and night I think of nothing else ... All is strange and all is miserable to me.' He again asked her to let him know if he could do anything: 'All this army – every individual mourns his loss – all felt his great influence – so kind, so gentle, yet so firm and noble.' Airey explained that 'all is broken up here – and the whole thing a mess – poor Colonel Vico and Mr Calvert both dead'. The Quartermaster-General had asked to return home; and, though the letter was hardly cheerful, he indicated how devastating the loss of Raglan was to him personally. In a strange way, it was the most moving and personal tribute of all. Airey could not go on in the Crimea without Raglan.[7]

Other more public tributes in statements and obituaries abounded. *The Illustrated London News* referred to 'the venerable and illustrious soldier' and lauded his 'fearless discharge of duty' amid 'the rifle-bullets of the Russians'. He knew, the paper claimed, 'how to inspire affection, as well as respect and obedience'. 'Among the many merits of Lord Raglan it is not least that he taught the English and French soldiers to love and respect each other.' But the obituary was equivocal about attacks on him: 'Though the impatience of ignorant criticism at home may at times have done him an injustice ... folly, if not malevolence may have launched its shafts against his venerable head'. *The Illustrated London News*, after all, had not been a wholehearted supporter of the late field marshal. Nor, patently, had *The Times*. Its obituary declared that 'he dies without an enemy, and his memory is unstained by a single act of selfishness, inhumanity or unkindness.' However, it also held that he 'did not possess the highest qualities of military genius' and hoped that, as command of the army had now changed, 'more decisive operations and more thorough measures will be taken'. Not exactly an editoral road to Damascus. *The Morning Post* somewhat flamboyantly played upon the nature of Raglan's greatness and goodness, maintaining, with obvious inaccuracy, that 'the hero and the man were alike estimable, and the nation loved him in both characters' – a severe case of journalistic amnesia.

The *Morning Chronicle* caustically, but accurately, exclaimed: 'All the classes of the community have united in honouring the virtues of the veteran soldier who died in the cause of his country, and who, when living, was the victim of undeserved malevolence.' When 'false, or exaggerated statements, prejudicial to the good name of Lord Raglan were daily issued to the public, we rejoice that in *The Morning Chronicle* the British Commander found a zealous and a sincere champion.' The paper felt sure that the verdict of History would look more favourably upon Raglan than had the pens of his contemporary detractors: 'Humane and merciful, he was respected and beloved by his troops, whilst his love of honour, his fearless gallantry, and unassuming gentleness, conquered the affection and admiration of his officers.'

A provincial publication, *The Wolverhampton Journal*, also castigated Raglan's critics, naming *The Times* in particular which had been guilty of 'flagrant falsehoods' and 'great injustice', while reminding the *Journal*'s readers that it had consistently supported the late field marshal: 'Lord Raglan was, in our estimation, one of those few men who are made the abodes of genius – not the genius of Napoleon which dazzled with meteoric brilliance and then *scorched*; but a genius alike elevated and beneficent, both in the hour of prosperity and adversity; both as a rival and a conqueror.' In theatrical terms, the reviews were 'mixed', but enough contained genuine plaudits to comfort the family.[8] A great number of poems, dedicated to Raglan's memory, were universal in their praise, and many of them are preserved in the Raglan Papers. From the St Petersburg correspondent of *Le Nord*, a pro-Russian Belgian newspaper, came an unexpected eulogy: 'He will be personally regretted in Russia by all who had the opportunity of knowing and appreciating the nobleness of his sentiments and the uprightness of his character ... even in the execution of his [military] duty he preserved unblemished to his death his own personal dignity and that of his country.'[9]

According to Lady Westmorland, the Queen proposed to Lady Raglan that her late husband's body go to Portsmouth, so the fleet and the army could 'pay him the most impressive honours; but my sister in thanking Her Majesty, asked that she would allow the ceremony to be in *private*, for she knew her incomparable husband's way of thinking, and knew how he would have wished it'. The Queen agreed to a private burial at Badminton; and Panmure subsequently wrote to Lady Raglan explaining that embarkation of Raglan's body had taken place on 3 July, *Caradoc* had sailed the same day and was expected to reach England 'in under sixteen days' after leaving Constantinople, coaling at Malta and Gibraltar. Now that the funeral had been arranged at Badminton, Panmure telegraphed to Marseilles in the hope that *Caradoc* could be contacted at Malta and diverted to Bristol. None of this could, nor in reality did, preclude a formal reception for the body at Bristol, a solemn procession through its streets and further demonstrations of respect on the way to Badminton, fifteen miles to the north-east. Initial expectation, expressed in the local press, that Lord Raglan's remains would be interred in Bristol Cathedral with those of his brothers John and William, were thus dashed; and rumours that the Prince Consort would be on the quayside likewise proved unfounded.[10]

Caradoc left Malta on 10 July before Panmure's message had been received. She subsequently coaled at Malaga and the changed destination was made known at Gibraltar. The 650-ton paddle steamer was sighted off Clevedon in the Severn estuary at 8 a.m. on Tuesday 26 July, and she dropped anchor in King Road at the mouth of the River Avon shortly after 9 a.m. News was immediately sent to the Mayor of Bristol and Richard, Lord Raglan. At 9.45 an 18pdr cannon from Brandon Hill in Bristol officially signalled the arrival off Clevedon. While anchored, *Caradoc* took on board the coffin in which Raglan's body would be buried. Meanwhile Richard, Colonel Bagot, Colonel Kingscote (Nigel's father) and Captain Price made their way to Shirehampton intending to join *Caradoc*, only to discover that the ship had already left under tow; so they boarded her en route. Burghersh had the 'painful duty' to hand him Raglan's personal effects, 'watch and keys and other things'.

Caradoc reached the great entrance dock just before 1 p.m. and moored in the centre of Cumberland Basin at 1.10. The weather had not been kind to those ashore, waiting to greet her beneath the towering cliffs close to the Hotwell Tavern. Umbrellas were much in evidence, for intermittent showers since noon had now given way to a torrential downpour.

Fortunately the elements had relented by 6 a.m. the following day, Wednesday 27 July, when the English oak coffin, covered with rich purple velvet studded with matted 'gold-like' nails and matching handles, was transhipped to the deck of *Star*. The lid of the coffin bore the family arms emblazoned on an engraved escutcheon, with an inscribed plate beneath: 'Field Marshal FitzRoy James Henry Baron Raglan G.C.B./ Commander of the British Forces in the East / Born, September 30th., 1788; Died, June 28th, 1855'. On top of it were Raglan's swords and cocked hat. Athwart the deck of *Star*, the coffin was placed on a 'bier covered with black cloth and crêpe and surmounted by a catafalque of the same materials'. As the transfer took place, 'the firing ... of the dismal minute-gun, and the melancholy chiming of the muffled bells' were heard throughout the city. Just before 11 a.m. a group of mourners, including

Richard, Colonels Bagot and Kingscote, Lieutenant-Colonels Somerset, Burghersh and Nigel Kingscote, Captain Calthorpe, Lord Calthorpe and other naval and military officers boarded *Star*. At precisely 11 a.m. the vessel began to steam slowly upstream, escorted by 'about fifty boats, all uniformly manned', other anchored vessels along the route firing minute-guns. The escort boats were painted in funereal black and blue stripes, flew ensigns at half-mast and formed line-astern on each side of *Star*, stretching away astern of her. Their crews rowed with muffled oars and, when *Star* reached the quay-head near Prince's Street, they formed two sides of a triangle around her to prevent unauthorized boats from approaching.

On the quay, which had been barricaded on the landward side, in 'a spacious shed' stood the bier decorated with 'festoons and draperies of black cloth and velvet, interspersed with rosettes of black crêpe'. Disembarkation commenced just before noon, the coffin being borne ashore by artillerymen, as befitted a former Master-General. The Mayor and Corporation, clergy and civic leaders waited in Queen Square to take their part in the proceedings, guarded by a strong body of police. Military personnel, enrolled pensioners (including six wounded Crimean veterans) and the entire depot of the Land Transport Corps from Horsfield Barracks were drawn up at the end of Prince's Street, with the artillery detachment on the Grove opposite Redcliff Parade. The masts and decks of ships, the windows and roof-tops of buildings in the vicinity were crowded, with every ship flying its ensign at half-mast. Churches also flew flags at half-mast and tolled their muffled bells. The large *Morning Star* under whose stern *Star* had slowly steamed 'was placed in maritime mourning, and formed a grand termination to the angle of the quay'. As the coffin was landed the gunners opposite Redcliff Parade, in position near the Sailors' Home, fired a nineteen-gun salute at minute intervals, 'the heavy booming of which was heard reverberating amongst the distant hills'. This demonstration, though, and the discharge of other artillery pieces was not without cost. A sailor in *Morning Star*, which continued to fire her minute-guns throughout the day, was taken to hospital after having been injured by wadding discharged from a cannon; and 'some hundreds of panes of glass' were shattered in Messrs Bush's warehouse close by.

As the coffin was placed in the hearse on the quay, a trumpeter of the Horse Guards 'sounded a blast of honour', and shortly afterwards the cortège moved off towards Prince's Street to be joined by civic dignitaries, military personnel and other representatives. 'The procession ... of immense length', 'both solemn and imposing' in appearance, began to wend its way through Bristol. At its head rode a body of police, followed by a detachment of artillery with howitzers, the band of the 15th Hussars 'with their picturesque uniforms and bright red shakos' playing the Dead March from *Saul* and a troop of Royal Horse Guards Blue in 'dazzling cuirasses and helmets'. The hearse, drawn by six horses whose mourning plumes waved gently in the breeze, was placed about one-third of the way down the cortège and was followed immediately by the family's mourning coaches. Towards the rear, representatives of such organizations as the Society of Merchant Venturers (of which Raglan had been the senior honorary member) and Ancient Order of Foresters walked in front of citizens of Bristol walking six abreast. The entire cavalcade was flanked by mounted escorts, each man, horse and vehicle displaying mourning dress or emblems. Every thoroughfare along the route was packed. *The Illustrated London News* reported: 'The shops, the banks, and the warehouses of the city were closed, the bells of the different churches chime muffled, and of the thousands of ladies and gentlemen and members of the middle class, who thronged the windows in the line of route, very few were to be seen who did not wear partial or entire mourning.' The streets of the suburbs were also densely packed, stands having been erected at vantage points, for seats in which 5s. a head was 'a very common charge'. An officer in the cortège estimated that no fewer than 150,000 people lined the route, which a reporter thought quite possible given that spectators came not only from Bristol and its immediate vicinity: 'special trains were run from Bath, from Weston, Clevedon, and other parts of the Great Western and Bristol and Exeter line, while there was scarcely a market town or village within reach of our old city which did not contribute its quota to the grand aggregate'.

Official military and civic representatives left the procession at the road leading to Fishponds Church, where a band played the Dead March, filing back towards Bristol through the village of Stapleton. The hearse and mourning coaches continued 'at an accelerated pace' towards Badminton. Although the progress was strictly private, marks of respect were still shown. All shops and other places of business were closed at Downend, where the church bell tolled throughout the morning, houses and the Green Dragon were draped with 'appropriate banners', inhabitants lined the road, the vicar and his curate in their robes 'saluted' the cortège as it passed the gates of the churchyard. Similar demonstrations occurred at Coalpit Heath, Yate, Chipping Sodbury, Old Sodbury and Cross Hands. Farmers on horseback joined the procession to form 'an appropriate guard' behind it, and by the time that Badminton was reached some 60-70 horsemen were at the scene. At the Bath Lodge entrance to Badminton Park the cortège was met at approximately 6 p.m. by the Dodington and Badminton Troops of the Royal Gloucestershire Hussars.

The procession halted at the main door of Badminton House, where the mourners alighted and entered. The coffin was carried into the Great Hall by the Badminton Hussars and received by the family. The spectators outside dispersed and details of Hussars kept guard in rotation throughout the night; all shutters and blinds of the mansion remained closed. Next morning (28 July) the public were admitted to the lying in state. The windows of the hall had been darkened and the walls suitably draped. Wax lights lit the room from three glass chandeliers suspended from the ceiling, and candelabra placed throughout the hall. People were admitted at one door, passed through the hall and out of another guarded by the Hussars. In the centre of the room on a dais opposite the main fireplace and covered with black cloth, lay the coffin partly encased in a rich pall of velvet and gold. On a table lay the late Lord Raglan's different orders and decorations on a cushion. Cushions on two other tables were laden with his coronet and field marshal's baton (never seen by him, it was covered with crimson-velvet, studded with small lions rampant in gold; each end was of beautifully wrought gold and the gold carved top had a representation of St George and the Dragon), his swords and hat.

On the coffin lay Pélissier's wreath of immortelles and a laurel wreath placed there by Bagot. On a carved sideboard at the end of the hall were Raglan's cuirasses worn as Colonel of the Royal Horse Guards. Throughout the morning and until 1 p.m. large numbers of people filed past the coffin. As the *Bristol Gazette* explained: 'The *coup d'oeil* was most solemn and affecting, the semi-darkness of the hall and the perfect stillness and silence maintained conspiring to invest the mind with awe and reverence.' At 1.30 the family paid their last respects, before the burial service in the church attached to Badminton House at 2 p.m. The small size of the Grecian-style building precluded any but the family and a few close friends; the capacity congregation being 'chiefly ladies, and almost universally attired in mourning habiliments'. At 1.45 the bell began to toll and shortly afterwards the funeral procession made its way across the garden from the Great Hall. The coffin, on which lay the cocked hat and swords of the late field marshal, was borne by twelve troopers of the Royal Gloucestershire Hussars, flanked by eight pallbearers including the Duke of Richmond, Major-General W. Cator, Lieutenant-General Sir John Burgoyne, Lieutenant-General Sir George Brown and General Lord Downes on the right. Family mourners led by Richard, Lord Raglan, and 'family attendants' followed behind. In front of the coffin Raglan's 'favourite valet' carried Raglan's orders and Pélissier's tribute on a cushion. After the procession up the aisle, the two officiating clergymen (Revds Joseph Buckley and Digby Wrangham) conducted the service for the dead in accordance with Church of England ritual and the responses were taken up 'strongly' by the congregation. 'At the proper point of the service' the coffin was lowered into the vault, a task that, because of its great weight, was not accomplished without some difficulty: Richard then threw down Pélissier's wreath and the service was concluded. Family and friends gazed for the last time on the coffin in the vault and then returned to the house.[11]

Elsewhere on Thursday 28 July 1855 Lord Raglan was also being remembered. The great 3½-ton bell of Gloucester Cathedral, requiring eight men to raise it, tolled during the morning and other muffled peals were heard in the city during the afternoon. In St James's parish, Westminster, small shopkeepers were urged to 'close a shutter or two at convenience, from the time the late Lord Raglan's remains are landed until he is buried'. In Bristol, a pamphlet sketching Raglan's military career and outlining details of the procession, noted that a considerable number of distinguished people would mourn his passing, including the Wellington, Beaufort, Cholmondeley, Westmorland, Codrington and Calthorpe families. Within days of the interment Count de Persigny called to convey to Lady Raglan the deep condolences of the Emperor and Empress of France.[12]

Efforts were soon in hand to present Lady Raglan with a tangible memorial to her late husband. In May 1853 a Testimonial Fund had been founded by 'numerous friends of Lt Gen Lord Raglan to present to him a token of their esteem and affectionate regard', which by 27 June 1854 had acquired a board of trustees and an administrative committee, the £4,800 collected being invested pending acquisition of 'a Landed Estate'. On 7 August 1855 the appeal was renamed 'The Raglan Memorial Fund'. At this meeting the Duke of Richmond revealed that it was hoped to secure land adjoining Raglan Castle, from which 'the deceased lord' had taken his title. Shortly afterwards the estate became available 'on reasonable terms' and a committee was established in London to supervise its purchase. 'Kefntilla [sic] Estate', situated in the parish of Landenny, hamlet of Gwohellog, and in the parish of Usk, County of Monmouthshire, bordering on land owned by the Duke of Beaufort, was handed over to Richard, Lord Raglan on 13 March 1856. Final accounts, published on 25 June 1858, showed that 1,550 subscribers from home and abroad had, from May 1853 to July 1855, realised a total of £12,540.14s.8d., which with interest came to £13,060.2s.8d.[13]

Although Richard formally took possession of Cefntilla in 1856, he and his family did not take up residence for another four years. During the English Civil War the house had belonged to Roger Oates. Contrary to popular legend Fairfax did not occupy Cefntilla while besieging Raglan Castle, but when the Marquis of Worcester surrendered the fortress, Parliamentary commissioners met Worcester's representatives 'in the dining room of Mr Roger Oates' house of Kefntilla' to sign the terms of capitulation. During the next 200 years the house passed into different hands, fell into decay and at the time of purchase in 1855 was little more than a poor farmhouse in need of extensive renovation. The house had been stripped 'so that the inside exhibits in many places a perfect skeleton'. Much therefore had to be done, and the Memorial Committee dealt with the task in an imaginative manner. Writing from the Isle of Wight on 4 August 1856 General Lord Downes assured Richard that Cefntilla was an 'excellent choice ... one I am sure your dear father would have highly approved of'. Downes had 'lately' been in touch with Sir Matthew Digby Wyatt, 'respecting the plans and estimates for the farm house and farm buildings to replace the old ones at Kefntilla'. Downes reproached Wyatt for tardiness, but the architect pleaded need to await completion of the railway from Monmouth to Usk so that building materials could be more easily transported. An inscription was placed over the porch of Cefntilla: 'This house, with 238 acres of land attached, was purchased by 1,623 of the Friends, Admirers and Comrades-in-arms of the late Field Marshal Lord Raglan G.C.B, and presented by them to his Son and his Heirs for ever as a lasting memorial of Affectionate Regard and Respect. 1858'.

Quite independently of the purchase of Cefntilla, pressure built up for a public monument. On 24 July 1857 Earl Fortescue noted in the Lords that 'above eighteen months' had elapsed since the close of the Crimean War, but nothing had been decided. Fortescue drew attention in detail to Raglan's achievements in the Crimea, not least his co-operation with his allies under trying circumstances, and underlined his 'calm and imperturbable gallantry in the field ... cheerful fortitude amid reverses and distresses ... frank courtesy of manner ... [and] singular modesty'. He concluded: 'My Lords, I beg to ask whether it is the intention of Her Majesty's Government, or whether they will be prepared at a more favourable time, to consider the question of erecting a public monument to the late Lord Raglan?', a call that was supported immediately by Brougham and Derby and whose sentiment was acknowledged by Granville, Lord President of the Council. Panmure, replying on behalf of the Government, proved less enthusiastic. The fact that the Government had not proposed 'a marble monument' did not mean that 'they under-value the services he rendered to the country ... With regard to public monuments, however, a Government is compelled to be cautious how they distribute those honours'. He did not rule out 'at some future period' a public monument, but 'I cannot trace a soldier who has a monument, with the exception of Lord Heathfield, who did not die before the enemy or of wounds received in battle'. Subsequent angry and petulant exchanges over the contents of Panmure's speech probably reinforced his determination not to accede to Fortescue's request. In the House that day the Secretary of State gave a public glimpse of the irrational reaction he was wont to display and with which Raglan had had so patiently to deal.

Next day *The Times* printed the short debate, with the bleak addendum: 'The subject was allowed to drop.' On 27 July 1857 *The Morning Herald* commented more directly and unfavourably on the Ministers' performance. 'For some reason or other the bare mention of this illustrious soldier's name is enough to throw them into convulsions.' Panmure was guilty of 'one of the most disgraceful exhibitions of temper ever witnessed in either House', and, despite his other encouraging remarks, Granville sought unreasonably to excuse his colleague's behaviour. 'The plea that public monuments are in this country only raised in honour of military commanders who have fallen in the execution of their duty is a wretched subterfuge.' Raglan had, indeed, died at his post; Wellington, Napier and Collingwood were among those granted monuments without falling in battle. The paper left no doubt as to where its sympathy lay. On 9 November 1857, Westmorland wrote to Fortescue in firm support, and the following year the Earl published the full text of his speech with a lengthy extract from Raglan's penultimate letter to his wife on 16 June 1855.

To no avail. No public monument was forthcoming, and it was left to localities and organizations to honour him by naming countless thoroughfares and hostelries 'Raglan', many of which survive to this day. At Edgbaston, home of Warwickshire County Cricket Club and one of England's test match grounds, a century after his death appeared the 'Raglan Stand', a fitting tribute to one who, as Military Secretary, had encouraged the development of cricket grounds for soldiers.[15] The Government did, however, approve pecuniary awards to Raglan's family. An annual pension of £1,000 was granted to Lady Raglan (who died 6 March 1881), £2,000 a year to the second Lord Raglan and to his heir. Panmure also gave Lady Raglan a verbal undertaking, through an intermediary, that a military pension of £500 per annum would be paid in addition to the Parliamentary grant.[16]

A number of memorials were, in fact, erected to Raglan's memory, though not in the form of monuments. Lady Mary Farquhar, daughter of the 6th Duke of Beaufort and Raglan's niece, gave the Perpendicular east window of the Slyfield Chapel in Great Bookham Church, Surrey to his memory; and a brass tablet (7 feet long and 18 inches deep) on the south wall of the aisle also commemorates him. His widow, Emily Harriet, erected a tablet 'to his beloved and revered memory' in the church at Badminton where his body was interred. Elsewhere, the officers of the Land Transport Corps subscribed to a window 'as their humble testimony to the late Field Marshal Lord Raglan'; and a stall in the Garrison Church at Portsmouth was dedicated to him. A tablet on the memorial designed by Sir Gilbert Scott to former pupils of Westminster School who fell during the Crimean War and Indian Mutiny, situated outside Westminster Abbey, commemorates him too. Belatedly, in 1911, a memorial plaque was fixed to the wall of 5 Great Stanhope Street, Mayfair.[17]

Before the troops left the Crimea three other memorials were completed there. A marble tablet, approximately 14 inches square, was fixed to the wall of Raglan's bedroom, bearing the inscription: 'In this room died F.M. Lord Raglan G.C.B. Commander of the British Army in the Crimea on the 28th. June 1855'. Russian troops took over the old farmhouse after the peace and these words were translated for a slightly larger slab, fashioned by British sappers, of stone quarried from in front of the 3rd Division's former position on the upland. On 3 July 1856, under orders from Leicester Curzon, Lieutenant Frederic Brine RE ensured that the Russian slab was fixed below that of the British and cemented to it. That day, too, a third memorial, also of quarried stone, was placed in the middle of the vineyard in front of the former British headquarters beneath a willow tree by the well. Brine chose the site, which overlooked the slope towards the ravine of the Monastery of St George, and Curzon 'furnished' the inscription: 'To the memory of Field Marshal Lord Raglan G.C.B. Commander in Chief of the British Army in the Crimea. Died 28th. June 1855'. There was a postscript. Brine and his men then completed three other 'great public monuments' for the Battles of Inkerman, Balaclava and the Redan, before marching down to Balaclava prior to embarkation on 9 July. Next day (10 July) Brine secured two volunteers to return to the farmhouse once more to blacken the letters on the outside slab. The Russians lent Privates Thompson and Dickson tallow candles and a lantern to complete the task, which they did by 11 p.m. As Brine explained to Lord Raglan's widow, this 'was the last thing executed by the British soldier on that blood-stained land'.[18]

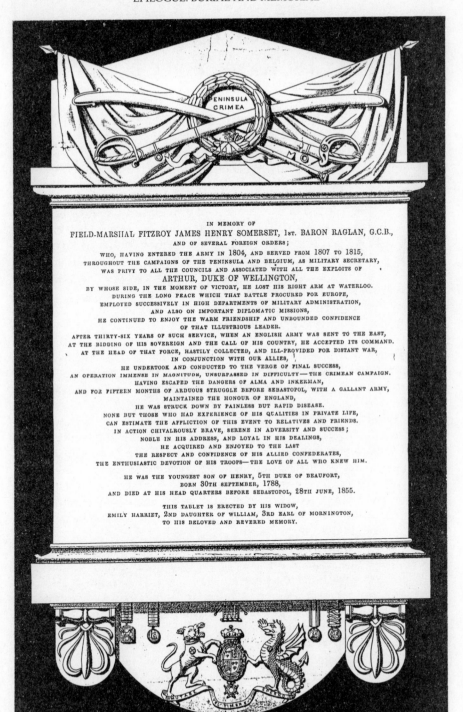

IN MEMORY OF

FIELD-MARSHAL FITZROY JAMES HENRY SOMERSET, 1ST. BARON RAGLAN, G.C.B.,

AND OF SEVERAL FOREIGN ORDERS;

WHO, HAVING ENTERED THE ARMY IN 1804, AND SERVED FROM 1807 TO 1815,
THROUGHOUT THE CAMPAIGNS OF THE PENINSULA AND BELGIUM, AS MILITARY SECRETARY,
WAS PRIVY TO ALL THE COUNCILS AND ASSOCIATED WITH ALL THE EXPLOITS OF

ARTHUR, DUKE OF WELLINGTON,

BY WHOSE SIDE, IN THE MOMENT OF VICTORY, HE LOST HIS RIGHT ARM AT WATERLOO.
DURING THE LONG PEACE WHICH THAT BATTLE PROCURED FOR EUROPE,
EMPLOYED SUCCESSIVELY IN HIGH DEPARTMENTS OF MILITARY ADMINISTRATION,
AND ALSO ON IMPORTANT DIPLOMATIC MISSIONS,
HE CONTINUED TO ENJOY THE WARM FRIENDSHIP AND UNBOUNDED CONFIDENCE
OF THAT ILLUSTRIOUS LEADER.
AFTER THIRTY-SIX YEARS OF SUCH SERVICE, WHEN AN ENGLISH ARMY WAS SENT TO THE EAST,
AT THE BIDDING OF HIS SOVEREIGN AND THE CALL OF HIS COUNTRY, HE ACCEPTED ITS COMMAND.
AT THE HEAD OF THAT FORCE, HASTILY COLLECTED, AND ILL-PROVIDED FOR DISTANT WAR,
IN CONJUNCTION WITH OUR ALLIES,
HE UNDERTOOK AND CONDUCTED TO THE VERGE OF FINAL SUCCESS,
AN OPERATION IMMENSE IN MAGNITUDE, UNSURPASSED IN DIFFICULTY — THE CRIMEAN CAMPAIGN.
HAVING ESCAPED THE DANGERS OF ALMA AND INKERMAN,
AND FOR FIFTEEN MONTHS OF ARDUOUS STRUGGLE BEFORE SEBASTOPOL, WITH A GALLANT ARMY,
MAINTAINED THE HONOUR OF ENGLAND,
HE WAS STRUCK DOWN BY PAINLESS BUT RAPID DISEASE.
NONE BUT THOSE WHO HAD EXPERIENCE OF HIS QUALITIES IN PRIVATE LIFE,
CAN ESTIMATE THE AFFLICTION OF THIS EVENT TO RELATIVES AND FRIENDS.
IN ACTION CHIVALROUSLY BRAVE, SERENE IN ADVERSITY AND SUCCESS;
NOBLE IN HIS ADDRESS, AND LOYAL IN HIS DEALINGS,
HE ACQUIRED AND ENJOYED TO THE LAST
THE RESPECT AND CONFIDENCE OF HIS ALLIED CONFEDERATES,
THE ENTHUSIASTIC DEVOTION OF HIS TROOPS—THE LOVE OF ALL WHO KNEW HIM.

HE WAS THE YOUNGEST SON OF HENRY, 5TH DUKE OF BEAUFORT,
BORN 30TH SEPTEMBER, 1788,
AND DIED AT HIS HEAD QUARTERS BEFORE SEBASTOPOL, 28TH JUNE, 1855.

THIS TABLET IS ERECTED BY HIS WIDOW,
EMILY HARRIET, 2ND DAUGHTER OF WILLIAM, 3RD EARL OF MORNINGTON,
TO HIS BELOVED AND REVERED MEMORY.

CONCLUSION:
IN RETROSPECT

'Poor dear Lord Raglan, he is an honourable man and gallant to a fault, but he is no General.' (Duke of Cambridge)

'No public man ever left to the care of his surviving friends a more spotless reputation.'(Sir John McNeill)[1]

Mainly as a consequence of a single incident near Balaclava that lasted twenty minutes, FitzRoy James Henry Somerset, first Baron Raglan, is the best-known British Army commander of the mid-nineteenth century. Others, such as Sir Charles Napier and Lord Clyde, achieved greater military success. Raglan's name has survived more readily in popular memory because of what he did – or, allegedly, did not do – during the morning of 25 October 1854. He has, it is true, bequeathed the sartorial elegance of the 'Raglan sleeve', but few now directly associate that with the one-armed Crimean commander. His reputation over the years has been determined by the fate of Tennyson's 'noble six hundred', masticated in haste by contemporaries and picked over at leisure by later commentators.[2]

Shortly before his death Raglan protested to Panmure: 'My lord, I have passed a life of honor. I have served the Crown for above fifty years.' Would it be true to say that during his long career he had been shielded by the patronage of such powerful men as Wellington, only for his inherent incompetence to be exposed under the spotlight of independent command in the Crimea? Were the obituary writers merely following a conventional formula of insincere decency? In short, was Raglan incompetent or has he been ill-used by posterity?[3]

Personal qualities, admired throughout Lord Raglan's life, were underlined in the strain and stress of the Crimean campaign. In this sense his 'spotless reputation' remained unchallenged. His kindness and consideration for others, recognized by establishment of the Testimonial Fund in 1853, are illustrated by his compassionate visits to the soldier's wife with her new-born child, and to Florence Nightingale during her debilitating illness. While billeted in Reigate in 1868, Corporal Proudfoot sought out Lady Raglan to tell her how kind her late husband had been to him and others of the Field Marshal's personal guard at British headquarters. Years later the Duke of Beaufort showed a group of Crimean veterans around Badminton. Jack Smith from Bristol stopped before a portrait of Raglan: 'If it had not been for that officer I should have been dead and buried fifty years ago.' Worn out with fatigue and hunger one day in the trenches, he had struck an officer, been court-martialled and sentenced to death for mutiny. When the sentence was laid before Raglan for confirmation, he ordered Smith to be brought before him. Sitting at his desk, Raglan stared at Smith for some time and eventually said: 'He is only a boy; let him go back to his regiment and do his duty.'[4]

His urbanity and his ability to communicate sensibly with others had been displayed in the Peninsula, when he established good working relationships with divisional and battalion staff as a young Military Secretary; qualities subsequently underscored during his brief diplomatic career, at the Horse Guards and Ordnance and, not least, in the Crimea. W.H. Russell, no unqualified admirer, referred to 'the handsome face, the sweet smile and kindly glance, the courteous and gracious, gentle manner ... [which] attracted attention and conciliated favour'. Raglan's charm, he concluded, 'fascinated those around him ... [and] captivated strangers'.[5]

Raglan was a committed, though unostentatious, Anglican High-Churchman. According to the Revd H.P. Wright, principal Chaplain in the Crimea, two-thirds of the headquarters staff usually joined their CinC 'at the Lord's Supper' and Raglan encouraged regular services in the hospitals and in the camps. 'He [Raglan] was a pattern of holiness to his army. Never was the Holy Communion celebrated, but he was there, strengthening and refreshing his own soul, and upholding those of others by his good example.' A correspondent of Charlotte's referred to 'the fervour of Lord Raglan's responses, when our beautiful liturgy was first uttered on the shores of the enemy's land'.[6]

His devotion to his family remained self-evident to the end, his paternal authority never fully relaxed. Thus, from the Crimea he reproved Richard for taking up smoking and issued detailed instructions to his grown-up daughters on issues of minor domestic importance. He cared passionately for his children, and he was wounded when both boys got deeply into debt. If he had a tendency to fuss over family matters, it was partly because Lady Raglan grew increasingly unable to cope with the running of the household as she got older and became increasingly neurotic. Lady FitzRoy's excursions outside London were usually for health reasons, to the coast or the Isle of Wight or, latterly, to take the waters at Ems. Yet, as in his professional career, Raglan saw it his duty to care for her. One of his nieces observed that 'at home he sacrificed every wish and thought of his own to Lady FitzRoy's wishes and caprices!' In his correspondence, Lord Raglan frequently betrayed an eye for a pretty woman; but there was never a hint of extra-marital dalliance.[7]

Nor were fundamental professional qualities in doubt. The fortitude displayed at Badajoz and Waterloo was seen again at the Alma, on the flank march, when the trenches were being bombarded and during the assault on the Great Redan. Sir Edmund Lyons – a frequent eye-witness – observed that while others were 'glad to be behind embrasures', if 'there was any object to be gained, or any information to be obtained' Raglan was wont to 'take up a glass' and go to a convenient spot 'as if he were walking across a room ... it was as if he were totally unconscious of danger, as if he truly did not know what Fear was'. Given Raglan's sensitivity, it is more likely that he rigidly controlled his fear to project a calm exterior – the mark of a brave man. Raglan's reputation as a shrewd tactician, founded in the Peninsula, was enhanced in the Crimea. He swiftly adjusted the British landing beach on 14 September 1854, noting the defensive attributes of the new location. His experienced eye saved the forward troops at the Bulganek. After the enemy had begun to retreat at the Alma and Inkerman, Raglan discerned that rapid pursuit would have produced a rout, but his allies failed to respond.[8]

Above all, perhaps, Raglan's sense of duty received wide recognition; whether in the narrow sense of the conscientious performance of a specific task or the broader commitment to Queen and Country. His own dignified response to Panmure's first critical dispatch in February 1855 underlined Raglan's dedication to the Crown. Richard Airey further pointed out that, as a soldier, he regarded it as his duty to obey the orders of the Queen's ministers in government; and this was seen in both his determination to invade the Crimea and to move on Sevastopol despite his own grave reservations. Shortly after Sir George Brown returned from sick leave in the spring of 1855, Raglan – 'cheerful notwithstanding the annoyance and cares he had undergone' – told him that he believed he had done his duty. After his death *The Economist* justifiably referred to him as 'a brave general who has died in the service of his country'.[9]

Without recent battle experience, like Hardinge in India, or even responsibility for a large field exercise, like Seaton on Chobham Common in 1853, Raglan was appointed to command because, in the words of *The Naval and Military Gazette*, 'the Duke of Wellington made Lord FitzRoy Somerset the depository of his opinions and his sentiments on ... military topics'. He had been Wellington's pupil and, in practice, he closely though not slavishly followed the Duke's style of command. Wellington was a cautious general as advice to Marshal Beresford during the Peninsular War showed: 'Remember that you are a commander-in-chief of an army, and must not be beaten; therefore do not undertake any thing with your troops, if you have not some strong hopes of success.' The Duke relied upon thorough preparation and insisted on the flank of any advance being covered by cavalry. He did not always praise the performance of that arm of the Service, but he recognized its vital role to protect the line of march or launch telling charges as at Salamanca or Waterloo. Raglan's insistence on preserving the integrity of the British cavalry – the only effective mounted troops on the progress south of Calamita Bay – almost certainly owed much to his years in the Peninsula.[10]

For, in the Crimea, he clearly did follow Wellington's example. Like Wellington he abhorred ostentation, preferring to ride with a single

ADC in preference to a cavalcade, and chose a frock coat, cravat and cocked hat rather than uniform in the field. Similarly he adapted Wellington's daily routine. In the words of one of his ADCs: 'He [Raglan] often sat up till two in the morning writing and was on horseback by *six* in the morning and seldom had above three hours rest.' Wellington usually rode before breakfast, dealt with correspondence after the meal before conducting interviews and visiting the lines. After dinner he wrote dispatches until a late hour. W.H. Russell, confirming Raglan's commitment to routine administration, condemned him for 'exhausting his energies in secretary's work' without apparently being aware of Wellington's pattern of life or the multitude of documents, official returns, reports and dispatches which demanded a CinC's personal attention in the field. Lord Stratford de Redcliffe, for example, wrote 210 letters to Raglan from April 1854 to June 1855; Raglan sent 150 replies. Apart from official and private correspondence with Newcastle and Panmure, other politicians such as Aberdeen, Palmerston, Graham, Wood, Clarendon and Sidney Herbert claimed Raglan's time. So did the Horse Guards and Ordnance. A British commander could not escape this labour. Not appreciating the bureaucratic burdens placed upon his CinC, Colonel C.A. Windham condemned him as 'a good red-tapist'. However Colonel J.M. Sherer remarked that 'Lord Wellington was much and closely occupied by his bureau ... He answered all important communications with his own hand.' Simpson, when he succeeded Raglan, discovered that the agony was by no means self-inflicted: 'This dreadful writing kills me ... This is one of the points on which most men will break down in commanding this army', adding that he must be at his desk 'from daylight in the morning until near sunset'. Referring to Raglan's correspondence with Newcastle, the Duke's biographer later wrote: 'It would be hard in English literature to find letters possessing more interest, written as they usually were, far into the night at the end of a day of increasing toil and perhaps of absorbing anxiety ... always, whatever the subject, in a calm, concise language and with penmanship without a correction or an erasure.'[11]

Yet despite his close adherence to Wellington's style of command, Raglan's generalship became a major focus of criticism. In January 1855 Sir William Molesworth reflected Cabinet opinion when he accused Raglan of 'incompetency'; and this view was then, and has been later, widely expressed. Arising mainly from disappointment over failure to take Sevastopol, especially when its capture had been announced and celebrated in London during December 1854, adverse comment gathered pace during the last six months of his life. Critics began to look back at other actions, like the Alma and Inkerman, to judge him in a less favourable light. A pamphlet, published before his death, proclaimed: 'He was late at the Alma ... he gave a rash order at Balaclava. He neglected to intrench the right of his position before Sebastopol.'[12]

Raglan was certainly not late at the Alma, and the pamphleteer may have been alluding to the false allegation that the British were dilatory in moving off from the Bulganek that morning. Others, though, have harshly castigated his actions during the battle, in particular his chosen position south of the river. Had he remained behind his troops north of the Alma, the battlefield would have been obscured from him by the smoke of cannon and the burning village of Bourliouk: his dispatch referred to 'a continual blaze for 300 yards, obscuring their [Russian] position'. In riding across the river to the exposed knoll, he could clearly see the course of the battle and call up reserves at a decisive moment; through his ADCs he kept in contact with the divisional commanders. Wellington had always been careful to obtain an unobstructed view of the battlefield and maintain communication with his subordinate commanders. Of the charge that he neglected the area of Mount Inkerman, reference need only be made to his attempts to persuade the French to plug this gap before 5 November, inability to spare troops from the siege lines or from the defences of Balaclava and efforts by British engineers to strengthen the Allied right. Raglan was fully aware of the problem. He simply did not have the resources to remedy deficiencies independently.

The Battle of Balaclava, and especially the Charge of the Light Brigade, has attracted constant and sharp controversy almost continuously ever since the day. However a more than cursory glance at the recorded story will reveal inconsistencies and inaccuracies often fostered at the time by individuals seeking self-justification. Raglan's dispatches to the Secretary of State for War were, in truth, reasonable. He could legitimately have expected the cavalry's divisional commander to read his orders in conjunction with Lucan's own experiences earlier in the morning. Lucan had seen the Russians capture Turkish-manned redoubts on the Woronzov (Causeway) Heights and then witnessed enemy cavalry being twice thrown back in confusion. Raglan was entitled to assume that he would recognize an enemy in disarray, appreciate a likely withdrawal from exposed forward positions and, therefore, that the captured guns would be towed away in accordance with accepted military practice. Lucan's subsequent words in speech and writing, if closely examined, do nothing to dispel the firm impression that the cavalry commander did, in fact, err. Furthermore, concentration on the Light Brigade's Charge of 25 October shows lack of perception and appreciation of the total effect of the encounters of that day. The Russians failed to take Balaclava or cut communications with the trench lines before Sevastopol. Nor did loss of the redoubts seriously influence supplies. The Woronzov Road had never been used as a major route to the upland, the shorter one via the Col being preferred. After the Russians withdrew across the Tchernaya in December, food and ammunition still went that way.[13]

The flank march, too, prompted much adverse comment. But the French were reluctant to move against the north side of Sevastopol Bay because of the perceived strength of the enemy defences; and, professionally, Sir John Burgoyne strongly favoured an attack from the south. Practically, unless the northern fortifications could be reduced and rapid reduction of the dockyard defences south of the bay be swiftly achieved, investment from the south constituted the only viable option. Once on the Chersonese upland, detractors claim that Raglan should have launched an immediate assault, not mounted a regular siege. Wellington had suffered at Badajoz and Burgos through having insufficient heavy artillery; and this was conceivably in Raglan's mind in September 1854. If a premature assault had brought disaster, there was no possibility of retreat other than ignominious withdrawal across the Black Sea. Similarly Raglan's strong opposition to dividing the Allied forces in front of Sevastopol for field operations in 1855, just as they were establishing strong numerical superiority over the garrison, was eminently justified.[14]

Lieutenant-Colonel E.B. Hamley at the time and W.B. Pemberton with hindsight are among those to emphasize the large number of French troops used against the Malakov and condemn Raglan for deploying too few British against the Great Redan. The French trenches, however, were much closer to the Russian defence work and the parallel British advance had to be made across open ground swept by enemy flank fire. It is a moot point whether a massed attack would have brought success or simply more casualties. Practically, however, the approaches to the British trenches and the trenches themselves did not allow for a greater concentration of troops without exposure to withering enemy bombardment. Raglan opted for a small initial force, followed by a reserve wave. His plan failed, but mainly because the flank fire had not been silenced as expected. Simpson fared no better on 8 September.[15]

A belief that Raglan did not favour the use of spies is categorically wrong; for Cattley (Calvert) ran a complicated and useful network from British headquarters. Nor has the charge that he failed to visit the camps any greater credibility. To this, Captain Harry Keppel RN, Lushington's successor in command of the Naval Brigade, reacted angrily: 'Those who say that he did not take an interest in the comforts and welfare of those under him, *lie* ... he was often in the Sailors' as well as Soldiers' camp'.[16]

The Duke of Cambridge and Sir Richard England deplored Raglan's lack of consultation with his divisional commanders; and Admiral Stewart recorded that after one conference Bruat asked him whether he had ever heard Raglan advance his own opinion or plan. The British CinC's experience, the French admiral felt, fitted him to give a lead. Stewart himself wrote: '... admitting all Lord Raglan's wonderful equanimity, courtesy, tact and temper, I have sometimes wondered whether more *firmness* (and by that I mean decisive opinion) displayed on his lordship's part might not have led to better results.' Raglan was undoubtedly secretive in conferences. But it is quite unreasonable to assume that he was therefore empty-headed, as Palmerston concluded: 'Raglan seldom gave opinion and never stated plans, because, with all their merits, he was not much of a hand at forming opinions or inventing plans.' Wellington neither consulted nor prematurely revealed his thoughts. Decision rested with the commander, discussion shifted the weight of responsibility. Bruat, Stewart and Palmerston failed to appreciate this. For the commander, however, sensitivity and loneliness are dangerous bedfellows.[17]

Raglan's most severe critic would be hard-pressed to gainsay his invaluable contribution to the alliance of the armies in the Crimea. In this sense his effectiveness as a general cannot be faulted. Lyons held that Raglan, through his calm personality, not only retained coherence between the Allies, but also ensured the independence of the British force despite its numerical inferiority, preventing it from becoming merely a 'contingent' of the larger French army. The three successive French commanders – St Arnaud, Canrobert and Pélissier – all acknowledged Raglan's persuasive skills. His support for the Turks, and in particular his influence with Omar Pasha, proved crucial in Bulgaria and once the Turkish commander reached Eupatoria. *The Monthly Review* not inaccurately lauded his ability to cope with 'brave but jealous allies'. Henry Clifford made much the same point: '... his pleasing but gentlemanly manners kept the commanders of the allied armies on good terms, often being the mediator between the French and the Turks'. Similarly, Harry Keppel argued that no other general would 'keep as he did the good understanding that existed between the French Army and ours'. Lieutenant-Colonel John Adye believed that following Raglan's death, British influence in the Crimea sank: 'The overbearing swagger of the French generals had only been kept within bounds by his high bearing, superior intellect and great moral courage.'[18]

In a broader context, apart from his military duties in peace and war, suggestions that Raglan lacked culture do not bear close scrutiny. It is true that he attended the London season, country house and shooting parties as an accepted part of life. This was no different from other political, military and professional figures of his social circle. Although only passing references to literature occur in his correspondence, he evidently read the whole of Dumas' *The Count of Monte Cristo* and owned a private library. Specifically, he was familiar with the works of the High-Church philosopher Henry Longueville Mansel, one of whose books he instructed Charlotte to obtain from his library for Lord Stratford de Redcliffe. As early as 1807, while with Arthur Paget, he had studied James Beattie's philosophical writings. The Westmorlands would not have maintained so familiar a relationship with an uncultured kinsman. Both were accomplished literary figures: Lord Westmorland being a composer and writer, his wife Priscilla an artist. Lord FitzRoy Somerset certainly attended the theatre in London with Priscilla or Kitty or, sometimes, alone; and while in St Petersburg he showed a lively interest in art and architecture, which must reasonably be assumed to have survived after 1826 without special comment in letters.

Lord Raglan does not appear to have read about, or otherwise studied, developments in warfare, but in fact there was little change in the conduct of war after 1815 – the Minié rifled musket and longer-range artillery pieces did not fundamentally alter the way that wars were fought. Hence Raglan and his contemporaries relied upon their own experience. Essentially he, and they, fought according to practical lessons from the past. Theoretical treatises were neither popular nor abundant in Britain during the first half of the nineteenth century. Jay Luvaas, in his study of British military thought, identifies only Sir William Napier, Sir Henry Torrens and Major-General John Mitchell as relevant writers. Napier and Torrens, he concluded, were only reinforcing past opinions, not making a positive contribution to forward thinking. Mitchell attacked the ultra-conservatism of military thinking, but chose a wider platform on which to fight social inequity. There was no atmosphere of constructive critical thought, therefore. The low esteem in which the Royal Military College Sandhurst (as distinct from the Royal Military Academy Woolwich with its scientific syllabi) was held serves to emphasize the lack of interest in theoretical training. Experience in the field was best for the young infantry and cavalry officer. Lord FitzRoy cannot be criticized for not reading works that did not exist.[19]

In July 1855 Sir John Walsh confidently predicted in Parliament that 'history would do him justice, and he would live enshrined in the annals of British glory amongst the highest and noblest of those who had been the associates of Wellington'. From 'the camp' Lieutenant-Colonel Maxwell in March 1856 reacted strongly to continuing criticism of Raglan in London: 'The perfect gentleman, the chivalrous, the kind friend, lies in his honored grave and the cowardly sneers fall harmless before the shield of Honor which guards Raglan's memory.' Nine months later the Duke of Argyll said at a public dinner: 'I think I can tell you that the history of the war has not yet been written, and that it will be for another generation to judge entirely of the conduct of the late Lord Raglan.'[20]

Two tributes to Raglan are worth recording at length. The *Life of Lord Raglan*, published in 1855, provided an interesting assessment: 'Whether we view him as a patriot or a soldier, as a gentleman or a Christian, he exhibits at all times the same heroic stature, the same high standard, the same noble aspect ... there was a classic severity in his rectitude of purpose; but so kind and captivating was his nature, that one looked not beneath the closed vest for the corselet of steel' – private authority similarly identified by Airey to Charlotte, 'so kind, so gentle, yet so firm and noble'. 'The mildness and equanimity of his [Raglan's] temper' meant that he was 'not all things to all men, but to all the same equally estimable as a husband, a father, and a friend ... his religious convictions were unobtrusive, but they were deeply rooted'. In a striking phrase, recalling that he was 'the especial pupil, disciple, and confidant of Wellington ... during a half century of daily personal intercourse', Raglan was 'the Elisha of our military Elijah'. 'Brave to a fault', he was 'an admirable horseman, possessing a vigorous constitution, unsurpassed powers of endurance, and a frame capable of sustaining the greatest fatigue'. His 'administrative talents' were so well illustrated that 'during a peace of forty years, he preserved to England the nucleus of an army ' – an oblique reference to the acknowledged frailties of Hill and Wellington at the Horse Guards. 'As a tactician, he will rank with the highest names in history ... [and] he was loved by his soldiers'.[21]

G.R. Emerson, another contemporary writer, concluded: 'Amateur generals disapproved of his tactics, and virulent journalists charged him with cruelty and neglect of his men, in the terrors of the winter before Sebastopol; but those who knew him best, exalted his prudence, his tact and heroic courage; and the soldiers knew that he shared their dangers and privations, and deeply sympathised with their sufferings.' A successful general is not one who necessarily wins spectacular victories, but like Sir John Moore in the Peninsula makes the best use of resources in prevailing conditions. In the Crimea, Raglan did just that.[22]

Controversy still surrounds the nature of Raglan's death. Medical evidence shows that on 28 June 1855 Raglan was suffering neither from dysentery nor cholera, but diarrhoea. Except for physical tiredness and mental strain, that would not have killed him. On 20 July Priscilla Westmorland noted that her sister had the doctors' report and 'a sort of diary that his secretary kept': 'they do not understand this illness, for he only had slight diarrhoea for two days'. Thus, the conclusion of *The United Service Magazine* seems reasonable: 'He succumbed to an attack of diarrhoea, which easily subdued a frame weakened by anxiety.' Just how significantly the press had contributed to this is debatable. According to one of his ADCs, Raglan had 'no time' to read newspapers, and relied upon his staff to point out important items; and Sir George Brown held that 'he does not ... allow the attacks of the newspapers to weigh upon his mind'. However this may be another example of Raglan's keeping his own counsel as a military commander, for correspondence with his family revealed undoubted traces of personal irritation. But the press could not be held primarily responsible for Raglan's death.[23]

Raglan admitted to being extremely upset at the disbanding of a separate Ordnance Department, and his widow believed that it did contribute directly to his state of mind and subsequent demise. It is clear, too, that the failure against the Great Redan on 18 June and the heavy loss of life deeply affected him, as did the death of close friends like Estcourt. But Lady Raglan declared unequivocally that her late husband had been profoundly distressed by the constant attacks of successive Secretaries for War, who not only appeared to doubt his every action and perceived inaction but failed miserably to protect him at home. The day after Raglan's death, Simpson wrote: 'I think Lord Raglan has suffered – perhaps died – in consequence of the continued injuries he met with. A Mail never arrived without bringing him insult!'. Lyons reinforced this view. Lack of support from the home government had greatly depressed him: 'The painful letters which Lord Raglan received from Lord Panmure and others, which he felt more deeply than any thing else.' The Secretary of State himself observed to Queen Victoria: 'Lord Raglan seems to be much hurt by the plain expressions in Lord Panmure's dispatch of the 12th February [1855].' Lieutenant-Colonel J.M. Adye, claiming that Raglan had expressed to him 'his great disgust at the conduct of the War Minister' exclaimed that he had 'always been of opinion that his [Raglan's] death was hastened – if not caused – by ... the coldness and silence of the Ministers whose duty it was to defend him from the ignorant abuse and calumny to which he was subjected'. The attitude of government ministers became all the more significant in the context of Raglan's commitment to duty and his belief that his loyalty lay with the Crown and the Government. In an uncharacteristic outburst to one of his nephews, he wrote: 'Sometimes I think Lord Panmure believes I am either criminally negligent or a lunatic'; and to his sister-in-law, Lady Westmorland, he confessed that, unlike Wellington who 'could stand alone' because of 'his great superiority of mind and firmness', Raglan felt in need of support which had not been forthcoming.[24]

Having listened to a carillon of eulogies in the House of Lords on 3 July 1855, the Earl of Galloway regretted that 'the sentiments now spoken had [not] been uttered while he was yet in life ... Lord Raglan fell a victim to the ingratitude of his countrymen, and, I regret to add, the coldness and neglect of that Government of whom he was so able and so zealous a servant.' His family most certainly believed that; and, in the closing phase of his life, Raglan clearly sensed it. Yet, what Sir John Fortescue disparagingly termed the 'skulking and shuffling of scared politicians' bent on personal self-preservation does not fully explain the persistence of adverse comment, which did not actually originate in 1854. During Wellington's last years the Duke, his Military Secretary and the Horse Guards as a whole suffered from the restless tongues and pens of would-be reformers. For FitzRoy James Henry Somerset, first Baron Raglan, had the misfortune to live and serve when the social system into which he was born was coming under increasingly sharp attack. Criticisms of his activity on the battlefield thus provided a convenient and emotive vehicle for anti-aristocratic frustration at home. *The Times* admitted as much. In that respect, Raglan was a whipping-boy, as well as a scapegoat.[25]

FitzRoy, Lord Raglan, displayed the traditional qualities of integrity, duty and loyalty expected of a late eighteenth-century officer and gentleman. Fifty years on, these proved less acceptable, less attractive to impatient radicals. He was, too, unfortunate to encounter the swifter communication with England afforded by steamships and the electric telegraph, and to assume active military command when the novelty of press reporters in the theatre of war generated an insatiable public demand for detailed accounts of everything connected with the Crimean campaign. The near-hysteria enflamed by regular, sensational and colourful articles reinforced by acerbic editorial comment scarcely made for balanced judgement in dwelling-house, hostelry or Cabinet office.

As his sister-in-law observed, Raglan was 'the most modest and least vain of men', which prompted him to focus more on the needs of others than to promote his own image. Harry Keppel aptly remarked: 'Poor Lord Raglan, if he had a fault it was that of having too good and kind a heart.' In peace and war, whether faced by an ailing chief in London or prickly allies at Sevastopol, FitzRoy, Lord Raglan, provided quiet, undemonstrative leadership, which all but a jaundiced few who came into close professional contact with him recognized.[26]

'Spotless' in his private life, certainly. 'Honourable' and 'gallant' in the field, undoubtedly. In practice, this kindly man of medium height and, perhaps, a trifle portly in middle age, was a better general than his critics allow.

NOTES

Frontispiece
Earl Westmorland to Earl Fortescue, 9 Nov 1857, Raglan Private Papers (hereinafter RPP), 10.

Preface
1. 7 July 1855, officer before Sevastopol, RPP, 7/296.
2. Ibid.; report from 'Our Artist and Special Correspondent, Camp before Sebastopol, 6 July 1855' in *The Illustrated London News* (hereinafter *TILN*), 21 July 1855; Lt-Gen Sir James Simpson to Lord Panmure, 7 July 1855, RPP, 10; sketch and report in *TILN*, 29 Sept 1855; Kennaway, C. *The War and the Newspapers*, 1856, p. 77; Kinglake, A. *The Invasion of the Crimea*, viii, 1887, pp. 296–9; Anon (ed.). *The Diary of Sergeant William McMillan*, 1990, p. 33, diary entry, 3 July 1855. Any military personnel standing behind the official representatives lining the route were there without permission. No doubt concerned about an enemy attack against weakened lines, 'all those who were not actually engaged in the ceremony were confined to camp', Duberly, Mrs H. *Journal Kept during the Crimean War*, 1855, p. 230.
3. *TILN*, 21 July 1855; Kinglake, op. cit., viii, pp. 299–300; Officer before Sevastopol, 7 July 1855, RPP, 7/296.
4. 5 July 1855, Captain R.B. Hawley to his father, 'The Hawley Letters' ed. S. Ward, in *Society for Army Historical Research Special Publication No 10*, 1970; Kinglake, op. cit., viii, pp. 298–300; *Annual Register*, 1855, pp. 287. Kinglake's contention, op. cit., viii, p. 299, that neither side fired 'whilst the mournful solemnity lasted' was contradicted by the dispatch of 7 July 1855 from its 'Artist and Special Correspondent' who maintained that 'as the funeral procession wound its way slowly along the hills and hollows ... the boom of great guns from the walls of Sebastopol [were] answered in quick response from the English batteries', *TILN*, 21 July 1855.
5. Lord Burghersh, Poulett Somerset, Nigel Kingscote and Somerset Calthorpe, Raglan's close relatives and ADCs, together with Joseph Prendergast, the doctor, accompanied the body in *Caradoc*, Royal Archives (hereinafter RA): QVJ 5 July 1855.

Chapter 1
1. Duke of Wellington, *Supplementary Despatches and Memoranda of Arthur, Duke of Wellington*, v, 1873, p. 453.
2. Lee, S. (ed.). *Dictionary of National Biography* (hereinafter DNB), liii, 1898; Somerset, W. *The Descendants of Henry Somerset, Fifth Duke of Beaufort*, 1936.
3. Anon. *Short History of Cefntilla Court and the Raglan Family*, nd, p.3; Anon. *Life of Field-Marshal Lord Raglan*, 1855, pp. 5–6; Simpson, W. The Life of Field-Marshal the Lord Raglan, p.6, unpublished typescript, University of Aberdeen Library.
4. *Gentleman's Magazine*, ii, 1855; DNB, op. cit.;

Annual Register, 1855. A serious carriage accident in 1769 left the Duchess of Beaufort permanently lame and may have contributed to the 'rheumatism' which caused such additional discomfort, and Lord Fitzroy's concern in later years; Durant, H. *The Somerset Sequence*, 1951, pp. 36, 124, 161, 163.
5. Badminton Muniments (hereinafter Bad Mun), Fm L 5/13; ibid., RA 2/1/18–21; Durant, op. cit., 1951, pp. 36, 124, 161, 163. Troy does not appear to have been visited regularly by the family during Lord FitzRoy's youth. After 1789 either the Duke or his eldest son used the house in connection with militia business or parliamentary elections. Stoke Park passed to Lord FitzRoy's mother after her husband's death, and she died there in 1828. The Beaufort family lived in London for approximately three months each year: e.g., 13 Mar–13 July 1798 and 14 Mar–29 June 1799. Accounts reveal that the London season proved expensive. Those for the year ending 30 Jan 1801 noted the following: Blandford Park £1,507.3s.0d.; Badminton £1,810.10s.8d.; Stoke 'House' £416.9s.10d.; London £4,399.2s.4d. This proportion of expenditure appears normal. During some years additional short leases were taken, possibly for holidays: e.g., Dawlish, Worthing or Brighton, averaging £2–300. Lord FitzRoy may, therefore, have visited these locations as well. I am indebted to Mrs Margaret Richards for her help with the above details. When staying at Badminton Lord FitzRoy's maternal grandmother, Mrs Boscawen, did not join the other ladies on their daily walks, instead 'I sit very quiet the while amidst 3,000 books', further underlining the cultural atmosphere in which her grandson grew up: 30 Sept 1893, Mrs Boscawen to Miss Frances Sayer (her god-daughter), Aspinall-Oglander, C. *Admiral's Widow: Being the Life and Letters of the Hon Mrs Edward Boscawen from 1761 to 1805*, 1942, p. 154.
6. Bad Mun,, RA 2/1/18; RPP, contain cuttings of FitzRoy Somerset's hair at different times of his life; Durant, op. cit., pp. 167, 172; 7 Aug 1835 (transcript) Fitzroy Somerset (hereinafter FS) to his brother William, RPP, 10; 30 Sept 1893, Mrs Boscawen to Frances Sayer; Aspinall-Oglander, op. cit., p. 154; Bagot, J. *George Canning and His Friends*, ii, 1909, p. 7. Mrs Boscawen's letter contains an intriguing reference to 'notre souverain' staying at Badminton 29–30 Sept 1793, which raises the possibility that George III attended Lord FitzRoy's fifth birthday party. 'Notre souverain' may well, however, have been the nickname of a member of the family or a friend. An unsubstantiated legend persists that in his youth FitzRoy jumped over a cedar sapling at Badminton (information supplied by Brig P.H.C. Hayward). In 1838 Charles Apperley remarked on the magnificence of Badminton's 116 rooms and that from his room to the billiards room was almost 1/8th of a mile. The library proved 'a room of vast comfort', 34 regular hunters were in

the stables and another ten 'able to go a-hunting'. Small wonder then that Badminton attracted so many visitors and the 'meets' regularly drew devotees from Bath and Bristol. The children's parties were also lavish affairs – 58 attended Worcester's 13th birthday celebrations, Durant, op. cit., pp. 167, 185, 187.

7. Family records show that on 13 May 1796 £357.0s.6d. was paid to Dr Goodenough for the brothers' schooling up to Christmas 1795, though the date on which FitzRoy started is not indicated, Bad Mun,, Fm L 5/13(7). Only John and FitzRoy were still at Goodenough's on 8 June 1801, when £267.12s.0d. was paid for the year ending Christmas 1800, ibid., Fm L 5/13(9). Mrs Boscawen died on 26 Feb 1805, and the possibility that FitzRoy had stayed with her – perhaps during short leaves from Goodenough's – is raised by the fact that, on their return to Ealing on 7 June 1801, the Duke gave his sons 10s.6d. 'for the maid of Mrs Boscawen', Bad Mun,, Fm M 5/2. Mrs Boscawen lived at 14 South Audley Street, Mayfair – close to Great Stanhope Street, where Lord and Lady FitzRoy would live – but had a summer residence, Rosedale, facing Deer Park near Richmond, about four miles south of Ealing over Kew Bridge.

8. Bad Mun,, Fm L 5/2 and Fm M 5/2; 25 Aug 1854, de Redcliffe to Raglan, Raglan Military Papers (hereinafter RMP), 6807/291; Smith, É. *Life of Stratford Canning, Lord Stratford de Redcliffe*, 1933, pp. 22–3. The Goodenough estate contained the following: in front of the house, 50 lime trees, four elms, one oak; in the kitchen garden, a mulberry, walnut, quince, medlar, three cherries, seven plums; in the shrubberies, 350 firs and 250 beeches. According to Dr Goodenough's *DNB* entry, his school catered for 'the sons of many noblemen and gentlemen of position'. Pupils certainly included a future prime minister (Henry Addington, Lord Sidmouth), the diplomat Thomas Bruce, the Earl of Elgin, and the distinguished antiquary Barre Charles Roberts. Goodenough House was demolished in 1858 and replaced by The Limes. I am indebted to Miss M. Gooding of Ealing's Local History Library for her assistance with the above material.

9. Bad Mun,, Fm M 5/2; entry books for Feb 1781, Aug 1800, July 1802, Aug 1803 and 1804, Westminster School Archives; Field, J. *The King's Nurseries*, 1987; 'Terms of Westminster School, 1803', Westminster School Archives, D4 NA1: Clapham's House is now called Rigaud's.

10. Miscellaneous papers, RPP, 10; letter from a contemporary at Westminster to *The Morning Post*, RPP, 8; Royal United Service Institution, *Field-Marshal Fitz-Roy J. H. Lord Raglan, G.C.B.*, nd, p.1.

11. Lennox, W. *Fifty Years' Biographical Reminiscences*, 1863, i, p. 112; Diary of Lord John Russell, 1803–4, Westminster School Archives, D4 FH5; 'Customs of Westminster School', ibid., D6; Simpson, op. cit., pp. 8–9; Sargeaunt, J. *Annals of Westminster School*, 1898, chapter XI.

12. Bad Mun,, Fm M 5/2 and L 5/13 (9).

13. *History of Cefntilla*, p. 3; *DNB*, op. cit.; *Army List*, 1805–7; *TILN*, 5 Feb 1853. FitzRoy's brothers Charles Henry, William, Edward and John already held regular commissions in 1807.

14. *Life of Lord Raglan*, p. 20; *DNB*, op. cit. On 16 Feb 1809 Paget married Lady Augusta Jane Fane, whose brother would marry FS's future sister-in-

law, Priscilla.

15. 16 and 17 May 1807, Canning to Paget, Paget, A. (ed.). *The Paget Papers: Diplomatic and Other Correspondence of the Rt Hon Sir Arthur Paget OBE*, ii, 1896, pp. 290 and 293; 19 June 1807, Paget to Canning, ibid., p. 298.

16. 13 July and 15 Aug 1807, Canning to Paget, ibid., pp. 320 and 323; 22 Aug, 29 Aug and 5 Sept 1807, Paget to Canning, ibid., pp. 324, 331 and 345; 30 Aug 1807, Paget to Countess of Uxbridge, ibid., p. 335.

17. 25 Sept 1807, Paget to Duchess of Beaufort, ibid., p. 361.

18. Ibid.; Simpson, op. cit., pp. 15–16.

19. 8 and 22 Oct 1807, Paget to Canning, Paget, op. cit., pp. 369 and 373. Paget's mission had been undermined from the outset by an abortive attempt by Adm Duckworth to coerce the Turks with a display of naval force off Constantinople.

20. *DNB*, op. cit.; *Life of Lord Raglan*, p. 1; 12 July 1808 (two letters), FS to William, RPP, 1/4–5.

21. Wellington, *Supplementary Despatches*, op. cit., vi, p. 80; 14 June 1808, Duke of York to Wellesley, Gurwood, J. *The Dispatches and General Orders of Field-Marshal the Duke of Wellington*, iv, 1838, p. 10; Goodspeed, D. *The British Campaigns in the Peninsula 1808–1814*, Ottawa, 1958, pp. 1–25; Gurwood, op. cit., iv, pp. 2–5.

22. Longford, Lady E. *Wellington: The Years of the Sword*,1971, p. 188; Wellington, *Supplementary Despatches*, op. cit., p. 453; Kinglake, op. cit., ii, p. 15; undated, FS's own handwritten summary of the Peninsular campaign, RPP, 1/6; Goodspeed, op. cit., p. 34; 4 Aug 1808, Wellesley to Cotton, Gurwood, op. cit., iv, p. 61; 8 Aug 1808, Wellesley to Burrard, ibid., p. 69.

23. 26 Oct 1808, Wellesley to Castlereagh (Sec of State for War and the Colonies), ibid., p. 161; 11 Aug 1808, Wellesley to Mil Sec in London, ibid., p. 81; Goodspeed, op. cit., p. 34.

24. Ibid., pp. 34–8; Longford, op. cit., pp. 192–3; supply problems, 13 Aug 1808, Wellesley to Gen Freire, Gurwood, op. cit., iv, p. 87; 17 Aug 1808, Wellesley to Castlereagh, ibid., p. 96; *Life of Lord Raglan*, p. 1; *DNB*, op. cit.; *Army List*, 1809. Lord Fitzroy's brother Edward was a lt-col in the 43rd.

25. Longford, op. cit., pp. 197–201; Goodspeed, op. cit., pp. 40–4; 21 Aug 1808, Wellesley to Burrard, Gurwood, op. cit., iv, p. 108; artillery losses, ibid., p. 113.

26. 22 and 24 Aug 1808, Wellesley to William Wellesley-Pole, RPP, Wellington A/3 and 4; 22 Aug 1808, Wellesley to HRH the Duke of York (CinC in London), Gurwood, op. cit., iv, p. 114; 22 Aug 1808, Wellesley to Castlereagh, ibid., p. 115; ceasefire, ibid., p. 117.

27. 27 Aug 1808, Wellesley quoted in *DNB*, op. cit.; 5 Sept 1808, Wellesley to Capt Pulteney, Gurwood, op. cit., iv, p. 139; cf., 6 and 16 Sept, 23 and 29 Oct 1808, Wellesley to Wellesley-Pole, RPP, Wellington A/5–8. Wellesley did not see the full terms of the convention until their publication in *The London Gazette*, 16 Sept 1808.

Chapter 2

1. 15 Dec 1812, Napier to his wife, RPP, 7/285.

2. 2 Mar 1809, memo by Wellesley, Gurwood, op. cit., iv, p. 261.

3. 13 April 1809, Wellesley to Wellesley-Pole, RPP, Wellington A/11; *Surveillante* captain's and master's logs, Public Record Office (hereinafter PRO), ADM 51/1984 and ADM 52/4350. Longford, op.

cit., p. 223, notes slightly contradictory stories about the alleged near-shipwreck, quoting books by Lord Broughton and A. Dyce and giving the wrong date of 14 April.

4. *Life of Lord Raglan*, p. 8; FS's Peninsula summary, RPP, 1/6; Gurwood, op. cit., iv, pp. 291–5 and 348–9; War Dept, *General Orders: Spain and Portugal, April 27th to December 28th 1809*, i, 1811.

5. 5 May 1809, Wellesley to Dom Miguel Pereira Forjaz, Gurwood, op. cit., iv, p. 301; 11 May 1809, Wellesley to Rt Hon John Villiers, ibid., p. 320; 12 May 1809, Wellesley to Castlereagh, ibid., p. 322; Longford, op. cit., pp. 226–33; FS's Peninsula summary, RPP, 1/6.

6. 18 May 1809, Wellesley to Beresford, RPP, Wellington C/4; 11 June 1809, Wellesley to Valliers, Gurwood, op. cit., iv, p. 412; 5 June 1809, Wellesley to Dep Comm-Gen Dalrymple, ibid., p. 389; 7 June 1809, Wellesley to Vice-Adm the Hon G. Berkeley, ibid., p. 391; General Order, 26 June 1809, *General Orders*, op. cit.

7. 3 June 1809, Wellesley to Beresford, Gurwood, op. cit., iv, p. 384.

8. Draft account of Baker's recollections concerning 'the summer of 1809', undated and unsigned, RPP, 1/7. This memo was obviously written long after the event, though added comments suggest that Baker died in 1852 before the predictions relevant to the Crimean War. Almost certainly the officer concerned was Maj Charles Massey Baker (14th Light Dragoons): *see* Blackburne, H. *Historical Record of the 14th (King's) Hussars 1715-1900* , 1901, pp.490-1, and *Army List*, 1809!

9. Longford, op. cit., pp. 240 *et seq.*; Bryant, A. *The Great Duke or the Invincible General*, 1971, pp. 158 *et seq*; Griffiths, A. *Wellington, His Commanders and Contemporaries*, 1897, pp. 53 *et seq*; Percival, V. *The Duke of Wellington*, 1969, p. 26; 1 Aug 1809, Wellesley to Wellesley-Pole Wellington, A/16; 29 July 1809, Wellesley to Castlereagh, Gurwood, op. cit., iv, pp. 532 *et seq*.

10. 25 Mar 1811, Wellington to Adm Berkeley, ibid., p. 40; FS's Peninsula summary, RPP, 1/6; 22 Aug 1809, Wellesley-Pole to Wellesley, RPP, Wellington B/93.

11. 25 Aug 1809, Edward Somerset to Duke of Beaufort, Bad Mun, Fm 4/1/6; 6 Oct 1809, Wellington to Wellesley-Pole, RPP, Wellington A/25; 21 Sept 1809, Wellesley-Pole to Wellington, RPP, Wellington B/96; 22 Oct 1809, Wellington to Wellesley-Pole, RPP, Wellington A/26; 6 Oct 1809, Wellington to Castlereagh, Gurwood, op. cit., v, p. 212.

12. 3 Nov 1809, FitzRoy to Edward Somerset, Bad Mun, Fm 4/1/4; Bryant, op. cit., pp. 211 *et seq*; Griffiths, op. cit., p. 82; Hay, L. (ed.). *Memoirs of Lt-Gen Sir James Leith GCB*, 1821, pp. 36–8; Percival, op. cit., p. 27; Sabine, E. (ed.). *Letters of Colonel Sir Augustus Simon Frazer KCB*, 1859, pp. 56–7; 30 Sept 1810, Wellington to Liverpool, Gurwood, op. cit., vi, p. 471, Longford, op. cit., pp. 279–89.

13. *Life of Lord Raglan*; 30 Sept 1810, Wellington to Liverpool, Gurwood, op. cit., vi, p. 472; 4 Oct 1810, Wellington to Wellesley–Pole, RPP, Wellington A/35; General Orders 28 Nov 1810 and 1 Jan 1811, *General Orders*, op. cit.; Ward, S. *Wellington's Headquarters*, OUP, 1957, p. 61; Oman, C. *Wellington's Army 1809–1814*, 1913, p. 153.

14. 8 Jan 1813, Maj-Gen F.S. Rebow to FS, RA 20434; Oman, op. cit., p. 153; *Life of Lord Raglan*, p. 11.

15. 20 Feb 1811, Liverpool to Wellington, RPP, Wellington C.

16. FS's Peninsula summary, RPP 1/6; Kincaid, J. *Adventures in the Rifle Brigade in the Peninsula, France and the Netherlands 1809–1815*, 1830, p. 53; Bryant, op. cit., p.250.

17. 1 May 1811, Wellington to Wellesley-Pole, RPP, Wellington A; Griffiths, op. cit., pp. 89 and 214; Bryant, op. cit., pp. 252 *et seq*; *Life of Lord Raglan*, pp. 9–10; Hay, op. cit., p. 56; FS's Peninsula summary, RPP, 1/6; 3 Mar 1813 entry, Larpent, G. (ed.). *The Private Journal of Judge Advocate Larpent*, 1854, p. 65; Fraser, E. *The Soldiers whom Wellington Led*, 1913, p. 127; Kincaid, op. cit., p. 73.

18. Longford, op. cit., pp. 312–15; FS's Peninsula summary, RPP, 1/6.

19. Ibid.

20. Bell, D. *Wellington's Officers*, 1938, p. 176; Griffiths, op. cit., p. 93; Kincaid, op. cit., pp. 101, 107 *et seq*; Bryant, op. cit., pp. 289–309; FS's Peninsula summary, RPP, 1/6; 7, 15 and 20 Jan 1812, Wellington to Liverpool, Gurwood, op. cit., viii, pp. 536, 540, 547, 549; 8 Jan 1812, Wellington to Maj Dickson RA, ibid., p. 539; Longford, op. cit., p. 329.

21. 12 and 19 Feb 1812, Wellesley-Pole to Wellington, RPP, Wellington B/116 and 117; Warrant No 585, RPP, 1.

22. Griffiths, op. cit., p. 94; Kincaid, op. cit., pp. 96 *et seq* ; 13 Mar 1812, Wellington to Liverpool, Gurwood, op. cit., viii, p. 8; 20 and 27 Mar, 3 and 7 April 1812, Wellington to Liverpool, Gurwood, op. cit., ix, pp. 1, 12, 27, 36; 24 Mar 1812, Wellington to Lord William Bentinck, ibid., p. 6; 28 Mar 1812, Wellington to Rt Hon Henry Wellesley, ibid., p. 16; 1 April 1812, Wellington to Lt-Gen Sir T Graham, ibid., p. 22; 6 April 1812, memo for the attack on Badajoz, ibid., p. 32.

23. 7 April 1812, Wellington to Torrens, ibid., p. 45; Warre, E. (ed.). *Letters from the Peninsula 1808–1812 by Lt-Gen Sir William Warre CB*, 1909, pp. 229 *et seq*; Badajoz Order, 6 April 1812, RPP, Wellington C; post-war draft handwritten 'narrative of the surrender of Badajoz', with marginal questions to FS and clearly based upon Lord Fitzroy's account to the author, RPP, 1/9; Warre, op. cit., xxii.

24. 29 April 1812, Wellington to Wellesley-Pole, RPP, Wellington A/46; 8 April 1812, Wellesley to Torrens, Camp at Badajoz, RPP, 10.

25. Griffiths, op. cit., p. 211; Bryant, op. cit., pp. 319 *et seq*; Kincaid, op. cit., p. 161; *Life of Lord Raglan*, p. 14; Longford, op. cit., pp. 246–56.

26. Wellington quoted in Fraser, op. cit., p. 109, and Griffiths, op. cit., p. 125; Ryan, G. *Our Heroes of the Crimea*, 1855, p. 2; 24 July 1812, Wellington to Bathurst, Gurwood, op. cit., ix, p. 299.

27. Bryant, op. cit., p. 326; Anon (ed.). *The Personal Narrative of a Private Soldier in the 42nd Highlanders*, 1821, pp. 154–5; Griffiths, op. cit., pp. 332 *et seq* .

28. FS, quoted in Longford, op. cit., p. 268; Griffiths, op. cit., p. 214; Kincaid, op. cit., p. 199; 19 and 26 Nov 1812 entries, Larpent, op. cit., pp. 21–8.

29. 15 Dec 1812, Napier to his wife, RPP, 7/285; 16 Jan 1813 entry, Larpent, op. cit., p. 41; Fraser, op. cit., p. 113; *Blackwood's Magazine*, xxvi, p. 925.

30. 15 Mar 1813 entry, Larpent, op. cit., p. 70; 12 April 1813, Larpent to his mother, ibid., p. 87; 1 May 1813 entry, ibid., p. 100.

31. 5, 10, 15, 17 May 1813 entries, ibid., pp. 104, 108, 113, 115.

32. 3, 11, 14, 23, 29 June 1813 entries, ibid., pp. 131,

142, 148, 157, 169; 18 June 1813, Larpent to his mother, ibid., p. 153; Bryant, op. cit., pp. 357–91; Kincaid, op. cit., pp. 217 *et seq*.

33. 22 June 1813, Wellington to Bathurst, Gurwood, op. cit., ix, pp. 446 *et seq*; 29 June 1813 entry, Larpent, op. cit., p. 169; Longford, op. cit., pp. 396–7; 27 July 1813, Torrens to FS, quoted ibid., p. 397. Raglan's nephew, Henry (future 7th Duke of Beaufort), also distinguished himself at Vitoria.

34. 17 July 1813, Wellington to Lt-Gen Sir T Graham, Gurwood, op. cit., ix, p. 534; 1 Aug 1813, Wellington to Bathurst, op. cit., p. 576; Glover, M. *Wellington's Peninsular Victories*, 1963, p. 136; 3 Sept 1813, Wellington to Wellesley-Pole, RPP, Wellington A/58.

35. Aldington, R. *Wellington*, 1946, pp. 188–9; 1 Aug 1813, Wellington to Bathurst, Gurwood, op. cit., ix, p. 576; Bryant, op. cit., p. 373; Beatson, F. *With Wellington in the Pyrenees*, 1914, pp. 155 *et seq*; 3 Aug 1813, Wellington to Wellesley-Pole, RPP, Wellington A/56; Glover M, op. cit., p. 140.

36. *Life of Lord Raglan*, pp. 16–18; Glover, op. cit., p. 133.

37. 26 June 1813, Wellington to Lt-Col Bourke, Gurwood, op. cit., ix, p. 461; 28 June and 14 July 1813, Wellington to Lt-Gen Sir Rowland Hill, ibid., pp. 469, 527; 2 July 1813, Wellington to Lt-Gen the Earl of Dalhousie, ibid., p. 489.

38. *Life of Lord Raglan*, pp. 18–19; Ryan, op. cit., p. 3; 1 Nov 1813, Wellington to Wellesley-Pole, RPP, Wellington A/63; 13 Nov 1813, Wellington to Bathurst, Gurwood, op. cit., xi, p. 280; Larpent, op. cit., pp. 201 *et seq*. An undated and unsigned paper in RPP, notes a similar (but evidently different) incident, when an encoded enemy dispatch was brought to Lord FitzRoy, who deciphered it in the presence of staff officers, RPP, 2/92a.

39. Bryant, op. cit., pp. 375 *et seq*; Griffiths, op. cit., pp. 152–3; 13 Nov 1813, Wellington to Sir Henry Wellesley, Gurwood, op. cit., xi, p. 278; 13 Nov 1813, Wellington to Bathurst, ibid., p. 280 *et seq*; Larpent, op. cit., p. 307.

40. 2 Dec 1813, Larpent to his mother, op. cit., p. 309; Bryant, op. cit., p. 380; Griffiths, op. cit., pp. 153–5; 14 Dec 1813, Wellington to Bathurst, Gurwood, op. cit., xi, p. 370; 27 Dec 1814 entry, Larpent, op. cit., p. 338.

41. 4 Jan 1814 entry, ibid., p. 343; 11 Jan 1814, Larpent to his mother, ibid., p. 354; 'Slender Billy' episode, RMP, 6807/428.

42. Sabine, op. cit., viii; Griffiths, op. cit., pp. 156–7; 5 Mar 1814 entry, Larpent, op. cit., p. 421; 1 Mar 1814, Wellington to Bathurst, Gurwood, op. cit., xi, p. 421; Bryant, op. cit., p. 387.

43. 6 April 1814 entry, Larpent, op. cit., p. 476; Percival, op. cit., p. 41; Bryant, op. cit., pp. 392–3; Griffiths, op. cit., p. 158; 12 April 1814, Wellington to Bathurst, Gurwood, op. cit., xi, p. 637.

44. 13 April 1814 entry, Larpent, op. cit., pp. 486–9; Gurwood, op. cit., v, p. 327n, concerning Coghlan.

45. 18 April 1814 entry, Larpent, op. cit., p. 494; Broughton, Lord J. *Recollections of a Long Life*, 1909, i, p. 112; Simpson, op. cit., pp. 30–1; 9 May 1814, Wellington to Lord Liverpool, Gurwood, op. cit., xii, p. 4; 14 May 1814, Wellington to Rt Hon Sir Henry Wellesley, ibid., p. 5.

46. 21 May 1814, Wellington to Castlereagh, ibid., p. 27; 25 May 1814, Wellington to Sir Charles Stuart, and Wellington to Castlereagh, ibid., p. 28; 26 May 1814, Wellington to Maj-Gen Pack, ibid., p.

29; Bryant, op. cit., pp. 396–7; *Hampshire Telegraph and Sussex Chronicle*, 27 June 1814.

47. Cf., *Army List*, 1842; *Life of Lord Raglan*, p. 20.

Chapter 3

1. 19 June 1815, Wellington to Duke of Beaufort, Gurwood, op. cit., xii, p. 489.

2. Percival, op. cit., p. 9; Bryant, op. cit., p. 400. 28 Aug 1814, Wellington to Castlereagh, Gurwood, op. cit., p. 84, noted that his predecessor had bought Princesse de Borghese's house, its contents and stables for 863,000 francs for the British Ambassador's official residence.

3. *Annual Register*, 1855; Fortescue, J. *A Gallant Company*, 1927, p. 210; *Life of Lord Raglan*, p. 20; Hibbert, C. *The Destruction of Lord Raglan*, 1961, p. 3; 7 Aug 1814, Wellington to Wellesley-Pole, RPP, Wellington A/70. In 1814, possibly at the time of his wedding, Lord FitzRoy opened an account with Hoare's Bank, which endured until his death, and in which there was never a hint of financial embarrassment. The account remained 'steady ... with a fairly regular credit balance of about £800 and an annual turnover of from £3,400 to £4,500', 9 Mar 1955, Messrs Hoare to Julia, Lady Raglan, RPP, Misc Papers.

4. *Life of Lord Raglan*, p. 19; *History of Cefntilla*, p. 4. Portraits in the possession of the present Lord Raglan of the young Lady FitzRoy in fancy dress as a Gordon Highlander and, more formally, with her sisters, illustrate Emily's vivacity and physical attractiveness.

5. Undated (1855), memo by Lady Westmorland, Weigall, R. (ed.), *The Correspondence of Lady Burghersh with the Duke of Wellington*, 1903, pp. 216–7.

6. 12 Dec 1814, Wellington to Prince of Orange, Gurwood, op. cit., xii, p. 211, noting FS's arrival; but 30 Nov 1814, Wellington to Castlereagh, ibid., p. 197, reveals that he had already begun serious work.

7. 28 and 30 Nov 1814, Wellington to Castlereagh, ibid., pp. 195–6, 197.

8. Longford, op. cit., p. 460; 4 Nov 1814, Wellesley-Pole to Wellington, RPP, Wellington B/128; 18 Dec 1814, Castlereagh to Wellington, noted in 27 Dec 1814, Wellington to Castlereagh, Gurwood, op. cit., xii, p. 226; 27 Dec 1814, Wellington to Liverpool, ibid., p. 227; 17 Jan 1815, Wellington to Lady Burghersh, Weigall, op. cit., p. 9.

9. 3 Jan 1815, Duke of York (CinC) to FS, RPP, 1/2; 9 Jan 1815, Wellington to William Hamilton, Gurwood, op. cit., xiii, p. 238; 18 Jan 1815, Prince Regent to Louis XVIII, RPP, 1/4: although FS officially started on 18 January, Wellington claimed four days earlier that he had surrendered the office, 14 Jan 1815, Wellington to Wellesley-Pole, RPP, Wellington A/79; 24 Jan 1815, Wellington to Henry Wellesley, Gurwood, op. cit., xii, p. 259; 25 Jan 1815, FS to William Hamilton, PRO,, FO 27/113; 7 Feb 1815, FS to Castlereagh, RPP, Wellington A/79.

10. 12 Mar 1815, Castlereagh to FS, RPP, 1/16.

11. 30 and 31 Jan 1815, Earl Bathurst to FS, PRO,, FO 27/113; 31 Jan 1815, Hamilton to FS, ibid.; 13, 17 and 22 Feb 1815, Bathurst to FS, ibid.; 22 Feb 1815, FS to Comte de Jaucourt, ibid.; 30 Jan 1815, FS to Castlereagh, ibid.

12. 26 Jan 1815, FS to Castlereagh, enclosing copy of *Le Moniteur Universal*, 23 Jan 1815, with an account of the previous day's reburial, ibid.; 9, 13,

20 Feb 1815, FS to Castlereagh, ibid.

13. 1 Mar 1815, Lord Burghersh, British Minister in Florence, to Wellington, Gurwood, op. cit., xii, p. 266; 9 Mar 1815, FS to Castlereagh, PRO, FO 27/113; Nicolson, H. *The Congress of Vienna*, 1948, pp. 227 *et seq*; 14 Mar 1815, FS to Wellington, quoted in *DNB*; 15 Mar 1815, Prince of Orange to FS, RPP, 1/17.

14. 12, 16, 19 Mar 1815, Castlereagh to FS, PRO, FO 27/113.

15. 18 and 27 Mar 1815, Wellington to Castlereagh, Gurwood, op. cit., xii, pp. 273, 284.

16. 20, 21, 22 Mar 1815, FS to Castlereagh, PRO, FO 27/113; 20 Mar 1815, Jancourt to FS, ibid.; 'Statement of my conduct at Paris', Whichwood Park, 19 Mar 1816, RPP, 1/20.

17. 28, 29, 30, 31 Mar, 1 April 1815, FS to Castlereagh, PRO, FO 27/113.

18. 6 April 1815, Wellington to Bathurst, Gurwood, op. cit., xii, p. 291; 12 April 1815, Wellington to Campbell, ibid., p. 300; 6 May 1815, Wellington to Hardinge, ibid., 355; 6 May 1815, Wellington to Bathurst, ibid., p. 356; 20 May 1815, Wellington to Prince of Orange, ibid., p. 407; 9 May 1815, FS to Hamilton, PRO, FO 27/113; 24 April 1815, Duke of York to FS, RPP, 1/22; 14 May 1815, Castlereagh to FS, RPP, 1/23.

19. Diary entries 20 May 1814 (referring to 'my friend' Lord FitzRoy), 8, 9, 10, 13 April 1815, Broughton, op. cit., i, pp. 127, 240, 246, 250. *See* also Chapter 4 below.

20. 6 June 1815, Wellington to Wellesley-Pole, RPP, Wellington A/82; Saunders, E. *The 100 Days*, 1964, pp. 104–5, quoting 12 June 1815, Maj-Gen Sir William Dörnberg to FS from Mons.

21. 11 June 1815, FS to Bagot, Bagot, op. cit., ii, p.3. The Hon Charles Bagot married William Wellesley-Pole's eldest daughter Mary in 1806; later he served as British Ambassador to St Petersburg and The Hague during a distinguished diplomatic career, being awarded the KCB in 1819 on his return from the USA.

22. Bell, op. cit., p. 263; 15 June 1815, FS to Hamilton, PRO, FO 27/113; Griffiths, op. cit., p. 174; 15 June 1815, Dörnberg to FS, Robinson, C. *Wellington's Campaigns, Peninsula-Waterloo 1808–1815*, 1907, p. 504.

23. 'Lord FS's account of the Battle of Waterloo, etc.', written at Badminton in 1816, RPP, 1/24; Bell, op. cit., p. 238.

24. FS's account, RPP, 1/24; 26 Nov 1842, FS to Lt W. Siborne, recalling Quatre Bras action, Siborne, H. (ed.). *Waterloo Letters*, 1891, p. 3; *Life of Lord Raglan*, pp. 16–17; Howarth, D. *A Near Run Thing*, 1968, pp. 83; Griffiths, op. cit., p.212; Ryan, op. cit., p. 4; Fitchett, W. (ed.). *Wellington's Men: Some Soldiers' Autobiographies*, 1960, p. 120, quoting FS to Barnard; Ward, B. (ed.). *A Week at Waterloo in 1815*, 1906, pp. 20–1. The timings have been taken from FS's account, although other sources sometimes differ; e.g., Ward, op. cit., places Gordon's departure at between 6 and 7 a.m., his return shortly after 10 a.m.

25. Raymond, J. (ed.). *The Reminiscences and Recollections of Captain Gronow*, 1964, p. 186; Howarth, op. cit., pp. 25–8.

26. FS's account, RPP, 1/24; Sir Augustus Frazer's report of Wellington's remark to FS – presumably before 7 p.m. – quoted in Brett-James, A. (ed.), *Wellington at War. A Short Selection of his Wartime Letters*, 1961, p. 310n; June 1815, Lord Edward Somerset to Beaufort, Somerset, op. cit., App.

27. Gunning obit, *Press*, 17 Jan 1863; versions of FS's words: Hibbert, op. cit., p. 3; *History of Cefntilla*, p. 4; 'The Empire Calendar' in *The Daily Sketch*, 27 June 1914; '100 Years Ago: Lord Raglan' (trans), *Le Monde*, 30 Sept 1954.

28. 19 June 1815, Wellington to Bathurst, Gurwood, op. cit., xii, pp. 482 *et seq*; 19 June 1815, Wellington to Lady Frances Webster, quoted in Ward, op. cit., p. 18: the same day he wrote in a similar vein to his brother, William Wellesley-Pole, RPP, Wellington A/83: 'It was the most desperate business I ever was in, I never took so much trouble about any Battle; and never was so near beat'; 19 June 1815, Wellington to Beaufort, Gurwood, op. cit., xii, p. 489; June 1815, Lord Edward Somerset to Beaufort, Somerset, op. cit., App; Simpson, op. cit., p. 45.

29. *History of Cefntilla*, p. 5; *The Globe*, 14 Jan 1858; loose papers in RPP, 10 include the dedication and a note of the gift, June 1815; 20 June 1815, FS to his mother, RPP, 1/27: it should be remembered, however, that Lord FitzRoy's natural childhood preference for writing left-handed may have been forcibly curbed.

30. 23 June 1815, Wellesley-Pole to Lady FS, RPP, 1/28; 28 June 1815, FS to his mother, RPP, 1/29.

31. 3 July 1815, Dowager Duchess of Beaufort to Lady FS, RPP, 1/30.

32. 23 July 1815, Wellington to FS at Savile Row, RPP, 1/34; 29 July 1815, FS to Fanny, RPP, 5/1; undated (July 1854), Lady Elizabeth Orde to Lady Mary Farquhar, 7/294. Arthur suffered almost constant ill-health, went to Portugal and died in Lisbon in 1816.

33. 21 Aug 1815, Wellington to FS, RPP, 1/39A; 23 July 1815, Wellington to Torrens, RPP, 1/33; Griffiths, op. cit., p. 229.

34. 2, 8, 19 Aug, 6 Sept, 17 Dec 1815, Wellington to FS, RPP, 1/36, 38, 39, 40, 42; 7 July 1815, Freeman of City of Gloucester, RPP, 1/31.

35. 13, 23 July, 8, 21 Aug, 12 Oct 1815, Wellington to FS, RPP, 2/32, 35, 37, 39A, 41.

Chapter 4

1. Revd Dr Cardew, supporting FS for election as MP for Truro, quoted in the *Royal Cornwall Gazette*, 10 June 1820.

2. 21 April 1816, FS to Wellington, RPP, 1/44; 7 May 1816, FS to Wellington, noted in 10 May 1816, Wellington to FS, RPP, 2/47.

3. 21 April 1816, FS to Wellington, RPP, 2/44; 30 April 1816, Wellington to FS, RPP, 2/46.

4. 7 July 1816, Castlereagh to FS, RPP, 2/48; Wellington wrote to FS at No 1 Avenue des Champs Elysées, 25 Oct 1816, RPP, 1/50; 'Statement of my conduct at Paris', 19 Mar 1816, RPP, 1/20, discussed in Chapter 3 above; 4 June 1816, Hobhouse to Ponsonby, RPP, 1/21a; 20 June 1816, Ponsonby to Hobhouse, RPP, 1/21b; 25 June 1816, Ponsonby to FS, RPP, 1/21. Despite this agreement, in his subsequent *Recollections*, op. cit., i, p. 250, Hobhouse (Lord Broughton) quoted an interview with Mrs Bailly Wallis in Paris on 13 April 1815, in which she described the panic among Englishmen at Napoleon's arrival: 'Somerset's fright was the worst'.

5. 18 Dec 1816, Wellington to FS, RPP, 2/52; 9 April 1817, Wellington to the Hon Mrs Bagot, Bagot, op. cit., p. 43; 2 June 1817, Wellington to FS, RPP, 2/56; 28 June 1817, indecipherable (possibly Burghersh, his brother-in-law) to FS, mentioning

Lord FitzRoy's letter of 18 June, RPP, 2/58; 12 Dec 1817 and 15 Feb 1818, Wellington to Priscilla, Weigall, op. cit., pp. 22–3.

6. 9 July, 31 Oct, 30 Nov 1817, 19 Sept, 21, 22 Dec 1818, Wellington to FS, RPP, 2/59, 2/71, 1/74, 2/68, 1/75–7; 12 Feb 1818, FS to Wellesley-Pole, Bagot, op. cit., p. 71.

7. For a fuller discussion of the duties of the Master-General, Board of Ord and Ord Dept, see Sweetman, J. *War and Administration*, Edinburgh, 1984, pp. 59–64.

8. 3 Jan 1819, Wellington to FS, RPP, 2/78; *TILN*, 5 Feb 1853; RPP, H/1; 29 July 1824, FS to Burghersh, ibid., p. 7.

9. Simpson, op. cit., p. 65; 29 July 1824, FS, RPP, 7; Buchan, S. *The Sword of State: Wellington after Waterloo*, 1928, p. 79; Oct 1825, Napier to FS, RPP, 2/92a.

10. 29 July 1824, FS to Burghersh, RPP, 7; Aldington, op. cit., pp. 263–4; *TILN*, 5 Feb 1853; mob incident, Durant, op. cit., p. 174.

11. Ibid., p. 183; 16 May 1826, FS to Charlotte, and 31 July 1826, Lady FitzRoy to Charlotte, RPP, 5.

12. *Life of Lord Raglan*, pp. 25–7; Smith, H. *The Parliaments of England, 1715–1847*, Chichester, 1973: in 1818 the tory candidates FS and William Tomline polled 12 votes each, their whig opponents Sir Hussey Vivian and Lt-Col William Gossett 11 each; two years later, Vivian polled 12, FS and Gosset each 11 and Tomline 10; in 1826, FS and Tomline were elected, though neither contested the 1829 election; *Royal Cornwall Gazette*, 10 June 1820.

13. On Tuesday 13 May 1828 FS voted against the motion for consideration of 'a final and conciliatory adjustment ... of the State of Laws affecting his Majesty's Roman Catholic Subjects in Great Britain and Ireland', which was carried 272–266. Lord FitzRoy is shown as being elected for the Parliaments which met on 14 Jan 1819 and 14 Nov 1826. On 31 Mar 1829, Viscounts Encombe and Nathaniel Peach represented Truro.

14. Extract from Foreign Office List, Jan 1856, RPP, 10/4.

15. Percival, op. cit., p. 10; *Annual Register*, 1855; *History of Cefntilla*, p. 5; Buchan, op. cit., pp. 53–63. References in several secondary sources to FitzRoy accompanying Wellington to 'The Congress of Vienna' should not be misinterpreted. These refer to the same congress as Verona in 1822, not the peace conference of 1815.

16. Buchan, op. cit., pp. 65–7; *History of Cefntilla*, p. 5; *Life of Lord Raglan*, p. 25; *Annual Register*, 1855.

17. Jan 1823, Wellington to FS, Simpson, op. cit., p. 71; 6 Jan 1823, Canning to FS, quoted in Temperley, H. *The Foreign Policy of Canning 1820–1827*, 1923, p. 288.

18. FS's reports to Wellington from Madrid Jan-Mar 1823, noted in Simpson, op. cit., p. 70, 75–7.

19. 7 April 1823, à Court to FS, RPP, 2/83.

20. Buchan, op. cit., pp. 81 *et seq*.

21. 6 Mar 1826, FS to Lady Frances Somerset, RPP, 2/93. In his correspondence FS referred to St Petersburg simply as 'Petersburg'.

22. 6 Mar 1826, FS to 'my dearest Cuddy' (Charlotte), RPP, 5/1a.

23. 16 Mar 1826, FS to Lady Frances Somerset, RPP, 2/94; FS to Bagot, quoted in Simpson, op. cit., p. 83.

24. 27 April 1826, FS to Lady Frances Somerset, RPP, 2/75.

25. 6 Aug 1826, Wellington to Priscilla, Weigall, op. cit., p. 37.

Chapter 5

1. 9 Aug 1842, Hill to FS, Sidney, E. *Lord Hill GCB*, 1845, p. 375.

2. 24 July 1827, FS to (illegible), RPP, 3/98: Wellington, Duke of (ed.). *The Conversations of the First Duke of Wellington with George Willian Chad*, Cambridge, 1956, pp. 8–9, records Wellington's assertion on 10 April 1828 that Canning wanted him out of the Cabinet, though the Duke protested: 'I beg your Pardon ... the Commander-in-Chief ought not to be in the Cabinet, but the Office of Master Genl. is one that makes it proper that the holder should'; extract from the Foreign Office List, Jan 1856, RPP, 10/4; Stocqueler, J. *A Personal History of the Horse Guards 1750–1872*, 1873, p. 143. Moore Smith, G. *The Life of John Colborne, Field-Marshal Lord Seaton*, 1903, pp. 251–2, claims that two days before Canning died, Colborne had agreed to become Mil Sec to Palmerston with the post of CinC discontinued.

3. Torrens quoted in Glover, R. *Peninsular Preparation*, Cambridge, 1963, p. 44. FS's pay as Mil Sec is not clear, but a memo by Lord Palmerston on 16 Mar 1817 put the salary then at £2,500 per annum, PRO, WO 43/95/151483. For a full discussion of the Mil Sec's work, see Sweetman, op. cit., Chapter 5.

4. Final report of the Select Committee on Army and Ord Expenditure, 21 July 1851, Parliamentary Papers (hereinafter PP), 1851, vii, p. 790; Lord Wolseley writing in Ward, T. (ed.). *The Reign of Queen Victoria*, i, 1887, p. 198. For note of the various establishments connected with army administration, see Sweetman, op. cit., p.8.

5. The *Army Lists* record that officially these two periods were 22 Jan–5 May 1827 and 27 Aug 1827–14 Feb 1828.

6. Rowland, Lord Hill (1772–1842), commanded the 90th Regt during the invasion of Egypt (1801), served with distinction in the Peninsula and at Waterloo, acted as second-in-command to Wellington with the Allied Army of Occupation in France (1815–18) and had been promoted full general only in 1825.

7. Sidney, op. cit., p. 323; 1 Feb 1828, Wellington to Hill, ibid., p. 335.

8. 24 Sept 1830 and 10 Jan 1834, FS to Charlotte, RPP, 5/4a and 5; 26 Dec 1836, Horse Guards, FS to Hill, noting deep snow; 24 Dec 1837 20 Jan 1834, FS to Hill, ibid.; Badminton, FS to Hill, RPP, 5; 3 Sept 1836, FS to Wellington, Wellington Papers. When consulted, the Wellington Papers were being catalogued at the National Register of Archives.

9. 29 Dec 1834, H. Goldsmith to Egerton, and 5 Jan 1835, FS to Egerton, RPP, 5; 28 Dec 1840, Hill to FS, including Mrs Weal's plea; 2 Jan 1841, FS to Mr Fortescue, RA MP 36/80 and 81; *Life of Lord Raglan*, pp. 27–8.

10. 9 Mar 1833, Nicholls to FS, Wellington Papers; Brown, 17 Jan 1837, FS to Hill, RPP, 5; 20 June 1854, FS to Hill, 30 Nov 1854, FS to Egerton, 5 Jan 1837, FS to Hill and 9 Jan 1837, Hill to FS, RPP, 5; 30 Aug 1829, FS to Hill, RPP, 3/105; 1 Sept 1829, Hill to FS, RPP, 3/106; 9 Sept 1829, Taylor to Macdonald (Adj Gen), RPP, 3/107; 10 Sept 1829, FS to Hill, RPP, 3/108; 7 Jan 1842, FS to Hill, RPP, 6.

11. 26 Sept 1835, FS to Hill, and 28 Sept 1835, Hill to

William IV, RPP, 3/139; 16 and 20 Jan 1837, FS to Hill, 17 Jan 1837, Hill to FS, RPP, 5.

12. 12 Dec 1838, FS to Egerton, RPP, 6; 26 Dec 1840, 31 July and 3 Aug 1841, FS to Hill, RPP, 6; 3 Aug 1841, Hill to FS, RPP, 6.

13. 5 Nov 1835, FS to Hill, RPP, 5; Moore Smith, op. cit., pp. 254 *et seq*.

14. 7 Aug 1837 and 14 April 1838, FS to Hill, RPP, 5; 9 Feb 1828 and 14 Mar 1838, FS to Widdrington, RA MP 7/64 and 64a; 15 June 1837, Howick to Melbourne, RA MP 7/63.

15. 31 July 1834, Hamilton to Mil Sec, Wellington Papers; 22 April 1835, Goldie to Egerton, and 1 May 1835, FS to Hill, RPP, 5; 7 Aug 1834, 27 Nov 1835 and 1 Jan 1836, FS to Wellington, Wellington Papers.

16. 1 Oct 1837, FS to Hill, RPP, 3/160; 19 Oct 1837, FS to Hill, and 21 Oct 1837, Hill to FS, RPP, 3; 11 Oct 1838, Woodford to FS, RA Add. E1/5; 18, 20, 23 Sept 1830, FS to Hill, RPP, 3/115; 9 Oct 1830, FS to Hill, RPP, 3/116; 12 Oct 1830, Hill to FS, RPP, 3/117.

17. Ci-devant Cavalry Officer, a. *Army Reform: a practical method of reducing the Army Estimates a million without diminution of its numerical force*, 1833, p 2; 5 Oct 1832, FS to Hill, RPP, 3/129; 23 Sept 1836, FS to Hill, RPP, 3/145; 9 Nov 1835, Wellington to FS, Wellington Papers; 23 Sept 1836, FS to Egerton, RPP, 3/146.

18. Report of the Commissioners appointed to inquire into the practicability and expediency of the civil administration of the army (Howick Report), PP, 1838, v, Pt 1, app 105 *et seq*, published the Richmond Report for the first time; Howick's conclusion on Richmond, ibid., p. 8; Ellice, 30 Dec 1833 and 2 Jan 1834, FS to Hill, RPP, 3/135–6.

19. Howick Report, op. cit., I *et seq*. Howick was not altogether a disinterested figure, being Sec at War April 1835–Sept 1839.

20. 25 Mar 1837, memo by Wellington for FS, Sidney Herbert Papers, 'Cabinet and other memoranda 1837–61'. Jan 1838, Wellington to Howick, aand 4 Jan 1838, Wellington memo, reinforce the Duke's position in detail, RA MP 17/71 and 72.

21. 27 Mar 1837, Taylor to FS, Wellington Papers; 29 Dec 1837, FS to Wellington, RPP, 3/153a; 30 Dec 1837 and 1 Jan 1838, FS to Wellington, Wellington Papers.

22. 3 Jan 1838, Hill to Howick, 4 Jan 1838, Wellington to Melbourne, and Melbourne to Howick, Grey Papers.

23. Head letter, *The Times*, 16 Feb 1855.

24. 14 Feb 1834, Brudenell to FS, and 22 Feb 1834, FS to Brudenell, quoted in Thomas, D. *The Hero of Balaclava*, 1987, p. 56; 16 Sept and 14 Oct 1835, FS to Hill, RPP, 5; Molesworth's motion defeated 42–322, 3 May 1836.

25. 29 Sept 1840, Macdonald to Egerton, and 29 Sept 1840, FS to Egerton, RPP, 6; anon letter (soon revealed as from Tuckett), *The Morning Chronicle*, 4 Sept 1840.

26. Woodham-Smith, C. *The Reason Why*, 1957, p. 75; anon letter, *The Morning Chronicle*, 16 Oct 1840; Hill to Lady Langdale, quoted in *Alligator*, 30 Jan 1841; Thomas, op. cit., pp. 90–1.

27. Woodham-Smith, op. cit., pp. 80–3; 16 Nov 1840, FS to Egerton, and 26 Dec 1840, FS to Hill, RPP, 6; 16 Jan 1841, FS to Egerton, RPP, 6; Thomas, op. cit., pp. 133–43.

28. *The Times*, 21 April 1841; Woodham-Smith, op. cit., pp. 94–7; 24 and 25 April 1841, Melbourne to

Queen Victoria, Benson, A. and Esher, Viscount (eds.). *The Letters of Queen Victoria 1837–1861*, i, 1908, pp. 262–4; 26 April 1841, Wellington to Lady Wilton, Wellington, Duke of (ed.). *Wellington and His Friends: Letters of the First Duke of Wellington*, 1965, p. 161; Paget letter to *The Times*, 11 Sept 1841; 29 Mar 1842, FS to Egerton, RPP, 6. Woodham-Smith, op. cit., p. 102, claims that Wellington was overruled.

29. 29 Oct and 7 Nov 1828, Wellington to FS, RPP, 3/102–3.

30. 4 Dec 1830, FS to Melbourne, RA MP 89/32: details of troops movements April-Oct 1831, RA MP 89/37, 39–46 and 93; Petrie, C. *Wellington*, 1956, p. 243; 5 Dec 1830, Wellington to FS, RPP, 3/119; Longford, Lady E. *Wellington: Pillar of State*, 1975, p. 335; 26 May 1831, Wellington to FS, RPP, 3/122; 22 Nov 1831, Wellington to FS, RPP, 3/124; Scots Greys, Ziegler, P. *King William IV*, 1973, p. 216; 21 Mar 1832, FS to Hill, RPP, 3/125.

31. 11 June 1840, King of Prussia to Queen Victoria, Benson and Esher, op. cit., i, p. 225; 7 Jan 1842, FS to Egerton, RPP, 6; Anon. *The Origins and History of the First or Grenadier Guards*, 1874, with a 'Corrigenda and Addenda' pamphlet, 1877, contained in RPP, 10.

32. 5 Dec 1830, Wellington to FS, Wellington Papers; 19 May 1831, Wellington to FS, RPP, 3/121; 17 Sept 1832, FS to Hill, and 19 Sept 1832, Hill to FS, RPP, 3/127; 23 Oct 1840, FS to Egerton, RPP, 6. Louis Phillipe succeeded Charles X as King of France following the 1830 revolution.

33. 25 July 1830, Wellington to FS, RPP, 3/114; 17 Sept 1832, FS to Hill, RPP, 3/127; 11 May 1836, FS to Hill, RPP, 3/144; 17 Aug 1836, Woodford to FS, Wellington Papers; 5 Dec 1837, Fraser to Vivian, enclosing 'Notes Relating to Ceuta and Gibraltar', Dec 1826, with a further covering note of 29 Oct 1837, RPP, 3/162A.

34. 10 Oct 1835, FS to Hill, RPP, 3/140; 24 Oct 1836, FS memo, RPP, 3/150; 28 Jan 1838, FS to Egerton, and 20 Aug 1838, FS to Egerton, RPP, 5.

35. 20, 25, 28 Aug, 4 Sept 1838, FS to Hill; 9 Oct, 20 Nov 1838 and 11 Sept 1839, FS to Egerton, RPP, 5; 23 Oct 1838, FS to Hobhouse, RPP, 5.

36. 5 Jan 1838, Wellington to FS, Wellington Papers; 24 Jan 1838, FS to Egerton, RPP, 5; 26 April 1838, FS to Wellington, enclosing extracts from Taylor's letter of 25 Mar 1838, Wellington Papers.

37. 19 July 1838, FS to Hill, RPP, 5; 19 Oct 1838, FS to Hill, noting Kempt's illness and Colborne's agreement to continue in command, dated 29 Sept 1838, RPP, 5; 7 and 21 Nov 1838, FS to Egerton, RPP, 5.

38. 19 Sept 1841, FS to Wellington, Wellington Papers.

39. 19 Oct 1838, FS to Hill, quoting Wellington about bayonets, RPP, 5; 7 Feb 1842, FS to Egerton, RPP, 6; 29 Dec 1833, Wellington to FS, Wellington Papers; 6, 8, 9 April 1833, Taylor to FS, and 10 April 1833, FS to Taylor, RA 36106–8, 36120–2, 36123–4 and 36125–7.

40. Somerset, op. cit.

41. Letters from FS to 'Angelica' and 'Angeline' appear among family correspondence. Simpson, op. cit., p. 107, without supporting evidence, suggests that the former applied to Charlotte but admits no idea of the latter. The context of the references do suggest one or both of the daughters. The information on Arthur is contained in the relevant Register of Gentlemen Cadets at the Royal Military College now kept in the archives

at Sandhurst; and I am particularly grateful to the curator (Dr T.A Heathcote) for his assistance in tracing and interpreting it. Edward A Somerset, Arthur's cousin, entered the RMC on 19 Aug 1831, passed all subjects, received a College recommendation on 31 Dec 1835 and joined the Rifle Brigade on 29 Jan 1836.

42. I am indebted to Mark Curthoys, Librarian and Archivist of Christ Church, for details of Richard's time at Oxford. *See* also Christ Church Archives, Chapter Book 1838–1857, entry 27 Mar 1839, and Oxford University Archives, Register of the Chancellor's Court 1835–1840, ref Hyp. A. 70: 26 June 1838 Richard Smith, cordwainer, claimed £26.8s.2d. and on 18 April 1839 a further £17.3s.8d., and on the latter date the assignees of a bankrupt (George Cole) claimed £39.15s.7d. Boase's *Contemporary Biography* makes no reference to Richard's residence at Christ Church, which Mr Curthoys concludes 'rather confirms that it was not entirely creditable', and the *University Calendar* makes no reference to Richard's sojourn at New Inn Hall, mentioned in the actions of April 1839, which suggests that his stay there was brief.

43. 8 Nov 1841, Charlotte to Richard, RPP, 9. Summary of FS's financial affairs contained in 9 Mar 1855, Messrs Hoare to Julia, Lady Raglan, RPP, Misc Papers.

44. 14 and 22 Feb, undated (Mar) and 25 April 1842, Arthur to Richard, RPP, H.

45. 2, 5, 24 June 1842, Arthur to Richard, RPP, H.

46. 4 June 1828, FS to Charlotte, RPP, 5/3; 20 July 1829, FS to Charlotte, RPP, 5/4.

47. 24 Sept 1830, FS to Charlotte, RPP, 5/4a; 20 Nov 1833, Katherine to FS, RPP, 1; undated (1833), (illegible) from Bishops Hale, Essex, to Charlotte, RPP, 6. Lady Harriet Blanche (19) and Lady Mary Octavia (16), Lord FitzRoy's nieces, married the Earl of Galloway and Sir Walter Farquhar respectively.

48. 10, 13 Jan 1834, FS to Charlotte, RPP, 5/5 and 6; 10 Jan 1841, FS to Kitty, RPP, 5/9; 4, 12 Dec 1841, FS to Charlotte, RPP, 5/10 and 11; 21 May 1842, FS to Charlotte, RPP, 5/12; 23 May 1842, FS to Angelina, RPP, 5/13.

49. 14 Jan 1834, Gordon to FS, RPP, 5; 13 Jan 1834, FS to Charlotte, RPP, 5/6; 19 Aug 1837, FS to Hill, RPP, 5; 30 Sept 1838, FS to Duke of Cambridge, RA Add. E/1/3; 30 Sept 1838, Wellington to Priscilla, Weigall, op. cit., p. 107; 9, 11, 25, 28 Oct 1838, FS to Egerton, RPP, 5.

50. 25 June 1839, Louise Dessoulavy to Charlotte, RPP, 6.

51. 23, 24 Sept 1835, FS to Hill, RPP, 5; 4 Mar 1836, FS to brother William, RPP, 10; 17 Jan 1837, FS to Hill, RPP, 5; 27 Mar 1837, FS to Wellington, Wellington Papers; Weigall, op. cit., p. 85; 22 Dec 1838, FS to Egerton, RPP, 5; 29 Mar 1842, FS to Egerton, RPP, 6.

52. 10 Jan 1841, FS to Kitty, RPP, 5/9; 12 Dec 1841, FS to Charlotte, RPP, 5/11; 4 June 1836, FS to William, RPP, 10; 17 Mar 1842, FS to Egerton, and 7 Jan 1842, FS to Egerton, RPP, 6.

53. 22 Sept 1840, Wellington to Priscilla, Weigall, op. cit., p. 127; 24 Sept 1830, FS to Charlotte, RPP, 5/4A; 10 Jan 1834, FS to Charlotte, RPP, 5/5; 10 Dec 1839, FS to Hill, and 14 Dec 1839, FS to Egerton, RPP, 6; note of following party season, 23 May 1842, FS to (illegible), RPP, 5/13; Cirencester, 4 Mar 1836, FS to William, RPP, 10; races, 4 June 1828, FS to Charlotte, RPP, 5/3; RA

QVJ: 21 Aug 1837; 22 Aug 1837, FS to Hill, RPP, 1/158; Thomas, op. cit., p. 85.

54. 19 Nov 1830, Hill to FS, RPP, 3/118: curiously, Sir Herbert Taylor's letter to Hill making the offer is dated 20 Nov 1830, but the *Army List* gives the appointment as 19 Nov 1830; Cannon, R. *Historical Record of the 53rd or the Shropshire Regt of Foot,* 1849, pp. 26–7; 14 July 1842, Royal Warrant, RPP, 3/167; *Army List,* 1840.

55. Percival, op. cit., p. 69; 19 June 1834, Beaufort to William, RPP, 10; translation of Philimore's Latin speech, RPP, 3/137.

56. Sidney, op. cit., pp. 369–78; 7 April, Hill to his brother, Sir Rowland, 29 July, Wellington to Hill, and 9 Aug 1842, Hill to FS, Wellington Papers; 31 Aug 1842, FS to Richard, RPP, 9.

57. Stocqueler, op. cit., p. 167. Hill officially served at the Horse Guards 25 Feb 1828–14 Aug 1842.

58. 9 Aug 1842, Hill to FS, RPP, 3/168.

Chapter 6

1. Fortescue, op. cit., p. 208.

2. 10 Aug 1842, Peel to Queen Victoria, Benson and Esher, op. cit., i, p. 420: Murray (*b.*1772), former Quart-Gen in the Peninsula, governor of the RMC Sandhurst and CinC Ireland, was currently Master-Gen of the Ord; Paget (*b.*1775), another Peninsula veteran, had commanded during the Burmese War (1824–5); Londonderry (*b.*1775) – Charles William Stewart – yet another Peninsula veteran with later extensive diplomatic experience; Combermere (*b.*1773), also a Peninsula veteran, an ex C-in-C Ireland (1822–5) and India (1825–30); Beresford (*b.*1768), commander of the Portuguese army during the Peninsular War and Master-General (1828–30); 22 Feb 1842, RPP, H/4.

3. 10 Aug 1842, Peel to Queen Victoria, and 12 Aug 1842, Benson and Esher, op. cit., i, pp. 420-1; Buchan, op. cit., pp. 186–9; Aldington, op. cit., p. 331; Wellington's patent, Sidney Herbert Papers, Misc Papers; 31 Aug 1842, FS to Richard, RPP, 9; 30 Aug 1841, Queen Victoria to Melbourne, Benson and Esher, op. cit., i, p. 309: 'The Duke of Wellington's health is too uncertain, and himself too prone to sleep coming over him ... to admit of his taking an office in which he would have much to do but be in the Cabinet.'

4. 27 Feb 1843, Hansard, lxvi, pp. 1347–9; 4 July 1843, Hansard, lxx, pp. 611–5; 12 Dec 1845, Queen Victoria to Wellington and Wellington to Queen Victoria, Benson and Esher, op. cit., ii, p. 55.

5. 23 Sept 1842, FS to Kitty, RPP, 5/14; 24 Oct 1842, FS to Charlotte, RPP, 5/15; 29 Dec 1842, Wellington to FS, RPP, 6; 21, 22 Jan 1845, Wellington to FS, RPP, 6; 1 Aug 1845, FS to Charlotte, RPP, 5/30; 10 Nov 1846, Wellington to FS, RPP, 6; 28 Dec 1846, FS to Wellington, RPP, 6; 3 Oct 1849, Wellington to FS, RPP, 6; 7 Aug 1849, FS to Charlotte, RPP, 5.

6. 13 Jan 1847, FS to Charlotte and Kitty, RPP, 5/44; 27 Nov 1850, FS to Charlotte, RPP, 5/62.

7. 16 Feb, 26 Mar, 6 Dec 1843, 15 Mar 1844, Wellington to FS, RPP, 6. For examples of the Mil Sec's involvement in such matters as length of military service, military pensions, formation of the pensioners into a reserve militia, etc., see PRO, WO 30/112.

8. 19, 29 Sept 1845, Wellington to FS, RPP, 6.

9. 29 Dec 1845 and 3 Nov 1846, Wellington to FS, RPP, 6; Chelsea correspondence 1845–50, PRO, WO 30/113.

10. Wheeler, O. *The War Office Past and Present*, 1914, pp. 125–6; 31 Mar 1850, FS to Brown, Brown Papers, MS 1848/26; Stocqueler, op. cit., pp. 180–1, 193; Maurice, quoted ibid., 125.

11. Ibid., 131; a formal examination for first commissions was introduced in 1849, invol.ving the following subjects: history, geography, algebra and logarithms, Euclid, French, Latin, field fortification, orthography and caligraphy; undated (1855), memo by Lady Westmorland, Weigall, op. cit., p. 218.

12. Wilson, P. (ed.). *The Greville Diary*, 1927, ii, pp.223–4; Granville quoted in Fitzmaurice, E. *The Life of Granville George Leveson Gower, Second Earl Granville*, 1905, i, p. 10.

13. 17 Aug 1842, Melbourne to Queen Victoria, and 18 Aug 1842, Graham to Queen Victoria, Benson and Esher, op. cit., i, pp. 425-6.

14. 3 April 1848, Horse Guards' memo, PRO, WO 30/111; 8 April 1848, DAG to Mil Sec, ibid.; 6 April 1848, Lt-Col Tulloch, memo concerning the deployment of pensioners, ibid.

15. 9 April 1848, Horse Guards' memo, ibid.; 9 April 1848, FS to Tulloch, ibid.; 9 April 1848, FS to Officer Commanding at Bethlehem Hospital, ibid.; 9 April 1848, Tulloch to FS, ibid.; 11 April 1848, Brotherton to FS, ibid.

16. FS, 'Memo showing troop dispositions for 10 April', ibid.; 'Stations of Police on Monday 10 April 1848', ibid.; 11 April 1848, FS to Tulloch, ibid.; 13, 14 April 1848, FS to Le Marchant, ibid.

17. 10 April 1848, FS to Warre, and FS to Gordon, ibid.; 10 April 1848, Lord FitzClarence from Gosport to Horse Guards, ibid.; 9 April 1848, Mil Sec to Lt-Gen Sir Thomas Arbuthnot, troops to Weeden, ibid.

18. 10 June 1848, Wellington to FS, RPP, 3/178; 17 June 1848, Wellington to Anglesey, PRO, WO 30/111.

19. 27, 30 May, 6 June 1844, Wellington to Thomas Raikes, Raikes, H. (ed.). *Private Correspondence of Thomas Raikes with the Duke of Wellington*, 1861, pp. 367–9; undated (1843), Monteagle to FS, RA M 52/26; 12 Jan 1848, Wellington to FS, RPP, 3/177; Queen Charlotte's funeral, 3, 5, 7, 11 Dec 1849, Wellington to FS, RPP, 3/180–3. Anglesey, Burgoyne, Palmerston, Grey and Russell were among those to express fears about coastal defences.

20. Williams, 4 April 1845, Hansard, lxxix, p. 213; *Annual Register*, vol. 86, p. 64; 28 Sept, 4, 9 Nov 1846, FS to Grey, Grey Papers; 12 April 1849, FS to Westmorland, RPP, 3/85.

21. 3 Nov 1842, FS to Richard, RPP, 6; *see* also 6 May 1842, FS to Buckingham, 21 May 1842, Revd Fisher to FS, 31 May 1842, FS to Richard, RPP, 6; 6 Mar 1850, FS to Cambridge, 8 Mar 1850, Cambridge to FS, 14 Dec 1851, FS to Cambridge, 6 Jan 1852, FS to Cambridge, and 8 July 1852, FS to Cambridge, RA Add. A8/909, 910, 986, 991, 1006; 24 Aug 1845, FS to Wellington, RPP, 6.

22. 21 Jan 1843, FS to Charlotte and Kitty, 13 Jan 1843, FS to Charlotte, RPP, 5/19 and 18; 22 Nov 1843 and 1 Jan 1845, FS to Angelina, RPP, 5/25 and 28; 2 Jan 1845, FS to (illegible), RPP, 5/29; 14 Dec 1845, FS to Charlotte, 20 Dec 1845, FS to Kitty, 21 Dec 1845, FS to Charlotte, RPP, 5/35, 36 and 37.

23. 24 Oct 1842, 29 July 1847, 27 Nov 1850, FS to Charlotte, RPP, 5/15, 46, 62; *Monte Christo* ref, 31 Jan 1846, FS to Kitty, RPP, 5/38. Lord FitzRoy's abortive visit to the Adelphi appears to reveal a musical, as well as dramatic, interest, possibly indicating that the childhood tuition in the Beaufort household had not been entirely wasted on him. 'Norma' was almost certainly Vincenzo Bellini's opera first performed in Milan in 1831.

24. 23 Sept 1842, FS to Kitty, RPP, 5/14; 30 Nov 1845, FS to Charlotte, RPP, 5/34; 10 May 1846, FS to Charlotte and Kitty, RPP, 5/42; 8 Aug 1851, FS to Kitty, RPP, 5/65; 19 Dec 1850, FS to Charlotte, RPP, 5/63; 14 Feb 1850, FS to Puggins (Charlotte), RPP, 5/57; 22 Nov 1851, FS to Charlotte, 5/64.

25. 31 Jan 1844, FS to Richard, RPP, 9; 12 Jan 1843, FS to Charlotte and Kitty, RPP, 5/17; 13 Jan 1843, FS to Charlotte, RPP, 5/18; 16 Jan 1845 and 23 Mar 1845, FS to Richard RPP, 9; 22 Nov 1851, FS to Charlotte, RPP, 5/64; 2 Nov 1851, Cambridge to Richard, RPP, 10/25. John Robert Hume had been Wellington's physician in the Peninsula.

26. *The United Service Gazette* (hereinafter USG), 25 Sept 1852; 8 Dec 1845, Wellington to FS, quoted in Stanmore, Lord. *Sidney Herbert: Lord Herbert of Lea*, 1906, i, pp. 74–6; Two Mounted Sentries, *The Horse Guards – a satire upon the Duke of Wellington*, 1850, pp. 1 *et seq*; 16 Feb 1852, Russell to Prince Albert, Benson and Esher, op. cit., ii, p. 365.

27. 12 April 1849, FS to Westmorland, RPP, 7/85.

28. 29 Jan 1842, FS to Richard, RPP, 9; (illegible) 1842, FS to Richard, ibid.; 7 Dec 1844 and 7 June 1845, FS to Richard, RPP, 9.

29. 14, 21 Dec 1845, FS to Charlotte, RPP, 5/35 and 37; 19 Dec 1850, FS to Charlotte, RPP, 5/63; 30 Jan 1843, FS to Charlotte, RPP, 5/20; 20 Nov 1843, FS to Kitty, RPP, 5/24; 17 Jan 1844, FS to Charlotte, RPP, 5/26; 28 Jan 1844, FS to Kitty, RPP, 5/27; 21 Feb 1848 and 7 Aug 1852, FS to Charlotte, RPP, 5/51 and 67; 5 Aug 1843, FS to Richard, RPP, 9.

30. Samples of hair from Lord and Lady FitzRoy at various times are contained in a packet marked Raglan K, RPP, 9.

31. 5 Dec 1842, 4 Mar 1843, 5 Aug 1843, FS to Richard, RPP, 9; 28 Jan 1844, FS to Kitty, RPP, 5/27; 24 Feb, 23 Mar, 24 June, 24 Oct 1845, FS to Richard, RPP, 9; 1 Aug 1854, FS to Charlotte, RPP, 5/30.

32. 3 Jan 1842, 31 Mar, 5 Aug, 5, 29 Dec 1843, 7 July 1844, 7 Mar, 7 May, 7 June 1845, 24 Dec 1846, FS to Richard, RPP, 9; 17 Jan 1844, FS to Angelina, RPP, 5/25.

33. 7 June 1844, 7 June, 24 Oct 1845, 3, 31 Jan 1842, FS to Richard, RPP, 9; 30 May 1842, Paget to Richard, RPP, 9; 8 Nov 1856, Gore to Richard, RPP, 9; Freemasonry certificate, RPP, 9: his grandfather, the 5th Duke of Beaufort, had been Grand Master of Freemasons 1767–72. Richard was formally engaged to Lady Georgiana on 31 July 1856.

34. 7 Nov 1845, 24 July 1845, 6 July 1843, 31 Aug 1842, 7 Mar 1845, FS to Richard, RPP, 9.

35. 3, 31 Jan, 4 July, 5 Dec 1842, 31 Mar 1843, 31 Mar 1844, FS to Richard, RPP, 9.

36. 7 Oct, 7 Dec 1844, 7, 23 Mar, 24 April, 7 June, 24 July, 7 Nov 1845, 7 Feb, 9 April, 7 May 1846, 6 Jan, 8 Mar 1847, FS to Richard, RPP, 9.

37. 4 Sept 1842, 6 Mar, 7 Sept 1844, 7 Feb 1846, FS to Richard, RPP, 9.

38. 4 Sept, 5 Dec 1842, 7 Aug, 7 Sept 1844, FS to Richard, RPP, 9.

39. 24 July 1845, FS to Richard, RPP, 9; Cruchley's New Plan of London and its Environs, PRO, FQ 925/4040: Great Stanhope Street is now called Stanhope Gate, and No 5 houses commercial businesses.

40. 5 Dec 1842, FS to Richard, RPP, 9; 8 Aug 1851, FS to Kitty, RPP, 5/56. Details of FS's financial transactions contained in 9 Mar 1955, Messrs Hoare to Julia, Lady Raglan, RPP, Misc Papers.

41. 5, 31 Dec 1842, 31 Mar, 8 May 1843, 6 Mar, 7 Aug 1844, 16 Jan, 24 Feb, 7 Mar 1845, FS to Richard, RPP, 9.

42. 1 Aug, 23, 27 Sept 1845, FS to Charlotte, RPP, 5/30, 32 and 33; 24 Aug 1845, FS to Wellington, RPP, 5; 29 July, 17 Nov 1847, FS to Charlotte, RPP, 5/46 and 48; 2 Aug 1849, FS to Kitty, RPP, 5/55; 25 Aug 1850, FS to Charlotte, RPP, 5/60.

43. 24 Oct 1842, FS to Charlotte, RPP, 5/15; 4 Nov 1843, 24 April 1845, FS to Richard, RPP, 9; 20 Aug 1850, FS to Anglesey, RPP, 5/58; 27 Nov 1850, FS to Charlotte, RPP, 5/62.

44. 31 Aug, 4 Sept 1842, 8 June, 24 July, 24 Sept, 27 Oct 1846, FS to Richard, RPP, 9; 27 Sept 1850, FS to Charlotte, RPP, 5/61; 2 June 1848, FS to Westmorland, RPP, 2/61.

45. 7 Feb, 24 Oct 1845, 7 Dec 1844, 27 Oct 1842, 5 Aug 1843, FS to Richard, RPP, 9.

46. 8, 16 Feb, 3 Mar, 12 April 1849, RPP, 2/69, 73, 81 and 85.

47. 5 Aug, 5 Dec 1843, 24 April, 24 Oct 1845, 7 Sept 1844, FS to Richard, RPP, 9. 'Lady Georgiana' may have been his brother John's daughter, who eventually married in 1854.

48. 29 Dec 1843, FS to Richard, RPP, 9; 14 Sept 1848, FS to Charlotte, RPP, 5/54; 13 Jan 1847, FS to Charlotte and Kitty, RPP, 5/44; 5 Oct 1842, FS to Egerton, RPP, 6; 29 Dec 1851, FS to Charlotte, RPP, 5/66.

49. Anon. *The King's Shropshire Light Infantry, 1755–1955*, 1955; Rogerson, W. *Historical Records of the 53rd (Shropshire) Regiment*, 1890, pp. 145–7; 5 April 1843, Metternich to FS, 6 May 1843, Wellington to FS and 12 May 1843, FS to Metternich, RPP, 1/170; *Annual Register*, 1855, pp. 287–8; 6 May 1848, Adolphus (Cambridge) to FS, RPP, 7.

50. 12 May 1843, Arthur to Kitty, RPP, Raglan H; 8 Aug 1843, Arthur to Richard, RPP, Raglan H; 31 Mar 1844, FS to Richard, RPP, 9.

51. 9 Jan, 1 May 1844, Arthur to Richard, RPP, Raglan H; 18 Mar 1844, Arthur to FS, noted in 5 May 1844, FS to Richard, RPP, 9; 7 June 1844, FS to Richard, RPP, 9; 14 April 1844, Arthur to FS received 5 June 1844; 7 July 1844, FS to Richard, noting 7 May 1844, Arthur to FitzRoy Somerset, RPP, 9.

52. 6 Mar, 6 May, 7 June 1844, FS to Richard, RPP, 9; 22 July 1844, Arthur to FS, noted in 7 Oct 1844, FS to Richard, RPP, 9.

53. 5 July, 1 Sept 1845, Arthur to Richard, RPP, Raglan J; 24 Oct 1845, FS to Richard, RPP, 9. Capt Dietrich George Alexander Frederich Henry Mellish, senior capt in the 10th Regt Lt Cav of the Bengal Presidency died at Meerut, the regiment's station, on 4 Oct 1844. Wood was commissioned on 30 Dec 1834, Arthur Somerset, 18 May 1832.

54. 5 Nov 1845, Arthur to FS, RPP, Raglan H/6; 30 Nov 1845, Arthur to Richard, RPP, Raglan H.

55. 24 Dec 1845, FS to Richard, RPP, 9.

56. 7 Feb 1846, FS to Richard, RPP, 9; 24 Feb 1846, FS to Richard, RPP, 3/174; 23 Dec 1845, Hardinge to FS, RPP, 3/171; 25, 30 Dec 1845, Gough to FS, RPP, 3/173; 27 Dec 1845, Hardinge to FS, RPP, 3/172.

57. Undated, Ryan to Sir John Macdonald, and undated, letter from Col Reed, 62nd Regt, RPP, Raglan H.

58. 17 Oct 1847, Hardinge to FS, RPP, Raglan H/9, enclosing Arthur Hardinge's testimony dated 16 Oct 1847.

59. Unsigned and undated account of Arthur's death, RPP, Raglan H/10; 5 May 1846, Cambridge to Charlotte, RPP, 6; 8 Mar 1846, FS to his nephew, Boscawen, RPP, 10.

60. Peel, 2 April 1846, Hansard, lxxxv, p. 446; Glenelg, 5 May 1846, Hansard, lxxxvi, p. 107.

61. 8 June, 24 Aug 1846, FS to Richard, RPP, 9; 7 Mar 1846, FS to Richard, RPP, 1/175: received 16 April, answered 22 April. 'Bob Wood' was probably Lt Col RB Wood.

62. 9 April, 7 May 1846, FS to Richard, RPP, 9; 8 May 1846, Richard to FS, RPP, Raglan H/12.

63. 8, 24 June, 24 July, 24 Aug, 5, 24 Sept, FS to Richard, RPP, 9; 27 Aug 1846, FS to Charlotte, RPP, 5/43; *Annual Register*, 1855, p. 288. Arthur's widow married Henry Boddington Webster on 19 Mar 1850 and died without issue on 25 Dec 1865, precisely 20 years after her second husband's death in India. Lord FitzRoy wrongly referred to Melfort's sister as 'Mrs Davis'.

64. 31 Dec 1845, Gladstone to FS, and 1 Jan 1846, FS to Gladstone, British Library (hereinafter BL) Add MS 44363; undated (1855), memo by Lady Westmorland, Weigall, op. cit., pp. 218–20. Lady Westmorland claimed that, from devotion to Wellington, he also turned down 'high situations in India [and] in Ireland.' Sir Charles Bagot died in office as Governor-General of Canada in 1843.

65. 15 Sept 1852, Charlotte to Beaufort, and 16 Sept 1852, FS to Beaufort, Bad Mun, Fm 3/4/1; 14, 16 Sept 1852, Lady Westmorland to Westmorland, Weigall, op. cit., pp. 202, 204; 28 Sept 1852, FS to Cambridge, RA Add. A8/909; RA QVJ: 16, 30 Oct 1852.

Chapter 7

1. 23 Sept 1852, FS to Richard, RPP, 3/184.

2. *USG*, 18 Sept 1852; 6 April 1850, Prince Albert in Wellington, enclosed in 22 Jan 1854, memo by Prince Albert, Aberdeen Papers, BL Add MS 43048; 17 Sept 1852, memo by Prince Albert, Benson and Esher, op. cit., ii, pp. 392 *et seq*.

3. *USG*, 18 Sept 1852.

4. 17 Sept 1852, memo by Prince Albert, Benson and Esher, op. cit., ii, pp. 392 *et seq*. Hardinge acted as second to Wellington in his duel with Lord Winchelsea in Battersea Fields, 21 Mar 1829, Colby, R. *The Waterloo Despatch*, 1965, p. 33; Percival, op. cit., p. 65.

5. 17 Sept 1852, Derby to FS, RPP, 7; RA QVJ: 21 Sept 1852; 22 Sept 1852, General Order, PRO, WO 43/152,444.

6. 23 Sept 1852, FS to Richard, RPP, 3/184; 22 Sept 1852, FS to Beaufort, Bad Mun, Fm 3/4/1.

7. *USG*, 18, 25 Sept 1852; Strachey, L. and Fulford, R. (eds.), *The Greville Memoirs 1814–1860*, iv, 1938, p. 365.

8. Ibid.; Ridley, J. *Lord Palmerston*, 1970, p. 98; 25 Sept 1852, Benjamin Hawes to FS, RPP, 3/185.

9. FO List, Jan 1856, RPP, 10/40; 23 Sept 1852, FS to Richard, RPP, 3/184; *USG*, 25 Sept 1852; *Army List*, 1853.

10. Anglesey, Marquis of. *One Leg, The Life and Letters of the First Marquis of Anglesey*, 1961, p. 387; *Army List*, 1853. For a summary of the work of the Master-General and Board of Ord, see Chapter 4 above.

11. 22 Sept 1852, Prince Albert to Derby, Benson

and Esher, op. cit., ii, p. 395; FO List, Jan 1856, RPP, 10/40; *History of Cefntilla*, p. 5; *TILN*, 5 Feb 1853; 30 Sept 1852, FS to the Marchioness of Cholmondeley, RPP, 3/186; 18 Oct 1852, Addington to Richard, RPP, 3/187.

12. 20 Nov 1852, Raglan to Marchioness of Cholmondely, RPP, 3/188. The Second Report from the Select Committee on Army and Ordnance Expenditure, 2 July 1849, estimated the gross Ord expenditure 1849–50 as £2,654,270 and detailed the barracks, PP, 1849, ix, pp. 5 *et seq*; Abstract of Returns of Troops, PP, 1852, xxx, 2; for added Ord responsibility in Britain, *see* Forbes, A. *A History of the Army Ordnance Services*, 1929, p. 189.

13. Cf., 7 Nov 1846, Burgoyne memo to Master-General, and 17 Dec 1846, Palmerston memo to Cabinet, quoted in Wrottesley, G. (ed.). *The Military Opinions of Sir John Fox Burgoyne*, 1873, i, pp. 434, 436; 9 Jan 1847, Wellington to Burgoyne, ibid., p. 444; 4 Jan 1848, Burgoyne memo to Master-General, ibid., p. 467; 29 May 1859, confidential memo by Burgoyne: 'Remarks on the Military Condition of Great Britain', Grey Papers; *see* also 13 June 1845, Sir Charles Napier, Hansard, lxxxi, p. 532; 22, 24 Jan 1851, Palmerston to Sir Charles Wood, Ashley, E. *The Life and Correspondence of Henry John Temple, Viscount Palmerston*, 1876, i, pp. 252, 253; 30 Aug 1852, Hardinge memo on coastal defences of Britain, PRO, WO 46/89/371.

14. 23 Oct 1852, Queen Victoria to Derby, Benson and Esher, op. cit., ii, p. 396; 8 Nov 1852, Prince Albert to Hardinge, ibid., p. 398; 31 Oct 1852, journal entry, Grey Papers, C 3/17; 16 Nov 1852, Grey to his brother Charles, ibid., F 7(i); 25 Nov 1852, Ord Minute, PRO, WO 46/43/9.

15. 29 Nov 1852, Raglan to Prince Albert, RA E44/61, enclosing a copy of his analysis, 20 Nov 1852, RA E44/62; 17 Jan 1853, Raglan to Prince Albert, RA E44/87.

16. *USG*, 18, 25 Dec 1852, 8, 12 Jan 1853, Burgoyne memo, Palmerston Papers, 'National Defences' file; Feb 1853, Herbert to Palmerston, quoted in Stanmore, op. cit., p. 180.

17. 23 Oct 1852, Queen Victoria to Derby, Benson and Esher, op. cit., ii, p. 396; 9 Jan 1853, Hardinge to Palmerston, Palmerston Papers; 10 Jan 1853, Palmerston to Aberdeen, and 10 Jan 1853, Aberdeen to Panmure, Aberdeen Papers, BL Add MS 43069; Hardinge, 7 April 1854, Hansard, cxxxii, p. 655; Sweetman, op. cit., p. 34.

18. *TILN*, 5 Feb 1853.

19. 13 Dec 1852, Ord Minute, PRO, WO 46/87/151; Devonport, 22 April, 4 May 1853, PRO, WO 46/43/65 and 70; 19 Oct 1852, Adj-Gen to Sec to Board of Ord, PRO, WO 3/318/288; 17 June 1853, Ord Minute, PRO, WO 46/43/90; Falmouth, 7 Mar 1853, Master-General to Sir Charles Lennon MP, PRO, WO 46/87/325; Western District, 18 Dec 1852, PRO, WO 46/43/13; Palmerston, 13 Jan 1853, noted in PRO, WO 46/87/216.

20. 1 Dec 1852, Master-General to Buccleuch, PRO, WO 46/87/117; 23 June 1853, Ord Minute, PRO, WO 46/43/93; Oct 1853, Ord report on North British forts, PRO, WO 44/277; Newhaven, 12 April 1853, PRO, WO 90/17; other southern ports, 23 May 1853, PRO, WO 90/101, 20 Sept 1852, PRO, WO 47/2745, and Feb 1854, PRO, WO 44/286; Channel Islands, PRO, WO 44/514, and PRO, WO 46/42/15; *USG*, 17 Dec 1853.

21. Hardinge, 29 June 1855, Hansard, cxxxvi, p. 1108; *USG*, 25 Dec 1852; Pechell, 7 Dec 1852, Hansard, cxxiii, p. 1088; Smith, ibid., p. 1019;

Hume, ibid., p. 1020; 15 July 1853, FS to Emily (his niece), RPP, 10.

22. Report from the Select Committee on Small Arms, PP, 1854, xviii, iii-iv; 25 April 1853, Adj-Gen to Sec to Board of Ord, PRO, WO 3/319/416; Anglesey, 20 May 1850, PRO, WO 43/92/120,486; Select Committee report, PP, 1849, ix, 28; 18 Mar 1852, Treasury to Sec at War, and 12 Dec 1852, Raglan to Hardinge, PRO, WO 46/88/148; 1853, Hardinge memo and 14 Feb 1853, Royal Warrant, ibid.

23. Cf., Hume, 28 Feb 1853, Hansard, cxxiv, p.1743, and 2 Mar 1854, Hansard, cxxxi, p. 223; Ord estimates, WO A Papers 1/53; Ord Minutes, 19 Jan, 7 Feb 1854, PRO, WO 47/2748.

24. *USG*, 1 Jan 1853; Report of the Select Committee on Small Arms, PP, 1854, xviii, iv *et seq* ; Treasury committee report, 17 Dec 1853, W(ar) O(ffice) A Papers 1/53; William Monsell, 27 Feb 1854, Hansard, cxxx, pp. 1393 *et seq* ; establishments noted in PRO, WO 43/103/159,744.

25. 29 Sept, 11 Oct 1852, 24 Jan 1853 (2), FS to Brown, Brown Papers, MS 1848, 79, 82A, 95 and 96; 11 Dec 1853, Brown in Hardinge, ibid., p. 176.

26. 'The Order of the Proceeding in the Public Funeral of the late Field-Marshal Arthur Duke of Wellington KG', RPP, Wellington C.

27. 21, 23 Nov 1853, Raglan to Charlotte, RPP, 6/79 and 80; 22 Nov 1853, Raglan to Priscilla, RPP, 7. Howe was the new Duke of Beaufort's father-in-law.

28. 31 Mar, 21 Nov, 14 Dec 1853, Raglan to Charlotte, RPP, 5/73, 79 and 81.

29. 12 Nov, 5 Dec 1853, Aberdeen to Lord John Russell, Aberdeen Papers, BL Add MS 43067; 6 Dec 1853, Aberdeen to Queen Victoria, ibid., Add MS 43048.

30. 13, 14 Jan, 24 Mar 1853, Raglan to Charlotte, RPP, 5/69, 72 and 70.

31. 20 Nov 1852, 14 Jan 1853, Raglan to Charlotte, RPP, 5/68 and 70.

32. 24 Mar, 17 Oct 1853, Raglan to Charlotte, RPP, 5/72 and 74. Both Raglan's father and younger son were Freemasons, see Chapter 6 above.

33. 31 Oct 1853, Raglan to Kitty, RPP, 5/75; 8 Nov 1853, Raglan to Charlotte and Kitty, RPP, 5/76; 9 Nov, 14 Dec 1853, Raglan to Charlotte, RPP, 5/78 and 81; copy of letter to *The Morning Chronicle*, RPP, 8/339.

34. Ibid.; *TILN*, 5 Feb 1853.

35. 29 Sept 1853, Aberdeen to Queen Victoria, Aberdeen Papers, BL Add MS 43047; 6 Oct 1853, Aberdeen to Queen Victoria, ibid.; 5 Oct 1853, Queen Victoria to Aberdeen, ibid.; 5, 10, 20 Nov 1853, Aberdeen to Queen Victoria, Aberdeen Papers, BL Add MS 43048.

36. Dec 1853 (undated but after 19 Dec), Queen Victoria to Aberdeen, Benson and Esher, op. cit., ii, p. 469.

Chapter 8

1. 22 Aug 1854, Raglan to Richard, RPP, 7/208.

2. 24 Dec 1853, Clarendon to Lord Stratford, government instructions to the fleet, quoted in Temperley, H. *England and the Near East: the Crimea*, 1936, p. 378.

3. Burgoyne left England on 28 Jan 1854 and returned on 7 April, 22 April, 1855, Burgoyne to Newcastle, Newcastle Papers, NeC 10315; 18 Jan 1854, Graham to Burgoyne, 22 Jan 1854, Burgoyne to Graham, and 26 Jan 1854, Graham to

Raglan, Wrottesley, op. cit., ii, pp. 2, 5.

4. 24 Dec 1853, Graham to Dundas, quoted in Lambert, A. *The Crimean War: British Grand Strategy against Russia, 1853–6*, 1990, p. 64; ibid., pp. 65–71; 12 Jan 1854, Graham to Raglan, and 20 Jan 1854, Burgoyne to Graham, quoted in Conacher, J. *The Aberdeen Coalition, 1852–1855*, Cambridge, 1968, pp. 251–4; 14 Jan 1854, Newcastle to Lord John Russell, Russell Papers, PRO, 30/22/11C.

5. *The Morning Chronicle*, 15 Feb 1854; 9 Nov 1857, Westmorland to Fortescue, reprinted for *USG*, RPP, 10; *TILN*, 5 Feb 1853; Feb 1854, Hardinge to Newcastle, Newcastle Papers, NeC 10,058; extract from *The Morning Chronicle*, undated, RPP, 8/339; *The United Service Magazine* (hereinafter *USM*), Aug 1855, recalling its declared position of early 1854; Kinglake, op. cit., ii, pp. 18–21.

6. Fortescue, op. cit., p. 226; 9 Nov 1857, Westmorland to Fortescue, RPP, 10; 15 Feb 1854, Lady Westmorland to Comtess Pauline Néale (a Prussian confidante), Weigall, op. cit., p. 191; 27 Feb 1854, Lady Westmorland to Revd W. Hood (former tutor to her children), ibid., p. 192; 19 Feb 1854, Newcastle to Queen Victoria, Newcastle Papers, NeC 9785; 8 Feb 1855, Hardinge to Newcastle, RA G10/3; 18 Feb 1854, court-martial authority, RMP 6807/280; extract from FO List, Jan 1856, RPP, 10/4; Martineau, J. *The Life of Henry Pelham, Fifth Duke of Newcastle, 1811–1864*, 1908, p. 136.

7. Kennaway, op. cit., p. 18; 21 Feb 1854, Cambridge to Richard, RPP, 10/29; 12 Feb 1854, Hardinge to Newcastle, Newcastle Papers, NeC 10,061. On 2 Aug 1854, Hansard, cxxxv, p. 1179, Capt Laffan claimed that Burgoyne had been actively considered as second in command.

8. 8, 10 Feb 1854, Newcastle to Queen Victoria, Newcastle Papers, NeC 9785; 10 Feb 1854, Newcastle to Hardinge, ibid., 10,059c.

9. Commissariat Minute, 17 Feb 1854, PRO, WO 59/75/3294; 20 Feb 1854, Trevelyan to Raglan, informing him of Filder's appointment, RMP 6807/290; 15 Feb 1854, Lady Raglan to Westmorland, RPP, 7; *The Morning Herald*, 15 Feb 1854; Cambridge quoted in Sheppard, E (ed.), *George, Duke of Cambridge*, 1906, i, p. 114; RA QVJ: 13 Feb 1854; Cardigan, Earl of. *Eight Months of Active Service*, 1855, p. 3.

10. Staff establishment, 21 Feb 1854, RMP 6807/280; 7 Mar 1854, de Ros to Raglan, RMP 6807/292; 17 Feb 1854, Estcourt to his brother Tom, Estcourt Papers, D 1571/33. Once an expedition was mounted, its senior administrative staff mirrored the Horse Guards with the commander having his own Mil Sec, Quart-Gen and Adj-Gen fulfilling a similar range of duties on campaign. Burghersh was Lady Westmorland's son; Poulett Somerset the son of Raglan's brother Charles by his second wife; Somerset Calthorpe the son of Charlotte, daughter of Raglan's brother Henry (6th Duke of Beaufort) and Nigel Kingscote, her sister Arabella's son. Leicester Curzon was the son of Earl Howe by Harriet, Lord Cardigan's sister, and Curzon's sister married Nigel Kingscote in 1856. Cardigan therefore had a nephew at Raglan's headquarters in the Crimea. Another of Curzon's sisters, Georgiana, married Raglan's nephew (later 8th Duke of Beaufort), so Leicester Curzon was distantly related to Raglan.

11. Undated, Hardinge to Newcastle, Newcastle Papers, NeC 10,075; 13 Mar 1854, Newcastle to Ellenborough, Ellenborough Papers, PRO,

30/12/18; Martineau, op. cit., pp. 136–7: 'My authority for this statement (about Lucan and Cardigan) is General the Hon. Somerset Gough Calthorpe, who had it from Lord Raglan himself', ibid., p. 137n. The usual practice for the appointment of generals of divisions and brigades was for Hardinge to consult Raglan, then submit names to Newcastle for the Government's approval, before (as CinC) sending them to the Queen for her sanction.

12. 21 Feb 1854, Raglan to Queen Victoria, RA B13/19; 15 Feb 1854, Lady Raglan to Westmorland, RPP, 7.

13. 1, 8 Feb 1854, Cambridge to Richard, RPP, 10/27 and 28; 3 Feb 1854, de Redcliffe to Clarendon, RMP 6807/291; 24 Feb 1854, memo by Rose, ibid. Interestingly, in 1828 Lt-Col George de Lacy Evans (one of Raglan's divisional commanders in the Crimea) had written *The Design of Russia*, in which he forecast need for military and naval action against Sevastopol.

14. Brown to Airey, Brown Papers, MS 1849; de Ros note, 31 Jan 1854, RMP 6807/291; 25 Feb 1854, Addington to Raglan, enclosing Macintosh's memo of 9 Jan 1854, RMP 6807/280: Lambert, op. cit., p. 85, notes Raglan in Paris 26–8 Feb 1854.

15. Aberdeen, 10 Feb 1854, Hansard, cxxx, pp. 395–6; Chesney, K. *Crimean War Reader*, 1960, pp. 16–19; 24 Feb 1854, Queen Victoria to Aberdeen, BL Add MS 43048; 24 Feb 1854, Aberdeen to Queen Victoria, ibid.

16. *Gentleman's Magazine*, Aug 1854; *The Times*, 28 Mar 1854.

17. *Life of Lord Raglan*, pp. 30–1; 7, 11 Feb 1854, Raglan to Gladstone Papers, BL Add MS 44377; 14 Feb 1854, Dep Adj-Gen to Sec Board of Ord, PRO, WO 3/322/97. Raglan was so busy that he did not attend farewell dinners, such as that arranged at Boodle's on 4 Mar, to which Cambridge and Cardigan went, Thomas, op. cit., p. 182.

18. 13 Feb 1854, Newcastle to Queen Victoria, Newcastle Papers, NeC 9785; 2 Aug 1854, debate on the Ord estimates, Hansard, cxxxv, pp. 1175 *et seq*; Kennaway, op. cit., p. 102n. In her journal, Queen Victoria merely recorded: 'Lord Raglan has accepted command of the whole expedition but will not at present give up his command at the Ordnance', RA QVJ: 13 Feb 1854.

19. 10 Mar 1854, Foreign Office to Raglan, RMP 6807/290; 27 Mar 1854, Athens consul to Raglan, RMP 6807/302; 29 Mar 1854, Cowley to Clarendon, RMP 6807/294; 30, 31 Mar 1854, Newcastle to Raglan, WO 6/69/12 and 13.

20. 2 Mar 1854, de Redcliffe to Raglan, RMP 6807/292; 11 Mar 1854, Cowley to Clarendon (and copy Clarendon to Raglan, 15 Mar 1854), RMP 6807/294.

21. 3 Mar 1854, Raglan to de Redcliffe, RMP 6807/292; 8 Mar 1854, Burgoyne to Raglan, Newcastle Papers, NeC 10308; 16 Mar 1854, Prince Albert to Newcastle, ibid., NeC 9687; 10 Mar 1854, Burgoyne to Lt-Col (later Col) E. Matson, Ass Adj-Gen to the Corps of Royal Engineers, Wrottesley, op. cit., ii, p. 16; 22 Mar 1854, Burgoyne to de Redcliffe, ibid., p. 20.

22. 17 Mar 1854, Newcastle to Raglan, PRO, WO 6/69/4; Chesney, op. cit., p. 71.

23. 22 Mar 1854, Newcastle to Queen Victoria, Newcastle Papers, NeC 9785; 21 Mar 1854, Newcastle to Lt-Gen Sir George Brown and copy to Raglan, PRO, WO 6/69; 29 Mar 1854, Newcastle

to Fergusson, ibid. Each infantry division comprised two brigades of three regiments (each nominally 1,000 men in a single battalion) and thus totalled 6,000 infanteers, exclusive of attached specialist troops such as engineers and gunners. Each cavalry regiment had an establishment of 150 men.

24. Brown, G. *Memoranda and Observations on the Crimean War, 1854–5,* 1879, pp. 7, 10; 24, 27, 30 Mar 1854, Brown to Raglan, and 29 Mar 1854, Raglan to Brown, RMP 6807/292.
25. April 1854, Adj-Gen's list of staff officers, RMP 6807/280; 22 Mar 1854, commission contained, RMP 6807/280; 6 Mar 1854, Kirkland to Raglan, RMP 6807/305.
26. 19 Mar 1854, Raglan to Countess of Westmorland, RPP, 7.
27. 2 Mar 1854, Raglan to Cowley, RMP 6807/294; 12 Mar 1854, treaty noted, RMP 6807/281; 29 Mar 1854, Cowley to Clarendon, RMP 6807/294.
28. *Annual Register,* 1854, pp. 54–5 and App 531–2; *The London Gazette,* 28 Mar 1854; *The Times,* 28 Mar 1854; Conacher, op. cit., p. 281. News of the declaration of war was greeted by the British Black Sea fleet with six cheers, Wood, E. *The Crimea in 1854 and 1894,* 1895, p. 5.
29. 5 April 1854, Raglan's letter of appointment, WO A Papers 14/55; 5 April 1854, Hardinge to Raglan, RMP 6807/289.
30. 10 April 1854, Newcastle to Raglan, PRO, WO 6/69/22; 10 April 1854 (secret) Newcastle to Raglan, PRO, WO 6/74/1: a copy is also contained in RA G12/5. Newcastle listed the units and the total number of men, exclusive of siege train and ambulance corps, as 26,006 rank and file plus officers (c.30,000 in all).
31. Kinglake, op. cit., ii, pp. 24–9; 20 April 1854, Duchess of Gloucester to Lady Westmorland, Weigall, op. cit., p. 201; 11 April 1854, Cambridge to his mother, RA Add. A8/150; 11 April 1854, Raglan to Hardinge, RMP 6807/289; 17 April 1854, Raglan to Richard, RPP, 7/192; 13 April 1854, Raglan to Ross, RMP 6807/289. Because of the presence of Cambridge the visit to Paris was very much a royal occasion. Much of the pomp would not have been staged for Raglan alone.
32. 13 April 1854, Newcastle to Raglan, Newcastle Papers, NeC 9973; 13 April 1854, Newcastle to Queen Victoria, ibid., NeC 9785.
33. 21 April 1854, Raglan to Countess of Westmorland, RPP, 7; 14 April 1854, Raglan to Brown, RMP 6807/292. Interestingly, having met them in Dresden en route to Vienna, Cambridge observed that the Saxon royal family were 'very affable, but [they] are terribly pro-Russian', 25 April 1854, Cambridge to his mother, RA Add. A8/152.
34. Simpson, op. cit., p. 136; Lambert, op. cit., p. 106; 25 April 1854, Raglan to Cowley, RMP 6807/291; 30 April 1854, Kingscote to Richard, RPP, 7/193. HMS *Caradoc,* an 'iron paddle gunboat' built in 1847, mounted a single 2pdr gun, Colledge, J. *Ships of the Royal Navy,* Newton Abbot, 1969. Once repaired *Caradoc* was sent by Raglan to convey the Duke of Cambridge, after his diversion to Vienna, from Corfu to Turkey, 6 May 1854, Cambridge to his mother, RA Add. A8/154. Simpson, op. cit., p. 136, claims that the Sultan offered Raglan a palace overlooking the Bosporus, subsequently occupied by Prince Napoleon, the emperor's cousin; but Raglan opted to cross to Scutari.
35. *The Times,* 5 May 1854; 30 April 1854, Kingscote

to Richard, RPP, 7/193.
36. 15 April 1854, Newcastle to Raglan, PRO, WO 6/69/35; 10 April 1854, Smith to Trevelyan, Newcastle Papers, NeC 10511b; 17 April 1854, de Redcliffe to Raglan, RMP 6807/291.
37. Lambert, op. cit., pp. 101–2; 11 April 1854, Burgoyne to Raglan, Newcastle Papers, NeC 10310b, quoting Tylden; 20 April 1854, Prince Albert to Newcastle, Newcastle Papers, NeC 9689; 27 Mar 1854, Athens consul to Raglan, and 10 April 1854, Raglan to Athens consul, RMP 6807/302; 30 April 1854, de Fonblanque to Raglan, ibid.
38. 12 April 1854, Raglan to Kitty, RPP, 5/82; 17 April 1854, Raglan to Richard, RPP, 7/192; 21 April 1854, Raglan to Priscilla, RPP, 7; 10 April 1854, Raglan to Emily, RPP, 9; undated (1855), memo by Lady Westmorland, Weigall, op. cit., pp. 217–18.
39. 17 April 1854, Burgoyne to Raglan, Newcastle Papers, NeC 10311a; 30 April 1854, General Order No 1, Gordon, A (ed.), *General Orders issued to the Army of the East 30 April 1854 – 31 December 1855,* 1856.
40. 1 May 1854, Burgoyne to Raglan, RMP 6807/292; MacMunn, G. *The Crimea in Perspective,* 1935, p. 32; 13 April 1854, Rose to Raglan, RMP 6807/294; Kinglake, op. cit., ii, pp. 33–40; 15 May 1854, Raglan to Newcastle, RMP 6807/284; 23 May 1854, de Redcliffe to Raglan, RMP 6807/291; 29 May 1854, Raglan to Newcastle, RMP 6807/284.
41. 3 May 1854, Raglan to Charlotte, RPP, 5/194; 24 May diary entry, McMillan, op. cit., p. 12; 27 May 1854, Raglan to Newcastle, RA G13/51.
42. 1 May 1854, General Order, PRO, WO 28/47/1; 2 May 1854, Raglan to Newcastle, RMP 6807/289; 13 May 1854, Raglan to Monsell, RMP 6807/289; 13 May 1854, Boxer to Capt Christie, copied to Raglan, RMP 6807/300; 22 May 1854, Boxer's warrant, RMP 6807/300; 30 May 1854, Kingscote to Richard, RPP, 7/195.
43. 1 May 1854 (completed 5 May), Raglan to Charlotte, RPP, 7/194.
44. Ibid.; 30 May 1854, Kingscote to Richard, RPP, 7/195. In contrast to Raglan's accommodation, Cambridge had 'a fine castle' placed at his disposal, which Stratford de Redcliffe declared it 'necessary' for him to accept, 10 May 1854, Cambridge to his mother, RA Add. A8/155. William Cator was FS's contemporary at Westminster.
45. 19 May 1854, Simmons to Raglan, RMP 6807/295; 25 May 1854, Raglan to Hardinge, RMP 6807/289.
46. 30 May 1854, Kingscote to Richard, RPP, 7/195. Omar Pasha was born Michael Lattas, the Greek Orthodox son of a Croatian soldier in the Austrian Army. Later converted to Mohammedism, he joined the Turkish Army, commanded forces in Moldavia and Wallachia 1848–9 and in 1852–3 operated against Christian rebels in Montenegro.
47. 25 May 1854, Raglan to Hardinge, RMP 6807/289; McMillan, op. cit., p. 12; 27 May 1854, Raglan to Newcastle, RA G13/51.
48. 8 May 1854, Hardinge to Queen Victoria, RA B13/77; 16 May 1854, appointment to be colonel of The Blues from 8 May, RPP, 10.
49. 1 May 1854, Raglan to Charlotte, RPP, 7/194.
50. 10, 30 May 1854, Cambridge to his mother, RA Add. A8/156 and 157. Cambridge would endure a lengthy illness two months later in Bulgaria and effectively suffer a nervous breakdown after the Battle of Inkerman (Nov 1854), not finally aban-

doning plans to return to the front until Jan 1855. During these periods Raglan remained solicitous: cf., 30 Nov 1854, Cambridge to his mother, RA Add. A8/172: 'My nerves ... are still affected', and similarly on 7 Jan 1855, RA Add. A8/176, he made further allusion to 'my nerves'.

51. 24 June 1854, Raglan to Newcastle, RMP 6807/282.

52. 8 June 1854, Newcastle to Raglan, PRO, WO 6/69/94; 14 June 1854, Raglan to Boxer, RMP 6807/300; 29 June 1854, de Redcliffe to Boxer, RMP 6807/300; 29 June 1854, de Redcliffe to Raglan, RMP 6807/291; 29 June 1854, War Office to Admiralty, PRO, WO 6/76.

53. 9 June 1854, Raglan to Kitty, RPP, 7/196; 20 June 1854, Raglan to Richard, RPP, 7/198.

54. Kinglake, op. cit., ii, pp. 40 et seq; 5 June 1854, Raglan to Newcastle, RMP 6807/284; 8 June 1854, Raglan to Newcastle, ibid.; 23 June 1854, Newcastle to Raglan, PRO, WO 6/69/102.

55. 20 June 1854, Raglan to Richard, RPP, 7/198; 23 June 1854, Raglan to Charlotte, RPP, 7/199. 18 June 1854, Cambridge to his mother likewise dubbed Varna 'a dreadful place', RA Add. A8/160.

56. 23 June 1854, Raglan to Charlotte, RPP, 7/199.

57. Woodham-Smith, op. cit., pp. 150 et seq; 2 June 1854, Lucan to Cardigan, quoted ibid., p. 151; 11 June 1854, Lucan to Cardigan, quoted ibid., 155; 15 June 1854, Cardigan to Lucan, quoted ibid., p. 158; 20 June 1854, Estcourt to Lucan, quoted ibid., 159; 22 June 1854, Lucan to Estcourt, quoted ibid., p. 159; 28 June 1854, Kingscote to Kitty, RPP, 7/201.

58. Sweetman, op. cit., p. 118; 13 June 1854, Newcastle to Raglan, NeC 9973; Newcastle, 26 Jan 1855, Hansard, cxxxvi, p. 959; 1 June 1854, Drummond to Grey, Grey Papers; 5 June 1854, Grey to Drummond, ibid.; 15 June 1854, Raglan to Priscilla, RPP, 7; 28 June 1854, Newcastle to Raglan, PRO, WO 6/69/106.

59. 24 June 1854, Omar Pasha to Raglan, RMP 6807/295; 27 June 1854, Raglan to Kitty, RPP, 7/200; 29 June 1854, Cambridge to Duchess of Gloucester, Sheppard, op. cit., p. 130.

60. 27 June 1854, Wood to Grey, Grey Papers; cf., The Times, 15 and 22 June 1854; 8 June 1854, Newcastle to Raglan, Newcastle Papers, NeC 9973; 29 June 1854, memo by Prince Albert, ibid., NeC 9694b.

61. 29 June 1854, Aberdeen to Queen Victoria, Aberdeen Papers, BL Add MS 43049; Kinglake, op. cit., ii, pp. 93 et seq; 29 June 1854, Newcastle to Raglan, PRO, WO 6/74/5.

62. 10 June 1854, Kingscote to Richard, RPP, 7/197; 28 June 1854, Kingscote to Kitty, RPP, 7/201; 27 June 1854, Wood to Grey, Grey Papers; 29 June 1854, Cowley to Raglan, RMP 6807/294.

63. McMillan, op. cit., pp. 12–15; 27 June 1854, Raglan to Kitty, RPP, 7/200; 26 June 1854, Raglan to Cardigan, RMP 6807/292; 30 June 1854, Cardigan to Raglan, ibid.

64. The New York Tribune, 9 June 1854; 15 June 1854, Raglan to Priscilla, RPP, 7; 26 June 1854, Westmorland to Raglan, RMP 6807/295; 28 June 1854, Baron de Hess to Raglan, ibid.

65. 5 June 1854, Raglan to Charlotte, RPP, 5/83; 9 June 1854, Raglan to Kitty, RPP, 7/196.

66. 20 June 1854, Raglan to Richard, RPP, 7/198; 23 June 1854, Raglan to Charlotte, RPP, 7/199; 27 June 1854, Raglan to Kitty, RPP, 7/200; 28 June 1854, Bellerophon concert programme, RPP, 10.

The regular dispatch of £50 to Richard mirrored the same sum sent to Raglan's brother Edward by his father: cf., 19 Jan and 18 April 1896, Bad Mun, Fm L 5/2.

67. 15 June 1854, Raglan to Priscilla, RPP, 7.

68. 30 June, 3, 11 July 1854, Cardigan to Raglan, RMP 6807/292; July 1854, Raglan to Cardigan, quoted in Eight Months of Active Service, op. cit., p. 4. Correspondence with Cambridge, including such matters as the Duke's health, sickness among his troops and the acquisition of forage, show that Raglan was similarly concerned about the condition of all his subordinate commands. No wonder that Raglan excused himself from visiting Cambridge on 4 Aug, as he was 'very busy'; 27, 30 July, 1, 5 Aug 1854, RA Add. E1/177, 180, 181 and 182.

69. Cardigan conversation, Duberly, op. cit., p. 57; 28 June 1854, Newcastle to Raglan, RMP 6807/283; 14 July 1854, Raglan to Newcastle, Newcastle Papers, NeC 9796; 19 July 1854, journal entry, Calthorpe, S. Letters from Headquarters, By an officer on the staff, 1856, i, p. 93; 29 June 1854, Newcastle to Raglan, RMP 6807/281; Kinglake, op. cit., ii, pp. 101 et seq; 3, 18 July 1854, Newcastle to Raglan, Newcastle Papers, NeC 9973.

70. Kinglake, op. cit., ii, pp. 100 et seq; 14 July 1854, Raglan to Cowley and Cowley to Raglan, RMP 6807/294; 12 July 1854, Raglan to Charlotte and Kitty, RPP, 7/204; 26 July 1854, Simmons to Raglan, RMP 6807/295; 28 July 1854, Raglan to de Redcliffe, concerning warning to Omar Pasha, RMP 6807/291; 29 July 1854, Kingscote to Richard, RPP, 7/206.

71. Kinglake, op. cit., ii, pp. 123–5; 18 July 1854, Raglan to de Redcliffe, RMP 6807/291.

72. 14, 29 July 1854, Newcastle to Raglan, PRO, WO 6/69/144 and 129; 17 July 1854, Newcastle to Raglan, RMP 6807/281.

73. 28 July 1854, Burgoyne memo quoted in Wrottesley, op. cit., ii, pp. 58–60; 29 July 1854, Tylden to Burgoyne, quoted ibid., pp. 52–3; 24 July 1854, Cambridge to his mother, RA Add. A8/164. Cambridge was, as a lt-gen, 'employed on a particular service under the command of Gen the Rt Hon Lord Raglan GCB, with two paid Aides de Camp and an Extra unpaid Aide de Camp'. He was to 'obey such orders as you shall receive from Her Majesty, the General Commanding in Chief, or any other [of] your superior officers', 28 July 1854, Sidney Herbert to Cambridge, RA Add. El/178.

74. Kinglake, op. cit., ii, pp. 125–7; 23 or 24 July, Clifford diary entry, Fitzherbert, C. (ed.). Henry Clifford VC: his letters and sketches from the Crimea, 1956, p. 40; 29 July 1854, Kingscote to Richard, RPP, 7/206; 29 July 1854, Kingscote to Kitty, RPP, 7/207; 29 July 1854, Raglan to Newcastle (secret), RMP 6807/182.

75. 27 July 1854, Clifford diary entry, Fitzherbert, op. cit., p. 42; Kinglake, op. cit., ii, pp. 127–132; 31 July 1854, Newcastle to Queen Victoria, Newcastle Papers, NeC 9785; 29 July 1854, Cambridge to the Duchess of Gloucester (his aunt), Sheppard, op. cit., pp. 131; 18 July 1854, de Redcliffe to Raglan, RMP 6807/291.

76. 29 July 1854, Cattley memo, RMP 6807/301.

77. 14 July 1854, Estcourt to Henry Addington, Estcourt Papers, D 1571/32/17; 14 July 1854, Brown to Raglan, Brown Papers, MS 1849; The Daily News, 10 July 1854; 24 July 1854, Raglan to Newcastle, RMP 6807/282; 13 July 1854, Monsell to

Raglan, RMP 6807/289; 27 July 1854, Raglan to Monsell, RMP 6807/289; 6 July 1854, General Order, Gordon, op. cit.; 31 July 1854, Filder to Raglan, RMP 6807/293. A broadsheet printed in Newcastle-upon-Tyne by J. Todd on 25 July 1854, made an interesting but unsubstantiated claim: 'Lord Raglan's life has been attempted. The assassin, a Greek who fired at him, has been shot, and four of his companions were flogged then discharged', John Johnson Collection, 1f. If this incident has any basis, the Greeks might have been disaffected transport drivers. Quoting French Sources, Gooch, B., *The New Bonapartist Generals in the Crimean War*, 1959, p.91. dismisses reports of the episode as 'unfounded rumours'.

78. Sickness figures, 9–15 and 23–29 July 1854, RMP 6807/293; 21 July 1854, Col Cobbe to Raglan from Gallipoli, RMP 6807/305; 25 July 1854, Raglan to Cardigan, RMP 6807/292; 24 July 1854, Airey to Raglan, RMP 6807/292. Cambridge had been plagued with gout for some time, at one stage being confined to bed for a fortnight: 19, 30 Aug 1854, 7 Jan 1855, Cambridge to his mother, RA Add. A8/167 and 168; 30 July, 1 Aug 1854, Raglan to Cambridge, RA Add. E1/180 and 181.

79. 19, 26 July 1854, Raglan to de Redcliffe, RMP 6807/291; 19 July 1854, Raglan to Newcastle, RMP 6807/182.

80. 29 July 1854, Kingscote to Richard, RPP, 7/206; 1 July 1854, Raglan memo, RMP 6807/280; troop dispositions in July 1854 shown in Sayer, F. (ed.). *Campaign in Turkey, Asia Minor and the Crimea, 1854-6, Despatches and Papers*, 1857, App.

81. 15 July 1854, Raglan to de Redcliffe, RMP 6807/291; 14 July 1854, Estcourt to his brother Henry, Estcourt Papers, D 1571/33; 2 July 1854, Raglan to Trevelyan, RMP 6807/290; *Life of Lord Raglan*, p. 33.

82. 10 July 1854, Omar Pasha to Raglan, RMP 6807/295; 12 July 1854, Raglan to Charlotte and Kitty, RPP, 7/204; 21 July 1854, Raglan to de Redcliffe, RMP 6807/291; Herbert, 2 Mar 1854, Hansard, cxxxi, p. 240 and 17 July 1854, Hansard, cxxv, pp. 335–6.

83. 29 July 1854, Kingscote to Richard, RPP, 7/206; 29 July 1854, Kingscote to Kitty, RPP, 7/207.

84. 4 Aug 1854, Raglan to Priscilla, RPP, 7; 9 Aug 1854, Cowley to Raglan, RMP 6807/294; 5 Aug 1854, Raglan to Cambridge, RA Add. E1/182; 19 Aug 1854, Raglan to Priscilla, RPP, 7; Conacher, op. cit., p. 434; *The Times*, 5 Aug 1854; 22 Aug 1854, Raglan to Richard, RPP, 7/208.

85. 3, 15, 17 Aug 1854, Newcastle to Raglan, Newcastle Papers, NeC 9973; 15 Aug 1854, Newcastle to Raglan, PRO, WO 6/74.

86. Lambert, op. cit., pp. 117–18; 22 Aug 1854, Burgoyne to Col Sandham, RE (Dep Insp-Gen of Fortifications); Wrottesley, op. cit., ii, p. 64; 29 Aug 1854, Burgoyne memo, ibid., p. 69.

87. 9 Aug 1854, Cambridge to Duchess of Gloucester, Sheppard, op. cit., p. 131; 10 Aug 1854, Tylden to Raglan, Wrottesley, ii, p. 55; 20 Aug 1854, Tylden to Matson, ibid., p. 53; 29 Aug 1854, de Ros to Raglan, RMP 6807/292.

88. Aug sickness figures, RMP 6807/293; MacMunn, op. cit., p. 48; 22 Aug 1854, Raglan to Richard, RPP, 7/208; 21 Aug 1854, Raglan to de Redcliffe, RMP 6807/291.

89. 29 Aug 1854, Raglan to Charlotte, RPP, 7/210; 29 Aug 1854, Kingscote to Kitty, RPP, 7/211; 20, 29 Aug 1854, de Redcliffe to Raglan, RMP 6807/292.

90. 3 Aug 1854, Col Mundy to Trevelyan, RMP 6807/301; Cattley's activities summarized 20 Sept 1854–21 June 1855, RMP 6807/301; 25 Aug 1854, de Redcliffe to Raglan, RMP 6807/291.

91. 20, 29 Aug 1854, de Ros to Raglan, RMP 6807/292; 24 Aug 1854, Raglan to Charlotte and Kitty, RPP, 7/209.

92. Ibid.; 4, 19 Aug 1854, Raglan to Priscilla, RPP, 7.

93. 22 Aug 1854, Raglan to Richard, RPP, 7/208; 24 Aug 1854, Raglan to Charlotte and Kitty, RPP, 7/209; 29 Aug 1854, Raglan to Charlotte, RPP, 7/210.

94. 16 Aug 1854, Aberdeen to Queen Victoria, RA A23/136, recommended that the offer of Cowes Castle be made forthwith because 'in the event of success attending the great operation in which Your Majesty's troops are now engaged, Lord Raglan would probably receive some more signal mark of Your Majesty's favour'; 17 Aug 1854, Aberdeen to Raglan, RMP 6807/290; 24 Aug 1854, Raglan to Charlotte and Kitty, RPP, 7/209.

95. Kinglake, op. cit., ii, p. 137.

96. Ibid., pp. 138 *et seq*; McMillan, op. cit., pp. 18–19; 29 Aug 1854, Kingscote to Kitty, RPP, 7/211; 24 Aug 1854, Raglan to Charlotte and Kitty, RPP, 7/209.

97. 22 Aug 1854, Newcastle to Raglan, Newcastle Papers, NeC 9973; 4 Sept 1854, Cambridge to his mother, RA Add. A8/169.

Chapter 9

1. 18 Nov 1854, Queen Victoria to Raglan, Benson and Esher, op. cit., iii, p. 52.

2. Kinglake, op. cit., ii, pp. 140–1; *TILN*, 23 Sept 1854.

3. Kinglake, op. cit., ii, pp. 142–9; 7 Sept 1854, St Arnaud to Raglan, RMP 6807/294. The bulk of the Allied armada appears to have left Balchik 6–7 Sept. The Duke of Cambridge sailed in *Triton* on Wednesday 6 Sept, anchoring at the rendezvous on Saturday the 9th at 6 p.m. and remaining there during Sunday: 13 Sept 1854, Cambridge to his mother, RA Add. A8/170.

4. Kinglake, op. cit., ii, pp. 151–7. Later Raglan revealed that St Arnaud had a long-standing heart condition, 'was attacked by it more than once when at Varna', and suffered 'greatly' during the crossing of the Black Sea so 'as to be unable to reconnoitre the coast with me', 24 Aug 1854, Raglan to Lady Westmorland, quoted in Simpson, op. cit., p. 245b.

5. Kinglake, op. cit., ii, pp. 157–8; Lambert, op. cit., p. 120; 12 Sept 1854, Raglan to de Redcliffe, RMP 6807/291; McMillan, op. cit., p. 19; Calthorpe, op. cit., i, p. 131; Hardinge, quoted in Hardinge, Viscount. *Viscount Hardinge*, 1891, p. 186; 23 Sept 1854, Hardinge to Airey, Airey Papers, G/IV/A/385. Lambert, op. cit., p. 120, puts Raglan's return to the armada at 7.10 a.m. on 11 Sept, though Kinglake, op. cit., ii, p. 158, gives 'the night' of 10/11 September.

6. McMillan, op. cit., p. 19; Kinglake, op. cit., ii, pp. 159–60; 13 Sept 1854, Cambridge to his mother, RA Add. A8/170; Lambert, op. cit., p. 120, puts the fleet's departure from the RV on 12 September at precisely 3.50 a.m. Duberly, op. cit., p. 77, observed that as ships left the RV, Odessa or Sevastopol was the expected detination.

7. Kinglake, op. cit., ii, p. 163; Lambert, op. cit., p. 120.

8. Kinglake, op. cit., ii, pp. 167–73; McMillan, op.

cit., diary entries 14–18 Sept 1854, pp. 19–20; 'Notes added to the Second and Third Editions of Mr Kinglake's History of the Invasion of the Crimea', RPP, 8. The British landing orders were reproduced in full in *The Glasgow Herald*, 20 Sept 1954.

9. Hibbert, op. cit., p. 44; Kinglake, op. cit., ii, pp. 182–3, 190.

10. Ibid., pp. 192, 200, 202–8; St Arnaud quoted in *DNB* (FS entry); 23 Sept 1854, Raglan's dispatch quoted in *The Times*, 9 Oct 1854.

11. Kinglake, op. cit., ii, pp. 211–15; Kinglake, 'Notes on Second and Third editions', op. cit., RPP, 8; *The Times*, 9 Oct 1854; McMillan, op. cit., p. 20.

12. Kinglake, op. cit., ii, pp. 216–18; General Order, 19 Sept 1854, RA G17/21.

13. Lambert, op. cit., p. 122; Kinglake, op. cit., ii, pp. 219–26.

14. Ibid., pp. 227–37: precise figures are impossible to define, because of constant losses through death and sickness on the march from Calamita Bay. Prior to the landing on 14 Sept, the Duke of Cambridge had expressed fears that the purpose and destination of the armada could not be concealed and that the Russians would oppose the landing. They had not done so, but these strong defensive positions proved his point, 13 Sept 1854, Cambridge to his mother, RA Add. A8/170.

15. Kinglake, op. cit., ii, pp. 240–8; Jocelyn, J. *The History of the Royal Artillery (Crimean Period)*, 1911, p. 126. Simpson, op. cit., pp. 187–8, states that Trochu reached Raglan's headquarters at 7.30 a.m. to find the British about to move off.

16. Kinglake, op. cit., ii, pp. 250–1.

17. Ibid., pp. 254 et seq; Hibbert, op. cit., pp. 55 et seq; McMillan, op. cit., 20 Sept 1854 entry, p. 21; 22 Sept 1854, 'Rough datum on the battle of Alva [sic]', by J.A. Lloyd, RMP 6807/288; Calthorpe, op. cit., i, p. 170; 20 Sept 1854, Cambridge to his mother, RA Add. A8/171; *The Times*, 9 Oct 1854. A week after the battle Duberly, op. cit., p. 87, recorded: 'Our cavalry being so weak we were unable to follow up our advantage.'

18. Kinglake, op. cit., ii, pp. 498–9; Lyons, quoted ibid., iii, p. 16; casualties, ibid., ii, p. 503; 'The Crimean Journal of Col R.N.F Kingscote', Gloucestershire Record Office, D 471/F22; Lyons remark on 15 Feb 1856, RPP, 7/276. *The Record*, 10 April 1856, referred to an unidentified letter from Raglan to Lady Raglan explaining that St Arnaud had refused to advance with him after the Alma.

19. General After Order, 22 Sept 1854, RPP, 8/212; Paget, Lord G. *The Light Brigade in the Crimea*, 1818, p. 28; 23 Sept 1854, Dundas' dispatch No 487, printed in *The Times*, 9 Oct 1854.

20. Alma dispatch No 73, RMP 6807/288.

21. McMillan, op. cit., 23 and 24 Sept entries, p. 22; Kinglake, op. cit., iii, pp. 27–9.

22. Ibid., pp. 30–3.

23. Ibid., pp. 35–79; Lambert, op. cit., p. 125; 9 Jan 1854, Drummond report, Kinglake, op. cit., iii, p. 35; 28 Sept 1854, Raglan to Newcastle, ibid., p. 62n; 21 Sept 1854, Burgoyne memo, quoted ibid., p. 67; 22 Sept 1854, *Sampson*'s report, and 23 Sept 1854, Dundas' dispatch to Admiralty, printed in *The Times*, 9 Oct 1854.

24. Lambert, op. cit., p. 130; Calthorpe, op. cit., i, p. 220; 28 Sept 1854, Raglan to Newcastle, RMP 6807/282; Hibbert, op. cit., pp. 101–2; Woodham-Smith, op. cit. 208–9; Russell's despatch, 20 Oct 1854, printed in *The Times*, 14 Nov 1854. Simpson,

op. cit., p. 204, states that Raglan's meal, eaten off a tin plate and with cutlery provided by a hussar officer, came from the captured Russian baggage train. The Mackenzie Heights were named after an admiral of Scottish descent, who commanded Russian naval forces in Sevastopol during the eighteenth century and had farmed there.

25. Kinglake, op. cit., iii, pp. 96–104; McMillan, op. cit., 26 Sept entry, p. 23; 1 Oct 1854, Raglan to de Redcliffe, RMP 6807/291; Russell's dispatch, 25 Oct 1854, *The Times*, 14 Nov 1854.

26. Kinglake, op. cit., iii, pp. 105, 117; Simpson, op. cit., p. 206.

27. Kinglake, op. cit., iii, pp. 121 et seq; ibid., p. 129, estimates that Menshikov's total force in Sept 1854 comprised: 51,500 army, 1,000 militia, 2,666 Marines, 2,708 coastal artillery and 18,510 seamen; 31 Aug 1855, Romaine quoted in Kinglake, op. cit., iii, p. 237; 20 Nov 1854, memo by Burgoyne, quoted ibid., p. 244; 28 Sept 1854, Cathcart/Raglan exchange, ibid., 252n; (28) Sept 1854, Cathcart to Raglan (draft), ibid., p. 238; 2 Oct 1854, Cathcart to Lady Georgiana, his wife, ibid., p. 239n; *The Times*' leader, 23 June 1855.

28. McMillan, op. cit., 28 Sept 1854 entry, p. 23; Lambert, op. cit., p. 132; 26, 27, 28, 30 Sept 1854, Dundas to Raglan, 26, 30 Sept 1854, Raglan to Dundas, RMP 6807/298; 29 Sept 1854, Burgoyne to Col E. Matson, RE, Ass Adj-Gen at the Ord Office, Wrottesley, op. cit., ii, p. 97.

29. 28 Sept 1854, Raglan to Cardigan and Lucan, Kinglake, op. cit., iv, p. 70; Woodham-Smith, op. cit., p. 175.

30. 1 Oct 1854, Gen Grey (Prince Albert's private sec) to his wife, RPP, 7/287; 9 Oct 1854, Hardinge to Raglan, RMP 6807/298; 9, 10 Oct 1854, Newcastle to Raglan, Kinglake, op. cit., iv, p. 13; 2 Oct 1854, Queen Victoria to Raglan, and 27 Oct 1854, Raglan to Queen Victoria, RMP 6807/280; 21 Sept 1854, St Arnaud's dispatch, printed in *The Times*, 9 Oct 1854; Kinglake, op. cit., iv, pp. 31–8; 10 Oct 1854, Cowley to Raglan, RMP 6807/294; 12 Oct 1854, Combermere to Raglan, RPP, 7/217.

31. 3 Oct 1854, Airey to Hardinge, Kinglake, op. cit., iii, p. 270; Kinglake, op. cit., iii, pp. 272 et seq; 8 Oct 1854, Raglan to Newcastle, ibid., p. 305; 6, 7, 8 Oct 1854, Burgoyne to Matson, Wrottesley, op. cit., ii, pp. 98–101.

32. 1 Oct 1854, Aberdeen to Queen Victoria, Aberdeen Papers, BL Add MS 43049; Kinglake, op. cit., iv, pp. 10, 20–5; 8 Oct 1854, Graham to Raglan, RMP 6807/290; *The Times*, 3, 4, 5 Oct 1854. Burghersh reached the War Dept in Downing St at 7 a.m. on 8 Oct with private letters and dispatches from Raglan about the Alma battle, 8 Oct 1854, Newcastle to Queen Victoria, quoted in Martineau, op. cit., p. 160. Without a precise date as supporting evidence, Kinglake, op. cit., vi, p.211, notes that, unwell one night, Raglan asked Odo Russell (recently arrived from the British Embassy in Constantinople) to talk to him until he felt better. Kinglake believed that this revealed Raglan under strain.

33. 18 Oct 1854, Raglan to Newcastle, Kinglake, op. cit., iv, p. 29; 9 Oct 1854, Newcastle to Raglan, Newcastle Papers, NeC 9973; 25 Oct 1854, Newcastle to Raglan, PRO, WO 6/69/119.

34. Kinglake, op. cit., iii, p. 294; Bentley, N. (ed.). *Russell's Despatches from the Crimea, 1854–1856*, 1966, p. 109; 24 Oct 1854, Raglan to Lady Westmorland, quoted in Simpson, op. cit., p. 245a; 1 Oct 1854, Raglan to de Redcliffe, RMP 6807/291;

3 Oct 1854, Kingscote to Richard, RPP, 7/215.

35. Kinglake, op. cit., iv, p. 6; 23 Oct 1854, Raglan to Newcastle, ibid.; McMillan, op. cit., p. 23: ibid., 25, 28 Oct 1854 entries, pp. 26–7.

36. 23 Oct 1854, Kingscote to Kitty, RPP, 7/219; Bentley, op. cit., p. 107; 12, 20 Oct 1854, Raglan to Newcastle, RMP 6807/288; 10 Oct 1854 diary entry, Duberly, op. cit., p. 104; Kinglake, op. cit., vi, p. 136; 19 Oct 1854, Raglan to Brown, RMP 6807/292; 24 Oct 1854, Raglan to Lady Westmorland, quoted in Simpson, op. cit., p. 244.

37. 4, 14 Oct 1854, Cathcart to Raglan, RMP 6807/292; 13 Oct 1854, Newcastle to Cathcart, ibid.

38. 4 Oct 1854, Boxer to Raglan, RMP 6807/300; 16 Oct 1854, Raglan to Hall, RMP 6807/293; McMillan, op. cit., 4 Oct 1854 entry, p. 24; 3 Oct 1854, Kingscote to Richard, RPP, 7/215; 23 Oct 1854, Raglan to Hardinge, RMP 6807/289; 23 Oct 1854, Raglan to Newcastle, Kinglake, op. cit., iii, p. 504; The Times, 12 Oct 1854; Russell's dispatches quoted in Woodham-Smith, op. cit., p. 98; 25 Oct 1854, Menzies to Smith, Sidney Herbert Papers, 'Miscellaneous correspondence about hospitals'; 13 Oct 1854, Smith to Menzies, ibid.; Russell dispatch, 24 Oct 1854, The Times, 14 Nov 1854. Kinglake, op. cit., iii, App XII, put French strength at 46,000 men, 5,500 horses and 5,000 Turks. Raglan also had 4,400 Turks under command.

39. 2 Oct 1854, Newcastle to Raglan, RMP 6807/281; Life of Lord Raglan, p. 44; 13 Oct 1854, Newcastle to Raglan, PRO, WO 6/69/121; 19 Oct 1854, Newcastle to Raglan, acknowledging Raglan's objection to Beatson's force dated 16 Aug 1854, RMP 6807/281; 13 Oct 1854, Newcastle to Raglan, Newcastle Papers, NeC 9973; 9 Oct 1854, Newcastle to Raglan, PRO, WO 6/69/113.

40. Simpson, op. cit., p. 163 a-g, quoting 'Papers relative to Military Affairs in Asiatic Turkey and the Defence and Capitulation of Kars, presented to both Houses of Parliament by Command of Her Majesty, 1856.' Williams' letter of 23 June 1854 would arrive after Raglan's death.

41. Kinglake, op. cit., iii, pp. 353 et seq; Airey quoted in Monthly Review, Mar 1857, p. 163; 22 Oct 1854, report of the interrogation of Polish sailors, RMP 6807/301; The Times, 14 Nov 1854.

42. Ibid.; 24 Oct 1854 diary entry, Duberly, op. cit., p. 115.

43. Bentley, op. cit., pp. 113, 116; Kinglake, op. cit., iv, pp. 3–4.

44. Woodham-Smith, op. cit., pp. 220 et seq; Hibbert, op. cit., pp. 132–153; Kinglake, op. cit., iv, pp. 89 et seq; Nov 1854, unidentified extract from the sister of a serving officer noting Raglan's distressed reaction, RPP, 7/246; 20 Oct 1854, Campbell report, quoted in Kinglake, op. cit., iv, p. 89; Cardigan and Lucan exchanges over Heavy Brigade Charge, quoted ibid., p. 210; 27 Oct 1854, Lucan to Raglan, quoted ibid., p. 236n; 27, 29 Oct 1854, Clifford letters, Fitzherbert, op. cit., pp. 69, 78; Russell dispatch, 25 Oct 1854, The Times, 14 Nov 1854. In it he listed 'as well as I can ascertain' 607 sabres going into action, not the correct 673. Elsewhere in The Times, 14 Nov 1854, Russell referred to an exposed track on the upland before Sevastopol, along which ammunition must be transported to the siege batteries, as 'The Valley of Death'. Reading Russell's report of the Charge in conjunction with this and other reports in The Times, 14 Nov 1854, the basis for Tennyson's poem seems clear.

45. Kinglake, op. cit., iv, p. 224 and 224n; 16 Dec 1854, Raglan to Newcastle, ibid., App VIII; Life of Lord Raglan, p. 52.

46. Kinglake, op. cit., iv, p. 364; 26 Oct 1854, Lucan to Airey, ibid., App VII, p. 415; 16 Dec 1854, Raglan to Newcastle, ibid., App VIII, p. 419.

47. 30 Nov 1854, Lucan to Raglan, ibid., App VIII, p. 416; First Order, ibid., p. 117n; Life of Lord Raglan, p. 52.

48. 25 Oct 1854, Raglan to Newcastle, quoted in Woodham-Smith, op. cit., p. 268; 28 Oct 1854, Raglan to Newcastle, Kinglake, op. cit., iv, p. 415; Airey visit, Woodham-Smith, op. cit., p. 269; Paris correspondent's dispatch, 12 Nov 1854, The Times, 14 Nov 1854.

49. Kinglake, op. cit., iv, p. 380; Capt H. Montgomery, quoted in Pemberton, W. Battles of the Crimean War, 1962, p. 168; 7 Oct 1854, Raglan to Queen Victoria, RMP 6807/280; General Orders, 13, 15, 27 Dec 1854, Gordon, op. cit. After enemy withdrawal from the redoubts, the Allies did not immediately re-occupy them. On 20 December Fanny Duberly accompanied a French reconnaissance party 'to try to recover the batteries abandoned by the Turks on the 25th of October', but enemy small-arms fire frustrated the effort. However, a Zouave reconnaissance ten days later confirmed that the Russians had fully retired from the area, 20, 30 Dec 1854 journal entries, op. cit., pp. 152, 155.

50. McMillan, op. cit., 26 Oct 1854 entry, p. 27; Todleben, E., Défense de Sebastopol, i, St Petersburg, 1863, p. 404; Kinglake, op cit, iv, pp. 3 et seq; The Times, 14 Nov 1854; Annual Register, 1855, p. 287.

51. 24 Oct 1854, Raglan to Lady Westmorland, quoted in Simpson, op. cit., p. 245.

52. 8 Oct 1854, Raglan to Richard, RPP, 9; 16 October 1854, Raglan to Aberdeen, RMP 6807/290. Raglan may not always have been fully informed about his wife's ill-health, for 6 Oct 1854, Duchess of Gloucester to Lady Westmorland, Weigall, op. cit., p. 241, acknowledged that Lady Raglan had been too sick to join her sister at Cologne.

53. Calthorpe, op. cit., i, pp. 334, 343; Life of Lord Raglan, p. 55; McMillan, op. cit., 2, 4 Nov 1854 diary entries, p. 27; unidentified letter, Nov 1854, RPP, 7/246.

54. Kinglake, op. cit., v, pp. 33 et seq; Russell, W. The British Expedition to the Crimea, 1858, p. 205; 3, 8 Nov 1854, Raglan to Newcastle, Kinglake, op. cit., v, pp. 35, 43; extract from The Morning Chronicle, Mar 1855, RPP, 8/339.

55. Kinglake, op. cit., v, pp. 185 et seq; 27 Nov 1854, Newcastle to Raglan, and 18 Dec 1854, Raglan to Newcastle, ibid., 185; 6 Nov 1854, Menshikov's dispatch, quoted ibid., p. 411n; Life of Raglan, pp. 54–6.

56. Ibid., p. 56; Sept 1855, memo by Lady Louisa Perry following conversations with Sir John McNeill, RPP, 7/245; 15 Feb 1856, summary of visit by Lyons to unknown diarist, RPP, 7/276; 6 Feb 1855, Kingscote to Richard, RPP, 7/232, noted that Ferdinand had taken Raglan his lunch at the Battles of Balaclava and Inkerman.

57. 29 Nov 1854, Raglan to Charlotte and Kitty, RPP, 7/224; The Times, 14 Nov 1854; Sept 1855, summary of McNeill's opinion, op. cit., RPP, 7/245; 26 Feb 1856, record of Lyons' words, op. cit., RPP, 7/276.

58. Airey's evidence to the Board of General Offi-

cers, quoted in *Monthly Review*, Mar 1857, pp. 163–4; Report of the Board of General Officers appointed to inquire into the Statements contained in the Reports of Sir John McNeill and Colonel Tulloch, PP, xxi, p. 242; Calthorpe, op. cit., i, p. 355; 7 Nov 1854, Burgoyne to Dep Insp–Gen of Fortifications, Wrottesley, op. cit., ii, p. 118.

59. 22 Nov 1854, Kingscote to Richard, RPP, 7/222; Lambert, op. cit., p. 52; 10, 17 Nov 1854, memos by Burgoyne, RMP 6807/288; Kinglake, op. cit., vii, p. 21; 25 Nov 1854, Raglan memo, RMP 6807/288; McMillan, op. cit., 26 Nov 1854 entry, p. 30.

60. Hibbert, op. cit., pp. 199–204; Russell, W. *The War in the Crimea*, 1855, pp 270–1; Kinglake, op. cit., vi, pp. 163–5; 15, 16 Nov 1854, Raglan to Newcastle, ibid., pp. 164, 165; McMillan, op. cit., 14 Nov 1854 diary entry, p. 29; 18 Nov 1854, Raglan to Newcastle, RMP 6807/284; Calthorpe, op. cit., i, pp. 426, 428; *Monthly Review*, Mar 1857, p. 165; 17 Nov 1854, entry in Kingscote's journal, op. cit., D 471/F22. The disjointed nature of administrative responsibility, which involved the Ord Office, War Office, War Dept and Admiralty in London, had delayed dispatch of clothing originally ordered on 21 July 1854, Forbes, op. cit., i, p. 263.

61. 10 Nov 1854, Aberdeen to Queen Victoria, Aberdeen Papers, BL Add MS 43050; 3 Nov 1854, Raglan to Newcastle, RMP 6807/284; Duberley, op. cit., p. 31; 23 Nov 1854, Sidney Herbert memo quoted in Conacher, op. cit., pp. 339–40; 29 Nov 1854, Vicars to Lady Raleigh, Anon. *Memorials of Captain Hedley Vicars, 97th Regiment*, 1856, p. 219; RA QVJ: 3 Dec 1854; 23 Nov 1854, Kingscote to Richard, RPP, 7/222.

62. 18 Nov 1854, Queen Victoria to Raglan, RPP, 10; 18 Nov 1854, Aberdeen to Raglan, RMP 6807/290; 27 Nov 1854, King Leopold to Raglan, RMP 6807/280; 23 Nov 1854, Yorke to Airey, Airey Papers, G/IV/A/391; 27 Nov 1854, Newcastle to Raglan, RPP, 8/220.

63. 8 Nov 1854, Russell to Delane, quoted in Atkins, J. *The Life of Sir William Howard Russell*, i, 1911, p. 174; 13 Nov 1854, Raglan to Newcastle, Kinglake, op. cit., vi, p. 240; 23 Nov 1854, Kingscote to Kitty, RPP, 7/223.

64. Ibid.; 30 Nov 1854, Lt-Gen Lucan to His Excellency the Commander of the Forces, Kinglake, op. cit., iv, pp. 416–8; 24 Nov 1854, Kingscote to Richard, RPP, 7/222; 28 Nov 1854, Kingscote to Kitty, RPP, 7/223.

65. 30 Nov and 9 Dec 1854, Cambridge to his mother, RA Add. A8/172 and 173.

66. 12 Dec 1854, Raglan to Charlotte and Kitty, RPP, 7/225; 17 Dec 1854, Kingscote to Kitty, RPP, 7/226; RA QVJ: 4 Dec 1854.

67. 14 Dec 1854, Messrs Hoare to Raglan, RPP, 9; 14 Dec 1854, RF Burnett to Raglan, ibid.: both mentioned Raglan's letter of 28 Nov 1854.

68. 1 Dec 1854, Thanks of the Inhabitants of Melton Mowbray, and 28 Dec 1854, Raglan's reply, RMP 6807/305; 12 Dec 1854, Raglan to Charlotte and Kitty, noting letter to Lady Raglan, RPP, 7/225; 18 Nov 1854, Queen Victoria to Raglan, and 7 Dec 1854, Raglan to Queen Victoria, RMP 6807/280; 18 Dec 1854, votes of both Houses of Parliament, RMP 6807/280; 21 Dec 1854, fieldmarshal's commission, ibid. Aberdeen initiated the promotion, which had originally been planned for the fall of Sevastopol, but success at Inkerman made 'this

moment favorable'; and Queen Victoria immediately concurred. So did Newcastle and Hardinge, who deemed it 'most opportune ... and conferred after such brillant success is a compliment to that Army which he so ably led', 17, 18 Nov 1854, Aberdeen to Queen Victoria; 18 Nov 1854, Queen Victoria to Aberdeen, and 19 Nov 1854, Hardinge to Queen Victoria, RA G19/65, 71, 68 and 76.

69. 17 Dec 1854, Kingscote to Kitty, RPP, 7/226; General Order, 24 Dec 1854, including 27 Nov and 2 Dec 1854, Newcastle to Raglan, RPP, 8/220.

70. 8 Dec 1854, Raglan to Queen Victoria, Newcastle Papers, NeC 9926b; 9, 12 Dec 1854 diary entries, Anglesey, Marquis of (ed.). *Little Hodge: extracts from the diaries and letters of Colonel Edward Hodge written during the Crimean War, 1854–56*, 1971, pp. 63, 64; 13 Dec 1854, Estcourt to Henry Addington, Estcourt Papers, D 1571/32/17; 14 Dec 1854, Raglan to Filder, RMP 6807/292; 18 Dec 1854, Kingscote to Kitty, RPP, 7/226.

71. 5, 11 Dec 1854, Paulet to Raglan, RMP 6807/293; 29 Dec 1854, Cambridge to Raglan, RMP 6807/292; 30 Dec 1854, Estcourt to Henry Addington, Estcourt Papers, D 1571/33; 28 Dec 1854, Hall to Raglan, RMP 6807/293; 31 Dec 1854, Florence Nightingale to Herbert, quoted in O'Malley, I. *Florence Nightingale 1820–1856*, 1931, p. 267; General Order, 15 Dec 1854, Gordon, op. cit.; 5 Dec 1854, Raglan to Romaine, RMP 6807/292; 15 Dec 1854, Hall to Smith, Sidney Herbert Papers, 'Miscellaneous Correspondence concerning Hospitals'.

72. 22 Dec 1854, Treasury Minute, PRO, WO 43/103/159,744; 1 Dec 1854, Aberdeen to Queen Victoria, Aberdeen Papers, BL Add MS 43050; 2 Dec 1854, Raglan to Newcastle, RMP 6807/282. For a fuller account of the Civil Engineering Corps, see Sweetman, J. 'Ad Hoc Support Services in the Crimea' in *Military Affairs*, July 1988.

73. 2 Dec 1854, three-power treaty, Conacher, op. cit., p. 439; 6 Dec 1854, Palmerston to Clarendon, ibid.; 12 Dec 1854, Newcastle to Raglan, PRO, WO 6/70/172; 12 Dec 1854, Raglan to Charlotte and Kitty, RPP, 7/225; 18 Dec 1854, Newcastle to Raglan, Newcastle Papers, NeC 9995; 22 Dec 1854, Newcastle to Raglan, Kinglake, op. cit., vi, pp. 294; 22, 25, 29 Dec 1854, Newcastle to Raglan, Newcastle Papers, NeC 9996, 9997 and 9998.

74. 23, 29 Dec 1854, Aberdeen to Queen Victoria, Aberdeen Papers, BL Add MS 43050; 23 Dec 1854, Granville note, Granville Papers, PRO, 30/22/11; 1 Dec 1854, Grey to his brother Charles, Grey Papers, F7 (i).

75. 16 Dec 1854, Raglan to Newcastle, Kinglake, op. cit., iv, pp.418–21.

76. 17 Dec 1854, Kingscote to Kitty, RPP, 7/226; 30 Dec 1854, Kingscote to Richard, RPP, 7/228.

Chapter 10

1. 2 Mar 1855, Raglan to Panmure, RMP, 6807/287/185.

2. 30 Dec 1854, Kingscote to Richard, RPP, 7/228.

3. 20 Jan 1855, Raglan to Queen Victoria, RMP 6807/280; 23 Jan 1855, Estcourt to Herbert, Estcourt Papers, D 1571/32/18; 20 Jan 1855, Lucan to Raglan, RMP 6807/292. When visiting the Russian lines under flag of truce on 29 Jan 1855, Burghersh was told by an enemy officer that this was the finest of the nine winters that he had spent in the Crimea: 'If this is so, I do not envy them their climate', 29 Jan 1855, Raglan to New-

castle, RA G24/23.

4. 9 Jan 1855, Newcastle to Palmerston, Palmerston Papers under 'Hardinge'; 20 Jan 1855, Newcastle to Raglan, PRO, WO 6/70/212; 22 Jan 1855, Newcastle to Raglan, Newcastle Papers, NeC 1000b; McMurdo's memo, 18 Jan 1855, Ellenborough Papers, PRO, 30/12/18. For a fuller consideration of the Land Transport Corps see Sweetman, J. 'Military Transport in the Crimean War 1854–1856' in *English Historical Review*, Jan 1973.

5. 8 Jan 1855, de Redcliffe to Raglan, RMP 6807/291. For details of the Civil Engineering Corps, see Sweetman, op. cit., *Military Affairs*, July 1988.

6. 20 Jan 1855, Raglan to Queen Victoria, Benson and Esher, op. cit., iii, p. 69; 30 Jan 1855, Raglan to Newcastle, RMP 6807/282; 4 Jan 1855, Newcastle to Raglan, PRO, WO 70/196; 5 Jan 1855, Raglan to Herbert, Sidney Herbert Papers, 'Crimea and China 1854–1861'; 8 Jan 1855, Herbert to Lansdowne, ibid., 'Miscellaneous Political Correspondence 1834–1861'; 12 Jan 1855, Herbert to Estcourt, ibid., 'Crimea and China 1854–1861'; 13, 23 Jan 1855, Raglan to Newcastle, quoted in Kinglake, op. cit., vi, pp. 390–1; 30 Jan 1855, Raglan to Newcastle, RMP 6807/282.

7. 1 Jan 1855, Newcastle to Raglan, Newcastle Papers, NeC 9999; 1 Jan 1855, Newcastle to Raglan, PRO, WO 6/70/193; 6 Jan 1855, Newcastle to Raglan, RMP 6807/281; 6 Jan 1855, Raglan to Newcastle, RMP 6807/282.

8. 8 Jan 1855, Newcastle to Raglan, RMP 6807/283; 12 Jan 1855, Newcastle to Raglan, RMP 6807/281; 15 Jan 1855, Raglan to Newcastle, RMP 6807/282; 22 Jan 1855, Newcastle to Raglan, PRO, WO 33/1/73/213; 29 Jan 1855, Newcastle to Raglan, RMP 6807/281; 30 Jan 1855, Raglan to Newcastle, PRO, WO 33/1/167/164.

9. RA QVJ: 9, 10, 13 Jan 1855.

10. 26 Jan 1855, unaddressed note, Granville Papers, PRO, 30/29; letter from Sir Howard Douglas, *The Times*, 13 Jan 1855; 4 Jan 1855, Raglan to Herbert, Newcastle Papers, NeC 9948a; Herbert to Raglan, RMP 6807/289; 1 Jan 1855, Newcastle to Raglan, quoted in Kinglake, op. cit., vi, p. 296. On his return to England Sir George Brown roundly condemned *The Times'* behaviour as 'a scandal' to Queen Victoria during a dinner at Osborne, RA QVJ: 31 July 1855. Despite his own earlier reservations, the Duke of Cambridge believed that *The Times* 'goes too far' in attacking Raglan, 16 Jan 1855, Cambridge to his mother, RA Add. A8/179.

11. 26 Jan 1855, Clarendon to de Redcliffe, quoted in Anderson, O. *A Liberal State at War*, New York, 1967, p. 75; 26 Jan 1855, Newcastle to Raglan, RMP 6807/283; 27 Jan 1855, Cowley to Raglan, RMP 6807/294; Roebuck's motion, 26 Jan 1855, Hansard, cxxxvi, p. 979.

12. 5 Jan 1855, Windham to his brother-in-law, quoted in Chesney, op. cit., p. 145; 10 Jan 1855, Cambridge to Louisa, quoted in St Aubyn, G. *The Royal George – The Life of the Duke of Cambridge*, 1963, pp. 86–7; 7 Jan 1855, Cambridge to his mother, RA Add. A8/176; 9, 17, 18 Jan 1855, Hawley to his father, Ward, op. cit.; 25 Jan 1855, Hawley to his sister Ellen, ibid.; 20 Jan 1855, Palmerston, undated (Jan 1855), Argyll, and 22 Jan 1855, Molesworth memos, Dalhousie Muniments, 8/171; 14 Jan 1855, Greville, quoted in Hibbert, op. cit., p. 255; RA QVJ: 12 Jan 1855; 11 Jan 1855, Raglan to Cambridge, RA Add. E1/214.

13. *John Bull*, 20 Jan 1855; extracts from a letter by Lyons (Jan 1855), 'a sergeant' (19 Jan 1855) and 'an officer' (Jan 1855), RPP, 7/252–4; 25 Jan 1855, Kinglake to Talbot, RPP, 7/230.

14. 4 Jan 1855, Newcastle to Raglan, PRO, WO 6/74; 2 Jan 1855, Raglan to Newcastle, quoted in Kinglake, op. cit., vii, p. 23.

15. 18 Jan 1855, Canrobert to Raglan, RMP 6807/294; 23 Jan 1855, Raglan to Newcastle, and 10 Feb 1855, Raglan to Russell, quoted in Kinglake, op. cit., vi, p. 388; 30 Jan 1855, Burgoyne to Maj-Gen H.H. Rose, RMP 6807/290; 31 Jan 1855, Burgoyne memo, ibid.; 29 Jan 1855, Raglan to Newcastle, RA G24/23.

16. 15 Jan 1855, Burgoyne memo, RMP 6807/288; 8 Jan 1855, Graham to Raglan, RMP 6807/290; 21 Jan 1855, Russell to Raglan, RMP 6807/290; 31 Jan 1855, Lt-Col L. Simmons RE to Raglan, RMP 6807/295.

17. 8 Jan 1855, Raglan to Richard, RPP, 9.

18. 2, 5, 8 Feb 1855, memos by Burgoyne, RMP 6807/288; Calthorpe, op. cit., ii, p. 100.

19. Kinglake, op. cit., vii, pp. 74, 107; 20 Feb 1855, de Redcliffe to Raglan, RMP 6807/291; 25 Feb 1855, Brown to Raglan, RMP 6807/292; 16 Feb 1855, Vicars to his mother, *Vicar's Memorials*, op. cit., p. 253; 20 Feb 1855, Panmure to Raglan, Douglas G. and Ramsay, G. (eds.). *The Panmure Papers*, 1908, i, p. 79.

20. Kinglake, op. cit., vii, pp. 118-120; RA QVJ: 17 Feb 1855.

21. 6, 7, 11, 22 Feb 1855, Simmons to Raglan, RMP 6807/295; 16 Feb 1855, de Redcliffe to Raglan, RMP 6807/291; Kinglake, op. cit., vii, pp. 57, 59; 18, 24 Feb 1855, Omar Pasha to Raglan and Canrobert, RMP 6807/295.

22. 10 Feb 1855, Neale to Raglan, RMP 6807/302; Feb 1855, Bizot to Vaillant, quoted in Rousset, C. *Histoire de la Guerre de Crimeáe*, Paris, 1894, ii, p. 32.

23. 12 Feb 1855, Panmure to Raglan (private), quoted in Kinglake, op. cit., vi, p. 335; 12 Feb 1855, Panmure to Raglan (official), PRO, WO 33/1/95/1; 13 Feb 1855, Queen Victoria to Panmure, RA L19/80: as with Newcastle's critical dispatch of 6 Jan, Raglan did not know that 'the Queen was much pleased with the dispatch which Lord Panmure has addressed to Lord Raglan painful as it must be to have to write or to receive it, the truth of everything stated therein and the directions given if attended to can alone produce an improvement'.

24. 2 Feb 1855, Hardinge to Airey, Airey Papers, G/IV/A/412; *The Times*, 3, 9, 12, 17 Feb 1855.

25. 10 Feb 1855, Palmerston to Queen Victoria, quoted in Connell, B. *Regina versus Palmerston 1837–1865*, 1962, p. 167; 28 Feb 1855, Estcourt diary entry, Estcourt Papers, D 1571/33; 30 Jan 1855, Raglan to Newcastle, PRO, WO 33/1/167/164; 7 Feb 1855, Burgoyne memo to Raglan, Wrottesley, op. cit., ii, p. 212; 18 Feb 1855, Burgoyne to Matson, ibid., p. 229; Kinglake, op. cit., vii, p. 112.

26. 10 Feb 1855, Palmerston to Queen Victoria, Connell, op. cit., p. 167; 12 Feb 1855, Palmerston 'Memo of Measures to Establish a better order of things in the Crimea', Douglas and Ramsay, op. cit., i, pp. 53–4; 19 Feb 1855, Panmure to Simpson, Dalhousie Muniments, 8/192; 19 Feb 1855, Panmure to Raglan, Douglas and Ramsey, op. cit., i, p. 70; 19 Feb 1855, Hardinge to Raglan, RMP 6807/289; *USG*, 24 Feb 1855; RA QVJ: 17 Feb

1855.

27. 23 Feb 1855, 'Report upon the State of the Hospitals of the British Army in the Crimea and Scutari', Dr A. Cumming, Mr P. Benson-Maxwell and Dr P. Sinclair Laing, PP, 1854–5, xxxiii, 1; 16 Feb 1855, Panmure to Raglan, PRO, WO 6/70; Palmerston, 22 Feb 1855, Hansard, cxxxvi, 1732; instructions to McNeill and Tulloch, PP, 1856, xl, p. 375, and PP, 1856, xx, 2; USG, 24 Feb 1855.

28. 19 Feb 1855, Russell dispatch, quoted in Chesney, op. cit., p. 195; Bentley, op. cit., p. 195; Estcourt diary entries, 21–3 Feb 1855, Estcourt Papers, D 1571/33; Kinglake, op. cit., vi, p. 392; Hibbert, op. cit., p. 259.

29. 1, 7 Feb 1855, Burgoyne memo, RMP 6807/288; 1 Feb 1855, McPherson to A. Tongue of Greenock, RPP, 7/267; The Globe, 5 Feb 1855, remarks of 'a general' in the Crimea to an unidentified correspondent in England, RPP, 7/233.

30. Undated, Wilbraham to his sister, quoted by Mrs Selwyn (wife of the Bishop of New Zealand), 5 Feb 1855, RPP, 7/257; 28 Feb 1855, Charlotte to Lady Elizabeth Orde, RPP, 7/255. Calthorpe, op. cit., ii, p. 62, gives more details without essentially contradicting Charlotte's version. The wife of a corporal in the 23rd gave birth to a daughter on 15 January, in 'a small dog-kennel tent' and Raglan 'with his usual kindness' sent his own doctor to attend her. The following day, 'amid a high wind driving the frozen snow before it, and a temperature at 20[deg]' Raglan made his visit accompanied by two ADCs. On 17 January, he sent a staff officer with a rubber sleeping-bag lined with flannel, which had been sent to him from England. When Florence Nightingale became ill with fever on a visit to the Crimea, Raglan made a similar long journey up to the Castle Hospital on the wet and stormy afternoon of 24 May 1855. Announcing himself as 'only a soldier', he was almost turned away but Miss Nightingale recognized his voice. Removing his mackintosh cloak, he sat by her bedside talking to her for some time, despite the danger of infection, and according to the medical staff this visit aided Miss Nightingale's recovery, O'Malley, op. cit., pp. 307–9; Simpson, op. cit., p. 414. Mrs Duberly was piqued, however, when Raglan personally rejected her request on 24 Jan 1855 to live ashore 'in any house, however small'. He no doubt considered that she was already adequately accommodated aboard ship in Balaclava harbour, and houses were in short supply, journal entry, 24 Jan 1855, Duberly, op. cit., p. 163.

31. 6 Feb 1855, Kingscote to Richard, RPP, 7/232; 10 Feb 1855, Charlotte to Lady Farquhar, RPP, 7/231; 28 Feb 1855, extract from letter by Charlotte to unknown correspondent of 'a general' in the Crimea, RPP, 7/233.

32. 10 Feb 1855, Charlotte to Lady Mary Farquhar, RPP, 7/231; 6 Feb 1855, Raglan to Richard, RPP, 9.

33. 24 Feb 1855, Raglan to Hardinge, RMP 6807/289; 18 Feb 1855, Herbert to Palmerston, Sidney Herbert Papers, 'Cabinet and other Memoranda 1837–1861'.

34. 2, 10 Mar 1855, Russell dispatches, quoted in Chesney, op. cit., pp.196–8; Mar 1855, Fenton quoted ibid., p. 200; 7 Mar 1855, Kingscote journal entry, D 471/F22; 24 Mar 1855, Duberly, op. cit., p. 177.

35. 26 Mar 1855, Panmure to Raglan, PRO, WO 6/74; 23 Mar 1855, Panmure to Raglan, ibid.; 24

Mar 1855, Raglan to Queen Victoria, RMP 6807/280; 26 Mar 1855, Raglan to Lord John Russell, RMP 6807/290.

36. Kinglake, op. cit., vii, pp. 77, 80, 87 et seq; Todleben, op. cit., ii, pp. 34–5; 24 Mar 1855, Raglan to Queen Victoria, RMP 6807/280; 24 Mar 1855, Jones' memo, RMP 6807/288; 29 Mar 1855, Raglan to R. Colquhoun, RMP 6807/302.

37. 4 Mar 1855, note of Allied conference, RMP 6807/288; 6 Mar 1855, Jones' record of Allied council of war, ibid.; 7, 8 Mar 1855, Burgoyne memos, ibid.; Kinglake, op. cit., vii, pp. 74 et seq; 10 Mar 1855, Raglan to Panmure, quoted in Kinglake, op. cit., vii, p. 76; 16 Mar 1855, Bizot memo, RMP 6807/288; 17 Mar 1855, Burgoyne note, Wrottesley, op. cit., ii, p. 277; 13 Mar 1855, Raglan to Panmure, quoted in Kinglake, op. cit., vii, p. 84; Houston Stewart, quoted in Hibbert, op. cit., p. 271.

38. 11 Mar 1855, Simmons to Raglan, RMP 6807/295; 12 Mar 1855, Raglan to Paulet, RMP 6807/293; 19, 22, 23 Mar 1855, Simmons to Raglan, RMP 6807/295.

39. 2, 5 Mar 1855, Panmure to Raglan, RMP 6807/283/25 and 31; 2 Mar 1855, Raglan to Panmure, RMP 6807/286/185; 15 Mar 1855, Panmure to Brown, Brown Papers MS 2854/93.

40. 16 Mar 1855, Panmure to Raglan, Douglas and Ramsay, op. cit., i, p. 103; 19 Mar 1855, Panmure to Raglan, RMP 6807/283/49; 24 Mar 1855, Raglan to Panmure, RMP 6807/286/216 and 219; 5 Mar 1855, Herbert to Raglan, Sidney Herbert Papers, 'Crimea and China 1854–1861'; 30 Mar 1855, Panmure to Simpson, Douglas and Ramsay, op. cit., i, p. 135; 17 Mar 1855, Queen Victoria to Panmure, RA L19/80.

41. 12, 26 Mar 1855, Raglan to Lady Westmorland, quoted in Simpson, op. cit., pp. 418–421; 6 Mar 1855, Brown to Miss Somerset, ibid., p. 422.

42. 10 Mar 1855, diary entry, Estcourt Papers, D 1571/33; 24 Mar 1855, Raglan to Queen Victoria, RMP 6807/280; 26 Mar 1855, Raglan to Lord John Russell, RMP 6807/290.

43. 2 Mar 1855, Hardinge to Raglan, RMP 6807/289; Lucan, 19 Mar 1855, Hansard, cxxxvii, pp. 731–3; Woodham-Smith, op. cit., p. 276; 31 Mar 1855, Filder to Raglan, RMP 6807/286/231; 13 Mar 1855, Burgoyne letter, Wrottesley, op. cit., ii, p. 277.

44. 26 Mar 1855, Raglan to Richard, RPP, 9.

45. 5 Mar 1855, Curzon to Miss Somerset, RPP, 7/276; 15 Mar 1855, extract from McNeill letter, RPP, 7/265.

46. 25, 29 Mar 1855, Jones' memos, RMP 6807/288; 26 Mar 1855, Raglan to Lord John Russell, RMP 6807/290.

47. 3 April 1855, Raglan to Panmure, quoted in Kinglake, op. cit., vii, p. 21; 5 April 1855, Simmons to Clarendon, RMP 6807/295; 15 April 1855, memo on Allied conference, RMP 6807/288.

48. Kinglake, op. cit., vii, pp. 218–21; 18 May 1855, Simmons to Clarendon, RMP 6807/295; undated, Napoleon III to Canrobert, quoted in Kinglake, op. cit., vii, p. 220n.

49. Ibid., pp. 106–7, 223–30; 17, 21 April 1855, Raglan to Panmure, quoted ibid., p. 223; 21 April 1855, Raglan to Cowley, RMP 6807/294; 24 April 1855, Raglan to Panmure, quoted in Kinglake, op. cit., vii, p. 222, and 23 April 1855 meeting noted in Rousset, op. cit., ii, 154; 28 April 1855, Raglan to Panmure, quoted in Kinglake, op. cit., vii, p. 228.

50. 3 April 1855, Raglan and Canrobert to Omar Pasha, 6, 8 April 1855, Simmons to Raglan, 5, 16, 20 April 1855, Simmons to Clarendon, 25 April 1855, unsigned note 'from headquarters' on English numbers, RMP 6807/295.

51. 16 April 1855, Panmure to Raglan, quoted in Kinglake, op. cit., vii, p. 296; Rousset, op. cit., ii, p. 145; Kinglake, op. cit., vii, pp. 237–45; 20 April 1855, Panmure to Raglan, quoted ibid., p. 239; Lambert, op. cit., p. 218; 9 April 1855, Airey to Raglan, RMP 6807/292.

52. 23 April 1855, Panmure to Raglan, PRO, WO 6/74; 7 April 1855, Estcourt to Tom, Estcourt Papers, D 1571/33; Lambert, op. cit., p. 236; 16 April 1855, Simpson to Panmure, Douglas and Ramsey, op. cit., i, p. 150; 26 April 1855, Simpson to Panmure, quoted in Kinglake, op. cit., vi, p. 350.

53. Smith, op. cit., p. 291.

54. 6 April 1855, Panmure to Raglan, PRO, WO 6/70/75; 6 April 1855, Ass Surgeon Ricketts to Lt Stopford RE, RMP 6807/305; 27 April 1855, Beatty to Messrs Peto, Dalhousie Muniments 8/202; 6 April 1855, General Order, Gordon, op. cit.; 25 April 1855, Simmons to Raglan, RMP 6807/295.

55. 9 April 1855, Queen Victoria to Raglan, RMP 6807/280; 7 April 1855, Estcourt to Tom, Estcourt Papers, D 1571/33; 7 April 1855, Airey to Miss Somerset, RPP, 7/235.

56. Ibid.; 24 April 1855, Raglan to Charlotte, RPP, 7/236.

57. 30 April 1855, Raglan to Brown, RMP 6807/292.

58. *Life of Lord Raglan*, op. cit., p. 57; Lambert, op. cit., pp. 225–6; Kinglake, op. cit., pp. 256–71; 30 April and 1 May 1855, Canrobert to Raglan, RMP 6807/294; 1 May 1855, Raglan to Canrobert, ibid.; 2 May 1855, Raglan to Brown, RMP 6807/292; 4 May diary entry, McMillan, op. cit., p. 31; 4 May 1855, Raglan to Lyons, quoted in Kinglake, op. cit., vii, p. 261; 8 May 1855, Raglan to Panmure, ibid., p. 269.

59. 19 May 1855, Canrobert to Raglan, RMP 6807/294; Kinglake, op. cit., vii, pp. 291–3 and viii, pp. 1–5; 19 May 1855, Raglan to Panmure, and 21 May 1855, Panmure to Raglan, ibid., vii, pp. 294, 298; 26 May 1855, Kingscote to Kitty, RPP, 7/238.

60. 5 May 1855, Raglan to Panmure, quoted in Kinglake, op. cit., vii, p. 207; 26 May 1855, Kingscote to Kitty, RPP, 7/238; 9, 13 May 1855 entries, McMillan, op. cit., pp. 31–2; Kinglake, op. cit., vi, p. 405; 10 May 1855, Jones memo, RMP 6807/288.

61. Kinglake, op. cit., viii, p. 7; 5 May 1855, Jones memo, RMP 6807/288.

62. Kinglake, op. cit., vii, pp. 278 *et seq*; 5 and 8 May 1855, Raglan to Panmure, quoted ibid., pp. 278-9.

63. Kinglake, op. cit., vii, pp. 284–96, Raglan to Panmure, quoted ibid., p. 285.

64. Kinglake, op. cit., viii, pp. 10, 13, 18; Lambert, op. cit., p. 288; 21 May 1855, Pélissier to Vaillant, quoted in Kinglake, op. cit., viii, p. 28; 28, 29 May 1855, Jones memos, RMP 6807/288.

65. 21 May 1855, Pélissier to Vaillant, quoted in Kinglake, op. cit., viii, p. 28; Lambert, op. cit., p. 228; 21 May 1855, Raglan to Brown, RMP 6807/292; 22 May 1855, Raglan to Panmure, quoted in Kinglake, viii, p. 27; Kinglake, op. cit., viii, pp. 27–31, 39–49; 25 May, Brown to Raglan, 27, 31 May 1855, Raglan to Brown, RMP 6807/292; 29 May 1855, Raglan to Queen Victo-

ria, RMP 6807/280.

66. 3 May 1855, Hansard, cxxxviii, pp. 5 *et seq*; 25 May 1855, Panmure to Raglan, RMP 6807/285/144; 12, 26, 28 May 1855, Raglan to Panmure, RMP 6807/286/281, 297, 298 and 302; 31 May 1855, Raglan to Panmure, RMP 6807/293.

67. 8 May 1855, Palmerston to Panmure, Douglas and Ramsay, op. cit., i, p. 190; 15 May 1855, Stewart to Duchess of Somerset (extract), RPP, 7/237; 11 May 1855, Raglan to Lord Kilmaine, RMP 6807/305; 22 May 1855, Raglan to Egerton and Tower, quoted in Kinglake, op. cit., vi, p. 404.

68. 26 May 1855, Kingscote to Kitty, RPP, 7/238.

69. 7 May 1855, Panmure to Raglan, Douglas and Ramsay, op. cit., i, p. 183; 18 May 1855, Hansard, cxxxviii, pp. 736 *et seq*; 21 May 1855, Raglan to Panmure, RMP 6807/287; 25 May 1855, Panmure to Raglan, Douglas and Ramsay, op. cit., i, p. 210; 29 May 1855, Hastings to Raglan, RMP 6807/289; 30 May 1855, Raglan to Ross, ibid.; 2 May 1855, Panmure memo, PRO, WO 33/1/35; 10 May 1855, Panmure to Queen Victoria, Douglas and Ramsay, op. cit., i, p. 194; extract from the Foreign Office list, Jan 1856, RPP, 10/40.

70. 17, 24 May 1855 diary entries, McMillan, op. cit., p. 32; 24 May 1855, journal entry, Duberly, op. cit., pp. 202–3; 31 May 1855, note by Raglan on Jones memo, RMP 68 7/288; 29 May 1855, Simmons to Clarendon, RMP 6807/295.

71. 4, 10 June 1855, Brown to Raglan, quoted in Kinglake, op. cit., viii, pp. 53-4, 75–86; 12 June 1855, Raglan to Panmure, ibid., p. 80. The potential problem of delayed communication between the Allied commanders and their governments was illustrated by Raglan's telegraph message to Panmure concerning the success of the remounted Kertch expedition being sent from his headquarters at 1.05 p.m. on 14 June, but not reaching the War Dept until 10.30 p.m. on 15 June: RA G33/12.

72. 1 June 1855, Jones memo, 2 June 1855, Jones to Raglan, RMP 6807/288.

73. June 1855, Pélissier to Min of War, 5 June 1855, Napoleon III to Pélissier, and 5 June 1855, Pélissier to Napoleon III, quoted in Kinglake, op. cit., viii, pp. 36, 89; ibid., pp. 88–90; 9 June 1855, Kingscote to Richard, RPP, 7/241; 15 Feb 1856, Lyons' remarks summarized, RPP, 7/276; 4 June 1855, Wood to Raglan, and 21 June 1855, Raglan to Wood, RMP 6807/290; 5 June 1855, Raglan to de Redcliffe, RMP 6807/291.

74. 7 June 1855, Simpson's orders, RMP 6807/288; Paget, op. cit., pp. 99–100; Kinglake, op. cit., viii, pp. 90–126; 6, 8 June 1855, diary entries, McMillan, op. cit., p. 32; 8 June 1855, Raglan to Brown, RMP 6807/292; 8 June, Tylden memo, 9, 10 June 1855, Jones memos, RMP 6807/288; 9 June 1855, Kingscote to Richard, RPP, 7/241.

75. 10, 16 June 1855, Jones memo, RMP 6807/288; 17 June 1855, Raglan memo, ibid.; 15 Feb 1856, summary of Lyons' words, RPP, 7/276.

76. Kinglake, op. cit., viii, pp. 138–151, 162; Rousset, op. cit., ii, p. 255; 19 June 1855, Raglan to Panmure, quoted in Kinglake, op. cit., viii, p. 144; 17 June 1855, Canrobert to Raglan, RMP 6807/288; 21 June 1855, Jones memo, ibid.

77. Kinglake, op. cit., viii, pp. 152–217; 19 June 1855, Raglan to Panmure, quoted ibid., pp. 161–2; *History of Cefntilla*, p. 7; *Life of Lord Raglan*, pp. 57–8; extract from Maj Malan 'A Soldier's Experience', RPP, 7/289; 18, 19 June 1855 diary entries, McMillan, op. cit., p. 33.

78. 19 June 1855, Raglan to Lady Raglan, reproduced in *The Globe*, 14 Jan 1858 and Kinglake, op. cit., viii, pp. 309–10.
79. 21 June 1855, Raglan to Wood, RMP 6807/290; 19 June 1855, Raglan to Panmure, RA G34/9; Raglan's alleged words in Harris, J. *The Gallant 600: A Tragedy of Obsessions*, 1973, p. 280, and Pemberton, op. cit., p. 217; Calthorpe, op. cit., ii, p. 351; Kinglake, op. cit., viii, p. 261. Queen Victoria declared, later, that 'his letters show *how* it [failure] distressed him, and I fear that it helped to kill him', RA QVJ: 2 July 1855.
80. 9 June 1855, Kingscote to Richard, RPP, 7/241; 23 June 1855, Hardinge to Airey, Airey Papers, G/IV/A/379; *USG*, 23 June 1855.
81. 1 June 1855, Ross to Raglan, RMP 6807/289; 4 June 1855, Panmure to Raglan, RMP 6807/287; 5 June 1855, Raglan to Richard, RPP, 7/240; Order in Council, 6 June 1855, PP, 1854–5, xxxii, 677; 7 June 1855, Hardinge to Raglan, RMP 6807/289.
82. 12 June 1855, Raglan to Panmure, RA Add. F2/105; 2 June 1855, Raglan to Mrs Carpenter, RMP 6807/305; 19 June 1855, extract from letter by Stewart, RPP, 7/239; 8 Dec 1855, letter from Mrs Fremantle, RPP, 7/272; 8 July 1855, letter from Mr Cumberbatch, RPP, 7/273; anon extract, RPP, 7/250; Brown, *Memoranda*, op. cit., p. 86; 25 June 1855, Raglan to Thomas Tower, noted in Kinglake, op. cit., vi, p. 404n.
83. 26 June 1855, Airey to Miss Somerset, RPP, 7/242; 2 July 1877, Dr H.F. Smith to Kinglake, NAM 6305/162. Shepherd, J. *The Crimean Doctors: a history of the British Medical Services in the Crimean War*, Liverpool, 1991, ii, p. 509, doubts whether Raglan would have been strong enough, given his known medical condition, to visit Estcourt's grave on 24 June. Dr H.F. Smith served at the British headquarters throughout the Crimean campaign, but does not seem to have attended Raglan during his last illness. Nevertheless he would have been fully aware of the relevant medical details. In his letter to Kinglake, 2 July 1877, he firmly stated that Raglan did visit the grave, his last excursion from the headquarters building.
84. 29 June 1855, report of Dr J. Prendergast, Staff Surgeon 1st Class, RMP 6807/280; Shepherd, op. cit., ii, p. 509; Mitra, S. *The Life and Letters of Sir John Hall*, 1911, pp. 381–2.
85. Kinglake, op. cit., viii, pp. 263–80; 23, 26 June 1855, Raglan to Panmure, ibid., pp. 271, 278; 25 June 1855, Raglan to Hardinge, RMP 6807/289; 26 June 1855, Airey to Miss Somerset, RPP, 7/242; 12 July 1855, Calthorpe's mother to an unidentified niece, RPP, 7/298. Hibbert, op. cit., pp. 293–4, maintains that Steele was the last to speak to Raglan, in words similar to those of Airey's. When Raglan's final dispatch arrived in England, Queen Victoria noted that it had been 'signed with a feeble hand' (RA QVJ: 9 July 1855); and Panmure observed that his signature to the last 'few official documents too truly betrays his severe illness', 9 July 1855, Panmure to Queen Victoria, RA G34/43. These comments were made, however, with the benefit of hindsight after Raglan's death.
86. 20, 25 July, Lady Westmorland to Comtesse Néale, Weigall, op. cit., pp. 267, 268.
87. Extract from Revd Wright's notebook, RPP, 7/288; Kinglake, op. cit., viii, pp. 280–1; Calthorpe quoted in Kinglake, op. cit., vii, p. 313; *Gentleman's Magazine*, Aug 1855; 29 June 1855,

General Order, Gordon, op. cit. The lock of Raglan's hair is contained in RPP, 9.
88. 7 July 1855, extract from unidentified officer 'before Sebastopol', RPP, 7/296; 12 July 1855, (illegible) correspondent noting Baillie's reaction, RPP, 7/298; 30 June 1855, Clifford to his father, Fitzherbert, op. cit., p. 28; 'an officer', quoted by Sir Hew Ross, 17 July 1855, Hansard, cxxxix, p. 971.
89. Pélissier's General Order, 29 June 1855, RPP, 7/243; Calthorpe, op. cit., ii, p. 363; 29 June, Pélissier to Lady Raglan, 30 June, Napoleon III to Lady Raglan, 30 June, Panmure to Dundas, and 30 June 1855, Steele to Lady Raglan, RMP 6807/280; 30 June 1855, Stewart extract, RPP, 7/295; 30 June 1855, Curzon to Miss Somerset, 7/293; 4 July 1855, Hardinge's General Order No 648, and Hardinge to Richard, RPP, 7/244; 5 June 1855, Raglan to Richard, RPP, 7/240.
90. Archdeacon Wright, in a book describing the garrison church at Portsmouth, where Raglan was commemorated, RPP, 7/288; for cholera allegation, cf., Pemberton, op. cit., p. 217, and *History of Cefntilla*, p. 7; 28 June 1855, with an enclosure of 29 June, Hawley to his father, Ward, op. cit.; *The Wolverhampton Journal*, 7 July 1855; 2 July 1877, Dr H.F. Smith's analysis, NAM 6305/162. Interestingly, Dr Robert Lyons, appointed in March 1855 'to investigate the pathology of diseases' with Raglan's army, held that a particular, virulent strain of diarrhoea was prevalent in the Crimea, Shepherd, op. cit., ii, p. 582. A later commentator, Compton, P. *The Last Days of General Gordon*, 1974, p. 17, used another expressive non-medical term: Raglan died of 'tear and wear'. Referring to 'his honourable conduct', and that he had been 'done so little justice by the country, and by those who ought to have supported him', the Duchess of Gloucester referred to 'the idea that he died (as I am sure he did) from a broken heart', 14 Feb 1856, Duchess of Gloucester to Lady Westmorland, Weigall, op. cit., p. 283.

Burial and Memorial

1. Lady Raglan's words on the memorial tablet to her late husband in Badminton church.
2. 29, 30 June 1855, Dundas to Lady Westmorland, RPP, 7. With appalling timing, a broadsheet published by John Jones in Newcastle-upon-Tyne on 29 June 1855 declared, utterly without foundation: 'It is said that Lord Raglan has requested to be relieved of his command to return home to recruit his health', John Johnson Collection, 1f.
3. 3 July 1855, Dundas to Lady Westmorland, and details of medication on loose sheet, RPP, 7; details of legal documents and leases, RPP, 9.
4. 5 July 1855, Emily to Priscilla, RPP, 8/310A; 13 July 1855, Kitty to Aunt Priscilla, RPP, 8. Neither Charlotte nor Kitty, who after their mother's death shared a succession of lodgings, married. Both suffered bouts of illness, with advice to 'take the waters' at Bath. Charlotte, in thanking a niece for an electric clock as a 90th birthday present, still showed a clear firm hand in 1905. Cf., 26 Nov 1889, A.W. Kinglake to Kitty, RPP, 6; 19 Mar 1891 and 14 Sept 1898, Capt R Somerset to Aunt Kitty, RPP, Raglan J; 20 May 1905, Aunt Charlotte to [possibly] Louise, RPP, 7.
5. RA QVJ: 28, 29, 30 June 1855; 2 July 1855, J(ulian) to Lady Westmorland, RPP, 7; 30 June, Queen Victoria to Lady Raglan, RA F2/148.

6. 3 July 1855, Lady Raglan to Queen Victoria, RA Add. F3/1; 12 Aug 1855, Lady Raglan to Queen Victoria, RA F3/75.

7. McNeill to Lady Rose (Fane), RPP, 7; 6 July 1855, Codrington to his wife, RA F3/12; 2 July 1855, letter from King Leopold, RA Y79/115; 16, 30 July 1855, Cambridge to Richard, RPP, 10/30 and 31; 20 July 1855, Spanish testimonial to G.H. Gibbs Esq, The Horse Guards, RPP, 8/311; undated (July) 1855, Lady Elizabeth Orde to Lady Mary Farquhar, RPP, 7/294; 14 July 1855, Airey to Miss Somerset, RPP, 7/297.

8. TILN, 7 July 1855; The Times, 2 July 1855; The Morning Post, 28 July 1855; The Morning Chronicle, 26 July 1855.

9. Cf., 'Lines on the Death of Lord Raglan', by J. Casmey, Boroughbridge, RPP, 8/340; 'Ode on the Death of Lord Raglan', by J. Butler, July 1855, RPP, 8; Anon 'Lines on Lord Raglan', ibid.; 9 July 1855, dispatch from correspondent of Le Nord, RPP, 7/275.

10. 20 July 1855, Lady Westmorland to Comtess Neale, Weigall, op. cit., p. 268; 5 July 1855, Dundas to Lady Westmorland, RPP, 7; History of Cefntilla, p. 7; 13 July 1855, Hardinge to Col the Hon Charles Phipps, RA A24/148; 15 July 1855, Beaufort to Phipps, RA F3/24; The Bristol Mirror, 21 July 1855. Undated (July) 1855, Lady Elizabeth Orde to Lady Mary Farquhar, RPP, 7/294, however, indicated that at least some of the family favoured a public funeral. Tablets to Col Lord John Thomas Henry Somerset, Lord William George Henry Somerset and Lord William's second wife, Frances Westby, are in Bristol Cathedral.

11. 30 July 1855, Lady Westmorland to Comtess Neale, Weigall, op. cit., p. 261; TILN, 4 Aug 1855; various unidentified newspaper cuttings, RPP, 10; Bristol Gazette, 26 July, 2 Aug 1855; The Bristol Mirror, 21 July 1855. The Bristol Gazette, 2 Aug 1855, named Gen Sir Henry Ross as a pallbearer, but this was an apparent misprint for 'Hew Ross'. The Duke of Cambridge did not attend the service, although he had offered to be a pallbearer. He subsequently regretted his inability to 'pay my humble tribute', which etiquette as a member of the royal family may have prevented: 16, 30 July 1855, Cambridge to Richard, RPP, 10/30 and 31.

12. Press cuttings in RPP, 10; Anon. The Life, Military Career and death of Lord Raglan with a programme of the Procession, Bristol, 1855.

13. History of Cefntilla, pp. 5, 7; Raglan memorial, Cefntilla estate papers, RPP, E; The Times, 26 July 1853.

14. History of Cefntilla, pp. 2–3; 4 Aug 1856, Downes to Richard, RPP, 9.

15. 24 July 1857, Hansard, cxlvii, pp. 336 et seq; The Times, 25 July 1857; The Morning Herald, 27 July 1857; 9 Nov 1857, Westmorland to Fortescue, RPP, 10; Westmorland, Earl of. A Letter to Earl Fortescue on his speech in the House of Lords, Friday 24 July 1857, 1858. I am indebted to Mr A.S. Oakman, Chief Executive of Warwickshire CCC, for his help; and to Col R. Brennan, formerly of the Army Sport Control Board, for information concerning FS's official support for the provision of a cricket pitch for every barracks noted in General Order No 551, 8 Mar 1841. Raglan's name continues to be commemorated. On 17 Oct 1992, a Royal National Lifeboat Institution boat dedicated by the Bishop of Portsmouth in a formal ceremony was named 'Lord Raglan' at the Portsmouth (Langstone Harbour) Lifeboat Station by the Crimean commander's great-great grandson. The £12,000 for it had been raised voluntarily at an inn, 'The Lord Raglan', in Wokingham.

16. Lady FitzRoy died at 5 Great Stanhope Street and was buried at Badminton. Richard died suddenly on 3 May 1884 at his sisters' house, 8 Chesterfield Street, London, being succeeded by his son, George FitzRoy Henry, who died in 1921 when the government pension thus ceased. Charlotte died in London 3 July 1906, Kitty on 15 Oct 1915. Queen Victoria's papers indicate that Palmerston, rather than Panmure, was instrumental in securing the Parliamentary grant. 'A little after 7' on 30 June 1855, after a preliminary letter suggesting a procedure, he visited the Queen at Buckingham Palace to discuss a royal message to Parliament 'proposing 1,000 a year should be given to Lady Raglan, besides her pension as Field-Marshal's widow, and 2,000 for the present Lord and his next male heir.' With Queen Victoria's approval, the Prime Minister thus proceeded and, on 3 July, reported that Parliament had 'unanimously agreed', RA QVJ: 30 June 1855; 30 June, 3 July 1855, Palmerston to Queen Victoria, RA A24/91 and 97; message to Parliament, RA G34/13.

17. Skinner, B. St Nicolas Church, Great Bookham, Leatherhead, 1957; Carleton, J. Westminster School: a History, 1965; Land Transport Corps memorial, unidentified letter from Dublin to Richard, Lord Raglan, RPP, 8/350; Portsmouth memorial noted, RPP, 7/288.

18. Notes on Crimean memorials, RPP, 8; concerning outside memorial, undated letter from Col Frederic Brine to The Morning Post, RPP, 8/341; 25 Mar 1857, Brine to dowager Lady Raglan, RPP, 8/343A. On his way to Sevastopol after the Yalta Conference with Joseph Stalin and President Roosevelt in February 1945, Winston Churchill studied the scene of the Light Brigade Charge from the Sapoune Ridge: 'We had visited his [Lord Raglan's] tomb in the morning [13 Feb])', he recorded. A mysterious assertion. Either he had seen Cathcart's grave or the garden memorial at the old British headquarters: Churchill, W. The Second World War, 1965, xii, p. 59.

In Retrospect

1. 10 Jan 1855, Cambridge to Louisa, quoted in St Aubyn, op. cit., pp. 86–7; 2 July 1855, McNeill to Lady Rose Fane, RPP, 7.

2. Precisely how 'the Raglan sleeve' emerged is in dispute. The fifth Lord Raglan has been told that the fashion dated from approximately 1857. However, a centenary article in Le Monde, 30 Sept 1954, described how Raglan himself developed the new style with the aid of a regimental tailor in time for a review of Anglo-French troops in 1854.

3. 2 Mar 1855, Raglan to Panmure, RMP 6807/286.

4. Aug 1868, Proudfoot (4th Dragoons) incident noted by Charlotte, RPP, 7/286; Smith incident, RPP, 7/340: this probably occurred on 29 June 1895, when veterans from a Bristol ex-servicemen's club laid a wreath at Badminton in Raglan's memory.

5. Russell, W. The Great War with Russia, 1895, p. 306.

6. Feb 1857, Wright at a 'Meeting for the Propaga-

tion of the Gospel in Foreign Parts', RPP, 7/281; 13 Feb 1857, Mrs Fountain to Charlotte, RPP, 7/282; *see* also *Life of Lord Raglan*, pp. 60–1, for acknowledgement of Raglan's Christianity.

7. 25 July 1855, Lady Rose (Fane) to Arthur Somerset, RPP, 7. 20 July 1855, Lady Westmorland to Comtess Néale, Weigall, op. cit., p. 267, noted that Raglan's letters to his wife 'never failed her twice a week'.

8. Lyon's words recorded by an unidentified diarist, 15 Feb 1856, RPP, 7/276.

9. 2 Mar 1855, Raglan to Panmure, RMP 6807/286; Airey quoted in 'Lord Raglan and the Press', *Monthly Review*, Mar 1857, p. 168n; Brown's report, RPP, 7/268; *The Economist*, 7 July 1855.

10. *The Naval and Military Gazette*, 7 July 1855; 11 May 1809, Wellesley to Beresford, Gurwood, op. cit., iv, p. 320.

11. 19 Feb 1855, views of 'a general' in the Crimea to an unknown correspondent in England, RPP, 7/233; evidence of an ADC, RPP, 7/250; Russell, W. *The War: From the Landing at Gallipoli to the Death of Lord Raglan*, 1856, i, p. 364; Stratford de Redcliffe's correspondence, RMP 6807/290; Horse Guards and Orde correspondence, RMP 6807/289; Sherer, J. *Military Memoirs of Field-Marshal the Duke of Wellington*, 1930, ii, p. 293; Windham quoted in Pemberton, op. cit., p. 171; Simpson quoted in Godwin-Austen, A. *The Staff and the Staff College*, 1927, p. 89; Martineau, op. cit., vi.

12. 22 Jan 1855, Molesworth memo, 20 Jan 1855, Palmerston memo, undated (Jan 1855), Argyll memo, Dalhousie Muniments 8/171; Ryan, op. cit., p. 13.

13. Raglan's Alma dispatch, RMP, 6807/288. Tennyson's poem had a swift effect in the Crimea. Duberly, op. cit., p.206, noted on 27 May 1855: 'Rode this evening all over the valley of the Balaclava charge – the valley of death, as Tennyson calls it'. Most authorities, following Raglan's letter to the Queen on 7 Dec 1854, place Russian withdrawal from the redoubts on 6 December. However, entries in Mrs Duberly's journal, 20 and 30 Dec 1854, suggest that not until the latter date did French Zouaves establish total enemy withdrawal from the Plain of Balaclava and the Woronzov Heights, Duberly, op. cit., pp. 152, 155.

14. An editorial comment in *Press*, 17 Jan 1863, castigated those who used Cathcart's pressure for an immediate assault on Sevastopol against Raglan: 'No one asks or cares what was the opinion of Sir George Cathcart. Never very brilliant, his judgement was easily swayed ... ... Why is the spectre of Sir George Cathcart brought up to shake his greying locks?'

15. Hamley, E. *The Story of the Campaign of Sebastopol, written in camp*, 1855, p. 262; Pemberton, op. cit., p. 192.

16. Wrottesley, op. cit., i, p. 31; 18 July 1855, Keppel to Sir Henry Stevenson, RA G35/47.

17. Stewart 'off Sevastopol', quoted in Simpson, op. cit., p. 528; (July) 1855, Palmerston to Panmure, quoted ibid., p. 530.

18. Lyon's words recorded by an unknown diarist, RPP, 7/276; *Monthly Review*, Mar 1857, p. 157; 24 Oct 1855, note by Lady Ellesmere that St Arnaud's letters 'lately published' contained generous tributes to Raglan of 'respect and esteem', RPP, 7/301; 7 July 1855, Clifford to his father, Fitzherbert, op. cit., p. 231; 18 July 1855, Keppel to Sir Henry Stevenson, RA G35/47; 22 June 1857, comments by Adye, RPP, 7/302.

19. Luvaas, J. *The Education of an Army. British Military Thought 1815–1940*, 1965, pp. 21 *et seq.*

20. Walsh, 17 July 1855, Hansard, cxxxix, p. 992; 22 Mar 1856, Maxwell to his brother Sir William Maxwell, RPP, 7/251; Argyll at a public dinner for Adm Stewart, quoted in *Monthly Review*, Mar 1857, p. 160n. 16 July 1855, Prince Metternich to Lady Westmorland, Weigall, op. cit., p. 266, similarly implied the favourable verdict of history.

21. *Life of Lord Raglan*, pp. 59–63; 14 July 1855, Airey to Miss Somerset, RPP, 7/297.

22. Emerson, op. cit., p. 157.

23. 20 July 1855, Lady Westmorland to Comtess Néale, Weigall, op. cit., p. 267; *Life of Lord Raglan*, p. 58; ADC's words, RPP, 7/250; Spring 1855, Brown quoted in RPP, 7/268.

24. 29 June 1855, Simpson to Brown, Brown Papers, MS 1850; Lyons quoted in diarist's summary, RPP, 7/276; 16 Mar 1855, Panmure to Queen Victoria, Douglas and Ramsay, op. cit., i, p. 103; 22 June 1857, Adye quoted in RPP, 7/302; undated, Raglan to a nephew, and Raglan to Lady Westmorland, quoted in Hibbert, op. cit., pp. 264, 268. King Leopold of the Belgians was among those to argue that 'the way in which the press abused him must have done him harm', RA Y79/115.

25. Galloway, 3 July 1855, Hansard, cxxxix, p. 401; Fortescue, J. *History of the British Army*, 1930, xiii, p. 204; *The Times*, 23 Dec 1854.

26. Undated memo (1855) by Lady Westmorland, Weigall, op. cit., p. 219; 18 July 1855, Keppel to Sir Henry Stevenson, RA G35/47.

SELECT BIBLIOGRAPHY

1. Manuscript Sources

Aberdeen Papers: British Library, Additional Manuscripts

Airey Papers: Herefordshire Record Office, Hereford

Badminton Muniments: Badminton, Gloucestershire

Brown Papers: National Library of Scotland, Edinburgh

Clarendon Deposit: Bodleian Library, Oxford

Codrington Papers: National Army Museum, Chelsea

Dalhousie Muniments (Panmure Papers): Scottish Record Office, Edinburgh

Ellenborough Papers: Public Record Office, Kew

Estcourt Papers: Gloucestershire Record Office, Gloucester

Gladstone Papers: British Library, Additional Manuscripts

Granville Papers: Public Record Office, Kew

Grey Papers: Durham University

Kingscote Papers: Gloucestershire Record Office, Gloucester

Lyons Papers: West Sussex Record Office, Chichester

Newcastle Papers: Nottingham University

Palmerston Letterbooks: British Library, Additional Manuscripts

Palmerston Papers: Southampton University

Peel Papers: British Library, Additional Manuscripts

Royal Archives: Windsor Castle

Raglan Private Papers: Cefntilla, Usk

Raglan Military Papers: National Army Museum, Chelsea

Registers of Gentlemen Cadets: Royal Military Academy Sandhurst

Scovell Papers: Public Record Office, Kew

Sidney Herbert Papers: Wiltshire Record Office, Trowbridge

Strathnairn Papers (Henry Rose): British Library, Additional Manuscripts

Stratford Canning Papers (Lord Stratford de Redcliffe): Public Record Office, Kew

War Office 'A' Papers: Ministry of Defence Library

Wellington Papers: Southampton University

Westminster School Archives: Westminster School

2. Official Publications

Hansard

Parliamentary Debates

Parliamentary Papers

1833: Report from the Select Committee on Army and Navy Appointments, vii, 1

1837: Report of the Commissioners appointed to inquire into the practicability and expediency of consolidating the different Departments connected with the Civil Administration of the Army, xxxiv, Pt 1, 1

1849: Interim Report from the Select Committee on Army and Ordnance Expenditure, ix, 1

1850: Interim Report from the Select Committee on Army and Ordnance Expenditure, x, 1

1851: Final Report from the Select Committee on Army and Ordnance Expenditure, vii, 753

1852: Reports of the Committee appointed to inquire into the Naval, Ordnance and Commissariat Establishments, xxx, 361

1852: Report from the Commission of Inquiry into Ordnance and Commissariat Establishments abroad, lix, 395

1854–5: Report from the Select Committee on the Army before Sebastopol, ix, Pt I, II, III

1854–5: Report upon the State of the hospitals of the British Army in the Crimea and Scutari, with an Appendix, xxxiii, 1

1854–5: Order in Council regulating the Establishment of the Civil Departments, xxxii, 677

1854–5: Copies of Correspondence relating to the state of the Harbour of Balaclava, xxxiv, 107

1856: Reports from the Commission of Inquiry into the Supplies of the British Army in the Crimea, xx, 1

1856: Report of the Board of General Officers appointed to inquire into the Statements contained in the Reports of Sir John McNeill and Colonel Tulloch, xxi, 1

1857: Return of casualties in the Crimea, (Sess 1), ix, 7

1857: Report to the Minister of War of the proceedings of the Sanitary Commission despatched to the Seat of War in the East, 1855–6, (Sess 1), lx, 241

3. Official Records: PRO, Kew

ADM 51: Logs of Ships' Captains

ADM 52: Logs of Ships' Masters

FO 27: Papers of the Paris Embassy

FO 925: Maps of London

WO 3: Commander-in-Chief's out-letters

WO 4: Secretary at War's out-letters

WO 6: Secretary of State for War's out-letters

WO 12: General Muster Books and Pay Lists

WO 14: Scutari Depot Minute Books and Pay Lists, 1854–6

WO 28: Headquarters Records of the Crimea

WO 30: Miscellanea, including 1848 Chartist dispositions

WO 31: Commander-in-Chief's memoranda papers, including appointments and promotions

WO 33: Miscellaneous Papers, 1853–1930

WO 43: A collection of papers subdivided into VOS (very old series) and OS (old series)

WO 44: Ordnance Office in-letters

WO 45: Ordnance Office Reference Books

WO 46: Ordnance Office out-letters

WO 47: Ordnance Office Minutes, including Board's Minute Books, 1809–1855

WO 54: Ordnance Office Registers

4. Miscellaneous pamphlets and unpublished works

Anon. Observations upon the Peace Establishment of British Army, 1822.

Anon. Some Observations on the War in the Crimea, 1855.

Anon. Life of Field-Marshal Lord Raglan, 1855: reprinted from *The United Service Magazine*, Aug 1855.

Anon. The Life, Military Career and Death of Lord Raglan with a programme of the Procession, Bristol, 1855.

Anon. The Royal Artillery, 1855.

Anon. Short History of Cefntilla Court and the Raglan Family, nd.

Anon. The Origins and History of the First or Grenadier Guards, 1874.

Bristol Central Library *Old Bristol*, 1930, II.

Ci-devant Cavalry Officer, a. Army Reform: a practical method of reducing the Army Estimates a million without diminution of its numerical force, 1833.

Hoad, M. and Patterson A. (eds.). Portsmouth and the Crimean War, Portsmouth, 1973.

John Johnson Collection of Printed Ephemera, The Bodleian Library, Oxford

Kennaway, C. The War and the Newspapers, 1856.

Maxwell, P. Whom Shall We Hang? The Sebastopol Inquiry, 1855.

Officer, an. Observations on the Army, 1825.

Royal United Service Institution. Field-Marshal Fitz-Roy J. H. Lord Raglan, G.C.B., nd.

Simpson, W. The Life of Field-Marshal the Lord Raglan, c.1955, unpublished, copy in RMA Sandhurst Library.

Skinner, B. St Nicolas Church, Great Bookham, Leatherhead, 1957.

Somerset, W. The Descendants of Henry Somerset, Fifth Duke of Beaufort, privately published, 1936.

Two Mounted Sentries. The Horse Guards – a satire upon the Duke of Wellington, 1850.

Ward, S. (ed.). The Hawley Letters, Society for Army Historical Research Special Publication No 10, 1970.

Weale, J. An open letter to the Right Honourable Lord John Russell, First Lord of the Treasury, on the Defence of the Country, 1847.

Westmorland, Earl of. A Letter to Earl Fortescue on his speech in the House of Lords, Friday 24 July 1857, 1858.

5. Maps and Illustrations

Anon. Environs of Bristol and Bath, Bristol, 1850.

Ashmead, G. Map of the City and Borough of Bristol, Bristol, 1855.

Bassett, A. An Actual Survey and Plan of the Parish of Ealing, 1777.

Biddulph, M. A Series of Topographical Sketches of the Ground before Sevastopol, nd.

Cruchley. New Plan of London and its Environs, 1830.

Fortescue, J. Maps and Plans illustrating the History of the British Army, 1930, xiii.

Kinglake, A. Maps connected with Lord Raglan's activities contained in The Invasion of the Crimea, 1868-87, iii-viii.

Resident, a. A Street View of Bristol, Bristol, 1853.

Rousset, C. Histoire de la Guerre de Crimée Atlas, Paris, 1877.

Stanford. Bird's Eye View of the Seat of War in the Crimea, 1855.

6. Published Books
(All published in London unless stated)
Adye, J. *The Crimean War 1854–5*, 1860.
Aldington, R. *Wellington*, 1946.
Anderson, O. *A Liberal State at War*, New York, 1967.
Anglesey, Marquis of. *One Leg. The Life and Letters of the First Marquis of Anglesey*, 1961.
— *Little Hodge*: Extracts from the diaries and letters of Colonel Edward Hodge written during the Crimean War, 1854–6, 1971.
Anitschkof, V. *La Campagne de Crimée*, Fr. trans, Paris, 1858.
Anon (ed.). *The Personal Narrative of a Private Soldier in the 42nd Highlanders*, 1821.
Anon. *The Battle of Waterloo*, 1852.
Anon. *Memorials of Captain Hedley Vicars, 97th Regiment*, 1856.
Anon. *The King's Shropshire Light Infantry, 1755–1955*, 1955.
Anon (ed.). *The Diary of Sergeant William McMillan*,1990.
Ashley, E. *The Life and Correspondence of Henry John Temple, Viscount Palmerston*, i and ii, 1876.
Aspinall, A. (ed.). *Three Early Nineteenth Century Diaries*, 1952.
Aspinall-Oglander C. *Admiral's Widow: Being the Life and Letters of the Hon Mrs Edward Boscawen from 1761 to 1805*, 1842.
Atkins, J. *The Life of Sir William Howard Russell*, i, 1911.
Bagot, J. *George Canning and His Friends*, i and ii, 1909.
Bapst, C. *Le Maréchal Canrobert, souvenirs d'un siècle*, i-vi, Paris, 1989–1913.
Barker G. and Stenning, A. *The Records of Old Westminsters*, ii, 1928.
Bazancourt, Baron César de. *Cinq Mois devant Sebastopol, L'Expédition de Crimée jusqu' à la prise de Sébastopol*, Paris, 1855.
Beatson, F. *With Wellington in the Pyrenees*, 1914.
Bell, D. *Wellington's Officers*, 1938.
Bell, H. *Lord Palmerston*, ii, 1936.
Benson, A. and Esher, Viscount (eds.). *The Letters of Queen Victoria, 1837–1861*, i-iii, 1908.
Bentley, N. (ed.). *Russell's Despatches from the Crimea, 1854–1856*, 1966.
Bill, E. and Mason, J. *Christ Church and Reform*, Oxford, 1970.
Blackburne, H. *Historical Record of the 14th (King's) Hussars 1715-1900*, 1901.

Booth, J. *Battle of Waterloo*, 1852.
Bonham-Carter, V. (ed.). *Surgeon in the Crimea: The Experiences of George Lawson recorded in his letters to his family, 1854–1855*, 1918.
Bonner-Smith, D. (ed.). *The Russian War 1854. Baltic and Black Sea Official Correspondence*, 1943.
Bosquet, P. *Lettres du Maréchal Bosquet, 1830–1858*, Paris, 1894.
Brett-James, A. (ed.). *Wellington at War. A Short Selection of his Wartime Letters*, 1961.
Briggs, A. *Victorian People*, Harmondsworth, 1967.
Broughton, Lord J. (J. Cam Hobhouse). *Recollections of a Long Life* , i and ii, 1909–1911.
Brown, G. *Memoranda and Observations on the Crimean War, 1854–5*, 1879.
Bryant, A. *The Great Duke or the Invincible General*, 1971.
Buchan, S. *The Sword of State: Wellington after Waterloo*, 1928.
Burke, B. *A Genealogical and Heraldic Dictionary of the Peerage and Baronetage together with Memoirs of the Privy Councillors and Knights*, 1887.
Calthorpe, S. *Letters from Headquarters. By an officer on the Staff*, i and ii, 1856–7.
Cannon, R. *Historical Record of the 53rd or the Shropshire Regt of Foot*, 1849.
Cardigan, Earl of. *Eight Months on Active Service*, 1855.
Carleton, J. *Westminster School: a History*, 1965.
Chandler, D. (ed.). *Great Battles of the British Army*, 1991.
Chesney, K. *Crimean War Reader*, 1960.
Churchill, W. *The Second World War*, xii, 1965.
Clark, F. (ed.). *The East-India Register and Army List for 1845* , 1845.
Clode, C. *The Military Forces of the Crown*, ii, 1869.
Colby, R. *The Waterloo Despatch*, 1965.
Colledge, J. *Ships of the Royal Navy*, Newton Abbot, 1969.
Compton, P. *Cardigan of Balaclava*, 1972.
Conacher, J. *The Aberdeen Coalition, 1852–1855*, Cambridge, 1968.
Connell, B. *Regina versus Palmerston 1837–1865*, 1962.
Cook, E. *Delane of The Times*, 1915.
Curling, H. (ed.). *Recollections of Rifleman Harris*, 1929.
Curtiss, J. *The Russian Army under Nicholas I, 1825–1855*, Durham NC, 1965.
Dalton, C. *The Waterloo Roll Call*, 1971.

Derrecagaix, G. *Le Maréchal Pélissier*, Paris, 1911.

Dewar, A. *The Russian War 1855, Black Sea Official Correspondence*, 1945.

Douglas, G. and Ramsay G. (eds.). *The Panmure Papers*, i and ii, 1908.

Duberly, Mrs H. *Journal kept during the Crimean War*, 1855.

Durant, H. *The Somerset Sequence*, 1951.

Eardley-Wilmot, S. *Life of Vice-Admiral Edmund, Lord Lyons*, 1898.

Emerson, G. *Sebastopol: the Story of its Fall*, 1855.

Evans, G de Lacy. *The Designs of Russia*, 1828.

Fergusson, J. *The Perils of Portsmouth*, 1851.

Field, J. *The King's Nurseries*, 1987.

Fitchett, W. (ed.). *Wellington's Men: Some Soldiers' Autobiographies*, 1960.

Fitzherbert, C. (ed.). *Henry Clifford VC: his letters and sketches from the Crimea*, 1956.

Fitzmaurice, E. *The Life of Granville George Leveson Gower, Second Earl Granville*, i, 1905.

Forbes, A. *A History of the Army Ordnance Services*, i and ii, 1929.

Forshall, F. *Westminster School. Past and Present*, 1884.

Fortescue, J. *History of the British Army*, xiii, 1930.

— *A Gallant Company*, 1927.

— *Wellington*, 1925.

Fraser, E. *The Soldiers Whom Wellington Led*, 1913.

Gernsheim H. and Gernsheim, E. (eds.). *Roger Fenton, Photographer of the Crimean War. His photographs and letters from the Crimea*, 1954.

Gibbs, P. *The Battle of the Alma*, 1963.

Glover, M. *Wellington's Peninsula Victories*, 1963.

Glover, R. *Peninsula Preparation*, Cambridge, 1963.

Godwin-Austen, A. *The Staff and the Staff College*, 1927.

Gooch, B. *The New Bonapartist Generals in the Crimean War*, The Hague, 1959.

Gooch, G. (ed.) *The Later Correspondence of Lord John Russell 1840–1878*, i and ii, 1925.

Goodspeed, D. *The British Campaigns in the Peninsular War 1808–1814*, Ottawa, 1958.

Gordon, A. (ed.). *General Orders issued to the Army of the East 30 April 1854–31 December 1855*, 1856.

Gordon, H. *The War Office*, 1935.

Gowing, T. *A Voice from the Ranks*, 1954.

Griffiths, A. *Wellington, His Commanders and Contemporaries*, 1897.

Guedalla, P. *The Duke*, 1931.

Gurwood, J. *The Dispatches and General Orders of Field-Marshal the Duke of Wellington*, iv-xii, 1837–8.

Hamilton, F. *The Origin and History of the First or Grenadier Guards*, 1874.

Hamley, E. *The Story of the Campaign of Sebastopol, written in camp*, 1855.

— *War in the Crimea*, 1891.

Hardinge, Viscount Charles. *Viscount Hardinge*, 1891

Harris, J. *The Gallant 600: A Tragedy of Obsessions*, 1973.

Hay, L. (ed.). *Memoirs of Lieutenant-General Sir James Leith GCB* , 1821.

Head, F. *The Defenceless State of Great Britain*, 1850.

Hibbert, C. *The Destruction of Lord Raglan*, 1961.

Hodasevich, R. *A Voice from within the Walls of Sebastopol*, Eng. trans., 1856.

Hodson, V. *List of the Officers of the Bengal Army 1758–1834*, iii, 1946.

Howard, M. *Studies in War and Peace*, 1970.

Howarth, D. *A Near Run Thing*, 1968.

Jocelyn J. *The History of the Royal Artillery (Crimean Period)*, 1911.

Jocelyn, J. *The Correspondence and Diaries of the late Right Honourable J.W. Croker*, i-iii, 1884.

Jones, H. *Journal of the Operations conducted by the Corps of Royal Engineers*, i, 1859.

Kincaid, J. *Adventures in the Rifle Brigade in the Peninsula, France and the Netherlands 1809–1815*, 1830.

Kinglake, A. *The Invasion of the Crimea*, i-viii, Edinburgh and London, 1863–87.

Lambert, A. *The Crimean War: British Grand Strategy against Russia, 1853–6*, 1990.

Larpent, G. (ed.). *The Private Journal of Judge Advocate Larpent* , 1854.

Lee, S. (ed.). *Dictionary of National Biography*, 1898.

Lennox, P. *Fifty Years' Biographical Reminiscences*, i, 1863.

Longford, Lady E. *Wellington: the Years of the Sword*, 1971.

— *Wellington: Pillar of State*, 1975.

Luvaas, J. *The Education of an Army. British Military Thought 1815–1940*, 1965.

MacKenzie, G. *The Royal Naval and Military Calendar and National Record*, 1821.

MacMunn, G. *The Crimea in Perspective*, 1935.

Martin, T. *The Life of His Royal Highness The Prince Consort*, ii, 1876.

Martineau, J. *The Life of Henry Pelham, Fifth Duke of Newcastle 1811–1864*, 1908.

Maxwell. H. (ed.). *A Selection from the Correspondence and Diaries of the late Thomas Creevey MP*, 1903.

— *The Life of Wellington*, 1907.

Mitra, S. *The Life and Letters of Sir John Hall*, 1911.

Moore Smith, G. *The Life of John Colborne, Field-Marshal Lord Seaton*, 1903.

Napier, W. *History of the War in the Peninsula and South of France*, i–vi, 1828–40.

— *The Life and Opinions of General C.J. Napier*, iv, 1857.

Nicolson, H. *The Congress of Vienna*, 1948.

Niel, A. *Siège de Sébastopol: Journal des Opérations de Génie*, Paris, 1858.

Nolan, E. *The Illustrated History of the War against Russia*, i and ii, 1857.

O'Malley, I. *Florence Nightingale 1820–1856*, 1931.

Oman, C. *Wellington's Army, 1809–1814*, 1913.

— *A History of the Peninsular War*, i–vii, Oxford, 1902–30.

Paget, A. (ed.). *The Paget Papers: Diplomatic and Other Correspondence of the Rt Hon Sir Arthur Paget OBE*, ii, 1896.

Paget, Lord George. *The Light Brigade in the Crimea*, 1881.

Parker, C. *Life and Letters of Sir James Graham 1792–1861*, i and ii, 1907.

Pemberton, W. *Battles of the Crimean War*, 1962.

— *Lord Palmerston*, 1954.

Percival, V. *The Duke of Wellington*, 1969.

Petrie, C. *The Victorians*, 1960.

— *Wellington*, 1956.

Poole, S. *The Life of Lord Stratford de Redcliffe*, 1888.

Raikes, H. (ed.). *Private Correspondence of Thomas Raikes with the Duke of Wellington*, 1861.

Raymond, J. (ed.). *The Reminiscences and Recollections of Captain Gronow*, 1964.

Reeve, H. *The Greville Memoirs*, 1903.

Ridley, J. *Lord Palmerston 1784–1865*, 1970.

Robinson, C. *Wellington's Campaigns, Peninsula – Waterloo 1808–1815*, 1907.

Robinson, F. *Diary of the Crimean War*, 1856.

Rogerson, W. *Historical Records of the 53rd (Shropshire) Regiment*, 1890.

Rousset, C. *Histoire de la Guerre de Crimée*, i and ii, Paris, 1894.

Russell, W. *The War in the Crimea*, 1855.

— *The British Expedition to the Crimea*, 1858.

— *The War: From the Landing at Gallipoli to the Death of Lord Raglan*, i and ii, 1855–6.

— *The Great War with Russia*, 1895.

Ryan, G. *Our Heroes of the Crimea*, 1855.

Sabine, E. (ed.). *Letters of Colonel Sir Augustus Simon Frazer KCB*, 1859.

Sargeaunt, J. *Annals of Westminster School*, 1898.

Saunders, E. *The Hundred Days*, 1964.

Sayer, F. (ed.). *Campaign in Turkey, Asia Minor and the Crimea, 1854–6*

— *Despatches and Papers*, 1857.

Scarfe, N. *Letters from the Peninsula: the Freer Family Correspondence 1807–18*, Leicester, 1953.

Schroeder, P. *Austria, Great Britain and the Crimean War*, New York, 1972.

Seaton, A. *The Crimean War: a Russian Chronicle*, 1977.

Shadwell, L. *Life of Colin Campbell, Lord Clyde*, 1881.

Shand, A. *The War in the Peninsula 1808–1814*, 1898.

Shepherd, J. *The Crimean Doctors: a History of the British Medical Services in the Crimean War*, i and ii, Liverpool, 1991.

Sheppard, E. (ed.). *George, Duke of Cambridge*, i, 1906.

Sherer, J. *Military Memoirs of Field-Marshal the Duke of Wellington*, ii, 1830.

Siborne, H. (ed.). *Waterloo Letters*, 1891.

Sidney, E. *Lord Hill GCB*, 1845.

Simpson, F. *Louis Napoleon and the Recovery of France 1848–1856* , 1930.

Smith, E. *The Life of Stratford Canning, Lord Stratford de Redcliffe*, 1933.

Smith, H. *The Parliaments of England 1715–1847*, Chichester, 1973.

Spiers, E. *Radical General: Sir George de Lacy Evans*, Manchester, 1983.

Stanhope, Earl. *Notes of Conversations with the Duke of Wellington 1831–1851*, 1888.

Stanmore, Lord. *Sidney Herbert: Lord Herbert of Lea*, i, 1906.

St Aubyn, G. *The Royal George – The Life of the Duke of Cambridge*, 1963.

Staunton, H. *The Great Schools of England*, 1865.

Stocqueler, J. *A Personal History of the Horse Guards 1750–1872* , 1873.

Strachey, L. and Fulford, R. (eds.). *The Greville Memoirs 1814–1860*, iv, 1938.

Stuart, B. (ed.). *Soldier's Glory, Being Rough Notes of an Old Soldier* (Sir George Bell), 1956.

Sweetman, J. *War and Administration: the Significance of the Crimean War for the British Army*, Edinburgh, 1984.

Temperley, H. *The Foreign Policy of Canning 1820–1827*, 1923.
— *England and the Near East: the Crimea*, 1936.
Thomas, D. *The Hero of Balaclava* (Cardigan), 1987.
Thompson, J. *Louis Napoleon and the Second Empire*, 1954.
Todleben, E. de. *Défense de Sébastopol*, i, St Petersburg, 1863.
Trevelyan, G. *The Life and Letters of Lord Macaulay*, 1889.
Tyrell, H. *The History of the War with Russia*, i and ii, 1855–6.
Verner, W. *The Military Life of George, Duke of Cambridge*, i, 1905.
Vieth, F. *Recollections of the Crimean Campaign*, Montreal, 1907.
Vulliamy, C. *Crimea, The Campaigns of 1854–1856*, 1939.
Wake, J. *The Brudenells of Deane*, 1953.
War Department. *General Orders: Spain and Portugal*, 27 April to 28 December 1809, i, 1811.
Ward, B. (ed.). *A Week at Waterloo in 1815*, 1906.
Ward, S. *Wellington's Headquarters*, Oxford, 1957.
Ward, T. (ed.). *The Reign of Queen Victoria*, i, 1887.
Warre, E. (ed.). *Letters from the Peninsula 1808–1812 by Lieutenant-General Sir William Warre CB*, 1909.
Weigall, R. (ed.). *Correspondence of Lady Burghersh with the Duke of Wellington*, 1903.
— *The Correspondence of Priscilla, Countess of Westmorland 1830–1870*, 1909.
Wellesley, M. *Wellington in Civil Life (through the eyes of those who knew him)*, 1939.
Wellington, (Second) Duke of. (ed.). *Supplementary Despatches and Memoranda of Arthur, Duke of Wellington*, v and vi, 1873.
Wellington, (Seventh) Duke of. *The Conversations of the First Duke of Wellington with George William Chad*, Cambridge, 1956.
— *Wellington and his Friends: Letters of the First Duke of Wellington*, 1965.
Wheeler, O. *The War Office Past and Present*, 1914.
Wolseley, G. *The Story of a Soldier's Life*, i, 1903.
Wood, E. *The Crimea in 1854 and 1894*, 1895.
— *From Midshipman to Field-Marshal*, 1907.
Wilson, P. (ed.). *The Greville Diary*, i and ii, 1927.
Woodham-Smith, C. *The Reason Why*, 1957.
— *Florence Nightingale*, 1964.
Woodward, E. *The Age of Reform 1815–1870*, Oxford, 1962.
Wrottesley, G. (ed.). *The Military Opinions of General Sir John Fox Burgoyne*, i and ii, 1873.
Ziegler, P. *King William IV*, 1973.

7. Newspapers, periodicals and other publications

Alligator
Annual Register
Army List and *Hart's Army List*
Blackwood's Magazine
Bristol Gazette
Bristol Mirror
British Army Review
Bury Post
Churchman's Magazine
Daily News
Daily Sketch
Economist
English Historical Review
Examiner
Gentleman's Magazine
Glasgow Herald
Globe
Hampshire Telegraph and Sussex Chronicle
The Illustrated London News
John Bull
Journal of the Society for Army Historical Research
Le Monde
London Gazette
Military Affairs
Morning Avertiser
Morning Chronicle
Morning Herald
Morning Post
Monthly Review
Naval and Military Gazette
New York Tribune
The Observer
Press
Punch
Royal Cornwall Gazette
Standard
The Sunday Times
The Times
United Service Gazette
United Service Magazine
Wolverhampton Journal

INDEX